T0318938

Banking Law

Banking regulation and the private law governing the bank–customer relationship came under the spotlight as a result of the global financial crisis of 2007–2009. More than a decade later UK, EU and international regulatory initiatives have transformed the structure, business practices, financing models and governance of the banking sector. This authoritative text offers an in-depth analysis of modern banking law and regulation, while providing an assessment of its effectiveness and normative underpinnings. Its main focus is on UK law and practice, but where necessary it delves into EU law and institutions, such as the European Banking Union and supervisory role of the European Central Bank. The book also covers the regulation of bank corporate governance and executive remuneration, the promises and perils of FinTech and RegTech, and the impact of Brexit on UK financial services.

Although detailed, the text remains easy to read and reasonably short; pedagogic features such as a glossary of terms and practice questions for each chapter are intended to facilitate learning. It is a useful resource for students and scholars of banking law and regulation, as well as for regulators and other professionals who are interested in reading a precise and evaluative account of this evolving area of law.

Andreas Kokkinis is Senior Lecturer in Corporate Law and Financial Regulation at the University of Birmingham. Before that he was an Associate Professor at the University of Warwick, and he has also taught at University College London (UCL) and the University of Kent. He holds a PhD from UCL (2014), an LLM (Master of Laws) from the London School of Economics (2009) and an LLB from the National University of Athens (2008).

Andrea Miglionico is Lecturer in Banking and Finance Law at the University of Reading. Prior to joining Reading he was an Associate Lecturer, a Research and Teaching Fellow at the Centre for Commercial Law Studies (CCLS) at Queen Mary University of London. He received his LLM from the London School of Economics and his PhD from Queen Mary University of London.

Banking Law

Private Transactions and Regulatory Frameworks

**Andreas Kokkinis and
Andrea Miglionico**

LONDON AND NEW YORK

First published 2021
by Routledge
2 Park Square, Milton Park, Abingdon, Oxon OX14 4RN

and by Routledge
605 Third Avenue, New York, NY 10158

Routledge is an imprint of the Taylor & Francis Group, an informa business

© 2021 Andreas Kokkinis and Andrea Miglionico

British Library Cataloguing-in-Publication Data
A catalogue record for this book is available from the British Library

Library of Congress Cataloging-in-Publication Data
Names: Kokkinis, Andreas, author. | Miglionico, Andrea, author.
Title: Banking law: private transactions and regulatory frameworks /
Andreas Kokkinis and Andrea Miglionico.
Description: Milton Park, Abingdon, Oxon; New York, NY: Routledge, 2021. |
Includes bibliographical references and index. |
Identifiers: LCCN 2020055416 (print) | LCCN 2020055417 (ebook) |
ISBN 9780367679804 (hardback) | ISBN 9780367679064 (paperback) |
ISBN 9781003133636 (ebook)
Subjects: LCSH: Banking law—Great Britain.
Classification: LCC KD1715 .K65 2021 (print) |
LCC KD1715 (ebook) | DDC 346.41/082—dc23
LC record available at https://lccn.loc.gov/2020055416
LC ebook record available at https://lccn.loc.gov/2020055417

ISBN: 978-0-367-67980-4 (hbk)
ISBN: 978-0-367-67906-4 (pbk)
ISBN: 978-1-003-13363-6 (ebk)

Typeset in Galliard
by codeMantra

Contents

Table of cases

English cases

European cases

American cases

Table of legislation

Acts of Parliament – UK

Statutory instruments – UK

European Union (EU) Treaties

EU Directives

EU Regulations

EU Decisions

European (Italian)

Acts of Congress – USA

Preface

The inception of a banking law manuscript seems overambitious particularly at the age of innovation and digital technologies. The rapid evolution of securities markets and the radical changes in bank payments pose challenges for financial regulators and public authorities. The process towards disintermediation favoured by the proliferation of virtual platforms raises concerns among policymakers and supervisory bodies. Customers are often disoriented through the myriad of complex products that face challenges for the stability of the banking sector. This book aims to shed light on the recent developments in the financial industry taking a holistic view both from a practitioner and academic perspective. The overarching objective is to provide a critical overview of the current architecture of banking law and regulation in the UK, and of the EU framework. The analysis seeks to examine the intricacies of the business of banks addressing the main issues behind private transactions and regulatory policies. The role of credit institutions in the FinTech revolution shows critical aspects in terms of risk assessment and prudential treatment of lending mechanisms: the digitisation of bank services makes individual investors unskilled regarding loan transactions even when they have obtained full information about the products.

The work provides a comprehensive coverage of issues in the areas of systemic risk, corporate governance, payment methods and prudential supervision. It addresses themes that are intimately related, such as bank capital, deposit insurance, money laundering and terrorist financing, resolution tools, executive remuneration and senior managers' accountability. The first part of the book sets the context of the analysis, by exploring the main features of the banking system taking into consideration the major problems involving banks and their regulators. This part introduces the reader to the notion of a credit institution and the different types of banks operating within the UK and EU regulatory framework. The first part also focuses on the regulatory architecture of the UK banking sector and harmonisation process of the EU financial regime. It discusses the transformation of UK regulation brought by the Banking Act 2009; the Financial Services Act 2012 and 2016, which abolished the FSA and introduced the PRA and FCA; and the Banking Reform Act 2013. This part also examines the creation of the EU 'Banking Union', a process facing important legal and political hurdles concerning the European Central Bank and its new supervisory role in the Eurozone.

The second part of the work examines the (mostly) private law aspects of the relationship between banks and their customers such as bank accounts, bank lending and the prevention of financial crime. This analysis explores the evolution of the UK bank–customer relationship along with the scope of banks' fiduciary obligations and duty of care applicable when giving advice. In this context, it discusses the ways in which regulatory interventions seek to ensure that banks treat their customers fairly and that customers have access to a satisfactory range of appropriate products. This part also discusses the relationship between depositors and banks, and illustrates the mechanics of clearing and settlement under the applicable relevant rules. In considering banks' business and consumer lending, this part provides suggestions for clarifying the legal techniques available to transfer a claim arising from a loan agreement and the typical structure of loan securitisation. Finally, the role of banks against money laundering and terrorist financing is addressed by examining the international standards and domestic criminal legislation to prevent financial crime.

The third part of the book analyses the principal regulatory tools that aim to prevent banking crises in terms of capital, liquidity, risk-taking and governance. It also examines the new senior managers regime and emerging structures of digital banking which may potentially threaten financial stability. This part further discusses the phenomenon of RegTech and its main effects in the area of banking compliance: particular emphasis is devoted on blockchain and automated mechanisms as well as virtual currencies and crypto assets.

The fourth part of the book examines regulatory tools to deal with failing banks in a way that prevents contagion and ensures the continuity of critical services. It discusses the two main pillars of the European Banking Union, namely, the Single Supervisory Mechanism and Single Resolution Mechanism. Managing bank failures has become the main challenge for regulators and supervisory authorities: the incomplete third pillar of the Banking Union – the Single Deposit Guarantee Scheme – raises concerns on the adequate protection of depositors and the credit system. The discussion of banking failures is interlinked with the regulatory and accounting treatments of non-performing loans which represent the crux of the matter in the context of the asset quality of banks. This part also provides an overview of the potential impact of Brexit on the banking sector: the possible scenarios of the withdrawal from the European Union are explored in the light of the recent developments of negotiations that will affect the UK-based banks and inherently the resolution regimes.

Overall, the book analyses the articulations of the banking industry in connection with the evolution of regulatory trajectories and the implications of digital technologies for customers and investors. The methodological approach adopted in the book aims to reach the interest of scholars and practitioners in this area as well as to encounter the favour of postgraduate research students in law and business institutions. The manuscript follows a pedagogical layout to enable the reader to understand the rationale of presented concepts. This first edition of the book provides a practical analysis of the latest changes in banking services and engages with doctrinal debates on the current policy measures. The materials covered bring readers up to date in a very dynamic research area that has recently undergone substantial modifications due to the 2007–2009 financial crisis. The intended objective is to critically enlighten specific topics of banking law, aiming to render this book a point of reference for academics and early career researchers. It is an ambitious project that reflects joint conversations and insightful thoughts that the authors have shared during the long journey that culminated with the present work.

This book has benefitted from the effort and support of several scholars in the field including the anonymous reviewers that have generously spent a considerable amount of time reading and commenting on the manuscript. The authors owe a debt of gratitude to, and acknowledge the welcome assistance of Russell George, the Commissioning Editor at Routledge, and Chloe James, the Senior Editorial Assistant, for their perceptive suggestions and advice at early stages of the process. Their constructive feedback and rigorous competence significantly enhanced the content of this work. We are also heavily indebted to Daniel Osei Agyekumhene for his valuable editorial assistance. Furthermore, the authors are particularly grateful to the Centre for Law, Regulation & Governance of the Global Economy (GLOBE) at the University of Warwick and the Centre for Commercial Law and Financial Regulation (CCLFR) at the University of Reading, for their intellectual and institutional support.

A final note is due on the input and knowledge on this intellectually stimulating research that has been a significant source of inspiration for the authors in their academic collaboration. This book is a result of joint research. Chapters 6, 7, 9, 10 and 12 have been written by Andreas Kokkinis. Chapters 4, 8, 13, 15 and 16 have been written by Andrea Miglionico. Chapters 1, 2, 3, 5, 11, 14, 17 and the *post scriptum* are the result of joint work.

Part I
Banks and their regulators

This part introduces the reader to the notion of a bank and the different types of credit institutions before examining the UK and the EU regulatory framework within which banks operate.

1 The banking system

1.1 Introduction

This chapter serves as an introduction to the book and intends to familiarise the reader with the nature and specificities of banks' business, and the rationales for and types of regulation that banks are subjected to. The discussion starts with a brief account of the historical development of the banking sector in the UK including the development of the legal forms used by banking firms. It then examines the legal definition of credit institutions in EU law; the main types of banks, including virtual banks; and the economic functions and special characteristics of banks. Furthermore, the chapter explains why banking regulation is necessary, and it distinguishes between conduct of business regulation and prudential regulation, further elaborating on the distinction between macro-and micro-prudential regulations. The chapter concludes with a broad assessment of recent and current regulatory trends in the financial markets which canvasses the key challenges facing banking regulators and supervisors in the UK and the EU.

1.2 The historical development of banks and the global financial crisis

Banks and other financial institutions have played a major role for a long time in the economy of the UK. After the establishment of the Bank of England in 1694 and the Bank of Scotland in 1695, banking grew steadily in tandem with industrial capitalism. Originally, all private sector banks operated as partnerships without separate legal personality and limited liability. The history of the introduction of limited liability in the UK is interesting in its own right,[1] but here we will focus on the adoption of limited liability by banking firms, which followed a slightly different path from other companies. This largely reflects the early recognition of the special features of the banking sector that make limited liability a potential threat to the public interest. Indeed, limited liability became available for companies in general by virtue of the Limited Liability Act 1855, while the possibility to incorporate and acquire separate legal personality by registration was introduced by the Joint Stock

---

1 See e.g. Robert A. Bryer, 'The Mercantile Laws Commission of 1854 and the Political Economy of Limited Liability' (1997) 50 *Economic History Review* 37. From the perspective of banks, see e.g. Lucy A. Newton, 'The Birth of Joint-Stock Banking: England and New England Compared' (2010) 84 *Business History Review* 27. From a US perspective, see Stephen M. Bainbridge and M. Todd Henderson, *Limited Liability: A Legal and Economic Analysis* (Edward Elgar Publishing 2016) 21–43.

Companies Act 1844. Both Acts excluded banks from their scope, as did the Joint Stock Companies Act 1856 which codified and expanded company legislation.[2]

In England until 1826, banks could only operate as common law partnerships with an upper limit of six partners that had been introduced in the early 18th century.[3] The Banking Copartnerships Act 1826 allowed banks to become joint stock companies for the first time which had been common practice in other sectors for years.[4] Joint stock companies had no separate legal personality, and their shares were only a share of the joint stock assets and were not transferable without the approval of the directors. The Joint Stock Banks Act 1844 clarified that the Joint Stock Companies Act did not apply to banks which could only obtain legal personality via a royal charter for a maximum duration of 20 years.[5] It was only when the Joint Stock Banking Companies Act 1857 was enacted that banks were allowed to incorporate as companies with legal personality without a Charter and still with unlimited liability and a requirement of a minimum denomination of shares at £100, a significant amount at the time, thus rendering banks' shares illiquid. Limited liability first became available to banking companies in 1858 by virtue of the Joint Stock Banks Act 1858. The minimum share denomination requirement was abolished by the Companies Act 1862, thus integrating the company law framework for banks within the general company law framework, albeit with some special provisions.[6]

Nevertheless, banks were initially reluctant to adopt the legal form of a limited liability company, as depositors continued to rely heavily on bank shareholders' personal wealth as a reassurance that their deposits were safe. Indeed, by the mid-1870s only seven English banks (out of a large number of banks in existence) had incorporated as limited liability companies, although the Act was being adopted by the most newly established banks.[7] This trend changed only after the infamous collapse of the City of Glasgow Bank in 1878, which led to catastrophic financial losses for its shareholders, many of whom were middle-class individuals.[8] By 1884 nearly all UK banks had adopted limited liability. Still, most of them issued high amounts of uncalled share capital, thus maintaining the liability of certain shareholders to contribute up to that amount in case of insolvency and made use of the possibility introduced by the Companies Act 1879 to issue reserve share capital,[9] which was similar to uncalled capital but could only be called by the company in case of insolvency. Thus, in late 19th-century Britain, a large portion of the total value of deposits were covered

---

2 John D. Turner, *Banking in Crisis: The Rise and Fall of British Banking Stability, 1800 to the Present* (CUP 2014) 39–41.

3 Ibid., 36.

4 Ibid., 38.

5 See Bishop C. Hunt, *The Development of the Business Corporation in England, 1800–1867* (Harvard University Press 1936) 96.

6 On the application of the Act on insurance companies and companies formed 'for the purpose of carrying on the business of banking', see Companies Act 1862, ss 3–4. The full text of the Act can be found online at <http://www.irishstatutebook.ie/eli/1862/act/89/enacted/en/print.html?printonload=true> (accessed 1 August 2020).

7 Turner (above n 2) 41 and 124.

8 An account of the events surrounding the bank's failure can be found in Leo Rosenblum, 'The Failure of the City of Glasgow Bank' (1933) 8 *The Accounting Review* 285, esp. 289–291. See also Turner (above n 2) 120–123.

9 The difference between uncalled share capital and reserve share capital was that reserve capital was not callable at the directors' discretion but, rather, only if the bank went insolvent and had inadequate funds to repay depositors. On this generally, see Lewis T. Evans and Neil C. Quigley, 'Shareholder Liability Regimes, Principal-agent Relationships, and Banking Industry Performance' (1995) 38 *Journal of Law and Economics* 497.

by banks' called-up share capital, uncalled capital and reserve capital.[10] This practice faded gradually until the 1950s when the level of coverage of deposits by capital reached the very low level of around 5% at which it has more or less remained.[11] It was only during the 1980s that the majority of investment banks, originally operating as partnerships, completed the same process of adopting the corporate form, or were acquired by retail banks.

Furthermore, during the 1980s and 1990s, most of the UK's building societies, which are co-operative banks functioning as mutual institutions, transformed into public companies or merged with banking corporations. Thus, since the 1990s the greatest part of retail and investment banking activity is being carried out by financial conglomerates, which are structured as groups of companies ultimately owned by a parent public company which has its shares listed on the London Stock Exchange. The abolition of foreign exchange controls in 1979 and deregulation of the 1980s, culminating in the so-called 'Big Bang' of 1986, allowed banks to engage in securities trading, and generally to adopt risky business strategies of their own choice under the generally liberal supervision of the relevant authorities: the Bank of England until 1998, the Financial Services Authority from 1998 to 2013, and currently the Prudential Regulation Authority and Financial Conduct Authority.[12] The late 1990s and early 2000s witnessed a steep increase in financial sector activities, which up until the 2008–2009 financial crisis grew at a significantly faster pace than the rest of the economy. Indeed, financial intermediation contributed 9% of the UK's GDP in 2008,[13] and the assets of the banking sector amounted to more than 500% of GDP in 2006.[14]

This period of rapid development came to an end with the first run on a UK bank after more than a century, namely the run of depositors on Northern Rock in September 2007. The cataclysmic events that followed, including the partial nationalisation of the Royal Bank of Scotland (RBS) and Lloyds Banking Group in 2009,[15] have left a lingering legacy of public distrust in the UK financial system.[16] Lloyds has now returned to 100% private sector ownership, while the government still owns a controlling stake in RBS, which made its first profit since 2007 only in 2017.[17] Considering the prominence of the banking sector, it was unsurprising that the UK felt the consequences of the global financial crisis more severely than most continental European countries, and that its economy entered a deep recession. The UK government's support to the banking sector peaked at £1,162 billion in

10 Indeed, shareholder capital in a broad sense covered 70% of deposits in 1885, but only 40% in 1900. See Turner (above n 2) 128–129.

11 Ibid., 129–131.

12 For a discussion of the evolution of financial regulation architecture in the UK, see Chapter 3.

13 See Stephen Burgess, 'Measuring Financial Sector Output and Its Contribution to UK GDP' (2011) 234 *Bank of England Quarterly Bulletin* 234–235.

14 The data is taken from a conference speech given by Mr Haldane, Bank of England Executive Director for Financial Stability. See Andrew Haldane, 'The Contribution of the Financial Sector: Miracle or Mirage?' (Future of Finance Conference, London, 14 July 2010) 14–15 <http://www.bis.org/review/r100716g.pdf> (accessed 15 July 2020).

15 Immediately after injecting public funds in 2009, the government owned approximately 82% of the share capital of RBS and 43% of the share capital of Lloyds. See Emma Dunkley, 'Lloyds Back in Private Ownership after Government Sells Out' *Financial Times* (London, 17 May 2017).

16 For a succinct discussion of the five main banking failures in the UK during the 2007–2009 crisis, see Edward Walker-Arnott, 'Company Law, Corporate Governance and the Banking Crisis' (2010) 7 *International Corporate Rescue* 19, 19–20 and 24–26.

17 The total losses that RBS incurred from 2008 to 2016 amounted to £58 billion. See Kamal Ahmed, 'RBS Reports First Profit in 10 Years' *BBC News* (London, 23 February 2018) <https://www.bbc.co.uk/news/business-43166560> (accessed 5 August 2020).

2009, while the direct cost of bank rescues to the Treasury stood at £51 billion at the end of March 2013.[18] The final direct cost to the Exchequer will depend on the price at which the remaining government shares in RBS are eventually sold.

During the years that followed the crisis, several UK banks have faced serious scandals and regulatory scrutiny of their actions, which has often led to an enforcement action. Most notably, in 2012 Barclays was fined by the FSA, the Commodity Futures Trading Commission and the US Department of Justice for manipulation of the London Interbank Offered Rate (LIBOR).[19] In 2013 Barclays and RBS were among the six global financial institutions fined by the European Commission, and the Co-operative Bank faced serious losses and was recapitalised partially via bailing in bondholders whose bonds were converted to equity.[20] Finally, several major UK banks – among other large companies – have attracted widespread opposition to their executive remuneration policies and packages from institutional investors since 2011, a phenomenon described by the financial press as the 'shareholder spring'.

1.3 The economic functions of banks

Banks are essential for a modern economy as they perform several vital functions. Like financial intermediaries, banks efficiently transfer funds from depositors, bondholders and other capital market investors to individual, corporate and sovereign borrowers, allowing for economic growth and expansion. In fact, banks generate liquidity, to the extent that they fund illiquid assets (e.g. term loans) using monies deposited in them (which is typically available on demand).[21] Bank lending may also affect the total supply of real money, which explains the need for central banks responsible for monetary policy to supervise the total level of lending in the economy.[22] A similar intermediation function is performed when banks fund loans via the capital markets e.g. by securitising obligations. In such cases, they transfer funds from those who invest in the relevant financial instruments to those who borrow from banks. Moreover, banks operate a complex payment services system which facilitates transactions via cash machines, cheques, credit cards, debit cards, cash cards, electronic purses, money transfers and standing orders. The fast and secure execution of transactions

---

18 Considering the share prices of RBS and Lloyds on 31 March 2013, the loss to the Treasury stood at £28 billion. Another £3 billion was the cost of resolving Northern Rock and Bradford & Bingley. The additional interest paid by the Treasury to fund its investments in the banking sector amounts to £20 billion in four years. See H.M. Treasury, *Annual Report and Accounts 2012–13* (2013–2014, HC 34).

19 For an overview of the relevant events and a discussion of regulatory lessons learnt from them, see David Hou and David R. Skeie, 'LIBOR: Origins, Economics, Crisis, Scandal, and Reform' (2014) Federal Reserve Bank of New York Staff Report 667 <https://papers.ssrn.com/sol3/papers.cfm?abstract_id=2423387> (accessed 4 August 2020). It is worth noting that several Barclays traders have been prosecuted and three have been found guilty of conspiring to fraudulently manipulate global benchmark interest rates. See Simon Bowers, 'Libor-Rigging Scandal: Three Former Barclays Traders Found Guilty' *The Guardian* (London, 4 July 2016).

20 On this, see below note 47 and accompanying text.

21 Of course, it has been demonstrated that the financial intermediation role of banks is nowadays less important than in the past, as their main sources of income are fees and trading activities rather than the margin between interest rates paid by borrowers and interest rates paid to depositors. See e.g. Franklin Allen and Anthony Santomero, 'What Do Financial Intermediaries Do?' (2001) 25 *Journal of Banking & Finance* 271.

22 In the UK, monetary policy is independently administered by the Bank of England (and the Bank's Monetary Policy Committee) within the inflation target set by the Treasury. See Bank of England Act 1998 s 10 which abolishes the power of the Treasury to give directions to the Bank in relation to monetary policy, and s 11 which lexically prioritises the Bank's objective to maintain price stability vis-à-vis its duty to support the economic policy of the government.

and settlement of debts reduces transaction costs and increases economic efficiency. In this way, banks resemble public utility firms providing an intangible network of essential importance for society that is used effectively by all economically active persons and firms. We will see in Chapter 14 that the continuation of critical functions is a key goal of bank resolution.

Banks and other financial institutions are also large employers, especially in countries like the UK where the financial sector accounts for nearly 10% of the GDP. In parallel, financial institutions exert a significant influence on the corporate governance of other large companies. Banks influence the business models and governance of companies they lend funds to through loan facility covenants, through informal monitoring of financed companies, and by screening companies before loans are advanced. In this context, they also play a major role in debt restructuring and corporate rescue, particularly in the UK, where insolvency law is mostly creditor oriented. In most cases, whether the business of an ailing company can be rescued and the way to achieve this is decided in practice by the ailing company's major creditors, which are typically banks.

1.4 The special nature of banks

Investor protection and financial stability policies are the cornerstones of the financial sector. Systemic risk constitutes the main threat to financial stability.[23] The failure of a financial institution of significant size and complexity tends to have spill-over effects on the entire system. Other major institutions are likely to suffer losses, and a string of failures may be triggered. Problems in a few institutions can thus infect the whole financial system and lead to macro-instability. Institutions whose failure can cause negative effects on the financial system are described in regulatory terms as systemically important financial institutions (SIFIs),[24] and include not only banks but also large insurance companies and investment companies, even if only acting on the wholesale market.[25]

Economic literature identifies as the main cause of systemic risk the high interdependence of financial institutions which conduct a large part of their business among themselves.[26] UK regulators have identified two types of systemic risk, namely, cyclical risk and structural risk.[27] Banks, for instance, rely on the inter-bank lending market to ensure that they have adequate liquidity to meet their liabilities, especially in times of low depositor confidence as will be explained below. Activities on the derivatives and foreign exchange markets are other examples of the interconnected nature of banking as banks are the major players in these markets.

---

23 For a detailed examination of the various components of systemic risk, see Steven L. Schwarcz, 'Systemic Risk' (2008) 97 *Georgetown Law Journal* 193 and Steven L. Schwarcz and Lucy Chang, 'The Custom to Failure Cycle' (2012) 62 *Duke Law Journal* 767.

24 The Basel Committee has identified five features of systemically important financial institutions, namely, their size, linkages, global footprint, complexity and substitutability of services.

25 As evinced by the state rescue of American wholesale insurer AIG in 2008, which is discussed briefly in the introduction to this volume. On this, see Mads Andenas and Iris H.-Y. Chiu, *The Foundations and Future of Financial Regulation: Governance for Responsibility* (Routledge 2014) 93 and 305.

26 See Peter O. Mulbert, 'Corporate Governance of Banks after the Financial Crisis—Theory, Evidence, Reforms' (2010) ECGI Working Paper No. 130/2009, 11–12 <http://papers.ssrn.com/sol3/papers.cfm?abstract_id=1448118> (accessed 4 August 2020).

27 See Bank of England and Financial Service Authority, 'Instruments of Macroprudential Policy' (December 2011) <http://www.bankofengland.co.uk/publications/Documents/other/financialstability/discussionpaper 111220.pdf> (accessed 20 July 2020).

Another component of systemic risk is the reputational one. The failure of a large bank can cause a crisis of confidence in the system as a whole, and depositors' runs may affect other banks. Due to the maturity mismatch between deposits that are typically payable on demand and loans, that are to be repaid after a fixed period, it follows that no bank can repay a significant fraction of its deposits at any given time. Banks cannot raise large amounts of liquidity without incurring large losses, as many of their assets (especially loans) are illiquid and cannot therefore be sold at short notice, other than at very low prices. If a large number of depositors believe that their bank is in a precarious position and rush to draw their funds, they will cause the collapse of the bank to the detriment of depositors themselves. The inability of depositors to co-ordinate their actions allows creditors' runs to happen, in a typical collective action problem situation. Therefore, all deposit-taking institutions are dependent on the continuous confidence of depositors and can be diminished to cash flow insolvency as a result of a crisis of confidence. Furthermore, the opacity of the banking sector is a cause of systemic risk.[28] Opacity of assets refers to the difficulty in valuing loan portfolios which constitute the biggest part of banks' balance sheets. The inability of other financial institutions to value the assets of an ailing institution precipitates the collapse of the latter. In parallel, the inability of financial markets to distinguish between sound and unsound banks in times of crisis can paralyse the inter-bank lending market and make it more difficult for banks to raise equity capital. Similarly, the general inability of depositors to distinguish between good and bad banks precipitates a crisis of confidence once one major bank collapses.[29]

To appreciate the magnitude of the threat that systemic risk poses to financial stability, it is pertinent to examine a further special feature of banks, that is, their heavy reliance on debt financing. In financial institutions, as in all limited liability companies, insolvency risk increases in tandem with the company's leverage. If a company's activities are mostly funded by equity, there is a large buffer to absorb losses and hence insolvency is unlikely. Conversely, if a company relies primarily on debt capital, it runs a higher risk of insolvency.[30] This can happen if for any reason the company becomes unable to pay its debts as they fall due (e.g. due to a reduction in the income of the company or a failure to roll over short-term debt), or if the value of the company's assets decreases to the extent that it becomes lower than the company's liabilities.[31] Unlike most other large companies, banks rely heavily on debt capital, as their core business activity is to incur debt by accepting deposits and

---

28 An empirical study on banks found evidence that opacity causes contagion by exacerbating the cycles of bubbles and crashes. In other words, more opaque banks benefit in times of euphoria and then suffer in times of crisis. See Jeffrey Jones, Wayne Lee and Timothy Yeager, 'Opaque Banks, Price Discovery, and Financial Instability' (2012) 21 *Journal of Financial Intermediation* 383.

29 For instance, evidence suggests that US immigrants who experienced a bank crisis in their home country are less likely to open a bank account. See Una Okonkwo Osili and Anna Paulson, 'Bank Crises and Investor Confidence: An Empirical Investigation' (2009) Federal Reserve Bank of Chicago Policy Discussion Paper No. PDP2009-9 <http://www.chicagofed.org/webpages/publications/policy_discussion_papers/2009/pdp_9. cfm> (accessed 3 August 2020).

30 If markets were perfect and there were no taxes, agency costs and administrative costs associated with insolvency, the capital structure of a company would not matter for its profitability, as posited by the Modigliani-Miller Theorem which proves that in perfect market conditions, the additional cost of borrowing would fully outweigh any benefits accruing to the shareholders from increased leverage. See Franco Modigliani and Merton Miller, 'The Cost of Capital, Corporation Finance and the Theory of Investment' (1959) 48 *American Economic Review* 261.

31 The two main tests of insolvency, namely, the cash flow test and the balance sheet test, are set out in the Insolvency Act 1986, s 122.

lending the funds out to borrowers. A typical bank is approximately 95% debt financed[32] and only 5% equity financed. This equates to a gearing ratio[33] of 19:1 which is remarkably higher than the gearing ratios of typical non-financial companies, which are considered to be highly geared as soon as the ratio exceeds the level of 1:1. The reason why banks are far more highly leveraged than other companies is that, in general, their profitability rises as their equity-to-assets ratio falls.[34]

1.5 The classification of banks and the business of banks

The banking system comprises the network of institutions responsible for providing banking services: general public banks (multi-branched 'high street' banks or merchant banks specialising in financing capital market transactions or foreign trade), such as universal banks and specialist institutions dealing with particular types of banking business; higher-level institutions (not involved in direct contact with the general public) such as central banks (i.e. bankers and government bank responsible for monetary policy and macroeconomic management of the monetary system); and supervisory authorities that oversee other banks and check their probity, liquidity and solvency.[35] Banks are crucial for the functioning of market economies. However, there is no generally accepted definition of a banking system: the concept relates to the legal rules concerning to banks, finances and financiers (i.e. the rules relating to the process of raising or providing funds or capital or granting credit to another person). Banking system is therefore a broad concept that may include the legal framework applicable to investors, depositors or lenders, financial intermediaries, borrowers and issuers, financial instruments, transactions and contracts, markets and exchanges, and even public authorities overseeing that process.[36]

1.5.1 The banking system, business of banks and legal definition of banks

To understand the business of banks, it is pertinent to examine the conventional distinction between retail/commercial banking, on the one hand, and investment/merchant banking, on the other. The traditional business of retail/commercial banking involves accepting deposits and lending money from/to individuals and firms, as well as providing means of payment. Meanwhile, the business of investment/merchant banking consists of trading in various securities, either on behalf of the bank's clients (portfolio management) or on the banks' own behalf (proprietary trading); underwriting issues of securities by companies; and advising companies on their capital structure, mergers and acquisitions, and other financial matters. In this context, the German model of 'universal banking' has spread around the world and

---

32 See Jonathan Macey and Maureen O'Hara, 'The Corporate Governance of Banks' (2003) 9 *Federal Reserve Bank of New York Economic Policy Review* 91, 92.

33 The gearing ratio of a company is equal to the ratio of its total liabilities to its total equity. It must be kept in mind that in accounting terms equity = assets – liabilities. So, a company where assets = 100 and liabilities = 95 has equity = 5 and a gearing ratio of 95:5, which can be arithmetically simplified to 19:1. A company where assets = 100 and liabilities = 50 has equity = 50 and a gearing ratio of 50:50, which can be simplified as 1:1.

34 An economic explanation of the reason why banks are so highly leveraged can be found in Harry DeAngelo and Rene M. Stulz, 'Liquid-Claim Production, Risk Management, and Bank Capital Structure: Why High Leverage Is Optimal for Banks' (2013) Fisher College of Business Working Paper 2013-03-08 <http://papers.ssrn.com/sol3/papers.cfm?abstract_id=2254998> (accessed 18 July 2020).

35 For a general overview see Kern Alexander, *Principles of Banking Regulation* (CUP 2019) 28.

36 Roy C. Smith, Ingo Walter and Gayle DeLong, *Global Banking* (OUP 2012) 27–28.

influenced the development of national banking systems in Europe and elsewhere.[37] A 'universal bank' is a bank that accepts deposits and lends money, but it also carries out a large range of financial activities, including investment services, property services and insurance services.[38] Thus, a universal bank combines retail and investment banking activities. A further line of banking business is what is known as 'private banking' which consists of retail banking, wealth management and other financial services provided to high-net-worth individuals.

Most financial institutions that accept deposits and grant loans are 'banks' for the purposes of law and regulation. For specific legal purposes (e.g. taxation, or the rights of the customer or financial regulation), a certain financial institution may be considered a 'bank' in some legal context and a 'non-bank' in another legal context.[39] What constitutes a 'bank' is defined differently at common law, in statutory legislation and for the purposes of international or European law. In *United Dominion Trust*, Lord Denning stated that a bank is '[a]n establishment for the custody of money received from, or on behalf of, its customers. Its essential duty is to pay their drafts on it: its profits arise from the use of money left unemployed by them'.[40] EU law uses the term 'credit institution' which is defined as 'an undertaking whose business is to receive deposits or other repayable funds from the public and to grant credits for its own account'.[41]

The activity of banking includes the provision of payments facilities, credit and capital to individuals, firms and the government. Customers have trust in the banking system, and they trust that state-sponsored networks and legal relationships add value to that promise. Customers know that the bank will pay if asked, or, otherwise, the operation of the law and the intervention of other institutions such as the central bank and supervisory authorities will result in the swift satisfaction of the debt. It is their trust in legal and political institutions that induces individuals to place their money in the bank in return for a mere promise to be repaid later.[42]

A firm wishing to raise funds has two options: go to a bank and get a loan, or go to the capital markets and receive funds from potential investors in exchange of equity or debt securities. An increase in the share of capital markets is followed by a decline in the share of bank lending. A new issue of securities to the public is a lost opportunity for a bank loan to the firm. This competitive relationship between banks and capital markets jointly with the ongoing decline of bank lending has prompted banks to explore other business opportunities and steadily engage in fee-generating activities in capital markets. The role of banks in capital markets has become increasingly important as banks more and more broaden their securities and capital markets activities.[43]

---

37 Theodor Baums and Michael Gruson, 'The German Banking System—System of the Future?' (1993) 19 *Brooklyn Journal of International Law* 101–102.

38 See among other the seminal work of George J. Benston, 'Universal Banking' (1994) 8 *Journal of Economic Perspectives* 124–125.

39 E. Peter Ellinger, Eva Lomnicka and C.V.M. Hare, *Ellinger's Modern Banking Law* (5th edn, OUP 2011) 79–80.

40 *United Dominions Trust Ltd v Kirkwood* [1966] 2 Q.B. 431.

41 According to the First EU Banking Directive (77/780/EEC). The UK Banking Act 1987, the Financial Services Act 1986 and the Consumer Credit Act 1974 regulated the deposit-taking business of credit institutions. In the US, the Dodd-Frank Act 2010 repealed the whole banking statutory laws set in the Banking Act 1933 and Gramm-Leach-Bliley Act 1999.

42 Pauline W.J. van Esterik-Plasmeijer and W. Fred van Raaij, 'Banking System Trust, Bank Trust, and Bank Loyalty' (2017) 35 *International Journal of Bank Marketing*, 99–100.

43 Howard Davies and David Green, *Banking on the Future. The Fall and Rise of Central Banking* (Princeton University Press 2010) 52–53.

The general classification of banks involves the distinction between primary and secondary markets. Banks in primary markets are permitted to underwrite security issues either directly or through subsidiaries (if this is not permitted, underwriters will often turn to banks for credit in order to finance their activities). In secondary markets, a commercial bank may simply apply for a regulatory license to provide broker-dealer services to its clients, purchasing financial instruments on the customers' behalf. Investment bankers and brokers will, on occasion, need to accumulate large amounts of stock in order to satisfy a block purchase and high customer demand, for which they may need short-term credit from a commercial bank in the inter-bank market. Dealers demand credit in order to finance their proprietary positions and to facilitate the buying and selling required of them in their role as market makers. Most financial institutions involved in capital markets normally need access to bank lines of credit to manage settlement delays or failures.

1.5.2 Co-operative banks, building societies and virtual banks

In this context, it is worth mentioning the role of mutual banks or co-operative banks. In the UK, the Co-operative Bank founded in 1872 (called "Loan and Deposit Department of the Cooperative Wholesale Society") was a company controlled by the Co-operative Banking Group (known as "Co-operative Financial Services") part of a financial conglomerate which provided insurance services and pension funds.[44] The Co-operative Bank experienced a turmoil after the merger with Britannia Building Society in 2009, a transaction that caused huge losses and led to the recapitalisation of the institution.[45] Co-operative banks include credit unions and building societies. Credit unions are regulated by the Credit Unions Act 1979 Chapter 34, as amended by the Legislative Reform (Industrial and Provident Societies and Credit Unions) Order 2011 (UK), SI 2011/2687, which define the main aim of these banks in 'the promotion of thrift among the members of the society by the accumulation of their savings'. Building societies are regulated by the Building Societies Act 1986 Chapter 53 (BSA), as amended by the Financial Services Act 2012 (Mutual Societies) Order 2013 (SI 2013/496). Article 5, paragraph 1 of the BSA 1986 provides that main objective of the building societies 'is that of raising, primarily by the subscriptions of the members, a stock or fund for making to them advances secured on land for their residential use'. Specifically, the building societies are mutual financial institution and take part of the Building Societies Commission.[46] The Co-operative and Community Benefit Societies Act 2014 regulates the whole sector: this statute has reordered the co-operative banks as a type of banks.[47]

Among credit institutions particular attention is dedicated to central banks which are primarily concerned with three main and interconnected aspects of stability: (1) domestic

---

44 First models of co-operative bank are Friend of Labour Loan Societies, Funding Clubs, Slate Clubs, Self-help Societies, Co-operative People's Bank, Community Cooperatives and Cooperative Workshops. For an overview, see H.W. Wolff, *Co-operative Banking. Its Principles and Practice* (BiblioBazaar, LLC 2008) 8–9.

45 Sir Christopher Kelly, 'Failings in Management and Governance. Report of the Independent Review into the Events Leading to the Co-operative Bank's Capital Shortfall' (30 April 2014) 2–3 <https://robllewellyn.com/wp-content/uploads/2017/02/kelly-review.pdf> (accessed 28 July 2020).

46 In doctrine, see Lorraine E. Talbot, 'Keeping Bad Company: Building Societies—A Case Study' (2009) 60 *Northern Ireland Legal Quarterly* 444–445.

47 See Co-operative and Community Benefit Societies Act 2014 Chapter 14 <https://www.legislation.gov.uk/ukpga/2014/14/contents> (accessed 29 July 2020).

price stability; (2) external stability of the value of the currency; and (3) overall systemic stability in the financial system.[48] Central banks are typically established by law or statute, but beyond this initial act which gives them legitimacy and generally sets out the goals, functions and governance in generic terms, there is little detailed law governing their operational aspects.[49] The provision of lending facilities to the government has been a traditional rationale for the establishment of central banks.[50] The main rationale for central banking is the twin mandate of monetary stability and financial stability.[51] The privilege of issuing money is considered the first rationale of a central bank, a task generally associated with financing the government, particularly in war times.[52] It is also this privilege that lets it act as 'lender of last resort': this is an instrument of banking supervision in a 'crisis-situation' stage.[53] As part of its micro-prudential functions, the central bank via the lender of last resort provides assistance to a bank suffering from a liquidity crisis.

Most recently, financial technologies have spread the use of virtual platforms to negotiate banking services: digital devices, cloud computing and automation characterise the commercial business of banks. The traditional channels of banking services have mutated into an electronic system of payments. Virtual banks represent the new frontiers of lending and money deposits: e-banking refers to any activity carried out by using electronic devices and digital services provided through pre-loaded computer programs.[54] Internet banking refers to the provision of any banking services placed online, while e-money consists of stored value on prepaid payment devices that allow payment to be made.[55] E-trading refers to the conduct of market making (as principal) or brokerage (as agent) dealing in securities using electronic devices. The new technologies have determined a revolution in the banking industry that makes financial services more efficient and profitable, reinforcing investment options and ensuring credit access. As Lord Hodge noted 'banks are using AI and machine-learning to maximise profits from scarce capital, to improve their models for risk-management and stress-testing, and to carry out market impact analysis, by creating so-called "trading robots" which evaluate the impact of the business's own trading on the market in which it operates'.[56]

48 Rosa M. Lastra, *International Financial and Monetary Law* (2nd edn, OUP 2015) 31–33.
49 Patricia S. Pollard, 'A Look Inside Two Central Banks: The ECB and the Federal Reserve' *Federal Reserve Bank of St Louis* (January–February 2003) <https://research.stlouisfed.org/publications/review/03/01/Pollard.pdf> (accessed 8 July 2020).
50 Milton Friedman, 'The Role of Monetary Policy' (1968) 58 *American Economic Review* 2–3.
51 Monetary policy refers to the actions taken by the monetary authorities to affect the supply and cost of money and credit. A legal definition is generally absent in central bank statutes.
52 Marvin Goodfriend and Robert G. King, 'Financial Deregulation, Monetary Policy and Central Banking' (1988) 74 *Economic Review Federal Reserve Bank of Richmond* 5–6. See also Charles Goodhart, *The Evolution of Central Banks* (MIT Press 1988).
53 Glenn Hoggard, Patricia Jackson and Erlend Neir, 'Banking Crises and the Design of Safety Nets' (2005) 29(1) *Journal of Banking and Finance* 143–144.
54 Anita K. Pennathur, '"Clicks and Bricks": e-Risk Management for Banks in the Age of the Internet' (2001) 25 *Journal of Banking and Finance* 2013–2014.
55 Electronic money (e-money) is defined as an electronic store of monetary value on a technical device that may be widely used for making payments to entities other than the e-money issuer. The device acts as a prepaid bearer instrument which does not necessarily involve bank accounts in transactions.
56 Lord Hodge, 'The Potential and Perils of Financial Technology: Can the Law Adapt to Cope?' (The First Edinburgh FinTech Law Lecture, University of Edinburgh, 14 March 2019) <https://www.supremecourt.uk/docs/speech-190314.pdf> (accessed 27 July 2020).

1.6 The rationales for regulating banks

Financial regulation comprises the legislative, regulatory and soft-law rules, and principles that apply to financial institutions and their senior managers.[57] In this sense, the regulatory framework includes both the applicable rules and principles and the process of supervision. It is conventional to distinguish between prudential regulation, on the one hand, and conduct of business regulation, on the other.[58] The former has two interconnected objectives, namely to protect the stability of the financial system as a whole (macro-prudential regulation) and to safeguard the safety and soundness of each financial institution (micro-prudential regulation).[59] Conduct of business regulation encompasses consumer protection, market integrity, maintaining market confidence, and reducing financial crime. The need to protect the consumers of financial products arises due to information asymmetry between banks and consumers and the weaker negotiating position in which consumers are placed. In that sense, its rationale is not fundamentally different from the general rationale for consumer protection and market regulation. Chapter 8 provides a detailed discussion and critique of the policy rationales for conduct of business regulation in the financial services context.[60]

1.7 Banks and financial markets

It is generally considered that the banking sector and capital markets require transparency, fairness, equal access, competition and financial soundness. The banking collapses such as Lehman Brothers and Northern Rock showed that the financial industry had underestimated the value and importance of investor protection (e.g. money market fund).[61] For instance, in the LIBOR scandal, information disclosure pre-crisis was extensive and it was the market's failure to interpret that information properly that led to mispricing.[62]

Rapid changes affecting the regulatory structure of banking sector in the aftermath of 2007–2009 global crisis and Brexit vote (as discussed at length in Chapter 17) have revealed an important question, namely, how far are we from ensuring market activity is conducted safely and legally.[63] On the one hand, the UK system has responded with a series of measures reflecting a principles-based approach and tending to consider investor protection as the cornerstone of future regulatory developments. On the other hand, the Continental system has sought to protect consumers through a series of directives that have introduced a form of mixed regulation (rules-based regime with the MiFID (Markets in Financial Instruments

---

57 For a general discussion of banking regulation and supervision globally, see James Barth, Gerard Caprio Jr. and Ross Levine, *Rethinking Bank Regulation: Till Angels Govern* (CUP 2006).

58 David Llewellyn, 'The Economic Rationale for Financial Regulation' (FSA Occasional Paper Series 1, April 1999) 10 <https://www.researchgate.net/publication/247849804_The_Economic_Rationale_for_Financial_Regulation> (accessed 10 July 2020).

59 See Markus Brunnermeier et al., *The Fundamental Principles of Financial Regulation: Geneva Reports on the World Economy 11* (Center for Economic Policy Research 2009) Chapter 3.

60 For a discussion of the economic rationales for financial regulation, see Llewellyn (above n 58). A brief discussion on why banks should be regulated can be found in Kenneth Spong, *Banking Regulation: Its Purposes, Implementation and Effects* (5th edn, Federal Reserve Bank of Kansas City Publications 2000) 5–13.

61 Robert Schiller, *The Subprime Solution* (Princeton University Press 2008) 87–88.

62 Gregg Fields, 'Common Cause: Institutional Corruption's Role in the Libor and the 4pm Fix Scandals' (2014) 8 *Law and Financial Markets Review* 9–10.

63 Barnabas Reynolds and Thomas Donegan, 'Brexit—Opportunity for a Reboot of Financial Regulation' (2016) 31 *Journal of International Banking Law and Regulation* 613.

Directive) II and a mixed system of principles and rules with the Banking Union). The principles-based approach is implemented by a mechanism of voluntary provisions as firms and market participants have a responsibility to act in the interest of market growth and success, with a clear division of accountability and roles. As Sants observed, 'a principles-based approach does not work with individuals who have no principles'.[64]

The main challenge is moving from regulation based only on observable facts to regulation based on judgements about the future.[65] As Paulson pointed out, 'a new regulatory architecture accountable to investors, with flexibility to adapt to changing markets and clarity of responsibility to interact with international counterparts to forge a seamless global market infrastructure, would inspire the confidence for the financial system to create prosperity in all sectors once again'.[66] Particular attention should be paid to the information gap to which business transactions are generally subject. The imbalanced relationship between managers and investors is principally determined by lack of financial knowledge and causes a distortion of consumers' choices at the time when the investment is executed.[67] Indeed, the global financial crisis showed that customers were too trusting of banks with little understanding of the risks of commercial transactions. Market credibility can be measured in terms of intermediaries' accountability, not only from the point of view of the suitability of market actors, but also of effective enforcement. In this context, the role of internal controls, such as the function of internal audit and audit committees, represents the best expression for the adoption of forms of self-regulation in terms of detailed duties and improved reputations.

What has been achieved ensues from the Banking Union[68] and the numerous financial directives that the EU Institutions have adopted with a view to reforming the banking and securities sectors.[69] It appears that the perceived need for better regulation and consumer protection has driven the EU's strategy, also under the influence of the real integration of the markets. Particularly, evidence of a desire to remove the existing national barriers as between Member States has marked certain directives, for example, the MiFID Directive.[70] This assumption can be measured by the growing need for harmonised securities regulation, a common set of rules at the international level have definitively replaced the former local rules and administrative burdens (costs of cross-border financial activities, such as permissions, licenses and authorities' approvals). The effective consequence is the adoption of shared rules and forms of soft law,[71] the current activity of the financial markets has

---

64 Peter Thal Larsen and Jennifer Hughes, 'Sants Signals More Muscular Regulatory Era' *Financial Times* (12 March 2009) 19.

65 A simple principle must be accompanied by a strong judgement of the facts in short, moving to an outcomes-based regime is considered the most appropriate way of resolving the recent regulatory failures.

66 Henry Paulson, 'Reform the Architecture of Regulation' *Financial Times* (18 March 2009) 13.

67 Alessio M. Pacces, 'Financial Intermediation in the Securities Markets Law and Economics of Conduct of Business Regulation' (2000) 20 *International Review of Law and Economics* 499.

68 Communication from the Commission to the European Parliament and the Council. A Roadmap towards a Banking Union COM (2012) 510 final.

69 Directive 2014/59/EU establishing a framework for the recovery and resolution of credit institutions and investment firms.

70 The fifth recital in the preamble to MiFID states that 'it is necessary to establish a comprehensive regulatory regime governing the execution of transactions in financial instruments irrespective of the trading methods used to conclude those transactions so as to ensure a high quality of execution of investor transactions and to uphold the integrity and overall efficiency of the financial system'.

71 Soft law signifies a form of non-binding rules constituted by legal opinions, statements, guides, protocols and commentaries. These forms have no legal force but can influence the Courts and market participants.

permitted the development of new methods of regulation, such as the principles-based regime and the outcomes-based regime.[72] These new forms of regulation have been reflected in a self-regulation regime[73] characterised by internal controls, best practices, compliance and 'treat customers fairly' programmes.[74]

At first glance, the complexities of the regulatory system result in fragmentation and a substantive confusion of accountability; indeed, the principles adopted to regulate the markets do not seem to operate in a clear manner. In the last few decades, rule-making (specifically normative activity) has been considered too slow to keep up with innovation in the sphere of financial instruments (as in the case of derivatives) and has been relegated to the same level as principles, with the inevitable confusion of their respective roles.[75] The former UK Financial Services Authority (today Financial Conduct Authority) put greater stress on the use of principles-based regulation, while affirming that this kind of approach 'means moving away from dictating through detailed prescriptive rules and supervisory actions how firms should operate their business'.[76] In addition, technological innovation and the transformation of the financial markets have brought about huge changes in terms of regulation, particularly in comparison between the EU and the UK strategies. On the one hand, the EU approach has laid the foundation for a new way of dealing with the securities sector, which is characterised by consumer protection and an investor-disclosure system. On the other, the UK approach has adopted the outcomes-based regime governed, not only by rules but also by principles. In the post-crisis regime, there is an increased emphasis on the use of rules and judgement but without abandoning principles-based regulation and meta-regulation.[77] Adopting principles-based regulation does not mean jettisoning the rules. It gives legislatures the power to set high-level regulatory goals and outcomes, and leaves the articulation of processes and details to front-line regulators in collaboration with the industry itself.

Glossary of terms

- Bank: Firm that engages in the business of accepting deposits from the public, operating payment systems and giving out loans; banks may also engage in capital markets business, investment advice, insurance and other financial business.
- Credit institution: The term used for a bank in EU legislation; the key feature of a credit institution is the deposit-taking function.
- Financial institution: Term that encompasses banks and other financial firms such as investment firms.
- Retail banking: The core banking activity of accepting deposits, operating payment systems and giving out loans also referred to as commercial banking. In the UK, large retail banks are also referred to as high street banks.

---

72 The Economist, 'Bolting the Stable Door' (21 March 2009) 35.
73 Julia Black, 'Decentring Regulation: Understanding the Role of Regulation and Self-Regulation in a "Post-Regulatory" World' (2001) 54 *Current Legal Problems* 112–113.
74 FSA, 'Treating Customers Fairly: Towards Fair Outcomes for Consumers' (July 2006).
75 Erik F. Gerding, 'Code, Crash, and Open Source: The Outsourcing of Financial Regulation to Risk Models and the Global Financial Crisis' (2009) 84 *Washington Law Review* 132–133.
76 FSA, 'Principles Based Regulation: Focusing on the Outcomes that Matter' (April 2007).
77 Andromachi Georgosouli, 'The FSA-PRA Coordination Scheme and the Challenge of Policy Coherence' (2013) 8 *Capital Markets Law Journal* 62–63.

- Investment banking: Banking activities in the capital markets including advising corporations that seek to raise capital or engage in mergers and acquisitions, acting as sponsor and/or underwriter when a corporation issues equity or debt securities to the market, and trading in securities either on behalf of customers or on the bank's own behalf.
- Co-operative bank: Bank that is not legally organised as a corporation and hence has no shareholders but rather is a social enterprise organised democratically as an association of persons; it may be part of a broader co-operative organisation.
- Building society: Type of co-operative bank owned by its members which engages in savings accounts and residential mortgage lending; members typically include those with savings and those with a mortgage from the society.
- Virtual bank: Bank that has no physical presence such as branches but rather transacts the entirety of its business online and by phone.

Practice questions

Although the role of banks has changed in recent decades, with much greater emphasis on capital markets activities, banks still play a pivotal economic role as financial intermediaries, which explains the importance of a comprehensive and effective regulatory regime. Critically discuss.

You may also find it useful to review the chapter through the following questions:

- Briefly explain the development of the UK banking sector from the late 17th century until the global financial crisis.
- What are the key economic functions performed by banks?
- In what ways are banks different from other large corporations?
- What is a bank according to English law and a credit institution according to EU law?
- What are the main different types of banks, and why do such distinctions matter?
- What are the main rationales for regulating banks?
- Explain the difference between prudential regulation and conduct of business regulation.

2 Systemic risk and systemic stability in the prudential banking framework

2.1 Introduction

This chapter examines the regulatory and institutional issues relating to the management of systemic risk in the UK and the EU, and the concept of macro-prudential supervision in financial markets. It defines accordingly the concept of systemic risk in the financial system. It then outlines the rationale for prudential supervision taking into account the experience of the 2007–2009 global financial crisis and considers the specificity of the UK and EU banking sectors to that regard. It also addresses the dichotomy between micro-and macro-prudential supervisions, and the instruments that are commonly used to monitor credit institutions. The following two chapters will explore regulatory architecture in the UK and the EU, respectively.

2.2 Systemic risk and the prudential regulation of banks

The 2007–2009 global crisis showed that the central problem for financial regulation is to manage and mitigate systemic risk. As seen in Chapter 1, systemic risk can be defined as the risk that the failure of one significant financial institution can cause, or significantly contribute to, the failure of other significant financial institutions as a result of their linkages to each other.[1] However, understanding the notion of systemic risk is not straightforward.

At the EU level, the 'Lamfalussy Report' defined systemic risk as 'the risk that the illiquidity or failure of one institution, and its resulting inability to meet its obligations when due, will lead to the illiquidity or failure of other institutions'.[2] But systemic risk also related to 'the relative propensity of payment and settlement systems to transmit exposures suddenly or unexpectedly from one participant to another—and from one market to other markets—in ways that increase the difficulty all participants will have in managing and containing their exposures'.[3] Article 2 of the Regulation No 1092/2010 defines systemic risk as, 'a risk of disruption in the financial system with the potential to have serious negative consequences for the internal market and the real economy. All types of financial

---

1 Hal S. Scott, 'The Reduction of Systemic Risk in the United States Financial System' (2010) 33 *Harvard Journal of Law and Public Policy* 673. The author implies that 'the threat of systemic risk (whether real or imagined) results in both the need for government bailouts at taxpayer expense and in an increase in moral hazard'. See also Ian Ayres and Joshua Mitts, 'Anti-herding Regulation' Yale Law & Economics Research Paper No. 490 <http://ssrn.com/abstract=2399240> (accessed 22 March 2020).
2 Bank for International Settlements, Report of the Committee on Interbank Netting Schemes of the Central Banks of the Group of Ten Countries (Lamfalussy Report) (Basel, November 1990) 6–7.
3 Ibid., 7.

intermediaries, markets and infrastructure may be potentially systemically important to some degree'.[4] Systemic risk looms large in the regulation of banking and financial institutions; in particular, it can derive from the inter-bank linkages and from the linkages between banks through the payment system.[5]

In 2001, the report 'Core Principles for Systemically Important Payment Systems' defined systemic risk as 'the risk that the inability of one of the participants to meet its obligations, or a disruption in the system itself, could result in the inability of other system participants or of financial institutions in other parts of the financial system to meet their obligations as they become due'.[6] As a result, systemic risk can arise because of the public perception that other banks are in the same position as the suspect or failed bank: the default by one institution can spread to undermine other institutions. Systemic risk oversight looks at the risks to the overall financial system and the interactions between institutions and markets. Such oversight has the potential to broaden the regulatory view from the traditional 'micro-prudential' supervision focus on individual institutions to a broader 'macro-prudential' supervision focus on the financial system and on the potential for contagion in the financial system.

As mentioned, systemic risk refers to the risk or probability of breakdown of the entire financial system, as opposed to breakdowns in individual parts or components.[7] But a widely accepted definition is still missing. Eatwell and Taylor argued that 'systemic risk is created by individual financial institutions and the aggregate amount of risk created by all financial institutions in global financial markets'.[8] All classes of financial intermediaries, markets and infrastructures can be systematically important in some level. Any risk (not only credit risk, but also liquidity risk, interest rate risk, exchange rate risk, etc.) can grow into systemic proportions when its negative impact extends beyond an individual institution, affecting or threatening to affect by contagion other institutions (externalities), often creating a disruption in the monetary or financial system and which depending on the severity of the downturn will then mutate into economic paralysis. Systemic risks seldom occur alone; they usually spread to other risks, causing a cascade of defaults that can trigger systemic instability.

Successful financial regulation, particularly in the attempted management of systemic risk, should be based on a coherent understanding of the relationship between microeconomic risk, macroeconomic contagion and macroeconomic consequences. However, it has been observed that 'systemic risk should not be monitored solely by existing prudential regulators. A sounder approach to regulating current financial markets is to ensure that the securities regulatory mandate can and does cover all aspects of capital market activity'.[9]

The ability of the banking system to withstand unforeseen shocks is recognised by central banks as the key indicator of financial stability. In negative terms, financial stability is the

---

4 Article 2 of the Regulation (EU) No. 1092/2010 of the European Parliament and of the Council of 24 November 2010 on European Union macro-prudential oversight of the financial system and establishing a European Systemic Risk Board.

5 Daniel Tarullo, 'Regulating Systemic Risk' (Speech at '2011 Credit Markets Symposium', Charlotte, NC, 31 March 2011).

6 Bank for International Settlements, Committee on Payment and Settlement Systems, 'Core Principles for Systemically Important Payment Systems' (January 2001) 5.

7 Steven L. Schwarcz, 'Systemic Risk' (2008) 97 *Georgetown Law Journal* 198.

8 John Eatwell and Lance Taylor, *Global Finance at Risk: The Case for International Regulation* (New York Policy Press 2000) 15.

9 Anita A. Anand, 'Is Systemic Risk Relevant to Securities Regulation?' (2010) 60 *University of Toronto Law Journal* 980.

absence of crisis. In positive terms, the achievement of this objective encompasses a variety of elements such as good supervisory techniques, adequate capital and liquidity, competent and honest management, internal controls, early warning systems, effective regulation, transparency, accountability and an efficient payment system. What makes a crisis of a systemic nature is not so much the trigger event (*causa proxima*) but the transmission mechanisms, domestically and internationally. If the linkages are strong, the potential for systemic instability increases. If the connections are weak, there is less of a threat of systemic risk: no chain is stronger than its weakest link. The transmission mechanisms can be classified into at least four categories: (1) the inter-bank, inter-institution, inter-instrument channel; (2) the payment systems channel; (3) the information channel; and (4) the psychological channel.

The loss of confidence in an institution or market (whether informed or uninformed, rational or irrational) will undermine the functioning of that institution or market. Interestingly, the resolution of a crisis also presents a psychological component: the mere belief that the problem has been solved will bring investors back to the market. It is not so much the ability to lend but the willingness to do so that really counts in the resolution of a financial crisis. Financial stability aims to prevent financial turbulences and reduce the severe risks of financial problems which do occur from time to time.[10] It also refers to the safety and soundness of the financial system and to the stability of the payment and settlement systems.[11] In other words, financial stability 'encompasses a variety of elements…such as a good licensing policies, good supervisory techniques, adequate capital and liquidity, competent and honest management, internal controls, early warning systems, transparency, and accountability. It also refers to the smooth operation of the payment systems'.[12]

The bank collapses (Northern Rock, Royal Bank of Scotland, Bear Stearns and Lehman Brothers) revealed a lack of control by the authorities delegated to monitor and prevent the financial risks.[13] As Schwarcz noted, 'once a failure occurs, there may already be economic damage, and it may be difficult to stop the failure from spreading and become systemic'.[14] Consequently, in response to those failures the regulators have made a significant switch from a principles-based regime towards a more intrusive and systemic regulatory approach. Alexander observed that 'systemic risk often occurs because banks have an incentive to under-price financial risk, which can lead to too much of it being created in the financial system'.[15] The institutional challenges involved in creating arrangements at the international, regional and domestic levels represent a radical shift towards the development of systemic regulatory approach.[16] However, international co-operation and co-ordination of policies are necessary

---

10 Douglas W. Arner, *Financial Stability, Economic Growth, and the Role of Law* (CUP 2007) 73. See also Andrew Crockett, 'Why Is Financial Stability a Goal of Public Policy?' in *Maintaining Financial Stability in a Global Economy* (Symposium sponsored by the Federal Reserve Bank of Kansas City Jackson Hole, WY 28–30 August 1997) 9.

11 Rosa M. Lastra, *Legal Foundations of International Monetary Stability* (OUP 2006) 92 and 302.

12 Ibid., 93.

13 Marc Labonte, 'Systemically Important or "Too Big to Fail" Financial Institutions' Congressional Research Service Report (19 September 2014) 34–36 <https://www.fas.org/sgp/crs/misc/R42150.pdf> (accessed 10 July 2020).

14 Steven L. Schwarcz, 'Keynote Address: Ex Ante versus Ex Post Approaches to Financial Regulation' (2011) 15 *Chapman Law Review* 258.

15 Kern Alexander, Rahul Dhumale and John Eatwell, 'Managing Systemic Risk. The Rationale for International Financial Regulation' in Kern Alexander, Rahul Dhumale and John Eatwell (eds), *Global Governance of Financial Systems. The International Regulation of Systemic Risk* (OUP 2005) 15.

16 See Article 70 ('Transmission of information to central banks, monetary authorities, payment systems overseers and the European Systemic Risk Board') of the Directive 2014/51/EU of the European Parliament and of

for realising effective domestic and regional institutional frameworks for macro-prudential policy. In this context, the deregulation and liberalisation of domestic financial markets, combined with advances in technology, have resulted in a substantial increase in cross-border trade in financial services and portfolio capital flows.[17] Consequently, the changing structure of global financial markets not only has created more opportunities for profits but also has introduced a higher level of risk in financial transactions that may impact systemic stability.

The effective regulation of systemic risk in global financial markets requires a multilateral framework treaty that sets broad standards of good regulatory practice, which States will be generally obliged to observe. In this regard, it has been proposed to replace the notion of 'systemically important institution' with that of 'systemically important platform'.[18] Such platforms would only be directly accessible to a group of 'officially recognized financial institutions' that would have to comply with special regulatory requirements and would be directly supervised by the central bank. The status of 'officially recognized financial institution' could be revoked by the central bank if these special regulatory requirements are not satisfied. On this view, traditional prudential regulation is targeted at financial firms: it plays an important role to enhance the soundness of the financial system by inducing financial institutions (banking and non-banking institutions) to act prudently.[19] The regulation and supervision of systemic risk would instead be targeted at infrastructures. Prudential regulation relates to three distinct types of service providers: (1) systemic infrastructure such as central counterparties and payment and settlement systems; (2) prudentially significant firms such as deposit takers and insurers; and (3) other financial service providers such as most investment firms, insurance brokers and fund managers.

In the banking sector, prudential regulation protects the consumers of banking products but also increases moral hazard on the financial condition of the firms. The rationale for regulating the banking industry is to diminish efficiently the banker's ability (or that of their intermediaries) to distort their promises at the moment of selling their products and to default on their duties (by insolvency or deficient sinister compensation).[20] In this regard, the banking function of safety nets and moral hazard are relevant issues: ill-designed safety nets can be a significant cause of financial instability if they fail adequately to counteract the loss of market discipline that they induce (the 'moral hazard' problem).[21] A macro-prudential orientation in financial stability policies requires safety nets whose structure and functioning address systemic risk.

---

the Council of 16 April 2014 amending Directives 2003/71/EC and 2009/138/EC and Regulations (EC) No. 1060/2009, (EU) No. 1094/2010 and (EU) No. 1095/2010 in respect of the powers of the European Supervisory Authority (European Insurance and Occupational Pensions Authority) and the European Supervisory Authority (European Securities and Markets Authority).

17 Kern Alexander, 'Bank Capital Management and Macro-Prudential Regulation – A Law and Finance Perspective' (2012) 24 *Journal of Banking Law* 331.

18 Jean-Charles Rochet, 'Systemic Risk: Changing the Regulatory Perspective' (2010) 6 *International Journal of Central Banking* 273.

19 See Isaac Ofoeda, Joshua Abor and Charles K.D. Adjasi, 'Non-bank Financial Institutions Regulation and Risk-Taking' (2012) 20 *Journal of Financial Regulation & Compliance* 435–436.

20 Fernando Castagnolo and Gustavo Ferro, 'Could We Rely on Market Discipline as a Substitute for Insurance Regulation? (2013) 21 *Journal of Financial Regulation & Compliance* 5–6. The authors observe that 'the regulation of the insurance market is based on the existence of market failures which affect the social welfare maximization otherwise achieved under perfect competition'.

21 John Breckenridge, James Farquharson and Ruth Hendon, 'The Role of Business Model Analysis in the Supervision of Insurers' (2014) 54 *Bank of England Quarterly Bulletin* 49–50.

Prudential regulation may act as a system of implicit banking conditions: (1) financial requirements, especially when risk-related, limits on range of banking activities; (2) prompt declaration of insolvency; (3) imposition of costs on depositors by way of reduced coverage and coinsurance element (this, however, preserves the incentive to run on the bank); and (4) imposition of *ex post* direct costs on owners. It can be observed that the changing structure of global financial markets not only has resulted in a substantial increase in cross-border trade in financial services and portfolio capital flows but also has introduced a higher level of risk in financial transactions that may impact on systemic stability.[22] The EU financial system has thus developed a systemic regulatory approach where the role of prudential supervision is to ensure the financial stability of the whole securities sector and the conduct of business supervision.

2.3 Macro-prudential vs micro-prudential regulation

As a result of systemic risk, financial crises have detrimental effects on the real economy. In a typical crisis scenario, bank lending is curtailed as ailing banks seek to reduce their loan portfolios. The resulting credit crunch undermines the ability of firms to raise debt and expand, and can thus cause the economy as a whole to enter into a recession[23] and unemployment to rise.[24] Government spending to prevent the failure of large banks (and thus the collapse of the financial system) and to stimulate the economy leads to increasing public debt with serious long-term economic consequences.[25] Thus, serious negative externalities are generated when a large financial institution fails, and the losses are borne not only by other financial institutions but also by the taxpayers. The consequences of financial crises are so severe that it is highly unlikely that any benefits accruing from profitable risk-taking during the period leading up to a crisis outweigh the cost of a crisis.

Indeed, due to systemic risk and the impact of financial crises on the real economy, the protection of the stability of the financial system becomes a matter of public policy reflecting the nature of financial stability as a public good in the strict sense of the term.[26] That being said, financial stability, although intuitively appealing, is an elusive concept and one that is hard to give a precise definition to or measure.[27] The immediate response of

---

22 Kern Alexander, 'Bank Capital Management and Macro-Prudential Regulation – A Law and Finance Perspective' (2012) 24 *Journal of Banking Law* 331.

23 For instance, in 2009, UK GDP declined by 4% as a result of the 2008 financial crisis.

24 For example, the UK unemployment rate increased dramatically from around 5.3% in 2007 to 8% in 2011. See European Economic Forecast Autumn 2013 (Commission, August 2013) 101 <http://ec.europa.eu/economy_finance/eu/forecasts/2013_autumn_forecast_en.htm> (accessed 1 August 2020).

25 The UK national debt to GDP ratio increased from 43.3% at the end of the 2007–2008 fiscal year to 88.1% at the end of 2012–2013. Ibid.

26 According to economic literature, public good is defined as good or service that is both non-excludable (i.e. no person can be excluded from its use) and non-rivalrous (i.e. use by one individual does not diminish its value for others). Public goods are an example of market failure, as markets tend to under-produce them. See Paul Samuelson, 'The Pure Theory of Public Expenditure' (1954) 36 *Review of Economics and Statistics* 387. For a discussion of financial stability as a 'framework-type' public good, see Mads Andenas and Iris HY Chiu, *The Foundations and Future of Financial Regulation: Governance for Responsibility* (Routledge 2014) 5–6, 8–10 and 18–20. See also David S. Bieri, 'Regulation and Financial Stability in the Age of Turbulence' in Robert W. Kolb (ed), *Lessons from the Global Financial Crisis* (John Wiley & Sons 2010) 327.

27 Davies and Green argue that it is very hard to assess *ex ante* if a given financial system is stable or not, but with the benefit of hindsight one can define instability as loss of normalcy and resilience. See Howard Davies and David Green, *Banking on the Future: The Rise and Fall of Central Banking* (Princeton University Press 2010) Chapter 3.

governments to financial crises tends to be the provision of liquidity support (normally by the central bank)[28] and the setting up of deposit insurance schemes that guarantee bank deposits (up to a limit) to prevent creditors' runs on banks as will be discussed in Chapter 15.[29] These tools of crisis management protect the financial system from immediate collapse, but come at the cost of exacerbating the problem in the long run, as explicit or implicit state support strengthens the incentives of financial institutions' managers and clients to take excessive risks.[30] This problem is known as moral hazard[31] and is due to the expectation of bank shareholders and senior managers that government intervention will rescue ailing institutions or at least prevent the collapse of the financial system, thus mitigating the negative externalities generated by risk-taking. Moral hazard prompts governments to introduce rules that constrain risk-taking by financial institutions, such as rules on minimum capital ratios, rules on liquidity, structural rules separating retail from investment banking activities and rules relating to their corporate governance and senior management accountability. In parallel, to mitigate the risk that public funds will be required if a major bank fails, governments introduce rules that require banks to plan their own resolution and structure their liabilities in a way that there have sufficient loss-absorbing liabilities that can be written down or converted to equity if a bank faces difficulties.

Moreover, it is worth noting that legislative emphasis on financial stability in the UK is relatively recent and has clearly been a response to the 2007–2009 global financial crisis. Indeed, the Banking Act 2009 added to the list of the statutory objectives of the Bank of England a financial stability objective.[32] Similarly, the Financial Services Act 2010 included financial stability to the objectives of the former Financial Services Authority.[33] Furthermore, the Financial Services Act 2012 amended the formulation of the financial stability objective by asserting that the Bank ought to 'protect and enhance the stability of the financial system of the UK' rather than merely to contribute 'to the protection and enhancement' of financial stability, as the previous statutory formulation was.[34]

The macro-prudential objective can be defined as limiting the costs to the economy from financial distress, including those that arise from any moral hazard induced by the policies pursued, whereas the micro-prudential objective can be seen as limiting the likelihood of

---

28 For an analysis of the lender of last resort function of the Bank of England, its history and its recent evolution, see Andrew Campbell and Rosa Lastra, 'Revisiting the Lender of Last Resort – The Role of the Bank of England' in Iain MacNeil and Justin O'Brien (eds), *The Future of Financial Regulation* (Hart Publishing 2010) 161–170.

29 For a critical discussion of the relationship between deposit protection and moral hazard, see Jenny Hamilton, 'Depositor Protection and Co-insurance after Northern Rock: Less a Case of Moral Hazard and More a Case of Consumer Responsibility?' in Johanna Gray and Orkun Akseli (eds), *Financial Regulation in Crisis? The Role of Law and the Failure of Northern Rock* (Edward Elgar 2011) 19–24.

30 For instance, Picciotto argues that the existing regulatory and institutional framework (including limited liability, the lender of last resort function and tax avoidance through offshore vehicles) resulted in ineffective hyper-regulation, regulatory arbitrage, perverse incentives and market distortions. See Sol Picciotto, *Regulating Global Corporate Capitalism* (CUP 2011) 288–290.

31 The concept of moral hazard originated from insurance contracts. Arrow's seminal work on the medical care market explored the effects of moral hazard in that context. See Kenneth Arrow, 'Uncertainty and the Welfare Economics of Medical Care' (1963) 53 *The American Economic Review* 941, 961–962. See also Mark Pauly, 'The Economics of Moral Hazard: Comment' (1968) 58 *The American Economic Review* 531.

32 Banking Act 2009 s 238(1) inserting s 2A to the Bank of England Act 1998.

33 Financial Services Act 2010 s 1(3) inserting s 3A into the Financial Services and Markets Act 2000.

34 Financial Services Act 2012 s 2(2).

failure of individual institutions.[35] The 2011 Report *A New Approach to Financial Regulation: Building a Stronger System* explained that 'macro-prudential policy seeks to augment the existing regulatory framework by focusing on systemic risk. Systemic risk can be broadly defined as risks to the stability of the whole or a large part of the financial sector'.[36] The institutional challenges involved in creating arrangements at the international, regional and domestic levels represent a radical shift towards the development of systemic regulatory approach.[37] However, international co-operation and co-ordination of policies are necessary for realising effective domestic and regional institutional frameworks for macro-prudential policy.[38]

The global financial crisis highlighted the urgency of establishing a clear separation between macro- and micro-prudential regulations as well as macro- and micro-prudential supervisions. According to the House of Lords Report on the Future or EU Supervision and Regulation:

> macro-prudential supervision is the analysis of trends and imbalances in the financial system and the detection of systemic risks that these trends may pose to financial institutions and the economy. The focus of macro-prudential supervision is the safety of the financial and economic system as a whole – the prevention of the materialization of systemic risk. Micro-prudential supervision is the day-to-day supervision of individual financial institutions. The focus of micro-prudential supervision is the safety and soundness of individual institutions and consumer protection.[39]

In general terms, macro-prudential regulation encompasses the oversight of the whole banking sector, while micro-prudential regulation aims to monitor individual firms. Macro-prudential regulation is empowered to target the causes of systemic risk and ensure the integrity, stability of the financial system.[40]

Systemic risk oversight looks at the risks to the overall financial system and the interactions between financial institutions and between markets.[41] Such oversight has the potential

---

35 Andrew Crockett, 'Marrying the Micro- and Macro-prudential Dimensions of Financial Stability' (International Conference of Banking Supervisors, Basel, 21 September 2000) 2.

36 H.M. Treasury, *A New Approach to Financial Regulation: Building a Stronger System* (The Stationery Office 2011).

37 See Article 70 ('Transmission of information to central banks, monetary authorities, payment systems overseers and the European Systemic Risk Board') of the Directive 2014/51/EU of the European Parliament and of the Council of 16 April 2014 amending Directives 2003/71/EC and 2009/138/EC and Regulations (EC) No. 1060/2009, (EU) No. 1094/2010 and (EU) No. 1095/2010 in respect of the powers of the European Supervisory Authority (European Insurance and Occupational Pensions Authority) and the European Supervisory Authority (European Securities and Markets Authority). The Directive 2014/51/EU (so-called 'Omnibus II') has replaced Directive 2009/138/EC (so-called 'Solvency II') by introducing specific rules on 'risk-based capital requirements across all EU Member States'.

38 Stijn Claessens, Swati R. Ghosh and Roxana Mihet, 'Macro-prudential Policies to Mitigate Financial System Vulnerabilities' (2013) 39 *Journal of International Money and Finance* 153–154.

39 House of Lords – European Union Committee – Fourteenth Report 2008–2009, 'The Future of EU Financial Regulation and Supervision' (9 June 2009) <https://publications.parliament.uk/pa/ld200809/ldselect/ldeucom/106/10609.htm> (accessed 29 June 2020).

40 Dimensions of macro-prudential supervision include (1) horizontal – interdependence and connections; (2) vertical – criticality of certain institutions by size or by function; (3) temporal – economic cycle, evolution of business models, bubbles; (4) legal – gaps, overlaps and inconsistencies, pro-cyclicality, crisis; and (5) international – the "external" risk in a global financial world.

41 Viral V. Acharya, 'A Theory of Systemic Risk and Design of Prudential Bank Regulation' (2009) 5 *Journal of Financial Stability* 224–225.

to broaden the regulatory view from the traditional 'micro-prudential' supervision on individual institutions to a broader 'macro-prudential' supervision on the financial system and on the potential for contagion in the banking industry.[42] Successful prudential regulation, particularly in the attempted management of systemic risk, should be based on a coherent understanding of the relationship between microeconomic risk and macroeconomic contagion.[43] In the UK regulatory system, the Financial Conduct Authority (FCA) is entrusted with the responsibility for market conduct to all those who provide to the public financial services (this covers both prudentially significant and all other financial service providers), whereas the Prudential Regulation Authority (PRA) is established and charged with the prudential regulation of the prudentially significant firms.[44] However, it has been observed that 'systemic risk should not be monitored solely by existing prudential regulators. A sounder approach to regulating current financial markets is to ensure that the securities regulatory mandate can and does cover all aspects of capital market activity'.[45]

From an institutional perspective, the exercise of macro-prudential regulation is given either to newly created councils for financial stability, such as the Financial Stability Oversight Council in the US,[46] or to the central bank, such as the Bank of England in the UK, where the Financial Policy Committee is in charge of this task.[47] The Turner Review was published to provide the first, in-depth response to the evident gaps in banking supervision. Its recommendations were based on a macro-prudential approach rather than focusing solely on specific firms.[48] In the EU, the European Systemic Risk Board shares macro-prudential supervisory responsibilities with national authorities, and according to the Banking Union architecture, also with the European Central Bank for those Member States that become part of the Single Supervisory Mechanism (SSM).[49] Ongoing discussions are trying to identify the powers and instruments macro-prudential authorities should have.[50] Given the lack of a commonly accepted theoretical paradigm on the definition of systemic risk, this is not an easy task.[51]

42 Matthias Thiemann, Mohamed Aldegwy and Edin Ibrocevic, 'Understanding the Shift from Micro- to Macro-prudential Thinking: A Discursive Network Analysis' (2018) 42 *Cambridge Journal of Economics* 935–936.

43 Kern Alexander, 'Bank Resolution Regimes: Balancing Prudential Regulation and Shareholder Rights' (2009) 9 *Journal of Corporate Law Studies* 63–64.

44 Simon Debbage and Stephen Dickinson, 'The Rationale for the Prudential Regulation and Supervision of Insurers' (2013) 53 *Bank of England Quarterly Bulletin* 216–217.

45 Anita A. Anand, 'Is Systemic Risk Relevant to Securities Regulation?' (2010) 60 *University of Toronto Law Journal* 980.

46 Edward V. Murphy, 'Financial Stability Oversight Council: A Framework to Mitigate Systemic Risk' Congressional Research Service Report R42083 (21 March 2013) 1–2 and 4–6 <http://fas.org/sgp/crs/misc/R42083.pdf> (accessed 27 July 2020). It is underlined that 'the FSOC is expected to facilitate communication among existing financial regulators intending to identify sources of financial instability that cross agency regulatory jurisdiction, or that reside in gaps in the financial regulatory framework'.

47 H.M. Treasury, 'Remit and Recommendations for the Financial Policy Committee' Letter from the Chancellor, George Osborne to the Governor of the Bank of England Mervyn King (30 April 2013).

48 FSA, 'The Turner Review. A Regulatory Response to the Global Banking Crisis' (March 2009) 2 and 18–20. See also Iain MacNeil, 'The Trajectory of Regulatory Reform in the UK in the Wake of the Financial Crisis' (2010) 11 *European Business Organization Law Review* 487.

49 Valia Babis, 'Single Rule Book for Prudential Regulation of EU Banks: Mission Accomplished?' (2015) 26 *European Business Law Review* 781–782.

50 Pierre Schammo, 'EU Day to Day Supervision or Intervention-Based Supervision: Which Way Forward for the European System of Financial Supervision' (2012) 32 *Oxford Journal of Legal Studies* 771–772.

51 Financial Stability Board, 'Policy Measures to Address Systemically Important Financial Institutions' (4 November 2011) <https://www.fsb.org/2011/11/r_111104bb/> (accessed 25 July 2020).

Prudential regulation plays an important role to enhance the soundness of the financial system by inducing financial institutions (banking and non-banking institutions) to act prudently.[52] Prudential regulation refers to three distinct types of service providers: systemic infrastructures such as central counterparties and payment and settlement systems; prudentially significant firms such as deposit takers and insurers; and other financial service providers such as most investment firms, brokers and fund managers.[53] In the banking sector, prudential regulation protects the consumers of banking products but also increases moral hazard on the financial condition of the firms.[54] The rationale for regulating the banking industry is to diminish efficiently the banker's ability (or that of their intermediaries) to distort their promises at the moment of selling their products and to default on their duties (by insolvency or deficient compensation).[55] On this view, banking function of safety nets and moral hazard are relevant issues; ill-designed safety nets can be a significant cause of financial instability if they fail adequately to counteract the loss of market discipline that they induce (the 'moral hazard' problem).[56] A macro-prudential orientation in financial stability policies requires safety nets whose structure and functioning address systemic risk.

Macro-prudential regulation follows a top-down approach, working out the desirable safety standard for the system as a whole and, from there, deriving that of the individual institutions within it.[57] Macro-prudential regulation focuses on risks to the financial system as a whole, with a view to protecting the real economy from severe disruptions in the provision of financial services. In contrast, micro-prudential supervision focuses on strengthening individual financial institutions with a view to protecting their creditors, particularly depositors and retail investors.[58] Macro-prudential policies are designed to deal with two types of systemic risk: 'resiliency risks' are those that reflect a concentration of risk that can arise at a point in time because the interconnectedness and similar exposures of financial institutions and markets reduce the resiliency of the financial system to shocks and stresses, while 'procyclical risks' are those that cumulate over time and reflect the tendency of the financial system to procyclical behaviour that exacerbates economic booms and busts.[59] By addressing systemic risk, macro-prudential policy endeavours to contribute to financial stability. Indeed, the focus of macro-prudential supervision is the safety of the financial and economic system as a whole; it consists of the analysis of trends and imbalances in the financial system and the detection of systemic risks that these trends may pose to financial institutions and the economy.[60]

52 Isaac Ofoeda, Joshua Abor and Charles K.D. Adjasi, 'Non-bank Financial Institutions Regulation and Risk-Taking' (2012) 20 *Journal of Financial Regulation & Compliance*, 435–436.
53 Benjamin Geva, 'Systemic Risk and Financial Stability: The Evolving Role of the Central Bank' (2013) 28 *Journal of International Banking Law and Regulation* 413.
54 Mathias Dewatripont and Jean Tirole, *The Prudential Regulation of Banks* (MIT Cambridge Press 1994) 13–14.
55 Fernando Castagnolo and Gustavo Ferro, 'Could We Rely on Market Discipline as a Substitute for Insurance Regulation?' (2013) 21 *Journal of Financial Regulation & Compliance* 11, 5–6. The authors observe that 'the regulation of the insurance market is based on the existence of market failures which affect the social welfare maximization otherwise achieved under perfect competition'.
56 John Breckenridge, James Farquharson and Ruth Hendon, 'The Role of Business Model Analysis in the Supervision of Insurers' (2014) 54 *Bank of England Quarterly Bulletin* 49–50.
57 Geva (n 53) 408.
58 Paul Jenkins and Gordon Thiessen, 'Reducing the Potential for Future Financial Crises: A Framework for Macro-Prudential Policy' in Canada Commentary No. 351 (C.D. Howe Institute, May 2012) 2.
59 Steven L. Schwarcz, 'The Functional Regulation of Finance' (Paper presented at 3rd CCLS Roundtable on Financial Regulation: 'Financial Markets: Impossible to Govern?', London, 26–27 June 2014) 38–39.
60 House of Lords, 'The Future of EU Financial Regulation and Supervision' Volume I, London (17 June 2009) 12.

2.4 The enhanced role of macro-prudential supervision

Macro-prudential supervision takes an inductive rather than deductive perspective that follows a top-down approach, working out the desirable safety standard for the system as a whole and, from there, deriving that of the individual institutions within it.[61] Macro-prudential supervision focuses on risks to the financial system as a whole, with a view to protecting the real economy from severe disruptions in the provision of financial services. In contrast, micro-prudential supervision focuses on strengthening individual financial institutions with a view to protecting their creditors particularly depositors and investors.[62] In this regard, macro-prudential supervision is analogous to the oversight of the forest, whereas micro-prudential supervision is analogous to the oversight of individual trees.[63]

As mentioned above, macro-prudential policies are designed to deal with two types of systemic risk, resiliency risk and procyclical risks. The macro-prudential objective can be defined as limiting the costs to the economy from financial distress, including those that arise from any moral hazard induced by the policies pursued, whereas the micro-prudential objective can be seen as limiting the likelihood of failure of individual institutions.[64] The 2011 Report *A New Approach to Financial Regulation: Building a Stronger System* explained that 'macro-prudential policy seeks to augment the existing regulatory framework by focusing on systemic risk. Systemic risk can be broadly defined as risks to the stability of the whole or a large part of the financial sector'.[65]

In the aftermath of the global financial crisis, a consensus has emerged regarding the difference between macro- and micro-prudential supervisions. According to the House of Lords Report on the future of EU supervision and regulation, macro-prudential supervision is the analysis of trends and imbalances in the financial system and the detection of systemic risks that these trends may pose to financial institutions and the economy.[66] The focus of macro-prudential supervision is the safety of the financial and economic system as a whole – the prevention of the materialisation of systemic risk. Micro-prudential supervision is the day-to-day supervision of individual financial institutions. The focus of micro-prudential supervision is the safety and soundness of individual institutions and also depositor protection. The same or a separate supervisor can carry out these two functions. If different supervisors carry out these functions, they must work together to provide mechanisms to counteract macro-prudential risks at a micro-prudential level. On this view, macro-prudential supervision should target the causes of systemic risk.

Prudential supervision plays an active role in regulation of systemically important financial institutions (SIFIs) 'whose disorderly failure, because of their size, complexity and systemic interconnectedness, would cause significant disruption to the wider financial system

---

61 Geva (n 53) 408.

62 Paul Jenkins and Gordon Thiessen, 'Reducing the Potential for Future Financial Crises: A Framework for Macro-Prudential Policy' in Canada Commentary No. 351 (C.D. Howe Institute, May 2012) 2.

63 Rosa M. Lastra, 'Systemic Risk, SIFIs and Financial Stability' (2011) 6 *Capital Markets Law Journal* 198.

64 Andrew Crockett, 'Marrying the Micro- and Macro-prudential Dimensions of Financial Stability' (International Conference of Banking Supervisors, Basel, 21 September 2000) 2.

65 H.M. Treasury, *A New Approach to Financial Regulation: Building a Stronger System* (The Stationery Office 2011).

66 House of Lords, 'The Future of EU Financial Regulation and Supervision' Volume I, London (17 June 2009) 12.

and economic activity'.[67] It also plays a significant role in globally active and systemically important banks (G-SIBs), in particular in the creation of a special recovery and resolution framework for failing credit institutions.[68]

The supervisory framework for G-SIBs is based on three pillars: (1) the identification of those activities that bear the potential of triggering systemic risk in the event of the disorderly failure of the bank; (2) the designation of certain banks with global presence as G-SIBs; and (3) the adoption of policy measures that are geared towards the recovery of the financially distressed G-SIB or – where this is no longer feasible – its orderly resolution. In substance, the main goals of the supervisory regime are ongoing resolvability assessments; identification of recovery and resolution plans; mandatory restructuring; and a soft law framework for co-ordinating measures for the orderly recovery and resolution of G-SIBs. However, the success of this proposed framework depends on policy and legal reform at domestic and regional level, the progress of harmonisation and the willingness of the relevant authorities to share burdens and co-operate at a global level, ideally by legally committing themselves to a forward-looking plan of action.[69]

2.5 Significant banks and G-SIBs

One important lesson from the 2007–2009 global financial crisis was that individual banks can be systemically important, even banks that are not very large or that only engage in investment banking activities. In other terms, the failure or financial distress of these entities can produce negative externalities and spillover effects that can cause disruptions to both the real and the financial economies, across jurisdictions. The case of Lehman Brothers (investment bank with no retail depositors) and Northern Rock (medium-sized deposit taker and mortgage lender) are noteworthy examples.[70]

In 2011, the Financial Stability Board (FSB) issued a set of guidelines to regulate global systemically important financial institutions (G-SIFIs) with the aim to ensure a level playing field for cross-border banking activities.[71] The supervisory policies applicable to G-SIFIs have been extended to 'Global systemically important banks' (G-SIBs). G-SIBs are defined as bank-dominated conglomerates, banking groups and any banks whose distress or disorderly failure (because of their size, complexity and interconnectedness) would cause significant disruption to the global financial system and financial stability. Financial stability is a central banking objective, heir to the objective of bank soundness. Recent events have proven that in times of crises it also becomes a government objective, since governments can afford neither bank runs nor a collapse in the mortgage market.

---

67 Financial Stability Board, 'Reducing the Moral Hazard Posed by Systemically Important Financial Institutions – FSB Recommendations and Time Lines' (20 October 2010) 1.

68 Financial Stability Board, 'Global Systemically Important Insurers and the Policy Measures That Will Apply to Them' (18 July 2013).

69 Financial Stability Board, 'Key Attributes of Effective Resolution Regimes for Financial Institutions' (15 2014).

70 Roman Tomasic and Folarin Akinbami, 'The Role of Trust in Maintaining the Resilience of Financial Markets' (2011) 11 *Journal of Corporate Law Studies* 381–383.

71 Financial Stability Board, 'Key Attributes of Effective Resolution Regimes for Financial Institutions' (October 2011). The guidelines have been amended in the Key Attributes of 2014 <http://www.fsb.org/wp-content/uploads/r_111104cc.pdf> (accessed 28 May 2020).

The case of Banca Monte dei Paschi di Siena (MPS), recently in the spotlight for distress scenario,[72] has highlighted the concern for classifying a credit institution as a G-SIB or as a domestic systemically important bank (D-SIB)[73] or 'other systemic important institution or O-SII authorized to operate'.[74] Although MPS is not globally systemically important, it has been identified as a domestic significant bank and its failure can produce a serious impact in other fragile financial institutions. It can be noted that under the SSM Regulation,[75] the SSM supervises significant institutions. The test of significance is open-ended though some criteria are established in article 6.4 of the SSM Regulation.[76] The procedures for classifying entities as 'significant' are outlined in articles 43–44 of the SSM Framework Regulation.[77] The latest list of 119 significant supervised entities was published by the ECB in August 2018.[78] The case of MPS tested the suitability of the SSM and the new resolution regime to resolve failing banks in an orderly fashion.[79] However, the case of MPS demonstrated that banks rely on government policies and it is difficult to predict a change in the regulatory approach to national measures.

The effects of a distressed D-SIB are assessed by the domestic authorities, in conjunction with the EU authorities. This would allow a margin of discretion for the national authorities in the assessment and application of restructuring tools.[80] Within the EU, the categorisation as D-SIB is not, as such, relevant for the need for recovery and resolution plans, which, in fact, apply across the board, but with some relaxations for smaller institutions. This means that a D-SIB could be subject to the recovery and resolution plans, and

---

72 MPS represented a real concern to the Italian Central Bank and the European Central Bank, and it demonstrated that banks rely on government bailout, something that it is difficult to change in the regulatory approach to failing credit institutions. European Commission, *State Aid: Commission Authorises Precautionary Recapitalisation of Italian Bank Monte dei Paschi di Siena* (Press Release 4 July 2017) 2. See also Monte dei Paschi di Siena, *BMPS: European Commission Approves the 2017–2021 Restructuring Plan* (Press Release) <http://english.mps.it/media-and-news/press-releases/2017/Pages/press_release_20170705.aspx> (accessed 21 June 2020).

73 Although D-SIBs are not significant from an international perspective, they could have an important impact on their domestic financial system and economy compared to non-systemic institutions. See Basel Committee on Banking Supervision, 'A Framework for Dealing with Domestic Systemically Important Banks' (October 2012) 1.

74 The Bank of Italy has identified MPS banking groups as domestic systemically important institutions or 'other systemically important institutions' (O-SII) authorised to operate in Italy. The decision to identify MPS (jointly with UniCredit and Intesa Sanpaolo) as O-SII was taken pursuant to Bank of Italy Circular No. 285/2013 on prudential regulations for banks, which implements Directive 2013/36/EU (Capital Requirements Directive, CRD IV) in Italy and specifies the criteria on which the methodology for identifying the O-SIIs is based. The assessment was carried out following the European Banking Authority Guidelines (EBA/GL/2014/10), which set out the criteria and the data required to identify O-SIIs in EU jurisdictions. The Guidelines are consistent with the rules set by the Basel Committee on Banking Supervision to identify systemically important banks at a national level, the goal being uniformity in the identification process at an international level. See release by the Bank of Italy, dated 22 January 2016 <https://www.bancaditalia.it/compiti/stabilita-finanziaria/politica-macroprudenziale/documenti/OSII_2016_comunicato_en.pdf?language_id=1>.

75 Council Regulation EU No. 1024/2013 of 15 October 2013.

76 Regulation EU No. 468/2014 of the European Central Bank adopted on 16 April 2014.

77 Ibid.

78 See <https://www.bankingsupervision.europa.eu/ecb/pub/pdf/ssm.list_of_supervised_entities_201807.en.pdf> (accessed 2 May 2020).

79 Matthias Haentjens, *New Bank Resolution Regime as an Engine of EU Integration* (Oxford Business Law Blog 14 June 2017) <https://www.law.ox.ac.uk/business-law-blog/blog/2017/06/new-bank-resolution-regime-engine-eu-integration> (accessed 19 June 2020).

80 Basel Committee on Banking Supervision (n 73) 2.

any other available rescue mechanism suitable for the bank. The Basel Committee issued specific provisions for dealing with distressed G-SIBs,[81] while the D-SIB framework is regulated by high-level principles.[82] These principles, which are not binding and not enforceable, determine uncertainty on the applicable procedures for D-SIBs due to the potentially systemic and cross-border nature of these institutions.

Paradoxically, the margin of discretion left to national authorities to categorise non-G-SIBs or D-SIBs, and the involvement of the ECB and the Commission make the dividing line between the bank categories rather obscure. This lack of consistency creates a grey area in which the loopholes for public financial support can affect the reorganisation actions among failing banks.[83] The suitable solution would be a set of harmonised standards for resolving non-globally systemic bank institutions and tighter State aid regulation, rather than the extension of the resolution toolbox to all cases of bank distress, irrespective of the systemic relevance of the failing institution.[84]

2.6 Conclusions

This chapter demonstrated the emergence of financial stability as a key objective of banking and financial regulation as a response to the traumatic experience of the global financial crisis which highlighted the significance of systemic risk and the inadequacy of micro-prudential supervision to ensure sound financial systems. It has also explained the core position of macro-prudential regulation and supervision within the financial systems of the UK and the EU. These changes, alongside the shift from principles-based and market-oriented regulation to intrusive monitoring, are reflected on the new regulatory architecture in the UK and EU, as will be examined in Chapters 3 and 4.

Glossary of terms

- Systemic risk: Risk that the failure of one significant financial institution can cause, or significantly contribute to, the failure of other significant financial institutions as a result of their linkages to each other.
- Financial stability: The term refers to the safety and soundness of the financial system and to the stability of the payment and settlement systems.
- Macro-prudential supervision: This focuses on risks to the financial system as a whole, with a view to protecting the real economy from severe disruptions in the provision of financial services.
- Micro-prudential supervision: This focuses on strengthening individual financial institutions with a view to protecting their creditors, particularly depositors and retail investors.

---

81 Basel Committee on Banking Supervision, 'Global Systemically Important Banks: Updated Assessment Methodology and the Higher Loss Absorbency Requirement' (June 2013).

82 Basel Committee on Banking Supervision (n 73). It is stressed that 'these principles allow appropriate national discretion to accommodate structural characteristics of domestic financial systems, including the possibility for countries to go beyond the minimum D-SIB framework'.

83 James R. Barth, Chris Brummer, Tong Li and Daniel E. Nolle, 'Systemically Important Banks (SIBs) in the Post-Crisis Era: "The" Global Response, and Responses Around the Globe for 135 Countries' in Allen N. Berger, Philip Molyneux and John O.S. Wilson (eds), *The Oxford Handbook of Banking* (2nd edn, OUP 2015) 617.

84 Jens-Hinrich Binder, *Proportionality at the Resolution Stage: Calibration of Resolution Measures and the Public Interest Test* (3 July 2017) 20 <https://ssrn.com/abstract=2990379> (accessed 13 January 2020).

- Systemically important financial institutions (SIFIs): Financial institutions whose disorderly failure because of their size, complexity and systemic interconnectedness would be likely to cause significant disruption to the wider financial system and economic activity.
- Globally active and systemically important banks (G-SIBs): Bank-dominated conglomerates, banking groups and any banks whose distress or disorderly failure (because of their size, complexity and interconnectedness) would cause significant disruption to the global financial system and financial stability. EU law uses the term 'Global Systemically Important Institutions' (G-SIIs).

Practice questions

At the aftermath of the 2007–2009 global financial crisis, a new core principle has emerged in banking law and regulation, namely, safeguarding financial stability and managing systemic risk. Critically discuss.

You may also find it useful to review the chapter through the following questions:

- What is systemic risk, and how is it transmitted across financial institutions and systems?
- Explain the rationales for prudential banking regulation.
- Explain the difference between macro-and micro-prudential regulations.
- How has the importance of macro-prudential supervision changed financial systems since the global financial crisis?
- Which financial institutions are considered to be G-SIBs, and what are the consequences of this characterisation?

3 The regulatory architecture of the UK banking system

3.1 Introduction

It is universally accepted nowadays that the regulation of financial markets should strive to achieve transparency, fairness, equal access, effective competition and financial soundness. Currently, a very strong case, substantiated by, *inter alia*, the 2007–2009 global financial crisis (GFC), can be made for asserting that the financial industry had underestimated the value and importance of consumer protection. For instance, in bank collapses such as Northern Rock and Halifax Bank of Scotland, consumers were exposed to a continuous lack of transparency and information asymmetries, which reflect a fundamental imbalance between market participants.[1] Consequently, it can be argued that investors find it difficult to choose the right business transaction because there is no appropriate system of disclosure and they lack proper financial knowledge; this gap is made worse by the absence of co-operation between the parties to financial contracts (i.e. managers and investors, bankers and customers) and a lack of adequate rules on internal controls. On this view, regulators realised the need to establish more robust prudential supervision to prevent the spread of systemic risk into the financial sector in order to avoid the use of taxpayers' money for resolving failing credit institutions.

This chapter provides a brief historical account of the evolution of bank supervision and regulation over the last half century. Then, the discussion focuses on the main regulatory techniques prevalent at the time the 2007–2009 financial crisis happened, namely, principles-based regulation. The rest of the chapter tracks the transformation of UK regulatory architecture since the onset of the GFC focusing particularly on the Banking Act 2009; the Financial Services Act 2012, which abolished the Financial Services Authority (FSA) and introduced the Prudential Regulation Authority (PRA) and Financial Conduct Authority (FCA); and the post-crisis approaches to financial regulation and supervision.

3.2 The evolution of the UK banking regulation until the 2007–2009 financial crisis

3.2.1 The bank of England and HM treasury: the moral suasion tool

Most accounts of the history of banking regulation and supervision in the UK place its inception in the late 1970s and emphasise the fact that a formal licensing requirement and

---

1 See House of Lords, House of Commons, Parliamentary Commission on Banking Standards, 'An Accident Waiting to Happen: The Failure of HBOS' Fourth Report of Session 2012–2013 (4 April 2013) available at <https://publications.parliament.uk/pa/jt201213/jtselect/jtpcbs/144/144.pdf> (accessed 26 July 2020).

supervisory regime for all banking institutions was only introduced by the Banking Act 1987.[2] However, if a broader notion of regulatory function is adopted, it is evident that the Bank of England had been exercising a proto-regulatory function since much earlier. Indeed, since the onset of World War I, the Bank of England stopped competing against other banks and assumed effective leadership of the banking system.[3] This took place despite the absence of any formal licensing, regulatory or supervisory powers of the Bank and is hence frequently described as 'the moral suasion tool'. According to anecdotal evidence, it was common at the time for the Bank of England to invite the senior management of a bank for an informal conversation and to suggest them the need to change their business policy, for instance, by reducing lending to a particular economic sector or type of business.[4]

The persuasive authority of the Bank of England was based on the fact that commercial banks relied on the Bank of England to restrict entry to the market thus insulating them from effective competition.[5] This informal regulatory ecosystem was facilitated by the social and geographical proximity between the Bank and major UK banks, and by the strong interventionist role of the state in the economy between 1945 and the early 1970s. Ultimately, an omnipresent implicit threat of nationalisation, existing during the whole period from the 1930s until the 1970s, ensured compliance with the instructions and guidance provided by the Bank of England.[6] By the 1930s, the Bank's informal control over major banks encompassed crucial corporate decisions such as the payment of dividends and amalgamations.[7] Thus, historically, the development of effective regulatory arrangements in the UK closely followed the full adoption of limited liability and the discontinuation of the practices of using reserve capital and uncalled capital in the early 20th century.[8] This is unsurprising, as it is exactly the practice of limited liability banking that poses great risks of externalities and thus necessitates the establishment of effective regulatory and supervisory arrangements.

3.2.2 Financial Services and Markets Act 2000: the Financial Services Authority

The introduction of statutory supervisory arrangements since 1979 marked the beginning of an era of relatively frequent overhauls of regulatory architecture. The Banking Act 1979 was a response to the secondary banking crisis of 1973–1975.[9] The original 1979 structure put in place a two-tier system whereby banks of high reputation and standing were not

---

2 See e.g. Mads Andenas and Iris HY Chiu, *The Foundations and Future of Financial Regulation: Governance for Responsibility* (Routledge 2014) 5–6 and Christopher Ryan, 'Transfer of Banking Supervision to the Financial Services Authority' in Michael Blair et al. (eds), *Blackstone's Guide to the Bank of England Act 1998* (Blackstone Press 1998) 39–40.

3 See Charles A.E. Goodhart, *The Evolution of Central Banks* (MIT Press 1988) 44–55.

4 A detailed account of the history of the UK financial industry in the 20th century can be found in David Kynaston, *The City of London – Volume IV: A Club No More, 1945–2000* (Pimlico Publications 2002).

5 See Fred Hirsch, 'The Bagehot Problem' (1977) 45 *The Manchester School of Economic & Social Studies* 241, 248.

6 See John D Turner, *Banking in Crisis: The Rise and Fall of British Banking Stability, 1800 to the Present* (CUP 2014) 175.

7 Ibid., 176–177.

8 Such practices effectively made bank shareholders liable to some extent in the case of a bank's insolvency and thus reduced incentives to take excessive risk.

9 For a concise discussion of the crisis, see Margaret Reid, *The Secondary Banking Crisis, 1973–75: Its Causes and Course* (Macmillan Publishers 1982).

subject to licensing and supervisory requirements, whereas smaller deposit-takers were.[10] A formal deposit protection scheme was also introduced.[11] This structure attracted heavy criticism after the collapse of Johnson Matthey, an established bank, in 1984. As a result, the Banking Act 1987 introduced a comprehensive regime of authorisation and supervision for all deposit takers[12] as well as the requirement that both firms and senior persons are fit and proper to engage in banking.[13] At the same time, insurance companies were regulated by the Department of Trade and Industry and other financial sector firms were regulated by five self-regulating organisations,[14] which were overseen by the Securities and Investment Board (SIB). The SIB was a statutory body under the Financial Services Act 1986, which, as we will see, in due course evolved into the FSA, and eventually into the present-day FCA.

By the mid-1990s, the heavily fragmented and partially self-regulatory nature of financial supervision was perceived as highly problematic, especially in the light of the collapse of the Bank of Credit and Commerce International in 1991 and Barings Bank in 1995.[15] It is of little surprise that the Labour administration which came into power in 1997 set out to rectify this problem by creating a single financial regulator, especially given the trend of integration in the financial services sector.[16] Indeed, the SIB was renamed in October 1997 as the FSA,[17] and assumed the *de facto* role of regulating investment firms and insurance companies. In June 1998, the responsibility for regulating banks was transferred from the Bank of England to the FSA by virtue of section 21 of the Bank of England Act 1998. At the same time, the Act made the Bank of England independent from the Treasury in matters of monetary policy.[18] Eventually, in December 2001, the FSA was given full regulatory and supervisory authority over the whole financial industry sector – including banking, insurance and investment business – by virtue of the Financial Services and Markets Act 2000 (FSMA 2000).[19] This was a period characterised by a profound belief in the ability

10 See Andenas and Chiu (n 2) 5.
11 Banking Act 1979, s 29 (as originally enacted) provided for a protection limit of £10,000 of which 75% could be claimed.
12 Banking Act 1987, ss 8–14 (as originally enacted).
13 A detailed examination of the Act can be found in Graham Penn, *Banking Supervision: Regulation of the UK Banking Sector under the Banking Act 1987* (Butterworths 1989).
14 The five self-regulating organisations, known as SROs, were the following: the Association of Futures Brokers and Dealers (AFBD); the Financial Intermediaries, Managers and Brokers Regulatory Association (FIMBRA); the Investment Management Regulatory Organisation (IMRO), the Life Assurance and Unit Trust Regulatory Organisation (LAUTRO), and The Securities Association (TSA). In 1991, the AFBD and TSA were replaced by the Securities and Futures Authority (SFA), and in 1994, the FIMBRA and LAUTRO were replaced by the Personal Investment Authority (PIA), thus reducing the number of SROs to three. On this point, see Eilís Ferran, 'Examining the UK's Experience in Adopting the Single Financial Regulator Model' (2003) 28 *Brooklyn Journal of International Law* 257, 266–267.
15 For a discussion of the events surrounding the failure of these banks and especially Barings, see Christos Hadjiemmanuil, 'The Bank of England and the Lessons from Barings: UK Banking Regulation under Parliamentary Scrutiny' (1996) 1 *Yearbook of International Financial and Economic Law* 333.
16 For an analysis of the policy rationales for the creation of the FSA, see Eilís Ferran (n 14) 270–271.
17 See E. Peter Ellinger, Eva Lomnicka and Christopher V.M. Hare, *Ellinger's Modern Banking Law* (5th edn, OUP 2011) 28.
18 Bank of England Act, ss 10–19. An in-depth discussion of the concept of independent regulatory agencies can be found in Kirti Datla and Richard Revesz, 'Deconstructing Independent Agencies (and Executive Agencies)' (2013) 98 *Cornell Law Review* 769.
19 FSMA 2000, s 19 contains a general prohibition for any person to carry on a regulated activity unless it is authorised and Sch 2 provides a list of regulated activities covering *inter alia* deposit taking, insurance and dealing in financial instruments as principal or agent.

of market discipline – in most circumstances – to ensure customer protection and financial stability, and hence by a dominant conception of the appropriate role of regulation as one exclusively concerned with tackling market failures.[20]

The FSA was conceived as a comprehensive regulator for the whole of the financial services sector and for all purposes. It was envisaged that its creation would enhance the effectiveness of supervision, reduce cost due to economies of scale and scope and enable the Bank of England to focus exclusively on monetary policy. This model proved popular internationally and was followed, to a greater or lesser extent, by countries such as Japan, Germany, Ireland and Austria. It reflected the increasing integration of the financial services industry with firms' activities spanning across the conventional boundaries of retail banking, investment banking, insurance and investment management. In modern integrated financial sectors, having multiple sectoral regulators has been argued to make little sense, as it is necessary for regulators to be able to monitor the overall level of risk taken by each financial conglomerate.[21] For instance, Alan Greenspan, Chairman of the US Federal Reserve Board, stated in 1998 that 'Risks managed on a consolidated basis cannot be reviewed on an individual legal entity basis by different supervisors'.[22] However, as the 2008–2009 financial crisis revealed, regulating firms for all purposes including both prudential regulation and conduct of business regulation came at the cost of diluting emphasis on prudential concerns. This issue will be discussed further in Section 3.5.

3.3 Principles-based regulation and reliance on market discipline

Prior to the GFC, the approach the FSA took to financial regulation was described as principles-based regulation. The principles-based regime represented the cornerstone of UK financial and securities regulation strategy and was characterised by broadly worded high-level principles that regulated entities were free to operationalise and implement. As such, this regulatory approach was reliant on market discipline in the form of effective monitoring by market players, and reflected the great confidence placed at the time in efficient markets.

In substance, a principle is regarded as a general rule, or a second level of statutory norm that deploys its legal force under the risk of misconduct and a risk of non-compliant behaviours. Whereas the principle ensues from a decision by the regulator, market participants have to play an active role in ensuring that it is effective. In other words, the UK system was characterised by self-induced regulation through flexibility of principles, monitoring of management behaviours and a system of internal controls.[23] However, the principles-based regime, as a pre-crisis approach, proved to have limits and weaknesses.[24] The most important aspect had to do with the legitimacy of this regime as a regulatory strategy. A principle

20 See Harry McVea, 'Financial Services Regulation under the Financial Services Authority: A Reassertion of the Market Failure Thesis?' (2005) 64 *Cambridge Law Journal* 413.
21 A detailed evaluation of the introduction of the FSA as a single regulator from the perspective of regulatory effectiveness, which is supportive of the idea of single financial regulators, can be found in Richard Dale and Simon Wolfe, 'The UK Financial Services Authority: Unified Regulation in the New Market Environment' (2003) 4 *Journal of International Banking Regulation* 200.
22 See Alan Greenspan, *Statement before the Subcommittee on Financial Institutions and Consumer Credit, Committee on Banking and Financial Services* (United States House of Representatives 13 February 1998) 10.
23 See Robert Baldwin and Julia Black, 'Really Responsive Regulation' (2007) LSE Law, Society and Economy Working Papers No. 15, 3–4.
24 See Julia Black, 'Paradoxes and Failures: "New Governance" Techniques and the Financial Crisis' (2012) 75(6) *Modern Law Review* 1042–1045.

in itself does not ensure a correct application of rules because, often, it is synonymous with escaping enforcement and a lack of certainty.[25] In this respect, it has been observed that 'a principles-based approach does not work with individuals who have no principles'.[26]

A principles-based regime needs internal controls to strengthen its enforcement and must be accepted by market participants as a flexible, yet binding, legal regime. Adopting principles-based regulation does not mean jettisoning the rules. It gives legislatures the power to set high-level regulatory goals and outcomes, and leaves the articulation of processes and details to front-line regulators in collaboration with the industry itself.[27] Therefore, a principles-based regime can be considered as a form of self-regulation in which the markets can be regarded as rule-makers and governance rules as a surrogate for detailed statutory norms.[28] In general, the positive aspects of implementing self-regulatory measures are speed, cost-efficiency and, more importantly, industry acceptance and cross-border application. However, to bring about these benefits, self-regulation needs to be properly integrated into the overall normative framework and must have adequate and effective enforcement regimes.[29]

The real shortcoming was determined by a failure to appreciate that 'principles [do] not simply act in combination with more detailed rules, but... play a more informing and influencing role in enabling and inducing compliance with the rules'.[30] It has been argued that principles represent a form of soft law, albeit not readily translatable into a legal paradigm of reference.[31] Practices such as 'treating customers fairly' or '[a] firm must pay due regard to the interests of its customers and treat them fairly', placing responsibility on firms' senior management to deliver fair outcomes for consumers and offering firms the flexibility to deliver these outcomes in the way which best suits their business[32] do not make sense in the absence of a proper level of enforcement managed by compliance bodies which inculcate legal and ethical values into the corporate organisation and assume an active role in the day-to-day regulation of the firm.[33]

---

25 See Julia Black, 'Using Rules Effectively' in Christopher McCrudden (ed.), *Regulation and Deregulation* (OUP 1998) 101.

26 See Peter Thal Larsen and Jennifer Hughes, 'Sants Signals More Muscular Regulatory Era' *Financial Times* (13 March 2009) 19. In particular, Sants pointed to the fragility of the 'light touch' approach, while announcing more intensive supervision characterised by macro-prudential and sector analysis.

27 See Cristie Ford, 'Principles-Based Securities Regulation in the Wake of the Global Financial Crisis' (2010) 55 *McGill Law Journal* 261.

28 See Julia Black and David Rouch, 'The Development of the Global Markets as Rule-Makers: Engagement and Legitimacy' (2008) 2(3) *Law and Financial Markets Review* 223–225; see also Joanna Benjamin, Paul Bowden and David Rouch, 'Law and Regulation for Global Financial Markets: Markets as Rule-makers – Enforcement, Dispute Resolution and Risk' (2008) 2 *Law and Financial Markets Review* 322–323; Joanna Benjamin and David Rouch, 'The International Financial Markets as a Source of Global Law: The Privatisation of Rule-making?' (2008) 2(2) *Law and Financial Markets Review* 82–83.

29 See Niamh Moloney, *How to Protect Investors. Lessons from the EC and the UK* (CUP 2010) 104. In particular, Moloney pointed to the fragility of the self-regulation in the retail markets observing that 'investors are poorly equipped to monitor market actors and to price protections'.

30 See Julia Black, '"Which Arrow?": Rule Type and Regulatory Policy' (1995) 1 *Public Law* 94–95.

31 See Steven L. Schwarcz, 'The "Principles" Paradox' (2008) Duke Law School Legal Studies Paper No. 205.

32 The 'Treating Customers Fairly Initiative' represents the clearest example of the FSA's principles-based regime. It consists of a set of best practices by which firms are to ensure market confidence and consumer protection. See Andromachi Georgosouli, 'The FSA's "Treating Customers Fairly" (TCF) Initiative: What Is So Good about It and Why It May Not Work' (2011) 38(3) *Journal of Law and Society* 406–407.

33 See Christine Parker, 'The Ethics of Advising on Regulatory Compliance: Autonomy or Interdependence?' (2000) 28(4) *Journal of Business Ethics* 346.

Principles are better understood as incentives for good faith and compliant behaviour in which corporate management assumes the role of regulator through its everyday conduct of the business.[34] In this regard, internal regulation could represent a social benefit for the company and not an onerous burden which is managed by rational regulators and improves the interests of market participants through an effective and efficient regulatory system (in terms of disclosure, allocation of resources and market success). Principles can yield effectiveness, durability, flexibility, accessibility, efficiency and congruence: they are not an alternative to detailed rules but represent a different method of regulation, deriving from management choices and not from statutory decisions.[35]

In the context of principles, questions of legitimacy and accountability are linked to the utmost degree with consumer protection policy.[36] The UK system has set out in section 2(2) of the Financial Services and Markets Act 2000 (FSMA 2000) significant regulatory objectives, such as market confidence, public awareness, consumer protection and reduction of financial crime.[37] Market confidence can be considered the key objective, in terms of investor protection, on account of its fundamental role in achieving the soundness of the financial markets. A controversial question is whether the UK legislation affords an adequate level of consumer protection; indeed, it is argued that, whilst, on the one hand, section 5(1) of FSMA 2000 ensures 'an appropriate degree of protection for consumers', on the other, section 5(2) provides that 'in considering what degree of protection may be appropriate, the Authority must have regard to (d) the general principle that consumers should take responsibility for their decisions'. As observed, 'an evident lack of certainty and clarity underscores the limits of the UK consumer protection system'.[38]

Legitimate and accountable regulation prevents the potential risk of confidence failure and promotes a clear understanding of consumer protection law. An innovative challenge has been set by the Office of Fair Trading, a government agency appointed to enhance consumer protection through informative leaflets or booklets, guidance and publication of best practices.[39] In this context, the English courts have made appreciable advances in terms of investor protection by confirming the tendency to consider consumers as an active part of financial markets, particularly in the banking sector.[40]

3.4 The Northern Rock crisis and the Banking Act 2009

The GFC revealed the distortions involved in managing securities products and altered the prevailing sentiment with regard to regulatory approaches questioning the predictability of market actors' behaviour (i.e. managers, shareholders, stakeholders). The corporate and banking collapses such as Lehman Brothers and Northern Rock showed that the financial

---

34 See Mark W. Nelson, 'Behavioural Evidence on the Effects of Principles-and Rules-Based Standards' (2003) 17(1) *Accounting Horizons* 100–101.

35 See Michael Power, *Organized Uncertainty. Designing a World of Risk Management* (OUP 2007) 48–49.

36 See Niamh Moloney 'Confidence and Competence: The Conundrum of EC Capital Markets Law' (2004) 4(1) *Journal of Corporate Law Studies* 11–12.

37 See Jonathan Fisher, Jane Bewsey, Malcolm Waters and Elizabeth Ovey, *The Law of Investor Protection* (Sweet & Maxwell 2003) 18.

38 See Joanna Benjamin, *Financial Law* (OUP 2007) 590.

39 See Brain W. Havey Harvey and Deborah L. Parry, *The Law of Consumer Protection and Fair Trading* (Butterworths 2000) 50–51.

40 *Office of Fair Trading v Abbey National and Others* [2009] EWCA Civ 116.

industry had underestimated the value and importance of investors.[41] The failures of co-ordination and communication that characterised the early handling of Northern Rock caused the passing of emergency legislation, but, most importantly, revealed weaknesses in the UK regulatory structures because the Authorities relied for too long on informal arrangements in allocating responsibilities and powers.[42] In response to the Northern Rock crisis, the UK Government introduced a set of regulatory initiatives. In particular, some banks were offered government funding or central bank liquidity insurance schemes, others received capital injections or were nationalised outright, and some were offered no support at all.[43]

In January 2008, a consultation document – 'Financial Stability and Depositor Protection: Strengthening the Framework' – was presented to Parliament by the Chancellor of the Exchequer.[44] It contained recommendations to enhance depositor protection arrangements principally focused on the following: (1) strengthening the stability and resilience of the financial system, both in the UK and globally; (2) reducing the likelihood of individual banks facing difficulties; (3) reducing the impact if, nevertheless, a bank gets into difficulties; (4) providing effective compensation arrangements in which consumers have confidence; and (5) strengthening the Bank of England, ensuring effective co-ordinated actions by authorities, both in the UK and internationally.[45] Subsequently, Parliament enacted the Banking (Special Provisions) Act 2008 to provide a temporary and expedient measure of last resort for failing banks and building societies (in the form of public ownership).[46]

The Act included wide-ranging powers for HM Treasury to effect transfer of securities issued by, and property of, a failing bank – overriding the private law rights of shareholders, bondholders and counterparties to the bank, who are to be compensated for their losses

41 See Robert Schiller, *The Subprime Solution* (Princeton University Press 2008) 87–88.
42 It has been reported that the FSA systematically failed in its regulatory duty to ensure that Northern Rock would not pose a systemic risk. Also, the 'tripartite authorities' at deputies level failed to plan in advance for the announcement of the Government guarantee on Northern Rock deposits that proved necessary to stop the run. See on this matter House of Commons Treasury Committee, 'The Run on the Rock' Fifth Report of Session 2007–08, Volume I (26 January 2008).
43 See Andrew K Rose and Tomasz Wieladek, 'Too Big to Fail: Some Empirical Evidence on the Causes and Consequences of Public Banking Interventions in the United Kingdom' (August 2012) Bank of England, Working Paper No. 460, 3–4.
44 The document included a wide range of proposals on national matters such as the introduction of a special insolvency framework for banks and building societies and improvements to depositor protection systems and matters requiring international co-operation such as the introduction of an early warning system on global financial risks and a review of the functioning of the securitisation markets. See for a general comment Richard Stones, 'The Special Resolution Regime: A Cherrypicker's Charter?' (2008) 23 *Journal of International Banking and Financial Law* 523–524.
45 See Bank of England, HM Treasury and FSA, 'Financial Stability and Depositor Protection: Strengthening the Framework' (January 2008) 8.
46 The Banking (Special Provisions) Act, passed in February 2008 in order to nationalise Northern Rock, provided the Treasury with powers to facilitate an orderly resolution to maintain financial stability and protect the public interest. The main objective was to enhance financial stability and improve depositor protection; it also provided a raft of new powers, including tools the UK tripartite authorities (HM Treasury, the Financial Services Authority and the Bank of England) can use to deal with failing and failed banks. The Banking (Special Provisions) Act 2008 clearly defined the FSA's role in deciding upon the need for bank resolution. The purposes of the statute are indicated in the preamble: 'An Act to make provision to enable the Treasury in certain circumstances to make an order relating to the transfer of securities issued by, or of property, rights or liabilities belonging to, an authorised deposit-taker; to make further provision in relation to building societies; and for connected purposes'.

arising by virtue of the exercise of the powers.[47] The Act also contained wide-ranging 'Henry VIII clauses' giving significant powers to the Treasury to make orders for the purposes of the Act.[48] This statute was incorporated into the Banking Act 2009 as part of the Special Resolution Regime (SRR)[49] and marked an important change in the institutional, legal and insolvency arrangements in the UK system.

The Banking Act 2009 established a permanent SRR in the UK financial system, providing the Authorities with tools to deal with banks that get into financial difficulties.[50] It was designed to improve the resilience of the UK financial system and to support financial stability by strengthening depositor protection. According to Section 4 of the Banking Act 2009, the special resolution objectives are as follows: (1) to protect and enhance the stability of the financial systems of the UK, (2) to protect and enhance public confidence in the stability of the banking systems of the UK, (3) to protect depositors, (4) to protect public funds and (5) to avoid interfering with property rights in contravention of a Convention right (within the meaning of the Human Rights Act 1998). To achieve these objectives, the SRR introduced three 'stabilisation options' to be used when a financial institution is failing, allowing the Bank of England to make 'share transfers' or 'property transfers' from the failing institution. The stabilisation options – that can be achieved through the use of so-called 'stabilisation powers' conferred on the Bank and the Treasury – are as follows: (1) transfer of all or part of the business of the bank to a private sector purchaser, (2) transfer to a Bank of England-owned bridge bank and (3) transfer to temporary public ownership. In addition, the SRR introduced two insolvency procedures, namely, bank insolvency and bank administration.

The temporary SRR set up in the wake of the Northern Rock rescue highlighted the importance to minimise the disruption of a troubled bank and ensure continuation of business functions to safeguard the interests of creditors and counterparties. Precisely, the deficiencies of the UK insolvency regime (the Insolvency Act 1986) to deal with banks in distress have underlined the questions of emergency liquidity assistance, deposit insurance and pre-insolvency arrangements. The Banking Act 2009 has tackled these concerns reforming the supervision powers of the FSA and challenging the regulatory framework for

---

47 Bob Penn and Daniel Measor, 'A Guide to the Banking Bill 2008' (2009) 3 *Law and Financial Markets Review* 35.

48 The Banking (Special Provisions) Act 2008 was used to manage the failure of Bradford and Bingley and to transfer deposits from two Icelandic banks to ING. The Act was also used in relation to Northern Rock Plc and in two later instances, relating to Heritable Bank Plc and Kaupthing Singer & Friedlander Ltd.

49 The Banking Act came into force on 21 February 2009. The Act is structured into seven Parts dealing with different areas: Special resolution regime, Bank insolvency, Bank administration, Financial Services Compensation Scheme, Inter-bank payment systems, Banknotes: Scotland and Northern Ireland and Miscellaneous. Further, the statutory instruments dealing with safeguards for partial property transfers (the 'Safeguards Order') and 'no creditor worse off' provisions (the 'NCWO Order' together with the Safeguards Order, the 'Orders') came into effect. The Banking Act 2009 represents the most important legislative response in the UK to the issues raised by the Crisis. It replaces and extends the Banking (Special Provisions) Act 2008, which was introduced as a temporary and emergency measure in the wake of the Northern Rock default. The Financial Services Bill 2012 introduced the schedule 17 into the Banking Act 2009. This new schedule makes a number of organisational consequential amendments to the Banking Act 2009 as a result of the conferral of the FSA's functions on the FCA and the PRA.

50 It should be noted that the Banking Act 2009 has been used once in relation to the rescue of Dunfermline Building Society at the end of March 2009. For a general review of the Act, particularly the Special Resolution Regime, see Andrew McKnight, 'The Banking Act 2009' (2009) 3 *Law and Financial Markets Review* 325–331.

banking crisis.[51] Lastra observed that 'the efficiency of bank insolvency law and procedures would be greatly enhanced by the adoption of a formal system of prompt corrective action linking the intensity of supervision to trigger ratios related to the level of capitalisation, and to other indicators of liquidity and sound banking (including risk management)'.[52]

The Banking Act provided a permanent set of measures to manage bank failures but has also raised questions on how it would deal with banks that operate with branches or subsidiaries in other countries, and likewise how foreign banks operating in the UK would be sorted out.[53] In particular, the Act introduced a new 'investment bank insolvency regulations' according to sections 233 and 234. As a result, the Treasury issued the 'Investment Bank Special Administration Regulations 2011' to tackle the problems associated with the default of Lehman Brothers.[54] It can be argued that these legislative initiatives aimed to preserve the stability of the financial system and ensure the integrity of markets. In this context, effective bank resolution proceedings may prevent the spread of systemic risk and ensure the protection of depositors, as will be discussed in Chapter 14.

3.5 The Financial Services Acts 2012 and 2016

The Financial Services Act 2012 (FSA 2012)[55] received Royal Assent on 19 December 2012, and most of its provisions came into force on 24 January 2013.[56] The Act marked an extensive restructuring of the UK's financial regulation regime by (a) transferring the micro-prudential regulation functions of the FSA to a new PRA, established as a subsidiary company of the Bank of England, and (b) transforming the FSA into the FCA. In addition, the Act established a new Financial Policy Committee within the Bank of England and amended the corporate governance of the Bank to strengthen scrutiny and accountability. As discussed in Section 3.4, the Banking Act 2009 had already introduced a SRR comprising three stabilisation options and granted the relevant powers to the Bank thus making it the primary player in crisis management. This paved the way for the revival of the Bank's banking supervision role and the partial reversal of the 1998 reforms. The reform initiative was taken by the Chancellor of the Exchequer in his 2010 Mansion House speech.[57] Subsequently, the Treasury published two consultation papers.[58] The Financial Services Bill

---

51 See Michael Krimminger and Rosa M. Lastra, 'Early Intervention' in Rosa M Lastra (ed), *Cross-border Bank Insolvency* (OUP 2011) 62.

52 See Rosa M. Lastra, 'Northern Rock, UK Bank Insolvency and Cross-Border Bank Insolvency' (2008) 9 *Journal of Banking Regulation* 171.

53 See Andrew Bailey, 'The UK Bank Resolution Regime' (Speech delivered to the ICAEW Financial Services Faculty Breakfast, London, 26 November 2009).

54 The special administrative regime should reduce the disruption of an investment firm failing and ensure continuation of business functions to protect the interests of creditors.

55 This part is based on Andreas Kokkinis, *Corporate Law and Financial Instability* (Routledge 2017) 78–82.

56 According to section 122 (3) of the Act, the majority of its provisions are to come into force on such day as the Treasury appoints by order. The first of these orders was made on 23 January 2013 and brought into force most of the crucial provisions of the Act with effect from the 24th of January. The order provides that the provisions of the Act that require the Treasury to make appointments have effect from the 19th of February. See the Financial Services Act 2012 (Commencement No. 1) Order 2013, SI 2013/113.

57 For a detailed discussion of the initial stages of the reform process, see Philip Rawlings, 'Bank Reform in the UK: Part II- Return to the Dark Ages?' (2011) 8 *International Corporate Rescue* 55. See also Eilís Ferran, 'The Break-Up of the Financial Services Authority' (2011) 31 *Oxford Journal of Legal Studies* 455.

58 See HM Treasury Consultation Papers: A New Approach to Financial Regulation: Judgement, Focus and Stability (2010) and A New Approach to Financial Regulation: Building a Stronger System (2011).

2012 was introduced in the House of Commons in January 2012, and the Act was finally passed in December after the two Houses agreed on amendments. The Bank of England started preparing for the transition in 2011 and published two policy documents in 2012 delineating the regulatory approach of the new PRA.[59] Subsequently, the Bank of England and Financial Services Act 2016 abolished the PRA as a separate body corporate and transferred its functions to the Bank of England which currently acts as the PRA.[60] This part aims to summarise the most crucial reforms introduced by the new Act, to explain how the new structure works and to assess the new regime on the basis of past experience from the UK and abroad.

3.5.1 An overview of the new regulatory architecture

The Financial Services Act 2012 abolished the FSA as a single financial regulator and transformed it into the 'FCA', while bestowing micro-prudential regulation on the Bank of England in its capacity as the 'PRA'. A new Financial Policy Committee of the Bank ('FPC') was created to be responsible for macro-prudential regulation. In this way, the Act reversed the main effect of the regulatory reform of the late 1990s that created the FSA as a unified regulator of the whole UK financial industry, responsible for both prudential regulation and conduct of business regulation. It is necessary here to reiterate that prudential regulation has two core objectives,[61] namely to protect the stability of the financial system as a whole (macro-prudential regulation) and to safeguard the safety and soundness of individual systemic financial institutions (micro-prudential regulation).[62] Conduct of business regulation deals with consumer protection, market integrity and competition.[63] An in-depth analysis of these different types of financial regulation and their rationales took place in Chapter 1.

The FPC operates as a committee of the Bank's court of directors with two main objectives: to contribute to the achievement of the financial stability objective of the bank and to support the economic policy of the Government, as specified by the Treasury.[64] The main functions of the FPC are as follows: (1) to monitor the stability of the financial system with a view to identifying systemic risks, (2) to prepare financial stability reports and (3) to give binding directions to the FCA and PRA in order to ensure the implementation of its macro-prudential policies.[65]

The PRA (Bank of England) is the new micro-prudential regulator for all systemic financial institutions. This category includes all deposit takers (banks, building societies and credit unions), all insurance firms and major investment firms.[66] The common characteristic of these firms is that their potential failure poses a threat to the stability of the financial

---

59 The PRA's Approach to Banking Supervision (2012) and the PRA's approach to Insurance Supervision (2012) are available at <http://www.fsa.gov.uk/about/what/reg_reform/pra> (accessed 15 July 2020).

60 Financial Services and Markets Act 2000 s 2A and s 2AB, as substituted by the Bank of England and Financial Services Act 2016 s 12.

61 See Markus Brunnermeier et al., 'The Fundamental Principles of Financial Regulation; Geneva Reports on the World Economy 11' (2009) International Centre for Monetary and Banking Studies (ICMB), at xvi, available at <http://www.princeton.edu/~markus/research/papers/Geneva11.pdf> (accessed 17 July 2020).

62 See FSMA 2000, s 2B (inserted by FSA 2012, s 6).

63 FSMA 2000, ss 1A–1D (inserted by FSA 2012, s 6).

64 Bank of England Act 1998, ss 9C and 9D (inserted by Financial Services Act 2012, s 4).

65 FSMA 2000, s 9G (inserted by Financial Services Act 2012, s 4).

66 Overall, the PRA is currently responsible for the prudential regulation and supervision of 1,700 financial institutions. See <http://www.bankofengland.co.uk/pra/Pages/default.aspx> (accessed 19 July 2020).

system and could disrupt the continuity of the provision of financial services. The particular activities that fall within the scope of PRA's prudential regulation were specified by the Treasury according to the Act.[67] Firms that seek to engage in such activities will have to be licensed by the PRA, while all other financial firms will be licensed by the FCA.[68] A second objective of the PRA focuses on insurance firms regulated by it. The PRA is thus required to ensure an appropriate degree of protection for present and potential policy-holders.

The FCA is the authority regulating and supervising the market conduct of all financial institutions whether they are licensed by it or by the PRA. It is responsible for securing an appropriate degree of consumer protection, enhancing the integrity of the financial system and promoting effective competition in the interests of consumers. The FCA has discretion to determine the level of consumer protection but must have regard to a list of matters specified in the Act, including the general principle that consumers should take responsibility for their decisions.[69] The integrity of the financial system includes its resilience, the avoidance of financial crime and market abuse, its orderly operation and transparency in price formation.[70] The FCA is also the UK Listing Authority (UKLA), and as such it is the UK's securities regulator which maintains the official list of securities admitted to trading on the Main Market of the London Stock Exchange.[71] The UKLA is responsible for making, amending and enforcing the Listing Rules, Prospectus Rules and Disclosure and Transparency Rules.[72] These sets of Rules transpose into domestic law relevant EU directives.

It is worth noting that the PRA has a veto power over the exercise of the FCA's regulatory powers with respect to firms authorised by the former. The PRA may exercise its veto power where the FCA is proposing to exercise its regulatory powers in a way that the PRA considers to be threatening the stability of the UK financial system or likely to result in the failure of a systemic institution.[73] Finally, the Treasury has the power to give binding directions to the Bank of England in circumstances where the Treasury provides financial assistance to a financial institution, incurs expenditure in connection with the Banking Act 2009 or provides financial assistance or a loan to the Financial Services Compensation Scheme manager. As a result, in any case where public funds are committed to the rescue of a financial institution, or where the failure of an institution results in public funds being used to

---

67 FSMA 2000, s 22A (inserted by Financial Services Act 2012, s 9). The Financial Services and Markets Act 2000 (PRA-regulated Activities) Order 2013 (SI 2013/556) came into force on 1 April 2013: accepting deposits, effecting or carrying out a contract of insurance and acting as a managing agent at Lloyd's fall automatically within the regulatory scope of the PRA (art 2). Dealing in investments as principal is a PRA-regulated activity only if the relevant firm is designated by the PRA after consulting with the FCA (art 3). Art 8 of the Order requires the PRA to issue a statement of policy with respect to its exercise of the power to designate investment firms. In its Statement, the PRA identified the following factors that will be considered to decide whether or not to designate an eligible investment firm: (i) the firm's balance sheet exceeding an average of £15 billion in gross assets over four quarters; (ii) the balance sheet of all firms in the same group exceeding the above threshold; and (iii) if the firm is part of the group of a PRA-regulated firm, whether its revenues, balance sheet and risk-taking is significant relative to those of the group as a whole. See PRA, 'Designation of Investment Firms for Prudential Supervision by the Prudential Regulation Authority' (Statement of Policy, March 2013) paras 8–12, available at <http://www.bankofengland.co.uk/publications/Documents/other/pra/designationofinvestmentfirms.pdf> (accessed 18 July 2020).
68 FSMA 2000, s 55A (inserted by FSA 2012, s 11).
69 FSMA 2000, s 1C (2) (d) (inserted by FSA 2012, s 6).
70 FSMA 2000, s 1D (inserted by FSA 2012, s 6).
71 FSMA 2000, s 74.
72 FSMA 2000, s 73A.
73 FSMA 2000, s 3I (inserted by FSA 2012, s 6).

compensate its depositors, the Treasury can give directions to the Bank of England, with a view to protecting the public interest. This, in a way, creates a hierarchy of decision-making with the Treasury at the top followed by the Bank of England, which includes the PRA, and with the FCA at the bottom. Georgosouli, for instance, argues that the concept of resilience, in the sense of capacity to adapt, can be used to ensure that the FCA and PRA share a common umbrella policy objective and work together in a coherent manner.[74]

3.5.2 *The governance of the regulatory bodies*

The corporate governance structure of the new regulatory authorities reflects the hierarchy established by the division of responsibilities among them, that is, the Treasury, FPC, PRA and FCA. The composition of the court of directors of the Bank of England (appointed by the Treasury) was amended to include four Deputy Governors, namely, for financial stability, monetary policy, markets and banking, and prudential regulation. The non-executive members of the court shall be no more than nine, a reform that was first introduced by section 239 of the Banking Act 2009. The FPC consists of the Governor and Deputy Governors of the Bank, the CEO of the FCA, one executive employee appointed by the Governor, four external members appointed by the Chancellor of the Exchequer and one non-voting representative of the Treasury.[75] A new committee of the court – the Oversight Committee – consisting of all the independent directors was introduced in 2012 to supervise the discharge of the functions of the FPC and was empowered to remove its members with the approval of the Treasury.[76] The Oversight Committee was abolished in 2016, and its functions were transferred to the court of directors.[77]

The PRA was originally headed by a board consisting of a majority of independent non-executive directors. The executive members of the board were prescribed by the legislation: the Governor of the Bank chairs it, the Deputy Governor for prudential regulation acts as the CEO of the PRA and the Deputy Governor for financial stability is also an executive director. The non-executive members are to be appointed by the court of directors of the Bank with the approval of the Treasury.[78] Currently, the relevant functions are exercised by the Bank's Prudential Regulation Committee (PRC) which consists of the Governor of the Bank of England, the Deputy Governor for prudential regulation who acts as the chief executive for prudential regulation, the Deputy Governors for financial stability and for markets and banking, the CEO of the FCA, a member appointed by the Governor with the Chancellor's approval and six external members appointed by the Chancellor.[79] The PRA is required to appoint a Practitioner Panel and to consult it before exercising its functions.[80]

Similarly, the board of the FCA is chaired by a non-executive chairman appointed by the Treasury; includes a CEO appointed by the Treasury; and also comprises the Bank's Deputy

---

74 See Andromachi Georgosouli, 'The FCA, the PRA and the Idea of Resilience as a Narrative for Policy Coherence' (2012) <https://papers.ssrn.com/sol3/papers.cfm?abstract_id=2094569> (accessed 10 July 2020).

75 Bank of England Act 1998, Sch 2A s 1 (inserted by FSA 2012, Sch 1).

76 Bank of England Act 1998, Sch 2A s 9, as it stood before the coming into force of the Bank of England and Financial Services Act 2016.

77 Bank of England and Financial Services Act 2016 s 3.

78 FSMA 2000, Sch 1ZB (inserted by FSA 2012, Sch 3), as it stood before the coming into force of the Bank of England and Financial Services Act 2016.

79 Bank of England Act 1998, Sch 6A, inserted by the Bank of England and Financial Services Act 2016, Sch 1.

80 FSMA 2000, ss 2L–2N (inserted by FSA 2012, s 6).

Governor for prudential regulation as a non-executive member, two non-executive members appointed by the Treasury and at least one further member appointed by the Treasury which must ensure that the majority of members are non-executive.[81] At the time of writing the board of the FCA consisted of nine members: a non-executive chair, six non-executive directors, the CEO and one other executive director.[82] The FCA is required to appoint four panels of stakeholders which it will have to consult the Practitioner Panel, the Smaller Business Practitioner Panel, the Markets Practitioner Panel and the Consumer Panel.[83]

Overall, the five key figures in the new regime – all appointed by the Treasury – are as follows: the Governor of the Bank, who chairs the FPC and sits on the PRC; the Deputy Governors for financial stability and markets and banking, who are members of the FPC and the PRC; the Deputy Governor for prudential regulation, who is a member of the FPC; the CEO of the PRA division and a member of the FCA's board; and the CEO of the FCA, who is also a member of the FPC and the PRC. These five persons dominate all three decision-making bodies, namely, the FPC, the PRC and the FCA. This overlap is intended to ensure the smooth co-operation and co-ordination of the authorities.

A particular concern of the 2012 Act was to ensure the existence of a sound information flow between the authorities and avoiding regulatory clashes. This is achieved by introducing a statutory duty on the part of the FCA and PRA to co-ordinate the exercise of their functions and prepare a relevant memorandum of understanding.[84] In addition, the two authorities must take steps to co-operate with the Bank of England,[85] and the Treasury is given the power to establish boundaries between the responsibilities of the two Authorities.[86] Furthermore, Part 4 of the Act is devoted to the collaboration between the Bank, the Treasury, the PRA and the FCA. The Bank, Treasury and PRA are expected to maintain a memorandum of understanding on crisis management, and all four entities have to maintain a memorandum with respect to the UK's representation on international organisations such as the European Supervisory Authorities.[87] This approach follows established practice since the enactment of the Banking Act 2009, which provided for the Treasury, Bank of England and FSA to adopt a memorandum of understanding with respect to the exercise of the stabilisation functions of the Bank.

3.5.3 An evaluation of the current UK regulatory architecture

The Financial Services Act 2012 marks the abandonment of the single financial regulator approach[88] and the adoption of a form of a 'Twin Peaks' approach,[89] whereby different

---

81 FSMA 2000, Sch 1ZA (inserted by FSA 2012, Sch 3).
82 FCA, 'The FCA Board' (13 June 2019) <https://www.fca.org.uk/about/fca-board> (accessed 26 July 2020).
83 FSMA 2000, ss 2M–2R (inserted by FSA 2012, s 6).
84 FSMA 2000, ss 3D–3E (inserted by FSA 2012, s 6). A draft memorandum was published immediately after the introduction of the Financial Services Bill 2012 in Parliament. The full text of the memorandum is available on the FCA's official website at <https://www.fca.org.uk/news/statements/fca-and-bank-england-agree-memorandum-understanding-supervision-markets-and-market> (accessed 20 July 2020).
85 FSMA 2000, s 3Q (inserted by FSA 2012, s 6).
86 FSMA 2000, s 3G (inserted by FSA 2012, s 6).
87 FSA 2012, ss 65–67.
88 This part is based on Andreas Kokkinis, 'The Financial Services Act 2012: The Recent Overhaul of the United Kingdom's Financial Regulatory Structure' (2013) *International Corporate and Commercial Law Review* 325.
89 The concept was developed by Michael Taylor in the early 1990s. See Mark Taylor, 'Twin Peaks: A Regulatory Structure for the New Century' Centre for the Study of Financial Innovation (CSFI), London (1995); ibid., 'Peak Practice: How to Reform the UK's Regulatory System' CSFI, London (1996); ibid., 'Twin Peaks Revisited' CSFI, London (2009).

regulators deal with the two main aspects of financial regulation, namely, prudential regulation and conduct of business regulation. The new regime draws a clear distinction between macro-prudential regulation (FPC), micro-prudential regulation (PRC) and conduct of business regulation (FCA). This is the main advantage of the new structure, as it ensures that prudential regulation of systemic financial institutions is the core function of an authority dedicated to this objective, rather than one of the responsibilities of an umbrella regulator such as the FSA.

A further synergy arises out of combining the rescue function of the Bank of England with its micro-prudential supervisory function. Given the strong complementarity between monitoring the safety and soundness of banks, and intervening to prevent crises, it makes sense to have both of these functions within the same institution, an objective that is achieved under the new regime, since the PRA is a subsidiary of the Bank. Finally, the power granted to the FPC to give instructions to the two authorities and the power of the PRA to veto a decision of the FCA, if it is likely to threaten the stability of systemic institutions, ensure that the objective of safeguarding the stability of the financial system will not be undermined by the activity of any regulator. For instance, the PRA can veto the imposition on a systemic bank of severe penalties proposed by the FCA due to a breach of conduct of business regulation, if such a measure would threaten the stability of the bank in question or of the financial system as a whole.

The actual potential of the new structure to deliver the expected results will depend on the dynamics that evolve between the regulators, and especially on the information flows among them.[90] To be sure, the main difficulty with the upcoming regime is the complexity that it inevitably leads to. There are now two potential authorities responsible for licensing financial institutions (namely, the PRA and the FCA), and three regulatory bodies with overlapping responsibilities. Furthermore, the competition objective of the FCA overlaps with the responsibilities of the Competition and Markets Authority. A related concern is the increased administrative costs that the new structure entails, and the loss of economies of scale and scope achieved through the introduction of the FSA a decade and a half ago. At any rate, the link between regulatory structure and the quality of regulation and supervision is only a tentative one, as there are many other factors that affect the quality of supervision. Therefore, it remains to be seen whether the benefits of the new structure will outweigh the increased complexity of the regime and the considerable implementation costs that it entailed.

3.6 Outcomes- and judgement-based regulations

Rapid changes affecting the regulatory structure of banking sector in the aftermath of GFC have revealed an important question, namely, how close are the UK financial markets to safety and soundness, and compliance with the law. The 2007–2009 financial crisis revealed evident failures of the UK regulatory regime in respect of legitimacy and accountability. Indeed, the bank collapses (e.g. Northern Rock, Royal Bank of Scotland and Halifax Bank of Scotland)[91] have revealed a lack of effective control by the supervisory authorities

---

90 For a discussion of competing regulatory models, see Charles Goodhart, 'The Organisational Structure of Banking Supervision' (2010) FSI Occasional Papers No. 1, available at <http://www.sa-dhan.net/Adls/Dl6/Baselcommittee/TheOrganisationalStructure.pdf> (accessed 15 July 2020).

91 See Eilís Ferran, 'Crisis-Driven Regulatory Reform: Where in the World Is the EU Going?' in Eilís Ferran, Niamh Moloney, Jennifer G. Hill and John C. Coffee, Jr. (eds), *The Regulatory Aftermath of the Global Financial Crisis* (CUP 2012) 24–25. See also Clare Chambers, 'The Turner Review: A Verbose Attempt at Curbing

delegated to monitor and prevent financial risks. In response to those failures, the regulators have made a significant switch from a principles-based regime towards a more intrusive and systemic regulatory approach.[92]

As mentioned, the principles-based regulatory approach was implemented by a mechanism of flexible provisions, while the FSA had the responsibility to act in the interests of market growth and success with a clear division of accountability and roles between the regulator and regulated entities. In this context, the Turner Review made a significant shift in the approach to the regulation of the UK financial and banking sector.[93] The document was issued by the FSA in 2009 as a response to the widening global crisis and the implications of bank collapses (such as Northern Rock). Its recommendations were based on a macro-prudential approach rather than focusing solely on specific firms.[94] The Review proposed a new type of regulatory regime, namely, a principles-based one.[95] Such a regime meant 'moving away from reliance on detailed, prescriptive rules and relying more on high-level, broadly stated rules or principles to set the standards by which regulated firms must conduct business'.[96]

According to the Review, such a regulatory regime involves the following: (1) a radical shift in supervisory style from focusing on systems and processes to focusing on key business outcomes and risks, and on the sustainability of business models and strategies; (2) a different approach to the assessment of approved persons, with a focus on technical skills as well as probity; and (3) an outstanding increase in resources devoted to sectoral and firm comparator analysis, enabling the FSA to identify emerging sector-wide trends which may create systemic risk.[97]

The main challenge was moving from regulation based only on observable facts to regulation based on judgements about the future.[98] As the Paulson Report stated, 'a new regulatory architecture accountable to investors, with flexibility to adapt to changing markets and clarity of responsibility to interact with international counterparts to forge a seamless global market infrastructure, would inspire the confidence for the financial system to create prosperity in all sectors once again'.[99] On this view, particular attention should be paid to the information asymmetry to which business transactions are generally subject. The imbalanced relationship between bank managers and customers is principally determined by the lack of financial knowledge of the latter and causes a distortion of customers' choices at

---

the Cycle' (2009) 30 *Business Law Review* 158; Simon Crown, 'Turner Review and Its Impact on the Future of Banking' (2009) 24(65) *Butterworths Journal of International Banking and Financial Law* 243; Stephen Platt, 'Why Turner Got it Wrong' (2009) 21(9) *Compliance Monitor* 1.

92 Black (n 24) 1042–1045.

93 See Financial Services Authority, 'The Turner Review. A Regulatory Response to the Global Banking Crisis' (March 2009) 18–20. See also Iain MacNeil and Justin O'Brien, 'Introduction: The Future of Financial Regulation' in Iain MacNeil and Justin O'Brien (eds), *The Future of Financial Regulation* (Hart Publishing 2010) 19–20; Iain MacNeil, 'The Trajectory of Regulatory Reform in the UK in the Wake of the Financial Crisis' (2010) 11 *European Business Organization Law Review* 497–499.

94 See MacNeil (n 93) 487.

95 The principles-based regime consists of a set of second-level norms, such as standards, guidance, voluntary codes, ethical and moral values, and best practices enhancing forms of self-induced legislation.

96 See Julia Black, Martin Hopper and Christa Band, 'Making a Success of Principles-Based Regulation' (2007) 1 *Law and Financial Markets Review* 191.

97 See Financial Services Authority (n 93) 88–92.

98 A simple principle must be accompanied by a strong judgement of the facts in short, moving to an outcomes-based regime is considered to be the most appropriate way of resolving the recent regulatory failures.

99 See Henry Paulson, 'Reform the Architecture of Regulation' *Financial Times* (18 March 2009) 13.

the time when the investment or transaction is executed.[100] For instance, the financial crisis showed that customers were too trusting of banks with little understanding of the risks of commercial transaction. Market credibility can be measured in terms of intermediaries' accountability, not only from the point of view of the suitability of market actors, but also of effective enforcement. In this context, the role of internal controls such as the function of audit committees represents the best expression for the adoption of forms of self-regulation in terms of detailed duties and improved reputations.

In July 2010, the UK Government issued a significant consultation document which identified failures in the supervision system to maintain financial stability and consumer protection.[101] The effective consequence was the adoption of shared rules and forms of soft law.[102] The current activity of the financial markets has permitted the development of new methods of regulation, such as the principles-based regime and the outcomes-based regime.[103] These new forms of regulation have been reflected in a self-regulation regime[104] characterised by internal controls, best practices, compliance and 'treat customers fairly' programmes.[105] In this context, the UK regulatory strategy has launched the 'outcomes-based' regime governed, not only by rules but also by principles, which have to be correctly interpreted. The 'outcomes-based' regime lies in the market's judgement where 'judgement-led regulation affords greater scope of discretion for regulators and presupposes that regulators have the capacity and the willingness to use that discretion'.[106] That is based on the idea of a self-regulation regime in the sense of market confidence. The banking and corporate failures need to be seen in terms of 'reputational value' on financial markets that means reputational risk and potential damages in the investment operations.[107]

For example, the intermediaries' behaviours in financial transactions are not only enforced by law, through mandatory disclosure, but also by reputation efficiency as it determines the correct business operation. By the same token, the importance of self-regulatory measures – having their origin in confidence, trust and right culture – lies in the role that they can play in bringing about sound financial stability and 'market efficiency', which requires a high quality of information together with a high degree of credibility on the part of the actors concerned.[108] In substance, whilst the disclosure regime reduces the costs of

100 See Alessio M. Pacces, 'Financial Intermediation in the Securities Markets Law and Economics of Conduct of Business Regulation' (2000) 20(4) *International Review of Law and Economics* 499.
101 See HM Treasury, 'A New Approach to Financial Regulation: Judgement, Focus and Stability' (July 2010). Following this consultation paper, the UK Government produced other consultation documents, namely, 'A New Approach to Financial Regulation: Building a Stronger System' (February 2011) and 'A New Approach to Financial Regulation: A Blueprint for Reform' (June 2011).
102 Soft law signifies a form of non-binding rules constituted by legal opinions, statements, guides, protocols and commentaries. These forms have no legal force but can influence the courts and market participants.
103 See The Economist, 'Bolting the Stable Door' (21 March 2009) 35.
104 See Julia Black, 'Decentring Regulation: Understanding the Role of Regulation and Self-Regulation in a "Post-Regulatory" World' (2001) 54 *Current Legal Problems* 103, 112–113.
105 See FSA, 'Treating Customers Fairly: Towards Fair Outcomes for Consumers' (July 2006).
106 See Andromachi Georgosouli, 'Judgement-Led Regulation: Some Critical Reflections' (Financial Services Authority conference 'Academic Input for Better Regulation', January 2012), available at <https://ssrn.com/abstract=2053505> (accessed 25 July 2020). See also Georgosouli, 'Judgement-Led Regulation: Reflections on Data and Discretion' (2013) 14 *Journal of Banking Regulation* 209–210.
107 See Charles A.E. Goodhart, 'The Regulatory Response to the Financial Crisis' (2008) LSE Financial Markets Group Paper Series, Special Paper 177, 9, available at <http://www.lse.ac.uk/fmg/documents/specialPapers/2008/sp177.pdf> (accessed 26 July 2020).
108 See Ronald J. Gilson and Reinier H. Kraakman, 'The Mechanisms of Market Efficiency' (1984) 70 *Virginia Law Review* 549.

capital and information, voluntary self-disclosure systems presuppose perfect alignment of manager and investor interests. To achieve allocative efficiency on the securities markets, firms should act fairly and compete on a level playing field.[109]

It can be argued that a set of agreed principles can allow a certain degree of rulebook simplification and provide the regulator with the needed flexibility to respond to market developments. It can also provide some greater flexibility for firms themselves but is not a substitute for a good understanding between regulators and regulated entities about what is not acceptable market practice, and it can only work effectively if supervisors are trained to focus on outcomes and system-wide risks.[110] Principles are used to treat the market fairly with a set of best practices; however, the complexities of the regulatory system result in fragmentation and a substantive lack of accountability. In addition, the principles adopted to regulate the markets do not seem to operate in a clear manner. As a result, rule-making (specifically normative activity) has been considered too slow to keep up with innovation in the sphere of financial instruments (as in the case of derivatives) and has been relegated to the same level as principles, with the inevitable confusion of their respective roles.[111] Thus, the UK regulatory system still relies on principles to regulate firms' behaviours, which means that the financial markets self-regulate through internal management controls under the monitoring of the FCA.

3.7 Conclusion

Predictability, legitimacy, accountability, certainty: these concepts constitute the benchmarks of an efficient market where consumer confidence and investor protection are the fundamental corollaries of transparent behaviours. However, a certain amount of effectiveness and integrity is lost if the supervisory authorities are not held accountable to monitor the business conduct of market players. In this context, the UK regulatory architecture has undergone two extensive overhauls in the last two decades: the first to reflect a highly interconnected financial industry sector and the second to respond to the deficiencies revealed by the GFC. As discussed in this chapter, UK banking regulation has configured a clear relationship between three paradigms, namely, the principles-based regime, the outcomes-based regime and the judgement-led approach. From the above analysis, it can be argued that a judgement-led response has replaced the self-regulation regime, addressing the shortcomings of a principles-based strategy that failed to regulate the conduct of financial actors.

Glossary of terms

* Principles-based regulation: Broadly worded high-level principles that regulated entities are free to operationalise and implement.
* Principle: General rule or second level of statutory norm that deploys its legal force under the risk of misconduct and of non-compliant behaviours.

---

109 See John C. Coffee Jr., 'Market Failure and the Economic Case for a Mandatory Disclosure System' (1984) 70 *Virginia Law Review* 734.
110 See Andromachi Georgosouli, 'The Revision of the FSA's Approach to Regulation: An Incomplete Agenda?' (2010) 7 *Journal of Business Law* 608–609.
111 See Erik F. Gerding, 'Code, Crash, and Open Source: The Outsourcing of Financial Regulation to Risk Models and the Global Financial Crisis' (2009) 84 *Washington Law Review* 132–133.

- Market confidence: Key regulatory objective, in terms of investor protection, on account of its fundamental role in safeguarding the soundness of the financial markets.
- Prudential regulation: Regulation protects financial stability and the consumers of banking products but also increases moral hazard on the financial condition of the firms.
- Macro-prudential regulation: Regulation aiming to protect the stability of the financial system as a whole.
- Micro-prudential regulation: Regulation aiming to safeguard the safety and soundness of individual systemic financial institutions.
- Prudential Regulation Authority (PRA): New micro-prudential regulator for all systemic financial institutions; an operational division of the Bank of England.
- Financial Conduct Authority (FCA): The authority regulating and supervising the market conduct of all financial institutions whether they are licensed by it or by the PRA.
- UK Listing Authority (UKLA): It is the UK's securities regulator which maintains the official list of securities admitted to trading on the Main Market of the London Stock Exchange.
- HM treasury: Government department that may provide financial assistance to a financial institution, incur expenditure in connection with the Banking Act 2009 or provide financial assistance or a loan to the Financial Services Compensation Scheme manager.
- Outcomes-based regulation: Regulatory approach based on rules and principles which prescribe a certain outcome while allowing firms to choose the means to achieve this outcome.

Practice questions

As a result of the enactment of the Financial Services and Markets Act 2000 and the many pieces of secondary legislation issued under its various provisions, the UK system of banking regulation has abandoned its emphasis on broad regulatory discretion and informal norm-setting, negotiation and enforcement; it now rests, instead, on formal legal provisions and detailed procedures. Critically discuss.

You may also it find useful to review the chapter through the following questions:

- What are the main features of the UK financial regulation architecture?
- What are the key responsibilities/tasks of the FCA and the sPRA?
- What does the Northern Rock scandal tell us about supervisory practices at the FSA in the run-up to the crisis?
- What does the 'Run on the Rock' report tell us about the operation of the tripartite structure in 2007?
- Why do governments set up independent regulators, and how do they attempt to balance independence with accountability? Is this balance appropriately struck in the new UK structure?

4 EU harmonisation of the banking regulatory framework

4.1 Introduction

This chapter examines the regulatory structures which exist at the EU level for regulating banks. The main focus of this chapter is on the historical background of EU banking regulation, on the broad policy goals which underlie it and on the recent reforms to the legislative framework at the EU level for bank products. This chapter will not address the implications of the UK's departure from the EU; these will be addressed in Chapter 17.

Over the last few years, technology has brought about a spectacular change in trade negotiations and cross-border transactions: although the 1957 Treaty of Rome looked forward to the creation of a single market in goods, services, capital and people, European countries maintained a wide range of barriers to the achievement of a single market.[1] Domestic reluctance to take over EU directives is best explained in terms of asymmetric vulnerability of domestic corporate governance systems and reforms: national differences in normative and the legal systems constituted a serious obstacle to the effective reform of the financial services sector. The normative rules governing financial services encompass two core elements: first, the free movement of financial services, and subsequently, the specific regulations under which those services circulate among the Member States.[2]

In the European Union (EU), banking integration can be considered a fundamental pillar of the financial regulatory framework. As part of the creation of a single market, the Commission launched a vast programme of harmonisation to ensure the free movement of financial services while reducing barriers between Member States. Specifically, the EU legislators aimed to develop an internal market in which banks could trade their products according to harmonised prudential standards and home State authorisation.[3] The free movement of financial services posed the basis of a mechanism for passporting and licensing of banks and financial institutions that was progressively implemented in the Financial Services Action Plan, as discussed at length in Section 4.4.

This chapter also examines the creation of the EU 'Banking Union' encompassing all Eurozone Member States, which was never joined by the UK. This process faces important legal and political hurdles. The chapter considers the new supervisory role of European Central Bank (ECB) as the regulatory authority of all large banks in the Eurozone. The chapter

---

1 Treaty of Rome (EEC) signed on 25 March 1957 (applied from 1 January 1958). The Treaty purported the idea 'to lay the foundations of an ever-closer union among the peoples of Europe'. In order to achieve this objective, a single or integrated market is to make the EU 'an area without internal frontiers in which the free movement of goods, persons, services and capital is ensured'.
2 See Article 49 EC of the Treaty of Rome.
3 The internal market is generally defined as an area without internal frontiers in which the free movement of goods, persons, services and capital is ensured according to the provisions of the Treaty of Rome.

concludes by arguing that co-operation and co-ordination between supervisory authorities are necessary for achieving effective harmonisation of macro-prudential policies.

4.2 The EU Banking Directives

The first legislative act towards the integration of financial services was the Banking Directive of 1977 which granted full responsibility for supervision of banks operating in a given country to national supervisors.[4] The Directive established the requirements for obtaining a licence to operate as a credit institution, i.e. separate and adequate own funds, effective management run by experienced persons, and adopted the host country model (of host country supervision). The Directive also provided that national supervisors should co-operate, and that foreign identity could not be a ground for refusing a banking licence. It allowed for cross-border branching under the host country rule, which signified that a bank had to obtain permission to operate in a foreign country by the supervisory agencies of that country. This marked a significant step towards the liberalisation of cross-border banking activity. Most importantly, the Directive introduced the concept of passport rights and home country control although it was initially only limited to freedom of establishment and did not confer any express passporting rights per se.[5]

The First Banking Directive was followed by the Second Banking Directive in 1989 which established the single banking licence to provide access to financial institutions established in Member States.[6] The Directive adopted the principle of home State authorisation and prudential supervision for credit institutions. It applied the principle of mutual recognition for banks which means access to the activity of credit institutions if they are recognised by the home State. In substance, a bank authorised as a credit institution in its home country can provide a wide range of banking and investment services throughout the Community area by opening branches or by supplying services in other Member States, without being subjected to any local licensing requirements.[7]

In this way, the Directive liberalised banking services, and credit institutions which are authorised to operate in any Member State are allowed to establish branches and to provide cross-border services throughout the community on the basis of the principle of home country supervision.[8] The Directive extended the licensing conditions to include minimum initial capital and own funds requirements, together with provisions allowing home State regulators to monitor the shareholders of banks.[9] Banks and other financial institutions were allowed to set up branches or provide services in other Member States, but they

---

4 First Council Directive 77/780/EEC of 12 December 1977 on the coordination of the laws, regulations and administrative provisions relating to the taking up and pursuit of the business of credit institutions.

5 George Walker, Robert Purves and Michael Blair, 'European Financial Services' in George Walker and Robert Purves (eds), *Financial Services Law* (4th edn, OUP 2018) 77.

6 Second Council Directive 89/646/EEC of 15 December 1989 on the coordination of laws, regulations and administrative provisions relating to the taking up and pursuit of the business of credit institutions and amending Directive 77/780/EEC.

7 The Second Banking Directive provides a definition of credit institution as 'whose business is to receive deposits or other repayable funds from the public and to grant credits for its own account'.

8 Ross Cranston, Emilios Avgouleas, Kristin van Zwieten, Christopher Hare and Theodor van Sante, *Principles of Banking Law* (3rd edn, OUP 2017) 9.

9 Communication from the Commission on Intra-EU Investment in the Financial Services Sector, C/2005/4080, 21 October 2005, reminding Member States of the relevant Treaty freedoms and their application to supervisory decisions in relation to cross-border consolidation.

were subject to the authorisation of host State of the branch that could impose additional regulatory requirements. The Second Banking Directive has been amended by the Credit Institutions Directive[10] which has now been replaced by the EU legislation on prudential requirements and supervision of banks and investment firms – Capital Requirements Regulation (CRR)[11] and Capital Requirements Directive (CRD IV).[12] The Banking Directives constitute the pillars of integration of financial services across Europe although the full harmonisation of rules among Member States is still far from complete.

4.3 The freedom of establishment and mutual recognition of banks

European banking integration aims to ensure freedom of establishment for credit institutions and mutual recognition of financial services. The Banking Directives adopted a 'minimum harmonisation approach' to regulate the legislative framework of investment firms.[13] These directives provide the right to circulate financial services on a cross-border basis. This model can be considered the first regulatory scheme in the EU banking sector and constitutes the basis for the principle of mutual recognition, formally launched in the Commission's White Paper on Completing the Internal Market.[14] The White Paper aimed to remove the obstacles, i.e. administrative barriers to the free movement of capital, and create a single market in banking and financial services.[15] However, the minimum harmonisation allowed Member States to impose more burdensome obligations on their own firms and on other European entities on public interest grounds. Mutual recognition gives effect to cross-border market access, i.e. freedom of establishment and services, on the basis of home country control system which purports ongoing supervision. This implies mutual trust and adoption of common rules among EU Member States on the basis of compliance with certain agreed minimum harmonisation standards and with supervision through the home country control.[16] The home country control and mutual recognition have been consolidated in the Single European Act of 1986[17] and Maastricht Treaty of 1992.[18] It can

---

10 Directive 2000/12/EC of the European Parliament and of the Council of 20 March 2000 relating to the taking up and pursuit of the business of credit institutions.
11 Regulation (EU) No. 575/2013 of the European Parliament and of the Council of 26 June 2013 on prudential requirements for credit institutions and investment firms and amending Regulation (EU) No. 648/2012.
12 Directive 2013/36/EU of the European Parliament and of the Council of 26 June 2013 on access to the activity of credit institutions and the prudential supervision of credit institutions and investment firms, amending Directive 2002/87/EC and repealing Directives 2006/48/EC and 2006/49/EC.
13 The 'minimum harmonization' approach finds its origin in the well-known decision *Cassis de Dijon* in 1979 (Case 120/78) which also developed the concept of 'mutual recognition'. See also Commission Communication on its interpretation of the decision in Cassis de Dijon (OJ C256, 3.10.80, 2) and Commission Communication to the Parliament, the Council and the Member States (COM (1980) 30 DEF, 24.1.80).
14 Commission of the European Communities, 'Completing the Internal Market. White Paper from the Commission to the European Council' (Brussels, 14 June 1985) COM(85) 310 final.
15 The aim to remove all obstacles to free trade and to secure the effective operation of the single market based on a mutual recognition policy was the foundation of the Commission's White Paper. However, the effective free movement of financial services began with the Treaty of Maastricht of 1992 and Financial Services Action Plan of 1998.
16 Walker, Purves and Blair (n 5) 78.
17 Single European Act of 1986 [OJ L 169, 29.6.1987, 1].
18 See the Treaty on European Union, as signed in Maastricht on 7 February 1992 <https://europa.eu/european-union/sites/europaeu/files/docs/body/treaty_on_european_union_en.pdf> (accessed 24 March 2020).

be argued that the road towards securities market integration exhibited the same contours as the monetary integration which culminated in the achievement of the single currency (the euro) in 1999.[19]

Notwithstanding the recent process of legislative integration, there is a lack of uniformity among Member States, as Member States maintain internal barriers that frustrate the EU financial reforms: an example can be found in the Services Directive[20] with the *vexata quaestio* whether the rule to be applied is the one of the countries of origin or the one of the countries of destination. It can be argued that the Single European Market may represent an illusion, when it comes to the effective integration of the rules on financial instruments.[21] Political obstacles hampered by the recent financial and sovereign debt crises show reluctance to implement harmonised rules and open the internal frontiers. These obstacles create a significant gap with extra-European States (the US, China, India, Japan) in terms of governance and consumer and investor rights. The lack of the information necessary to access services has created asymmetric conditions within the internal market: this negative consequence determines restrictions and abusive behaviours as between stakeholders and policymakers. For EU financial markets, effective competition with clear liberalisation would make a contribution towards reducing prices and improving the level of service.

The freedom of establishment and mutual recognition of banks remain anchored to the domestic and national legislation: the recent banking scandals[22] demonstrated that the objectives 'to assess the current conditions for implementation of the regulation of the securities markets in the European Union; to assess how the mechanism for regulating the securities markets in the European Union can best respond to developments under way on the securities markets; and in order to eliminate barriers and obstacles, propose as a result scenarios for adapting current practices in order to ensure greater convergence and co-operation in day-to-day implementation and take into account new developments on the markets'[23] proved to be overambitious.

4.4 The Financial Services Action Plan

The financial markets can be seen as the major cornerstone of the EU's strategy in terms of policy efforts. Given the importance of capital markets for the future of the Eurozone and the devastating consequences of the global financial crisis, the need for adequate regulation of financial markets and institutions has become the main objective of the European reforms in recent years. What has been achieved ensues from the Financial Services Action

---

19 Council Regulation (EC) No. 1103/97 of 17 June 1997 on certain provisions relating to the introduction of the euro. For a commentary see Rosa M. Lastra, *International Financial and Monetary Law* (2nd edn, OUP 2015) 234–236.

20 Directive 2006/123/EC of the European Parliament and of the Council of 12 December 2006 on services in the internal market, OJ L 376, 27.12.2006, 36.

21 Jette Steen Knudsen, 'Is the Single European Market an Illusion? Obstacles to Reform of EU Takeover Regulation' (2005) 11(4) *European Law Journal* 507–508.

22 See the bank collapses namely Northern Rock, Royal Bank of Scotland and Halifax Bank of Scotland that revealed a complete lack of control by the UK authorities (principally the FSA) delegated to monitor and prevent financial risks.

23 Committee of Wise Men, 'Initial Report of the Committee of Wise Men on the Regulation of European Securities Markets' (Brussels 2000) <http://europa.eu.int/comm./internal_market> (accessed 20 June 2020).

Plan (FSAP)[24] and the numerous financial directives that the EU institutions have adopted with a view to reforming the securities sector.[25] The FSAP legislative package aimed to establish a single market in wholesale financial services, improve competition on retail markets and enhance prudential supervision. The EU legislator adopted this complex financial architecture to ensure free access to capital markets and implement financial regulation among Member States.

First, it appears that the perceived need for better regulation and consumer protection has driven the EU's strategy, also under the influence of the real integration of the markets which has occurred. Particularly, evidence of a desire to remove the existing national barriers as between Member States has marked certain directives, for example, the MiFID Directive which is considered to be the centrepiece of the FSAP.[26] This assumption can be measured by the growing need for harmonised securities regulation; a common set of rules at international level have definitively replaced the former local rules and administrative burdens (costs of cross-border financial activities, such as permissions, licenses and authorities' approvals). The effective consequence is the adoption of shared rules and forms of 'soft law'[27]; in short, the current activity of the financial markets has permitted the development of new methods of regulation, such as the principles-based regime and the outcomes-based regime.[28]

Second, these new forms of regulation have been reflected in a self-regulation regime[29] characterised by internal controls, best practices, compliance and 'treat customers fairly' programmes.[30] At first glance, the complexities of the regulatory system result in fragmentation and a substantive confusion of accountability; indeed, the principles adopted to regulate the markets do not seem to operate in a clear manner. In the last few decades, rule-making (specifically normative activity) has been considered to be too slow to keep up with innovation in the sphere of financial instruments (in the case of derivatives, for example) and has been relegated to the same level as principles, with the inevitable confusion of

---

24 In general terms, the Financial Services Action Plan (FSAP) was adopted by the Commission in 1999 to improve the single market in financial services. The programme is divided into four broad areas: (1) retail markets; (2) wholesale markets; (3) prudential rules and supervision and (4) other aspects necessary to complete the financial market. Briefly, the FSAP is inserted into the 'Lamfalussy Reform' that provides a single set of rules for Member States through a complex structure of four levels. See the analysis of Jane Welch, 'European Financial Services' in Michael Blair and George Walker (eds), *Financial Services Law* (OUP 2006) 762.

25 See the Prospectus Directive, the Financial Conglomerates Directive, the Credit Rating Agency Regulation, the Insider Trading Directive, the Market Abuse Directive, the Capital Requirements Directive, the Markets in Financial Instruments Directive (MiFID).

26 The fifth recital in the preamble to MiFID provides that 'it is necessary to establish a comprehensive regulatory regime governing the execution of transactions in financial instruments irrespective of the trading methods used to conclude those transactions so as to ensure a high quality of execution of investor transactions and to uphold the integrity and overall efficiency of the financial system'.

27 Soft law signifies here a form of non-binding rules constituted by legal opinions, statements, guides, protocols and commentaries.

28 In the Turner Review (2009), the former Financial Services Authority launched a new type of principles regime, namely, an outcomes-based regime characterised by the improvement of enforcement and prudential supervision.

29 On the significance of self-regulation regime, see Julia Black, 'Decentring Regulation: Understanding the Role of Regulation and Self-regulation in a "Post-Regulatory" World' (2001) 54(1) *Current Legal Problems*, 112–113.

30 For an overview of this matter, see Financial Services Authority, 'Treating Customers Fairly: Towards Fair Outcomes for Consumers' (July 2006).

their respective roles. For instance, in its document[31] the former Financial Services Authority (FSA) put greater stress on the use of principles-based regulation, while affirming that this kind of approach 'means moving away from dictating through detailed prescriptive rules and supervisory actions how firms should operate their business'.[32]

Within the FSAP architecture, the 'Lamfalussy process' has imposed a new common ground of provisions, while adopting a practical and flexible approach to rule-making; in particular, 'all rulemaking bodies within the Lamfalussy framework (adopting both binding and non-binding rules) commit to 'regulatory self-restraint' which is consistent with the principles of better regulation'.[33] The Lamfalussy model adopted a four-level approach: Level 1 – Framework principles to be decided by the normal EU legislative procedures (i.e. proposal by the European Commission to the Council of the European Union and the European Parliament for co-decision); Level 2 – Establishment of two new committees: (a) an EU Securities Committee and (b) an EU Securities Regulators Committee to assist the Commission in determining how to implement the details of the Level 1 framework; Level 3 – Enhanced co-operation and networking among EU securities regulators to ensure consistent and equivalent transposition of Level 1 and 2 legislation (common implementing standards); and Level 4 – Strengthened enforcement (greater role of the Commission to enforce Community law) and enhanced co-operation between the Member States, their regulators and the private sector.

The EU financial reforms are strictly characterised by investor protection measures, and most of them reflect a manifest preoccupation with consumers and their expectations. At this juncture, it is fundamental to observe that consumers cannot be dismissed as persons with little financial clout but must be regarded as an essential parameter of assessment for the whole financial sector. The FSAP architecture has constituted an important innovation in terms of regulatory approach and financial stability. The FSAP model improved the EU regulatory system through robust legislation culminating with the legal platform of the MiFID Directive and the subsequent MiFID II. The European legislation (specifically the FSAP Directives), with its normative system, has strengthened the existing principles-based regime for securities regulation, and the MiFID Directive has imposed a new legal platform where principles are provided within rules and the monitoring function of internal management organisations is strengthened through a need for reputational protection. It can be observed that the European dimension under the MiFID Directive has provided a system of provisions that afford a legal basis for the compliance function.[34]

The European strategies adopted to integrate and harmonise Member States' law, such as the Financial Action Plan and the Lamfalussy model, can be regarded as tools for promoting greater access to the markets via a rule-based system which removes regulatory

---

31 FSA, 'Principles Based Regulation: Focusing on the Outcomes that Matter' (April 2007).

32 Ibid., 4. For a critical view, see Carlos Conceicao and Rosalind Gray, 'Problems of Uncertainty' (2007) 26(6) *International Financial Law Review* 42–43.

33 Valuable evidence can be found for this in 'Inter-institutional Monitoring Group. Final Report Monitoring the Lamfalussy Process' (Brussels, October 2007) 8–13.

34 Europe Economics, 'Study on the Cost of Compliance with Selected FSAP Measures. Final Report' (London, January 2009). Specifically, it has been reported that 'the MiFID Directives have played an important role, giving the compliance function an opportunity to re-define itself in a positive way – even as a source of competitive advantage – whereas previously it had been seen as more of a 'necessary evil' or an afterthought. A concrete example of this would be an increased focus upon (new) product quality due to the implementation of MiFID that allowed the compliance function to present itself in a more positive way to senior management' (p. 25).

barriers.[35] Moreover, that rule-based system aims at establishing detailed rules on transparency, market integrity and investor protection, which should boost greater investment in EU capital markets.[36] However, as has been argued 'despite a sustained legislative drive at the European Union level towards the integration and harmonization of financial markets, by the end of 2008, significant barriers still remained to the integration of European retail banking markets (including banking services to small business)'.[37] The lack of harmonisation between Member States in terms of the legal rules governing financial instruments is a major obstacle to the creation of a single market for financial services.[38] In recent years, this lack has given rise to a significant gap in comparison with the extra-European States, in terms of cross-border transactions, consumer rights and corporate governance.[39] The critical point is that in the absence of full harmonisation, retail investor rights in respect of financial instruments are still determined by differing and sometimes conflicting private international law rules.[40]

4.5 The Lamfalussy report: the role of CEBS

The Lamfalussy report can be considered as the first component of EU financial architecture in terms of supervision and regulation. The report established three external, independent bodies: (i) the Committee of European Securities Regulators ('CESR')[41] which was replaced in 2011 by the European Securities and Markets Authority (ESMA); (ii) the Committee of European Banking Supervisors ('CEBS'),[42] which was replaced in 2011

---

35 Howard Davies and David Green, *Global Financial Regulation* (Polity Press 2008) 134.
36 Gráinne de Búrca, 'The Constitutional Challenge of New Governance in the European Union' (2003) 28(6) *European Law Review* 814–815.
37 John Goddard, Philip Molyneux and John O.S. Wilson, 'Banking in the European Union' in Allen N. Berger Philip Molyneux and John O. S. Wilson (eds), *Oxford Handbook of Banking* (OUP 2012) 833.
38 Three linked strategies have historically been employed to achieve the single market for financial services: harmonisation between Member States of the essential or minimum standards for the prudential supervision of financial institutions; the mutual recognition, by each Member State, of the competence of the respective national regulatory bodies to ensure compliance with those minimum standards; and finally the assignment to the home country, in those areas which have been harmonised between Member States, of the control and supervision of financial institutions (the footnote reproduces the analysis of Gerard Hertig and Robert Lee, 'Four Predictions about the Future of EU Securities Regulation' (2003) 3(2) *Journal of Corporate Law Studies* 368.
39 Kern Alexander, Eilis Ferran, Howell E. Jackson and Niamh Moloney, 'A Report on the Transatlantic Financial Services Regulatory Dialogue' (2007) Harvard Law Discussion Paper Series, John Olin Center for Law, Economics and Business, No. 1.
40 Herbert Kronke, *Capital Markets and Conflict of Laws* (Academie de droit international de la Haye 2001) 261–262; ID, 'Connected and Global Security Markets – With or Without Conflict of Laws?', in Theodor Baums, Klaus J. Hopt and Norbert Hörn (eds), *Corporations, Capital Markets and Business in the Law. Liber Amicorum Richard M. Buxbaum* (Kluwer Law International 2000) 363.
41 The Committee of European Securities Regulators, established by Commission decision in 2001, has replaced the previous Federation of European Securities Commissions (FESCO): it is organised as an independent body with its own rules of procedure and has members drawn from the national regulatory bodies.
42 The Committee of European Banking Supervisors was established by Commission decision in 2003 and focuses on the huge project for the introduction of risk-based capital requirements in the EU banking sector through the implementation of Basel II; 'it is formally charged with promoting convergence of banking supervisory practices and supervisory cooperation in Europe' (CEBS, 'Role, Programme and Challenges' June 2005). The Commission adopted Decision 2009/78/EC, of 23 January 2009 establishing the Committee of European Banking Supervisors and formally repealing Decision 2004/5/EC (Official Journal of the EU, L 25 of 29.1.2009, 23).

by the European Banking Authority (EBA); and (iii) the Committee of European Insurance and Occupational Pensions Supervisors (CEIOPS), which was replaced in 2011 by the European Insurance and Occupational Pensions Authority (EIOPA). In particular, under Level 3 of the Lamfalussy model, those committees played a huge role in ensuring supervisory convergence by laying down best practices, guidance, standards and non-legally binding principles; this prominent challenge affected the implementation of Level 1 and 2 decisions.

The CESR and the CEBS improved the dialogue among Member States and better regulation as regards the implementation of the EU legislation; indeed, CESR was given the task of contributing to the development of confidence and consumer protection.[43] In this regard, the CESR adopted a set of measures for the purposes of implementing EU securities law, namely, peer review, analysis of EU Lamfalussy acts (at Levels 1 and 2) and mediation processes in the event of a failure to implement directives involving a panel of members from other jurisdictions.[44] At this point, the key question has to do with the law-making process in the regulatory bodies: in fact, CESR decisions were based on qualified majority voting at Level 2 and on consensus at Level 3, which obviously means that this constituted an impediment in the event that one member is in disagreement. At the institutional level, the existence of European regulators should facilitate the adoption of EU measures based on a single financial regulatory strategy; on these lines, the creation of a single European supervisor or of an independent agency to control the national supervisors served as the premise to the current Banking Union structure.[45]

By the same token, banking regulatory convergence requires certain tools in order to ensure proper disclosure and adequate accountability on the part of the supervisory authorities[46]; the CEBS pointed out that 'the effectiveness of supervision is closely related to the legitimacy and credibility of the competent supervisory authorities; appropriate disclosure by supervisory authorities is desirable to ensure proper accountability, which in turn helps to promote sound governance practices on the part of the supervisors themselves'.[47] The work at Level 3 has recognised a need for incremental improvements: in particular, the CEBS has proposed a set of concrete improvements designed to deliver supervisory convergence on the basis of three different notions of convergence, namely, convergence in principles, group-specific convergence and hard convergence. The objectives of clear *ex ante* definition of the convergence target and ex post assessment of the results, development of new practical convergence tools and pursuance of hard convergence in certain areas entail phasing out options and national discretions, a proper implementation of the Lamfalussy structure in banking, the development of own-initiative advice by the CEBS and enhanced efforts at Level 4 to ensure consistent implementation of EU law.[48]

---

43 The major features of CESR objectives can be found in 'Which Supervisory Tools for EU Securities Markets' ('Himalaya Report'), CESR/04-333f (October 2004).
44 CESR, 'Mediation Mechanism' CESR/05-483d (January 2006).
45 Eddy Wymeersch, 'The Future of Financial Regulation and Supervision in Europe' (2005) 42(4) *Common Market Law Review* 1005–1009.
46 See generally, Basel Committee on Banking Supervision, *Core Principles Methodology* (October 2006). For an academic view, see Asli Demirgüç-Kunt, Enrica Detragiache and Thierry Tressel, 'Banking on the Principles: Compliance with Basel Core Principles and Bank Soundness' (2006) IMF Working Paper No. 242.
47 CEBS, 'Guidelines on Supervisory Disclosure – Updated' (March 2006) 4.
48 CEBS, 'Contribution to the Lamfalussy Review' (November 2007) 2–3.

Under this supervisory architecture, the unconvincing regulatory structure of committees is evidenced by an insufficient level of control with regard to the responsibility of members; for instance, the Commission exercises solely a role of 'light supervisor' over the CESR mandates. This uncertainty characterises what may be described as a soft law-making process that does not improve the mechanisms of EU legislation.[49] It can be argued that the acts of these regulators have resulted in an area of vague law; indeed, at the same time, the increasing development of activities and competence at Level 3 has determined a huge risk of vulnerability of legitimacy and accountability.[50] Manifestly, the regulatory creep entails a lack of proper monitoring of Community law by market members; at first glance, the total absence of controls would appear to make for ample discretion on the part of the bodies charged with overseeing EU financial legislation. However, better dialogue between external committees and EU institutions should have improved the understanding of Level 3 regulation.

In this connection, it has been argued that the EU institutions should take into account the fact that CESR was itself a fledgling body with a small staff, and that it would be unwise to delegate a large number of mandates for technical advice to it within a short time-scale. But also, 'further work was undertaken by CESR and the underlying Member State regulators to develop their approach to Level 3 work; there it has been strong emphasis on flexible regulation which did not stifle innovation and on consistency of implementation of EU rules and CESR standards and agreed processes'.[51] In order to avoid a lack of transparency and accountability with regard to the securities legislation process, which could favour a form of decentred regulation (i.e. indirect regulation), it has been observed that 'care needs to be taken not to allow law-making power to shift too far in CESR's direction because this could undermine positive features of the model that has emerged in which this power is shared between the Commission, the European Parliament and CESR'.[52] The Lamfalussy process offered a practical solution to the problem of different Member States having different regulations, whereas the European Commission's ambitious programme designed 'to align national regimes across all stages of the trading cycle' seems fragmented and difficult to realise. In this context, an efficient regulatory framework for integrated financial markets can be achieved only if there are certain rules designed to foster investor confidence and consumer protection.

49 An interesting criticism of the Lamfalussy law-making process, particularly focused on CESR, is to be found in Gerard Hertig and Ruben Lee, 'Four Predictions about the Future of EU Securities Regulation' (2003) 3(2) *Journal of Law Corporate Studies* 364–377.

50 Niamh Moloney, 'Innovation and Risk in EC Financial Market Regulation: New Instruments of Financial Market Intervention and the Committee of European Securities Regulators' (2007) 32(5) *European Law Review* 644–646. The author underlines the weaknesses in terms of transparency and accountability of CESR; she observes that 'CESR's formal accountability is minimal; it is not formally accountable to the Member States or the EU institutions and sits somewhat adrift in the institutional structure' (p. 650). At the same time, she points out that 'very little is known as to CESR's working and regulatory culture and how this influences its approach to market regulation'.

51 Michael McKee, 'The Unpredictable Future of European Securities Regulation: A Response to Four Predictions about the Future of EU Securities Regulation by Gerard Hertig and Ruben Lee' (2003) 18(7) *Journal of International Banking Law and Regulation* 282–283.

52 Eilís Ferran, *Building an EU Securities Market* (CUP 2004) 90. The author argues that 'The accountability of CESR members could be focused more on domestic issues than on agencies' supranational activities and such mechanisms are also subject to all of the vagaries that may affect different accountability structures within the Member States' (p. 103).

To set an efficient supervisory approach, the independent regulatory bodies should improve the network of co-operation with the EU institutions, by developing an effective and constructive dialogue with the Level 1 legislation, which will entail more efforts practically to enhance the monitoring function. The major objective of the Lamfalussy structure was to provide single regulation of financial markets for all Member States not only in terms of homogeneous rules but also in terms of co-operation and the implementation of EU legislation. It has been noted that the FSAP in combination with the Lamfalussy process has heavily diluted regulatory competition in the production of laws as a potential driver of optimal regulation and market integration.[53] While the FSAP and Lamfalussy procedure were characterised by a degree of innovation in the instruments of financial market intervention, as they provided a uniform set of rules in a self-regulatory context, a fragmented and incomplete securities market continued to prevail despite these initiatives.[54]

4.6 The MiFID Directive

The Markets in Financial Instruments Directive (2004/39/EC),[55] which replaced the Investment Services Directive (93/22/EEC),[56] constitutes the cornerstone of the scheme of regulatory frameworks launched by the FSAP.[57] The MiFID has been amended by Directive 2014/65/EU ('MiFID II') on markets in financial instruments as discussed at length in Section 4.8 of this chapter.

The MiFID Directive provides a unified framework for securities for (1) investment firms, (2) multilateral trading facilities (MTF), (3) regulated markets (i.e. exchanges) and (4) financial instruments (transferable securities, money market instruments, units in collective investment undertakings and derivatives, excluding bonds and securitised debt). Principally, the Directive is intended to reduce the transaction costs of trading securities; substantially, this objective is achieved by allowing trading to take place outside regulated exchanges and among Member States by awarding investment firms permits or passports to trade. MiFID, which became applicable in November 2007 – now replaced by MiFID II and MiFIR – enables the authorisation given by Member States to investment firms

---

53 Moloney (n 50) 631.
54 Yannis Avgerinos, 'The Need and the Rationale for a European Securities Regulator' in Mads Andenas and Yannis Avgerinos (eds), *Financial Markets in Europe: Towards a Single Regulator?* (Kluwer Law 2003) 146. The authors observe that 'centralization in supervision and more flexible regulation will be the only answer to the hurdles of inconsistencies and loopholes, systemic inflexibility, high-transaction cost, problematic cooperation and coordination and EU's failure to speak with one voice at international negotiations'.
55 Specifically, MiFID is a Lamfalussy Directive and its legal basis is Article 47(2) of EC Treaty.
56 The Investment Services Directive provided a first financial structure for investment firms although based on minimum harmonisation and limited competition between trading venues.
57 Generally speaking, the major impact of the FSAP is to maximise the pool of capital available to potential investors in the economy, through an adequate system of disclosure and an available flow of information which act in combination in order to avoid imbalance between management and consumers. In substance, the FSAP brings about a shift away from the double regulatory burden resulting from mutual recognition to an approach of effective European harmonisation. Seen in this light, it has been observed that 'with the FSAP the EU moved into a new and more aggressive phase of securities law-making' in which 'the Lamfalussy process can be considered an ongoing attempt to reduce the tensions between the need for an efficient regulatory system characterised by speed, expertise and adaptability and the need for a system that is legitimate and properly accountable' (Eilís Ferran, *Building an EU Securities Market* (CUP 2004) 125–126).

to specify what services and activities they are authorised to provide.[58] However, in implementing it, Member States have shown great reluctance to abandon local rules and dismantle normative barriers.[59] In addition, the Directive establishes that services and activities authorised by Member States may be provided throughout the EU; on this view, the Directive can be regarded as being the sole platform for selling wholesale securities cross-border.[60]

The Directive enables investment firms to operate in regulated markets whereby the home Member State ensures that the authorisation specifies the investment services or activities which the investment firm is authorised to provide; in this way, the authorisation is valid for the entire Community and allows an investment firm to provide services or perform the activities for which it has been authorised throughout the Community, either through the establishment of a branch or the free provision of services.[61] The outstanding feature of the MiFID is that it improves transparency and consumer protection. In this connection, it has been observed that 'the most significant change is that investment firms will no longer be required to route orders exclusively through stock exchanges'[62]; furthermore, other major changes concern, in particular, computer and compliance systems, investment advice, conflicts of interest, best execution and record keeping. It can be argued that the virtually complete definition of pan-European securities markets has posed new challenges in terms of legal analysis and regulation strategy. On the one hand, the concept of harmonisation has permitted the administrative costs of the duplication of provisions (i.e. home country and host country rules) to be reduced, thus favouring cross-border financial transactions. On the other hand, the introduction of self-regulation regimes has allowed for a flexible and innovative framework in which principles can take the place of norms by virtue of the internal controls managed by the compliance function, which reduces the reputational risk of enterprise.[63]

---

58 A detailed description of the spirit of the FSAP and, specifically MiFID, can be found in J. Said, R. Snook, D. McWilliams and M. Pragnell, 'The Importance of Wholesale Financial Services to the EU Economy 2007' *Centre for Economics and Business Research* (City of London, May 2007) <http://www.cityoflondon.gov.uk/economicresearch> (accessed 20 July 2020) 57–60.

59 See in this regard the judgement of the European Court of Justice (Seventh Chamber) of 25 September 2008 in Case C-87/08 *Commission of the European Communities v Czech Republic*, in which the Court declared that 'by failing to adopt all such laws, regulations and administrative provisions necessary to comply with Commission Directive 2006/73/EC of 10 August 2006 implementing Directive 2004/39/EC of the European Parliament and of the Council as regards organisational requirements and operating conditions for investment firms and defined terms for the purposes of that Directive, the Czech Republic has failed to fulfil its obligations under Article 53(1) of that directive'. In academic circles, it has been argued that domestic protectionism still exists and, in particular, that few States have adopted a complete pan-European harmonisation; consequently, 'the European legislation has never been a driving force for market developments, except in spurring avoidance, and is often experienced by the financial markets as burdensome and out of step' (Joanna Benjamin, *Financial Law* (OUP 2007) 579).

60 The EU measure allows wholesale services to be sold in other Member States, while also attempting to tackle the market failure caused by lack of information on the customer side of the transaction; in other words, MiFID seeks to ensure business investment growth and enhance market efficiency and the optimal allocation of securities resources.

61 A description of the main features of FSAP policy can be found in the Commission Communication of 11 May 1999 'Financial Services: Implementing the Framework for Financial Markets Action Plan' COM(1999) 232 final.

62 Stephen Valdez, *An Introduction to Global Financial Markets* (5th edn, Palgrave Macmillan 2007) 303.

63 The theme of regulatory harmonisation versus regulatory competition has been taken up by Guido Ferrarini, 'Securities Regulation and the Rise of Pan-European Securities Markets: An Overview' in Guido Ferrarini,

At first sight, MiFID introduced a rules-based approach designed to govern the conduct of investment firms (investment banks, fund managers and derivatives firms) and regulated markets; however, the provisions of the Directive are characterised by a mixed set of rules and principles, in which detailed norms are combined with self-regulation measures (for example, on the one hand, the suitability regime and appropriateness test, on the other, the reinforcement of the compliance function through best execution). In this regard, the investor protection system is fostered by the suitability requirement and investment advice disclosure (i.e. the 'know-your-customer' programme); the retail client is assisted by firms in her choice of financial product and by the capability to choose the best execution. The EU legislator provided, in articles 19–21 of MiFID, a set of practices to assess the suitability, appropriateness and execution of financial transactions, thereby improving the relationship between intermediaries and consumers.[64] To achieve this goal, the firm not only should put proper arrangements in place to ensure high standards of disclosure, but should also enable the client, by means of its financial knowledge, to comprehend the 'appropriate operation'. As regards the suitability regime, two questions arise: to what extent has the MiFID structure provided for a level of enforcement such as to impose personal liability for misleading statements and misconduct during the operation, combined with the quantum of compensation to the client for losses suffered, and what is the minimum degree of financial knowledge that will exonerate firms from liability where advice has been provided by intermediaries.

First of all, although the Directive does not lay down a specific norm regarding enforcement, it delegates this function to compliance, which has to monitor management behaviours and create strong incentives to reduce the risk of confidence failures.[65] In this way, compliance becomes the instrument of control for securities activities in order to monitor the regulation of financial markets (in terms of law-making process). The consequence is the powers of the compliance function to penalise a breach of the self-regulation regime adopted by MiFID and, consequently, to impose personal liability and sanctions on intermediaries in the event of negligence or misconduct.[66]

Second, the degree of investor competence constitutes the major theme for the retail regulatory strategy; while, on the one hand, article 153(1) of the EC Treaty promotes the right

---

Klaus J. Hopt and Eddy Wymeersch (eds), *Capital Markets in the Age of the Euro. Cross-Border Transactions, Listed Companies and Regulation* (Kluwer Law International 2002) 249–250. Specifically, the author observes that uniformity of rules can enhance proper harmonisation in terms of regulatory provisions by reducing transaction costs while, however, leaving room for different domestic norms; in this way, there is a critical perspective towards 'competition at the enforcement level as the application of harmonised rules and the sanctioning of non-compliance fall within the national authorities' competence'.

64 An exhaustive analysis of the suitability regime is set out in Niamh Moloney, *EC Securities Regulation* (OUP 2008) 614–615. In this context, the author argues that this innovation 'Reflects the Commission's concern to reinforce the positive duties imposed on the investment firm to de-emphasize disclosure'.

65 MiFID Directive, Article 13(2), in which is affirmed that 'an investment firm shall establish adequate policies and procedures sufficient to ensure compliance of the firm including its managers, employees and tied agents with its obligations under the provisions of this Directive as well as appropriate rules governing personal transactions by such persons'; see also MiFID Directive Level 2 (2006/73/EC), Articles 6 and 9(1).

66 In this context, cases of enforcing principles such as AWD Chase de Vere (November 2008), Credit Suisse (August 2008), BNP Paribas (May 2007), Deutsche Bank (April 2006) and Citigroup Global Markets (June 2005) involved FSA actions, where the suitability regime combined with the conduct of business was breached. Specifically in the above cases, the compliance function concerned the measure for the enforcement of the principles, by acting as a sort of watchdog that monitored the reputation risks of management, thereby bringing about a strict link with the normative rule and avoiding the legal risks of market failure.

to achieve an adequate financial education, on the other, consumer protection initiatives are, principally, a matter for the Member States.[67] The level of financial literacy in the business operation is monitored by firms, through ad hoc tests of client suitability; in particular, intermediaries must be ensured that the client has proper knowledge of the transaction and the capability to make an informed choice of product. In this way, co-operation between investors and intermediaries can arguably enhance the best execution by enabling consumers to make informed decisions about the use of financial products and by filling the gap of information asymmetries.

MiFID revolutionised the organisation, day-to-day operations and business strategies not only of investment firms but also of exchanges, asset managers and other financial markets intermediaries, such as brokers, data consolidators and business solutions providers. Specifically, 'MiFID accelerates some important ongoing changes in European financial markets that are driven primarily by technological improvements and enhanced competition in the provision of financial services arising from globalization'.[68] It can be argued that the MiFID Directive has mixed into its rules-based approach the regulatory strategy of a principles-based regime in the form of voluntary norms, such as the conduct of business and the suitability regime, that becomes on the facts hard law. As a result of the internal controls of management behaviours, the new EU securities framework has, in the final analysis, adopted the compliance culture.[69]

4.7 The de Larosière Report and the ESAs

The need for a proper supervision system in the securities sector has been manifest in the aftermath of the 2007–2009 financial crisis which has raised many concerns on how to enhance efficient regulation by EU regulators and domestic authorities. Financial instability has underscored the existence of a complex, confused structure characterising the approach to supervision, not only at European level but also at national level. In order to better appreciate how this could be resolved by moving towards a single financial supervisory system, fundamental developments should be taken into account.

---

67 In this connection, the Commission adopted a Communication (18 December 2007), which outlines its views on financial education and announced several concrete initiatives in this area; in fact, the Commission believes that programmes which improve the financial literacy and capability of consumers should be available at all stages of life and adapted to the needs of various social groups. However, it is observed that 'financial education should not be seen as the only means to address information asymmetries between consumers and providers, but rather as a complement to adequate consumer protection and to the responsible behaviour of financial services providers'.

68 Jean-Pierre Casey and Karel Lannoo, *The MiFID Revolution* (CUP 2009) 7.

69 From this point of view, MiFID Directive Level 2 (2006/73/EC), recital 3, states that 'it is necessary to specify concrete organisational requirements and procedures for investment firms performing such services or activities. In particular, rigorous procedures should be provided for with regard to matters such as compliance, risk management, complaints handling, personal transactions, outsourcing and the identification, management and disclosure of conflicts of interest', while recital 15 specifies that 'the fact that risk management and compliance functions are performed by the same person does not necessarily jeopardise the independent functioning of each function. The conditions that persons involved in the compliance function should not also be involved in the performance of the functions that they monitor, and that the method of determining the remuneration of such persons should not be likely to compromise their objectivity, may not be proportionate in the case of small investment firms. However, they would only be disproportionate for larger firms in exceptional circumstances'.

There was a constructive debate involving the EU institutions,[70] scholars and commentators[71] as a possible approach to supervision which could be capable of minimising the risk of market failures; in particular, various proposals showed a clear preference for establishing an integrated structure, namely, a European System of Financial Supervision (hereinafter 'ESFS').[72] This proposal stemmed from the past experience with different supervision models, such as the institutional model, the functional model and the integrated model.[73] The proposed scheme reflected the main purposes of the supervision function: prudential supervision, ensuring the financial stability of whole securities sector and the conduct of business supervision, combined with disclosure and investor protection systems incorporated in the internal management controls.[74]

In October 2008, the European Parliament adopted a resolution with recommendations to the Commission on the follow-up of the Lamfalussy report. This resolution requested that the Commission had to submit legislative proposals to the Parliament on three areas: (1) basic prerequisites for effective regulatory and supervisory arrangements, (2) financial stability and risk measures and (3) supervisory framework (including a recommendation on the need to strengthen and clarify the status and accountability of the Level 3 Committees). The EU Commission warned that the Lamfalussy model would create the risk of supervisory arbitrage in which lead supervisors would compete by easing the rules to favour their domestic undertakings. The President of the Commission conferred a mandate to the former Governor of the Banque de France (Jacques de Larosière) to chair a high-level group on financial supervision to make proposals to strengthen European supervisory arrangements covering all financial sectors, with the objective of establishing a more efficient, integrated and sustainable European system of supervision.

The 'de Larosière Group' focused on better supervision of EU financial institutions and aimed to ensure the prudential soundness of institutions; the orderly functioning of markets; and the protection of depositors, policy holders and investors. Specifically, the newly formed financial architecture was directed to strengthen EU co-operation on (1) financial stability oversight; (2) early warning mechanisms; (3) crisis management (including the

70 Commission Communication of 27 May 2009 'European Financial Supervision' COM(2009) 252 final.
71 European Parliament, High Level Conference 'Towards a New Supervisory Architecture in Europe' (Brussels, 7 May 2009).
72 Jaques de Larosière, 'The High-Level Group on Financial Supervision in the EU Report' (Brussels, February 2009) 47–48. Principally, the major change is the idea of creating a European System of Financial Supervision (ESFS) that 'should be a decentralised network: existing national supervisors would continue to carry-out day-to-day supervision; three new European Authorities have been set up, replacing CEBS, CEIOPS and CESR, with the role to coordinate the application of supervisory standards and guarantee strong cooperation between the national supervisors; colleges of supervisors would be set up for all major cross-border institutions'. In particular, it was proposed that 'the ESFS will need to be independent of the political authorities but be accountable to them; it should rely on a common set of core harmonised rules and have access to high-quality information' (p. 48).
73 Eddy Wymeersch, 'The Structure of Financial Supervision in Europe: About Single Financial Supervisors, Twin Peaks and Multiple Financial Supervisors' (2007) 8(2) *European Business Organization Law Review* 242–243. It is analysed the main supervision schemes: 'institutional, whereby the main line of business of the firm determines its supervisory regimes; functional, whereby similar activities developed by firms will be subject to the same type of supervision, irrespective of the legal status of that firm; integrated, in which all supervisory functions are concentrated in the hands of one single entity' (p. 250).
74 The distinction between prudential supervision and conduct of business supervision was formulated by Michael Taylor, *Twin Peaks: A Regulatory Structure for the New Century* (Centre for the Study of Financial Innovation 1995).

management of cross-border and cross-sectorial risks) and (4) co-operation with other major jurisdictions to improve safeguard financial stability at the global level. According to the 'de Larosière Group', effective macro-prudential supervision requires mandatory flow of information between EU national supervisors and the ECB/European System of Central Banks (ESCB) that means safeguards for confidentiality of the relevant information transmitted[75] and an effective early warning mechanism for identified weaknesses in the financial system. It can be observed that the 'de Larosière Group' advocated for upgrading European macro-prudential supervision of financial institutions and replacing the Banking Supervision Committee of the ECB by the European Systemic Risk Council (ESRC).[76] As a result, the de Larosière Report established an ESFS, an integrated network of European financial supervisors, working with enhanced Level 3 Committees known as European Supervisory Authorities (ESAs).[77]

In substance, the de Larosière architecture developed two main pillars: macro-prudential supervision and micro-prudential supervision, and moved towards more effective co-operation in which supervision remained at the national level. The new EU financial structure comprised the European Systemic Risk Board (ESRB)[78]; three ESAs: (1) the ESMA,[79] (2) the EBA,[80] (3) the EIOPA[81]; and the Joint Committee of the ESAs and the supervisory authorities of Member States as specified in the Regulations establishing the ESMA, EBA and EIOPA. It can be argued that the main tasks of the ESAs—laid down in three separate but largely identical regulations—are to develop common rules and ensure consistent application of EU law; act in emergency situations and supervise EU-wide entities/economic activities; collect information and undertake certain direct licensing; assess market developments and oversee supervisory colleges.[82] As such, the ESAs do not have direct regulatory and supervisory powers over market actors[83] but rather co-ordinate and supervise the work

---

75 The ECB and ESCB have no responsibility for micro-prudential supervision.

76 The ESRC aimed to (1) form judgements and make recommendations on macro-prudential policy; (2) issue risk warnings; (3) compare observations on macro-economic and prudential developments; and (4) provide directions on these issues.

77 The ESAs replaced the former CESR, CEBS and CEIOPS. On the one side, national supervisors continued to carry out day-to-day supervision and being the first point of contact for the firm; on the other side, ESFS coordinated the application of common high-level supervisory standards.

78 Regulation (EU) No. 1092/2010 on European Union macro-prudential oversight of the financial system and establishing a European Systemic Risk Board. Article 2 of the ESRB Regulation provides a definition of systemic risk as 'a risk of serious disruption in the financial system with the potential to have serious negative consequences for the internal market and the real economy. All types of financial intermediaries, markets and infrastructure may be potentially systemically important to some degree'.

79 Regulation (EU) No. 1095/2010 of the European Parliament and of the Council of 24 November 2010 establishing a European Supervisory Authority (European Securities and Markets Authority), amending Decision No. 716/2009/EC and repealing Commission Decision 2009/77/EC.

80 Regulation (EU) No. 1093/2010 of the European Parliament and of the Council of 24 November 2010 establishing a European Supervisory Authority (European Banking Authority), amending Decision No. 716/2009/EC and repealing Commission Decision 2009/78/EC.

81 Regulation (EU) No. 1094/2010 of the European Parliament and of the Council of 24 November 2010 establishing a European Supervisory Authority (European Insurance and Occupational Pensions Authority), amending Decision No. 716/2009/EC and repealing Commission Decision 2009/79/EC.

82 Article 21 of the ESMA Regulation provides that 'ESMA shall contribute to promoting and monitoring the efficient, effective and consistent functioning of the colleges of supervisors'. According to the Regulation, ESMA plays an active part in the development of a single European rule book.

83 An exception to that is the power of ESMA to regulate Credit Rating Agencies. See Andrea Miglionico, *The Governance of Credit Rating Agencies. Regulatory Regimes and Liability Issues* (Edward Elgar 2019) 136–138.

of National Competent Authorities (NCAs). It can be noted that ESMA's objective is to protect the public interest by contributing to the short-, medium- and long-term stability and effectiveness of the financial system.[84]

The structure of ESMA comprises a Board of Supervisors, a Management Board,[85] a Chairperson,[86] an Executive Director[87] and a Board of Appeal.[88] The Board of Supervisors is composed by a non-voting Chairperson, the heads of the Member State regulatory authorities responsible for the supervision of market participants, a non-voting representative from the Commission, a non-voting representative of the ESRB and a non-voting representative from each of the other two ESAs.[89] The main roles of the Board of Supervisors are guidance to ESMA and taking charge of the decisions made under Chapter 2 of the ESMA Regulation, and adopting opinions, recommendations and decisions (including settling cross-border issues). Decisions are taken by simple majority unless exceptions apply (e.g. qualified majority requested for actions specified in Arts 10–16 of the ESMA Regulation and decisions adopted under the third subparagraph of Art 9(5) and on budgetary and financial issues).

The structure of EBA includes a Board of Supervisors, a Management Board, a Chairperson, an Executive Director and a Board of Appeal.[90] The Board of Supervisors comprises the heads of the relevant competent authorities in each Member State and is chaired by the Chairperson of the Authority: its members act independently, and representatives of the Commission, the ESRB, the ECB, and the ESAs should participate as observers. Under the 'de Larosière Report', the financial supervision architecture moved from an institutional and functional model towards an integrated approach where the role of national authorities is co-ordinated by one independent single network of financial supervisors; in this manner, a clear distribution of roles and functions between financial regulators will make for integrity and uniformity of acts.[91] The 'de Larosière Report' created a single EU-level supervisor which would replace national supervisors for the supervision of cross-border entities and would leave no role for domestic supervisors in monitoring cross-border groups. In this context, there has been a strong call at EU level for an ongoing dialogue between institutions and a constant exchange of information among the individual supervisory authorities: manifestly, this objective could be achieved with an integrated supervision approach under which the supervisory function should be effective, transparent and accountable to the political institutions.

Concurrently, it has been argued that 'a single financial market needs a single financial supervisor with a set of harmonised supervision powers'.[92] It can also be observed that such a supervisory solution would supply a plausible, definitive solution to the risk of monitoring

---

84 Niamh Moloney, *The Age of ESMA. Governing EU Financial Markets* (Hart Publishing 2018) Chapter I.
85 See Arts 45–47 of the ESMA Regulation No. 1095/2010.
86 See Arts 48 and 50 of the ESMA Regulation No. 1095/2010.
87 See Arts 51 to 53 of the ESMA Regulation No. 1095/2010.
88 See Arts 58–60 of the ESMA Regulation No. 1095/2010.
89 See Arts 40–44 of the ESMA Regulation No. 1095/2010.
90 See Article 6 of the EBA Regulation No. 1093/2010.
91 Clive Briault, 'The Rationale for a Single National Financial Services Regulator' (1999) FSA Occasional Paper Series No. 2, 18–19; in the same vein, also Clive Briault, 'Revisiting the Rationale for a Single Financial Services Regulator' (2002) FSA Occasional Paper Series No. 16, 21–22.
92 Howard Davies and David Green, *Global Financial Regulation* (CUP 2008) 255–256. In particular, the authors argue that 'the existing legislative framework, enhanced by recent and prospective legal developments in relation to lead supervision, provides significant scope for effective co-operation between regulators so the mandate should be to produce the effect of unitary regulatory arrangements and decision-making'.

loopholes and provide a response to the emergent co-operation between national supervisors and European regulators. It can also be reasonably pointed out that a strong improvement of risk management, together with the enforcement of internal compliant behaviours, should be implemented when tackling the new challenge of the reform of supervision. In other words, in introducing a single supervisory body it will be necessary to implement continuing co-operation and co-ordination of functions with a permanent dialogue between national and European authorities.[93]

4.8 The MiFIR and MiFID II

The MiFID Directive has been replaced by MiFIR Regulation[94] and MiFID II Directive.[95] Acknowledging technological developments and drawing lessons from the 2008 financial crisis, the G20 agreed at the 2009 Pittsburgh summit on the need to improve the transparency and oversight of less regulated markets (derivatives and volatility).[96]

The EU legislation with MiFID has imposed a stringent assessment of investor guarantees through 'the fair presentation of investment recommendations and the disclosure of conflicts of interest'.[97] Specifically, the EU legislator has introduced a set of provisions clearly characterised by voluntary conducts on the part of business (for instance, the 'suitability regime' and 'best execution') that delegate to market participants the power of behaviour control. As observed in Section 3.5, one of MiFID's fundamental goals is harmonisation as between Member States and the introduction of an enhanced single framework of provisions. It can be observed that the Directive on financial instruments has created a single system for cross-border transactions with an efficient integration of securities products in which market participants are clearly accountable for their acts. In particular, the new classification of clients (i.e. retail, professional or eligible counterparty) has produced a remarkable disclosure regime, combined with a high level of consumer protection.

The reform of the MiFID Directive aims to remedy shortcomings in investor protection, functioning and transparency of financial markets.[98] On this view, MiFID II set rigid rules to (1) ensure more robust and efficient market structures, (2) take account of technological innovations, (3) increase transparency, (4) reinforce supervisory powers and a stricter framework for commodity derivatives markets and (5) enhance investor protection. MiFIR and MiFID II extend the transparency requirements already applicable to the equity market to non-equity markets (including organised trading in bonds and derivatives) and apply transparency requirements to a wide range of organised trading venues beyond the particular regulated markets previously covered by MiFID.[99]

---

93 Eilís Ferran, 'Capital Market Competitiveness and Enforcement' (2008) European Corporate Governance Institute (paper produced for the City of London Corporation) 2–5.
94 Regulation (EU) No. 600/2014 of the European Parliament and of the Council of 15 May 2014 on markets in financial instruments and amending Regulation (EU) No. 648/2012.
95 Directive 2014/65/EU of the European Parliament and of the Council of 15 May 2014 on markets in financial instruments and amending Directive 2002/92/EC and Directive 2011/61/EU.
96 See G20 Leaders Statement: The Pittsburgh Summit, Pittsburgh (24–25 September 2009) <http://www.g20.utoronto.ca/2009/2009communique0925.html> (accessed 18 May 2020).
97 MiFID Directive Level 2 (2006/73/EC) recital 28.
98 Danny Busch, 'MiFID II and MiFIR: Stricter Rules for the EU Financial Markets' (2017) 11(2–3) *Law and Financial Markets Review* 126.
99 A detailed overview of the MiFID II is found in Danny Busch and Guido Ferrarini (eds), *Regulation of the EU Financial Markets: MiFID II and MiFIR* (OUP 2017) Chapter 1, paras 1.07–1.13.

In terms of efficient market structures, MiFID II regulates the 'organised trading facility' (OTF) where standardised derivatives' contracts were increasingly traded without being regulated. It also introduces the concept of the provision of investment advice 'on an independent basis' and strengthens the role of management bodies in ensuring sound and prudent management of their firms, the promotion of market integrity and the protection of investors. Regarding technological innovations, MiFID II introduces new safeguards for algorithmic and high-frequency trading activities which have drastically increased the speed of trading and pose possible systemic risks, i.e. all algorithmic traders to become properly regulated; provide appropriate liquidity; and rule to prevent them from adding to volatility by moving in and out of markets. It also increases post-trading competition in services (i.e. clearing procedure). In terms of transparency, MiFID II organised trading facilities categories (trading activities in equity markets including 'dark pools')[100] and introduces new trade transparency regime for non-equities markets (i.e. bonds, structured finance products and derivatives).

Under the supervision head, MiFID II reinforces the roles and powers of regulators in co-ordination with ESMA, and enhances supervision of commodity derivatives markets. It introduces a position reporting obligation by category of trader and better evaluates the role of speculation in the markets. The directive reforms investor protection: in addition, MiFID II sets stricter requirements for portfolio management, investment advice and the offer of complex financial products such as structured products. The framework prevents potential conflicts of interest: independent advisors and portfolio managers are prohibited from making or receiving third-party payments or other monetary gains. Further, MiFID II introduces rules on corporate governance and managers' responsibility for all investment firms.[101]

On this view, the principles of good faith, trust and fairness are embodied in intermediaries' behaviours. The MiFID Directive established principles within its prescriptive provisions; the principle is inserted into the norm, thereby bringing about a mixed system where self-regulation is combined with normative regulation. For example, the conduct of business regulated by articles 19, 21 and 22 of the MiFID Directive provides for the 'investment advice or personal recommendations regime' and requires a set of ethical principles in order to ensure that 'an investment firm acts honestly, fairly and professionally in accordance with the best interests of its clients'.[102]

The principle is at the same time a statutory norm. The MiFID Directive represents the European legal framework for securities regulation, which institutionalises the principles-based regime within the statutory rules, whereas the principles are implemented under the legal basis of EU law. In other words, MiFID has created a mixed system of

---

100 See Thomas Clarke, 'High-Frequency Trading and Dark Pools: Sharks Never Sleep' (2014) 8 *Law and Financial Markets Review* 342, 347, where a dark pool is defined as 'an OTC (over-the-counter) venue for reporting purposes, which has the practical value that unmatched trade orders are not displayed on an open order book'. See also Kristin N. Johnson, 'Regulating Innovation: High Frequency Trading in Dark Pools' (2017) 42 *Journal of Corporation Law* 833, 864–866. As observed, 'dark pools mitigate information leakage, enabling institutional investors to execute large block trade transactions without fear that imitators will replicate or that predators may prey on their trades'.

101 Jens-Hinrich Binder, 'Governance of Investment Firms Under MiFID II' in Danny Busch and Guido Ferrarini (eds), *Regulation of the EU Financial Markets: MiFID II and MiFIR* (OUP 2017) Chapter 3, paras 3.21–3.24.

102 Niamh Moloney, 'Financial Market Regulation in the Post-Financial Services Action Plan Era' (2006) 55(4) *International & Comparative Law Quarterly* 986–988.

rules and principles in which principles exist because the EU provisions allow them to do so. On this view, compliance can be considered to constitute the direct link between rules and principles in the sense that it enables principles to be self-enforced. MiFID II has enhanced trading venues and strengthened the protection of traders.[103] It allows different traders to act in various market structures with respect to their needs; this incentivises the variety of market participants and their service requirements to compete in different trading venues.

The recent EU securities reforms introduced with MiFID II and MiFIR have constituted an important innovation in terms of regulatory approach and financial stability: these reforms can be seen as an instrument for harmonisation among Member States and for creation of a single system for cross-border transactions. This means effective integration of market infrastructures and clear accountability of investors which in turn lead to co-ordination of supervisory functions.

4.9 The European Systemic Risk Board

In the EU financial architecture, the ECB undertakes the role to ensure effective prudential supervision at the macro level. The intricate design of the supervisory structure of the single market in the EU (with the ESAs)[104] and the complex regulatory framework of Banking Union[105] constitute the pillars of financial markets across Europe. The ESRB shares macro-prudential supervisory responsibilities with national authorities, and according to the Banking Union architecture, also with the ECB for those Member States that become part of the Single Supervisory Mechanism (SSM).[106]

The ESRB is responsible for the macro-prudential oversight of the EU financial system in order to contribute to the prevention or mitigation of systemic risks to financial stability, which directly contributes to the smooth functioning of the internal market. In identifying, analysing and monitoring systemic risks the ESRB relies on information provided by ESAs, ESCB, the European Commission, national supervisory authorities and the national statistics authorities with whom the ESRB closely co-operates to fulfil its tasks. However, the ESRB's instruments are limited to warnings of systemic risks that are deemed to be significant and recommendations for the remedial action that should be taken to address

---

103 Guido Ferrarini and Paolo Saguato, 'Reforming Securities and Derivatives Trading in the EU: From EMIR to MiFIR' (2013) 13(2) *Journal of Corporate Law Studies* 349–351.

104 Jacques de Larosière, 'The High-Level Group on Financial Supervision in the EU Report' (Brussels, February 2009) 47–48. The major change was the idea of creating a ESFS, an integrated network of national and EU supervisors which comprises three ESAs: ESMA, EBA and EIOPA. Principally, the ESAs play the role to co-ordinate the application of supervisory standards and guarantee strong cooperation between the national supervisors.

105 European Commission, 'Communication from the Commission to the European Parliament and the Council: A Roadmap towards a Banking Union' COM (2012) 510 Final (September 2012) <http://eur-lex.europa.eu/LexUriServ/LexUriServ.do?uri=CELEX:52012DC0510:EN:NOT> (accessed 15 April 2020). The design of EU Banking Union has determined a transfer to the European level of the regulatory and institutional framework for safeguarding the robustness and stability of the banking sector. In particular, the EU Banking Union aims to introduce a common platform for the regulation of (a) supervision, (b) resolution mechanisms and (c) deposit insurance. From an academic view, see Charles Randell, 'European Banking Union and Bank Resolution' (2013) 7 *Law and Financial Markets Review* 30.

106 Eilís Ferran, 'European Banking Union: Imperfect, But It can Work' (2014) University of Cambridge Faculty of Law Research Paper No. 30 <http://ssrn.com/abstract=2426247> (accessed 1 May 2020).

the risks identified.[107] European supervisors can provide a more independent and objective assessment of the problems identified in the course of the supervisory process than national supervisors. At the institutional level, the existence of European regulators should facilitate the adoption of EU measures based on a single financial regulatory strategy; on these lines, the creation of a single European supervisor – as established in the European Banking Union – aims to control the national supervisors.[108]

Under this supervisory architecture, the unconvincing regulatory structure of authorities is evidenced by an insufficient level of control with regard to the responsibility of members; for instance, the Commission exercises solely a role of 'light supervisor' over the ESMA mandates. This uncertainty characterises what may be described as a soft law-making process that does not improve the mechanisms of EU legislation. It can be argued that the acts of these regulators have resulted in an area of vague law; indeed, at the same time, the increasing development of activities and competence has determined a huge risk of vulnerability of legitimacy and accountability.[109] Ongoing discussions are trying to identify the powers and instruments macro-prudential authorities should have.[110] Given the lack of a commonly accepted theoretical paradigm on the definition of systemic risk, this is no easy task.[111]

Debate about systemic risk is ubiquitous in the aftermath of the financial crisis. However, the definition of systemic risk still remains contentious, and this complicates the search for adequate instruments to prevent and contain it. In this regard, the weaknesses of the supervisory architecture put in place by the ESAs hampered the need to rethink the regulatory approach for retail financial services. The global financial crisis demonstrated that these bodies lacked authority, had insufficient independence and exerted only a marginal influence over the shape of primary legislation, with insufficient flexibility in the correction of legislative errors and inadequate funding and resources. In this respect, appropriate scrutiny and accountability mechanisms can enhance the ESAs consultation procedures and their engagement with practitioners and regulators. It is essential to develop a more flexible and expedited mechanism whereby the ESAs can improve their function in the law-making process.

4.10 The centralised system of supervision and financial stability

A new era for banking supervision in the EU has been achieved with a centralised supervisory system within the Banking Union, in which the ECB acts as a single regulator for significant credit institutions in the Eurozone.[112] A centralised supervision system finds

---

107 The recommendations can be either of a general or of a specific nature, and may be addressed to the EU as a whole, the European Commission (in relation to EU legislation), Member States, ESAs and national supervisory authorities. The ESRB has no legally binding powers and no powers to intervene or decide on emergencies. The ESRB does not have legal personality. Both ESRB warnings and recommendation can be kept confidential or made public; the ESRB decides this on a case-by-case basis.

108 Eddy Wymeersch, 'The Future of Financial Regulation and Supervision in Europe' (2005) 42(4) *Common Market Law Review* 1005–1006.

109 Niamh Moloney, *The Age of ESMA. Governing EU Financial Markets* (Hart Publishing 2018) Chapter II.

110 Pierre Schammo, 'EU Day to Day Supervision or Intervention-based Supervision: Which Way Forward for the European System of Financial Supervision' (2012) 32 *Oxford Journal of Legal Studies* 771–772.

111 Financial Stability Board, 'Policy Measures to Address Systemically Important Financial Institutions' (4 November 2011).

112 Communication from the Commission to the European Parliament and the Council – A Roadmap towards a Banking Union, COM(2012) 510 final.

its foundation in the SSM that enhances the process of harmonisation through the Single Rulebook.[113]

The Single Rulebook aims to ensure the consistent application of the regulatory banking framework across the EU.[114] It is an articulated package of the CRD IV and the corresponding technical standards, namely, (1) regulatory technical standards (RTS),[115] (2) implementing technical standards (ITS) and (3) EBA guidelines. On 4 November 2014, the ECB took over supervisory responsibility for large banks in the euro area; this means the ECB directly supervises the significant banks of the participating countries.[116] National supervisory authorities have responsibility for the supervision over all other institutions ('less significant') within the regulations, guidelines and instructions issued to them by the ECB.[117] The ECB can decide at any time to classify a bank as significant to ensure that high supervisory standards are applied consistently.

In the Banking Union, supervision is both micro and macro but responsibility for the latter is shared between ECB and national authorities (and ESRB). The ECB, in co-operation with the national supervisors, is responsible for the effective and consistent functioning of the SSM. It has the authority to (1) conduct supervisory reviews, on-site inspections and investigations; (2) grant or withdraw banking licences; (3) assess banks' acquisition and disposal of qualifying holdings; (4) ensure compliance with EU prudential rules; and (5) set higher capital requirements ('buffers') in order to counter any financial risks. In this context, converging towards a harmonised approach on supervision is the key issue at stake. As Nieto and Wall observed, 'given that the barriers to cross-border banking are likely to fall, the EU should consider what sort of banking structure would provide the best combination of an integrated financial system and a financial system in which the banks are neither too

---

113 Council Regulation (EU) No. 1024/2013 of 15 October 2013 conferring specific tasks on the ECB concerning policies relating to the prudential supervision of credit institutions. The Council, acting by means of regulations in accordance with a special legislative procedure, may unanimously, and after consulting the European Parliament and the ECB, confer specific tasks upon the ECB concerning policies relating to the prudential supervision of credit institutions and other financial institutions with the exception of insurance. Tasks are conferred to the ECB – at the same time the National Competent Authorities (NCAs) compose the SSM, and the ECB is responsible for its effective and consistent functioning. Article 127(6) of the TFEU constitutes the legal basis for the SSM.

114 For an overview, see Asen Lefterov, 'The Single Rulebook: Legal Issues and Relevance in the SSM Context' (October 2015) ECB Legal Working Paper Series 15, 31–33 <https://www.ecb.europa.eu/pub/pdf/scplps/ecblwp15.en.pdf?03b5c5c0a61bb0d01ab6067afa536f87> (accessed 20 May 2020).

115 Building on a technical standard the ECB adopted Decision ECB/2014/29 on the provision of supervisory data reported to the national competent authorities by the supervised entities pursuant to Commission Implementing Regulation (EU) No. 680/2014.

116 Article 6(5)(c) of Regulation (EU) No. 1024/2013. See also Article 6(5)(a) of Council Regulation (EU) No. 1024/2013 which empowers the ECB to issue regulations, guidelines or general instructions to national competent authorities regarding the supervision of less significant institutions. ECB has direct supervision for 'significant' credit institutions. Criteria for determining significance are (1) size – the total value of its assets exceeds €30 billion; (2) economic importance for the specific country or the EU economy as a whole; (3) cross-border activities – the total value of its assets exceeds €5 billion and the ratio of its cross-border assets/liabilities in more than one other participating Member State to its total assets/liabilities is above 20%; and (3) direct public financial assistance – it has requested or received funding from the European Stability Mechanism or the European Financial Stability Facility. A supervised bank can also be considered significant if it is one of the three most significant banks established in a particular country.

117 Articles 4–6 of the SSM Regulation. For less significant credit institutions, ECB may issue general instructions, guidelines or requests to the NCA under close co-operation.

large to supervise nor too large to safely fail'.[118] This means that rules will have an impact on where banks locate operations due to cost factors and that as a result risk will likely migrate to less regulated local subsidiaries.

The rules contained in the Banking Union are largely flexible to allow Member States to adopt the policy measures necessary to protect the public interest. Divergences in the supervisory rules and lack of co-operation pose serious risks for regulatory effectiveness and may create additional costs for financial institutions, which are likely to be passed on to retail investors. The centralised system of supervision culminating with the SSM should be able to deal efficiently with the proliferation of cross-border banking and any possible negative implications. However, the EU mechanism for supervising banks is still a work in progress and needs to be fully tested.

4.11 The structure of the Banking Union and the SSM mechanism

The global financial crisis has underscored the existence of a complex, obsolete structure characterising the approach to cross-border crisis management, not only at European level but also at national level. In order to better appreciate how this could be resolved by moving towards a single resolution system, fundamental developments in the structure of EU bank supervision have led to a centralisation mechanism under the SSM framework.[119]

The establishment of the Banking Union has determined a transfer to the European level of the regulatory and institutional framework for safeguarding the robustness and stability of the banking and financial sector.[120] In particular, the Banking Union introduces a common platform for the regulation of (1) supervision, (2) resolution mechanisms and (3) deposit insurance.[121] It aims to reduce the systemic effects of banking failures in the Eurozone. At macroeconomic level, the establishment of a single, unique safety net within the Banking Union addresses the 'vicious circle' between national governments and banks.[122] The SSM put the ECB directly in charge as the supervisor for the largest Eurozone banking groups.[123] The dominant part of the Eurozone banking system is monitored by a common

---

118 Maria Nieto and Larry D. Wall, 'Cross-Border Banking on the Two Sides of the Atlantic: Does It Have an Impact on Bank Crisis Management?' (2015) FRB Atlanta Working Paper No. 2015-11, 19.

119 For an overview see Guido Ferrarini, 'Single Supervision and the Governance of Banking Markets: Will the SSM Deliver the Expected Benefits?' (2015) 16(3) *European Business Organization Law Review* 523–524. Interestingly, the author notes that 'the SSM, despite being a remarkable step towards a single supervisor model, still represents a semi-strong form of centralisation for it still relies, to some extent, on supervisory cooperation'.

120 European Commission, 'Communication from the Commission to the European Parliament and the Council: A Roadmap towards a Banking Union' COM (2012) 510 Final (September 2012) <http://eur-lex.europa.eu/LexUriServ/LexUriServ.do?uri=CELEX:52012DC0510:EN:NOT> (accessed 10 February 2020). See Daniel Gros and Dirk Schoenmaker, 'European Deposit and Resolution in the Banking Union' (2014) 52(3) *Journal of Common Market Studies* 529.

121 European Commission, 'A Roadmap towards a Banking Union' COM (2012) 510 final, Brussels.

122 See 'European Banking Union' by Rosa Lastra, Bernd Krauskopf, Christos Gortsos and René Smits, MOCOMILA Report to the ILA Meeting in Washington, DC (April 2014) <http://www.ila-hq.org/en/committees/index.cfm/cid/22> (accessed 25 February 2020).

123 The SSM is composed of the ECB and the NCAs, with the ECB in charge of its effective and consistent functioning (Article 6.1). The scope of application of the SSM Regulation comprises all euro area Member States on a compulsory basis and also non-euro area Member States that voluntarily enter into a 'close cooperation' with the ECB (Article 7). The SSM Regulation confers 'specific tasks' related to the prudential supervision of credit institutions to the ECB. See Commission release Statement/14/77, 20 March 2014.

institution: in substance, the ECB is the direct supervisor of the significant banks for the entire Eurozone, and it has the right to inspect smaller banks that it does not supervise directly.[124]

With the launch of SSM, national supervisors continue to be responsible for Eurozone banks for certain functions related to consumer protection and some national legal requirements. However, the exact division of roles between the ECB and national supervisors within the SSM is still far from being clear. In this context, the relationship between Eurozone countries and non-Eurozone member countries that have elected to remain outside the SSM (for example, the UK) constitutes a significant issue. The SSM affects the balance of power within the EBA as the ECB takes the place of all the national supervisors of the countries that join the SSM. This implies that in many cases the ECB alone could push through decisions on the board of the EBA. The need to combine efficiency (to avoid a cumbersome and unduly complicated decision-making process and excessive bureaucracy) with democratic legitimacy (the interest of the citizens of the Member States) is fundamental for the future of Europe, and since democracy is considered the sole legitimate form of government in the EU, legitimacy equates to democratic legitimacy.[125]

The Banking Union as the name indicates centralises banking policy, but responsibility for other sectors of the financial system (securities, insurance) remains decentralised albeit subject to increasing 'federalisation' through ESMA and EIOPA. The creation of any agency or authority (be it a central bank, or any other type of governmental or intergovernmental entity) must be the result of a democratic act (an act of the legislator, a constitutional decision or a treaty provision). The more complex the activity, the more difficult it is to establish clear standards of conduct and specific outcomes. In which case accountability becomes ever more evasive. As Donnelly noted, 'Banking Union still relies significantly on national rather than European administrative and financial resources to ensure local financial stability, so that resilience remains asymmetric'.[126] The new regulatory framework established by the Banking Union seems far from being effective to deal with complexity and to provide accountability. This means that it is difficult to realise a co-existence between a Banking Union and the single market since the issues of 'jurisdictional domain' haunt the design of Banking Union.[127] As has been observed, 'the regulatory landscape of the Banking Union remains much more decentralized and still relies to some extent on national au-

---

124 Eilís Ferran and Valia Babis, 'The European Single Supervisory Mechanism' (2013) 13 *Journal of Corporate Law Studies* 255. The authors note that 'designing the SSM has been an exercise in sophisticated legal gymnastics to fit within the existing Treaty framework, as well as high stakes political manoeuvring and pragmatic decision-making'.

125 Accountability may be usefully defined as an obligation to give account of, explain and justify one's actions. In the sense of a clear definition of responsibility, accountability is made up of four components: (1) a holder of power, (2) an authority to whom accountability is owed, (3) the content of the obligation and (4) criteria of assessment. See Rosa M. Lastra and Fabian Amtenbrink, 'Securing Democratic Accountability of Financial Regulatory Agencies – A Theoretical framework' in Richard V. de Mulder (ed.), *Mitigating Risk in the Context of Safety and Security. How Relevant is a Rational Approach?* (Erasmus School of Law & Research School for Safety and Security 2008) 115–116.

126 Shawn Donnelly, 'Liberal Economic Nationalism, Financial Stability, and Commission Leniency in Banking Union' (2017) 21 *Journal of Economic Policy Reform* 170.

127 Rosa M. Lastra, 'Banking Union and Single Market: Conflict or Companionship?' (2013) 36(5) *Fordham International Law Journal* 1190–1191. In particular, the euro area, the SSM area, the EU and the EEA (European Economic Area) represent concentric circles of integration, subject to differentiation and conditionality. A major challenge for the EU is that the needs of a well-functioning single market in financial services cannot be disentangled from the design of the supervisory pillar.

thorities'.[128] The recent EU bank failures (Caixa Bank, Novo Banco, Banco Santander and Banca Monte dei Paschi di Siena)[129] represented a real concern to the ECB and highlighted that credit institutions rely on domestic regulatory intervention, a practice that is difficult to change in the supervisory actions of competent authorities.

4.12 The joint supervisory teams

One of the important features of the new EU banking supervision architecture is represented by the establishment of the joint supervisory teams (JSTs). JSTs are defined as teams of supervisors in charge of the supervision of a significant supervised entity or a significant supervised group.[130] JSTs are one of the main forms of co-operation between the ECB and the national supervisors: they play an important role in the micro-prudential supervision of significant supervised entities and groups. The SSM Framework Regulation governs their tasks and composition[131]: the main aim is to foster a common supervisory culture and promote consistent supervisory practices and approaches.

A JST is established for each significant institution: each JST is organised by a co-ordinator at the ECB who is responsible for the implementation of the supervisory tools as included in the supervisory review and evaluation process (SREP) for individual significant credit institution. This complex structure involves close co-operation among different supervisors and poses questions on the effectiveness of division of the supervisory tasks and participation as well as consultation mechanism in the supervision. Other questions regard 'the ability of a limited number of ECB supervisory staff to ensure adequate centralized control within the JSTs which could affect the credibility of ECB supervision of significant banks'.[132] However, the main concern raises on the presence of multiple voices in the JSTs, i.e. members from the ECB and NCAs, which may face divergent views on the applicable supervisory tool. In other terms, 'the fact that JSTs consist of staff members from different NCAs with different experiences, backgrounds and focus areas, may increase the chance that draft decisions are better challenged within the team'.[133] The important feature of JST's supervisory role manifests in the competences of its members to work closely with

128 François-Charles Laprévote and Amélie Champsaur, 'Hand in Hand or Parallel Paths? Reflections on the Future Coexistence of State Aid Control and Bank Resolution in the EU' in François-Charles Laprévote, Joanna Gray and Francesco De Cecco (eds), *Research Handbook on State Aid in the Banking Sector* (Edward Elgar 2017)538-539.
129 Martin Sandbu, 'Banking Union will Transform Europe's Politics' *Financial Times* (26 July 2017), who observed that in the recent banking failures 'Spain offered a glimpse into the future of bank regulation, while Italy clung to the bad habits of the past. On this discrepancy, Italy demonstrated greater ability to lobby for its case, however power is not all; it matters what one uses it for'. Further, banks in Italy are run by politically embedded foundations, a scenario that shows an incestuous relation between state and credit institutions. This phenomenon can determine the following effects: 'deep confusion between the national interest and that of the banking sector; hidden subsidies from taxpayers to banks, protecting both their managers and their investors; and gross inefficiencies in an allocation of capital driven more by political and personal priorities than economic logic'.
130 See Article 2, point (6) of the ECB Framework Regulation.
131 See Article 4(1)(2) of the SSM Framework Regulation.
132 Jakub Gren, David Howarth and Lucia Quaglia, 'Supranational Banking Supervision in Europe: The Construction of a Credible Watchdog' (2015) 53(S1) *Journal of Common Market Studies* 192.
133 On this point Laura Wissink, 'Challenges to an Efficient European Centralised Banking Supervision (SSM): Single Rulebook, Joint Supervisory Teams and Split Supervisory Tasks' (2017) 18 *European Business Organization Law Review* 445–446.

other relevant authorities involved in the prudential oversight of credit institutions. It can be noted that the JSTs supplement the work of the ECB in avoiding conflicts of interest among authorities and advising the suitable supervisory procedure.[134]

The JSTs carry out ongoing supervision of the significant banks; their main tasks are to (1) perform the SREP; (2) propose the supervisory examination programme, including a plan of on-site inspections; (3) implement the approved supervisory examination programme and any supervisory decisions; and (4) ensure co-ordination with the on-site inspection teams and liaise with the national supervisors. JSTs are formed of staff of the ECB and the relevant national supervisors, including the competent authorities of the countries in which credit institutions, banking subsidiaries or significant cross-border branches of a given banking group are established.[135] The size, overall composition and organisation of a JST is tailored to the business model and risk profile of the bank it supervises. JST supervision is done at the highest level of consolidation within the SSM, which means that the JST constitutes the main tool within which NCAs assist the ECB in the supervision of significant banking groups.

Article 3, para 1 of the SSM Regulation provides that 'a joint supervisory team shall be established for the supervision of each significant supervised entity or significant supervised group in participating Member States. Each joint supervisory team shall be composed of staff members from the ECB and from the NCAs appointed in accordance with article 4 and working under the co-ordination of a designated ECB staff member (hereinafter the "JST co-ordinator") and one or more NCA sub-co-ordinators, as further laid down in Article 6'.[136] The establishment of JST for the supervision of significant credit institutions complements the function of the ECB as a consolidating supervisor and the role of NCAs to adopt decisions in respect of significant supervised entities (upon the ECB's instructions). It can be argued that co-operation is essential among supervisory authorities: since the JSTs perform the day-to-day supervision which comprises staff from both NCAs and the ECB, it is essential that they are supported by the horizontal and specialised expertise divisions of directorates-general for micro-prudential supervision (DGMS).[137]

The mechanism of JSTs reflects a more intrusive and forward-looking supervision: the use of the best supervisory practices responds to effective and corrective monitoring measures. However, more independent and close supervision means macro-prudential expertise and homogeneity within the SSM (i.e. level playing field and simplification of processes).

134 Christos V. Gortsos, 'Competence Sharing between the ECB and the National Competent Supervisory Authorities within the Single Supervisory Mechanism (SSM)' (2015) 16 *European Business Organization Law Review* 410–411.
135 Article 31(2) of the Council Regulation No. 1024/2013 conferring specific tasks on the European Central Bank concerning policies relating to the prudential supervision of credit institutions (SSM Regulation).
136 Article 3, para 2 of the SSM Regulation states that 'Without prejudice to other provisions of this Regulation, the tasks of a joint supervisory team shall include, but are not limited to, the following: (a) performing the supervisory review and evaluation process (SREP) referred to in Article 97 of Directive 2013/36/EU for the significant supervised entity or significant supervised group that it supervises; (b) taking into account the SREP, participating in the preparation of a supervisory examination programme to be proposed to the Supervisory Board, including an on-site inspection plan, as laid down in Article 99 of Directive 2013/36/EC, for such a significant supervised entity or significant supervised group; (c) implementing the supervisory examination programme approved by the ECB and any ECB supervisory decisions with respect to the significant supervised entity or significant supervised group that it supervises; (d) ensuring coordination with the on-site inspection team referred to in Part XI as regards the implementation of the on-site inspection plan; (e) liaising with NCAs where relevant'.
137 ECB, 'Guide to Banking Supervision' (September 2014) 14–15 <https://www.ecb.europa.eu/pub/pdf/other/ssmguidebankingsupervision201409en.pdf> (accessed 30 March 2020).

On this view, the innovative supervisory activities of the JSTs should be co-ordinated with the EBA to ensure consistency within the single market. The supervisory mechanism established with JSTs shows a notable step forward in the EU banking supervision: the JSTs should facilitate the collaboration between the ECB and NCAs in the division of tasks and responsibilities. This function is more evident in the co-operation arrangements and joint supervisory powers of the ECB and NCAs within the SSM. As noted, the functionality of JSTs enables 'information sharing between the ECB and relevant national supervisors while providing a clear line of command and decision-making'.[138] This expedites the supervision of cross-border banking groups in the euro area previously carried out on country-by-country basis.

Further, the JSTs can prevent the concentration of powers of the SSM authorities playing the role of mediation in case of divergent decisions. In terms of governance of banking supervision, the JSTs allow for a systematic view of the banks which is relevant for financial disclosure and data collection.[139] It can be observed that the JSTs contribute to the process of harmonisation in the EU banking sector integrating the supervisory practices and consolidating the centralised day-to-day supervision. That would enhance the duty to co-operate in good faith and the obligation to exchange information between ECB and NCAs.

4.13 The principles of separation and co-operation between authorities

Under the European Banking Union, there has been a strong call for an ongoing dialogue between institutions and a constant exchange of information among individual supervisory authorities. This objective can be achieved with an integrated supervision approach under which the supervisory function should be effective, transparent and accountable to the political institutions. Concurrently, a single financial supervisor should foster collaboration between regulators. It can be observed that such a supervisory solution would supply a plausible, definitive solution to the risk of monitoring loopholes and provide a response to the need of co-operation between national supervisors and European regulators. However, the centralised system of supervision involves more intrusive oversight on risk management, together with the enforcement of internal compliant behaviours. On this view, it seems that the new challenge of the reform of supervision involves the clear separation of tasks and responsibilities in the monitoring function. In introducing a single supervisory body, it is necessary to implement continuing co-operation and co-ordination of functions with a permanent dialogue between national and European authorities.

Supervision may involve potential reputational damage particularly at times of crisis: resources and personnel shortages may raise governance issues that are likely to manifest in the absence of clear division of duties between authorities. Within the Banking Union, the SSM regulates the principle of separation that refers to different functions in the

---

138 Dirk Schoenmaker and Nicolas Véron (eds), *European Banking Supervision: The First Eighteen Months*, Bruegel Blueprint Series (Bruegel 2016) 4.

139 Vítor Constâncio, 'The Role of Stress Testing in Supervision and Macroprudential Policy' in Ronald W. Anderson (ed), *Stress Testing and Macroprudential Regulation: A Transatlantic Assessment* (Centre for Economic Policy Research 2016) 53, where it is observed that 'SSM Joint Supervisory Teams (JSTs) follow up with banks on their individual results, dig deeper into the issue of potential pockets of risk, and decide, where necessary, on additional bank-specific measures'.

supervisory procedures (i.e. Supervisory Board, separated Governing Council deliberations, separation at staff level, internal rules and mediation panel).[140] Further, it identifies the specific role assigned to various reporting lines involved in the supervision: this supports the decision-making structures and the establishment of priorities as part of exercising judgement. Typical governance issues manifest in the 'non-objection' procedure that gives the Governing Council the upper hand as it can reject (object to) a decision prepared by the Supervisory Board.[141] If the Governing Council of the ECB objects to a draft decision of a Supervisory Board, the reasons for the objection, in particular monetary policy concerns, must be clearly stated. Moreover, if the NCAs concerned have different views on such objection, a mediation panel must be in place to resolve such differences.[142] The principle of separation applies to the organisational level, including staff,[143] exchange of information and professional secrecy[144] and resources[145] and accountability.[146] Article 26(5) of the SSM Regulation prohibits appointing the ECB representatives who perform duties directly related to monetary function of the ECB to the Supervisory Board. In substance, the principle of separation means that the ECB role in the SSM is distinct from the basic monetary tasks, other central banks tasks and NCBs. This reflects an important change in the banking supervision because the separation between monetary and supervisory responsibilities within the ECB is ensured by the organisational separation of both categories of the staff involved.[147] However, it has been argued that 'the separation of ECB monetary policy operations from banking supervision limits its effectiveness as a banking supervisor as well as its conduct of monetary policy'.[148]

The separation between the ECB's monetary and supervisory mandates raises doubts in relation to the potential overlap and conflicts of interest that these tasks may face. The risk posed by the separation of functions, i.e. ECB and SSM, is evident given the inherently close relationship of the members of staff that work closely in the supervisory resources and budgetary process.[149] The fact that the ECB engages in various activities, namely, monetary, micro-prudential and macro-prudential supervision, resolution policies, reinforces concerns on the level of independence in the decision-making powers. In this context, the principle of independence is strictly related to the principle of separation between monetary policy and banking supervision under the SSM Regulation. This also implies different degrees of accountability in both activities since the legitimacy of the ECB actions has implications for the effectiveness of supervision.[150] The discussion is more complicated

---

140 See Arts 19(1), 25(2) and 25(5), 26(5) and 26(8) of the SSM Regulation.
141 See Article 26(8) of the SSM Regulation.
142 Article 25(5) of the SSM Regulation.
143 Article 28 of the SSM Regulation.
144 Arts 25(2) and 27 of the SSM Regulation.
145 Arts 29 and 30 of the SSM Regulation.
146 Arts 20, 21 and 25(2) of the SSM Regulation.
147 For an overview Kern Alexander, 'The ECB and Banking Supervision: Building Effective Prudential Supervision?' (2014) 33 *Yearbook of European Law* 421.
148 Kern Alexander, 'The European Central Bank and Banking Supervision: The Regulatory Limits of the Single Supervisory Mechanism' (2016) 13(3) *European Company and Financial Law Review* 467.
149 On this point see Nicolas Véron, 'Charting the Next Steps for the EU Financial Supervisory Architecture' Bruegel Policy Contribution, No. 2017/16, 9 <https://www.econstor.eu/handle/10419/173112> (accessed 31 May 2020).
150 Yves Mersch, 'Central Bank Independence Revisited' (2018) 18 *ERA Forum* 636. The author observes that 'when performing its supervisory tasks, the ECB is not shielded from external influences with the same level of independence as it is in its monetary policy function' (p. 639).

when looking at the different level of independence in the ECB as a supervisor and as a monetary authority: a clear mandate of tasks and responsibilities – as a Central Bank and as a bank supervisor – would help to clarify the interpretation of the principle of separation in the SSM provisions.

In the aftermath of the global financial crisis, the introduction of new supervisory mechanisms for EU banks has been lauded as a significant step forward in the banking regulatory framework. The rapid rise of cross-border transactions and the recent growth of virtual technologies have demonstrated the need to strengthen the harmonisation process of supervision to avoid inconsistency in the application of rules and discretion of authorities. The EU Banking Union represents a welcome approach in this direction: the SSM and the role of ECB establish innovative tools to prevent financial instability and systemic risk contagion.

Glossary of terms

- Principle of mutual recognition: Access of credit institutions to the market of another state, provided they are recognised and licensed by their home state.
- Principle of home country supervision: Banking services and credit institutions which are authorised to operate in any Member State are allowed to establish branches and to provide cross-border services throughout the EEA.
- Lamfalussy report: The first component of EU financial architecture in terms of supervision and regulation.
- Markets in Financial Instruments Directive (MiFID): Unified framework for securities across Member States which awards investment firms permits or passports to trade within the EEA.
- Compliance function: Instrument of internal control, e.g. for securities activities.
- De Larosière Report: Financial architecture focused on better supervision of EU financial institutions and aimed to ensure the prudential soundness of institutions, the orderly functioning of markets and the protection of depositors, policy holders and investors.
- MiFID II Directive: Amended the MiFID framework in the following ways: it regulates organised trading facilities (OTFs); it introduces investment advice on an independent basis; and it strengthens the role of management bodies in ensuring sound and prudent management of their firms, the promotion of market integrity and the protection of investors.
- Banking Union: Common platform for banking regulation, supervision, resolution mechanisms and deposit insurance in the Eurozone.
- Single Supervisory Mechanism (SSM): A centralised supervision system as part of the Banking Union that enhances the process of harmonisation through the Single Rulebook.
- Domestic systemically important bank (D-SIB): Banks that although are not significant from an international perspective, they could have an important impact on their domestic financial system and economy compared to non-systemic institutions. EU law uses the term Other Systemically Important Institutions (O-SIIs).
- Joint supervisory teams (JSTs): Teams of supervisors in charge of the supervision of a significant supervised entity or a significant supervised group.

Practice questions

The Lamfalussy reforms have streamlined the law-making process for EU financial regulation but have not led to any simplification in the regulatory regime. Critically discuss.

You may also find it useful to review the chapter through the following questions:

- To what extent do the reforms introduced under the de Larosière Report mark a shift in the way that regulatory policy and legislation is developed in the EU, and how effective have they been to date?
- What are the benefits and risks of financial regulation harmonisation?
- What role remains for Member States in the new European financial architecture?
- What are the implications of the MiFID Directive in the assessment of clients' risk profile?
- What is the MiFID passport system? What are the main reforms implemented by the MiFID II Directive?
- Explain the principles of freedom of establishment and mutual recognition of banks?
- What are the main features of ECB's supervision role?
- What are the benefits and risks of the EU Banking Union?
- What do you think some of the implications will be of the creation of a Eurozone Banking Union, and what are some of the pre-conditions for its effectiveness?
- What are the regulatory tools of the single resolution mechanism?

Part II
The business of banks

This part of the book examines the private law aspects of the relationship between banks and their customers and the relevant regulatory rules. Particular emphasis is placed on bank accounts, bank lending and the prevention of financial crime.

5 The relationship between banks and customers

5.1 Introduction

This chapter analyses the bank–customer relationship in English law and the main obligations that arise between banks and their clients. Particular attention is devoted to the identification of the notion of a bank customer at common law and to the common law duties of care and confidentiality. Although banks are not in general held to be in a fiduciary relationship with their customers, such relationship may arise in specific contexts, such as the giving of special financial or investment advice. The first part of the chapter explores the scope of banks' fiduciary obligations to customers, and legal techniques used to avoid them as well as the duty of care applicable when giving advice. The second part analyses the duty of confidentiality owed by banks to customers.

5.2 The bank–customer relationship

5.2.1 The bank customer

It is generally considered that banks are special because banking is crucial for the functioning of market economies.[1] Banks are financial intermediaries that collect funds from the customers (deposits) and use that source of liquidity to finance its lending business or invest in capital markets. Further, bank deposits play a very important role as value for the performance of payments, saving both time and money for all parties involved.[2] The activity of banking includes the provision of payments facilities, credit and capital to individuals, firms and the government. The traditional business of commercial banking consists in (1) accepting deposits and (2) lending. In this context, the German model of 'universal banking' has spread around the world and influenced the development of

---

1 In 1899, the United States Supreme Court (Austen) used these words to define a bank: '[as] an institution, usually incorporated with power to issue its promissory notes intended to circulate as money (known as bank notes); or to receive the money of others on general deposit, to form a joint fund that shall be used by the institution, for its own benefit, for one or more of the purposes of making temporary loans and discounts; of dealing in notes, foreign and domestic bills of exchange, coin, bullion, credits, and the remission of money; or with both these powers, and with the privileges, in addition to these basic powers, of receiving special deposits and making collections for the holders of negotiable paper, if the institution sees fit to engage in such business'. See *Auten v United States Nat'l Bank of New York*, 174 U.S. 125 (1899).

2 For an overview Ross Cranston et al., *Principles of Banking Law* (3rd edn, OUP 2017) 6–8.

national banking systems in Europe and elsewhere.[3] A 'universal bank' is a bank that accepts deposits and lends money, but it also carries out a large range of financial activities, including investment services, property services and insurance services.[4] In the light of these premises, it can be observed that customer is anyone with an account with a bank: the relationship is qualified by the counterparty, and it is generally not considered of advisory or fiduciary nature.[5]

In *United Dominions Trust Ltd v Kirkwood*, the court held that banks accept money from their customers in the form of deposits and they collect cheques on their behalf, placing those cheques to the customer's credit.[6] On this view, banks must honour the cheques or orders-to-pay drawn on them by their customers. To carry out their operations, banks maintain current accounts for their customers where they keep a record of the money debited and credited to the customers' accounts. The analysis pursued by the court in *United Dominion* represents a first attempt to define a bank's activity. In 1901 Justice Holmes argued, in the case *Re Shields Estate*, that 'the real business of the banker is to obtain deposits of money which he may use for his own profit by lending it out again'.[7] Interestingly in *Joachimson v Swiss Bank Corporation*, Justice Atkin held that 'the bank undertakes to receive money and to collect bills for its customer's account. The proceeds so received are not to be held in trust for the customer, but the bank borrows the proceeds and undertakes to repay them. The promise to repay is to repay at the branch of the bank where the account is kept, and during banking hours...'.[8] The 1948 Privy Council decision in *Bank of Chettinad* defined a bank as '... a company which carries on as its principal business the accepting of deposits of money on current account or otherwise, subject to withdrawal by cheque, draft or order...'.[9] From these decisions, it can be inferred that the bank–customer relationship is based on contract. The bank and its customer frequently enter into numerous separate contracts (acceptance of deposits, for the lending of money or the safe custody of valuables). The opening of the bank account creates per se certain legal rights and obligations even if no further transaction is ever initiated or agreed. As a result, the bank–customer relationship is governed by (1) the law of contracts, (2) the jurisprudence developed by English courts and (3) statutory legislation enacted by Parliament (either on its own initiative or under the mandate of European Union law or the influence of international initiatives for the

---

3 Gary Gorton and Frank A. Schmid, 'Universal Banking and the Performance of German Firms' (1996) NBER Working Paper No. 5453, 6, where universal banking is defined as 'banks allowed to offer the full range of commercial and investment banking services [...]'.

4 Jordi Canals, *Universal Banking: International Comparisons and Theoretical Perspectives* (OUP 1997) 102–103.

5 According to the FCA Banking Code of Business Sourcebook, a banking customer is defined as a consumer; a micro-enterprise (an enterprise that employs fewer than ten people and whose annual turnover and/or annual balance sheet total does not exceed €2m) or a charity that has an annual income of less than £1 million.

6 See *United Dominions Trust Ltd v Kirkwood* [1966] 2 Q.B. 431. Lord Denning stated that a bank is '[a]n establishment for the custody of money received from, or on behalf of, its customers. Its essential duty is to pay their drafts on it: its profits arise from the use of money left unemployed by them'. Justice Diplock noted: '[w]hat I think is common to all modern definitions of banking and essential to the carrying on of the business of banking is that the banker should accept from his customers loans of money on deposit, that is to say, loans for an indefinite period on running account, repayable as to the whole or any part thereof on demand by the customer...'.

7 *Re Shields Estate* [1901] 1 Irish Reports 182.

8 *Joachimson v Swiss Bank Corporation* [1921] 3 K.B. 110.

9 *Bank of Chettinad Ltd of Colombo v Income Tax Commissioner of Colombo* [1948] A.C. 378.

protection of consumers).[10] The central aspect in this relationship is the placement of the bank deposit which is based on contract between the bank and the depositor. Accepting the customers' deposits is what distinguishes banks from other financial institutions. The particular legal implications of that transaction raise several questions, whether (1) the bank is obliged to keep the customer's money safe in a vault and return the very same notes and coins on the customer's demand; (2) the bank is entitled to use the deposit in order to finance its lending business and simply return to the customer an equivalent amount (plus interest) and (3) the deposit is the customer's money or the banker's money.

In *Foley v Hill*, the court clarified the legal nature of the relationship between the bank and the customer.[11] It was held that the relationship created by a deposit of funds with the bank was a relationship of debtor and creditor. The deposit may be made either directly by the depositor or by a third party; may be carried out either in cash or by means of collection of payment from another account and may be payable either on demand or at the expiry of a notice period or after the lapse of a specific period of time and may or may not bear interest. The bank cannot be obliged to seek the customer in his home or business address to repay the deposit: banks operate during business hours from within their business premises and it is reasonable. In the *Joachimson* case, it was held that the obligation of the bank towards the customer is not a 'debt simple' but rather a debt for which demand has to be made by the customer at the branch where the account is kept and during normal business hours unless the parties agree otherwise. Under English law, the bank customer is entitled to have the deposit repaid to him or her indirectly by transferring funds to another party designated by the customer even if no special agreement was reached.[12]

In terms of contractual obligations, the bank–customer relationship consists of express as well as implied terms. Express terms are hardly ever negotiated (particularly in bank accounts offered to individual customers and small businesses). The terms are contained in standard-form contracts or contracts of adhesion, which normally reflect standard industry practice and tend to favour the bank rather than the customer.[13] However, some issues arise in the contracts of adhesion namely (1) services and functions available to the account holder; (2) fees and charges, possibly the electronic facilities available to the customer; (3) the question of liability in the event of fraud or negligent loss; (4) the requirements of security in using the bank's facilities; (5) the reasons for terminating the agreement; and (6) the operation of accounts held jointly by more than one person. English courts are very reluctant to accept that other terms are implied between the parties despite the lack of any explicit reference to these terms.

In *Tai Hing Cotton Mill Ltd v Liu Chong Hing Bank Ltd*, the bank argued that the bank–customer relationship automatically gives rise to a duty on the part of the customer

10 For an overview Charles Proctor, *The Law and Practice of International Banking* (2nd edn, OUP 2015) 297–298.
11 *Foley v Hill* (1848) 2 H.L. Cas. 28. The House of Lords held that 'money placed in the custody of a banker is, to all intents and purposes, the money of the banker, to do with it as he pleases; he is guilty of no breach of trust in employing it; he is not answerable to the principal if he puts it into jeopardy, if he engages in a hazardous speculation; he is not bound to keep it or deal with it as the property of the principal; but he is, of course, answerable for the amount, because he has contracted, having received that money, to repay to the principal, when demanded, a sum equivalent to that paid into his hands'.
12 E.P. Ellinger, Eva Lomnicka and C. Hare (eds), *Ellinger's Modern Banking Law* (5th edn, OUP 2011) 119–120.
13 The UK Unfair Terms in Consumer Contracts Regulations 1999 requires that contracts are expressed in a plain and intelligible language.

to exercise reasonable care to prevent forged cheques being presented to the bank, or at least to check its periodic bank statements to uncover any fraudulent or unauthorised activity.[14] The court was not keen to create an implied duty, and it held that in the absence of an express provision, there was no such duty. The customer was not under the law required to exercise reasonable care in view of avoiding the forgery and subsequent presentation of cheques. If the banks wanted protection against careless customers, they could have easily specified it in written terms with the customer there was no need for the court to discover implied terms of that nature.

Recently, the bank–customer relationship has assumed an international dimension due to several episodes of banking failure that raise the question of consumer protection and accountability for senior managers. The collapses of Lehman Brothers and Northern Rock are cases in point in terms of lack of transparency in the bank governance and weak system of internal controls. However, the main question at stake regards the banks and customers duties and their implications in the deposit relationship (i.e. a fiduciary relationship can arise due to status or relationship).[15] A range of duties arises in the bank–customer relationship, namely, a duty of loyalty, advisory duty or duty to advise and duty to act on customer's mandate which can involve conflicts of interest. The next sections discuss whether a bank owes a duty of care with respect to customers and how a bank's duty of care is regulated. These issues will be examined in further detail in Chapter 7.

5.2.2 The non-fiduciary nature of the standard relationship

In *Bristol and West Building Society v Mothew*, the court held that 'a fiduciary is someone who has undertaken to act for or on behalf of another in a particular matter in circumstances which give rise to a relationship of trust and confidence. The distinguishing obligation of a fiduciary is the obligation of loyalty. The principal is entitled to the single-minded loyalty of his fiduciary. This core liability has several facets. A fiduciary must act in good faith [...]'.[16] Fiduciary is all about selflessness (promoting the interests of beneficiary above his own). This reflects the fact that banks are not charitable institutions; however, a bank might be subject to fiduciary obligations when giving investment advice to its customers. In *Bank of Scotland v A Ltd*, the court reinforced the contractual nature of bank–customer relationship arguing that on the face of it the relationship between a bank and its customer is not a fiduciary.[17]

The fiduciary duty is inherently related to the duty of care and duty to act in good faith. As observed these duties arise depending on the circumstances of each bank–customer relation and generally the duty towards commercial clients is less than those towards inexperienced private client.[18] The challenge for the courts is to identify the relationship between parties that imposes the duty of care. This type of relationship may not only be a fiduciary or the relationship between principal and agent relation but also a trading during the ordinary course of business. In this context, the English courts held that there is no general duty to advise customer on wisdom of (1) transaction with bank or (2) third-party transaction

---

14 *Tai Hing Cotton Mill Ltd v Liu Chong Hing Bank Ltd (No. 1)* [1986] A.C. 519.
15 The UK courts traditionally are seen as reluctant to impose fiduciary duties, and banks are generally reluctant to have an extension to fiduciary duties.
16 *Bristol & West Building Society v Mothew (t/a Stapley & Co)* [1997] 2 WLR 436.
17 *Adris and Others v The Royal Bank of Scotland Plc and Others* [2010] EWHC 941 (QB).
18 Danny Busch and Cees van Dam (eds), *A Bank's Duty of Care* (Hart Bloomsbury 2017) Chapter 12.

with banking funding.[19] According to the UK Supply of Goods and Services Act 1982, any advice that is given must be provided with reasonable care and skill.[20] In the cases of *Titan Steel Wheels Ltd v Royal Bank of Scotland Plc (RBS)*[21] and *Peekay v Australia and New Zealand Banking Group*,[22] it has been observed that 'the relationship between professionals and their clients is inherently of a fiduciary nature…in which the core duty of loyalty of the fiduciary manifests itself in the "no conflict" rule, that the fiduciary should not put himself in a position where his duty to his client conflicts with his own interest or with his duty to another client'.[23] In *Nocton v Ashburton*, the court held that a fiduciary relationship arising out of a professional relationship supports a duty of care in tort for which ordinary tort damages are recoverable.[24] This ruling underlined the question of economic losses flowing from a fiduciary relationship such as that of principal and agent. The principal-agent nature of the bank–customer relationship underlines the question whether a duty of care arises in any contractual relationship between bank and client. This involves the duty to act on behalf of another without a conflict of interest: in the advisory relationship this duty can cross the boundary to become fiduciary, i.e. customer may believe it to be (e.g. best interests). In *Lloyds Bank v Bundy*, the court argued that the course of the relationship founds an expectation that advice will be given in the client's best interests.[25]

Customer due diligence, best advice, suitability of products have been discussed in *Woods v Martins Bank* that clarified where the advice is grossly negligent or bank has conflict of interest and how any advice volunteered must be skilled, even to non-customers.[26] Duty to advise at common law has been further examined in *Cornish v Midland Bank* where the court held that no duty to explain effect of mortgage, but any explanation given must be accurate,[27] and in *Verity and Spindler v Lloyds Bank* where a bank was recognised liable due to its marketing leaflet, actions of its staff, naivety of the customer.[28] However, there is no duty at common law to recommend the best account as has been held in the case *Suriya and Douglas v Midland Bank*.[29] Further, no duty to advise on this but if an outcome is predicted, it must be a reasonable prediction has been argued in *Box v Midland Bank*.[30]

The Lending Code provides that there is no duty at common law to advise on loans. Banks should lend money responsibly: lenders should deal quickly and sympathetically with things that go wrong and act sympathetically and positively when considering a customer's financial difficulties.[31] The Financial Services and Markets Act (FSMA 2000) regulates the advice on investments as a matter of public law: this only applies to

---

19 *National Commercial Bank (Jamaica) Ltd v Hew* [2003] UKPC 51.
20 Supply of Goods and Services Act 1982, Chapter 29 <http://www.legislation.gov.uk/ukpga/1982/29> (accessed 2 February 2020).
21 *Titan Steel Wheels Ltd v Royal Bank of Scotland Plc* [2010] EWHC 211 (Comm).
22 *Peekay v Australia and New Zealand Banking Group* [2006] 2 Lloyd's Rep 511.
23 On this point Colin Bamford, *Principles of International Financial Law* (2nd edn, OUP 2015) 247–248.
24 *Nocton v Ashburton* [1914] A.C. 932. See also *Arenson v Casson Beckman Rutley & Co* [1977] A.C. 405 and *Midland Bank Trust Co Ltd v Hett Stubbs & Kemp* [1979] Ch. 384.
25 *Lloyds Bank v Bundy* [1975] QB 326.
26 *Woods v Martins Bank* [1959] 1 QB 55.
27 *Cornish v Midland Bank* [1985] All ER 513.
28 *Verity and Spindler v Lloyds Bank* [1995] CLC 1557.
29 *Suriya and Douglas v Midland Bank* [1999] 1 All ER (Comm) 612.
30 *Box v Midland Bank* [1979] 2 Lloyds Rep 391.
31 See The Lending Code. Setting standards for banks, building societies, credit card providers and their agents, March 2011 (Revised 28 September 2015) <https://www.lendingstandardsboard.org.uk/wp-content/uploads/2016/06/The-Lending-Code-Mar-2011-revised-2015-1.pdf> (accessed 20 May 2020). The Lending

(1) individuals, (2) investments and (3) others acting outside course of business.[32] Banks must comply with the Financial Conduct Authority (FCA) Handbook: Section 138D(1) of the FSMA 2000 which grants a civil liability claim where the bank was in breach of its statutory duty to a private customer – such a breach must be actionable in a court of law.[33] This could include breach of the FCA Conduct of Business Sourcebook.[34] In the FCA Banking Conduct of Business Sourcebook, banks must provide a service in relation to a retail banking service which is prompt, efficient and fair, and pay due regard to the interests of its customers and to treat them fairly. In particular, a firm should deal fairly with a customer whom it has reason to believe is in financial difficulty.[35] According to the Perimeter Guidance Manual (PERG), the FCA provides that 'advice requires an element of opinion on the part of the adviser. In effect, it is a recommendation as to a course of action. Information, on the other hand, involves statements of fact or figures'.[36] The analysis of the above cases highlights the question whether a bank acts as adviser or counterparty. Sophisticated customers trading with bank in financial instruments may imply the advisory duty: in *JP Morgan Chase Bank v Springwell Navigation Corp*, the court held that sophistication of counterparty does not involve advisory service and assumption of responsibility for making an investment decision, therefore no fiduciary duty arises.[37]

5.2.3 Banks' duty of care and other duties

As discussed in the previous section, the course of the relationship creates an expectation that advice will be given in the client's best interests. One of the most controversial aspects in the bank–customer relationship is the analysis of banks' duty of care. In *Junior Books Ltd. Respondents v Veitchi Co. Ltd.*, Lord Denning noted that 'when a banker negligently gives a reference to one who acts on it, the duty is plain and the damage is not too remote'.[38] The *Junior Books* case elaborated the 'assumption of responsibility' rule in *Hedley Byrne & Co. Ltd. v Heller & Partners Ltd.*, where the House of Lords allowed a claim in negligence

---

Code has been replaced by the Standards of Lending Practice in July 2016: in March 2017, the Lending Standards Board published the Standards of Lending Practice for business customers.

32 Article 53(1) of the Financial Services and Markets Act 2000 (Regulated Activities) Order 2001 (SI 2001/544) (RAO).

33 *R (ex p British Bankers Association) v FSA* [2011] EWHC 999 (Admin).

34 Principle 2.1.1(1) of the Conduct of Business Sourcebook provides that 'a firm must act honestly, fairly and professionally in accordance with the best interests of its client (the client's best interests rule)'. Principle 2.2.1(1) states that 'the adviser must provide appropriate information in a comprehensible form to a client about the services and investments it is offering so that the client is reasonably able to understand the nature and risks of the service and of the specific type of investment that is being offered and, consequently, to take investment decisions on an informed basis'. Principle 9.2.1(1): 'a firm must take reasonable steps to ensure that a personal recommendation, or a decision to trade, is suitable for its client' <https://www.handbook.fca.org.uk/handbook/COBS.pdf> (accessed 30 March 2020).

35 Principle 5.1.4 of the Banking Conduct of Business Sourcebook 'Dealings with customers in financial difficulty' <https://www.handbook.fca.org.uk/handbook/BCOBS.pdf> (accessed 3 May 2020).

36 PERG 8.28 'Advice or Information' <https://www.handbook.fca.org.uk/handbook/PERG/8/28.html> (accessed 3 March 2020).

37 *JP Morgan Chase v Springwell Navigation Corp* [2006] EWCA 161. See also *Thornbridge Ltd v Barclays Bank* [2015] EWHC 3430, in which relevant factors considered by the court were: (1) bank did not receive advice fee; and (2) observations as to future interest rate movements were not 'advice'.

38 *Junior Books Ltd. Respondents v Veitchi Co. Ltd. Appellants* [1983] 1 A.C. 520.

for pure economic loss on the basis of the assumed responsibility of the defendant and the reliance of the claimant.[39]

The court argued that in a relationship of proximity the scope of the duty of care includes not only a duty to avoid causing foreseeable harm to persons, but also a duty to avoid causing pure economic loss consequential on defects. The court expanded the category of claims for damages for economic loss as a direct consequence of a negligent act and for economic loss unrelated to damage. Basically, the House of Lords agreed that damages could be recovered on the basis that the act should have been provided correctly. This decision provided grounds to cover the situation where pure economic loss is to be foreseen as likely to be suffered by persons in a relationship of proximity. The House of Lords explained that even in the absence of contract there is a special relationship of proximity which is similar to contract so that the scope of the duty of care extends to purely economic loss. The *Hedley Byrne* case affirmed that direct injury to the person is not necessary to support an action in negligence, and that the claimant is allowed to recover the indirect or consequential loss suffered. As a result, when a duty of care arises in giving advice irrespective as to whether there is a fiduciary or contractual relationship between the maker of a statement and the person relying thereon, the indirect or economic loss can be sufficient to support the claim. In the case of negligent misstatement, damages are recoverable, not for failure to give the right advice, but to compensate for damage arising out of reliance on the advice. However, negligent advice can cause economic loss irrespective of a relationship of proximity and it does not always entail floodgate risks as the giver of advice knows the class of person who will use the advice to make an investment decision.

The 'assumption of responsibility' rule and 'special relationship' of *Hedley Byrne* were considered in *Caparo Industries Plc v Dickman*, a landmark case where the courts held that a duty of care arises in the presence of three factors: (1) reasonable foreseeability, (2) proximity and (3) fairness.[40] Specifically, the existence of a duty of care is determined by a 'three-stage test': (1) whether the harm is foreseeable, (2) whether there is sufficient proximity between the parties, and (3) whether the imposition of a duty is just, fair and reasonable.[41] The *Caparo* case established that a duty of care is owed where the maker of the statement knew that his statement would be directed to an identifiable class of persons in connection with a particular transaction that would be very likely to rely on it for the purpose of deciding to enter upon that transaction.[42]

On this view, the imposition of any duty of care is limited to the specific transaction for which the maker of the statement knew that the information was to be available to a precise class of individuals. The court adopted a restrictive approach to the 'special relationship' in *Hedley Byrne* so as to avoid the potential 'floodgates' argument and indeterminate liability.[43] The 'three-stage' test refined the proximity between the parties as follows: (1) the

---

39 See the judgment of Lord Denning in *Hedley Byrne & Co. Ltd. v Heller & Partners Ltd.* [1964] A.C. 465.

40 *Caparo Industries Plc v Dickman* [1990] 2 A.C. 605.

41 See the conclusions of Lord Oliver in *Caparo* at 643.

42 See the observations of Lord Bridge in *Caparo* at 621.

43 On this argument see the landmark conclusions of Cardozo J in *Ultramares Corp v Touche, Niven & Co* (1931) 174 NE 441. See also the economic analysis carried out by William Bishop, 'Negligent Representation through Economists' Eyes' (1980) 96 *Law Quarterly Review* 360, where it is observed that 'liability should be restricted when (a) the information is of a type that is valuable to many potential users, (b) the producer of the information cannot capture in his prices the benefits flowing to all users of the information, and (c) the imposition of liability to all persons harmed would raise potential costs significantly enough to discourage information production altogether'.

defendant knew the statement would be communicated to the claimant; (2) the defendant's statement related to an identifiable transaction or particular type of transaction; and (3) the defendant reasonably anticipated the claimant would rely on statement and the claimant did rely on it.[44] This practical test endorsed the principle that a duty of care does not arise to an indeterminate class as the duty is limited to a limited class of persons. As a result, the 'three-stage' test faces challenges to identify the specific transaction where the class of persons use the information upon which they rely to enter in such transaction.

In *Customs & Excise Commissioners v Barclays Bank Plc*, the court examined whether it was fair, just and reasonable to impose a duty of care between parties not contractually bound.[45] This case questioned whether the assumption of responsibility rule was most appropriate to establish whether the duty of care should be imposed.[46] In a similar context *Riyad Bank v Ahli United Bank (UK)*, where the court adopted the *Hedley Byrne* rule.[47] *Ahli* advised *Riyad* on the creation of a mutual fund in Saudi Arabia that would be sharia compliant (it invested in leasing agreements). The leases proved to be worth much less than had been paid for them, but *Riyad* could not sue in contract due to lack of contractual nexus, so had to sue in tort: *Ahli* had made an 'assumption of responsibility' towards *Riyad*.

In *JP Morgan Chase Bank v Springwell Navigation Corp*, the English court made the distinction between the giving of advice ('salesman') and a relationship which is such that, by giving advice, a party accepts responsibility for that advice ('investment adviser').[48] The court argued that it is inevitable during the sales process for a salesman to provide comment, even opinion, on the product he is trying to sell. A similar approach is found in *Titan Steel Wheels v RBS*, where the English court put particular attention on the distinction between giving advice or making recommendations and giving advice in an advisory capacity.[49] These rulings addressed the controversial questions of whether a duty was owed and what the scope of that duty should be for a bank. In *McInerny v Lloyd's Bank Ltd*,[50] the courts applied the assumption of responsibility rule in recognising that there is a duty to exercise reasonable care in providing accurate statements.

In *Morgan Crucible Plc v Hill Samuel Bank Ltd.*, the House of Lords recognised a duty of care to the claimant for pure economic loss because the defendant (a financial adviser) was aware that the information provided would affect relying on third parties.[51] Specifically,

---

44 Lord Bridge observed, 'it is preferable…that the law should develop novel categories of negligence incrementally and by analogy with established categories, rather than by a massive extension of a prima facie duty of care restrained only by indefinable considerations which ought to negative, or to reduce or limit the scope of the duty or the class of person to whom it is owed' (*Caparo Industries Plc v Dickman* at 618).

45 *Customs and Excise Commissioners v Barclays Bank Plc* [2006] UKHL 28.

46 Ibid. Interestingly the court examined the 'assumption of responsibility' test, the 'three-stage test' and 'the incremental test' to establish whether a duty of care should be imposed. Regarding the incremental test, it was considered that 'new categories of negligence should be developed incrementally and by analogy with established categories, is of limited assistance since it does not provide any qualitative criteria by which to measure whether a duty should be held to arise' [at 184'. The adoption of these tests depends on the suitable cases where they can be applicable to demonstrate whether the imposition of a duty of care is fair, just and reasonable. For a commentary David Capper, 'No Tort Liability for Breaching Freezing Orders' (2006) 65 *Cambridge Law Journal* 484, 484–485.

47 *Riyad Bank v Ahli United Bank (UK)* [2006] 2 Lloyds Rep 292 CA.

48 *JP Morgan Chase Bank v Springwell Navigation Corp* [2008] EWHC 1186 (Comm).

49 *Titan Steel Wheels v RBS* [2010] EWHC 211 (Comm).

50 *McInerny v Lloyd's Bank Ltd* [1973] 2 Lloyd's Rep. 389 at 400.

51 *Morgan Crucible Plc v Hill Samuel Bank Ltd.* [1991] 1 All ER 148 where the House of Lords circumvented the decision in the *Caparo* case recognising third-party reliance on the defendant. It was held that 'if during the

the House of Lords affirmed that statements in the ordinary course of business raise a duty of care with respect to a third party who reasonably relied on such statements. The significance of this case lies in the recognition of financial information as capable of identifying a specific class of individuals that use the information for the purpose of making an investment decision. On this view, it can be observed that financial intermediaries owe a duty of care to third parties to provide correct statements of fact as to the suitability and quality of securities. In particular, the financial adviser knew in advance the potential user of the information and the potential effects of a misleading forecast. The observations made by the House of Lords diverged from the ruling in *Caparo* and refined the criteria established in the 'three-stage test'.

To determine whether a duty of care is owed under the *Caparo* test or *Hedley Byrne* test is a matter of interpretation for the courts but the existence of the elements that characterise these tests does not necessarily provide the answer in all situations. It can be argued that the 'assumption of responsibility' and 'three-stage test' are only benchmarks to establish a degree of liability for professionals and that whether the restrictive approach or the broad approach is to be applied should be assessed in each concrete situation. The risk of floodgates concern is avoided because the liability is restricted to a limited class only.

After examining the duty of care to non-customers in the tort of negligence, another interesting aspect is the duty on the bank to avoid undue influence. This analysis regards the following points: (1) when the matrimonial home is used as security; (2) mortgage of the jointly owned home to secure loan to husband or to his company and (3) presumption of undue influence in 'non-commercial' relationships. In this scenario, mortgage can be voided by undue influence as manipulation of trust and confidence so that the wife does not act on her own free will (renders the contract voidable at her option) and misrepresentation as false information given to wife so that she enters into a transaction that she otherwise would not have entered into (also renders the contract voidable at her option).[52] A lender can be affected under the following circumstances: (1) it exerts the undue influence itself; (2) it uses the exerter as its agent; (3) it has actual notice of the exertion and (4) it has constructive notice of the exertion.

In *Credit Lyonnais v Burch*,[53] the court held that different steps need to be taken by the lender depending on the degree of risk of undue influence. If risk is normal, a senior official of the lender should see wife on her own and explain the transaction to her and the risk,

---

course of a contested take-over bid the directors and financial advisers of the target company made express representations after an identified bidder had emerged intending that the bidder would rely on those representations, they owed the bidder a duty of care not to be negligent in making representations which might mislead him. Since on the assumed facts the defendants intended the plaintiff to rely on the pre-bid financial statements and profit forecast for the purpose of deciding whether to make an increased bid, and the plaintiff did so rely on those statements and the profit forecast, it was plainly arguable that there was a relationship of proximity between each of the defendants and the plaintiff sufficient to give rise to a duty of care' [at 149]. It can be noted that the *Morgan Crucible Plc* case distinguished the conclusions of the House of Lords in *Caparo* case where it was affirmed that 'in certifying a company's accounts for the purpose of the Companies Act 1985, an auditor owes no duty of care to a potential take-over bidder, whether or not he is already a shareholder of the company. [And] that foreseeability, no matter how high, that a potential bidder might rely on the audited accounts did not suffice to find a duty of care, since there was no sufficient relationship of proximity between auditor and potential bidder' [at 153].

52 See *Barclays Bank v O'Brien* [1994] 1 AC 180; *RBS v Etridge (No. 2)* [2001] 3 WLR 1021; *Barclays Bank v Coleman* [2002] 2 AC 273.
53 *Credit Lyonnais Bank Nederland NV v Burch* [1997] 1 All E.R. 144.

and the desirability of her taking independent advice (it is also sufficient for the wife to be advised by a solicitor). As discussed, the analysis of bank's duty of care involves various duties: duty to classify customers, duty to investigate (Know Your Customer rule), duty to disclose risks, duty to warn of unsuitable investments, duty to act in good faith and bank director duties. The next section examines the customer's duties in the light of the recent developments in the regulation of bank–customer relationship.

5.2.4 Customers' duties

Customers owe duties to banks in their contractual relationship, i.e. duties to inform the bank of compromise, duty to prevent forgery, duty to give notice and duty to pay demands. These duties are related to the bank's duty to act on the customer's mandate: they are two sides of the same coin (for example, in case of the rule on forgeries unless the customer is aware of the forgeries or facilitates them).[54]

In *Price Meats Ltd v Barclays Bank*, the court held that there must be actual knowledge of the transactions on a customer's account and constructive knowledge is not taken into account.[55] In *Libyan Arab Foreign Bank v Bankers Trust*, the court held that a customer must exercise care drawing cheques although no duty of confidentiality was recognised at that time.[56] The banking customer must not act fraudulently or intentionally or with gross negligence, failing to comply with his or her obligations. Further, the customer must take all reasonable steps to keep his personalised security features safe. Where the customer has notified the bank (unless he has acted fraudulently) liability does not arise if the bank has failed to ensure that appropriate means are available at all times to enable the customer to notify it.

The Payment Services Regulations on disputed transactions provide that a customer must use his card in accordance with the terms and conditions governing its issue and use, and notify the bank in the agreed manner and without undue delay on becoming aware of the loss, theft, misappropriation or unauthorised use of the card.[57] In the landmark case *Foley v Hill*, the court examined the nature of the bank–customer relationship arguing that '[...] The customer on his part undertakes to exercise reasonable care in executing his written orders so as not to mislead the bank or to facilitate forgery'.[58]

In *London Joint Stock Bank Limited v Macmillan and Arthur*, the House of Lords examined the obligations upon the customer in the following terms:

> in the first place his cheque must be unambiguous and must be ex facie in such a condition as not to arouse any reasonable suspicion. But it follows from that that it is the duty of the customer, should his own business or other requirements prevent him from personally presenting it, to take care to frame and fill up his cheque in such a manner that when it passes out of his, the customer's, hands it will not be so left that before presentation, alterations, interpolations, &c., can be readily made upon it without

54 *London Joint Stock Bank v MacMillan* [1918] AC 777. See also *Greenwood v Martins Bank* [1933] AC 51; *Tai Hing Cotton Mills v Liu Chong Hing Bank* [1986] AC 80.
55 *Price Meats Ltd v Barclays Bank* [2000] 2 All ER (Comm) 246.
56 *Libyan Arab Foreign Bank v Bankers Trust* [1989] QB 728.
57 See Regulation 72 of the Payment Services Regulations 2017 (SI 752/2017) that replaced the Payment Services Regulations 2009.
58 *Foley v Hill* (n 11).

giving reasonable ground for suspicion to the banker that they did not form part of the original body of the cheque when signed. To neglect this duty of carefulness is a negligence cognizable by law. The consequences of such negligence fall alone upon the party guilty of it, namely, the customer.[59]

In *Greenwood v Martins Bank Ltd*, the House of Lord held that a customer is bound to inform the bank if he knows that a fraud is taking or has taken place on his account.[60] Interestingly, it has been observed that 'despite the courts steadfast refusal to widen the ambit of the duties in *Macmillan* and *Greenwood*, banks have attempted to gain protection from customers seeking redress after fraud has been perpetrated on their accounts; principally by the use of standard terms and conditions'.[61]

In *Tai Hing Cotton Mill Ltd v Liu Chong Hing Bank Ltd*, the court mitigated the customer's duties arguing that the customer is required to 'take reasonable steps to check his periodic bank statements so as to be able to notify the bank of any items which were not, or might not, have been, authorised by him'.[62] These cases underline the customer's duties regarding the payment of a cheque and require customers to take "reasonable steps" and 'reasonable care' in fulfilling the contractual obligations with bank. However, these general requirements have been developed in the UK with the Banking Code[63] and in EU legislation with the Payment Services Directive 2,[64] implemented through the Payment Services Regulations 2017.[65] The Banking Code, although consisting of a voluntary set of principles and guidelines not binding and not enforceable, demonstrated an important change in policy towards consumers: on this view, the English courts have made appreciable advances in terms of consumer protection by confirming the tendency to consider consumers as an active part of financial markets.[66] The next part deals with relevant issues arising from the bank–customer's duty of confidentiality.

5.3 Banks' duty of confidentiality

One important aspect of the general law applicable to the relationship between banks and their customers is the duty of banks to keep customer information confidential. In English law this is known as the duty of confidentiality and is part of private law. In other jurisdictions the term used is duty of secrecy and occasionally the two terms are used interchangeably in the literature.[67] However, it is perhaps more accurate to reserve the terminology of

---

59 *London Joint Stock Bank Limited v Macmillan and Arthur* [1918] A.C. 777 at 824.
60 *Greenwood v Martins Bank Ltd* [1933] A.C. 51.
61 Bill Davies, 'What Is the Extent of the Customer's Duty Not to Facilitate Fraud?' (2009) 30(11) *Business Law Review* 242.
62 *Tai Hing Cotton Mill Ltd v Liu Chong Hing Bank Ltd* [1986] A.C. 80.
63 British Bankers Association, The Banking Code and Business Banking Code (31 March 2008). The Banking Code was replaced by the Payment Services Regulations 2009.
64 Directive (EU) 2015/2366 of the European Parliament and of the Council of 25 November 2015 on payment services in the internal market, amending Directives 2002/65/EC, 2009/110/EC and 2013/36/EU and Regulation (EU) No. 1093/2010, and repealing Directive 2007/64/EC.
65 The Regulations came into force partly on 13 August 2017 and partly on 13 October 2017.
66 *Office of Fair Trading v Abbey National and others* [2009] EWCA Civ 116. The High Court stressed the question of unfair commercial practices while affirming the centrality of reasonable consumer expectations.
67 See e.g. Dora Neo, 'Conceptual Overview of Bank Secrecy' in Sandra Booysen and Dora Neo (eds), *Can Banks Still Keep a Secret? Bank Secrecy in Financial Centres around the World* (CUP 2017) 4–6.

'duty of secrecy' to duties that are imposed by criminal law, for instance, in jurisdictions such as Switzerland and Singapore.[68]

The conventional account of the policy rationale for the duty of confidentiality of banks relies on the premise that banks need to be able to demonstrate to potential customers that their information will remain confidential. This encourages customers to do business with banks and to disclose relevant information. By implying a confidentiality term to the contract between banks and customers, the law saves parties the expense of including an express term to the same effect in every contract. This part will explain the current state of English law on banks' duty of confidentiality with particular attention to its legal nature, scope and qualifications. In doing so, it will briefly discuss how the requirements of General Data Protection Regulation (GDPR) relate to banks' handling of customer information.

5.3.1 Statement and legal nature of the duty of confidentiality

The duty originates from the well-known 1923 decision of the Court of Appeal in *Tournier v National Provincial and Union Bank of England*,[69] and has never been codified by statute, despite the recommendation of the Jack Committee Report in 1989.[70] However, the Banking Code, a voluntary code of best practice that applied until 2009, provided a statement of the duty and its qualifications according to the case law.[71]

The facts of *Tournier* concerned a person (T) holding an overdrawn account with the defendant bank. The bank demanded the plaintiff gradually to repay his overdraft, which he started doing but then payments stopped. After that, T found employment for three months as a salesman with a company. Then a cheque for a considerable amount of money, far greater than T's overdraft, was drawn to him by a company who was customer of the same bank. T did not pay the cheque into his account (at which point the overdraft would have been repaid) but instead endorsed it in favour of a third party. When the cheque was eventually returned to the defendant bank for payment (because the drawer company was their customer), the branch manager contacted the bank that had collected the cheque and enquired who their customer was in order to find out to whom T had paid the money. The other bank informed the plaintiff bank's branch manager that the cheque had been collected for an L who was a bookmaker. From that the branch manager deduced that T was gambling. He then contacted T's employers and informed them that T was indebted to the bank, that he was somehow receiving considerable amounts of money and that he saw a cheque being paid into a bookmaker's account, while T ought to have paid off some of his debt. As a result, T's employers refused to renew his employment when the three-month period expired.

---

68 This is the position taken by Chaikin who takes a negative view of the Swiss approach. See David Chaikin, 'Adapting the Qualifications to the Banker's Common Law Duty of Confidentiality to Fight Transnational Crime' (2011) 33 *Sydney Law Review* 265, 266.

69 [1924] 1 KB 461.

70 Review Committee on Banking Services Law, *Banking Services: Law and Practice Report by the Review Committee* (R.B. Jack, Cm 622, HMSO 1989). The committee, chaired by Professor Jack, was commissioned in 1987 by the Treasury and Bank of England to review the law on the banker-customer relationship, electronic banking developments and developments in the European Community and internationally.

71 On this, see Keith Stanton, 'The United Kingdom' in Sandra Booysen and Dora Neo (eds), *Can Banks Still Keep a Secret? Bank Secrecy in Financial Centres around the World* (CUP 2017) 344–346.

T brought an action against the bank on grounds of slander and breach of an implied contractual term of secrecy which gave rise to an absolute duty of non-disclosure. At first instance, the court found for the defendant bank, citing *Hardy v Veasey*.[72] The majority of the Court of Appeal found for the plaintiff and ordered a retrial. The lead judgement was delivered by Bankes LJ. For our purposes, we will limit the discussion to the question of breach of an implied term of non-disclosure of any information relating to the state of the customer's account and the customer's business and affairs with the bank.

Bankes LJ affirmed the existence of a qualified legal duty of confidentiality in contract: 'At the present day I think it may be asserted with confidence that the duty is a legal one arising out of contract, and that the duty is not absolute but qualified'.[73] Exploring further the nature of the duty, Bankes LJ referred to a range of similar relationships including counsels, solicitors and doctors,[74] observing that in each case the extent of the duty is different. Regarding the bank–customer relationship, his Lordship observed that:

> The case of the banker and his customer appears to me to be one in which the confidential relationship between the parties is very marked. The credit of the customer depends very largely upon the strict observance of that confidence.[75]

These accounts, which draw a parallel between banks, on the one hand, and doctors and lawyers, on the other, are consistent with the interpretation provided by Ellinger[76] that the duty arises out of the nature of the relationship between banks and their customers, which is one featuring elements of agency and of handling personal information. These elements give rise to the implied contractual duty of confidentiality the precise extent of which depends on the nature of the relationship. A breach of the duty gives rise to damages. Typically, these will cover the pecuniary loss that resulted from the breach, for example, loss of profits. It may also entitle the customer to terminate his contractual relationship with the bank.

5.3.2 *The scope of the duty of confidentiality*

In the case of banks, the duty is not limited to information supplied directly by the customer or deriving from the customer's account (e.g. customer's personal details, address, state of the account, payments into and out of the account). It also covers any information about the customer that the bank receives from third parties in its capacity as banker. Indeed, Bankes LJ emphasised: 'I cannot think that the duty of non-disclosure is confined to information derived from the customer himself or from his account'.[77] This approach was later affirmed by the Court of Appeal in *Barclays Bank Plc v Taylor*.[78] It appears that the duty does not cover information received after the end of the bank–customer relationship.[79]

---

72 LR 3 Ex 107.
73 *Tournier* (above n 68) 471–472.
74 A similar account was given by Diplock LJ in *Parry-Jones v Law Society* [1969] 1 Chapter 1 which concerned a solicitor unsuccessfully resisting a demand of the Law Society to allow it to inspect his accounts on the grounds of his duty to his customers.
75 *Tournier* (above n 68) 474.
76 On this, see Ellinger and others (above n 12) 171–172.
77 *Tournier* (above n 68) 474.
78 [1989] 1 WLR 1066 per Lord Donaldson MR. See also *Lipkin Gorman v Karpnale Ltd* [1989] 1 WLR 1340.
79 *Tournier* (above n 68) 481 and 485.

The duty does not extend to the disclosure of information to a person who is already aware of, or is entitled by law to be aware of the information. A case in point is *Christofi v Barclays Bank Plc*.[80] The facts of the case are quite complex and concern a disclosure by a bank to the trustee in bankruptcy of the husband of the bank's customer to the effect that a caution that the trustee had registered on a property belonging to the couple had been cancelled. Under the relevant legislation, a cancellation of such a caution could only take place upon the land registry's giving notice to the trustee. In other words, the trustee was already aware of the information that the bank revealed. The court took a sensible approach mindful of the need to preserve the coherence of the law:

> Accordingly, it seems to me right to look at the matter in broader terms. Is it a necessary obligation which must be implied into the relationship of banker and customer in the interests of commercial efficacy? I cannot persuade myself that it is necessary, as a matter of law, to impose on a bank an obligation not to disclose information to the very person who must be taken to have that information under a statutory scheme. For the law to impose such an obligation would, I think, be to invite ridicule. There is no sense in it.[81]

The duty applies to bank customers, and therefore, a bank–customer relationship must have been established – normally by the opening of an account or agreement to open an account. However, the duty does not expire upon termination of the relationship, i.e. when the account is closed, but rather it survives unless one of the qualifications applies.[82] Regarding the scope of entities that qualify as banks for the purposes of the duty, courts have taken a broad approach covering various deposit-taking institutions, including building societies.

It is worth noting, however, that the above discussion is limited to the implied duty of confidentiality in the absence of any express undertaking on behalf of the bank. If such an undertaking exists, it will be enforced strictly by the courts.[83] In such circumstances, the duty may apply outside a bank's deposit-taking role; for instance, it may relate to the bank's investment banking activities.

Furthermore, a bank may be under a duty of confidentiality to a non-customer, such as a person disclosing a business plan in the hope of obtaining a loan, under the general law on breach of confidence. Briefly speaking, a duty of confidence arises when confidential (secret) information which is not trivial comes to the knowledge of a person in circumstances where he has notice of the confidential nature of the information, unless there is a countervailing public interest which requires disclosure.[84]

A further observation of practical importance is that in recent years many cases involving alleged breaches of banks' duty of confidentiality vis-à-vis retail customers have been dealt with under the complaints procedure of the Financial Ombudsman.[85] Examples of cases that have been decided indicate that banks typically breach their duty accidentally. It is usual for the disclosure of confidential information to be made to a spouse, relative,

---

80 [1999] 2 All ER (Comm) 417 (CA).
81 Ibid., 426 per Chadwick LJ.
82 *Tournier* (above n 68) 473.
83 *Christofi* (above n 79).
84 On this, see *Attorney General v Guardian Newspapers Ltd (No. 2)* [1990] 1 A.C. 109, 281–282 per Lord Goff.
85 The role of the Ombudsman will be discussed in Chapter 10 of this volume.

partner or other person closely related to the customer, but also to neighbours or persons with similar addresses that are wrongly sent a bank statement.[86]

5.3.3 Banks and customer data: the GDPR and Data Protection Act 2018 framework

At this point, it is necessary to make some remarks regarding the positive obligations applicable to banks with regard to processing, storing and using information about their customers. The relevant statute is the Data Protection Act 2018 which repealed and replaced the Data Protection Act 1998. The new Act is fully in line with, and refers to, the General Data Protection Regulation[87] (to be abbreviated as 'GDPR') and will evidently continue to be in force after the UK's withdrawal from the European Union. A detailed discussion of this framework goes beyond the scope of the present text.[88] For our purposes, the discussion will be limited to a brief overview of how the relevant provisions relate to banks.

The GDPR framework applies to personal data which are defined as 'any information relating to an identified or identifiable natural person',[89] and it is therefore of principal importance for the relationship between banks and individual customers or, in the case of corporate customers, to the extent that information about natural persons managing or acting for the corporate customer is processed. GDPR stipulates six general principles on data processing,[90] largely in line with the now repealed Directive 95/46/EC. For banks the most important principle is principle (f) that requires data to be 'processed in a manner that ensures appropriate security of the personal data'. Processing personal data is lawful, if there is informed consent of the data subject, contractual necessity or necessity to protect the legitimate interests of the controller.[91] There are additional safeguards for the processing of sensitive data,[92] but such data is not commonly processed by banks.

Data subjects have a range of rights under GDPR: a right to be provided information at the point when data is collected[93]; a right of access to the data[94]; and rights to rectification, erasure and restriction of data processing.[95] We will discuss the right to object to automated decision-making in Chapter 9 on consumer lending. Where there is a personal data breach (e.g. accidental leaking of information or attack on the controller's electronic systems), the controller must notify the competent supervisory authority (which in the UK is the

---

86 See Financial Ombudsman Service, 'The Banker's Duty of Confidentiality to the Customer' (April 2005) 45 *Ombudsman News* 3 <https://www.financial-ombudsman.org.uk/publications/ombudsman-news/45/45.pdf> (accessed 25 January 2020).

87 Regulation (EU) 2016/679 of the European Parliament and of the Council of 27 April 2016 on the protection of natural persons with regard to the processing of personal data and on the free movement of such data, and repealing Directive 95/46/EC (General Data Protection Regulation) [2016] OJL 119/1.

88 For a detailed examination, see Paul Voigt and Axel von dem Bussche, *The EU General Data Protection Regulation (GDPR): A Practical Guide* (Springer 2017).

89 GDPR art 4(1).

90 GDPR, art 5.

91 GDPR, art 6. In the context of payment services, the Payment Services Regulations 2017, reg 97 requires the explicit consent of the payment services user or the provider to access, process or retain any personal data.

92 GDPR, art 9.

93 GDPR, arts 13–14.

94 GDPR, art 15.

95 GDPR, arts 16–18.

Information Commissioner)[96] without undue delay and normally not later than 72 hours from becoming aware of the event of the breach.[97] There is also a duty to notify the data subject without undue delay where the breach poses a high risk to the rights and freedoms of natural persons.[98]

As a result of the 2018 changes, UK banks have updated their databases, amended their privacy policies/notices and strengthened their cyber-security. Perhaps, the most important innovation introduced by GDPR from the perspective of banks is the duty to appoint a Data Protection Officer (DPO). The duty applies to banks because their core activities 'consist of processing operations which, by virtue of their nature, their scope and/or their purposes, require regular and systematic monitoring of data subjects on a large scale'.[99] Core activities are the primary business activities, so for banks they include operating accounts and payment systems and granting loans. As banks need to process customer data in the regular course of their business as deposit-takers, paymasters and lenders (including customers' names, addresses, income, transactions, etc.) and the scale of data is large, there is no doubt that they fall within the duty to appoint a DPO. The same applies to insurance firms that collect and process personal data which also includes sensitive data about individuals' health. A DPO must be involved in all matters relevant to personal data and must not receive any instructions regarding his tasks, neither be dismissed or penalised because of performing his tasks.[100] As such, the DPO has considerable independence from senior management, at least in theory, and resembles the function of the Chief Risk Officer. The core tasks of a DPO are as follows: provision of advice to the controller and its employees; monitoring compliance with GDPR; provision of advice on impact assessments and co-operating with and acting as a contact point for the Information Commissioner.[101]

Infringement of the basic principles for processing information or of the rights of individuals and non-compliance with an order of the Information Commissioner carries an administrative fine of up to the higher of 20,000,000 EUR or 4% of the entity's total worldwide annual turnover in the preceding financial year.[102] Moreover, 'any person who has suffered material or non-material damage as a result of an infringement of this Regulation shall have the right to receive compensation from the controller or processor for the damage suffered'.[103] The Data Protection Act 2018 also includes several criminal offences, for instance, an offence of unlawfully obtaining, disclosing or retaining personal data, knowingly or recklessly.[104] Where a body corporate, such as a bank, has committed an offence, any director or manager who consented or connived also commits an offence.[105] It is therefore evident that compliance with the GDPR framework is of crucial significance for banks and that these rules strengthen banks' incentives to comply with their duty of confidentiality, to the extent that breaches of the duty may also constitute infringements of GDPR.

---

96 Data Protection Act 2018, s 115. According to Schedule 12 to the Act, the Commissioner is a corporation sole, to be appointed following a competitive process and to be paid any salary determined by the House of Commons.
97 GDPR, art 33.
98 GDPR, art 34.
99 GDPR, art 37(1) (b).
100 GDPR, art 38.
101 GDPR, art 39.
102 GDPR, art 83.
103 GDPR, art 82(1).
104 Section 170.
105 Data Protection Act 2018, s 198.

5.3.4 The four qualifications to the duty of confidentiality

Contrary to the duty of confidentiality owed by solicitors to their clients, the duty owed by banks to customers is not absolute, which reflects the fact that overriding public interest concerns often trump the duty of confidentiality. In fact, there are four general qualifications to the duty which originate from Bankes LJ's judgement in *Tournier*:

> [I]t is necessary in a case like the present to direct the jury what are the limits, and what are the qualifications of the contractual duty of secrecy implied in the relation of banker and customer. There appears to be no authority on the point. On principle I think that the qualifications can be classified under four heads: (a) Where disclosure is under compulsion by law; (b) where there is a duty to the public to disclose; (c) where the interests of the bank require disclosure; (d) where the disclosure is made by the express or implied consent of the customer.[106]

These qualifications are not true exceptions to the duty but, rather, situations in which the duty does not apply.[107] Despite that and somewhat inaccurately, academic and practitioner commentary often refers to them as exceptions. We will now examine in detail each qualification, and, in particular, we will enquire whether the duty to the public and interests of the bank qualifications are still extant, in the light of legal change that has occurred since the decision in *Tournier*.

5.3.5 Compulsion by law

The compulsion by law qualification refers to an overriding duty to disclose information imposed on the bank by the general law of the land. This qualification reflects the coherence of the law and the non-absolute nature of the bank duty of confidentiality, contrary, for instance, to the duty owed by solicitors. Such duties to disclose information arise in two settings. First, legislation often requires banks to disclose certain information to particular parties, typically public authorities or regulatory bodies in order to protect some public interest. Second, banks may be compelled to disclose information by the court, either as part of proceedings that have already commenced or on the request of a party that seeks disclosure in order to initiate proceedings against a wrongdoer, typically the bank customer.

Starting from statutory duties to disclose, it must be noted that there is a multitude of such provisions in criminal, corporate, tax and insolvency law. The aim of the discussion herein is to provide a brief overview and some general comments. No doubt, the single most important area of legislation that imposes extensive duties of disclosure of information about bank customers is legislation relating to money laundering and terrorism financing. Banks are under extensive duties to report any suspicious activities to the relevant authorities and bank employees are at risk of criminal liability under several offences. The anti-money laundering and terrorism financing framework, and its impact of bank confidentiality, will be discussed in depth in Chapter 11 of the book. Furthermore, the relevant banking regulatory authorities, the PRA and the FCA, are equipped with a broad power

---

106 *Tournier* (above n 68) 473.
107 See e.g. Ross Cranston, Emilios Avgouleas, Kristin van Zwieten, Christopher Hare and Theodor van Sante, *Principles of Banking Law* (3rd edn, OUP 2018) 260–261.

to require banks to provide them with any information or documents upon reasonable notice.[108]

In the corporate context, the Secretary of State has the power to authorise an investigator to require a company, or any other person, to provide such documents or information as the investigator specifies.[109] A bank may thus be requested by the investigator of the affairs of a company to provide relevant information. It is worth noting that, if a person carrying on the business of banking – or a lawyer – provides such information without a request from an investigator, it is not excused from liability for breach of its duty of confidentiality, even if acted in good faith and in the reasonable belief that the disclosure was capable of assisting the Secretary of State.[110] Moreover, if there is reasonable cause to believe that an officer of a company is guilty of an offence in connection with the management of the company's affairs, the court may order a person carrying on the business of banking, who possesses or controls documents relating to the company's affairs, to produce the documents or allow an authorised person to inspect them.[111] In the case of a company in respect of which a winding-up order has been made, the court may summon any person whom the court thinks capable of giving information concerning the promotion, formation, business, dealings, affairs or property of the company and require any such person to submit an account of his dealings with the company or to produce any books, papers or other records in his possession or under his control.[112]

In the area of tax law, an HMRC officer has a general power to request a third party to provide information or produce a document insofar as it is reasonably required by the officer for the purpose of checking the tax position of another known person.[113] This can only take place with the permission of the relevant taxpayer or by approval of the First-tier (Tax) Tribunal.[114] As a result, an officer may require a bank to provide bank statements relating to an account held by a customer in order to check whether there is evidence of any untaxed payments being made into the account or for other similar purposes. There is a right to appeal against a third-party notice to the First-tier Tribunal, unless the document forms part of the taxpayer's statutory records. A business bank account of a self-employed person is invariably considered part of the taxpayer's statutory records, while a personal bank account is normally not, provided that it has not been in fact used extensively for business payments and transactions.[115] In the case of purely personal bank accounts, it is questionable whether their production can be considered as reasonably required, but further examination of this matter falls beyond the scope of the present discussion.

Turning to compulsion to disclose information by virtue of a court order in connection to ongoing proceedings, English courts have wide discretion to summon witnesses and

108 Financial Services and Markets Act 2000, s 165.
109 Companies Act 1985, s 447, as substituted for by the Companies (Audit, Investigations and Community Enterprise) Act 2004, s 21.
110 Companies Act 1985, s 448A, inserted by the Companies (Audit, Investigations and Community Enterprise) Act 2004, s 22.
111 Companies Act 2006, s 1132.
112 Insolvency Act 1986, s 236 (1)–(3), as amended.
113 Finance Act 2008, Sch 36, para 2. For a discussion of this provision and the international context on combatting tax evasion, see Stanton (above n 70) 355–358.
114 Finance Act 2008, Sch 36, para 3.
115 If it has been so used, it qualifies as business record. See *Jonathan Beckwith v HMRC* [2012] UKFTT 181 (TC).

require the disclosure of information by virtue of the Civil Procedure Rules.[116] For banks, a special procedure to produce evidence relating to a customer's account is provided for by the Bankers' Book Evidence Act 1879, the main effect of which is that bank clerks do not have to attend proceedings in person. The Act provides that an entry in a banker's book will qualify as *prima facie* evidence in all proceedings.[117] A banker is not compelled to produce any books other than by an order of a judge made for special cause.[118] Crucially, section 7 of the Act provides that:

> On the application of any party to a legal proceeding a court or judge may order that such party be at liberty to inspect and take copies of any entries in a banker's book for any of the purposes of such proceedings. An order under this section may be made either with or without summoning the bank or any other party, and shall be served on the bank three clear days before the same is to be obeyed, unless the court or judge otherwise directs.

When an order is made under section 7, an undertaking is implied on behalf of the plaintiff not to use the discovered documents other than for the purposes of the legal proceedings in question.[119] The jurisdiction of the court under section 7 includes accounts of third parties other than the defendant in the proceedings. But courts will exercise this power regarding accounts of third parties only if they are satisfied that either the account was in fact belonging to the defendant or that he was 'so much concerned with the account that items in it would be evidence against him at the trial'.[120] Furthermore, section 7 of the Bankers' Book Evidence Act 1879 can also be used before a trial, but in such cases the court must follow the general principles of the law on discovery of evidence in advance of proceedings.[121] This is the matter to which we will now turn our attention.

The starting point is to appreciate that it is occasionally necessary for a potential claimant to obtain some evidence from a third party before it can commence proceedings against another person. In the context of banks, if a bank customer is suspected of fraud, it may assist the party that is seeking to bring proceedings against the customer to obtain evidence on his account in order to establish the movements of the proceeds of the fraud. According to the leading case of *Norwich Pharmacal Co v Customs & Excise Commissioners*,[122] a court may order a third party who has been somewhat involved in the wrongful acts of another party to provide full information and identify the wrongdoer, the wrong being either a civil or criminal. It is not necessary for the third party to have notice of the wrongdoing – it may be entirely innocent. This power was used against a bank in the case of *Bankers Trust Co v Shapira*.[123] The claimant bank (an American bank) in that case sought to trace funds

---

116 The Civil Procedure Rules 1998 (SI 3132/1998), Rule 31.17. The power to order disclosure vis-à-vis persons that are not parties to the proceedings is based on section 34 of the Senior Courts Act 1981.
117 Bankers' Book Evidence Act 1879, s 3.
118 Bankers' Book Evidence Act 1879, s 6.
119 *Bhimji v Chatwani* [1992] 1 WLR 1158. The case concerned plaintiffs who disclosed the content of discovered documents to the police.
120 *South Staffordshire Tramways Co v Ebbsmith* [1895] 2 QB 669, 675.
121 Ibid., 674. In the context of the case, and following the practice of the Court of Chancery at the time, the court ruled that if the person against whom the order is sought makes an affidavit that there is nothing relevant to the dispute in the documents that are sought after, the order should not be made.
122 [1974] AC 133. See also *Ashworth Hospital Authority v MGN Ltd* [2002] UKHL 29.
123 [1980] 1 WLR 1274.

of which it had been fraudulently deprived by two individuals who presented to it forged cheques and paid much of the proceeds into an account that they held with a bank in London. The claimant bank applied for an order instructing the London bank to permit it to inspect the correspondence between the latter and the two fraudsters. Relief was refused at first instance but was granted on appeal in view of the fact that any delay in granting relief might result in the dissipation of the funds. However, the claimant was required to undertake that the information would only be used for the purposes of the action to trace the proceeds of the fraud and for no other purpose.

Regarding the way courts exercise their discretion to grant such relief, it is necessary for the court to balance the potential advantage that the order may bring to the claimant against the detriment that it may bring to the person against whom it is sought. The detriment may include liability for breach of confidentiality duties imposed under foreign laws. So, if there is no real prospect that the order will help the claimant locate or preserve assets, for instance, because substantial time has lapsed since the wrongdoing, an order will not be made.[124]

Before concluding the discussion of the compulsion by law qualification, it is necessary to make a brief reference to situations where a foreign court has ordered a bank, bank branch or bank officer under the jurisdiction of the English court to disclose confidential information. It is usual for such orders to originate from the US. In such cases, English courts may make an injunction restraining the bank from disclosing the information thus giving effect to the duty of confidentiality. A case in point is *X AG v A Bank*[125] where the High Court refused to discontinue an injunction that prevented the London branch of an American bank from complying with an order of the US District Court to produce information on a group of oil companies that was under investigation by the US Department of Justice. In general, English courts are reluctant to give effect to the orders of US courts and pay little attention to the policy of the US, unless the case involves international banking fraud.[126]

5.3.6 Public duty to disclose

The second qualification refers to disclosures in the public interest, which was originally conceived narrowly, as relating to national security, for instance, with regard to enemy aliens.[127] The continuing necessity of the public interest qualification was doubted by the Jack Committee, which recommended its abolition in view of the extensive statutory provisions compelling banks to disclose information.[128] However, there is arguably reason to retain it as a residual category to cover situations that are not captured by statutory duties to disclose information.[129] From a law and economics perspective, one could view the policy considerations as follows.[130] Bank customers are normally recognised by law as owners of their information, and therefore, banks cannot disclose it without their consent,

---

124 *Arab Monetary Fund v Hashim (No. 5)* [1992] 2 All ER 911.
125 [1983] 2 All ER 464. See also the decision of the Hong Kong Court of Appeal in *FDC Co Ltd v Chase Manhattan Bank* [1990] 1 HKLR 227.
126 See e.g. *Pharaon v Bank of Credit and Commerce International SA (liquidation)* [1998] 4 All ER 455. For a comprehensive discussion of this issue, see Ellinger and others (above n 12) 197–205.
127 *Tournier* (above n 68) 473 citing *Weld-Blundell v Stephens* [1920] AC 956.
128 Discussed in Tony Stockwell and Denis Petkovic, 'The Jack Committee Report on Banking Services: Law and Practice' (1989) 4 *Journal of International Banking Law* 134, 134.
129 Cranston and others (above n 106) 264.
130 For a law and economics analysis of the efficient allocation of property rights on private information, see Richard A. Posner, 'The Economics of Privacy' (1981) 71 *American Economic Review* 405. For a recent review of economic theory and evidence on privacy, see Alessandro Acquisti, Curtis Taylor and Liad Wagman, 'The Economics of Privacy' (2016) 54 *Journal of Economic Literature* 442.

unless there is some externality that justifies revoking this property right. So, the public interest qualification enables judges to engage in a cost-benefit analysis and reach efficient outcomes. Indeed, recent case law indicates that the concept of public interest is now viewed broadly and encompasses the effective regulation of banks, depositor protection and the investigation of the affairs of failed banks.[131] It remains unclear whether the public interest qualification also applies to disclosure of information to foreign law enforcement agencies with connection to foreign or international crimes.[132]

5.3.7 Disclosure in the bank's own interest

The third qualification concerns disclosures in the interest of the bank, for instance, where a bank brings proceedings against a customer to recover a debt. However, the qualification applies only to the bank itself as a legal person, not to other companies belonging the same group.[133] On that matter, the Jack Committee had recommended to allow banks to pass confidential information to entities of the same group that engage in banking business.[134] This qualification has been criticised as creating the false impression that banks have a right to disclose information whenever it is in their commercial interests to do so. No doubt, it is a very narrow qualification. Whether it is really an independent qualification has been doubted and it has been suggested that in fact all cases considered under this category can be justified on the basis of the public interest in effective administration of justice.[135] However, courts still consider it an independent qualification to the duty.[136]

An area where the interests of the bank qualification has significant practical relevance is the provision of customer information by banks to credit reference agencies. Such information may be negative (black) indicating that the customer has failed to honour his obligations to the bank, or positive (white) indicating that the customer has been fulfilling his obligations duly. Credit reference agencies are crucial for the efficient function of consumer lending and business lending markets, as they enable banks and other lenders to screen potential borrowers and estimate credit risk in an informed manner. This is also potentially beneficial for financial stability, as it facilitates the management of credit risk and the enhancement of the quality of banks' loan portfolios. In this context, the Jack Committee recommended that legislation allows the passing of black information by banks to credit reference agencies when the customer has defaulted on his debts, and there is a breakdown in the relationship between the bank and customer.[137] Taking into account the broader framework of data protection law and the public interest, it appears that banks can disclose black information without the customer's consent, whereas they have to obtain express consent prior to disclosing any white information to a credit referencing agency.[138]

---

131 See *Price Waterhouse v BCCI Holdings (Luxembourg) SA* [1992] BCLC 583.
132 An in-depth discussion can be found in Chaikin (above n 67) 273–284.
133 *Bank of Tokyo Ltd v Karoon* [1987] AC 45.
134 *Banking Services: Law and Practice Report* (above n 69).
135 Cranston and others (above n 106) 261.
136 See e.g. *El Jawhary v BCCI* [1993] BCLC 396 and *Christofi v Barclays Bank Plc* [1999] 2 All ER (Comm) 417.
137 *Banking Services: Law and Practice Report* (above n 69).
138 Cranston and others (above n 106) 265.

5.3.8 Disclosure with the customer's authority

The final qualification is that there is no breach of duty if confidential information is disclosed with the consent of the customer. The customer's consent may be express or implied. The breadth of circumstances that give rise to implied consent is evidently the crucial question in this area. The matter became of practical relevance in connection to the practice of banks providing references about their customers to other banks. Such references are known as bankers' references and come as a response to a status enquiry from another bank. Indeed, in the past, it was common for a person to make enquiries through their bank on the creditworthiness of another person, for instance, before providing goods on credit or advancing a loan. The bank of the prospective creditor would then seek a reference from the bank of the prospective debtor. This practice was justified on the grounds of implied consent and commercial usage. The Jack Committee recommended abolishing implied consent in this area, and requiring consent to be in writing.[139]

The leading authority on the matter is *Turner v Royal Bank of Scotland*.[140] The plaintiff held a business account with the RBS. Between 1986 and 1989, RBS responded to eight status enquiries from the National Westminster Bank Plc by providing unfavourable banker's references regarding the plaintiff's creditworthiness. The plaintiff, who later was declared bankrupt, sued RBS for damages for breach of its contractual duty of confidentiality. It is worth noting that by the time proceedings began, in fact since 1994, RBS and other major banks had abandoned the practice of giving such references without prior customer consent, as required by the voluntary Banking Code.[141] However, the legal issue in question was whether the prior practice of the banks was in breach of their common law duty of confidentiality. RBS based its argument on implied consent is as follows:

> [I]t was the general practice of banks in the ordinary course of business to respond to status inquiries made by other banks by giving information about the creditworthiness of customers. The bank contends that every customer opening an account with the bank must be taken to have agreed to this practice and to have authorised the bank to give references to third party inquirers based on information that would normally be confidential.[142]

The Court of Appeal rejected RBS's appeal and upheld the Country Court's order against RBS. The court ruled that there was no binding usage arising from the relevant bank practice because the element of notoriety was missing. This was due to the fact that such usage was not widely known among bank customers.

> How can the bankers' practice on which the bank relies be regarded as notorious? It is not to the point that all banks may have known of it. The question is whether it was also notorious among the customers, the ordinary members of the public who open accounts with banks. There is no evidence whatever that in that sense this banking practice was notorious. [...] Ordinary banking customers do not read Paget or any other banking textbooks. [...] There was no evidence of any documents put before

139 *Banking Services: Law and Practice Report* (above n 69).
140 [1999] 2 All ER (Comm) 664.
141 Ibid., 667.
142 Ibid., 666 per Sir Richard Scott V-C.

customers, when opening an account with banks, that drew attention to it. As I have said, the evidence in this case disclosed a policy on the part of the bank that customers should, if possible, be kept unaware of the practice. The law holds a person contractually bound by an established usage even if he does not know of it. But it cannot become an established usage unless it is notorious. How can a banking practice be notorious if the existence of the practice is kept from customers? The proposition that banks can agree among themselves upon a banking practice and put the practice into effect without the knowledge of their customers and then claim that, because the practice is common to all banks, it is binding upon their customers is, in my judgment, unacceptable.[143]

It is therefore clear that, as a matter of law, banks must ask for the express consent of their customers before providing a banker's reference.

5.4 Conclusion

This chapter analysed the legal nature of the relationship between banks and customers, and the main common law duties owed by banks to customers and by customers to banks. Traditional common law principles have been developed in recent years, in the light of changing public expectations, to ensure more robust protection for bank customers. At the same time, the statutory encroachments to the duty of confidentiality have grown significantly, thus undermining the duty and highlighting the modern use of banks by public policy as instruments in the fight against organised crime, terrorism and tax evasion.

Glossary of terms

- Fiduciary relationship: A relationship of trust and confidence between two parties that gives rise to fiduciary duties owed by the recipient of the trust and confidence to the other party.
- Lending code: Soft law code that sets out best practice expectations and guidance on banks' conduct in relation to lending money to retail customers and especially the processes to be followed and information that must be disclosed to prospective borrowers.
- Undue influence: Legal principle according to which a contract may be deemed unenforceable against a party if that party entered the contract as a result of undue influence (pressure) by another party.
- Duty of confidentiality: Duty to keep certain information about another person secret and refrain from disclosing it to anybody unless the law otherwise requires or the person in question consents to the disclosure.
- Personal data: Information about a specific natural person such as their name, address, age, occupation, transactions and health.
- General Data Protection Regulation (GDPR): Piece of EU legislation that sets out the general framework on data protection and free movement of data within the EU.
- Banker's reference: Reference written by one bank and addressed to another bank assessing the creditworthiness of a certain customer of the bank that is providing the reference.

---

143 Ibid., 670 per Sir Richard Scott V-C. Sir Richard cited with approval the decision of Bingham J in *Barclay's Bank Plc v Bank of England* [1985] 1 All ER 385.

Practice questions

There is no need to codify the duties owed by banks to their customers and vice versa, including the duty of confidentiality, as the present state of the case law is satisfactory and clear. In particular, the principle that banks do not automatically owe fiduciary duties to their customers is sound from a policy perspective. Critically discuss.

You may also find it useful to review the chapter through the following questions:

* When is a bank–customer relationship established in English law?
* Is the standard bank–customer relationship of fiduciary character?
* What is the scope and extent of banks' duty of care to their customers?
* Summarise the duties owed by customers to banks.
* Explain the nature and significance of the duty of confidentiality owed by banks.
* What are the qualifications to the duty? Are they justified?

6 Business conduct regulation and financial consumer protection

6.1 Introduction

Contrary to prudential regulation, which aims to protect financial stability, the objective of conduct of business regulation is to safeguard market integrity and achieve an appropriate level of consumer protection in the financial markets. The four original statutory goals of the former Financial Services Authority (FSA) were all relating to conduct of business matters: (1) market confidence, (2) public awareness, (3) the protection of consumers and (4) the reduction of financial crime.[1] Currently, conduct of business is the responsibility of the Financial Conduct Authority (FCA) as explained in Chapter 2. The statutory objectives of the FCA include its strategic objective of ensuring that the relevant markets function well[2] and three operational objectives: (a) securing an appropriate degree of protection for consumers,[3] (b) protecting and enhancing the integrity of the UK financial system[4] and (c) promoting effective competition in the interests of consumers.[5]

This chapter focuses on the consumer protection objective of the FCA, the relevant legal framework and the role of the Financial Ombudsman Service (FOS), the key alternative dispute resolution (ADR) mechanism for financial services consumers and the Money Advice Service. However, a brief discussion of the other two operational objectives is necessary. The market integrity objective encompasses the stability and resilience of the UK financial system (thus overlapping with the objectives of prudential regulation), the prevention of the use of the financial system for the purposes of financial crime (see Chapter 10 on money laundering and terrorist financing), the avoidance of insider dealing and market abuse, the orderly operation of markets and the transparency of the price formation process. The last three aspects relate closely to the role of the FCA as the UK Listing Authority. The competition objective requires the FCA to have regard to the need of consumers to have sufficient information, access to financial services, ease of changing provider, ease of entrance to the market and encouragement of innovation. The FCA has thus powers of investigation and

---

1 Financial Services and Markets Act 2000, ss 3–6, now abolished. To be abbreviated as FSMA 2000.
2 FSMA 2000, s 1B (2).
3 FSMA 2000, s 1C.
4 FSMA 2000, s 1D.
5 FSMA 2000, s 1E.

enforcement under the Competition Act 1998, concurrently with the Competition and Markets Authority (CMA).[6]

6.2 The consumer protection objective of the FCA

As discussed in the previous section, one of the operational objectives of the FCA is to secure an appropriate degree of protection for consumers in the financial services. The term consumer is defined broadly in the Financial Services and Markets Act (FSMA) as any person who uses, have used or may use regulated financial services; has invested or may invest in financial instruments; or has rights or interests in relation to financial services or instruments.[7] It is not therefore necessary for a person to not be acting in a business or professional capacity. FSMA lists a series of recommendations that the FCA must have regard to in determining the degree of consumer protection that is appropriate: (1) the level of risk involved in different types of investment or transaction; (2) the experience and expertise of consumers; (3) the need for timely provision of accurate and fit-for-purpose information; (4) the principle of consumer responsibility; (5) the principle that providers must provide consumers with a level of care reflecting the risk of each transaction and the capabilities of the consumer; (6) consumer expectations; (7) information provided to the FCA by the consumer financial education body (known as the Money Advice Service which, since January 2019, is part of the Money & Pensions Service); and (8) information provided to the FCA by the operator of the ombudsman scheme (the FOS).[8]

The FCA has stated that firms must 'have their customers at the heart of how they do business, give them appropriate products and services, and put their protection above the firms' own profits or income'.[9] In terms of the substantive standards of conduct expected of banks (and other FCA-regulated firms), the FCA Handbook contains 11 high-level principles, many of which are relevant to the protection of consumers.[10] Table 6.1 reproduces the full text of the 11 principles.

Principles 6–10 set out the key standards that must be observed by banks vis-à-vis their customers. Treating customers fairly, providing clear and fair information, fair management of conflicts of interest between the firm and customers and among customers, ensuring the suitability of advice and protecting clients' assets form the core regulatory expectations. In parallel, Principles 1 and 2, which are very general, are also broadly relevant to consumer protection as they can capture dishonest and negligent conduct that harms consumers' interests. It must be noted that contravention of the principles does

---

6 There is complementarity between competition and consumer protection law as effective competition benefits consumers. It has been argued that competition law and consumer protection law share a common overarching purpose of facilitating effective consumer choice, which presupposes the existence of a range of option and the ability to choose freely among them. See Neil W. Averitt and Robert H. Lande, 'Consumer Sovereignty: A Unified Theory of Antitrust and Consumer Protection Law' (1997) 65 *Antitrust Law Journal* 713.

7 FSMA 2000, s 1G (1).

8 FSMA 2000, s 1C (2).

9 See FCA, 'Protecting Consumers' (11 December 2017) <https://www.fca.org.uk/about/protecting-consumers> (accessed 11 April 2020).

10 The rule-making power of the FCA derives from FSMA, s 64A, which empowers the FCA to make rules if it appears to the Authority that doing so is 'necessary or expedient for the purpose of advancing one or more of its operational objectives'.

Table 6.1 The FCA principles for businesses[11]

1	Integrity	A firm must conduct its business with integrity.
2	Skill, care and diligence	A firm must conduct its business with due skill, care and diligence.
3	Management and control	A firm must take reasonable care to organise and control its affairs responsibly and effectively, with adequate risk management systems.
4	Financial prudence	A firm must maintain adequate financial resources.
5	Market conduct	A firm must observe proper standards of market conduct.
6	Customers' interests	A firm must pay due regard to the interests of its customers and treat them fairly.
7	Communications with clients	A firm must pay due regard to the information needs of its clients, and communicate information to them in a way which is clear, fair and not misleading.
8	Conflicts of interest	A firm must manage conflicts of interest fairly, both between itself and its customers and between a customer and another client.
9	Customers: relationships of trust	A firm must take reasonable care to ensure the suitability of its advice and discretionary decisions for any customer who is entitled to rely upon its judgement.
10	Clients' assets	A firm must arrange adequate protection for clients' assets when it is responsible for them.
11	Relations with regulators	A firm must deal with its regulators in an open and co-operative way, and must disclose to the FCA appropriately anything relating to the firm of which that regulator would reasonably expect notice.

not give rise to a private right of action for damages,[12] but can lead to the imposition of regulatory sanctions.

In general, the FCA has statutory power to impose the following types of sanctions to a regulated person who has contravened its rules[13]: financial penalty of such amount as it thinks appropriate, suspension or imposition of conditions on the performance of regulated activities for up to two years, limitation of the firm's authorisation and a public statement of misconduct.[14] Regarding measures that the FCA can take to offer relief to consumers, FSMA provides the FCA with two relevant tools: restitution orders and consumer redress schemes. The FCA can make a restitution order against an authorised person that has con-travened a relevant requirement provided that it made a profit as a result of the contraven-tion or one or more persons suffered loss as a result thereof.[15] The order will require the authorised person to make a payment to the appropriate persons in tandem with the profit made or loss caused. If it appears that 'there may have been a widespread or regular failure by relevant firms to comply with' relevant rules as a result of which consumers have suffered actionable loss or damage, the FCA may make rules requiring each relevant firm to estab-lish and operate a consumer redress scheme.[16] Such a scheme entails the firm investigating whether a breach has occurred, determining whether and to what extent consumers have suffered losses and make appropriate redress to the consumers.

11 FCA Handbook, PRIN 2.1 The Principles.
12 FCA Handbook, PRIN 3.4.4.
13 The conditions that must be present for the FCA to be able to impose a sanction are set out in FSMA 2000, s 66A. Failure to comply with a rule made by the FCA by an approved person is one such condition.
14 FSMA 2000, s 66 (3).
15 FSMA 2000, s 384. Apart from this, the FCA can also petition the court to make a restitution order under s 382.
16 FSMA 2000, s 404.

An interesting case, illustrating the FCA's approach to sanctions in relation to consumer protection breaches, is the imposition of a fine of £32,817,800 on Santander UK Plc in December 2018.[17] Santander UK was found to have breached Principles 3, 6 and 11 between 2013 and 2016 due to its failure to deal effectively with the assets of deceased customers. In particular, Santander's probate and bereavement processes were seriously flawed, thus limiting its ability to identify the funds of deceased customers, follow up communications with their representatives and monitor open cases. As a result, £183m were not transferred timely to beneficiaries, affecting 40,428 customers. It is worth noting that the *prima facie* amount of the fine was £46,882,500 but Santander UK benefited from a 30% discount, as it agreed to settle at an early stage of the investigation. In determining the amount of the penalty, the FCA took into account the fact that Santander displayed good co-operation with it throughout the investigation.

From a procedural perspective, FSMA requires the FCA to 'maintain effective arrangements for consulting practitioners and consumers' regarding the consistency of its policies and practices with its statutory duties.[18] In particular, the FCA is required to establish a Consumer Panel to represent the interests of consumers.[19] It can appoint to the panel consumers or organisations representing the interests of consumers as it deems appropriate, but must make sure that panel membership provides a fair degree of representation of the users of financial services. The FCA must appoint one panel member as its chair; the appointment and removal of the chair require the approval of the Treasury. Indeed, the Financial Services Consumer Panel is an independent statutory body, established in 1998 and currently consisting of 14 members. Members are often nominated by relevant trade associations. According to the Panel, current members have experience in the areas of consumer advice, campaigning, communications, market research, journalism, law, financial services, financial inclusion, European issues, financial regulation and compliance and later life issues.[20]

Looking forward, a consultation paper on the FCA approach to consumer protection was published in November 2017, and a final policy document was published in July 2018.[21] The document identifies two areas of significant harm for consumers, namely, the exploitation of consumers' behavioural biases and vulnerabilities by firms and deception as a result of scams. It also sets out the Authority's plan to issue guidance on the identification and fair treatment of vulnerable consumers. At the same time, the FCA issued a discussion paper on introducing an explicit duty of care to consumers, delineating different alternative models and launched a public consultation. A feedback statement was issued in April 2019, summarising the responses to the consultation, and further steps will be taken in the immediate future.[22] The reform options presented included a new statutory duty of care, a new regulatory duty of care within the FCA's Principles for Businesses, the creation of a private right of action for breach of the Principles and a fiduciary duty owed by firms to customers.

17 See FCA, 'Final Notice: Santander UK Plc' (19 December 2018) <https://www.fca.org.uk/publication/final-notices/santander-uk-plc-2018.pdf> (accessed 11 July 2020).

18 FSMA 2000, s 1M.

19 FSMA 2000, s 1Q.

20 See Financial Services Consumer Panel, 'Consumer Panel Members' (Financial Services Consumer Panel 2019) <https://www.fs-cp.org.uk/who-is-on-the-panel> (accessed 10 June 2020).

21 FCA, 'FCA Mission: Approach to Consumers' (2018) <https://www.fca.org.uk/publication/corporate/approach-to-consumers.pdf> (accessed 11 April 2020).

22 See FCA, 'A Duty of Care and Potential Alternative Approaches: Summary of Responses and Next Steps: Feedback Statement' (2019) FS19/2 <https://www.fca.org.uk/publication/feedback/fs19-02.pdf> (accessed 21 May 2020).

According to the respondents to the consultation, the main benefits of a new duty of care include its potential to lead to a change of culture in financial firms, increased clarity and emphasis on prevention of harm. The main argument against any reform is that the current system already provides adequate consumer protection, especially in the light of the strong language of Principle 6 and the introduction of the Senior Managers & Certification Regime. Regarding the introduction of a statutory or regulatory duty that would give rise to private actions, counterarguments include legal uncertainty, cost to firms, restriction of competition, innovation and access to the financial services, lack of deterrent effect, and that litigation is not in consumers' interests.

To evaluate these proposals and the overall idea of consumer protection in the financial services it is necessary to reflect on the purposes of consumer protection law in general and the specificities of the financial services context. The question of consumer protection illustrates the tension between the normative frameworks of market-individualism and consumer-welfarism that have occupied contract law theory in recent decades.[23] A market-individualism perspective emphasises classical freedom of contract and is likely to restrict consumer protection to the setting of favourable default rules, the construction of contractual terms and duties to disclose information. This view is largely consistent with the economic analysis of law, which accepts legal intervention to freedom of contract only in the face of a market failure, such as asymmetry of information.[24] The influence of these views is evident in FSMA's principle that consumers must take responsibility for their actions, and in the general emphasis on provision of information in the law and regulation. Contrary to that, a consumer-welfarism perspective advocates for a legal regime that maximises consumer wealth by addressing the imbalance of negotiating power between consumers and businesses.[25] This view allows for much broader legal intervention including scrutiny of contractual terms, imposition of mandatory terms and legally enforceable duties to treat customers fairly. Consumer-welfarism is supported by research in behavioural economics that highlights individuals' bounded rationality and evidences a series of decision-making biases.[26] Its influence is evident in FSMA's requirement for the FCA to have regard to the experience and expertise of consumers and in many EU-driven rules of consumer protection law.[27]

Historically and conceptually, it is possible to distinguish between a pre-intervention phase, in line with market-individualistic principles; an intervention phase, in line with consumer-welfarist principles; and the post-intervention (reflexive) phase, where rules structure the market in a way that its operation is conducive to the achievement of public policy

---

23 See e.g. Hugh Collins, *Regulating Contracts* (OUP 1999) Chapters 3–8; David Campbell, 'Reflexivity and Welfarism in the Modern Law of Contract' (2000) 20 *Oxford Journal of Legal Studies* 477; and Patrick S. Atiyah, *The Rise and Fall of Freedom of Contract* (OUP 1985) Chapters 18–22.

24 See e.g. Richard A. Posner, *Economic Analysis of Law* (8th edn, Wolters Kluwer 2011) Chapter 1.

25 For a discussion of consumer-welfarist policies in EU law, see Thomas Wilhelmsson, 'Varieties of Welfarism in European Contract Law' (2004) 10 *European Law Journal* 712.

26 There is a very rich literature on behavioural economics. See e.g. Daniel Kahneman and Amos Tversky, 'Prospect Theory: An Analysis of Decision Under Risk' (1979) 47 *Econometrica* 263; Christine Jolls, Cass R. Sunstein and Richard H. Thaler, 'A Behavioral Approach to Law and Economics' (1998) 50 *Stanford Law Review* 147; and Daniel Kahneman, 'New Challenges to the Rationality Assumption' (1997) 3 *Legal Theory* 105.

27 For instance, the MiFID rules on investor protection discussed in section 6.4 of this chapter. However, it should also be kept in mind that the EU consumer protection law developed as an instrument of achieving deep economic integration, as part of the Single Market, given that harmonising national laws removes regulatory obstacles to free trade.

goals.[28] The post-intervention phase broadly describes current law and policy, although there are evidently many elements from the previous phases still surviving. The reflexive approach is evident in the FCA's policy document that emphasises its commitment to ensure that markets have an effective choice architecture, that as many consumers as possible are active and able and that markets are working well for consumers.[29]

It is worth noting that a key argument against unfettered freedom of contract and in favour of interventionism is the lack of effective competition in many markets. Uncompetitive markets do not provide consumers with sufficient choice, and thus, consumers are placed in a dire negotiating position where they have to accept the terms offered by firms. It follows that, to a great extent, one's view on the appropriate level of consumer protection depends on one's attitude towards the chances of success of competition law in its mission to ensure that markets are competitive. Banking is a sector with high market concentration and oligopolistic features, especially in the UK,[30] which potentially justifies a higher level of consumer protection than in other parts of the economy. At the same time, the new competition objective of the FCA, in parallel to its consumer protection objective, highlights the complementarity between the two as components of a well-functioning market where consumers can make free and informed choices.

Further, financial contracts, especially those referring to credit and investment, are complex and involve risks and uncertainties that are hard for most non-expert individuals to process. A good example is the choice between different investment products and different types of mortgages. This argument supports the need for robust frameworks on the provision of information and the presentation of information in a clear, accessible and comparable manner.

6.3 Overview of consumer protection legislation applicable to banks

The purpose of this section is to provide an overview of applicable consumer protection legislation that is relevant to banks and their customers. To this effect, we will explain the development of the law since the 1970s. The Consumer Credit Act 1974 implemented the recommendations of the Crowther Committee[31] and applies to personal credit agreements made by consumers. Originally, a monetary limit of £5,000 was imposed[32] which was extended to £15,000 in 1985,[33] and to £25,000 in 1998.[34] The Consumer Credit Act 2006, which made several amendments to the 1974 Act, abolished the monetary limit for agreements not made for business purposes.[35] The Act covers both credit and hire

---

28　On this, see Norbert Reich, 'Diverse Approaches to Consumer Protection Philosophy' (1992) 14 *Journal of Consumer Policy* 257. For the concept of reflexive law in general, see Gunther Teubner, 'Reflexive Law' (1983) 19 *Law and Society Review* 239.

29　See 'FCA Mission: Approach to Consumers' (above n 21).

30　For an empirical analysis of the level of competition in the UK banking sector from 1980 to 2004, see Kent Matthews, Victor Murinde and Tianshu Zhao, 'Competitive Conditions among the Major British Banks' (2007) 31 *Journal of Banking & Finance* 2025.

31　Department of Trade and Industry, *Consumer Credit: Report of the Committee (Crowther Report)* (Cmd 4596, 1971).

32　Consumer Credit Act 1974 s 8.

33　The Consumer Credit (Increase of Monetary Limits) Order 1983 (SI. 1983/1878), Sch Part II.

34　The Consumer Credit (Increase of Monetary Limits) (Amendment) Order 1998 (SI 1998/996), art 2.

35　Consumer Credit Act 2006 s 2, amending Consumer Credit Act 1974 s 8, and inserting into the Act s 16B.

agreements, but the latter are not commonly entered into by banks. A detailed examination of the requirements of the Act regarding credit agreements and credit cards will take place in Chapter 9.

In relation to statutory controls of contract terms, the Unfair Contract Terms Act 1977 prohibited the restriction or exclusion of liability for death or personal injury resulting from negligence by virtue of a contract term or notice.[36] It also subjected any restriction or exclusion of liability for other loss or damage resulting from negligence to a requirement of reasonableness.[37] Regarding liability for breach of contract, the Act subjected to a requirement of reasonableness any term included in a party's written standard terms of business that purports to (1) exclude or restrict the liability of that party for breach of contract; (2) render performance substantially different from that reasonably expected by the other party; or (3) entitle that party to render no performance at all for the whole or any part of his contractual obligation.[38] Since 2015, the Act does not apply to consumer contracts as these are dealt with under the Consumer Rights Act 2015.

The next phase in the development of UK consumer protection law was heavily influenced by EU law. The 1993 Unfair Consumer Contract Terms Directive[39] is a minimum harmonisation directive that requires Member States to prohibit certain terms in consumer contracts and to subject to fairness review any non-individually negotiated term that does not pertain to the essential terms of a contract. The UK originally implemented the directive via the Unfair Terms in Consumer Contracts Regulations 1994[40] which were repealed and replaced by the Unfair Terms in Consumer Contracts Regulations 1999.[41] The main body responsible to enforce the Regulations was originally the Office for Fair Trading (OFT). The OFT was established in 1973 and was abolished in 2014. Its functions were transferred to a range of bodies, primarily the CMA[42] and, regarding the regulation of consumer credit, the FCA. The Consumer Rights Act 2015 (to be discussed later) was passed to consolidate and enhance UK consumer protection law. It supersedes the Regulations and, for the purposes of services and hence financial services, applies to any consumer contract entered into on or after 1 October 2015, while the Regulations continue to apply to any contract entered into before that date.[43] In terms of cancellation rights, the Financial Services (Distance Marketing) Regulations 2004[44] provide consumers with the right to cancel any distance financial services contract (e.g. bank account, credit card or portfolio management) within 14 calendar days starting from the day after the contract is made.[45] A distance contract is defined as 'any contract concerning one or more financial

---

36 Unfair Contract Terms Act 1977 s 2 (1).
37 Unfair Contract Terms Act 1977 s 2 (2).
38 Unfair Contract Terms Act 1977 s 3.
39 Council Directive 93/13/EEC of 5 April 1993 on unfair terms in consumer contracts [1993] OJ L95/29.
40 SI 1994/3159.
41 SI 1999/2083.
42 Enterprise and Regulatory Reform Act 2013 s 26 and Schs 5 and 6.
43 The Consumer Rights Act 2015 (Commencement No. 3, Transitional Provisions, Savings and Consequential Amendments) Order 2015 (SI 2015/1630), regs 3 and 6.
44 SI 2004/2095. The Regulations implemented Directive 2002/65/EC of the European Parliament and of the Council of 23 September 2002 concerning the distance marketing of consumer financial services [2002] OJ L271/16. It should be noted that the Consumer Contracts (Information, Cancellation and Additional Charges) Regulations 2013 (SI 2013/3134) do not apply to contracts for services of a banking, credit, insurance, personal pension, investment or payment nature (reg 6 (b)).
45 Distance Marketing Regulations 2004, regs 9–10.

services concluded between a supplier and a consumer under an organised distance sales or service-provision scheme run by the supplier or by an intermediary, who, for the purpose of that contract, makes exclusive use of one or more means of distance communication up to and including the time at which the contract is concluded'.[46]

Furthermore, the Enterprise Act 2002, Part 8[47] provides the CMA with certain enforcement powers as a general enforcer of consumer protection law,[48] while the FCA is listed as a CPC[49] enforcer.[50] The Act draws a distinction between domestic infringements (harming the collective interests of consumers in the UK)[51] and community infringements (contravening relevant EU law and EEA state laws, regulations or administrative provisions giving effect to EU law).[52] When a person has engaged in conduct that constitutes an infringement or is likely to do so, the CMA (and the FCA for community infringements only) can apply to the court for an enforcement order.[53] An enforcement order must specify the relevant conduct and direct the person against whom it is made not to continue or repeat that conduct and not to engage in such conduct as part of his business.[54] If an application is made by the FCA (or any other enforcer), the CMA must be notified[55] and can give directions to the FCA.[56] In terms of enforcement, the Consumer Protection from Unfair Trading Regulations 2008[57] prohibits unfair commercial practices which are defined as practices that contravene the requirements of professional diligence and are likely to materially distort the economic behaviour of the average consumer.[58] Knowingly or recklessly engaging in unfair commercial practices is an offence[59] punishable, on indictment, by a fine or imprisonment for a term not exceeding two years or both.[60] The Regulations also prohibit the promotion of unfair commercial practices, misleading actions and omissions and aggressive

---

46 Distance Marketing Regulations 2004, reg 2.
47 As amended by The Enterprise and Regulatory Reform Act 2013 (Competition) (Consequential, Transitional and Saving Provisions) Order 2014, Sch 1 which reflects the abolition of the OFT and transfer of its powers to the CMA.
48 Enterprise Act 2002 s 213 (1).
49 CPC stands for Consumer Protection Cooperation Framework, under the Consumer Protection Cooperation Regulation I. See Regulation (EC) No. 2006/2004 of the European Parliament and of the Council of 27 October 2004 on cooperation between national authorities responsible for the enforcement of consumer protection laws [2004] OJ L364/1. This Regulation was repealed and replaced by the Consumer Protection Cooperation Regulation II on 17 January 2020. See Regulation (EU) 2017/2394 of the European Parliament and of the Council of 12 December 2017 on cooperation between national authorities responsible for the enforcement of consumer protection laws [2017] OJ L345/1.
50 Enterprise Act 2002 s 213 5A (c), inserted by The Enterprise Act 2002 (Amendment) Regulations 2006 (SI 2006/3363), reg 11 and amended by the Financial Services Act 2012, Sch 18, para 95.
51 Enterprise Act 2002 s 211.
52 Enterprise Act 2002 s 212. But see The Consumer Protection (Enforcement) (Amendment etc.) (EU Exit) Regulations 2019 (SI 2019/203) in relation to Brexit.
53 Enterprise Act 2002 ss 215–217.
54 Enterprise Act 2002 s 217 (5) and (6).
55 Enterprise Act 2002 s 215 (9).
56 Enterprise Act 2002 s 216.
57 SI 2008/1277. To be abbreviated henceforth as 'CPUTR 2008'. The Regulations implemented the Unfair Commercial Practices Directive. See Directive 2005/29/EC of the European Parliament and of the Council of 11 May 2005 concerning unfair business-to-consumer commercial practices in the internal market [2005] OJ L149/22.
58 CPUTR 2008, reg 3.
59 CPUTR 2008, reg 8.
60 CPUTR 2008, reg 13.

commercial practices.[61] The latter are defined as practices that taken in their factual context are likely significantly to impair the average consumer's freedom of choice through the use of harassment, coercion or undue influence, and are likely to cause the consumer to take a transactional decision he would not have taken otherwise.[62]

It is now pertinent to discuss in some detail the Consumer Rights Act 2015. In drafting the relevant Bill, the Government took into account research findings that the UK consumer protection regime had two major weaknesses: uneven enforcement and excessively complex law.[63] Chapter 4 of the Act on services applies *inter alia* to financial services, as does Part 2 of the Act on unfair terms therefore imposing obligations to banks and empowering consumers to question the fairness of standard terms in contracts made with banks. Indeed, the Act applies to contracts for the supply of services from traders to consumers.[64] 'Trader' means a person acting for purposes relating to that person's trade, business, craft or profession.[65] 'Consumer' means an individual acting for purposes that are wholly or mainly outside that individual's trade, business, craft or profession.[66] There is an implied term that the trader has to perform the service with reasonable care and skill, and it is not permitted to exclude the trader's liability.[67] In parallel, it is not permitted for traders to exclude or restrict their liability for death or personal injury arising from negligence (i.e. breach of contractual or common law duty of care).[68] Consumers of services are also given special remedies: the right to request repeat performance and the right to require the trader to reduce the price.[69]

The most pivotal part of the Act is the requirement for terms in consumer contracts and notices pertaining to liability to be fair. Unfair terms and notices are not binding on the consumer.[70] A term or notice is unfair 'if, contrary to the requirement of good faith,[71] it causes a significant imbalance in the parties' rights and obligations under the contract to the detriment of the consumer'.[72] Fairness is to be determined taking into account the subject matter of the contract and by reference to all relevant circumstances.[73] There is a non-exhaustive list of terms of consumer contracts that may be regarded as unfair, including terms that limit the trader's liability or obligations to the consumer.[74] However,

---

61 CPUTR 2008, regs 4–7 and 9–12.
62 CPUTR 2008, reg 7.
63 Michael Harker et al., 'Benchmarking the Performance of the UK Framework Supporting Consumer Empowerment through Comparison against Relevant International Comparator Countries' (2008) <http://webarchive.nationalarchives.gov.uk/+/http://www.berr.gov.uk/publications/index.html> (accessed 21 April 2020).
64 Consumer Rights Act 2015 s 48 (1).
65 Consumer Rights Act 2015 s 2 (2).
66 Consumer Rights Act 2015 s 2 (3).
67 Consumer Rights Act 2015 ss 49 and 57 (1).
68 Consumer Rights Act 2015 ss 65–66.
69 Consumer Rights Act 2015 ss 55 and 56, respectively.
70 Consumer Rights Act 2015 s 62 (1) and (2).
71 The concept of good faith in the Act derives from the Directive and refers to objective good faith, which is a concept of civil legal systems, rather than to the more familiar concept of (subjective) good faith in English law. Objective good faith requires the observance of reasonable commercial standards of fair dealing. For a detailed discussion, see Martijn W. Hesselink, 'The Concept of Good Faith' in Arthur S. Hartkamp et al. (eds), *Towards A European Civil Code* (4th edn, Kluwer Law International 2010) 619–624.
72 Consumer Rights Act 2015 s 62 (4) and (6).
73 Consumer Rights Act 2015 s 62 (5).
74 Consumer Rights Act 2015 s 63 and Sch 2.

a transparent and prominent term cannot be assessed for fairness to the extent that it specifies the main subject matter of the contract or that the assessment would cover the appropriateness of the price payable under the contract.[75] This provision has generated landmark litigation involving major UK banks, which will be discussed in detail in Chapter 9.

6.4 Retail investor protection in the context of provision of investment advice

At the EU level, there is a special investor protection framework applicable to investment firms providing investment services and advice to retail clients under MiFID II[76] articles 24–30. In the UK, the competent authority for these purposes is the FCA, which authorises and supervises investment firms, and has implemented the Directive as part of its Handbook.[77] MiFID II, compared to its predecessor MiFID I (passed in 2004), strengthened investor protection through the introduction of new requirements on product governance and independent investment advice and the enhancement of requirements on the responsibility of management bodies, inducements, the provision of information and reporting to clients, cross-selling, investment firm staff remuneration and best execution. A brief overview will be provided for the purposes of this chapter.[78] 'Investment advice' is defined by MiFID II as 'the provision of personal recommendations to a client, either upon its request or at the initiative of the investment firm, in respect of one or more transactions relating to financial instruments'.[79]

Investment firms must act honestly, fairly and professionally in accordance with the best interests of their clients.[80] Marketing communications must be fair, clear, not misleading and clearly identifiable as such.[81] Firms are obliged to provide detailed information to clients including information on the relevant financial instruments, investment strategies and associated risks, and on costs and charges; firms must also specify whether their investment advice is independent or not.[82] If a firm purports to offer independent advice, it must assess a sufficient range of financial instruments available on the market and not only those offered by the firm itself and connected persons to it and must not accept fees, commissions or any other benefits by any third party.[83] Firms must also ensure that the design of variable remuneration for their staff does not undermine their duty to act in the best interests of clients e.g. by setting sales targets.[84] Relevant staff must have all necessary knowledge and

---

75 Consumer Rights Act 2015 s 64.
76 Directive 2014/65/EU of the European Parliament and of the Council of 15 May 2014 on markets in financial instruments (recast) [2014] OJ L173/349.
77 See FCA Handbook, Conduct of Business Sourcebook and Product Intervention and Product Governance Sourcebook.
78 For a comprehensive discussion of the legal and economic aspects of MiFID II, see Danny Busch and Guido Ferrarini (eds), *Regulation of the EU Financial Markets* (OUP 2017). See also Mario Comana, Daniele Previtali and Luca Bellardini, *The MiFID II Framework: How the New Standards Are Reshaping the Investment Industry* (Springer 2019).
79 MiFID II, art 4 (1) (4).
80 MiFID II, art 24 (1).
81 MiFID II, art 24 (3).
82 MiFID II, art 24 (4).
83 MiFID II, art 24 (7).
84 MiFID II, art 24 (10).

competence.[85] In order to fulfil their duty to act in the clients' best interests, firms must obtain information on every client's knowledge, investment experience, objectives, risk tolerance and capacity to bear losses, and must warn their clients if sufficient information is not provided or if the firm judges that a certain product or service is not appropriate for them.[86] Furthermore, firms are obliged to 'take all sufficient steps to obtain, when executing orders, the best possible result for their clients taking into account price, costs, speed, likelihood of execution and settlement, size, nature' and any other relevant consideration, unless the customer has provided a specific instruction on the way the order is to be executed.[87]

6.5 The Financial Ombudsman Service

In the UK, individual bank customers and small businesses that have a complaint against a financial firm can follow an alternative route to litigation. They can bring their complaint to the FOS in which case the dispute is decided based on broad principles of fairness rather than by reference to the relevant legal and regulatory rules.[88] If the FOS finds in favour of the customer, it can order a pecuniary award that is binding on the financial firm. Dispute resolution through the FOS brings to eligible financial services customers the benefits of speed, simplicity and low cost, as there is no need for them to seek legal advice and representation and use of the service is free.[89]

The FOS was established in 2000 and given statutory powers by FSMA 2000, Part XVI and Schedule 17, as an independent statutory dispute resolution scheme. The scheme operator, FOS, is a company limited by guarantee whose board of directors is appointed by the FCA; in the case of the board's chairman the approval of the Treasury is also needed.[90] At the time of writing, the board of the FOS consisted of six directors. The board is not involved in dispute resolution or executive functions. Its principal role is (1) to appoint the members of the ombudsmen panel, including the Chief Ombudsman (a responsibility delegated to the chairman); (2) adopt the FOS's annual budget; (3) oversee the way the service is operated by executive management; (4) approve the FOS's annual report and accounts; (5) maintain systems of internal financial controls and risk management and (6) make recommendations to the FCA on the appointment of new board members (this task is delegated to the nomination committee).[91] The panel of ombudsmen comprises the Chief Ombudsman, two Principal Ombudsmen and ten Lead and Managing Ombudsmen, and is effectively the senior management team of the FOS responsible for co-ordinating casework and investigations. The panel is supported by 455 ombudsmen who undertake the bulk of

---

85 MiFID II, art 25 (1).

86 MiFID II, art 25 (2) and (3).

87 MiFID II, art 27 (1).

88 Merricks argues that the FOS has developed a very different model from that of the civil courts and is the preferred alternative for most retail consumers of financial services. See Walter Merricks, 'The Financial Ombudsman Service: Not Just an Alternative to Court' (2007) 15 *Journal of Financial Regulation and Compliance* 135.

89 FOS is funded mostly via a levy on FCA-regulated firms which depends on each firm's size and complexity, and ranges from approximately £1,000 to £1,000,000.

90 FSMA 2000, Sch 17, para 3 (2).

91 FOS, 'Schedule of Matters Reserved for the Financial Ombudsman Service Board' (2018) <https://www.financial-ombudsman.org.uk/files/2481/schedule-of-matters-reserved-to-the-board-2018-02.pdf> (accessed 6 March 2020).

the casework. The FOS is expected to be independent from the FCA.[92] The FCA and FOS are required to co-operate with each other and to prepare a memorandum of understanding to that effect.[93] The FOS is also under a statutory duty to provide to the FCA any information it thinks may be useful in advancing the FCA's objectives.[94]

The jurisdiction of the FOS is distinguished by FSMA into two types: compulsory and voluntary. Compulsory jurisdiction encompasses complaints against acts or omissions that satisfy the following conditions: (1) the complainant is eligible, according to compulsory jurisdiction rules made by the FCA; (2) the complainant wishes to have the complaint dealt with under the scheme; (3) the respondent was an FCA-authorised person or electronic money issuer or payment service provider at the time the act or omission occurred; and (4) the relevant activity was at the time the act or omission occurred subject to compulsory jurisdiction rules made by the FCA.[95] Therefore, FSMA delegates to the FCA the determination of the scope of persons that are eligible to bring a complaint as well as the scope of activities to which compulsory jurisdiction applies, but only activities that are or could be made regulated activities under FSMA s 22 can be included.[96] The FCA rules are part of the Handbook. The activities to which compulsory jurisdiction applies are broadly defined and include regulated activities, lending, payment services, investment services, ancillary banking services and other ancillary activities.[97] FSMA also stipulates that, in the case the FCA has required a firm to set up a consumer redress scheme, consumers have a right to complain to the FOS if they are not satisfied with the scheme's decision and, in that case, the FOS must make its determination based on what the determination under the consumer redress scheme should have been.[98] In the case of voluntary jurisdiction, it is up to financial firms to opt into the scheme in which case the FOS has jurisdiction for any complaints made by eligible complainants that arise from acts or omissions occurring while a firm is part of the scheme.[99] Firms can withdraw from the scheme. Voluntary jurisdiction encompasses activities specified by the FOS with the FCA's approval,[100] but these activities can only be activities that are or could have been made subject to compulsory jurisdiction.[101]

Regarding the range of eligible complainants, it covers consumers and certain other persons. Consumers are defined as natural persons acting for purposes outside their trade, business or profession. Other eligible complainants include (1) charities with annual income of less than £6.5 million; (2) trustees of trusts with a net asset value of less than £5 million; (3) micro-enterprises; (4) small businesses; and (5) natural persons who have guaranteed or provided security for liabilities of micro-enterprises or small businesses. Micro-enterprises are defined as firms that employ less than ten persons and have an annual turnover of less than two million euros. Small businesses are defined as firms that are not micro-enterprises, have an annual turnover of less than £6.5 million and either employ less than 50 persons

---

92 FSMA 2000, Sch 17, para 3 (3).
93 FSMA 2000, Sch 17, para 3A.
94 FSMA 2000 s 232A.
95 FSMA 2000 s 226.
96 FSMA 2000 s 226 (4).
97 FCA Handbook, DISP 2.3.1 and 2.3.1A.
98 FSMA s 404B.
99 FSMA s 227.
100 See FCA Handbook, DISP 2.5.1.
101 FSMA s 227 (4).

or have assets less than £5 million. It is worth noting that small businesses have only been included in the range of eligible complainants since 1 April 2019.

FSMA stipulates that complaints brought under the FOS compulsory jurisdiction must be determined 'by reference to what is, in the opinion of the ombudsman, fair and reasonable in all the circumstances of the case'.[102] Therefore, previous decisions of the FOS are not binding precedent. Although not bound by them, the FOS must take into account relevant laws, regulations, regulatory rules, regulatory guidance and standards, codes of practice and good industry practice.[103] The FOS has the power to make money awards that it considers fair compensation for financial loss or other specified loss or damage, and to direct the respondent to take such steps in relation to the complainant as the ombudsman considers just and appropriate.[104] FSMA empowers the FCA to set an upper limit to money awards.[105] This limit is currently £350,000 for complaints about acts or omissions that occurred after 1 April 2019, and £160,000 for complaints about acts or omissions that occurred before that date.[106] It is worth noting that until 31 March 2019 the limit was £150,000 (having been £100,000 until the end of 2011). Its increase in 2019 was therefore significant and in line with the inclusion of small businesses within the scope of eligible complainants.[107] The Ombudsman may recommend that the respondent pay a higher amount than the upper limit.[108] In England and Wales, a money award is enforceable as if it were payable under a court order and a direction is enforceable by injunction.[109]

The process, which reflects the requirements of the ADR Directive,[110] is as follows.[111] Complainants must normally bring their complaints within six years from the date of the relevant act or omission.[112] Before bringing a complaint to the FOS, complainants must complain to the relevant financial firm and give it a reasonable opportunity to respond.[113] After the financial firm has responded a complaint must be brought within six months.[114] Complaints are, in the first instance, dealt with by case handlers who normally reach a decision within 90 days.[115] If dissatisfied with the case handler's decision, both the complainant and the respondent have the right to refer the case to an ombudsman. A hearing is not necessary.[116] The ombudsman has the power to request the parties to the dispute to

102 FSMA s 228 (2).
103 FCA Handbook, DISP 3.6.4.
104 FSMA 2000 s 229 (2) and (3).
105 FSMA 2000 s 229 (4) and (6).
106 FCA Handbook, DISP 3.7.4. Note that from 1 April 2020 onwards the limit will be adjusted annually to reflect inflation (CPI increase) rounder down to the nearest £5,000.
107 See FCA, 'SME Access to the Financial Ombudsman Service – Near-Final Rules' (2018) PS18/21; 'Increasing the Award Limit for the Financial Ombudsman Service' (2019) PS19/8.
108 FSMA 2000 s 229 (5).
109 FSMA 2000, Sch 17 para 16 and s 229 (9).
110 Directive 2013/11/EU of the European Parliament and of the Council of 21 May 2013 on alternative dispute resolution for consumer disputes and amending Regulation (EC) No. 2006/2004 and Directive 2009/22/EC [2013] OJ L165/63.
111 The FCA must ensure that the FOS at all times qualifies as an ADR entity and meet the ADR Directive's requirements. FSMA 2000, Sch 17 para 2 (2).
112 Time limits are set by the FOS according to FCA Handbook, DISP 3.5.13.
113 FSMA 2000, Sch 17 para 13 (3).
114 See FOS, 'Time Limits' <https://www.financial-ombudsman.org.uk/consumers/expect/time-limits> (accessed 31 January 2020).
115 ADR Directive, art 8 (c).
116 FCA Handbook, DISP 3.5.5.

provide information and produce documents within a reasonable time period.[117] In case a party refuses to provide information or produce documents, the ombudsman can notify the court which, if satisfied that a person defaulted without reasonable excuse, can treat them as if in contempt.[118]

The ombudsman's determination must be given in a written statement and contain reasons.[119] It must also request the complainant to notify the ombudsman within a specified time whether he accepts or rejects the determination.[120] Failure by the complainant to respond within the specified time leads to the determination being deemed to have been rejected.[121] If the determination is rejected by the complainant, the decision does not bind any of the parties and the complainant is free to bring legal action against the respondent. If the determination is accepted by the complainant, the ombudsman's decision is binding on both parties and final.[122] This means that the complainant can no longer bring legal action on that matter, and that the ombudsman's decision cannot be appealed; however, as the FOS is a public body, judicial review of its decisions is possible, but does not cover the decisions' substance.[123]

Examples of cases where the FOS made a positive determination for the complainant include a firm not providing sufficient information on the calculation of compensation for PPI[124] mis-selling, and a firm selling a pension annuity that was not entirely appropriate for the customer due to the latter's health problems.[125] Relevant FOS cases will be discussed in subsequent chapters on accounts and lending. The number of complaints brought to the FOS rose from 31,700 in 2000/2001[126] to 512,167 in 2013/2014 at the apex of the PPI saga. In 2018/2019, there were 388,392 complaints, of which 38% were upheld.[127] In 2018/2019, the FOS resolved 376,352 complaints, of which only 36,954 (9.8%) were resolved by an ombudsman. Therefore, around 90% of complaints were resolved by case handlers, a trend that has not changed significantly during the last five years.[128]

There is little research on the way the FOS uses its broad discretion in determining cases. The most comprehensive study to date was conducted by Gilad and involved non-participant observation research at the FOS office between November 2003 and December 2004. Gilad found that adjudicators, in their oral communication with complainants and in drafting their decisions, especially when dismissing complaints, took great care to use polite and compassionate language and to demonstrate that they had engaged with the points raised by the complainants and often that they acknowledge that the respondent firm had

---

117 FSMA 2000 s 231.

118 FSMA 2000 s 232.

119 FSMA 2000 s 228 (3) and (4) (a).

120 FSMA 2000 s 228 (4) (c).

121 FSMA 2000 s 228 (6). But see FSMA 2000 s 228 (6A).

122 FSMA 2000 s 228 (5).

123 For a discussion of the role of the court in judicial review in English administrative law, see Stephen Breyer, 'Judicial Review of Questions of Law and Policy' in Steven Cann (ed), *Administrative Law* (Routledge 2002).

124 PPI stands for payment protection insurance. It will be discussed in Chapter 9.

125 See FOS, 'Who We've Helped' <https://www.financial-ombudsman.org.uk/consumers/who-weve-helped> (accessed 11 June 2020).

126 The FOS reporting periods start on 1 April of each year and finishes on 31 March of the following year.

127 These figures have been taken from the FOS annual reviews. See FOS, Annual Reviews <https://www.financial-ombudsman.org.uk/publications/annual-reviews> (accessed 5 May 2020).

128 Ibid.

not acted entirely properly. She concluded that complainants had excessive expectations and that part of the role of the FOS was to manage and recalibrate such expectations by using customer-friendly and emotional language.[129] Furthermore, Gilad found that in its interaction with firms the FOS oscillated between co-operative informal strategies and adversarial precedent-based strategies. The FOS was likely to take an adversarial approach when facing risks to its autonomy and reputation, while firms were likely to do so when concerned that agreeing to compensate in an individual case might suggest that they had committed a regulatory breach and trigger regulatory enforcement or negative media coverage.[130]

It is worth noting that the UK's approach of establishing a FOS as an ADR mechanism for financial services consumers has been followed by other countries such as Australia which established the Australian FOS in 2008,[131] which alongside other similar schemes was merged into the Australian Financial Complaints Authority in 2018. The UK FOS has no doubt become the principal route of redress for individuals and very small businesses. The volume of cases handled grew dramatically and has now stabilised just below 400,000 per annum. It can therefore be surmised that the FOS is an effective consumer protection mechanism that offers an easily accessible services and is likely to take a more favourable approach to consumer grievance than English courts. At the same time, there is a risk that cases will continue to increase at an unsustainable rate, especially in view of the recent expansion of eligibility and increase of the monetary award limit. A further potential criticism is that, as the FOS is not required to follow its own precedent, decision-making can be inconsistent which does not facilitate firms in understanding how they are expected to behave and may also contribute to an excessive volume of complaints. However, Gilad's study suggests that significant efforts are made by the FOS staff to ensure a reasonable level of consistency of approach.[132]

6.6 The Money Advice Service

To complete the background of institutions that seek to protect financial services consumers it is pertinent to discuss the role of the Money Advice Service. The Money Advice Service was established in 2010 as the Consumer Financial Education Body, under the Financial Services Act 2010.[133] It was renamed as the Money Advice Service in 2011. At the beginning of 2019, the Money Advice Service was dissolved as a separate public body, and it now forms part of the broader Money & Pensions Service, which also encompasses Pension Wise and the Pensions Advisory Service. The amalgamation of the three entities into the new Money & Pensions Service was brought about by the Financial Guidance and Claims Act 2018.[134] However, the Money Advice Service brand is still being used as

---

129 Sharon Gilad, 'Accountability or Expectations Management? The Role of the Ombudsman in Financial Regulation' (2008) 30 *Law & Policy* 227.
130 Sharon Gilad, 'Juggling Conflicting Demands: The Case of the UK Financial Ombudsman Service' (2008) 19 *Journal of Public Administration Research and Theory* 661.
131 For a discussion of the effectiveness of the Australian FOS, see Vicki Waye and Vince Morabito, 'Collective Forms of Consumer Redress: Financial Ombudsman Service Case Study' (2012) 12 *Journal of Corporate Law Studies* 1.
132 Gilad (above n 129) 241–242.
133 Schedule 1 of the Act, inserting Schedule 1A in FSMA 2000.
134 Section 1. The Act uses the term 'single financial guidance body' and enables the Secretary of State to choose the final name of the new body by regulations. The renamed 'Money & Pensions Service' was launched on 6 April 2019.

an operational division of the Money & Pensions Service. The Money & Pensions Service is funded through financial assistance by the Department for Work and Pensions and via levies on financial firms under the Pension Schemes Act 1993 and FSMA 2000.[135]

The statutory objectives of the Money & Pensions Service are as follows: (1) to improve people's ability to make informed financial decisions; (2) to support the provision of information, guidance and advice in areas where it is lacking; (3) to do so in the clearest and most cost-effective way; (4) to allocate resources with a view to ensuring that information is provided to those that need it most, such as vulnerable individuals; and (5) to work closely with devolved administrations in Scotland, Wales and Northern Ireland.[136] Information, guidance and advice is defined as covering matters of occupational and personal pensions, debt and knowledge of financial matters and the ability to manage one's own financial affairs.[137] The Act specifies the six functions of the Service: pensions guidance, debt advice, money guidance, consumer protection, strategic function and advising the Secretary of State with regard to the other functions.[138] The consumer protection function involves a duty to notify the FCA if the Service becomes aware of practices by FCA-regulated firms that are detrimental to consumers.[139] The strategic function consists of developing a national strategy to improve the financial capability of the public, the public's ability to manage debt and the provision of financial education to children and young people.[140]

In terms of governance, the Money & Pensions Service could be described as a quasi-autonomous non-governmental organisation (QUANGO)[141] under the umbrella of the Department for Work and Pensions. It does not enjoy the status and immunities of the Crown, and its members and employees are not civil servants.[142] Its members[143] (equivalent to the board in a body corporate) include a non-executive chair, non-executive members, a chief executive and other executive members.[144] The chair and non-executive members are appointed by the Secretary of State. Regarding the chief executive and other executive members, the first ones were appointed by the Secretary of State but in the future their successors will be appointed by the body itself (i.e. by its members) with the approval of the Secretary of State.[145] The Secretary of State must ensure that the number of non-executive members exceeds at all times the number of executive members.[146] At the time of writing the Money & Pensions Service consisted of eight members, of which six (including the chair) were non-executive.

The CEO in his capacity as Accounting Officer performs the function of agreeing with the Director General of the Department for Work and Pensions, the Service's multi-year

135 Financial Guidance and Claims Act 2018 ss 11–14.
136 Financial Guidance and Claims Act 2018 s 2 (1).
137 Financial Guidance and Claims Act 2018 s 2 (3).
138 Financial Guidance and Claims Act 2018 s 3 (1) and (2).
139 Financial Guidance and Claims Act 2018 s 3 (7).
140 Financial Guidance and Claims Act 2018 s 3 (9).
141 For a critical discussion of the role of QUANGOs in the UK, see Matthew Flinders and Chris Skelcher, 'Shrinking the Quango State: Five Challenges in Reforming Quangos' (2012) 32 *Public Money & Management* 327.
142 Financial Guidance and Claims Act 2018, Sch 1, para 1.
143 Although the statute refers to members, the Service's website uses the terminology of "board".
144 Financial Guidance and Claims Act 2018, Sch 1, para 2 (1).
145 Financial Guidance and Claims Act 2018, Sch 1, para 6.
146 Financial Guidance and Claims Act 2018, Sch 1, para 2 (2).

Strategic Plan and annual Business Plan; these plans must also be approved by the board.[147] The current transitional business plan for 2019/2020 envisages a phase of detailed engagement with stakeholders such as consumers and financial firms, as well as with regulators; central, local and devolved governments; and parliamentarians.[148] It notes that in the UK 9 million adults are over-indebted, 10.7 million are not saving regularly and 22 million of working age people think they do not have sufficient knowledge to plan for their retirement.[149] During the 2019/2020 financial year, the Service expects that 560,000 over-indebted people will receive help and 170,000 calls and webchats will be served by its money guidance contact centre.[150] Indeed, the website of the Money Advice Service covers matters such as debt and borrowing, mortgages, budgeting and saving, social benefits, pensions, family matters, car costs and insurance.[151]

It is worth remarking that the education of financial services consumers and provision of impartial advice can play a vital role in reducing the asymmetry of information and imbalance of power between consumers and banks and other financial firms. It can enable consumers to make better choices and can limit the scope of exploitative practices by financial institutions. In the context of policy discussions around the potential imposition of a new duty of care owed to customers, discussed earlier in this chapter, it could be argued that investing resources in enhancing the capability and sophistication of the public is likely to be more effective than trying to enforce a duty on financial institutions to act in their customers' interests.

6.7 Conclusion

In the context of the financial services, consumer protection is one of the principal purposes of regulation and it is inextricably linked to public confidence in financial markets. The FCA has a broad role of supervising financial markets and regulated persons for the purposes of ensuring that there is an appropriate level of consumer protection. It has undertaken some of the functions of the now abolished OFT and works closely with the CMA which is the authority with the primary responsibility to enforce consumer protection legislation. Substantive consumer protection law in the UK has developed dramatically since the 1970s and has been heavily influenced by EU law. The implementation of the Consumer Rights Act 2015 marks a major step in simplifying the law and ensuring that there is more uniform enforcement. Apart from binding regulatory rules and consumer protection laws, bank customers can also make use of the FOS and raise complaints, free of charge, that are determined by reference to what is fair and reasonable in view of all the circumstances of each case. Financial consumer education and the provision of objective free advice is the ambit of the Money Advice Service, which is now an integral part of the Money & Pensions Service.

147 Money & Pensions Service, 'Board Terms of Reference' (2018) <https://moneyandpensionsservice.org.uk/wp-content/uploads/2019/04/MAPS-BOARD-TERMS-OF-REFERENCE.pdf> (accessed 14 June 2020).
148 Money & Pensions Service, 'Business Plan 2019/20' (2019) 10 <https://moneyandpensionsservice.org.uk/wp-content/uploads/2019/04/19-20-Business-Plan.pdf> (accessed 18 July 2020).
149 Ibid., 4.
150 Ibid., 6.
151 See The Money Advice Service <https://www.moneyadviceservice.org.uk/en> (accessed 4 March 2020).

Glossary of terms

- Ombudsman: Independent body acting as extra-judicial dispute resolution mechanism; hearing complaints relating to a certain industry, public authority or sector; and having certain powers to order remedies.
- Financial Ombudsman Service (FOS): UK's independent body having jurisdiction to hear complaints against financial services firms and power to order monetary remedies up to a limit; cases are decided based on fairness and reasonableness rather than the law; it is possible for a consumer to reject the FOS determination and bring a claim to the courts.
- Financial crime: Criminal activities relating to the financial markets and money such as money laundering, terrorist financing, insider dealing and financial fraud.
- Unfair term: A term in a consumer contract that is unenforceable because it is deemed to create a significant imbalance between the rights and obligations of the consumer and the rights and obligations of the business.
- Good faith: Subjective good faith refers to the honest belief of a person that their behaviour is lawful or in accordance with their duties or in the best interests of another party; objective good faith refers to expectations of fair dealing and reasonable behaviour and is a civil law concept that is alien to the common law.
- Investment advice: Advice offered by a financial intermediary (e.g. investment firm or bank) to an investor or prospective investor on the structure and management of their investment portfolio; other investment services include executing an investor's orders, trading on behalf of an investor and acting as a custodian for securities held by investors.
- Money & Pensions Service: Public body that provides free financial advice and pensions advice to individuals and undertakes financial education projects.

Practice questions

Strong consumer protection in the financial services comes at the cost of more expensive services and exclusion of certain groups of individuals. Consumer education on financial matters combined with effective competition law enforcement is a more efficient way to ensure good outcome for financial services consumers. Critically discuss.

You may also find it useful to review the chapter through the following questions:

- What is the role of the FCA in consumer protection?
- What are the main pieces of consumer legislation relevant to banks?
- How does MiFID II protect consumers in the context of investment advice?
- What is the jurisdiction of the Financial Ombudsman Service?
- How has the Financial Ombudsman Service used its broad discretion when resolving complaints?
- What are the objectives of the Money Advice Service?

7 Accounts and payment methods

7.1 Introduction

One of the core traditional functions of banks is to accept deposits from and offer bank accounts to their customers. As such, banks operate a complex payment system which allows individuals and businesses to make and receive payments in various ways and to draw cash. In the past, the main mechanism for non-cash payments was cheques, whereas currently, in the UK, debit cards are the most popular payment method. Bank accounts also offer customers the possibility of saving money and earning interest, albeit currently at a modest rate.[1]

This chapter examines the legal nature of the relationship between banks and depositors, which is one of debtor-creditor and examines the various common types of bank accounts: current accounts, joint accounts and savings accounts. It discusses the duties of the bank and the account holder and the consequences of fraudulent and other unauthorised transactions. It further analyses the right of banks to combine different accounts held by a customer, as a manifestation of the broader principle of set-off. The latter part of the chapter addresses common payment methods: cheques, debit cards, other payment cards and electronic transfers of funds, with an emphasis on the apportionment of liability in the case of unauthorised transactions.

This chapter will not cover aspects of the account relationship and payment methods that give rise to the provision of credit by banks to their customers. As a result, overdrafts, that is, the possibility of customers to reach a negative balance in their account, and credit cards will be discussed in Chapter 9 on lending. The clearing and settlement process and regulation of payment services in general will be discussed in Chapter 8.

7.2 The current account

7.2.1 Overview

The current account is the most common type of bank account which serves as the basis of most payment methods (as payments are made into and out of this account). In other words, the purpose of the current account is for the customer to be able to receive payments, such as her salary and other professional fees and claimed expenses, and to make payments, such

---

1 For example, as of 1 September 2019, the highest interest rate offered by HSBC UK for fixed term and fixed rate accounts was 0.85%, which was also the highest rate available on on-demand savings accounts. Higher rates were only available for accounts with low maximum subscription ceilings such as regular saver accounts (up to £3,000); children's accounts (up to £3,000) and help-to-buy accounts, under the relevant government scheme (up to £12,000). See HSBC, 'Savings Accounts' <https://www.hsbc.co.uk/savings/> (accessed 10 June 2020).

as for council tax, rent, mortgage repayments, credit card repayments, utility bills and daily life expenses. For a business, the current account is typically used to receive payments from customers and other forms of business income, and to make payments to cover all types of business expenditure, such as payments to suppliers, loan repayments and business taxes. The bank may agree with the customer that the latter can overdraw the account, up to a maximum amount. This facility is called an authorised overdraft. The balance of the current account shows the amount outstanding due to be paid to the customer at any time (or, if the account is overdrawn, the amount due to be paid to the bank).

The main terms of the current account relationship concern whether the account carries interest on the customer's credit balance, whether the customer has to pay a periodic fee to the bank for maintaining the account, whether the customer promises to pay a minimum amount monthly into the account and whether there is an arranged overdraft facility. By definition all current accounts offer the customer the option to withdraw their funds at any time. Regarding the other main terms, typically, a UK current account carries no interest on the customer's funds, and there is no periodic fee, insofar as a minimum amount of funds is paid into the account per month. In the case of a standard free account that is not overdrawn, the only financial benefit for the bank is the use of the credit balance of the account without paying interest for it. But this is a matter of freedom of contract and different sets of terms are not uncommon. For instance, some UK banks offer current accounts that cost a monthly fee, but that provide interest on the customer's balance (typically up to a maximum amount) and cashback on certain types of transactions, such as utility bill payments.

7.2.2 The legal nature of the current account relationship

Contrary to the general perception that money in a bank account belongs to the depositor, it is well established that the current account relationship is one of debtor-creditor: the bank being the debtor and the customer being the creditor. When funds are deposited into a current account or paid into it, they are lent by the customer to the bank. The bank acquires legal title to the funds and, as owner, can use the funds as it thinks fit, having a duty to repay the funds to the customer, according to the terms of their agreement. It follows that the money in an account is not held on trust for the customer, and that the bank is entitled to keep any profit it makes from using the money (e.g. from lending it). A case in point is *Foley v Hill*[2] where the House of Lords rejected a customer claim that the bank had to account for the profits made from the balance of an account. Lord Cottenham expressed in very clear terms the nature of the relationship created by a deposit: 'The money paid into the banker's, is money known by the principal to be placed there for the purpose of being under the control of the banker; it is then the banker's money; he is known to deal with it as his own…'.[3] The same applies to other types of bank accounts, such as savings accounts.[4] The reader is also referred to Chapter 5.1.1, which examines the nature of the bank-customer relationship in detail.

As a result, if a bank goes into liquidation, depositors are unsecured creditors. Until recently, depositors had the status of ordinary unsecured creditors in the context of bank

---

2 (1848) 2 HLC 28 (HL). The case was also discussed in Chapter 5.1.1.
3 Ibid., 36.
4 *Akbar Khan v Attar Singh* [1936] 2 All ER 545.

insolvency. However, as a result of EU law, deposits now have priority over other ordinary unsecured claims. Specifically, the part of deposits that is covered by deposit protection schemes (up to £85,000 or 100,000 euros per customer in the same banking group) has the highest priority among unsecured claims, followed by the part of deposits that exceeds the coverage limit.[5] Deposit protection will be discussed in detail in Chapter 15.

7.2.3 The core obligations of the parties

The main obligations undertaken by the bank are to repay the money on demand and to honour the customer's cheques and obey his payment instructions. The customer undertakes to exercise reasonable care when drawing cheques so as not to facilitate fraud. According to Atkin LJ's classic statement of the standard terms of the bank–customer contract:

> The bank undertakes to receive money and to collect bills for its customer's account. The proceeds so received are not to be held in trust for the customer, but the bank borrows the proceeds and undertakes to repay them. The promise to repay is to repay at the branch of the bank where the account is kept, and during banking hours. [...] [I]t is a term of the contract that the bank will not cease to do business with the customer except upon reasonable notice. The customer on his part undertakes to exercise reasonable care in executing his written orders so as not to mislead the bank or to facilitate forgery.[6]

The duty of the bank to honour the customer's cheques and make payments out of the customer's account when so instructed also implies that the bank acts as the customer's agent. These matters will be discussed in detail in Section 7.6 of this chapter. It is worth noting that the traditional requirement that the demand to repay is made on the branch where the account is kept is nowadays obsolete, as current banking practice permits customers to use any branch. In parallel, electronic banking, debit cards and cash cards enable customers to make bank transfers, use their account balance to make purchases and draw cash at any time of the day and on any day.

Once an appropriate demand is made on a bank to repay the balance of an account and the demand is not met the bank is in breach of contract. The statutory limitation period for the customer's claim against the bank starts running from the time of the bank's refusal of the customer's demand.[7] In other words, the limitation period does not run while an account is maintained even if the customer does not make any transactions for a long period of time. Nevertheless, inactive accounts pose a high risk of fraud, as they are not checked regularly by the account holder and may be used by fraudulent third parties. In such cases, the bank may give notice to the customer and freeze the account, which means that the account is blocked, and money cannot be paid into it or out of it. If the customer has another account with the bank, the bank may close the inactive account and transfer the balance to the other account. If not, and provided that the account has been dormant for at least 15 years, the bank has the right to close the account and pay the balance to Reclaim Fund

---

5 Bank Recovery and Resolution Directive art 108, as replaced by Directive 2017/2399. For the full citation of the Directive, see Chapter 14 (n 60).
6 *Joachimson v Swiss Bank Corporation* [1921] 3 KB 110 (CA), 127.
7 *Proven Development Sdn Bhd v Hong Kong and Shanghai Banking Corporation Plc* [1998] 6 MLJ 150, 154–155.

Limited,[8] under the Unclaimed Assets Scheme.[9] The former customer can still claim the funds from Reclaim Fund Limited at any time.

A further obligation of the bank is to provide regular written account statements free of charge. This is a regulatory obligation imposed by the FCA.[10] In the past, it was common for banks to issue passbooks where transactions were recorded by printing them onto the passbook. Customers visited branches from time to time to get their passbook updated with the latest transactions. However, passbooks are not used anymore, and therefore, the main means for customers to check their record of transactions is the bank statement.[11] For current accounts, statements are typically provided every month.

One of the main purposes of the bank statement is to enable the customer to scrutinise recent transactions and identify any fraudulent transactions not made by him. In principle, in the case of a fraudulent transaction, an innocent customer can demand a correction and dispute the incorrect debit. The bank will have to reverse the debit. The bank is also entitled to rectify any error in an account statement and reverse an incorrect debit or credit. Disputes may arise if a customer receives money by mistake, the bank does not reverse the credit for a long period of time and the customer uses the funds and then resists the bank's claim to return the relevant amount. Case law has established an estoppel in favour of the customer provided that (1) the bank does not reverse the credit within reasonable time; (2) the customer discovers the credit; (3) the customer is misled that he is entitled to the money; (4) the customer in reliance on the credit spends the money and (5) the customer did not ought to have known that the credit was incorrect (e.g. because the customer was not expecting any payment).[12]

In the more usual case, the customer's account is debited without his authority either by mistake or due to fraud. A bank making a payment in circumstances where it had reasonable grounds for believing that the payment instruction was an attempt to misappropriate the funds of its customer will be liable to the customer in negligence.[13] However, the bank is under no duty to investigate the authenticity of each payment instruction.[14] It is possible to exclude this common law duty of care by an express contractual term, but very clear wording must be used, as courts will interpret such terms *contra proferentem*.[15] If the customer is a consumer such terms are subject to fairness review under the Consumer Rights Act 2015, discussed in Chapter 6.

If the customer has actual notice of the erroneous entry and fails to dispute it, he can no longer do so.[16] Furthermore, a pertinent question is whether the customer owes a duty to

8 This is a not-for-profit organisation authorised and regulated by the Financial Conduct Authority.
9 The scheme was established by the Dormant Bank and Building Societies Act 2008.
10 FCA Handbook, BCOBS 4.2.1.
11 If the customer so wishes, they can opt out of receiving a hard copy statement and instead receive it only electronically.
12 The estoppel was established by *Skyring v Greenwood and Cox* (1825) 4 B&C 281. In *British and North European Bak Ltd v Zalzstein* [1927] 2 KB 92, the estoppel failed because the customer had not discovered the incorrect credit by the time of its reversal. In *United Overseas Bank v Jiwani* [1976] 1 WLR 964, the estoppel failed because the customer ought to have known that he was not entitled to the money.
13 *Barclays Bank Plc v Quincecare* [1992] 4 All ER 363.
14 *Federal Republic of Nigeria v JP Morgan Chase Bank N.A.* [2019] EWHC 347 (Comm) [31].
15 Ibid., [40].
16 In the context of cheques, this is well established. See *Greenwood v Martins Bank Ltd* [1933] AC 51 (HL). A New Zealand case is persuasive authority that the same applies to other account debits: *Bank of New Zealand v Auckland Information Bureau Inc* [1996] 1 NZLR 420 (NZCA).

the bank to check periodic account statements and whether a customer's failure to discover the incorrect debit within reasonable time bars his from disputing it at a later time. In the UK, the principle is that the customer does not have an implied contractual duty to check periodic bank statements and, therefore, that incorrect debits can be disputed at any time. The leading authority on the matter is *Tai Hing Cotton Mill Ltd v Liu Chong Hing Bank Ltd*[17] which confirmed earlier case law that the risk of the service of undertaking to honour cheques lies with the bank, that customers only have to draw cheques with care and need not organise their business in a way that facilitates the detection of fraud, and that there is no duty to check bank statements.[18] The Privy Council also rejected an argument that a duty was owed by the customer to the bank in tort to check account statements and ruled that relevant terms in the contracts that purported to render the statements conclusive evidence if not disputed within a time period were not expressed in clear enough language to change the default common law position.

Furthermore, the Privy Council emphasised that, contrary to the practice followed by Canadian banks that rely on verification clauses,[19] credit institutions in Hong Kong and in the UK do not return to customers cleared cheques that have been paid out of their accounts alongside bank statements:

> In Canada banks have for many years returned vouchers with the periodic statements and have had clauses in their contracts whereby if they are not notified within a stipulated time of errors the statements are conclusive [...] The defendant banks never returned cleared cheques to the company and the language of their terms of business is not sufficient to impose any obligation on the customer to examine statements and notify the banks of any error within the time stated, nor to make the statements conclusive in the absence of objection within the time limit. The notion that every customer would go to the bank within the time limit and there examine his cleared cheques is absurd, and so it is no answer for the banks to say that the company could have seen its cleared cheques if it had wished. No court anywhere has ever held that a customer who did not receive back his paid cheques was estopped from asserting that they were forged. All the case law in the United States is based upon the return of the cheques and vouchers with the statements.[20]

A consequence of this principle is that constructive notice is not sufficient to bar a customer from disputing a false debit, but shutting one's eyes to obvious means of knowledge, and thus being reckless, constitutes actual notice.[21] These principles apply to unauthorised transactions in general, but in the context of transactions made using payment cards there is an upper limit of 13 months for customers to dispute transactions, as will be explained in Section 7.7.

---

17 *Tai Hing Cotton Mill Ltd v Liu Chong Hing Bank Ltd* [1986] AC 80 (PC).
18 See e.g. *Kepitigalla Rubber Estates Ltd v National Bank of India Ltd* [1909] 2 KB 1010. A very different position has been taken by Canadian courts. For instance, in *Canadian Pacific Hotels Ltd. v Bank of Montreal* (1981) 122 D.L.R. (3d) 519, it was held that a customer owed a duty to the bank to operate an acceptable internal control system.
19 Such clauses were upheld in *Arrow Transfer Co. Ltd. v Royal Bank of Canada* (1972) 27 D.L.R. (3d) 81.
20 *Tai Hing Cotton Mill Ltd v Liu Chong Hing Bank Ltd* (above n 17), 85.
21 *Price Meats Ltd v Barclays Bank Plc* [2000] 2 All ER (Comm.) 346. An example of recklessness that led to the customer being estopped from disputing the debit is: *Brown v Westminster Bank Ltd* [1964] 2 Lloyd's Rep. 187.

The common law position has been criticised by Ellinger on the grounds that the obvious business purpose of account statements is for customers to scrutinise transactions.[22] However, a counterargument can be drawn from the perspective of law and economics. The default position taken by English courts that bank customers do not owe a duty to check statements can be described as an efficient 'penalty default' rule. A penalty default rule is different from most default rules that impose the outcome that would be contractually agreed by most parties. Instead, these are rules that would not have been wanted by one of the parties. Their function is to incentivise the stronger negotiating party to disclose information to the other party in order to contract around the penalty default rule.[23] In our context, the common law rule provides banks with an incentive to insert unambiguous verification clauses into their standard terms and conditions and return cleared cheques to customers (nowadays this could be done electronically), thus allowing them to inspect them, or alternatively bear the cost of late detection of fraudulent transactions.

It is worth remarking that if verification clauses were adopted by UK banks, they would be subject to judicial scrutiny under the Unfair Contract Terms Act 1977, which was discussed in detail in Chapter 6. As verification clauses would constitute contractual terms limiting banks' liability for breach of contract, they would only be binding to the extent that they are reasonable. For bank customers who qualify as consumers, such clauses would also be potentially challengeable as unfair under the Consumer Rights Act 2015.

7.3 The joint current account

A current account may be held jointly by two or more customers. In such cases, there is legal co-ownership of the debt (as a *chose* in action) that the account represents.[24] This is common in the case of spouses and other closely related individuals. In parallel, partnership accounts are also technically joint accounts, as the partnership firm is not a separate legal person, and therefore, the account is held by the partners jointly. In contrast, the accounts of limited liability companies are held by companies in their corporate capacity, but inevitably they can only act through authorised agents, thus giving rise to problems when authority is disputed.[25] Similar issues with agency are faced by partnership accounts. The rest of this section will focus on joint accounts held by individuals.

When opening the joint account, the account holders decide whether the authority of all of them, any of them or some of them is necessary to make payment instructions and draw cheques. If the joint holders stipulate that more than one signatures are needed and, in fact, a cheque is not signed by all parties that ought to have signed it and the bank honours it, any account holder who did not sign the cheque can demand the bank to repay him *prima facie* a proportional share of the amount of the cheque.[26] For instance, in the case of a joint

---

22 E.P. Ellinger, Eva Lomnicka and C. Hare, *Ellinger's Modern Banking Law* (5th edn, OUP 2011) 239.

23 See I. Ayres and R. Gertner, 'Filling Gaps in Incomplete Contracts: An Economic Theory of Default Rules' (1989) 99 *Yale Law Journal* 87; I. Ayres, 'Making a Difference: The Contractual Contributions of Easterbrook and Fischel' (1992) 59 *University of Chicago Law Review* 1391.

24 *National Provincial Bank Ltd v Bishop* [1965] Ch 450.

25 For an authoritative discussion of agency in company law, see Arad Reisberg and Anna Donovan, *Pettet, Lowry & Reisberg's Company Law* (5th edn, Pearson 2018) Chapter 6.

26 See *Jackson v White and Midland Bank Ltd* [1967] 2 Lloyd's Rep. 68 where the non-singing holder was in fact entitled to the whole amount of the cheque and the Australian case of *Vella v Permanent Mortgages Party Ltd* [2008] NSWSC 505 where the non-signing party was entitled to their share of the amount of the cheque.

account with two holders where only one signs a cheque, despite a stipulation that both must do so, the other holder can claim from the bank 50% of the value of the cheque. If the agreement is that each joint holder can operate and draw on the account individually, other holders have no ground to dispute any transaction made by any account holder. In the case of a joint account that has an authorised overdraft facility, the default position is that the account holders are jointly and severally liable,[27] which means that the bank can sue any of them for the whole amount due but can only recover once. Upon the death of one of the joint account holders, the legal title to the account vests in the surviving account holders, while the position in equity is more complicated and will not be investigated here in detail.[28]

7.4 The savings account

Savings accounts bear interest and are not used as a means of making and receiving payments. Thus, it is not possible to draw on a savings account by cheque, debit card or cash card, and a savings account can never be overdrawn. As some current accounts also bear interest, this chapter uses the term 'savings account' rather than 'interest-bearing account'. Usually funds are transferred to a savings account from a customer's current account. A savings account can also be held jointly by two or more persons in which case the principles discussed above apply.

There are many types of savings accounts in contemporary UK banking practice. Some accounts allow customers to withdraw funds at any time without any loss of interest. Other accounts reward customers with additional interest if they do not withdraw any funds within a given period of time. In other cases, the customer has to give notice to the bank and wait for a prescribed period of time before being able to withdraw the funds. Finally, certain savings accounts have a fixed term during which the customer either cannot withdraw funds at all, or can only withdraw funds at the cost of paying a penalty fee, usually equal to the interest that would have been earned within a period of time, or losing the whole interest earned or part thereof. Some savings accounts have a minimum funds requirement, while some have a maximum amount that can be deposited. Some savings accounts are aimed at customers who save regular amounts monthly, while others are aimed at customers with a lump sum. Interest rates offered by major UK banks have in the last decade been very low, in line with the low level of the Bank of England base rate, which at the time of writing stood at 0.75%, having previously been as low as 0.25%. Smaller and foreign banks offer higher rates in line with the higher risk of default that they pose.

As the balance in a savings account is a debt owed by the bank to the customer, and therefore a *chose* in action, it can be assigned at law provided that the requirements of section 136 of the Law of Property Act 1925 are met. An assignment that is not valid at law may be valid in equity. Legal and equitable assignments will be discussed in detail in Chapter 9. The deposit receipt provided by a bank with respect to a savings account is not a negotiable instrument,[29] which means that its delivery does not confer the title to the account to the

---

27 *Fielding v Royal Bank of Scotland Plc* [2004] EWCA Civ 64.

28 See *McEvoy v Belfast Banking Co* [1935] AC 24 (HL). For a detailed discussion of the law surrounding survivorship in the context of joint bank accounts, including the aspect of whether inheritance tax is owed, see Ellinger, Lomnicka and Hare (above n 22) 324–332.

29 A negotiable instrument is a piece of paper that incorporates a debt (promise to pay) to the effect that delivery of the instrument (for bearer instruments) or delivery and indorsement leads to transfer of the debt.

transferee (the person to whom it is delivered). In other words, deposit receipts, and in the past passbooks, are only paper evidence of the existence of the debt owed by the bank to the customer that the account represents.[30]

In the case of fixed term accounts a pertinent question is how the bank should treat the funds upon the maturity of the account, i.e. on the expiration of the fixed period. The bank can either pay the funds into the customer's current account (normally banks require a customer to hold a current account with them in order to open a savings account) or renew the account. Renewal cannot take place automatically, without the customer's authority. In the UK, banks do not have to remind customers when their fixed term account is approaching maturity and actively seek instructions on how to treat the funds. They only need to pay the funds into the customer's current account.[31] The opposite is the case in Singapore, where banks are expected to notify customers shortly before the expiration of a fixed term deposit and discuss available savings accounts options to place the funds in after the account in question matures.[32]

7.5 Combination of accounts

If a bank customer with an overdrawn account becomes bankrupt or insolvent[33] or is reluctant to repay the overdraft, it is crucial for the bank to be able to use any credit balance the customer has in other accounts held with the same bank in satisfaction of its claim against the customer. For example, if a customer holds two current accounts with the same bank one of which is overdrawn by £1,000 and the other has a credit balance of £2,000, the combination of accounts allows the bank to set off the debt of the customer against its own debt to the customer so that eventually the customer will hold one account with a credit balance of £1,000. This saves the bank from having to sue the customer for the amount due. If the customer is bankrupt (individual customer) or insolvent (corporate customer), the right to combine the accounts and set off the mutual obligations is particularly valuable. This is because it allows the bank to recover the whole amount due (provided that the credit balance is sufficient), rather than recovering through the bankruptcy or liquidation process, as the case may be, alongside other unsecured creditors who typically recover only a small fraction of the debts owed to them.

The basic position is that, even in the absence of bankruptcy/insolvency, a bank has a common law right to combine a customer's current accounts,[34] irrespective of the branch in which they are held,[35] provided that there is no contrary express term in the contract. The legal nature of the right to combine accounts is a right of set-off. It is not a lien, as suggested in the past, considering that the bank owns the funds that are deposited in it and therefore it cannot have a lien on its own property, according to a fundamental property law axiom.[36]

---

30 *Akbar Khan v Attar Singh* (above n 4).

31 *Suriya & Douglas v Midland Bank Plc* [1999] 1 All ER (Comm) 612 (CA).

32 *Bank of America National Trust and Savings Association v Iskandar* [1998] 2 SLR 265 (SGCA).

33 In the UK, the terms 'insolvency' and 'insolvent' are used with respect to bodies corporate, such as limited liability companies, whereas the terms 'bankruptcy' and 'bankrupt' are used with respect to natural persons. So, the relevant areas of law are known as 'corporate insolvency law' and 'personal bankruptcy law', respectively. On the contrary, in the US, the term 'bankruptcy' is used both for individuals and corporations.

34 *Re European Bank, Agra Bank Claims* (1872) LR 8 Ch App 41.

35 *Garnett v M'Keewan* (1872) LR 8 Ex 10.

36 *National Westminster Bank Ltd v Halesowen Presswork and Assemblies Ltd* [1972] AC 785 (HL).

The bank can exercise the right to combine accounts whenever the customer cannot discharge a current liability to the bank.[37] Notice needs to be given to the account holder. As the right to combine accounts is a right of set-off, it is required that the two obligations are mutual and that both debts are already due at the time of the set-off. Therefore, a bank cannot use the credit balance in a fixed term account that has not yet matured.[38] Furthermore, if an account is held on trust for another party or a special item of property is appropriated for a special purpose – in both cases known to the bank, the element of mutuality is absent, and thus, the trust account cannot be combined with other accounts held by the same customer.[39] But a mere mention of purpose e.g. in the account's name does not defeat mutuality of claims.[40]

In the context of individual bankruptcy and corporate insolvency, a special statutory right of set-off applies and can be used by banks to combine accounts.[41] This statutory right of set-off is a mandatory rule of law, and therefore, it is not possible to contract out of it.[42] In any case, if a bank has agreed with a corporate customer that two accounts will be kept separate and will not be combined, unless there is a material change of circumstances, this clause is construed as including the customer's insolvency, and the agreement not to combine accounts is deemed to be operative only as long as the corporate customer remains a going concern.[43] In cases where there is a material change of circumstances clause and the corporate customer has been wound up, no notice is required to be given by the bank in order to combine the accounts.

7.6 Cheques

A cheque is a written instruction given by a current account holder to the bank where the account is maintained to pay a designated third party a specified amount of money. The person giving the instruction is the drawer; the person to whom payment is to be made is the beneficiary (these days always the payee); the bank with which the payee keeps his account is the collecting bank and the bank with which the drawer keeps his account is the paying bank. So, the cheque moves from the drawer to the payee then on to the collecting bank when presented for payment, and finally, it is remitted to the paying bank.

Originally, cheques were negotiable instruments that could be transferred from the original payee to third parties and thus circulate in lieu of cash. The transfer was effectuated by the original payee writing a statement to that effect on the back of the cheque and signing it, a process known at law as indorsement. Cheques were also occasionally drawn to the bearer in which case they could be transferred by simple delivery. Although the law relating to indorsement and bearer cheques remains effective, it has been rendered obsolete due to the universal adoption by UK banks of the practice known as crossing which is provided for by the Cheques Act 1992 and renders cheques untransferable. A crossed cheque bears

---

37 *James Kirkwood & Sons v Clydesdale Bank Ltd* (1907) 15 SLT 413.
38 *Liverpool Freeport Electronics Ltd v Habib Bank Ltd* [2007] EWHC 1149 (QB).
39 *Greenwood Teale v William, Williams, Brown & Co Ltd* (1894) 11 TLR 56.
40 *National Westminster v Halesowen* (above n 36) 808.
41 For individual bankruptcy, the right is provided by section 323 of the Insolvency Act 1986. For corporate insolvency, the right is provided by rule 4.90 (1) of the Insolvency Rules 1986 (SI 1986/1925). These were preceded by section 31 of the Bankruptcy Act 1914 which also applied to companies by virtue of section 317 of the Companies Act 1948.
42 *National Westminster v Halesowen* (above n 36) 805.
43 Ibid., 807. The House of Lords followed *British Guiana Bank Ltd v OR* (1911) 27 TLR 454 (PC).

two parallel lines between which the following text must written: 'account payee' or 'a/c payee' with or without the word 'only'. This means that the cheque can only be paid into the account of the named payee, and cannot be transferred.[44] As a result, much of the statutory law and case law on indorsements and fraud related to forged indorsements has lost its practical significance and will not be discussed herein.

7.6.1 The decline in the use of cheques and the future of the cheque

In recent years, the use of cheques has declined considerably in tandem with the rise in the use of debit cards and electronic bank transfers. Whereas in 1990 four billion cheques were drawn in the UK, in 2018 there were only 346 million cheques drawn.[45] Still, as of 2018, 87% of charities and 75% of businesses had either made or received a payment by cheque within the last month, while 55% of personal account holders had either made or received a payment by cheque within the last year.[46]

As a result of the declining use of cheques, in 2009, the UK Payments Council proposed the abolition of cheques with effect from 2018. However, due to opposition by older customers, charities and small businesses, cheques were maintained.[47] In an attempt to bolster their use, a new system of image-based clearing will be introduced in the near future,[48] and customers will be able to present their cheques for payment not only physically at a branch, but also by scanning them on an electronic device and uploading them online.[49] Even when cheques will be presented in hard copy, the collecting bank will then scan them, so that all clearing will eventually be image-based. Image-based clearing will save the expense of having to physically send cheques from collecting banks to paying banks and will allow speedy clearing. Once the new system is fully operational, funds will be available by 23.59 on the next working day after presentation of the cheque.[50] Under the current paper-based clearing system, it takes two working days to start earning interest on the amount of a cheque (if the account bears interest), four working days to be able to withdraw the funds and six working days to be guaranteed that the credit will not be reversed. However, the option of presenting cheques for payment electronically, although convenient for customers, will probably increase the risk of fraud, as it will be possible to present the same cheque for payment more than once.

Booysen argues that the UK's attempt to reinvigorate the cheque is unlikely to reverse the trend of decline in their use. She also observes that UK policy on the matter is inconsistent with policy initiatives taken by other developed countries, such as the US and Singapore, and was motivated by short-term political considerations, as UK politicians wanted to side with public opinion during a time of great distrust towards the financial system, shortly

44 Bills of Exchange Act 1882 s 81A, inserted by Cheques Act 1992 s 1.
45 Cheque & Credit Clearing Company <https://www.chequeandcredit.co.uk/information-hub/facts-and-figures/key-facts-and-figures-0> (accessed 14 July 2020).
46 Ibid.
47 See Treasury Committee, *The Future of Cheques* (HC 2010–2012, 1147-I) and HM Treasury, *Speeding Up Cheque Payments: Summary of Responses* (2014).
48 The new system was launched in October 2017 on a gradual roll-out basis.
49 Electronic presentation of cheques is now permitted by sections 89A–89F of the Bills of Exchange Act 1882, inserted by section 13 of the Small Business, Enterprise and Employment Act 2015.
50 Cheque & Credit Clearing Company <https://www.chequeandcredit.co.uk/information-hub/history-cheque/what-next-cheque-clearing> (accessed 16 June 2020).

after the global financial crisis of 2007–2009.[51] At the same time, it is arguable that the planned abolition of cheques by 2018 was somewhat premature, as customers with lower digital literacy and small organisations still tend to find cheques a convenient payment system. If cheque use continues to decline heavily in the future, there will at some point come the time for their total abolition.

7.6.2 The obligation of the paying bank to honour the customer's cheques

Paying duly drawn cheques is one of the core obligations of banks, as a core part of the current account relationship. The paying bank is entitled to debit the account of the customer accordingly, even if the customer subsequently revokes the authority of the agent who authorised the cheque.[52] The only exceptions to the duty of the bank to honour the customer's cheques are the following: (1) absence of sufficient funds in the account or of an authorised overdraft facility; (2) the cheque being illegible or irregular[53]; (3) the cheque being out of date – normally if it is presented for payment more than six months after the drawing date; (4) the bank having reasonable grounds for believing that the cheque is not genuine[54]; and (5) payment of the cheque being prohibited by statute or court order.[55]

If the paying bank dishonours a cheque without one of the above exceptions applying, it is in breach of contract and strictly liable to pay damages to the customer covering any actual loss that is caused by the bank's refusal to honour the cheque. Such loss will normally flow from the fact that the customer's payee does not receive payment in time and might subsequently sue the customer, terminate their contract or charge the customer interest or a higher interest rate until payment is made. However, in many cases, there is no actual monetary loss but only the general loss to the customer's reputation and creditworthiness flowing from the refusal to honour the cheque.[56] Originally, only traders could recover reasonable compensation for injury to their credit and reputation,[57] while at present all customers can do so, the change of judicial approach having been prompted by the increased importance of credit ratings for non-traders in recent years, as an individual with a poor credit score is likely to lose access to bank credit.[58]

7.6.3 Consequences of wrongful payment of a cheque

A forged or materially altered cheque is void.[59] If the paying bank pays a cheque that was not authorised by the customer, usually because it was forged or altered by a fraudulent third party, it is not entitled to debit the customer's account and, if it so does, it must reverse the debit. The bank will normally have a claim against the fraudulent third party. However, the bank may have a defence that permits it to charge the customer's account for the amount of the forged or altered cheque.

51 Sandra A. Booysen, 'Cheques: To be or Not to Be?' (2018) 4 *Journal of Business Law* 283, 295–297.
52 *Sierra Leone Telecommunications Co Ltd v Barclays Bank Plc* [1998] 2 All ER 821.
53 *London Joint Stock Bank Ltd v Macmillan* [1918] AC 777.
54 *Lipkin Gorman v Karpnale & Co Ltd* [1989] 1 WLR 1340.
55 This usually occurs in the context of money laundering and terrorist financing. On these issues, see Chapter 10.
56 See Ellinger, Lomnicka and Hare (above n 22) 509–512.
57 See *Gibbons v Westminster Bank Ltd* [1939] 2 KB 882.
58 See *Kpohraror v Woolwich Building Society* [1996] 4 All ER 119.
59 Bills of Exchange Act 1882 ss 24 and 64, respectively.

At common law the paying bank has three defences. First, there is an estoppel if the customer breaches any of his two core duties of drawing cheques with due care,[60] and notifying the bank immediately once becoming aware of an unauthorised cheque.[61] Second, if a cheque lacks one required authorising signature but bears another genuine signature and thus is not a forgery, it can be ratified by the drawer (usually a company) either expressly or by conduct.[62] Third, the bank has a defence, if the customer's instructions were ambiguous, but not apparently so, and the bank acted in good faith in honouring the cheque. If the ambiguity is apparent the bank must not honour the cheque. In equity, the paying bank has a defence when the wrongful cheque payment discharges an existing debt owed by the customer to a third party, particularly where the cheque is defective only because it does not bear all necessary signatures.[63]

A further interesting matter is the potential liability of the collecting bank towards the true owner of a cheque where the collecting bank's customer falsely purports to be the true owner. As indorsement is no longer possible, this can only happen now if a cheque is forged or if another person impersonates the payee. In such cases, *prima facie*, the collecting bank is strictly liable in tort for conversion,[64] under the legal fiction that the property that is interfered with is the cheque as a piece of paper, not as a *chose* in action.[65] The bank is liable for the face value of the cheque.[66] The person who purports to be the payee is also liable to the true payee, but the true payee is likely to prefer to sue the collecting bank in view of the latter's much greater financial resources.

However, the collecting bank may be able to use the defence provided by section 4 of the Cheques Act 1957,[67] if it paid the cheque in good faith and without negligence. The defence does not apply in cases where the signature on a cheque is forged, as then the cheque is void and therefore it is not a cheque at all for the purposes of the Act. Thus, the defence primarily applies when another person impersonates the true payee. For the collecting bank to be able to claim that it was not negligent in paying the cheque, it must have verified that the person presenting the cheque was indeed its customer and that the customer appeared to be the cheque's payee. Bank clerks must thus check that the name of the payee on the cheque matches the customer's name as it appears on their debit card and current account. But provided that this has been done, 'the banker is entitled to assume that their customer is the owner of the cheque, unless there are facts which are, or ought to be, known to him which would cause a reasonable banker to suspect that the customer was not the true owner'.[68]

7.7 Debit cards and other payment cards

Modern banking practice makes use of various types of plastic cards the most important of which are credit cards, debit cards and charge cards. It is expected that by 2026, 53% of all

---

60 *London Joint Stock Bank Ltd v Macmillan* (above n 53).
61 *Greenwood v Martins Bank Ltd* (above n 16).
62 *London Intercontinental Trust Ltd Barclays Bank Ltd* [1980] 1 Lloyd's Rep. 241.
63 The defence was successful in *Ligget (Liverpool) Ltd v Barclays Bank Ltd* [1928] 1 KB 48, whereas it failed in *Crantrave v Lloyds Bank Plc* [2000] 3 WLR 877 where the payment was made by the bank entirely by mistake.
64 For a detailed account and appraisal of modern English law on conversion, see Sarah Green and John Randall, *The Tort of Conversion* (Hart Publishing 2009).
65 *OBG v Allan* [2007] UKHL 21.
66 *Marfani & Co Ltd v Midland Bank Ltd* [1968] 1 WLR 956.
67 Cheques Act 1957 c. 36.
68 Ibid., 972 per Diplock LJ.

payments in the UK will be made by cards.[69] It is common for the same card to act as both a debit card and a cash card. Credit cards will be discussed in Chapter 9. Payment cards are typically issued by banks, and it is normally a prerequisite that the card holder holds a bank account. However, payments are operated by specialist card provider companies, such as Visa, Mastercard and American Express.[70] The customer's bank is the card issuer (issuing bank) and is in a contractual relationship with the card provider. The card provider is in contractual relationship with participating banks (acquiring banks) that provide the relevant facilities and equipment to merchants (businesses) that accept the relevant card as a means of payment. The terms and conditions of the use of the card, including the interest rate in the case of credit cards and charges, are agreed between the bank and customer. Nevertheless, it is also possible to obtain certain cards directly from the card provider rather than via a bank, but not a debit card as debit cards are linked to current accounts.

Cash cards, also known as ATM cards, enable bank customers to draw cash from their current accounts using an ATM machine. It is standard practice for customers to be able to use any ATM machine and not only those belonging to the bank with which they keep their account. A PIN is required to make withdrawals, and there is typically a maximum daily withdrawal limit. A less common type of card is the prepaid card which can be purchased at certain outlets and is loaded with money by the customer either in store or by bank transfer, but – contrary to other types of card – it is not necessarily required that the customers have a bank account. Finally, a digital card is a card that is pre-loaded with monetary value in digital form which is then transferred in real time to merchants that participate in the relevant network.

Debit cards have become the most popular means of payment in the UK having overtaken cash in 2016. At the end of 2016, there were 100 million debit cards in the UK of which 70 million were contactless, while 51.1 million persons had a debit card, that is, 6% of the UK adult population.[71] The total value of debit card transactions in 2016 amounted to £715 billion, of which £530 billion represented purchases the remaining being cash withdrawals.[72] A debit card works as follows. When the customer makes a purchase from a participating merchant an electronic transfer of funds occurs from the account of the customer to the account of the merchant using the EFT-POS electronic system. Thus, no credit is provided by the bank. When a debit card is used at a point of sale the customer is required to enter her PIN number, unless the card is contactless and the transaction is up to £30, in which case it is only necessary to tap the card on the screen of the payment terminal. When a debit card is used to make purchases online, the customer is prompted to provide the card number, expiry date and an additional number written on the back of the card alongside the cardholder name and address. Banks provide customers the option to register their card

---

69 The UK Cards Association, 'UK Card Payments 2017' (2017) 12 <http://www.theukcardsassociation.org.uk/wm_documents/UK%20Card%20Payments%202017%20%20website%20FINAL.pdf> (accessed 18 May 2020).

70 These companies act as clearing houses for the card brand they administer. Together with the issuing and acquiring banks that process payments of the relevant card brand, they form card associations. The main purpose of a card association is to maintain and improve the card network, act as mediators between banks and set relevant fees between banks. Visa Inc is an American public listed company, since its public listing in 2006. From 2006 to 2016 Visa Europe Ltd was a separate company owned by European banks and other financial firms, but in 2016 it was acquired by Visa Inc. Mastercard Inc is also a public listed company since 2006, having before been a co-operative owned by banks and other financial institutions.

71 Ibid., 6.

72 Ibid., 6–7.

under a verification scheme operated by the relevant card provider company, which means that for certain transactions additional verification is required, such as a PIN.

The rights and duties of customers arising from any misuse of payment cards (including credit cards) are harmonised at the European level by virtue of the Payment Services Directive II.[73] The Directive has been implemented in the UK by the Payment Services Regulations 2017,[74] to be discussed further in Chapter 8. The Regulations apply to 'payment services providers' which includes credit institutions,[75] so in our discussion we will focus on their application to banks. In brief, cardholders are under a duty to notify the issuer without undue delay as soon as they become aware that the card has been lost or stolen, or that there has been an unauthorised transaction and must take reasonable steps to keep their credentials (e.g. PIN and passwords) secure.[76] In the case of unauthorised transactions, a cardholder is only entitled to redress if they notify the provider (the bank) without undue delay and, in any case, within 13 months from the date on which they were wrongly debited.[77] On their part, payment service providers must provide at all times and free of charge appropriate means for cardholders to make notifications of card loss, theft or misuse, and must ensure that the card cannot be used after such notification has been made.[78]

The fundamental principle is that an innocent cardholder should not be liable for unauthorised use of his card. When a cardholder claims that a transaction was not authorised or was improperly executed, it is for the bank 'to prove that the payment transaction was authenticated, accurately recorded, entered in the payment service provider's accounts and not affected by a technical breakdown or some other deficiency' (reversal of burden of proof).[79] In the case of unauthorised transactions, the bank is liable to refund the customer and restore the account to the position it was before being debited.[80] This must take place by the end of the following business day,[81] unless the bank has reasonable grounds to suspect that the customer has engaged in fraudulent behaviour, in which case the bank must report its suspicions, according to the Proceeds of Crime Act 2002,[82] discussed in Chapter 10. However, the customer will be liable for all the loss that results from the unauthorised use, if he has acted fraudulently or has failed to notify the bank of the card's loss, theft or unauthorised use or has failed to keep his credentials secure either intentionally or with gross negligence.[83] Furthermore, in standard cases where the bank is liable for an unauthorised transaction, it can still charge the cardholder up to £35 for any losses it incurred unless the loss or theft of the card was not detectable by the customer before the transaction or the loss was caused by an act or omission by an employee or agent of the bank.[84] Cardholders, however, cannot be charged at all: (1) for any losses that occurred after they notified the

---

73 Directive (EU) 2015/2366 of the European Parliament and of the Council of 25 November 2015 on payment services in the internal market, amending Directives 2002/65/EC, 2009/110/EC and 2013/36/EU and Regulation (EU) No. 1093/2010, and repealing Directive 2007/64/EC [2015] OJL 337/35.

74 SI 2017/752.

75 Payment Services Regulations 2017 reg 2 (1).

76 Payment Services Regulations 2017 reg 72.

77 Payment Services Regulations 2017 reg 74.

78 Payment Services Regulations 2017 reg 73.

79 Payment Services Regulations 2017 reg 75.

80 Payment Services Regulations 2017 reg 76 (1).

81 Payment Services Regulations 2017 reg 76 (2).

82 Payment Services Regulations 2017 reg 76 (3).

83 Payment Services Regulations 2017 reg 77 (3).

84 Payment Services Regulations 2017 reg 77 (1)–(2).

bank of the loss or theft of the card; (2) in cases where the bank failed to provide an appropriate means of notification; (3) when the card was used for a distance contract (e.g. online); and (4) when the bank did not require strong customer authentication for a transaction, although it had to do so under the Regulations.[85] Thus, the Regulations complement the common law principles on unauthorised payments that were analysed in Section 7.2.2 of this chapter.

7.8 The electronic transfer of funds

Modern banking practice allows customers to move funds electronically from their account to the account of another party, either by visiting a branch and by completing a form or online. The transfer of funds happens within a few hours or even instantaneously. The mechanics of electronic payment systems such as BACS[86] and CHAPS[87] will be discussed in detail in Chapter 8. Here it is sufficient to mention that transfer of funds from one UK bank account to another requires two identification elements: the account number which is an eight-digit number and sort code which implies three single digits. This section will set out the common ways in which bank customers use electronic fund transfers.

A distinction should be drawn between a credit transfer and a debit transfer. In the case of a credit transfer, the transaction is initiated by the payer. So, the bank customer who seeks to make a payment instructs the bank to credit the account of the payee. This facility is used by most employers to pay the monthly salaries of employees. It can also be used by individual bank customers to make regular payments of fixed sums, via a standing order. For instance, standing orders are commonly used to repay loans or to pay a person's rent. Conversely, a debit transfer is initiated by the payee who instructs the payer's bank to transfer funds into his account. Evidently, the authority of the payer must have been given in advance. The payer's bank will be presented by the payee with the payer's mandate. An example of debit transfer is the use of direct debits to pay various bills the amount of which changes from time to time.

There is an inevitable risk of fraud in electronic payments. A customer's mandate for a direct debit may be forged. In such cases, the principles on unauthorised debiting of a customer's account apply. Moreover, a customer making a credit transfer may be given the wrong bank account and sort code so that the payment does not reach the intended payee but is instead appropriated by a fraudulent third party. This happened in the case of *Tidal Energy Ltd v Bank of Scotland Plc*[88] where a company intended to make a substantial payment to a supplier but was provided fraudulently with the account details of another party. The relevant payment form mentioned the name of the intended beneficiary, and thus, the account details did not match the named beneficiary in the form. When the deceived company discovered the fraud and contacted its bank, its bank tried to stop the bank with which the recipient of the funds held its account from making the funds available for withdrawal. However, the bank of the recipient refused to prevent the recipient from withdrawing the funds. The customer sued its bank seeking to have the account recredited with the

---

85 Payment Services Regulations 2017 reg 77 (4).
86 BACS stands for Bankers' Automated Clearing Services. The current scheme operator is Bacs Payment Schemes Limited, which is a subsidiary of Pay.UK, the leading UK payments authority.
87 CHAPS stands for Clearing House Automated Payment System. The system is currently operated by the Bank of England (since 2017) and is used for high-value payments.
88 *Tidal Energy Ltd v Bank of Scotland Plc* [2013] EWHC 2780 (QB).

misappropriated funds. The court ruled that the defendant bank was not liable for sums paid into an account with the number and sort code provided by the customer, even if the name of the account holder did not match the payee name specified by the customer. This is because, according to normal banking practice, the identity of the beneficiary is irrelevant in processing a funds transfer: all that matters are the account number and sort code.[89]

The possibility to transfer funds electronically online opens up the risk that bank customers may fall victims of fraud. A typical technique used by fraudsters is to telephone their victim pretending to be officers of their bank and ask for the victim's online banking passwords. Having obtained the passwords, the fraudsters then log onto the victim's online banking account and execute a transfer of funds to their own account or to the account of an accomplice. The Payments Services Regulations 2017, discussed in Section 7.7, also apply to the use of online banking to make payments.[90] Therefore, the customer is liable for any loss, if he fails to keep his credentials secure due to gross negligence.[91] As in such cases the customer himself gives out the passwords to the fraudsters, it is arguable that the customer has behaved with gross negligence, especially in view of the fact that banks tend to warn customers regularly against the risk of fraud and explain that on no occasion will bank officers ask for a customer's password.

To the best of our knowledge, there are no decided cases on this matter, and it is hard to predict how a court would interpret gross negligence in this context. One of the reasons for the absence of decided cases is that bank customers who are defrauded in this manner can seek compensation through the Financial Ombudsman Service (FOS), discussed in detail in Chapter 6. Indeed, in a case of the type discussed above, where a bank refused to reimburse its customer for a fraudulent electronic payment of £7,000 on the grounds that the customer behaved grossly negligently by disclosing their personal security features to the fraudsters, the FOS found in favour of the customer.[92] The FOS's rationale was that the fraud was sophisticated, as the fraudsters imitated the security questions asked by the bank's officers, and therefore, the customer was not grossly negligent. This is an example of the function of the FOS as a substitute for private litigation and a vivid illustration of the inclination of the FOS to take a clearly customer-friendly approach.

The position of bank customers in the case of fraudulently elicited, but authorised, electronic payments, known as authorised push payment scams, have been significantly improved since May 2019 due to the adoption of a voluntary Contingent Reimbursement Model Code[93] by large UK banks and building societies. The Code imposes duties on signatories to take steps, educate consumers and provide regular information and warnings. It also recommends that firms reimburse victims of push payment scams unless there are special circumstances, e.g. the customer ignored effective warnings provided by the firm, or

---

89 For a discussion of the case, see Sandra A. Booysen, 'Payment Scams: Tidal Energy v Bank of Scotland and Recent Developments' (2018) 33 *Journal of International Banking and Financial Law* 405.

90 According to reg 2, payment instrument is defined as comprising not only devices such as cards but also any 'personalised set of procedures agreed between the payment service user and the payment service provider, used by the payment service user in order to initiate a payment order'.

91 Payments Services Regulations 2017 Regs 72 and 77 (3).

92 See Financial Ombudsman Service, 'Bank Said Victim of Text Message Scam Was Grossly Negligent and Won't Refund Lost Money' <https://www.financial-ombudsman.org.uk/case-studies/bank-said-victim-text-message-scam-grossly-negligent> (accessed 20 June 2020).

93 Lending Standards Board, 'Contingent Reimbursement Model Code for Authorised Push Payment Scams' (2019) <https://www.lendingstandardsboard.org.uk/wp-content/uploads/2019/05/CRM-code.pdf> (accessed 26 April 2020).

acted without a reasonable basis for believing that the payee was the intended person; that the payment was for genuine goods/services; or that the payee was a legitimate business. These provisions should increase customer protection from scums and incentivise banks to take steps to combat fraud, and are an example of the effectiveness of consumer advocacy and self-regulation prompted by reputational concerns.

7.9 Conclusion

This chapter provided an overview of current accounts, savings accounts and common payment methods such as cheques, debit cards and electronic fund transfers. It highlighted current trends in the use of payment methods and emphasised the respective duties of banks and customers and the apportionment of liability between the parties in the case of fraudulent and other unauthorised transactions. Maintaining customer confidence in the payment systems operated by banks and attributing losses to the party that can bear them more efficiently due to its size and financial strength are policy considerations that favour rendering banks liable for unauthorised transactions. At the same time, the principle that the loss must fall on the party that can do more to prevent it (in order to incentivise prevention) often militates in favour of the customer being liable. The common law balances these considerations by implying a duty on customers to draw cheques with care and a duty to notify their bank of any unauthorised transaction but does not imply a duty to check bank statements. The Payment Services Regulations follow a similar approach in the context of payment cards but impose an upper limit of 13 months for customers to report unauthorised transactions.[94]

Glossary of terms

- Current account: Account held with a bank by an individual or body corporate on the agreement that funds can be drawn without notice at any time; current accounts are used as the main payment mechanism of the account holder: the holder's income is paid into the account and their expenses are paid out of the account.
- Joint account: Account held jointly by two or more persons, natural or legal.
- Savings account: Account that bears interest and is used as a way to gain a return on the account holder's funds; withdrawal may be permitted at any time, by giving notice or may not be permitted for a fixed period of time.
- Combination of accounts: Legal principles that permit a bank to combine two or more accounts held with the bank by the same customer in cases where one of them is in debit but another is in credit; this permits the bank to set off the mutual obligations and hence gain effective priority if the customer is bankrupt or insolvent.
- Cheque: Written and dated order drawn by a customer who holds an account with a bank ordering the bank to pay a specified amount of money to a specified person (payee).
- Negotiable instrument: A written payment order that can be transferred from the original payee to other persons by indorsement and therefore can circulate (e.g. bill of exchange); cheques are not negotiable instruments in the UK anymore.

94 See above n 74 and the accompanying text.

- Account payee only: Written stipulation on a cheque that has the effect that the cheque is only payable into a bank account held by the specified payee and cannot be indorsed (transferred to another person).
- Debit card: Portable card issued by a bank that permits a customer to make payments at commercial outlets (e.g. shops) and online provided that the relevant business is part of the debit card network; payments are taken directly out of the customer's account.
- Cash card: Portable card issued by a bank that permits a customer to make cash withdrawals from ATMs of the same bank and of other banks; usually the same card acts as both debit card and cash card.
- Bankers' Automated Clearing Services (BACS): UK payment system used for low-value payments.
- Clearing House Automated Payment System (CHAPS): UK payment system used for high-value payments.

Practice questions

Cheques are increasingly redundant, and the UK government ought to have abolished them rather than encourage the introduction of electronic image processing. Policy efforts should rather focus on preventing fraud in relation to payment cards and bank transfers. Critically discuss.

You may also find it useful to review the chapter through the following questions:

- What is the legal nature of the current account relationship?
- What is the legal nature of the joint account?
- Explain the core obligations of the parties to the current account relationship.
- In what terms is a savings account different from a current account?
- What is the combination of accounts, and how does it protect the interests of banks in the context of customer insolvency or bankruptcy?
- What is a cheque? Are cheques negotiable instruments in the UK?
- When is a bank entitled to refuse paying a cheque?
- What are the consequences of wrongful payment of a cheque?
- Explain the function of debit cards and the electronic transfer of funds?
- To what extent are customers protected in the case of unauthorised use of their cash card or debit card?

8 Clearing and settlement process

8.1 Introduction: the evolution of the banking payment system

A payment is the transfer of funds from B (payer) to A (payee) which discharges an obligation on the part of the payer B vis-à-vis the payee A. Broadly speaking, payment systems comprise the institutions and technologies facilitating such transfer. A payment system involves one or more persons in the course of business for the purpose of enabling persons to make transfers of funds, and it is designed to facilitate the transfer of funds using another payment system.[1] It is relevant to distinguish between large-value (wholesale) payment systems, processing a small number of high-value and time-critical payments (e.g. CHAPS, Fedwire) and retail payment systems, processing large volumes of low-value payment orders, which are not time-critical (e.g. BACS, SEPA).[2]

Payments are made by transferring funds. For instance, SWIFT (Society for Worldwide Interbank Financial Telecommunication) is a communication network that supplies secure messaging services to the participants through which they can send instructions regarding the transfer of funds.[3] There are two principal settlement models: real-time gross settlement (RTGS) and deferred net settlement (DNS). Most large-value payment systems and some retail payment systems settle obligations directly in central bank money ('bankers' bank'). In this context, systemically important payment systems are an essential mechanism supporting the effectiveness of the financial markets.[4] They are subject to various risks, and if poorly designed, they can also transmit financial shocks and contribute to systemic crises. The banking payment system plays an important role in the process of 'money creation' since the on-demand deposits (current accounts) form the major part of money supply.[5] This characteristic of bank liabilities provides the rationale for several monetary and banking law rules and regulations. Specifically, the process of payment through the banking system involves credit relationships which require the establishment of an adequate degree of trust and availability of information. As discussed in Chapter 7, banking operations involve payments whether there is a credit transfer[6] or debit transfer.[7]

---

1 See Section 41 of the Financial Services (Banking Reform) Act 2013 Chapter 33.
2 Martijn Van Empel, 'Retail Payments in the EU' (2005) 42 *Common Market Law Review* 1426–1427.
3 Herbert F. Lingl, 'Risk Allocation in International Interbank Electronic Fund Transfers: CHIPS and SWIFT' (1981) 22 *Harvard International Law Journal* 621–623.
4 Rosa M. Lastra, 'Systemic Risk, SIFIs and Financial Stability' (2011) 6 *Capital Markets Law Journal* 199–200.
5 In this context, see the recent cases *Singularis Holdings Ltd (in liquidation) v Daiwa Capital Markets Europe Ltd* [2018] 1 WLR 2777 and *Nigeria v JP Morgan Chase Bank NA* [2019] EWHC 347 (Comm).
6 The payer instructs its bank to pay, and the payer's bank responds to debit the payer's account.
7 The payer authorises its bank to pay, but actual payment begins when the payee presents a debit instrument (e.g. cheque) or debit instruction to the payer's bank.

The evolution of payments and the international harmonisation efforts have provided a resilient normative (soft law) framework. The establishment by the Bank for International Settlements (BIS) in 1980 of the G10 Group of Experts on payment systems – to which in 1989 the ad-hoc Committee on Interbank netting systems[8] was added and the formalisation of this work via the establishment in 1990 of the Committee on Payments and Settlement Systems (CPPS), which was then renamed as Committee on Payments and Market Infrastructures in 2014[9] – has resulted into international soft law harmonisation of payment standards that worked rather efficiently during the global financial crisis. It is generally considered that the stability of the payment system has been a driver and a rationale of prudential banking regulation as the very definition of financial stability is in part related to the stability of the payment system (i.e. stability as resilience).[10] The function of money as means of payment and the legal categories that apply in this regard, as well as the differentiation between conduct of business and prudential considerations (with some conduct issues possibly becoming systemic), raise challenges for regulators. Payment arrangements involve record-keeping systems and can be distinguished by identification requirements into (1) account-based systems which are based on the individual owner of the account[11] and (2) token-based systems which are based on an object, real or counterfeit.[12]

The account vs token distinction arises for digital currencies as new technologies create a 'grey area' without a clear definition of both systems. Central banks provide some payments media: high-value payments systems (restricted access) and cash (universal access). However, the question is whether financial innovations such as distributed ledger technology (DLT) and mobile computing have changed the risk and efficiency trade-off in the public provision of centralised and decentralised payments media.[13] New technologies have potentially improved the trade-off regarding the issuance of digital tokens. Further, DLT could be used as a basis for a new system for the settlement of payments across jurisdictions. A consensus mechanism would be designed in a way that reflects the level of trust the respective participants are comfortable with. This new payment system would provide the following direct advantages over correspondence banking: reduction of any single point of failure, higher speed and lower cost of transactions, elimination of counterparty risk, better supervision and auditing of transactions, reduction of physical barriers to transactions and increase in some banks' profitability.[14]

---

8 In the netting system, contracts are converted into an obligation to pay an amount representing their present value.

9 See <https://www.bis.org/cpmi/> (accessed 20 June 2020).

10 Rosa M. Lastra, 'Systemic Risk and Macro-Prudential Supervsion' in Niamh Moloney, Eilís Ferran and Jennifer Payne (eds), *The Oxford Handbook of Financial Regulation* (OUP 2015) 313–314.

11 Account-based systems track individuals: issuer verifies identities, monitors behaviour and handles collateral. Liability usually lies on the issuer/operator and users relinquish some degree of anonymity.

12 Token-based systems track the history of objects: verification of cash is bilateral, issuer cares about the cost of counterfeiting tokens more than the cost of verification of transactions. Tokens are like 'mini-accounts' each segregated from the next.

13 Blockchain algorithms specifically allow transactions, or transfers, to be aggregated into blocks and added to existing chains using public and private key cryptography. For an overview, see Philipp Paech, 'The Governance of Blockchain Financial Networks' (2017) 80 *Modern Law Review* 1077–1078.

14 Priscilla Toffano and Kathy Yuan, 'E-shekels Across Borders: A Distributed Ledger System to Settle Payments between Israel and the West Bank' (2019) LSE Middle East Centre Paper Series, available at <http://eprints.lse.ac.uk/100470/> (accessed 3 July 2020).

In this context, the emerging shadow payment systems (peer-to-peer PayPal, mobile money platforms, such as M-Pesa in Kenya and crypto-currency exchanges, such as Mt Gox) pose concerns for credit institutions even if bank payment systems still dominate and are likely to dominate for the foreseeable future.[15] The main point for regulatory purposes is that since shadow payment systems function outside the regulatory perimeter, Emergency Liquidity Assistance, deposit insurance and special resolution regimes do not apply to them.[16] Dealing with shadow systems involves limitations which arise, on the one hand, from the cross-border geographic dimension and, on the other hand, from the design of the regulatory perimeter, the border between regulated and unregulated activities.[17] For instance, another limitation can be found between cyberspace and the traditional payment system which poses new challenges in the pursuit of financial stability.[18] It is interesting to observe that as innovation develops and expands, traditional regulatory concerns – from consumer/investor protection to prevention and containment of liquidity crises (runs) – become ever more relevant.

This chapter examines the mechanism of clearing and settlement in the context of the payment services system. It considers the relevant EU legislation [e.g. Payment Services Directive (PSD), EMIR (European Market Infrastructure Regulation) and Settlement Finality Directive] and the regulatory development, particularly on the publicly available information, portfolio transactions, definition of credit events and settlement practice. This chapter also discusses how market participants may understand and manage risk exposures on credit derivatives.

8.2 The dematerialisation of securities

In the past large amounts of paper had to be physically transferred as part of the settlement process: a practical problem raised in the context of channelling transactions. An investor's entitlement to specific securities was evidenced by a certificate: a certain number of the securities in question were registered in his/her name (in the case of registered securities) or a certificate to the bearer was issued (in the case of bearer securities). The transfer of securities was achieved by delivery from transferor to transferee of the appropriate certificate. Certificates were deposited with a central securities depository (CSD), holding them to the order, or for the account, of the ultimate investor with no need to be physically moved whenever they were transferred.[19]

To expedite the circulation of securities, certificates have been dematerialised by creating an appropriate entry on a (computer-based) register maintained by a CSD. Securities may

15 Dan Awrey and Kristin van Zwieten, 'The Shadow Payment System' (2018) 43 *Journal of Corporation Law* 796–797.

16 The arguments for dissociating banks from the provision of payments – for example the mutual fund banking proposals advocated by Goodhart in the Evolution of Central Banks and by others – are worth exploring further in a new post-global financial crisis regulatory framework in which the continuity of critical 'banking functions' is seen as an essential element of resolution policies.

17 Gary Gorton and Andrew Metrick, 'Regulating the Shadow Banking System' (2010) *Brookings Papers on Economic Activity* 269–271.

18 Rosa Maria Lastra and Jason Grant Allen, 'Virtual Currencies in the Eurosystem: Challenges Ahead' (July 2018) European Parliament, Monetary Dialogue, available at <http://www.europarl.europa.eu/cms-data/150541/DIW_FINAL%20publication.pdf> (accessed 26 July 2020).

19 Koen Vanderheyden and Tim Reucroft, 'Central Securities Depositories Regulation: The Next Systemic Crisis Waiting to Happen?' (2015) 7 *Journal of Securities Operations & Custody* 242–244.

be registered in the name of a CSD, which in turn records the entitlements of the ultimate investors (or their intermediaries) on computer records maintained by it.[20] CSDs do not want to deal with several small investors: one or more tiers of other intermediaries below a CSD exist each holding for lower-tier intermediaries or for the ultimate investors.[21] Regarding the role of intermediaries, broker-dealers carry out transactions for investors in whose name securities may be registered on behalf of their clients, while custodians provide safe-keeping and administrative services, such as monitoring the receipt of dividends and corporate actions.

In the process of a transfer of securities in a dematerialised system with intermediaries, the intermediary should hold an account recording the transferor as the owner; and an account in the name of the transferee.[22] If the transferee does not have (and does not wish to open) an account with that same intermediary, then the securities will need to be transferred into an account in the name of the transferee's intermediary (which will then record the transferee's entitlement in its own records). This will also entail changes in the records of another intermediary, one or more tiers higher up the chain of intermediaries, which holds accounts for both the transferor's and the transferee's intermediaries (or, in turn, their respective intermediaries).[23]

The payment services system has significantly developed in recent years as a result of major changes in the manner of holding securities.[24] In this context, immobilisation and dematerialisation represent the systems for settling transactions in publicly traded securities.[25] In the settlement of a purchase of privately held securities, the agreed price is to be paid against the transfer of the securities into the name of the purchaser. Dematerialisation of securities, the use of intermediaries to hold securities and closer linkages between securities settlement systems (SSSs) and payment systems are the current mechanisms to settle cross-border transactions.[26] Delivery versus payment (DvP) is an interlinked process involving a change of ownership of securities that occurs synchronically with the process of cash movement.[27] It involves checking whether the seller owns the appropriate securities and whether the buyer has sufficient funds in his settlement account. Settlement is only performed if both parties are granted confirmation.[28] The two main settlement components of a transaction are delivery of securities and delivery of funds. However, the

---

20 CSDs have a direct relationship with the issuer and may also provide clearance/settlement services.

21 Karel Lannoo and Diego Valiante, 'Europe's New Post-Trade Infrastructure Rules' (2012) ECMI Policy Brief No. 20, 5–6, available at <http://aei.pitt.edu/37320/1/ECMI_PB_No_20_Post-Trade_Market_ Infrastructure.pdf> (accessed 21 June 2020).

22 Steven L. Schwarcz and Joanna Benjamin, 'Intermediary Risk in the Indirect Holding System for Securities' (2002) 12(2) *Duke Journal of Comparative and International Law* 310–312.

23 Steven L. Schwarcz, 'Indirectly Held Securities and Intermediary Risk' (2001) 6(2) *Uniform Law Review* 284–286.

24 Richard Dale, 'Risk Management and Public Policy in Payment, Clearing and Settlement Systems' (1998) 1(2) *International Finance* 229–230.

25 David Henry, 'Clarifying and Settling Access to Clearing and Settlement in the EU' (2006) 17(4) *European Business Law Review* 1014–1015.

26 Pablo Iglesias-Rodríguez, 'The Regulation of Cross-Border Clearing and Settlement in the European Union from a Legitimacy Perspective' (2012) 13(3) *European Business Organization Law Review* 442–443.

27 Eddy Wymeersch, *Investor Protection in Europe: Corporate Law Making, the MiFID and Beyond* (OUP 2006) 467–468.

28 Settlement interval or the amount of time that elapses between the trade date (T) and the settlement date which is typically measured relative to the trade date. Settlement finality means that the settlement is irrevocable and unconditional.

question is how do you settle very large numbers of cross-border trades under pressures for quick settlement? Immobilisation and dematerialisation have led to the increasing use of intermediaries to deal with securities on behalf of the ultimate investors. DvP settlement systems seek to eliminate the risk of loss if one party fails to fulfil its obligations to pay or to deliver the securities (credit risk) within the system. DvP minimises this risk by ensuring that payment is made only if the securities are duly transferred and that the securities are transferred only if payment is duly made. However, DvP cannot eliminate all risks: if the seller of the securities does not receive payment when expected, then it may need to obtain funds from other sources (to make up the shortfall), or if the buyer of securities does not receive delivery when expected, he may need to obtain securities from other sources (e.g. by borrowing an equivalent quantity of the securities to meet its own obligations under other contracts).[29]

It is worth noting that a default by one institution may cause difficulties for other institutions, and thus have a 'knock-on' effect that may endanger financial markets much more widely. Because SSSs are so closely linked with, and dependent on, payment systems, regulators fear that a problem in one could have repercussions for another.[30] In this context, the replacement cost risk involves a counterparty that might default before settlement, with the result that the other party may incur a loss. If the seller defaults, and the price of the securities has risen, the buyer will have to pay more to acquire the securities in question. If the buyer defaults, and the price of the securities has fallen, the seller will lose an unrealised gain. Further, custody risk arises from the safekeeping and administration of securities and financial instruments on behalf of others. It refers to a potential loss of securities in the event that the holder of the securities becomes insolvent, acts negligently or commits fraud. Even if there is no ultimate monetary loss, the ability to transfer the securities might be temporarily impaired.

As far as legal risk is concerned, a party may suffer a loss because laws or regulations do not support the rules of the SSS, the performance of related settlement arrangements or the property rights, i.e. if the application of laws and regulations is uncertain (e.g. not knowing whether a contract would be valid and enforced, or which country's law would be applied). In parallel, operational risk encompasses unexpected losses as a result of deficiencies in systems and controls, human error or management failure: it includes errors or delays in processing, system outages, insufficient capacity or fraud by staff. In addition, the settlement bank failure risk involves any bank providing cash accounts to settle payment obligations for CSD members that could disrupt settlement and result in significant losses and liquidity pressures for those members (if a single settlement bank is required).[31] Settlement risk involves a counterparty failure to deliver a security or cash as per agreement when the security was traded after the other counterparty has already delivered the securities or cash. Settlement risk may comprise both credit and liquidity risks. Foreign exchange settlement risk is the greatest source of settlement risk for many market participants, as daily exposures amount to tens of billions of dollars for the largest banks and in some cases the amount at risk to even one counterparty can exceed a bank's capital.

29 Johan Devriese and Janet Mitchell, 'Liquidity Risk in Securities Settlement' (2006) 30(6) *Journal of Banking and Finance* 1807–1808.
30 Marc Vereecken, 'Reducing Systemic Risk in Payment and Securities Settlement Systems' (1998) 6(2) *Journal of Financial Regulation and Compliance* 107–108.
31 Charles M. Kahn, James McAndrews and William Roberds, 'Settlement Risk under Gross and Net Settlement' (2003) 35(4) *Journal of Money, Credit and Banking* 591–592.

8.3 The mechanics of payment services: the clearing houses

In December 2009, the European Council welcomed a paradigm shift in the approach to derivatives markets, namely, moving from the so-called 'light-handed regulation' to a more comprehensive regulatory policy aimed at reducing counterparty and operational risks, increasing transparency in derivatives markets and strengthening market integrity and oversight.[32] This radical change was intended to shift derivatives trading and clearing from predominantly over-the-counter (OTC) bilateral transactions towards centralised trading and clearing infrastructures.[33] A major weakness in the OTC derivative market is that there are relatively few players involved in a large number of trades; hedging can be cyclical with the result that if one counterparty fails there will be a domino effect.[34] According to the new regime, if trades are not centrally cleared, they are subject to a higher capital charge. A facility is available whereby clearing can be offered to non-members of the clearing house through members.[35] These rules have been reflected to changes in the capital requirements framework.

Central counterparty clearing (CCP) has been available for some years through swapclear which is part of LCH (London Clearing House) Clearnet.[36] A key innovation has been the development of a default management process whereby every member must participate in an auction of a defaulting member's portfolio. If there is a default of one clearing member, then positions can be transferred to another clearer. When securities are traded in the capital markets, ownership of the securities needs to pass to the buyer and payment for the securities to the seller, on the terms that they agree. Once a trade has been agreed, it is passed on to a clearing institution for reconciliation and confirmation – clearing – the process during which the identity and quantity of financial instruments, the date and price of the transaction and the identities of the counterparties are confirmed. Clearing services can be provided by a clearing house, a CSD or an international central securities depository (ICSD). The main challenges faced by Centralised Clearing are collateral intensive, relatively complex documentation and operational complexity.[37]

As previously mentioned, settlement is the actual delivery of the securities and the corresponding payment to the counterparties. Securities trades are settled in the books of a settlement system, which can be any of a CSD, an ICSD, or an intermediary. The main aim of clearing and settlement is to ensure the efficiency and safety of the financial markets. CSD is a facility or an institution for holding securities, which enables securities transactions to be

---

32 See Conclusions of the European Council of 2 December 2009 on the need to substantially improve the mitigation of counterparty credit risk and with the importance of improving transparency, efficiency and integrity for derivative transactions.

33 The Financial Services and Markets Act 2000 (regulated activities) order 2001 (SI 2001/544) as amended provides a definition of derivative instrument. At the EU level, Article 4(1)(2) of the MiFID II (Directive No 65 of 2014) regulates the derivatives. For an overview, see Joanne P. Braithwaite, 'OTC Derivatives, the Courts and Regulatory Reform' (2012) 7(4) *Capital Markets Law Journal* 364–365.

34 S.K. Henderson, 'Regulation of Credit Derivatives: To What Effect and for Whose Benefit?' (2009) 11 *Butterworths Journal of International Banking and Financial Law* 147. Credit derivative is defined as 'a financial arrangement the value of which is derived from another financial instrument index or measure of economic value'.

35 Edward Murray, 'Lomas v Firth Rixson: "As You Were!"' (2013) 8(4) *Capital Markets Law Journal* 395–396.

36 Adam W. Glass, 'The Regulatory Drive towards Central Counterparty Clearing of OTC Credit Derivatives and the Necessary Limits on This' (2009) 4(suppl. 1) *Capital Markets Law Journal* S79–S80.

37 Jeremy C. Kress, 'Credit Default Swaps, Clearinghouses, and Systemic Risk: Why Centralized Counterparties Must Have Access to Central Bank Liquidity' (2011) 48(1) *Harvard Journal on Legislation* 50–52.

processed by book entry. An ICSD is a CSD which clears and settles international securities or cross-border transactions in domestic securities (originally ICSDs were set up to settle Eurobond trades).[38] There are two ICSDs in Europe: Clearstream Banking and Euroclear Bank. At the international level, BIS and IOSCO published the 'Principles for Financial Market Infrastructures' which contain the international standards for payment, clearing and settlement systems, including central counterparties.[39] These standards are designed to ensure that the infrastructure supporting global financial markets is more robust and thus well placed to withstand financial shocks. In 2014 the EU legislature introduced the CSD Regulation, a set of common rules to increase safety in the settlement system and open up the market for securities settlement to improve efficiency.[40]

A CCP acts as a central provider of clearing services which interposes itself between the two parties. It also provides multilateral netting and centralised risk management. Contractual rights and obligations are transferred to the CCP by means of novation.[41] In the UK, the institutions wishing to provide CCP services must qualify as 'Recognised Clearing Houses' (RCH) under FSMA 2000 (major RCHs include LCH.Clearnet, Euroclear and others).[42] The Bank of England is responsible for the supervision of RCHs. As it will be discussed in Section 8.6 of this chapter, the EMIR introduced a regulatory framework for CCPs. As any other market participant, the CCP is exposed to a variety of risks. Direct access to CCP clearing is available only to the clearing members, the most creditworthy market participants who meet certain financial and operational requirements. There is a number of safeguards designed to minimise the losses incurred by a CCP as a result of default of its clearing member: article 45 of EMIR provides for margins to be posted by a defaulting clearing member, dedicated CCP own resources and contributions to the default fund by the non-defaulting clearing members.

In the UK, the Bank of England is responsible for oversight of the Recognised Payment Systems. Since 1 April 2015, the new Payment Systems Regulator (PSR), a subsidiary of the FCA, has become a competition-focused, utility-style regulator for retail payments systems in the UK.[43] SSSs established in the UK may be either RCHs or entities regulated under the Uncertificated Securities Regulations 2001 (USRs).[44] Currently only Euroclear which operates the CREST system is regulated under the USRs; the Bank of England is the regulator for the UK-incorporated SSSs.

---

38 Keith Dickinson, 'Securities Depositories (CSDs and ICSDs)' in Keith Dickinson (ed.), *Financial Market Operations Management* (Wiley & Sons 2012) 151–153.
39 Committee on Payment and Settlement Systems BIS/IOSCO, 'Principles for Financial Market Infrastructures' (April 2012), available at <https://www.iosco.org/library/pubdocs/pdf/IOSCOPD377-PFMI.pdf> (accessed 30 June 2020).
40 See EU Regulation No. 909 of 2014 on improving securities settlement in the European Union and on central securities depositories.
41 In the novation process, the bilateral contract is replaced by two opposing contracts with the counterparty. On this discussion, see Emilios Avgouleas and Aggelos Kiayias, 'The Promise of Blockchain Technology for Global Securities and Derivatives Markets: The New Financial Ecosystem and the "Holy Grail" of Systemic Risk Containment' (2019) 20(1) *European Business Organization Law Review* 82.
42 See Part 18 of FSMA 2000 that regulates Recognised Investment Exchanges (RIEs) and Recognised Clearing Houses (RCHs).
43 See Part 5 of the Financial Services (Banking Reform) Act 2013.
44 Uncertificated Securities Regulations 2001, available at <https://www.legislation.gov.uk/uksi/2001/3755/regulation/1/made> (accessed 30 May 2020).

8.4 The EU regulatory framework: the PSD 1 and the PSD 2

The EU legislature introduced common rules for payments with the adoption of the PSD 1 in 2007.[45] The PSD 1 has been implemented into the UK Payment Services Regulations 2009.[46] The PSD established the same set of rules on payments across the whole EEA, covering all types of electronic and non-cash payments such as credit transfers, direct debits, card payments, and mobile and online payments. The Directive laid down provisions on the information that payment services providers have to give to consumers and the rights and obligations linked to the use of payment services. In 2015, the EU legislature adopted the second Directive on Payment Services (PSD 2)[47] to improve the existing rules and take new digital payment services into account. The PSD 2 has been implemented into the UK Payment Services Regulations 2017.[48] PSD 2 includes rules to make it easier and safer to use internet payment services; to better protect consumers against fraud, abuse and payment problems; to promote innovative mobile and internet payment services; to strengthen consumer rights; and to strengthen the role of the European Banking Authority (EBA) in co-ordinating supervisory authorities and drafting technical standards.[49]

PSD 2 requires market-access for the benefit of new players, comprising regulated and unregulated entities. Regulated entities (i.e. authorised and supervised) include payment institutions, i.e. payment service providers other than credit institutions. Unregulated entities are considered payment initiation service providers – persons establishing a software bridge between the respective online banking platforms and initiating the desired transaction, and account information service providers – persons providing the payment service user with aggregated online information on one or more payment accounts held with one or more other payment service providers and accessed via online interfaces. PSD 2 limits the interchange fees for card-based transactions, i.e. consumer debit and credit cards, and bans retailers from imposing surcharges on customers for the use of these types of cards.[50]

Looking at the relevant provisions, article 36 of the PSD 2 regulates the access for payment institutions stating that 'Member States shall ensure that payment institutions have access to credit institutions' payment accounts services on an objective, non-discriminatory and proportionate basis. Such access shall be sufficiently extensive as to allow payment institutions to provide payment services in an unhindered and efficient manner'. The criterion of proportionality promotes greater access to payment institutions and facilitates competition in the distribution of services.[51] Article 66 of the PSD 2 regulates the access for payment

---

45 Directive 2007/64/EC of the European Parliament and of the Council of 13 November 2007 on payment services in the internal market amending Directives 97/7/EC, 2002/65/EC, 2005/60/EC and 2006/48/EC and repealing Directive 97/5/EC.

46 See <http://www.legislation.gov.uk/uksi/2009/209/contents/made> (accessed 6 June 2020).

47 Directive (EU) 2015/2366 of the European Parliament and of the Council of 25 November 2015 on payment services in the internal market, amending Directives 2002/65/EC, 2009/110/EC and 2013/36/EU and Regulation (EU) No. 1093/2010, and repealing Directive 2007/64/EC.

48 See <https://www.legislation.gov.uk/uksi/2017/752/contents/made> (accessed 5 June 2020).

49 Dirk Haubrich, 'The Development of Regulatory Requirements for Payment Services: The European Banking Authority and the Revised Payments Services Directive' (2018) 7 *Journal of Payments Strategy & Systems* 131–132.

50 For an overview, see Reinhard Steennot, 'Reduced Payer's Liability for Unauthorized Payment Transactions under the Second Payment Services Directive (PSD2)' (2018) 34 *Computer Law & Security Review* 954–956.

51 Guido Ferrarini, 'Regulating FinTech: Crowdfunding and Beyond' (2017) 2 *European Economy* 139, available at <http://european-economy.eu/wp-content/uploads/2018/01/EE_2.2017-2.pdf#page=123> (accessed 27 June 2020).

initiation service providers and specific obligations for them; article 67 of the PSD 2 addresses the access for account information service providers and specific obligations of payment information service providers. However, the PSD 2 left unresolved the problem of the enforcement of obligations. The Commission Delegated Regulation (EU) No. 389 of 2018 provides rules on security measures for the application of strong customer authentication in accordance with article 97 of the PSD 2; confidentiality and integrity of the payment service user's personalised security credentials; common and secure standards of communication; general obligations for access interfaces with respect to payment accounts.[52] In this context, the Single Euro Payments Area (SEPA) Instant Credit Transfer Rulebook (version 1.0) of 2018[53] has provided a set of (contractual) inter-bank rules applicable to credit transfers originated by a payer to a payee within SEPA up to a maximum amount of 15,000 euro.[54] The services based on the scheme are available 24 hours a day and on all calendar days of the year, and they target maximum execution time.[55]

8.5 The EU Settlement Finality Directive

Regulators are concerned about systemic risk due to interdependence between SSSs and payment systems and increasing links between different SSSs. This means that the same concerns about the effectiveness of netting, default procedures and the possible impact of other insolvency rules exist in relation to SSSs. The SSS includes contracts between the transferor (seller) and transferee (buyer) of the securities (also a lending transaction or a collateralised transaction); contracts between investors and the intermediaries whose services they use to carry out transactions in securities and who hold securities on the investors' behalf; contracts between the various intermediaries (a tier of two or more intermediaries) and contracts between those intermediaries that are direct participants in a settlement system and the system operator itself.[56] Basic requirements for settlement are the transfer of the entitlement to the securities by the transferor to the transferee and payment of the agreed price by the transferee to the transferor.

The Bank for International Settlements (BIS) has identified three different models of SSSs: (1) securities and funds transfers are both settled simultaneously (on a gross basis), i.e. trade-by-trade; (2) securities transfers are settled on a gross basis during the processing cycle, but funds transfers are settled on a net basis at the end of the processing cycle; (3) securities

---

52 Commission Delegated Regulation (EU) 2018/389 of 27 November 2017 supplementing Directive (EU) 2015/2366 of the European Parliament and of the Council with regard to regulatory technical standards for strong customer authentication and common and secure open standards of communication. The Delegated Regulation applies from 14 September 2019.

53 European Payments Council, '2019 SEPA Credit Transfer rulebook version 1.0' EPC125-05, available at <https://www.europeanpaymentscouncil.eu/sites/default/files/kb/file/2018-11/EPC125-05%202019%20SCT%20Rulebook%20version%201.0.pdf> (accessed 27 July 2020).

54 The rules took effect on 17 November 2019.

55 European Payments Council (n 53) 23. It is stated that 'latest at 10 seconds after the Originator Bank has put the Time Stamp [...] to the SCT Inst Transaction and Instantly sent the SCT Inst Transaction to the Beneficiary Bank, the Originator Bank must have received either the message that the Funds have been Made Available to the Beneficiary by the Beneficiary Bank (positive confirmation message), or the message that the SCT Inst Transaction has been rejected (negative confirmation message with the appropriate reason code)'.

56 D.C. Donald, 'Securities Settlement Systems' in Gerard Caprio (ed.), *Handbook of Key Global Financial Markets, Institutions, and Infrastructure* (Elsevier Science & Technology 2012) 558–559.

and funds transfers are both settled on a net basis at the end of the processing cycle.[57] Despite the differences between the three models, the degree of protection provided against the various risks outlined depends more on the specific risk management safeguards a system utilises than on which model is employed.[58]

At the EU level, payment systems and SSSs are considered side-by-side with regard to settlement finality. The Settlement Finality Directive (as amended) applies to (designated) SSSs and seeks to ensure that in case of default, the default rules of the system take priority over insolvency rules.[59] The Financial Markets and Insolvency (Settlement Finality) Regulations 1999 (Settlement Finality Regulations) implement the EU Settlement Finality Directive in the UK.[60] The Settlement Finality Regulations allow payment and settlement systems to apply for certain protections against the operation of normal insolvency law to ensure that transactions that have been settled in the system are final and irrevocable and to ensure the enforceability of collateral security. The FCA is the relevant authority for systems processing securities transfer orders and the Bank of England for payment transfer orders.

The Directive provides key definitions, i.e. system, system participant, transfer order and insolvency proceedings (article 2). Transfer orders of securities and cash shall be legally enforceable in the event of insolvency if entered into a 'system' (article 3(1)). When a transfer order has been entered into a system (see Part II of the Rules), it is protected from third parties in the event of bankruptcy of one or more participants in the system, to the effect that there is no rule of law that can lead to the unwinding of a netting (article 3(2)). The requisite for this 'super-protection' is that a transfer order has been entered into the system before the opening of insolvency proceedings, or on the same day as such proceedings were opened if the concerned parties can show that they were not aware and ought not to have been aware of these proceedings (article 3(1)). The moment of entry is defined by the rules of the system (article 3(3)) which does not determine any retroactive effect of insolvency proceedings (article 7). A system is a formal arrangement with common rules and standardised arrangements for the execution of transfer orders between the participants (as a general rule, normally three users – i.e. not performing a function), which is governed by the law of a Member State chosen by the participants.[61] System can include both a clearing house and a central counterparty.

The Settlement Finality Directive lays down a general rule about what law should be applied if a participant fails. Article 8 of the Directive states that 'in the event of insolvency proceedings being opened against a participant in a system, the rights and obligations arising from, or in connection with, the participation of that participant shall be determined by the law governing that system'.[62] This provision entails two limitations: it covers only

---

57 BIS Committee on Payment and Settlement Systems, 'Recommendations for Securities Settlement Systems' Report (November 2001), 8–10, available at <https://www.bis.org/cpmi/publ/d46.pdf> (accessed 29 June 2020).

58 Ibid., 2.

59 Directive 98/26/EC of the European Parliament and of the Council of 19 May 1998 on settlement finality in payment and securities settlement systems.

60 The Financial Markets and Insolvency (Settlement Finality) Regulations 1999, available at <https://www.legislation.gov.uk/uksi/1999/2979/made> (accessed 29 May 2020).

61 Pablo Iglesias-Rodríguez, 'The Regulation of Cross-Border Clearing and Settlement in the European Union from a Legitimacy Perspective' (2012) 13 *European Business Organization Law Review* 447–448.

62 See Article 8 of the Directive 98/26/EC.

direct participants in designated systems and applies only in the EU context.[63] The internationalisation of the securities markets involves more than one legal system that will be (potentially) relevant in relation to a given transaction, this creates legal risk in terms of conflicts of law.

The Hague Convention on the Law Applicable to Certain Rights in respect of Securities Held with an Intermediary ('Hague Securities Convention') is an international multilateral treaty intended to remove uncertainties as to the applicable law for cross-border securities held in electronic form with an intermediary.[64] The aim of this Convention is to provide a uniform code to determine which legal system will govern certain aspects of a particular holding of securities and of dealing in those securities. It adopts the PRIMA test ('place of the relevant intermediary approach') that requires parties to choose the applicable law so long as the intermediary has an office in the state concerned which administers securities accounts for customers.[65] The Convention establishes a conflict of law regime which states that the law applicable to holdings of securities is the one named in the account agreement with the relevant intermediary. The Convention does not standardise the substantive law applicable securities held with an intermediary. It specifies the legal issues that are to be governed by whichever legal system is found to apply according to the rules laid down by the Convention.[66] The UK position regarding the Convention is rather sceptical since the improvement of domestic rules and legal certainty are limited.[67]

In this context, the UNIDROIT (International Institute for the Unification of Private Law) Convention on Substantive Rules for Intermediated Securities is intended to complement the Hague Securities Convention.[68] Based on article 8 of the American Uniform Commercial Code (UCC),[69] the Convention aims to provide the basic legal framework for intermediated securities holding systems and reduce risk in cross-border transactions by ensuring systems are compatible and that all participants are operating under the same rules. The convention identifies the rights that arise from crediting securities to a securities account with a settlement system; explains the different methods of transferring securities; explains how to create security interests and other limited proprietary interests in securi-

---

63 Randall Guynn and Margaret Tahyar, 'The Importance of Choice of Law and Finality to Pvp, Netting and Collateral Arrangements' (1996) 4 *Journal of Financial Regulation and Compliance* 170–172.
64 Stephen J. Kozey, 'The Hague Securities Convention: An Opportunity to Take the UCC Global' (2015) 46 *Georgetown Journal of International Law* 1222–1224.
65 Luc Thevenoz, 'Intermediated Securities, Legal Risk, and the International Harmonization of Commercial Law' (2008) 13 *Stanford Journal of Law, Business & Finance* 393–394.
66 Each relationship in the chain will need to be considered separately. See C.S. Bjerre, 'A Transactional Approach to the Hague Securities Convention' (2008) 3 *Capital Markets Law Journal* 110–111.
67 Eva Micheler, 'Intermediated Securities and Legal Certainty' LSE Law, Society and Economy Working Papers 3/2014, 20–21, available at <http://eprints.lse.ac.uk/55826/1/WPS2014-03_Micheler.pdf> (accessed 5 May 2020). See also Jennifer Payne, 'Intermediated Securities and the Right to Vote in the UK' in Louise Gullifer and Jennifer Payne (eds), *Intermediated Securities. Legal Problems and Practical Issues* (Bloomsbury 2010) 212–213.
68 For an overview, see Hideki Kanda, Charles Mooney, Luc Thévenoz, Stéphane Béraud and Thomas Keijser, *Official Commentary on the UNIDROIT Convention on Substantive Rules for Intermediated Securities* (OUP 2012) Chapter III – 'Transfer of Intermediated Securities'.
69 Article 8 of the UCC introduced a new concept of 'property law', a 'security entitlement', describing the package of rights enjoyed by an investor who holds securities through an intermediary. These rights are both personal rights (against the intermediary) and property rights (to a proportionate share of a pool). For an overview, see Austin D. Keyes, 'Revised Article 8 of the Uniform Commercial Code: Investment Securities' (1998) 115 *Banking Law Journal* 346–347. See also Curtis R. Reitz, 'Reflections on the Drafting of the 1994 Revision of Article 8 of the US Uniform Commercial Code' (2005) 10 *Uniform Law Review* 364–366.

ties; clarifies the rules on the irrevocability of instructions to make book entries and the finality of the resulting book entries; establishes priority rules among competing interests in securities; protects a purchaser in good faith from adverse claims; sets out the rights of the account holder and the responsibilities of the intermediary in the event of insolvency; and defines the legal relationship between collateral providers and collateral takers where securities are provided as collateral.[70]

8.6 The EMIR regulation

In September 2009, G20 countries met in Pittsburgh and passed a resolution stating, 'all OTC derivative contracts should be traded on exchanges or electronic trading platforms, where appropriate, and cleared through central counterparties by end-2012 at the latest. OTC derivative contracts should be reported to trade repositories. Non-centrally cleared contracts should be subject to higher capital requirements'.[71] The European Parliament and the Council delivered the G20 commitments by adopting Regulation No. 648/2012 of 4 July 2012 on OTC derivatives, central counterparties and trade repositories ('EMIR').[72] The Regulation ensures that information on all European derivative transactions is reported to trade repositories and accessible to supervisory authorities. EMIR provided new requirements to improve transparency and to reduce the risks associated with the derivatives market. Further, EMIR establishes common organisational, conduct of business and prudential standards for CCPs and trade repositories. In substance, EMIR introduced a central clearing requirement for all standardised OTC derivatives, and risk mitigation requirements for non-centrally cleared derivatives; trade reporting obligations; and authorisation and supervision of CCPs and Trade Repositories. The new Regulation requires entities that enter into any form of derivative contract, including interest rate, foreign exchange, equity, credit and commodity derivatives to (1) report every derivative contract that they enter to a trade repository; (2) implement new risk management standards, including operational processes and margining, for all bilateral OTC derivatives, i.e. trades that are not cleared by a CCP; and (3) clear, via a CCP, those OTC derivatives subject to the mandatory clearing obligation.[73]

EMIR applies to any entity established in the EU that has entered into (is a legal counterparty to) a derivative contract and applies indirectly to non-EU counterparties trading with EU parties. EMIR identifies two main categories of counterparty to a derivatives contract: financial counterparties – which include banks, insurers, investment firms, fund managers, spread betting firms and pension schemes – and non-financial counterparties – which covers any counterparty that is not classified as a financial counterparty, including entities not involved in financial services. EMIR imposes requirements on all types and sizes of entities that enter into any form of derivative contract, including those not involved in financial

---

70 Philippe Dupont, 'Rights of the Account Holder Relating to Securities Credited to Its Securities Account' in Pierre-Henri Conac, Ulrich Segna and Luc Thévenoz (eds), *Intermediated Securities. The Impact of the Geneva Securities Convention and the Future European Legislation* (CUP 2013) 92–94.

71 See G20 Leaders Statement: The Pittsburgh Summit, Pittsburgh (24–25 September 2009), available at <http://www.g20.utoronto.ca/2009/2009communique0925.html> (accessed 29 June 2020).

72 Regulation (EU) No. 648/2012 of the European Parliament and of the Council of 4 July 2012 on OTC derivatives, central counterparties and trade repositories.

73 Dan Awrey, 'Complexity, Innovation, and the Regulation of Modern Financial Markets' (2012) 2 *Harvard Business Law Review* 267–268.

services. EMIR requires all counterparties with outstanding derivative contracts to report details of those contracts and any new contracts they enter into an authorised trade repository ('Reporting' requirements).[74]

In terms of risk management, European Securities and Markets Authority (ESMA) can require counterparties to clear OTC derivative contracts of a particular type once a CCP has been authorised under EMIR for that type of contract. For contracts that are not cleared, all counterparties are required to comply with operational risk management requirements. For financial counterparties, contracts not cleared through a CCP will also be subject to bilateral collateral requirements. Non-financial counterparties are only subject to clearing and bilateral collateral requirements if their OTC derivatives positions are large enough and are not directly reducing commercial risks or related to treasury financing activity.[75]

In May 2013, the EU Commission published a statement on the implementation of EMIR for non-EU CCPs.[76] A CCP established outside the EU may provide clearing services to EU clearing members where it has been recognised by the ESMA (article 25 of EMIR). The main conditions for the recognition of a non-EU CCP by ESMA are the EU Commission has adopted a positive equivalence decision with regard to the regulatory framework applicable to CCPs in the CCP's home country; the CCP is authorised and subject to effective supervision and enforcement in its home country; the CCP is established or authorised in a third country that is considered as having equivalent systems for anti-money laundering and combating the financing of terrorism to those of the Union; co-operation arrangements have been established between ESMA and the domestic supervisory authorities. Chapter 17 will examine how Brexit may affect the ability of UK CCPs to continue providing clearing services to EU-based clearing members.

8.7 Online banking and digital payment systems

The payment system has been reshaped by technological innovations: central bank virtual currencies and digital coin (e.g. Bitcoin) constitute a radical change to money as a means of payment. Financial innovations have also reshaped the mechanics of cheques, credit transfers, direct debits, card payments and, in terms of wholesale payments, the inter-bank transfers. This means a rapid increase of alternative forms of cash in the monetary system (e.g. digital token technology).[77] As will be discussed in Chapter 13, Fintech can facilitate reserve banking, transactions and monitor holdings: there is no need to reduce bank credit supply, banks can fund by 'pledging' loans onto the ledger, this creates an elastic supply of money for payment.[78] Potentially, Person-to-Person (P2P) lending could remove the need for deposit insurance on bank savings accounts. Retail savers could get access to low-risk fixed income savings products, through direct exposure, but it would require technology-supported transparency of underlying exposures.

---

74 Patrick Brandt, 'EMIR Regulations Continue to Impact Derivatives Markets in 2014' (2014) 131 *Banking Law Journal* 270–271.
75 Guido Ferrarini and Paolo Saguato, 'Reforming Securities and Derivatives Trading in the EU: From EMIR to MiFIR' (2013) 13 *Journal of Corporate Law Studies* 330–333.
76 EU Commission, 'Practical Implementation of the EMIR Framework to Non-EU Central Counterparties (CCPs)' (13 May 2013).
77 Agustín Carstens, 'The Future of Money and Payments' SUERF Policy Note, Issue No. 66 (April 2019) 5–6, available at <www.suerf.org/policynotes> (accessed 25 June 2020).
78 Alistair Milne, 'Fintech and RegTech as Tools for Financial Stability' Presentation at the Rebuilding Macroeconomics Finance Hub 2nd Workshop, London (24 January 2019).

In this context, the TARGET Instant Payment Settlement (TIPS) was launched, as a new component of the Eurosystem's TARGET Services.[79] In launching TIPS, the Eurosystem is acknowledging the changing reality that digitalisation is erasing the borders between whole-sale and retail payments. TIPS enables payment service providers to allow their customers to transfer funds across Europe timely and swiftly.[80] As pointed out, 'there is a growing gap between the transaction capabilities we need and expect in the digital economy – fast, convenient, and accessible to all – and the underlying settlement capabilities. Consumers and businesses increasingly expect to complete transactions with a simple keystroke, swipe, or tap'.[81] The legal bases of the TIPS are article 127 (2) of the TFEU (ECB and NCB promote 'smooth operation of payment systems') and Guideline (EU) No. 1626 of 2018.[82] TIPS has been developed by the ECB as an extension of TARGET2 in order to settle payments be-tween participants in central bank money.[83] It is based on the SEPA Instant Credit Transfer (24/7/365 clearing and settlement); participants need to fulfil the same eligibility criteria as for participation in TARGET2. Participants open TIPS-dedicated cash accounts with their respective central bank, from which instant payments can be settled (TIPS requires all payments to be pre-funded). It is only possible to add funds to these accounts during TARGET2 opening hours.[84]

The European Retail Payments Board has defined instant payments as 'electronic re-tail payment solutions available 24/7/365 and resulting in the immediate or close-to-immediate interbank clearing of the transaction and crediting of the payee's account with confirmation to the payer(within seconds of payment initiation'.[85] However, this system raises the following technical problems: (1) so far, payment systems were not set up to work in a 24/7, real-time world; instead, most payment systems settled funds between banks on a deferred basis; (2) instant payments processing means end of batch-oriented and cyclical processing; and (3) the challenge of secure integration of mobile/web applications via in-terfaces provided by payment service provides, including banks.

In terms of digitisation, the recent project 'Libra', a cryptoasset-based payment system launched by Facebook, has raised concerns among policymakers and stakeholders because

---

79 The Trans-European Automated Real-time Gross Settlement Express Transfer (TARGET) system constitutes the RTGS system for the euro. See European Central Bank, 'Overview of TARGET' (July 2005), available at <https://www.ecb.europa.eu/paym/pdf/target/current/targetoverview.pdf> (accessed 26 May 2020). The TARGET services are TARGET2 owned and operated by the Eurosystem for settling Europayments and EU monetary policy operations, TARGET2-Securities (T2S), the Eurosystem service for securities settlement in central bank money. Recently, the Eurosystem has issued a project to replace TARGET2 with a new RTGS system, a consolidated platform that should be launched in November 2021.

80 Yves Mersch, 'ECB Executive Board' (Speech at the TIPS launch event, Frascati, Rome, 30 November 2018) avail-able at <https://central-banks.economicblogs.org/ecb/2018/bank-yves-mersch-tips-future-retail-payment-solutions-europe> (accessed 26 July 2020).

81 Lael Brainard, 'Supporting Fast Payments for All' Federal Reserve Board (3 October 2018) available at <https://www.federalreserve.gov/newsevents/speech/brainard20181003a.htm> (accessed 25 April 2020).

82 Guideline (EU) 2018/1626 of the European Central Bank of 3 August 2018 amending Guideline ECB/2012/27 on a Trans-European Automated Real-Time Gross Settlement Express Transfer system (TAR-GET2) (ECB/2018/20).

83 Active since 30 November 2018.

84 For an overview, see Iris Chiu, 'A New Era in FinTech Payment Innovations? A Perspective from the Institu-tions and Regulation of Payment Systems' (2017) 9 *Law, Innovation and Technology* 211–212.

85 European Retail Payments Board, statement following the second meeting of the ERPB held on 1 December 2014 (ERPB/2014/018).

of the risk of altering the market of virtual currencies.[86] Libra will rely on a platform of 2.5 billion Facebook users and aims to have reserve backing and regulatory approval (principally to avoid systemic threats, e.g. speculative actions, privacy and money laundering issues).[87] It has possibly the greatest potential in financial inclusion terms of any current technological development, and hence it has huge significance in the financial inclusion debate. Libra will be supported by giant companies such as Visa, Mastercard, PayPal, eBay, Vodafone, Spotify and Uber, demonstrating the high credentials of this digital coin as a means of exchange.[88]

Despite all the criticism of Libra, it has the capacity to bring hundreds of millions of people into a better place on payments, particularly in relation to remittances although it can create a cartel in the monetary system due to the currency distribution network organised by the Libra Association.[89] Rival to Bitcoin, Libra is likely to become a global cryptocurrency and a strong competitor to dollar in the international legal framework of the monetary system. It has been argued that Libra will challenge the existing fiat money system through a decentralised, programmable blockchain technology[90] which will circulate as a 'crypto stablecoin' and 'smart contract platform'.[91] However, national jurisdictions will need to determine how, if at all, dealings with a Libra token effect change in property rights to the underlying financial assets.[92] Libra will operate outside the central banks arena bringing an innovative mechanism of lending and free money transfers that would certainly be a new frontier for cross-border payment systems.

8.8 Conclusion

The growth in prudential regulation has been closely linked to the role of banks as primary payment system providers. Digital payments infrastructure and open electronic payments systems have expanded the quality and range of services. Specifically, the digitisation of payments and provision of services have promoted a framework for inclusive financial transformation.[93] The recent years have seen an explosion of new financial technologies around the world, supporting the establishment of internet banks, the crowdfunding of both consumer lending and small business equity and debt, a range of innovative online and mobile-based payments and far-reaching change in business processes across the banking, insurance, investment advice and other financial services.

---

86 Gillian Tett, 'Facebook's "Stablecoin" Libra Raises Questions for Regulators' *Financial Times* (13 June 2019).

87 Dirk A. Zetzsche, Ross P. Buckley and Douglas W. Arner, 'Regulating LIBRA: The Transformative Potential of Facebook's Cryptocurrency and Possible Regulatory Responses' (August 2019) available at <https://papers.ssrn.com/sol3/papers.cfm?abstract_id=3414401> (accessed 24 July 2020).

88 Hannah Murphy, 'Facebook Unveils Global Digital Coin Called Libra' *Financial Times* (18 June 2019); see also Laura Noonan, 'Fintechs Face Libra Challenge' *Financial Times* (24 June 2019).

89 Yves Mersch, 'Money and Private Currencies: Reflections on Libra' (Speech at the ESCB Legal Conference, Frankfurt am Main, 2 September 2019) available at <https://www.bis.org/review/r190902a.pdf> (accessed 5 June 2020).

90 Libra Association Members, 'The Libra Blockchain' (July 2019) available at <https://developers.libra.org/docs/the-libra-blockchain-paper.Blockchain> (accessed 22 July 2020).

91 Libra Association Members, 'An Introduction to Libra' (July 2019) White Paper, available at <https://libra.org/en-US/wp-content/uploads/sites/23/2019/06/LibraWhitePaper_en_US.pdf> (accessed 23 March 2020).

92 Jason G. Allen and Rosa M. Lastra, 'Towards a European Governance Framework for Cryptoassets' (August 2019), SUERF Policy Note, available at <www.suerf.org/policynotes> (accessed 26 April 2020).

93 Dirk A. Zetzsche, 'Fintech, Financial Inclusion and Sustainable Investment' Presentation delivered at LSE Conference on Technology in Finance, Law and Regulation, London (16 May 2019).

Decentralised technologies such as 'blockchain' allow households and businesses to cheaply and conveniently exchange payments, provide loans and pool risks without the need for financial intermediaries at all. Where new services have become widely used, e.g. Paypal for online payments, this rests on a 'piggybacking' on existing financial services infrastructure. The sharp development of online credit in China (AliPay, Weipay) suggests that new technologies can reach previously underserved customer groups on a large scale. Payments technologies are closely linked to the broader impact of technology on industry and public services and to wider issues of identity and data infrastructure, for example, combat of fraud and financial crime.

Another interesting aspect is the willingness of consumers to adopt novel technologies for consumer financial services, whether in payments, savings products, insurance, household lending or other markets. A case in point is the first stage of implementation in June 2020 as required by the UK Competition and Markets Authority, of 'Open Banking' requiring the largest UK banks to offer standardised technical interfaces ('application programming interfaces' or APIs), allowing customers to securely share data with third parties competing in the provision of payments and other current account services.[94] This should be an effective competition remedy, substantially lowering barriers to entry in the market for personal current account and payments services, but its effectiveness depends critically on customer attitudes. Although financial technologies have revolutionised the banking payment system, the question is whether digital technologies can promote greater use of cryptocurrencies as a means of exchange expediting customer's purchases and cash payments. Technological change in bank delivery channels, e.g. through ATM, telephone or online banking (or on the network economics of card payments), and mobile payments technologies in emerging markets – mostly relating to the successful M-Pesa network in Kenya – raise concerns for legislators since the current regulatory framework seems incapable of addressing the spread of alternatives to traditional payment systems, such as shadow platforms.

Glossary of terms

- Derivative: A contract between two or more parties whose value is based on an agreed-upon underlying financial asset (like a security) or set of assets (like an index). Common underlying instruments include bonds, commodities, currencies, interest rates, market indexes and stocks.
- OTC Derivative: Derivatives can trade over-the-counter (OTC) or on an exchange. OTC derivatives constitute a greater proportion of the derivatives market. OTC-traded derivatives generally have a greater possibility of counterparty risk. Counterparty risk is the danger that one of the parties involved in the transaction might default. These parties trade between two private parties and are unregulated.
- Payment: The transfer of funds from B (payer) to A (payee) which discharges an obligation on the part of the payer B vis-à-vis the payee A.
- Payment system: System that involves one or more persons in the course of business for the purpose of enabling persons to make transfers of funds and is designed to facilitate the transfer of funds using another payment system.

---

94 See 'OBIE Publishes Version 3.1.6. of the Open Banking Standard' available at <https://www.openbanking. org.uk/about-us/latest-news/obie-publishes-version-3-1-6-of-the-open-banking-standard/>. See also Competition and Markets Authority, 'Retail Banking Market Investigation' Final Report (9 August 2016) available at <https://assets.publishing.service.gov.uk/media/57ac9667e5274a0f6c00007a/retail-banking-market-investigation-full-final-report.pdf> (accessed 30 March 2020).

- Large-value (wholesale) payment systems: Processing small numbers of high-value and time-critical payments (e.g. CHAPS, Fedwire).
- Retail payment systems: Processing large volumes of low-value payment orders which are not time-critical (e.g. BACS, SEPA).
- SWIFT (Society for Worldwide Interbank Financial Telecommunication): Communication network that supplies secure messaging services to participants through which they can send instructions regarding the transfer of funds.
- Payment account-based systems: Conventional systems that are based on the individual owner of the account.
- Token-based systems: Systems based on the object (token), real or counterfeit.
- Delivery versus payment (DvP): Interlinked process involving a change of ownership of securities that occurs synchronically with the process of cash movement.
- Clearing: The process during which the identity and quantity of financial instruments, the date and price of the transaction and the identities of the counterparties are confirmed.
- Settlement: The transfer of the entitlement to securities by the transferor to the transferee and payment of the agreed price by the transferee to the transferor.
- TARGET Instant Payment Settlement (TIPS): System that enables payment service providers to allow their customers to transfer funds across Europe timely and swiftly.

Practice questions

SSSs have developed significantly in recent years as a result of major changes in the manner of holding securities. The close linkages between SSSs and payment systems have further evolved into digital technologies and virtual platforms of trading. Critically discuss.

You may also find it useful to review the chapter through the following questions:

- What are the main elements of the EU clearing and settlement regulatory framework?
- What are the strengths and risks of the EMIR reform?
- What is the role of Centralised Securities Depositaries and Clearing Houses?
- What are the main aims of Payment Services Directive 2?
- What are the main objectives of the Hague Securities Convention?
- What are the main features of online banking and digital payment systems?

9 Business and consumer lending

9.1 Introduction

This chapter examines the role of banks in providing finance via lending. It explains the fundamental distinction between supplying credit in the form of an overdraft and in the form of a term loan. The chapter begins with some general legal principles that apply to all types of lending including the legal nature of overdrafts and term loans, security interests and the transfer of loans. After that, it focuses on business lending and examines common contract terms in credit facilities and loan syndication. Then the discussion focuses on consumer lending and covers the regulation of overdrafts, credit cards, personal loans and residential mortgages.

This chapter will not examine capital market-based techniques of corporate finance, such as the issuing of bonds and will only provide a brief overview of the concept of security rather than a detailed examination of the various types of security in English law. This is in line with the scope of this book which limits itself on core banking law and does not seek to cover capital markets law, corporate finance and commercial property law.

9.2 Bank lending in general

9.2.1 Overdrafts: legal nature and principal terms

As mentioned in Chapter 7, a current account is overdrawn when its balance is negative, and the customer owes a debt to the bank rather than the other way around. If there is express agreement between the bank and customer that she/he is entitled to overdraw his account up to a maximum amount, this is called an authorised overdraft. According to the agreement between the bank and its customer, interest may or may not be charged. If there is no such agreement, and the customer draws a cheque or attempts to make a payment in another way that, if honoured, would lead to a negative account balance, and the bank honours the cheque or completes the payment, this can be described as an unauthorised overdraft. When an unauthorised overdraft occurs, banks' standard terms and conditions typically impose certain charges and a (relatively high) rate of interest applicable to the account balance. As succinctly put by Wall J:

> If a current account is opened by a customer with a bank with no express agreement as to what the overdraft facility should be, then, in circumstances where the customer daws a cheque on the account which causes the account to go into overdraft, the customer, by necessary implication, requests the bank to grant the customer an overdraft

of the necessary amount, on its usual terms as to interest and other charges. In deciding to honour the cheque the bank, by implication, accepts the offer.[1]

This analysis explains how the contractual relationship of an unauthorised overdraft facility comes into existence: by implication, the drawing of the cheque constitutes the offer made by the customer, while the honouring of the cheque constitutes the acceptance by the bank. It is worth noting that it is common for UK banks to charge compound interest, which means that interest is charged not only on the original amount borrowed but also on accumulated unpaid interest from previous periods.[2] Typically, interest accrues daily and is applied to the borrower's current account in arrears on a quarterly basis.

Unless there is explicit agreement to the contrary,[3] an overdraft is repayable on demand by giving notice to the customer. However, until such notice has been given the bank is bound to honour any cheques drawn within the limit of the overdraft.[4] A crucial matter is the length of the notice period given by the bank. As the bank is entitled to be paid immediately, English law does not require banks to provide sufficient time for customers to raise the relevant funds. Before treating the debtor as in default, the bank needs only allow the time necessary to give the debtor 'a reasonable opportunity of implementing whatever reasonable mechanics of payment he may need to employ to discharge the debt'.[5] For instance, the court upheld the appointment of a receiver by a bank only one hour after demand was made on a company to repay all monies due to the bank under an overdraft facility. In *Sheppard & Cooper Ltd v TSB Bank Plc*,[6] the court ruled that the bank was entitled to appoint a receiver within 30 minutes from demanding repayment. Balckburne J provided additional *obiter* guidance on the application of the mechanics of payment test emphasising that the length of time that needs to lapse after demand before a debtor can be deemed to be in default is a practical question. Relevant factors include whether the debtor could reasonably be expected to hold the necessary amount in a bank account and whether the demand is made during normal banking hours or not.

9.2.2 Term loans

A term loan is a loan made for a fixed period of time. Unless the debtor defaults, the bank is not entitled to demand early repayment. It is common for term loans to be repaid gradually by monthly instalments. There is a huge variety of term loans depending on the nature of the borrower and the purpose of the loan. A crucial distinction is between loans to businesses (discussed in Section 9.3.1) and loans to individuals (discussed in Section 9.4.3). Loans can be either unsecured or secured (security will be discussed in Section 9.2.3,

---

1 *Lloyd's Bank Plc v Voller* [2000] 2 All ER (Comm) 978, 982.

2 The practice has been upheld by the courts and has been characterised as 'a usual and perfectly legitimate mode of dealing' (per Lord Atkinson in *Yourell v Hibernian Bank Ltd* [1918] AC 372, 385). It was also hailed as ordinary usage by the House of Lords in *National Bank of Greece (SA) v Pinios Shipping Co Ltd (No. 1)* [1990] 1 AC 637.

3 A case in point is *Titford Property v Cannon Street Acceptances Ltd* (Unreported, QBD, 22 May 1975). The bank, in a letter to the customer, had specified that it made available an overdraft of £248,000 for a period of 12 months for the customer to purchase and develop a property. It was held that the bank could not demand early repayment.

4 *Rouse v Barford Banking* [1894] AC 586, 596.

5 *Bank of Baroda v Panessar* [1987] CH 335, 348.

6 [1996] BCC 965. See also *Lloyd's Bank Plc v Lampert* [1999] BCC 507.

while residential mortgages, the most common type of secured loans for consumers, will be discussed in Section 9.4.4). Business loans can be either bilateral or syndicated (discussed in Section 9.3.2). The duration of term loans varies dramatically from months to several decades. In commercial parlance, loans for a term up to one year are typically described as short-term loans; loans for a term between one and ten years are medium-term loans and loans for a term exceeding ten years are long-term loans.

Term loans carry interest at a rate agreed between the bank and customer. In practice, banks' standardised terms specify the rates of interest for different types of loans and borrowers, so that the potential borrower has no option but to accept the rate offered. However, there may be alternative loan products whereby interest is calculated differently for the borrower to choose from. Interest rate can be fixed for the whole duration of the loan, variable or tracking a given base rate, such as the Bank of England base rate.[7] A variable rate is set unilaterally by the bank. As this is a case of exercising discretion under a contract, the bank is under a duty not to act in an arbitrary, irrational or capricious manner.[8] The duty entails following a proper decision-making process and precludes reaching an outcome that no reasonable person could reach. Apart from interest, a loan may carry an initial fee and various charges. It is usual for loan contracts to provide for a higher rate of interest to apply while the borrower is in default, known as default interest. As English law does not enforce penalty clauses, a question arises whether charging default interest constitutes a penalty. It is now established that, although charging a higher rate of interest after default retrospectively for the whole duration of the loan is an unenforceable penalty, doing so prospectively from the time of default and at a modest rate is not in the nature of penalty and can be fully enforced.[9]

In general, banks do not have to provide advice to customers on whether a loan is advantageous to them neither on whether the project that the customer seeks to finance with the loan is commercially sound: 'no duty in law arises upon the bank either to consider the prudence of the lending from the customer's point of view, or to advise with reference to it'.[10] Therefore, borrowers cannot successfully challenge the legality of loans and banks' rights of repayment on such grounds. However, if a bank actively engages with the merit of the business project to be financed, it undertakes a duty of care, under the principle of assumption of responsibility, and may be found to be liable in negligence.[11] The level of financial experience of the borrower is an important element that courts take into account in such cases.[12]

---

7 This is the interest rate that the Bank of England pays to commercial banks on the monies they hold with the Bank. It is set by the Bank's Monetary Policy Committee in view of maintaining the Bank's target inflation rate of 2%. At the time of writing, the Bank rate stood at 0.75%. See Bank of England, 'Interest rates and Bank Rate' <https://www.bankofengland.co.uk/monetary-policy/the-interest-rate-bank-rate> (accessed 16 May 2020).

8 *Braganza v BP Shipping* [2015] 1 WLR 1661.

9 See *Lordsvale Finance Plc v Bank of Zambia* [1996] 3 All ER 156 where the agreement provided for an increase in the rate of interest by 1%, while the debtor was in default. Ruling that the default interest was enforceable, Colman J observed that 'Given that money is more expensive for a less good credit risk than for a good credit risk, there would in principle seem to be no reason to deduce that a small rateable increase in interest charged prospectively upon default would have the dominant purpose of deterring default'. Ibid., 166.

10 *Williams & Glyns Bank Ltd v Barnes* [1981] Com LR 205, 207 per Gibson J.

11 In *Verity and Spindler v Lloyds Bank Plc* [1995] CLC 1557, a teacher and acupuncturist, who borrowed a sum to renovate a property and resell it, claimed successfully that Lloyds was liable in negligence because a branch manager visited potential investment properties and recommended the one to be purchased.

12 In *Woods v Martins Bank* [1959] 1 QB 55, the bank was found to owe a duty of care to the customer who was young and with little business experience, whereas in Barnes (above n 8), the customer was an experienced businessman.

9.2.3 *A brief overview of security interests in English law*

Security refers to the acquisition of a proprietary right by the creditor on property owned by the debtor (collateral), in addition to the personal claim the creditor has against the debtor, which normally gives the creditor the right to sell the collateral and use the proceeds in satisfaction of the debt in priority to the claims of the debtor's ordinary unsecured creditors. As Brown-Wilkinson VC eloquently put it:

> Security is created where a person (the creditor) to whom an obligation is owed by another (the debtor) by statute or contract, in addition to the personal promise of the debtor to discharge the obligation, obtains rights exercisable against some property in which the debtor has an interest in order to enforce the discharge of the debtor's obligation to the creditor.[13]

The main types of security interests in English law are the following: pledges, liens, mortgages and charges. From the perspective of banking, mortgages and charges are the security interests with the greatest practical significance, as they are both types of non-possessory security whereby the debtor retains possession of the collateral. A legal mortgage is effectively the transfer of the legal tile (ownership) to land or movable property from a debtor (mortgagor) to a creditor (mortgagee) under the agreement that the title will revert back to the mortgagor upon repayment of the debt and that in the meantime the mortgagor retains possession. At common law, in case of debtor's default, the mortgagor has rights to sell the property; appoint a receiver; take possession and a limited right to make the property his own, known as foreclosure. If the transfer of title is not effective in law but is recognised by equity, the mortgage will be an equitable mortgage. If the title of the mortgagor to the property is only an equitable title, this can only be transferred in equity and thus only an equitable mortgage is possible.[14]

A charge is an equitable interest created by the debtor (chargor) for the benefit of the creditor (chargee) which does not entail transfer of title or possession but merely that the charged property is appropriated to the discharge of a debt. If the chargor defaults, the chargee can apply to the court and seek an order to sell the property or appoint a receiver. Therefore, the distinguishing characteristic of a charge is:

> an intention that property, existing or future, shall be made available as security for the payment of a debt, and that the creditor shall have a present right to have it made available, there is a charge, even though the present legal right which is contemplated can only be enforced at some future date, and though the creditor gets no legal right of property, either absolute or special, or any legal right to possession, but only gets a right to have the security made available by an order of the Court.[15]

> Such a charge is created by an appropriation of specific property to the discharge of some debt or other obligation without there being any change in ownership either at law or in equity, and it confers on the chargee rights to apply to the court for an order for sale or for the appointment of a receiver, but no right to foreclosure (so as to make the property his own) or take possession.[16]

---

13 *Bristol Airport v Powdrill* [1990] Ch 744, 760.
14 For a detailed discussion, see Eilís Ferran and Look Chan Ho, *Principles of Corporate Finance Law* (2nd edn, OUP 2014) 315–316.
15 *National Provincial and Union Bank of England v Charnley* [1924] 1 KB 431, 449–450.
16 *Carreras Rothmans Ltd v Freeman Matthews Treasure Ltd (in liq.)* [1985] 1 All ER 155, 169.

Apart from a specific charge that applies to definite property, bodies corporate can also create what is known as a floating charge. Unlike fixed charges whereby the chargor cannot sell or charge the subject matter of the charge without the chargee's consent, floating charges attach to a shifting class of assets that changes from time to time, and the chargor is permitted to deal with them (e.g. sell them) in the ordinary course of business.[17] It is common for companies to create floating charges covering all their assets. Upon the occurrence of a specified event such as default on the loan or winding up of the debtor company, the floating charge crystallises and becomes akin to a fixed charge on the assets that belong to the relevant class at the time of crystallisation. For purposes of statutory priority rules among creditors in liquidation, crystallisation does not matter.[18] A floating charge remains subject to liquidation expenses and claims of preferential creditors, if there are no sufficient other assets for their satisfaction.[19] Moreover, to the extent that it encompasses substantially the whole of the assets, a floating charge is subject to the prescribed part of assets that is made available to unsecured creditors.[20]

Due to the weaker protection afforded by floating charges to creditors, bank had adopted a practice of creating charges on companies' book debts (i.e. receivables, monies owed to businesses by their customers) that purported to be fixed, while they required companies to pay the proceeds of the book debts into a specified account held with the bank and permitted them to draw freely on that account. The ability to draw on the account that contains the proceeds of the book debts is commercially inevitable, as most companies need to be able to do so to cope with business expenses. Originally, the courts upheld such charges as fixed charges.[21] However, in 2005 the decision of the House of Lords in *National Westminster Bank Plc v Spectrum Plus Ltd*[22] made it clear that for such charges to be fixed the proceeds of the book debts must be paid into a blocked account; if not, they will be floating irrespective of the intention of the parties.

With respect to land, the Law of Property Act 1925 abolished the common law legal mortgage and created two statutory types of legal mortgage of land: (i) by demise for a term of years absolute, subject to a provision for *cesser* on redemption, and (ii) by a charge by deed expressed to be by way of legal mortgage.[23] The second type, known as the charge by way of legal mortgage, is currently the most commonly used type of security over land. As its name suggests, it is truly a legal charge as it does not involve conveyance (transfer of title) of land. If the mortgagor defaults, the mortgagee has statutory powers to sell the property by public auction or by private contract, and appoint a receiver of the income of the mortgaged property.[24] The power to sell the land can only be exercised if the mortgagor has been served notice to pay the mortgage money and has failed to do so in three months, or if interest is unpaid for two months after, it is due or if the mortgagor has breached some non-financial provision contained in the mortgage deed or some provision of the Act.[25]

---

17 *Re Yorkshire Woolcombers Association* [1904] AC 355.

18 Insolvency Act 1986 s 251 defines a floating charge as a charge that was created as a floating charge.

19 Insolvency Act 1986 s 176ZA (1) for liquidation expenses; and s 175 (2) (b) for preferential debts.

20 Insolvency Act 1986 s 176A. The amount of the prescribed part is set by the Insolvency Act 1986 (Prescribed Part) Order 2003 (SI 2003/2097).

21 *Siebe Gorman & Co Ltd v Barclays Bank* [1979] 2 Lloyd's Rep 142.

22 [2005] 2 AC 680.

23 Law of Property Act 1925 s 85 for freeholds (fee simple estates); and s 86 for leaseholds (terms of years absolute).

24 Law of Property Act 1925 s 101 (1).

25 Law of Property Act 1925 s 103.

The mortgagee must sell fairly and take reasonable steps to obtain a proper price.[26] The proceeds of the sale shall be held by the mortgagee in trust to be applied 'first, in payment of all costs, charges, and expenses properly incurred by him as incident to the sale or any attempted sale, or otherwise; and secondly, in discharge of the mortgage money, interest, and costs, and other money, if any, due under the mortgage; and the residue of the money so received shall be paid to the person entitled to the mortgaged property'.[27]

As security rights are property rights, if there are two or more charges/mortgages on the same property, their priority is determined by the time of their creation. The prior right prevails and therefore monies will be applied first in satisfaction of the debt secured by the first charge/mortgage and then by the second and so on. In the case of a floating charge before crystallisation, a subsequent fixed charge on some of the assets covered by the floating charge will take priority.[28]

9.2.4 The transfer of loans

For various reasons, commercial or regulatory, banks frequently wish to transfer loans to other banks or financial institutions. The rights of a lender under a loan, i.e. the lender's claim against the borrower, can be transferred by novation or assignment, legal or equitable. The obligations of a lender under a loan contract cannot be transferred by assignment, but only by novation.[29] There are also agreements that transfer the economic risk the lender has undertaken under a loan to another party without affecting the parties to the loan contract.[30]

In general, novation is a new contract between all the parties to a pre-existing contract and a new party whereby it is agreed that the pre-existing contract is extinguished and a new contract on the same terms is made between the new party (the transferee) and the parties to the pre-existing contract except for the party that seeks to transfer its rights and obligations under the contract. Technically, there is no transfer as such but, rather, the creation of a new contract. In the context of a bilateral loan between a bank and a borrower, where the bank (old bank) wants to transfer the loan to another bank (new bank), a novation will require the agreement of the old bank, new bank and borrower. It will result in the discharge of the borrower's obligations to the old bank which is now entirely out of the picture and the creation of a new loan contract, on the same terms as the original loan, between the new bank and the borrower. The possibility of transferring obligations that novation offers is commercially significant when a loan is not fully drawn down yet, in which case the bank still has unfulfilled obligations under the loan contract. Novation is a legally secure way of transferring loans but it requires the consent of the borrower and in fact of all parties to the original contract so it can be cumbersome. As we will see under the section on loan syndication, however, the borrower's consent to novation can be granted *ex ante* as part of the terms of the original contract.

Assignment is the transfer of a contractual party's proprietary interest in its claim against the other party to the contract (which is a chose in action) to another person. Originally,

---

26 *Farrar v Farrars Ltd* (1888) 40 Ch D 395.
27 Law of Property Act 1925 s 105.
28 For a detailed analysis of priority rules amongst security interests, see Ferran and Ho (above n 14) 337–340.
29 *Tolhurst v Associated Portland Cement Manufacturers (1900) Ltd* [1902] 2 KB 660.
30 For an overview of the different techniques to transfer loans, see Philip Rawlings, 'Restrictions on the Transfer of Rights in Loan Contracts' (2013) 28 *Journal of International Banking and Financial Law* 543, 543–544.

the common law did not allow for the assignment of choses in action.[31] However, equity developed to recognise such transfers as valid in between the assignor and assignee but without impacting *prima facie* the legal position of the debtor under the original contract. An equitable assignment can be oral and may be addressed to the assignee or the obligee. There must be clear intention of the assignor to assign the right to the assignee.[32] As such, an equitable assignment has the effect that the assignee acquires a beneficial interest in the chose in action (the claim) while the assignor retains the legal interest. The assignee cannot bring an action directly against the debtor alone; he can request the assignor to do so, and if the assignor refuses, he must join the assignor in his action against the debtor.[33] The debtor is still *prima facie* required and entitled to render performance to the assignor who then holds the relevant property on trust for the assignee. However, the assignor may instruct the debtor to render performance to the assignee instead, in which case the debtor must do so.

The Law of Property Act 1925[34] permitted assignments to be valid in law insofar as the conditions laid down in the statute are satisfied. A statutory assignment has the effect of full transfer of the legal title to the chose in action (the claim), with all remedies, to the assignee who can thereafter bring an action against the debtor and to whom performance must be rendered. The requirements for a valid statutory assignment are as follows: (1) it must be absolute, so it cannot be by way of charge or only of a part of a debt; (2) it must be in writing; and (3) express notice must be given to the debtor.[35] Consideration is not required.[36] If one of these conditions is not met, but the assignment satisfies the requirements for an equitable assignment, it will be valid as an equitable assignment. It follows that defective legal assignments may be valid equitable assignments.

English law has never recognised a public interest in an active market for choses in action and, as a result, has upheld the validity of clauses restricting assignments.[37] Indeed, a contractual term restricting assignment (e.g. to a class of persons) and/or subjecting any assignment to the consent of the debtor is effective. If an assignment takes place against the stipulated restrictions and/or without the consent of the obligee, it will be invalid and hence, there will be no transfer of the chose in action. The debtor will still be entitled to render performance to the purported assignor (e.g. in the case of a loan, make repayments to the original bank) and will be able to assert any set-offs he has against the assignor. Further, the legal position of the debtor is not affected by the purported assignment. The purported assignee in such cases can bring a personal action against the purported assignor, but the latter has *prima facie* no obligation to account to the former for moneys received from the debtor, unless the contrary is clearly stipulated.[38]

31 As Holdsworth observes, in the medieval period, 'the assignment of such a right of action by the act of the two parties was unthinkable'. William S Holdsworth, 'The History of the Treatment of "Choses" in Action by the Common Law' (1920) 33 *Harvard Law Review* 997, 1003.
32 *William Brandt's Sons & Co v Dunlop Rubber Co Ltd* [1905] AC 454.
33 Iris H.-Y. Chiu and Joanna Wilson, *Banking Law and Regulation* (OUP 2019) 152–153.
34 Law of Property Act 1925 c. 20.
35 Law of Property Act 1925 s 136 (1).
36 *Re Westerton, Public Trustee v Gray* [1919] 2 Ch 104.
37 *Linden Gardens Trust Ltd v Lenesta Sludge Disposals Ltd* [1994] 1 AC 85. See also *Hendry v Chartsearch Ltd* [1998] CLC 1382.
38 Ibid., 108. See also *Helstan Securities Ltd v Hertfordshire County Council* [1978] 3 All ER 262 where the court rules that an assignment that contravenes a restrictive clause has no effective with respect to anyone. However, Rawlings argues that 'the disappointed transferee should be able to bring an action against the transferor'. Rawlings (above n 30) 543.

Contrary to novation and assignment, in the case of sub-participation a lender enters into an entirely separate contract with another party (usually another bank) with a view to transferring to the latter the risk that the debtor may default (credit risk), without affecting in any respect the relationship between the lender and debtor.[39] The original lender is called the 'grantor', whereas the party that assumes the credit risk is called the 'grantee'. The debtor need not be notified. This is the principal commercial advantage of sub-participation: it permits a bank to transfer credit risk under a loan without the knowledge of the debtor. There are two types of sub-participation: funded sub-participation and risk sub-participation. In the case of funded sub-participation, the grantee deposits funds with the grantor equal to the former's agreed participation in the loan and in exchange the grantor promises to pay the grantee a share of the monies repaid by the debtor under the loan. If the borrower defaults, the grantor is entitled to retain part of the deposited funds equal to the amount of the default. In the case of risk sub-participation, the grantee agrees to make a payment to the grantor if the debtor defaults on its obligations under the loan, the payment being equal to the amount of the default, and in exchange the grantor pays the grantee a fee. The main difference between funded sub-participation and risk sub-participation is, therefore, that in risk sub-participation the grantor bears the risk of insolvency of the grantee, as, if the grantee goes insolvent, it will not be able to meet its obligations under the contract.

9.3 Business lending

9.3.1 Common terms in business loans

Commercial loan agreements are highly standardised and, since 1999, the Loan Market Association (LMA)[40] has made available standardised forms for loan facilities.[41] There are two main types of facilities: term facilities and revolving facilities. In the case of the latter, within an agreed period of time a business can draw funds as the need arises up to a certain amount, so that its actual indebtedness changes from time to time, as funds are drawn and repaid. Commercial loan agreements typically contain (i) conditions precedent – these are conditions applicable to the obligation of the bank to make available the funds so that if they are breached the bank does not have to make the funds available; (ii) representations and warranties – of law and of fact (e.g. corporate capacity, accuracy of accounts, etc.): any inaccuracy is treated as an event of default; (iii) covenants – these are undertaking by the borrower to do something or to refrain from doing something (e.g. to maintain certain financial ratios, to provide information to the lender and not to grant any security interest in its property to other parties, known as a negative pledge): any breach is treated as an event of default; and (iv) default clauses – these specify what constitutes an event of default upon

---

39 *Lloyds TSB Bank Plc v Clarke & Chase Manhattan Bank Luxembourg SA* [2002] UKPC 27.

40 The LMA was established in 1996 with the objective of establishing widely accepted market practice in relation to primary and secondary syndicated loan markets in Europe, the Middle East and Africa. It currently comprises 700 member-organisations from more than 60 countries, including commercial and investment banks, institutional investors, law firms, service providers and rating agencies. See Loan Market Association, 'About Us' <https://www.lma.eu.com/about-us> (accessed 26 April 2020).

41 LMA documentation is not publicly available. The discussion herein is based on the exposition of some of the terms of LMA documentation in Chiu and Wilson (above n 33) 137–139 and, where indicated, on other primary and secondary sources. The views expressed herein are of the authors alone and do not represent the views of the LMA.

the occurrence of which the lender can accelerate the loan (demand the whole outstanding amount), and is not bound to make further advances. Cross-default clauses stipulate that any default of the borrower under another facility is deemed to be an event of default under the facility that contains the cross-default clause.[42]

Material adverse change (MAC) clauses stipulate that any MAC in the borrower's financial position constitutes an event of default.[43] MAC clauses have generated considerable litigation in recent years. It has been ruled that a borrower being investigated by a public authority, having its CEO arrested and its credit rating downgraded and being imposed a multi-billion tax bill clearly constituted a MAC.[44] Likewise, a large arbitration award made against the borrower was also upheld as a MAC.[45] In the latter case, the Privy Council clarified that for the event of default to be lawfully triggered the lender must be able to establish that it did in fact form the opinion that a MAC had occurred and the opinion must be honest and rational.[46] Further guidance was provided by the High Court in *Grupo Hotelero Urvasco SA v Carey Value Added SL*.[47] The burden of proof is on the lender. A state of affairs that existed at the time of the agreement and was known to the lender cannot give rise to a MAC. The borrower's financial condition must be ascertained by reference to its financial statements and any evidence that it has ceased paying its debts but does not encompass general economic or market changes. An adverse change is material only if it is not merely temporary and provided that it significantly affects the borrower's ability to perform its obligations.[48]

Regarding the interest rate charged on business loans, it can be fixed, quasi-fixed or floating. The most common arrangement is for the rate to be quasi-fixed: it is agreed that the rate will consist of a specified spread plus the higher of LIBOR or a given floor.[49] LIBOR stands for London Interbank Offered Rate and is a global benchmark that is broadly accepted by major financial institutions worldwide as the interest rate to lend to one another on a short-term basis. LIBOR is calculated on the basis of estimations provided by major banks and includes distinct rates for each of five major currencies (US Dollar, Euro, GB Pound, Japanese Yen and Swiss Franc) and for seven lengths of time ranging from overnight to 12 months. Until 2014, LIBOR was calculated by the British Bankers' Association. As a result of the LIBOR scandal, which involved large fines being imposed on Barclays, RBS and UBS by UK and US authorities,[50] LIBOR is now calculated by ICE Benchmark Administration (IBA), part of Intercontinental Exchange, a US company, under the regulation

---

42 For a discussion of events of default in financial contracts, see Alastair Hudson, *The Law of Finance* (2nd edn, Swett & Maxwell 2013) 558–560.

43 For a practical doctrinal analysis, see Travis Evens, 'A Brief Overview of Material Adverse Change Clauses in Credit Documents' (Lexology, 15 December 2016) <https://www.lexology.com/library/detail.aspx?g=8ad67d75-dccf-464e-a93b-b911956b6ba3> (accessed 12 May 2020).

44 *BNP Paribas SA v Yukos Oil Company* [2005] EWHC 1321.

45 *Cukurova Finance International Ltd v Alfa Telecom Turkey Ltd* [2016] AC 923.

46 Ibid., 950.

47 [2013] EWHC 1039.

48 Ibid., [348]–[363].

49 Robert Arscott, 'LIBOR Floors in Leveraged Loans' (2018) available at SSRN: <https://papers.ssrn.com/sol3/papers.cfm?abstract_id=3073156> (accessed 18 June 2020).

50 The relevant authorities are the FSA, the Commodity Futures Trading Commission and the US Department of Justice. For an overview of the relevant events and a discussion of regulatory lessons learnt from the scandal, see David Hou and David R Skeie, 'LIBOR: Origins, Economics, Crisis, Scandal, and Reform' (2014) Federal Reserve Bank of New York Staff Report 667 <https://papers.ssrn.com/sol3/papers.cfm?abstract_id=2423387> (accessed 8 May 2020). See also Martin Wheatley, 'The Wheatley Review of LIBOR:

and supervision of the Financial Conduct Authority (FCA). The FCA has indicated that it is considering alternatives to LIBOR from 2022 onwards.[51] It is worth noting that LIBOR is not only used as a benchmark for commercial loans and interest rate swaps, but also for credit cards and mortgages. Its manipulation by large banks is an incident of problematic culture in the financial sector and has undermined public confidence in finance.[52]

9.3.2 Syndicated loans

A syndicated loan is a transaction whereby two or more banks make legally separate loans to one borrower on common terms. Borrowers are typically large corporations or sovereigns. A syndicated loan may be either unsecured or secured. The reason why banks use syndicated loans is that for very large loans no single bank may be willing to advance the whole amount, for purposes of risk management and regulatory compliance. Most syndicated loans are made using the LMA's standard agreement. Both the rights and obligations of each party are separate and independent, and therefore, no party is responsible for the obligations of another party and each part can enforce its rights separately. However, a single set of documents is used thus saving costs. According to the terms of the LMA standard facility, matters relating to the administration of the loan, including the decision to accelerate the loan upon the occurrence of an event of default, are to be decided collectively by the participating banks by a qualifying majority of 2/3 of total commitments (amounts lent/ to be lent). Decisions such as varying the amounts due or releasing any security have to be taken unanimously by the participating banks.

A crucial art in the transaction is played by the arranging bank or arranger who puts together the syndicate. The arranger is usually a bank with an established relationship with the prospective borrower. On the basis of a mandate given by the borrower, the arranger undertakes to approach selected banks and provide them with a brief description of the borrower and the core terms of the proposed facility (term sheets). At a later stage a more detailed information memorandum is prepared by the borrower and disseminated by the arranger to recipient banks.

Another important function is that of the agent. Once the syndicated loan agreement has been agreed, the agent bank functions as the main point of contact with the borrower and representative of the participant banks. It undertakes to monitor compliance by the borrower with the terms of the agreement, to receive any notice from the borrower and to receive the loan funds from the banks to disburse to the borrower and, when repayments are made, to receive funds from the borrower and pass them on to the participating banks. Under the LMA standard agreement, there is a sharing clause that obliges the agent to share any amounts received by the borrower with other participants *pro rata*, according to the amount of outstanding debt owed to each participant. If a syndicated loan is secured, another function is that of the security trustee. The security trustee, which can be either

---

Final Report' (2012) <https://assets.publishing.service.gov.uk/government/uploads/system/uploads/attachment_data/file/191762/wheatley_review_libor_finalreport_280912.pdf> (accessed 28 June 2020).

51 As indicated in a speech by the FCA's CEO. See Andrew Bailey, 'The Future of LIBOR' (Bloomberg, London, 27 July 2017) <https://www.fca.org.uk/news/speeches/the-future-of-libor> (accessed 29 June 2020).

52 For an analysis of the LIBOR scandal from the perspective of social institutions theory, institutional corruption, and collective action problems, see Seumas Miller, 'The LIBOR Scandal: Culture, Corruption and Collective Action Problems in the Global Banking Sector' in Justin O'Brien and George Gilligan (eds), *Integrity, Risk and Accountability in Capital Markets* (Hart Publishing 2013) 111–128.

a participant bank or a third party, holds the legal title to any security provided by the borrower on trust for the benefit of the participating banks. This ensures that any changes in the membership of the syndicate do not affect the validity of the security. The roles of arranger, agent and security trustee may be performed by the same bank.

Regarding the possibility of participant banks to transfer their loans to other banks and exit the syndicate, the standard LMA terms provide that the borrower agrees *ex ante* to any future novation or assignment whereby the rights and obligations (in the case of novation) of any participant bank are transferred to a bank or other financial institution.[53] The provision of *ex ante* consent qualifies as an offer by the borrower to existing members to discharge their obligations and an offer to the whole world to create new loan contracts on the same terms as the original facility.[54] Acceptance of the offer by the transferee takes place by conduct, by complying with the transfer procedure stipulated in the agreement. The transfer procedure includes notification of the agent bank who collects repayments so that it can pass them on to the transferee. This practice has been upheld by the courts.[55]

An interesting legal question is the nature of the relationship between the participant banks and, in particular, the extent of any duties owed by the arranger to the other banks. It is accepted that the participant banks are not partners, as there is no net profit sharing: each bank makes a different rate of profit depending on its cost of funding the loan and other costs. The main legal risk for the arranger is that it might be held to owe fiduciary duties to other banks or perhaps a duty of care or to have made a misrepresentation to them. In practice, such questions arise in cases where the borrower defaults and there have been inaccuracies in the information provided to the lenders or some material information was not included. In such cases, participant banks may be tempted to bring legal action against the arranger claiming that it was aware of the inaccuracy or the omission. In short, the legal position is that the arranger, in view of the language commonly used in the loan agreements, does not *prima facie* owe fiduciary duties to the members of the syndicate, is not making any representations regarding the accuracy or completeness of information provided by the borrower and does not assume a duty of care to them.[56] A typical contractual formulation is the following:

The Recipient acknowledges and agrees that: (a) [The arranging bank] and its Affiliates, officers, employees, agents, and professional advisers do not make any representation or warranty, express or implied as to, or assume any responsibility for, the accuracy, adequacy, reliability or completeness of any of the Confidential Information. (b) [The arranging bank] and its Affiliates, officers, employees, agents and professional advisers shall be under no obligation to update or correct any inaccuracy in the Confidential Information or be otherwise liable in respect of the Confidential Information; and

53 The term 'other financial institution' was construed broadly by the court as including any institution that has some characteristics of a bank in *The Argo Fund Ltd v Essar Steel Ltd* [2006] EWCA Civ 241. At [49], Auld LJ opined that 'it is not a necessary characteristic of a transferee that its business should include bank-like activities, such as the lending of money, whether on the primary or secondary debt market or otherwise, or indeed that it should exhibit any particular standard of suitability or probity as a financial institution'.
54 The validity of an offer to the whole world was confirmed in *Carlill v Carbolic Smoke Ball Co* [1893] 1 QB 256.
55 *Habibsons Bank Ltd v Standard Chartered Bank (Hong Kong) Ltd* [2010] EWCA Civ 1335.
56 *Raiffeisen Zentralbank Osterreich AG v Royal Bank of Scotland Plc* [2010] EWHC 1392 (Comm); and *IFE Fund SA v Goldman Sachs International* [2007] EWCA Civ 811.

(c) The Confidential Information is not intended to provide the sole basis of any credit evaluation and should not be considered to be a recommendation that the Recipient participate in the Transaction.

This Information Memorandum (the 'Memorandum') has been prepared from Information supplied by the Company. The contents of this Memorandum have not been independently verified. No representation, warranty or undertaking (express or implied) is made, and no responsibility is accepted as to the adequacy, accuracy, completeness or reasonableness of this Memorandum or any further information, notice or other document at any time supplied in connection with the Facility. This Memorandum is being provided for information purposes only and is not intended to provide the basis of any credit decision or other evaluation and should not be considered as a recommendation that any recipient of this Memorandum should participate in the Facility.[57]

This judicial approach is based on the consideration that parties to syndicated loans are sophisticated commercial parties, and therefore, their explicit agreement regulating their relationship must be strictly adhered to. However, if an arranger goes beyond the role envisaged by the facility and actively recommends the merit of the transaction to other banks it may be held to owe them fiduciary duties, especially where the same bank is arranger, agent and security trustee.[58] Furthermore, if particular questions are asked of the arranger by other banks and the arranger answers such questions it assumes a duty of care and it will be liable if it fails to disclose relevant information.[59] Thus, the behaviour of the arranger may qualify as an assumption of responsibility for the accuracy of the information provided by the borrower.

9.4 Consumer lending

9.4.1 The regulation of overdrafts

Overdrafts, both authorised and unauthorised, are a common means for individual bank customers to obtain small amounts of short-term credit. This is particularly important for low-income and low-net worth individuals whose income fluctuates from time to time and who do not have substantial savings. At the same time, overdrafts can be costly, especially unauthorised (also known as unarranged) overdrafts. FCA research demonstrates that many consumers have been paying the equivalent of 10% per day for unarranged overdrafts and that 14% of account holders use overdrafts monthly and pay 69% of all overdraft fees.[60] In 2016 firms earned £2.3 billion from overdraft facilities.[61] As we will see, an attempt to control overdraft charges under consumer protection law failed at court, but the FCA has

---

57 *Raiffeisen* (above n 56) [64]–[65].
58 *UBAF Ltd v European American Banking Corporation* [1984] QB 713.
59 The arranger was held liable in negligence in the Australian case of *NatWest Australia Ltd v Tricontinental Corp Ltd* (1993) ATPR (Digest) 46.109. The possibility of voluntary assumption of responsibility was also accepted in *Sumitomo Bank Ltd v Banque Bruxelles Lambert SA* [1997] 1 Lloyd's Rep 487.
60 FCA, 'High-Cost Credit Review' (22 July 2019) <https://www.fca.org.uk/firms/high-cost-credit-consumer-credit/high-cost-credit-review> (accessed 8 April 2020).
61 See FCA, 'High-Vost Credit Review: Overdrafts' (2018) CP18/13 [1.1] <https://www.fca.org.uk/publication/consultation/cp18-13.pdf> (accessed 4 May 2020).

recently introduced bold reforms in the pricing of overdrafts, which came into effect on 6 April 2020.[62]

It is expedient to provide some further detail on the types of overdraft charges that are common in the UK market. For arranged overdrafts, interest is frequently charged for the debit balance of the account, normally at a rate ranging from 15% to 20%, although there are also certain accounts that offer arranged overdrafts free of charge, such as premier accounts and student and graduate accounts.[63] Also, a periodic (daily or monthly) fee is commonly charged and applies when an account is overdrawn – often depending on the amount of the overdraft. For unarranged overdrafts, there is typically a daily usage fee, and, in some cases, interest is also charged. Fees are also charged for unpaid transactions, i.e. in cases where a bank refuses to grant or extend an unauthorised overdraft and refuses a payment order or cheque due to lack of available funds. For instance, at the time of writing NatWest charges a £8 daily fee for unarranged overdraft use and a £8 fee for each transaction that the bank returns unpaid, but does not charge any interest on unarranged overdrafts and applies a monthly cap of use fees and unpaid transaction fees at £80.[64] The practice of charging fixed daily fees makes it more expensive to use overdrafts to borrow small amounts of money.

The practice of charging fixed fees for unarranged overdrafts was challenged by the Office of Fair Trading (OFT) in 2007 which brought an action against the main UK retail banks arguing that the charges were in the nature of penalties for breach of contract (and hence unenforceable) and that they were not excluded from fairness assessment under the Unfair Terms in Consumer Contract Regulations 1999.[65] The banks argued that the charges were part of the payment they receive for providing a complex package of services and, therefore, that they are excluded from fairness assessment, according to Regulation 6(2)(b).[66] The High Court rejected the penalty argument but ruled that the charges were not part of the price of the current account and were thus challengeable on grounds of fairness.

The Court of Appeal confirmed this ruling emphasising the fact that customers did not pay attention to these charges and did not view them as part of the price for the current account:

> The Court of Appeal accepted the following argument advanced by the OFT. The object of Regulation 6(2) is to exclude from assessment for fairness that part of the bargain that will be the focus of a customer's attention when entering into a contract, that is to say the goods or services that he wishes to acquire and the price he will have to pay for doing so. Market forces could and should be relied upon to control the fairness of this part of the bargain. Contingencies that the customer does not expect to involve him will not be of concern to him. He will not focus on these when entering into the bargain.[67]

Thus, it drew a distinction between, on the one hand, the core or essential terms of a contract that consumers can reasonably be expected to pay close attention to, and, on the other,

---

62 See n 74–75 below and the accompanying text.

63 Money Advice Service, 'Overdrafts Explained' <https://www.moneyadviceservice.org.uk/en/articles/overdrafts-explained> (accessed on 16 April 2020).

64 NatWest, 'Overdrafts' <https://personal.natwest.com/personal/current-accounts/overdrafts.html> (accessed on 26 April 2020).

65 Discussed in Chapter 6.3.

66 This has now been superseded by the Consumer Rights Act 2015 s 64 which mostly replicates the Regulations but makes it clear that to be excluded from assessment a term must be transparent and prominent.

67 *OFT v Abbey National Plc* [2009] UKSC 6, [79] per Lord Phillips.

secondary terms that consumers typically pay little attention to. This is a plausible interpretation of the Unfair Consumer Contract Terms Directive[68] and has traction from a policy perspective, as it is consistent with findings of behavioural economic research on bounded rationality and limitations on processing information. However, the Supreme Court, where the case was heard by five justices, unanimously reversed the Court of Appeal and ruled that:

> [T]he bank charges levied on personal current account customers in respect of unauthorised overdrafts (including unpaid item charges and other related charges) constitute part of the price or remuneration for the banking services provided and, in so far as the terms giving rise to the charges are in plain intelligible language, no assessment under the Unfair Terms in Consumer Contracts Regulations 1999 of the fairness of those terms may relate to their adequacy as against the services supplied.[69]

The Supreme Court's decision emphasised that these charges are an essential part of the reward that banks receive for offering a range current account services, such as 'the collection of cheques drawn in favour of the customer, the honouring of cheques drawn by the customer, payments on behalf of the customer pursuant to the use by the customer of credit or debit cards and cash distribution facilities'.[70] The judges were not oblivious to the negative reactions that this decision prompted and remarked that:

> Ministers and Parliament may wish to consider the matter further. They decided, in an era of so-called 'light-touch' regulation, to transpose the Directive as it stood rather than to confer the higher degree of consumer protection afforded by the national laws of some other member states.[71]

On the side or regulation, until recently, regulatory rules were limited to imposing disclosure obligations on banks as part of the current account agreement covering the rate of interest, and all charges under the agreement.[72] The FCA, however, kept these markets under close review and, in 2018, engaged in a comprehensive review of high-cost credit, including overdrafts.[73] As a result, new rules were introduced in 2019 on the pricing of overdrafts that took effect on 6 April 2020. Under the new rules, banks will be prohibited from charging daily or other fixed fees for all unarranged overdrafts and for arranged overdrafts up to £10,000: they will only be able to charge a single annual interest rate. Banks will still be able to charge unpaid transaction fees for refused payments, but guidance will be issued emphasising that such fees must reasonably correspond to the costs of refused payments. Moreover, banks will be prohibited from charging a higher rate of

---

68 Council Directive 93/13/EEC of 5 April 1993 on unfair terms in consumer contracts [1993] OJ L95/29.
69 Ibid., [51] per Lord Walker.
70 Ibid., [53] per Lord Phillips.
71 Ibid., [52] per Lord Walker.
72 FCA Handbook, Consumer Credit Sourcebook (CONC) 4.7.2. The information that must be included in an unsecured authorised overdraft agreement is specified by regulation eight of The Consumer Credit (Agreements) Regulations 2010 (SI 2010/1014) and includes the type of credit, identity and addresses of the parties, credit limit, duration of the agreement, total charge for credit, charges payable and an indication that the debtor may be requested to repay the amount of credit in full on demand at any time. Similar requirements apply to credit cards.
73 'High-Cost Credit Review: Overdrafts' (above n 61).

interest for unarranged overdrafts than the rate that they charge for arranged overdrafts. If an account does not have an arranged overdraft facility, the interest rate applicable for an unarranged overdraft will have to be no higher than the rate for arranged overdrafts that the bank applies to comparable accounts.[74] It is hoped that the new rules will embolden competition, as they make the cost of overdrafts more transparent, and that they will bring extensive financial benefits to unarranged overdraft users without limiting their access to credit.[75] Whether lowering the cost of unarranged overdrafts and maintaining unfettered access to credit by the individuals who are likely to use them are two compatible objectives remain to be seen.

9.4.2 Credit cards

The general contractual features of payment cards were discussed in Section 7.7. This section focuses on the regulation of credit cards as a type of consumer credit. Credit cards are regulated by the Payment Services Regulations 2017 which also apply to debit cards and have been discussed in Section 7.7. In addition, credit cards are regulated under the Consumer Credit Act 1974, as they are credit tokens.[76] The credit-token agreement must be in writing,[77] and the debtor must be informed of the amount of available credit, interest rate and charges, and of his rights under the Act.[78] In terms of unauthorised transactions, the debtor is not liable to the creditor for any losses, with the exception of losses up to £35 that arose while the card was not in the debtor's possession and before notice was given to the creditor that the card has been lost or stolen.[79]

Another significant provision of the Act is the imposition of what is known as 'connected lender liability' to card issuers (e.g. banks) for misrepresentations and breaches of contract committed by suppliers vis-à-vis cardholders.[80] For instance, when a cardholder uses her credit card to purchase goods from a supplier, if the goods are defective, the cardholder, apart from her claim against the supplier, also has a claim against the card issuer. The supplier and card issuer are jointly and severally liable.[81] The card issuer has a right to be indemnified by the supplier for any losses it incurs due to being liable to the cardholder including any costs reasonably incurred in defending proceedings instituted by the cardholder.[82] However, it must be noted that this provision only applies to purchased goods with a price that exceeds £100 and does not exceed £30,000,[83] and hence, it does not apply to small purchases and very large purchases. Connected lender liability also applies to

---

74 See FCA, 'High-Cost Credit Review: Overdrafts policy statement' (2019) PS19/16 [1.8] <https://www.fca. org.uk/publication/policy/ps19-16.pdf> (accessed on 2 May 2020).

75 Ibid., 11–13.

76 Consumer Credit Act 1974 s 14 (1). Credit cards are also debtor-creditor-supplier agreements falling within section 12 of the Act. Debit cards are arguably not within the scope of the Act, but this is less clear in the case of accounts with an overdraft facility. Chiu and Wilson argue that in such cases debit cards are regulated by the Act. See Chiu and Wilson (above n 33) 96.

77 Consumer Credit Act 1974 s 61 (1).

78 Consumer Credit Act 1974 s 61 (2).

79 Consumer Credit Act 1974 s 84.

80 Consumer Credit Act 1974 s 75.

81 Consumer Credit Act 1974 s 75 (1).

82 Consumer Credit Act 1974 s 75 (2).

83 Consumer Credit Act 1974 s 75 (3) (b), as amended.

transactions with a supplier that is based outside the UK, insofar as the card has been issued by a domestic issuer.[84]

Connected lender liability can be economically defended by reference to the superior ability of banks, compared to customers, to pursue legal action against suppliers and to monitor suppliers to ensure that rogues are not included within their credit card networks. Also, in case where the loss cannot be recovered by the supplier, the bank is more capable of bearing the loss than the average credit cardholder due to its size and resources. When the loss is avoidable via *ex ante* screening and monitoring, connected lender liability provides an efficient incentive for banks to screen and monitor suppliers. Thus, it functions as a signalling device for the reliability of suppliers, as unreliable suppliers are likely to be excluded from credit card networks.[85] However, as connected lender liability operates as an insurance policy in favour of the cardholder, it reduces the cardholders' incentives to assess the reliability of suppliers. It must also be noted that the benefit of connected lender liability for cardholders comes at a cost, as it tends to be reflected on the cost of credit.

9.4.3 Personal loans

This section discusses unsecured loans provided by banks to individual customers. Commercially, banks distinguish between personal loans, that are for general purposes, and special purpose loans, such as home improvements loans, car loans and debt consolidation loans. There are also unsecured loans for special categories of customers such as student loans and graduate loans. For our purposes all these loans will be referred to as personal loans. The most crucial terms of personal loans are the amount of the loan (usually between £1,000 and £25,000), the duration of the loan (usually between one and five years), the rate of interest and whether overpayments and early repayment are permitted without incurring any charges. It is common for banks to assess a prospective borrower's individual financial circumstances and adjust the rate of interest they charge accordingly. For instance, HSBC charges between 3.3% and 21.9% *per annum* for personal loans.[86] In deciding whether to grant a personal loan and at what rate of interest banks make use of credit reference agencies[87] and, in particular, credit scores. Before making a credit search, banks typically obtain the consent of the prospective borrower.

One matter that caused litigation was the fairness of a standard term in a loan contract to the effect that, in case of borrower default that leads to legal action by the bank, the contractual rate of interest continues to apply after judgement until the judgement debt is paid in full. Such terms are advantageous to banks in cases where the contractual rate of interest is higher than the statutory rate applicable to judgement debts, which currently stands at 8%.[88] In *DG of Fair Trading v First National Bank Plc*,[89] the House of Lords ruled that such terms are possible to be assessed for fairness under the Unfair Terms in

---

84 *OFT v Lloyds TSB Bank Plc* [2008] 1 AC 316.
85 In this way, it alleviates a market failure that is due to asymmetry of information between suppliers and buyers. On this, see Elisabetta Iossa and Giuliana Palumbo, 'Product Quality, Lender Liability, and Consumer Credit' (2004) 56 *Oxford Economic Papers* 331.
86 See HSBC, 'Personal Loans' <https://www.hsbc.co.uk/loans/products/personal/> (accessed 7 June 2020).
87 Discussed in Chapter 5.2.4.3.
88 Every judgement debt carries interest. For High Court judgements, this is pursuant to section 17 of the Judgments Act 1838, as amended.
89 [2002] 1 AC 481.

Consumer Contract Regulations 1999, as they do not pertain to the adequacy of the price of the contract. However, the House of Lords found that the particular term was not unfair and therefore it was fully enforceable.

Personal loans to individuals fall within the scope of Section 60 of the Consumer Credit Act 1974, which empowers the Treasury to make regulations as to the form and documents of the relevant agreements. The Consumer Credit (Disclosure of Information) Regulations 2004[90] specify the information that must be provided to prospective borrowers before the agreement is concluded, while the Consumer Credit (Agreements) Regulations 2010[91] prescribe the information that must be included in the agreement. Failure to comply with either set of Regulations leads to the debt being unenforceable by the bank without obtaining a court order.[92] In the event of borrower default, before the bank can terminate the agreement and demand immediate repayment of the whole amount due, it must give at least 14 days' notice to the borrower.[93]

As we discussed earlier in this chapter, banks are not under a general legal duty to consider whether a loan is suitable for a customer and to provide advice to that effect. However, the soft-law Standards for Lending Practice include a commitment on behalf of lenders to 'lend responsibly and aim to provide a product that is affordable' for each customer.[94] Customers who have been granted loans in circumstances where they were already over-indebted and unlikely to be able to repay the loans may raise a complaint with the Financial Ombudsman Service (FOS).[95] When resolving complaints the FOS takes into account soft-law best practice codes such as the Standards for Lending Practice. Indeed, in a case where a bank lent a customer £5,000 for 36 months which required a monthly repayment of £250 while the customer had an income of around £1,000 a month, most of which was spent in paying interest under payday loans, the FOS found against the lender and required it to refund all interest and charges that the customer had paid (the complaint having been brought after the loan had been fully repaid).[96] Banks must, therefore, be careful to establish prospective borrowers' financial circumstances diligently, and especially their true income and whether they have been using payday loans.

9.4.4 Residential mortgages

The most common type of secured debt raised by individuals is residential mortgages to fund the purchase of their main home, of an additional home or of a property to let. When

90 SI 2004/1481.
91 SI 2010/1014. According to Schedule 1, the agreement must specify *inter alia* the identity and geographical address of the creditor and debtor, the amount of the credit to be provided under the agreement, the duration of the agreement, how the credit is to be drawn down, the rate(s) of interest and, where available, any reference rate on which that rate is based, the total amount payable by the debtor, the annual percentage rate (APR) of interest, the timing and amount of repayments, the right to receive statements free of charge and any charges applicable.
92 Consumer Credit Act 1974 s 65 (1).
93 Consumer Credit Act 1974 s 87.
94 See Lending Standards Board, 'Standards for Lending Practice: Personal Customers' (2016) <https://www.lendingstandardsboard.org.uk/the-standards-for-personal-customers/#statement-of-lender-and-borrower-responsibilities> (accessed 8 June 2020).
95 Discussed in Chapter 6.5.
96 FOS, 'Case Studies: A Borrower Tells Us She Was Provided with a Loan She Couldn't Afford' <https://www.financial-ombudsman.org.uk/case-studies/borrower-tells-us-provided-loan-couldnt-afford> (accessed 9 July 2020).

an additional mortgage is raised on a property or when a mortgage is transferred to another bank (in which case the original mortgage is repaid and a new mortgage is created), the term 're-mortgage' is used in practice. Mortgages typically have a long duration which can reach up to 35 years and may be either interest-only or on a repayment basis. In interest-only mortgages, the borrower pays monthly the interest generated by the loan for the duration of the agreement and has to pay the capital amount in full at the end. In repayment mortgages, monthly payments cover both interest and capital, so that the outstanding amount under the mortgage gradually reduced and is fully repaid by the end of the agreed term. It is common for UK banks to charge a fee at the time of arranging a residential mortgage contract.

As is the case for personal loans, mortgages are also within the ambit of the Consumer Credit Act 1974 and there are specific requirements on the content of the mortgage agreement[97] and the information that must be provided to prospective borrowers in advance.[98] Furthermore, the bank is required to provide to the borrower an advance copy of the agreement and allow the borrower seven days to consider whether they want to proceed. At the end of the seven-day period the bank must send the borrower a copy of the agreement to sign allowing a seven-day consideration period.[99] These provisions aim to ensure that borrowers have ample opportunity to consider carefully whether they want to enter into a mortgage agreement or not.

Mortgages are regulated by a dedicated part of the FCA Handbook: Mortgages and Home Finance: Conduct of Business sourcebook. Among other rules, the Handbook has implemented the Mortgage Credit Directive[100] (with effect from 21 March 2016). The Directive applies to consumer credit agreements secured by a mortgage on residential immovable property.[101] It is a minimum harmonisation directive.[102] It requires Member States to designate a competent authority to ensure the enforcement of its provisions[103]; in the UK this is the FCA. It requires Members States to take measures to support consumer education on responsible borrowing and debt management, especially regarding residential mortgages.[104] Most importantly, article 7 of the Directive[105] requires banks to behave 'honestly, fairly, transparently and professionally, taking account of the rights and interests of the consumers' both when designing products and when offering services and advice to consumers. Furthermore, article 7 provides that, when designing remuneration policies for staff responsible for assessing the creditworthiness of prospective borrowers, banks must ensure that policies are consistent with sound risk management and do not give rise to conflicts of interest, and particularly that remuneration is not contingent on the number or proportion of accepted applications. This provision serves both consumer protection and prudential purposes, as granting mortgages to uncreditworthy borrowers was one of the causes of the 2008–2009 global financial crisis.

97 By virtue of the Consumer Credit (Agreements) Regulations 1983 (SI 1983/1553). Borrowers may, however, opt into the Consumer Credit (Agreements) Regulations 2010.
98 The Consumer Credit (Disclosure of Information) Regulations 2004 also apply to residential mortgage agreements.
99 Consumer Credit Act 1974 ss 58 (1) and 61.
100 Directive 2014/17/EU of the European Parliament and of the Council of 4 February 2014 on credit agreements for consumers relating to residential immovable property [2014] OJ L60/34.
101 Mortgage Credit Directive, art 3(1).
102 Mortgage Credit Directive, art 1.
103 Mortgage Credit Directive, art 5.
104 Mortgage Credit Directive, art 6.
105 Implemented by the FCA Handbook, MCOB 2A.1.1.

The FCA rules also expressly prohibit firms from entering into consumer mortgage contracts unless they can demonstrate that the mortgage contract is affordable for the customer.[106] To make the affordability assessment firms must take into account the net income of the customer, his committed expenditure and basic essential expenditure and quality-of-living cost of his household.[107] Income information must be verified, and self-certification by the customer is not sufficient.[108] Excessive charges must not be imposed on customers.[109] In particular, early repayment charges are only permitted to the extent that they constitute a reasonable pre-estimate of the costs to the firm of the customer repaying the amount due under the regulated mortgage contract before the contract's termination.[110] Regarding charges applicable in case of borrower default, known as payment shortfall charges, these are only allowed if firms can objectively justify that the charge is equal to or lower than a reasonable calculation of the cost of the additional administration required as a result of the customer's default.[111]

An issue that affected bank customer who obtained residential mortgages in previous years was the bundling of mortgage contracts with other financial products, such as Payment Protection Insurance (PPI), which led to customers being coerced into purchasing financial products that did not suit their needs and that they did not fully understand.[112] Nowadays, tying practices, that is, offering a mortgage contract in a package with other financial products or services are prohibited.[113] Many historical cases of PPI mis-selling have been dealt with by the FOS in recent years, and UK banks have been making large payments to compensate affected customers.[114] The FOS set a deadline of 29 August 2019 for customers to complain to businesses if they had been sold PPI until 29 August 2017.[115]

9.5 Conclusion

This chapter provided an overview of business and consumer lending. In the context of business lending, where all involved parties are sophisticated and there is no imbalance of bargaining power, English law has always focused on strict enforcement of contracts and regulatory interventions are rare. On the contrary, in the context of consumer lending, there is a range of common law, statutory, regulatory and soft-law rules and principles that seek to protect bank customers, for example, by requiring banks to disclose specified

---

106 FCA Handbook, MCOB 11.6.2 (1) (b).
107 FCA Handbook, MCOB 11.6.5.
108 FCA Handbook, MCOB 11.6.8.
109 FCA Handbook, MCOB 12.5.1.
110 FCA Handbook, MCOB 12.3.1.
111 FCA Handbook, MCOB 12.4.1.
112 For a detailed discussion of the PPI scandal and its implications for UK financial regulators, see Eilís Ferran, 'Regulatory Lessons from the Payment Protection Insurance Mis-selling Scandal in the UK' (2012) 13 *European Business Organization Law Review* 247.
113 Mortgage Credit Directive, art 12 (1), implemented by the FCA Handbook, MCOB 2A.2.1.
114 As of 2017, the total cost of payments to customers as a result of the PPI scandal was £9.1 billion for Barclays, £4.05 billion for HSBC, £18 Billion for Lloyds and £5 billion for RBS. See Amelia Heathman, 'This Is How Much the PPI Scandal Is Still Costing UK Banks' (Verdict, 28 July 2018) <https://www.verdict.co.uk/this-is-how-the-much-the-ppi-scandal-is-still-costing-uk-banks/> (accessed 10 June 2020).
115 FOS, 'Can You Look at Complaints about PPI, Now the Deadline Has Passed?' <https://www.financial-ombudsman.org.uk/faqs/questions-about-ppi/can-look-complaints-ppi-now-deadline-passed> (accessed 11 May 2020).

information and by limiting the ability of banks to impose certain fees and charges. The question of loan affordability remains crucial both from a consumer protection perspective and a prudential regulation perspective.

Glossary of terms

- Overdraft: Situation in which a current account has a negative balance and therefore the customer owes a debt to the bank; the debt can be called at any time.
- Authorised (arranged) overdraft: Overdraft that arose in line with a pre-exiting agreement between the bank and customer permitting the account to be overdrawn up to a certain limit and typically without imposing any charges.
- Unauthorised (unarranged) overdraft: Overdraft that arose in the absence of a pre-exiting agreement or beyond the limit imposes by such agreement as a result of the bank using its discretion to honour a payment order of the customer despite the absence of funds in their account; typically, it carries certain charges.
- Term loan: Agreement according to which an amount of money is lent from one part to another for a prescribed period of time; repayment is typically by instalments, but some loans provide only for payment of interest during the term of the loan and repayment of capital at the end.
- Secured loan: Loan that is secured on the property of the borrower; in such cases, the lender has a proprietary interest in certain assets belonging to the borrower in addition to its personal claim against the borrower.
- Unsecured loan: Loan that is not secured which means that the lender is an ordinary unsecured creditor and his claim ranks equally with the claims of other ordinary creditors in the debtor's insolvency or bankruptcy.
- Mortgage: Security interest that involves the transfer of ownership of an asset by the borrower to the lender on condition that the ownership of the collateral will be re-transferred to the borrower upon repayment of the debt secured by the mortgage.
- Charge by way of legal mortgage: Type of security interest created by the Law of Property Act 1925 which is the only possible way to create a mortgage on land; it does not involve transfer of ownership but grants the lender the right to take possession and sell the property.
- Charge: Equitable security interest whereby there is no transfer of ownership but certain property becomes available for the satisfaction of the secured debt; it can normally only be enforced by order of the court; a floating charge is a charge attaching to a class of assets that changes from time to time and can only be created by bodies corporate.
- Novation: Contract whereby a previous contract is extinguished, and a new contract is created; it can be used as a way to transfer both contractual rights and obligations, but it requires the involvement of all relevant parties.
- Assignment: Transfer of the rights under a contract by the original obligee (assignor) to another party (assignee); to be effective at law notice must be given to the obligor (debtor).
- Sub-participation: Contract between a party to another contract that is entitled to certain performance, typically payment of money, (grantor) and a third party (grantee) according to which the grantor undertakes to transfer the value it receives under the original contract to the grantee.
- London Interbank Offered Rate (LIBOR): Interest rate that is used broadly in finance (e.g. by setting the agreed interest rate by reference to LIBOR in lending contracts)

and is calculated on the basis of estimates provided by leading London banks on the prevailing market rate for them to borrow in the short-term from one another.

- Syndicated loan: A loan usually to a corporate or sovereign borrower made by a syndicate of bank; technically each loan by each bank is legally distinct, but all are on the same terms.
- Arranger bank: The bank that puts together the syndicate and leads the negotiations with the prospective borrower; it also typically acts as the agent bank receiving payments from the borrower and distributing them to the members of the syndicate and receiving notices from the borrower.
- Credit card: Portable card that permits a customer to make payments at commercial outlets (e.g. shops) and online provided that the relevant business is part of the credit card network; the customer borrows the sums spent by the bank and typically has the option of repaying the debt in full at the end of each statement period free of interest or to repay it gradually in which case the bank's credit card interest rate applies.
- Payment Protection Insurance (PPI): Contracts insuring borrowers against the risk of non-payment that were marketed in the UK to retail borrowers by several banks; as in many cases these contracts were not in the customers' interests, regulatory enforcement led to the abandonment of the practice by UK banks.

Practice questions

English law is excessively favourable to lenders. This is particularly problematic in the case of banks lending to retail customers and especially in relation to unauthorised overdraft charges. Critically discuss.

You may also find it useful to review the chapter through the following questions:

- Explain the legal nature of an overdraft and how it differs from a term loan.
- What are the main types of security interests in English law?
- Does English law permit the true transfer of (a) rights and (b) obligations under a contract, and, if yes, how?
- What is a syndicated loan, and why is syndication used in practice?
- Does the arranger bank owe any duties to the other banks that are parties to a syndicated loan transaction?
- Are the recent FCA rules sufficient to protect customers? Will they lead to negative unintended consequences?
- Explain the legal principle of connected lender liability and its justification.
- To what extent are credit card users protected in case of unauthorised use of their card?
- How does the law protect borrowers in the context of residential mortgages?

10 Money laundering and terrorist financing

10.1 Introduction

This chapter examines the impact on banks of the burgeoning framework against money laundering (AML) and counter terrorist financing (CTF). Adopting a general rather than a technical legal definition, money laundering (ML) is any act that seeks to disguise the criminal provenance of property so that it can be used and invested freely through the financial system without leading to the detection of the offence which generated the property (the predicate offence). Terrorist financing (TF) involves requesting or making available funds to be used to finance terrorist acts, often through the financial systems. The funds in question need not be connected with criminal activity.[1] AML and CTF laws and policies raise a myriad of pertinent questions in the areas of criminal justice policy, human rights and privacy.[2] However, in line with the scope of the book as a whole, this chapter will limit its discussion to the requirements that these policies impose on banks, the challenges banks and their employees are faced with and their impact on the bank-customer relationship.

The AML and CTF legal framework, as far as it concerns banks, consists of two elements: first, a set of criminal offences that target ML and TF activity in a very broad manner; second, a detailed set of rules that impose on banks obligations to adopt appropriate internal controls and procedures to prevent ML and TF. The criminal offences are not exclusively targeted at banks, but rather apply to a broad range of persons including the persons who have committed the predicate offence and a range of other professionals. For banks they become relevant as bank employees, including clerks and cashiers operating day-to-day transactions, can be held criminally liable. The regulatory framework has introduced obligations for banks to perform customer due diligence, to make suspicious activity reports (SARs) with respect to particular transactions, to appoint a dedicated nominated officer, to ensure that senior management has overall responsibility to prevent ML and TF and to conduct periodic risk assessments. The chapter will discuss the two frameworks in parallel: taking a functional approach and examining each step of the process followed by banks. Before doing so, it is necessary to provide an overview of evidence on ML and TF activity and a brief account of the evolution of the UK and EU legal regime to date.

---

1 On this, see E.P. Ellinger, Eva Lomnicka and C.V.M. Hare, *Ellinger's Modern Banking Law* (5th edn, OUP 2011) 93.
2 See M. Michelle Gallant, 'AML: Maintaining the Balance between Controlling Serious Crime and Human Rights' in Barry Rider (ed), *Research Handbook on International Financial Crime* (Edward Elgar 2015).

10.2　ML and TF activity and the UK financial system

It is generally difficult to quantify the extent and size of ML activity: most global figures are in the area of US$1–3 trillion annually,[3] but there is a scarcity of sound empirical academic work in the area, so they have to be taken with extreme caution. Indeed, a recent review of the economic literature on ML suggests that many studies present methodological limitations, such as the following: failure to adopt a clear definition of ML, imperfect transparency of data collection, lack of verification of the validity of shared databases, use of proxy variables of questionable relevance, lack of robust testing of the outcomes of theoretical models and undue generalisation of findings on small subpopulations.[4]

ML is typically described as comprising three phases: (1) placement of the illicit funds into the financial system (e.g. by depositing the proceeds of drug trade into the account of a third party, called a money mule); (2) distancing the funds from their origin through a number of transactions involving several accounts, legal entities and potentially jurisdictions (e.g. the money mule is instructed to send the money to an overseas account of an offshore company which transfers it further to another such entity and so on); and (3) reintegration into the legitimate financial system (e.g. the drug dealer receives a payment into his account from an offshore company for consulting services and can now use the funds without raising any suspicions).[5] TF, at least in the UK, typically consists of individuals raising modest funds, often as little as £300, to fund a terrorist attack, to travel abroad to join a terrorist group or to send funds abroad to a connected person who belongs to a terrorist group. In the UK, the most recent government risk assessment found that retail banking is at high risk of ML and medium risk of TF in absolute terms, but high compared to other financial sectors. Wholesale banking and capital markets transactions were found to be at high risk of ML but at low risk of TF. Wealth management and private banking were also assessed as being at high risk of ML and low risk of TF.[6]

10.3　The development of the UK, EU and international AML and CTF framework

Historically, the first countries that criminalised ML in connection with the proceeds of illicit drug trade were the US, by virtue of the Money Laundering Control Act 1986,[7] and the UK under the Drug Trafficking Offences Act 1986.[8] This was part of the 'war on drugs' strategy and responded to public outrage against conspicuous consumption by suspected drug dealers. In the UK, ML connected to other offences was criminalised by the Criminal Justice Act 1993[9] and the two distinct frameworks were integrated and strengthened by virtue of the

---

3　Petrus C. van Duyne, Jackie H. Harvey and Liliya Y. Gelemerova, *The Critical Handbook of Money Laundering: Policy, Analysis and Myths* (Palgrave Macmillan 2018) 202–205.

4　Ibid., 219–220.

5　See *Ellinger's* (above n 1) 92; Iris H.-Y. Chiu and Joanna Wilson, *Banking Law and Regulation* (OUP 2019) 679. This conceptualisation was first introduced by Angela Veng Mei Leong, 'Anti-money Laundering Measures in the United Kingdom: A Review of Recent Legislation and the FSA's Risk based Approach' (2007) 28 *Company Lawyer* 35.

6　HM Treasury and Home Office, *National Risk Assessment of Money Laundering and Terrorist Financing 2017* (2017) Chapter 4.

7　Money Laundering Control Act 1986 Public Law 99-570; 100 Stat. 3207-18.

8　Drug Trafficking Offences Act 1986 c. 32.

9　Criminal Justice Act 1993 c. 36.

Proceeds of Crime Act 2002 (to be abbreviated henceforth as 'POCA').[10] At the international level, an initiative taken by the US, UK, France and Australia led to the establishment in 1989 of the Financial Action Task Force (FATF) which is an intergovernmental body with no binding rule-making powers comprising 36 countries, including all major global economies.[11]

FATF's main output is its influential Recommendations, most recently published in 2012 and updated in 2018.[12] These set out minimum expectations for countries including criminalising ML and TF, having in place an appropriate regulatory framework for financial institutions and other professionals, having a national Financial Intelligence Unit (FIU) to receive reports from the private sector and co-ordinate responses and co-operating closely with other countries. Although the Recommendations are not legally binding, refusal of any country, be it a member of FATF or not, to comply with them leads to serious consequences as its banks may be excluded from international financial transactions. Indeed, FATF maintains a list of high-risk jurisdictions.[13] This has been criticised as an illegitimate imposition of rules by strong states on others.[14] TF rose to prominence after the 11 September 2000 attacks in New York and has since then been part of the FATF remit. In the UK, the Terrorism Act 2000[15] contains several provisions criminalising TF. The EU AML and CFT framework has developed through a series of directives that require Member States to prohibit ML and TF. The last comprehensive directive which abolished the previous ones was the Fourth Money Laundering Directive in 2015[16] which was amended in 2018 by the Fifth Money Laundering Directive.[17] The Fifth Directive enhanced customer due diligence and expanded the scope of the AML regime to virtual currency transactions. The UK has been implementing EU rules by amending POCA and the Terrorism Act and by adopting relevant Regulations. The Fourth Directive has been implemented by the Money Laundering Regulations 2017 which came into force on 26 June 2017.[18] The Fifth Directive was implemented in January 2020 heedless of the negotiations of Brexit and the government launched a consultation regarding the drafting of its implementing Regulations.[19]

10 Proceeds of Crime Act 2002 c. 29.
11 The FATF members at the time of writing are as follows: Argentina, Australia, Austria, Belgium, Brazil, Canada, China, Denmark, Finland, France, Germany, Greece, Hong Kong, Iceland, India, Ireland, Israel, Italy, Japan, Korea, Luxembourg, Malaysia, Mexico, the Netherlands, New Zealand, Norway, Portugal, Russia, Singapore, South Africa, Spain, Sweden, Switzerland, Turkey, the UK and the US.
12 FATF, 'International Standards on Combating Money Laundering and the Financing of Terrorism & Proliferation; The FATF Recommendations; Updated October 2018' (2018) <http://www.fatf-gafi.org/publications/fatfrecommendations/documents/fatf-recommendations.html> (accessed 16 April 2020).
13 These are currently the following: Bahamas, Botswana, Cambodia, North Korea, Ethiopia, Ghana, Iran, Pakistan, Serbia, Sri Lanka, Syria, Trinidad and Tobago, Tunisia and Yemen.
14 Peter Alldridge, *What Went Wrong with Money Laundering Law?* (Palgrave Macmillan 2016) 11–12.
15 Terrorism Act 2000 c. 11.
16 Directive (EU) 2015/849 of the European Parliament and of the Council of 20 May 2015 on the prevention of the use of the financial system for the purposes of money laundering or terrorist financing, amending Regulation (EU) No. 648/2012, and repealing Directive 2005/60/EC and Commission Directive 2006/70/EC [2015] OJ L141/73. From now on it will be referred to as the '4th Money Laundering Directive'.
17 Directive (EU) 2018/843 of the European Parliament and of the Council of 30 May 2018 amending Directive (EU) 2015/849 on the prevention of the use of the financial system for the purposes of money laundering or terrorist financing, and amending Directives 2009/138/EC and 2013/36/EU [2018] OJ L156/43. From now on it will be referred to as the '5th Money Laundering Directive'.
18 The Money Laundering, Terrorist Financing and Transfer of Funds (Information on the Payer) Regulations 2017, SI 2017/692. From now on, they will be referred to as the 'Money Laundering Regulations 2017'.
19 HM Treasury, 'Transposition of the Fifth Money Laundering Directive: Consultation' (2019) <https://www.gov.uk/government/consultations/transposition-of-the-fifth-money-laundering-directive> (accessed 6 April 2020).

10.4 The internal governance for AML and CTF compliance in banks and the role of the Financial Conduct Authority

The regulatory framework that applies to banks aims to enrol them to the fight against ML and TF and follows the model of a risk-based approach and of outcomes-focused regulation. The regulatory regime is encapsulated in the Fourth Money Laundering Directive, as amended by the Fifth Directive, the Money Laundering Regulations 2017 and the Financial Conduct Authority (FCA) Handbook.[20] The key concept is customer due diligence, and it encompasses measures that banks must apply to customers to prevent the use of the financial system for the purposes of ML and TF. As it will be discussed, the level of intensity of customer due diligence varies according to the risk that each customer poses. Standard customer due diligence is thus differentiated from simplified due diligence for low-risk customers, and from enhanced due diligence for high-risk customers, such as politically exposed persons.

10.4.1 Risk assessments and the duty to have adequate controls

The Directive, which is a minimum harmonisation instrument,[21] applies to credit institutions and financial institutions as well as to a range of professionals and firms that fall beyond the scope of this book.[22] The Commission was tasked to perform an initial risk assessment by 26 June 2017 and then every two years.[23] Member States are required to conduct national risk assessments and keep them up-to-date.[24] The Commission is empowered to adopt delegated acts to identify high-risk third countries with strategic deficiencies in their AML and CTF frameworks.[25] Consequently, the Commission adopted in February 2019 a draft delegated act listing 23 countries and territories,[26] but the Council rejected the delegated act in March 2019 apparently due to Member State concerns with the process and fears of trade retaliation by the US, four dependent territories of which were included in the list, and other major trade partners, such as Saudi Arabia.[27]

Obliged entities, such as banks, are also required to conduct risk assessments, keep them up-to-date and make them available to national competent authorities. In addition, obliged entities must have in place group-wide policies, controls and procedures to mitigate and manage effectively the risks of ML and TF, proportionate to their business nature and size.[28] Therefore, large UK banks are required to have highly sophisticated policies,

---

20 FCA Handbook, SYSC 6.3 Financial Crime.
21 Fourth Money Laundering Directive, art 5.
22 Fourth Money Laundering Directive, art 2 (1), and Money Laundering Regulations 2017, reg 8 (2).
23 Fourth Money Laundering Directive, art 6. The most recent EU-wide risk assessment was published in June 2019.
24 Fourth Money Laundering Directive, art 7. For the most recent UK risk assessment, see above n 6.
25 Fourth Money Laundering Directive, art 9.
26 European Commission Adopts New List of Third Countries with Weak Anti-money Laundering and Terrorist Financing Regimes (Strasbourg, 13 February 2019) <http://europa.eu/rapid/press-release_IP-19-781_ en.htm> (accessed 15 June 2020).
27 Money laundering and terrorist financing: Council returns draft list of high risk countries to the Commission (7 March 2020) <https://www.consilium.europa.eu/en/press/press-releases/2019/03/07/money-laundering-and-terrorist-financing-council-returns-draft-list-of-high-risk-countries-to-the-commission/?utm_ source=dsms-auto&utm_medium=email&utm_campaign=Money+laundering+and+terrorist+ financing%3a+Council+returns+draft+list+of+high+risk+countries+to+the+Commission> (accessed 14 June 2020).
28 Fourth Money Laundering Directive, arts 8 and 45.

controls and procedures. These must be approved and monitored by senior management and must include model risk management practices, customer due diligence, reporting, record-keeping, internal control, compliance management, the appointment of a compliance officer at management level, employee screening and an independent audit function. In particular, banks must ensure that their employees are aware of the provisions adopted pursuant to the Directive and participate in 'special ongoing training programmes to help them recognise operations which may be related to money laundering or terrorist financing', and must designate an individual member of the board responsible for compliance with the Directive.[29] This is an example of a process-oriented approach to regulation, where firms are required to put in place systems and internal processes to ensure compliance under the scrutiny of the regulator. Such an approach – which can be described as 'meta-regulation' or 'new governance' – is appropriate when an outcomes-oriented approach is not practicable due to the indeterminable nature of desired outcomes.[30]

10.4.2 Customer due diligence

Banks are required to apply customer due diligence when establishing a business relationship, when carrying out particular transactions (including any transaction exceeding 15,000 euros), when there is a suspicion of ML or TF, and when there are doubts about the veracity or adequacy of previously obtained customer identification data.[31] Anonymous customer accounts and safe deposit boxes must not be kept.[32] Customer due diligence includes the following components: (a) verifying the customer's identity using an independent source of data; (b) identifying the beneficial owner and verifying his identity and, in the case of customers who are legal persons or trusts, taking reasonable measures to understand their ownership and control structure; (c) assessing the purpose and intended nature of the business relationship; and (d) conducting ongoing monitoring of the relationship, including scrutiny of transactions, and ensuring that the documents, data or information held are kept up-to-date.[33] Although banks must apply all these measures, they are allowed to determine the extent of their application on a risk-sensitive basis, taking into account the following factors: the purpose of the account or relationship, the value of assets or transactions and the duration or regularity of the relationship.[34]

In certain cases, banks are permitted to apply simplified customer due diligence measures if they are satisfied that a relationship or transaction presents a lower degree of risk.[35] The factors that indicate lower risk include the following: (1) the customer being a listed public company; (2) the customer being a public body or state-owned enterprise; (3) the customer being resident within the EU or in a third country with an effective AML and CTF regime; and (4) certain low-risk products, such as low-premium life insurance policies, pension schemes and limited electronic money.[36]

---

29 Fourth Money Laundering Directive, art 46.
30 For a discussion and evaluation of the use of meta-regulation in financial institutions, see Iris H.-Y. Chiu, *Regulating (from) the Inside: The Legal Framework for Internal Control in Banks and Financial Institutions* (Hart Publishing 2015) 14–33.
31 Fourth Money Laundering Directive, art 11.
32 Fourth Money Laundering Directive, art 10 (1), as amended by Fifth Money Laundering Directive, art 1 (6).
33 Fourth Money Laundering Directive, art 13 (1).
34 Fourth Money Laundering Directive, art 13 (2)–(3) and Annex I.
35 Fourth Money Laundering Directive, art 15.
36 Fourth Money Laundering Directive, art 16 and Annex II.

Conversely, banks have to apply enhanced customer due diligence measures in the case of persons or legal entities established in high-risk third countries, cross-border correspondent relationships, politically exposed persons and in other cases of higher risk. In particular, banks must scrutinise the background and purpose of any transaction that is complex, unusually large, conducted in an unusual pattern or that does not have an apparent economic or lawful purpose.[37] High-risk factors to be taken into account include (1) business conducted in unusual circumstances; (2) customers resident in high-risk third countries; (3) customers which are legal persons (e.g. companies) that have the function of personal asset-holding vehicles; (4) customers that are companies that have nominee shareholders or bearer shares; (5) customers that are companies with an unusual or excessively complex ownership structure; (6) customers that are cash-intensive businesses; (7) private banking services; (8) products that favour anonymity; (9) non-face-to-face business relationships; (10) payments received from unknown third parties; and (11) new products and new business practices.[38]

We now proceed to examine the detailed rules on enhanced customer due diligence that apply to business relationships involving high-risk third countries, cross-border correspondent relationships and politically exposed persons. In the case of business relationships or transactions involving high-risk third countries a new provision introduced by the Fifth Directive requires banks to obtain additional information on the customer, the intended nature of the business relationship, the source of funds and wealth and the reason for the transactions; to obtain senior management approval; and to conduct enhanced ongoing monitoring. Additionally, banks must apply at least one of the following measures: (a) additional elements of enhanced due diligence; (b) enhanced reporting mechanisms of financial transactions; and (c) applying upper limits to such business relationships or transactions.[39] With respect to cross-border correspondent relationships with a third-country respondent institution, banks must collect information on the respondent institution, assess its AML and CTF controls, obtain senior management approval and document the responsibilities of each institution.[40] In the case of payable-through accounts, banks must make sure that the respondent institution has verified the identity of the customer and applied customer due diligence.

Furthermore, banks are obliged to have in place adequate risk management systems to identify customers that are politically exposed persons and must obtain senior management approval to deal with such persons, establish their source of funds and wealth and conduct enhanced ongoing monitoring of these relationships.[41] Politically exposed persons are defined as persons who are or have been entrusted with prominent public functions.[42] This category includes heads of state; heads of government; ministers; members of parliament; members of the governing bodies of political parties; members of supreme courts, of constitutional courts and of other courts whose decisions are not normally subject to appeal, ambassadors, *chargés d'affaires* and high-ranking officers in the armed forces; and members of the boards of central banks, state-owned enterprises and international organisations. A new provision introduced by the Fifth Directive requires Member States to draw up,

---

37 Fourth Money Laundering Directive, art 18 (2), as amended by Fifth Money Laundering Directive, art 1 (10) (b).
38 Fourth Money Laundering Directive, Annex 3.
39 Fourth Money Laundering Directive, art 18a, inserted by Fifth Money Laundering Directive, art 1 (11).
40 Fourth Money Laundering Directive, art 19.
41 Fourth Money Laundering Directive, art 20.
42 Fourth Money Laundering Directive, art 3 (9).

communicate to the Commission and publicise a list indicating the exact functions which, according to their national laws, regulations and administrative provisions, qualify as prominent public functions.[43] Banks must continue to apply enhanced due diligence on politically exposed persons after they leave office for a period of at least 12 months and in any case until they cease to pose increased risk.[44] The same measures apply to family members of politically exposed persons,[45] which are defined as their spouses, children and their spouses, and parents.[46] Banks are also prohibited from entering into a correspondent relationship with a shell bank.[47] A shell bank is a credit institution or financial institution, 'which is incorporated in a jurisdiction in which it has no physical presence, involving meaningful mind and management, and which is unaffiliated with a regulated financial group'.[48]

10.4.3 The supervisory role of the FCA

This section provides an overview of the UK supervisory arrangements with respect to ML and TF, as far as banks are concerned.[49] The Fourth Directive requires Member States to ensure that competent authorities monitor effectively and, in the case of banks, that they have enhanced supervisory powers.[50] The UK national competent authority for credit institutions and financial institutions is the FCA.[51] As such, the FCA is given broad powers to require information from banks, enter and inspect their premises and retain relevant documents.[52] For instance, the FCA is currently investigating HSBC's AML systems and compliance.[53] Regarding enforcement powers, the FCA is granted the usual toolkit of civil (administrative) sanctions: fines, public censure, withdrawal, suspension or limitation of authorisation and prohibitions on senior management, all of which may be applied for the

---

43 Fourth Money Laundering Directive, art 20a, inserted by Fifth Money Laundering Directive, art 1 (13).
44 Fourth Money Laundering Directive, art 22.
45 Fourth Money Laundering Directive, art 23.
46 Fourth Money Laundering Directive, art 3 (10).
47 Fourth Money Laundering Directive, art 24.
48 Fourth Money Laundering Directive, art 3 (17).
49 It must be noted that there are several professional bodies acting as supervisors for other firms and professionals that are subject to the AML and CTF framework. These are as follows: Association of Accounting Technicians, Association of Chartered Certified Accountants, Association of International Accountants, Association of Taxation Technicians, Chartered Institute of Legal Executives/ CILEx Regulation, Chartered Institute of Management Accountants, Chartered Institute of Taxation, Council for Licensed Conveyancers, Faculty of Advocates, Faculty Office of the Archbishop of Canterbury, Bar Standards Board, General Council of the Bar of Northern Ireland, Insolvency Practitioners Association, Institute of Certified Bookkeepers, Institute of Chartered Accountants in England and Wales, Institute of Chartered Accountants in Ireland, Institute of Chartered Accountants of Scotland, Institute of Financial Accountants, International Association of Bookkeepers, Solicitors Regulation Authority, Law Society of Northern Ireland, Law Society of Scotland. These bodies are overseen by the Office for Professional Body Anti-Money Laundering Supervision (OPBAS), which is part of the FCA, and which has been granted enforcement powers under the Oversight of Professional Body Anti-Money Laundering and Counter Terrorist Financing Supervision Regulations 2017 (SI 2017/1301).
50 Fourth Money Laundering Directive, art 48.
51 Money Laundering Regulations 2017, reg 7.
52 Money Laundering Regulations 2017, regs 65–74.
53 HSBC Holdings Plc, 'Annual Report and Accounts 2018' 290, <https://www.hsbc.com/investors/results-and-announcements/annual-report> (accessed 10 June 2020). It is worth noting that HSBC agreed to pay $1.9bn to the US authorities as part of a settlement of enforcement action in connection with money laundering. See Robert Peston, 'HSBC to Pay $1.9bn in US Money Laundering Penalties' *BBC News* (11 December 2012) <https://www.bbc.co.uk/news/business-20673466> (accessed 20 May 2020).

same breach.[54] In particular, the FCA can impose on any regulated person that has contravened a relevant requirement a fine of such amount as it deems appropriate and/or makes a public statement of censure.[55] This power (under the predecessor to the 2017 Regulations) was exercised in 2017 when the FCA fined Deutsche Bank AG £163 million for failing to maintain an adequate AML control framework between 2012 and 2015, the fine being the highest ever imposed by UK authorities in connection to ML.[56] Moreover, in the case of repeated or systematic failures, the FCA can cancel or suspend for up to 12 months or impose limitations for up to 12 months on any permission to carry on a regulated activity.[57] The FCA can also impose a temporary or permanent prohibition on having a management role within the regulated sector on any officer of a regulated firm who was knowingly concerned in a contravention of a relevant requirement.[58]

When deciding the type and level of sanction to impose, the FCA must take into account: (a) the gravity and the duration of the contravention or failure; (b) the degree of responsibility of the relevant person; (c) the financial strength of the relevant person; (d) the amount of profits gained or losses avoided by the relevant person; (e) the losses for third parties caused by the contravention or failure; (f) the level of co-operation of the relevant person with the FCA; (g) previous contraventions or failures by the relevant person; and (h) any potential systemic consequences of the contravention or failure.[59] A bank or bank manager who has been imposed a sanction by the FCA under this regime is entitled to appeal to the Upper Tribunal.[60] Finally, it must be noted that the Regulations also create three (minor) criminal offences of contravening a relevant requirement, prejudicing an investigation and providing false information, all of which are punishable on indictment by imprisonment of up to two years or a fine or both.[61]

10.5 The scope of banks' duty to report suspicions: the substantive ML and TF offences

To understand what types of customer behaviour or transaction can be relevant for banks it is necessary to examine the substantive criminal offences that penalise ML and TF in the UK. These offences can be committed by banks and bank employees in the course of their duties and thus represent part of the legal risk that banks and bank staff are exposed to, as the main consequence of failure to comply with the relevant reporting obligations.

10.5.1 The ML offences

POCA contains three substantive ML offences relating to criminal property: (a) concealing (Section 327); (b) entering into arrangements (Section 328) and acquisition; and (c) use

---

54 Money Laundering Regulations 2017, reg 79.
55 Money Laundering Regulations 2017, reg 76.
56 FCA, 'FCA Fines Deutsche Bank £163 Million for Serious Anti-money Laundering Controls Failings' (31 January 2017) <https://www.fca.org.uk/news/press-releases/fca-fines-deutsche-bank-163-million-anti-money-laundering-controls-failure> (accessed 25 May 2020).
57 Money Laundering Regulations 2017, reg 77.
58 Money Laundering Regulations 2017, reg 78.
59 Money Laundering Regulations 2017, reg 81.
60 Money Laundering Regulations 2017, reg 93.
61 Money Laundering Regulations 2017, regs 86–88.

and possession (Section 329). Central to all offences is the concept of criminal property, which applies to Part 7 of the Act. Criminal property is property that 'constitutes a person's benefit from criminal conduct or it represents such a benefit (in whole or part and whether directly or indirectly)' insofar as the defendant so knows or suspects.[62] Benefitting includes deriving any property or pecuniary advantage as a result of, or in connection with, criminal conduct.[63] Criminal conduct is defined as conduct that constitutes an offence in any part of the UK, or that would constitute an offence in any part of the UK, if it took place there.[64] Property is defined broadly as including money, real property, personal property, things in action and intangible property and encompassing both legal estates and equitable interests and powers.[65]

Thus, the UK adopts an 'all crimes approach' which means that any criminal offence can give rise to an ML offence, rather than only serious offences. This goes beyond the obligations of the UK under the Fourth Directive,[66] and indeed, many other EU Member States adopt a different approach whereby only crimes that can be punished by a prescribed period of imprisonment or only crimes belonging to a special list of serious crimes can give rise to ML offences.[67] There is also no time limit regarding the time the predicate offence was committed. This means, for instance, that any stolen goods or the proceeds of drugs trade constitute criminal property as well as any amounts that ought to have been paid as tax, if there is criminal tax evasion, and any monies or goods given to any person as reward for taking part in a criminal organisation.

Moreover, the definition of criminal conduct *prima facie* captures behaviours that occurred outside the UK, insofar as they are prohibited by the criminal law of any part of the UK, even if they are lawful according to the law of the country or territory where they occurred. This means, for instance, that the proceeds of trading in a substance, taking place in country X, that is lawful under the laws of country X, but would constitute an offence if committed in England, still constitute criminal property under POCA and may give rise to an ML offence, such as concealing, in the UK. In other words, there is no requirement for double criminality, that is, that for conduct taking place outside the UK, there is no requirement that it is criminal under the laws of both the UK and the country where the conduct took place.[68] However, since 2005 an exemption applies to all three substantive ML offences to the effect that no offence is committed if a person knows or reasonably believes that the relevant conduct occurred in a particular country outside the UK, and the conduct was not at the relevant time unlawful under the applicable criminal law of that country and is not of a type prescribed by the Secretary of State.[69] This is not the same as the double criminality standard as it depends on the knowledge of the person engaging in the act that may constitute an ML offence and only applies to offences not prescribed by the Secretary of State. The prescribed offences comprise any offence that would be punishable

62 POCA 2002, s 340 (3).
63 POCA 2002, s 340 (5)–(8).
64 POCA 2002, s 340 (2).
65 POCA 2002, s 340 (9)–(10).
66 On the notion of criminal activity under the Directive, see Fourth Money Laundering Directive, art 3 (4).
67 For an overview of the different approaches taken by major jurisdictions internationally, see van Duyne (above n 3) 171–174.
68 This is at odds with the approach taken in Part 5 of POCA on civil recovery of the proceeds of unlawful conduct, where a double criminality standard is adopted. See POCA, s 241(2).
69 See POCA 2002 s 327 (2A)–(2B), s 328 (3)–(4) and s 329 (2A)–(2B). These were inserted by the Serious Organised Crime and Police Act 2005, ss 102–103.

by imprisonment of a maximum term that exceeds 12 months in any part of the UK, if it occurred there.[70] So, the exemption applies only to behaviours that would constitute a very minor offence in the UK, e.g. any of the many minor offences included in the Companies Act 2006. For more serious offences committed abroad, their treatment by the law of the land where they were committed remains irrelevant.

We now proceed to examine the *actus reus* of the three offences. Under Section 327 it is an offence to conceal, disguise, convert, transfer or remove criminal property form any part of the UK, including concealing the property's nature, source, location, disposition, movement or ownership. Section 328 makes it an offence to enter into or become concerned in an arrangement that facilitates the acquisition, retention, use or control of criminal property. Section 329 penalises the acquisition, use and possession of criminal property other than for adequate consideration. Consideration is deemed inadequate if its value is significantly less than the value of, as the case may be, the property or of its use or possession. The adequacy of consideration limitation is a special one that applies only to the offence in Section 329 contrary to five general limitations applying to all substantive ML offences that will be discussed below.

The *mens rea* of all offences requires that the defendant knows or suspects that the property in question is criminal property. For instance, if A receives a piece of jewellery as a gift from B and has no idea and does not suspect that B has stolen it then A does not commit the offence in Section 329, as the property is not criminal property as far as A is concerned. For the offence in Section 328, there is an additional *mens rea* element: the defendant must know or suspect that the arrangement that he enters or gets concerned with facilitates the acquisition, retention, use or control of criminal property. In all cases, suspicion is sufficient as a mental state to ground criminal liability and it also triggers reporting obligations, as we will see in the next section. Suspicion is not defined in the statute, so it is necessary to examine the case law. The leading case is the decision of the Court of Appeal in *R v Da Silva*,[71] which interpreted the term suspicion used in Section 93A(1)(a) of the Criminal Justice Act 1988. The Court ruled that:

> It seems to us that the essential element in the word 'suspect' and its affiliates, in this context, is that the defendant must think that there is a possibility, which is more than fanciful, that the relevant facts exist. A vague feeling of unease would not suffice. But the statute does not require the suspicion to be 'clear' or 'firmly grounded and targeted on specific facts', or based upon 'reasonable grounds'.

This is a very low threshold which has been criticised by the Law Commission on the grounds that it is likely to lead to excessive reporting of suspicious conduct and is liable to be inconsistently applied.[72] It should also be noted that EU law only requires the criminalisation of intentional conduct that constitutes ML.[73] Bank employees are thus vulnerable to commit particularly the concealing and arrangements offences if they follow

---

70 See Proceeds of Crime Act 2002 (Money Laundering: Exceptions to Overseas Conduct Defence) Order 2006, SI 2006/1070. The Order, however, excludes from the scope of the exemption any offence under the Lotteries and Amusements Act 1976 and under Sections 23 and 25 of the Financial Services and Markets Act 2000.

71 [2006] EWCA Crim 1654, [2006] 2 Cr App R 35.

72 Law Commission, 'Anti-Money Laundering: The SARs Regime Consultation Paper' (Law Com No. 236, 2018) [2.64].

73 Fourth Money Laundering Directive, art 1 (3).

the instructions of a client in operating an account, while they suspect that the client's funds constitute criminal property insofar as it is indeed criminal property. In addition, bank employees may be held criminally liable for aiding or abetting the commission of an ML offence.[74]

Given the very broad scope of the three offences, it is unsurprising that there is a series of general exemptions. These are sometimes labelled as defences, although nothing in the statute imposes a reversed burden of proof on the defendant,[75] and for this reason the term 'exemptions' will be used herein. One of the exemptions refers to lawful overseas conduct and has already been discussed. Another exemption is of carrying out a law enforcement function, which is not relevant to banks and their employees.[76] For banks there are three significant exemptions: authorised disclosure, intention to disclose but failure due to a reasonable excuse and transactions below a threshold amount.

If the relevant person makes an authorised disclosure to the authorities and obtains consent before processing the relevant transaction, no offence is committed.[77] Disclosure must be to a constable, customs officer or nominated officer of the firm.[78] It must be made before the transaction or during a transaction as soon as suspicion arises, unless there is reasonable excuse. This means in practice that to avoid criminal liability a bank employee who suspects that a customer's account contains criminal property must block the account, report the suspicion to the bank's nominated officer and, if the nominated officer of the bank makes a SAR, wait for consent to be given by the FIU before unblocking the account and following any instructions of the customer. The reasonable excuse exemption is difficult to interpret as there is no guidance on what constitutes reasonable excuse in the banking context. Any threats or duress would no doubt suffice, but if the scope of reasonable excuse is so limited, then it adds little to the general principles of criminal law.

The threshold exemption is important for banks and, indeed, it only applies to deposit-taking bodies.[79] Currently, the threshold amount is £250.[80] As a result, a bank employee who suspects that funds in a customer's account constitute criminal property may continue to perform transactions without incurring criminal liability, if the value of the criminal property concerned is less than £250. In the case of a customer who is suspected of criminal activity, this permits small payments and cash withdrawals to be made out of the account, so that the customer can meet daily living expenses. In that sense, the threshold is low as it is insufficient for most mortgage repayments, especially in London, and it could be argued that a higher threshold is warrantied for mortgage repayments.[81]

---

74 See POCA 2002, s 340 (11).
75 In *Hogan v The DPP* [2007] 1 WLR 2944 the court ruled that, relating to the adequacy of consideration limitation under Section 329, once the issue is raised it is for the Crown to prove what consideration was advanced and its inadequacy. The Criminal Justice Act 1988 explicitly referred to defences, but POCA abandoned this language. The court found that the change of statutory language was deliberate and referred to the general principles that ambiguity in criminal statutes should be resolved in favour of the defendant, and that an opposite interpretation would offend the presumption of innocence right enshrined in article 6 (2) of the European Convention of Human Rights and implemented by the Human Rights Act 1998. For a detailed analysis, see Robin Booth et al., *Money Laundering Law and Regulation: A Practical Guide* (OUP 2011) 58–61.
76 POCA 2002, s 327 (2) (c); s 328 (2) (c); and 329 (2) (d).
77 POCA 2002, s 327 (2) (a); s 328 (2) (a); and 329 (2) (a).
78 POCA 2002, s 338 (1).
79 POCA 2002, s 327 (2C), s 328 (5) and s 329 (2C).
80 POCA 2002, s 339A (2).
81 'Anti-Money Laundering: The SARs Regime' (above n 72) [2.70].

The penalties under the three substantive ML offences are severe. On conviction on indictment, a person is liable to imprisonment up to 14 years, or to a fine or both. On summary conviction, a person is liable to imprisonment up to six months or to a fine up to the statutory maximum or both.[82] The maximum penalty of 14 years is higher than the maximum penalties provided for by the majority of other EU Member States but comparable to or lower than the penalties imposed by other common law countries.[83]

As we discussed, making an authorised disclosure and refraining from acting until consent has been given is necessary to avoid the risk of criminal liability. The duty to disclose that is indirectly imposed by the three offences is complemented by a direct duty to disclose, which is imposed by the offences of failure to disclose.[84] From the perspective of banks two of these offences are relevant: the regulated sector offence (Section 330) applying to all bank employees,[85] and the nominated officers in the regulated sector offence (Section 331) applying to banks' nominated officers. A disclosure made in compliance with these provisions is described as a required disclosure and is distinguishable from an authorised disclosure which constitutes an exemption under the three substantive offences.

The two offences are similar with the only differences reflecting that bank employees have to disclose to the nominated officer, while nominated officers have to disclose any information coming to them as part of required disclosures to the National Crime Agency (NCA). The *actus reus* elements of the offences are as follows: (a) the matter must have come to a bank employee in the course of a business in the regulated sector or to a nominated officer under a disclosure under Section 330[86]; and (b) a bank employee must have failed to disclose to the nominated officer – or a nominated officer must have failed to disclose to the NCA – as soon as possible the identity of the person suspected of ML, the whereabouts of the laundered property if known and any other relevant information.[87] There are two *mens rea* elements: (i) the defendant must know or suspect or have reasonable grounds for knowing or suspecting that another person is engaged in ML[88]; and (ii) the defendant must either be able to identify the person engaged in ML (or the whereabouts of the laundered property) or must believe or have reasonable grounds to believe that the information he has will or may assist in identifying the guilty person (or the whereabouts of the laundered property).[89] Having reasonable grounds for suspecting has been interpreted by the court as an objective test in the context of Section 17 of the Terrorism Act 2000,[90] and this interpretation is likely to apply also to the failure to disclose offences under POCA.

---

82 POCA 2002, s 334 (1).
83 The maximum custodial sentence for ML is ten years in Canada, France, Germany and Austria; six years in the Netherlands; and five years in Belgium and Switzerland. It is, however, 25 years in Australia and 20 years in the US. See van Duyne (above n 3) 167.
84 POCA 2002, ss 330–332.
85 Banking is part of the regulated sector as the regulated sector includes the acceptance by a credit institution of deposits and carrying of a board list of activities by a credit institution. See POCA, Schedule 9, s 1 (1) (a) and (b). It is worth noting that the disclosure offences cover many other professionals apart from bank employees and nominated officers such as lawyers, accountants, auditors and insolvency practitioners.
86 POCA 2002, s 330 (3) and s 331 (3).
87 POCA 2002, s 330 (4) and s 331 (4).
88 POCA 2002, s 330 (2) and s 331 (2).
89 POCA 2002, s 330 (3A) and s 331 (3A).
90 *R v Sally Lane and John Letts* [2018] UKSC 36. It is worth noting that the Supreme Court did not follow the approach taken in a different context by the House of Lords in *R v Saik* [2006] UKHL 18.

For both offences, there are exemptions of reasonable excuse and of lawful overseas conduct that are drafted exactly in the same manner as under the three substantive ML offences. The offence in Section 330 is subject to further exemptions. Of these only one is relevant to bank employees. A person does not commit an offence if they do not know or suspect that someone is engaged in ML (but had reasonable grounds for suspecting) and they have not been provided by their employer with appropriate training, as specified by the Secretary of State.[91] So, bank employees who act in good faith will not be penalised for failure to suspect despite having reasonable grounds of doing so, provided that they did not receive adequate training. Regarding the determination of criminal liability of nominated officers under Section 331, the court must consider whether the defendant officer followed relevant guidance which has been issued by a supervisory authority or appropriate body and approved by the Treasury.[92] For banks and the financial services in general[93] the relevant guidance is the guidance published by the Joint Money Laundering Steering Group (JMLSG). The latest approved guidance was issued on 21 December 2017 and received ministerial approval on 5 March 2018. Since then further revisions to the guidance have been made and ministerial approval is pending.[94] Failure to disclose is punishable on conviction on indictment by imprisonment up to five years or a fine or both, and on summary conviction by imprisonment up to six months or to a fine up to the statutory maximum or both.[95]

10.5.2 The terrorist financing offences

Having examined the disclosure obligations for banks triggered by the ML offences, we now turn our attention to the disclosure obligations triggered by offences relating to the financing of terrorism. The majority of the applicable statutory rules can be found in Part 3 of the Terrorism Act 2000. The Act contains five substantive TF offences: fund-raising (Section 15), use and possession (Section 16), funding arrangements (Section 17), insurance payments in response to terrorist demands (Section 17A), and money laundering of terrorist property (Section 18). All offences are based on the concept of terrorist property which is defined in Section 14. Terrorist property is any property which either is likely to be used for the purposes of terrorism (including all resources of proscribed organisations) or any property which represents the proceeds of acts of terrorism, or of acts carried out for the purposes of terrorism. Terrorism is defined as any act or threat of serious violence against the person, serious damage to property, endangering life, creating a serious risk to public health and safety or seriously interfering with an electronic system, insofar as it is designed to influence the government or intimidate the public and is made for the purpose of advancing a political, religious, racial or ideological cause.[96]

The *actus reus* of each of the four original substantive TF offences is as follows: for the fund-raising offence, to invite someone to provide property, receive property or provide property; for the use and possession offence, to use or possess property; for the funding

---

91 POCA 2002, s 330 (7).

92 POCA 2002, s 331 (7)–(9).

93 Outside the financial services, there are 22 relevant professional bodies issuing guidance, which are now supervised by the Office for Professional Body Anti-Money Laundering Supervision (OPBAS), which is part of the FCA.

94 See <http://www.jmlsg.org.uk/industry-guidance/article/jmlsg-guidance-current> (accessed 25 May 2020).

95 POCA 2002, s 334 (2).

96 Terrorism Act 2000, s 1.

arrangements offence, to enter into or become concerned in an arrangement as a result of which money or other property is made available to another person; and for the ML offence, to enter into or become concerned in an arrangement which facilitates the retention or control by or on behalf of another person of terrorist property by concealment, removal from the jurisdiction, transfer to nominees or in any other way. The *mens rea* component in Sections 15–17 is intending to use property for the purposes of terrorism or knowing or having reasonable cause to suspect that property will or may be used for the purposes of terrorism. For the money laundering offence, it is a defence to prove that the defendant did not know and had no reasonable cause to suspect that the arrangement is related to terrorist property. The reversed burden of proof is contrary to the approach taken for the substantive ML offences and raises questions of policy, as there appears to be no justification to differentiate between the two.

The offence of making insurance payments in response to terrorist demands warrants separate discussion. This offence was added in 2015[97] and targets situations where an insurance firm has offered insurance against kidnapping and ransom, including cyber ransom. The policy behind the offence is to prevent terrorists from obtaining ransoms as a result of kidnapping, cyber-attacks or other acts by prohibiting insurance firms from making payments to policy holders who either have already transferred funds or property to terrorists or will hand over the payment to terrorists. The *mens rea* element is that the insurer or the person authorising the payment on the insurer's behalf knows or has reasonable cause to suspect that the money or other property has been, or is to be, handed over in response to a demand made wholly or partly for the purposes of terrorism. Typically, insurance firms are limited liability companies and therefore they will be criminally liable, insofar as their employee who authorised payment has the relevant knowledge or cause of suspicion. If any director, company secretary or manager of the insurance company consented to, connived to or neglected to prevent the commission of such offence by the company, that person is also guilty of the same offence.[98] The penalties for the substantive TF offences are the same as for the substantive ML offences (on indictment, imprisonment up to 14 years or a fine or both).[99]

Similar to the ML offences, a series of exemptions apply to TF offences, which have the effect of compelling relevant persons to make disclosures to the authorities. A person does not commit an offence under Sections 15–18 if the person is acting with the express consent of a constable.[100] Once a person has become involved in a transaction and he becomes aware or suspect that property is terrorist, to avoid committing an offence the person must disclose his belief or suspicion and the information on which it is based to a constable on his own initiative and as soon as is reasonably practicable, unless there is reasonable excuse.[101] If the person is an employee and the organisation has established a procedure for such disclosures, then disclosure can also be made following the internal procedure.[102] However, if a constable forbids a person from continuing with a transaction and the person so does, the exemption from criminal liability ceases to apply.[103] In addition, a person who has relevant

97 It was inserted by the Counter-Terrorism and Security Act 2015, s 42.
98 Terrorism Act 2000, s 17A (2).
99 Terrorism Act 2000, s 22.
100 Terrorism Act 2000, s 21 (1).
101 Terrorism Act 2000, s 21 (2), (3) and (5).
102 Terrorism Act 2000, s 21 (6).
103 Terrorism Act 2000, s 21 (4).

knowledge or suspicion does not commit an offence if, before becoming involved in a transaction or arrangement, he makes a disclosure to the agent designated by the NCA of his suspicion or belief that property is terrorist and the information on which the suspicion or belief is based.[104] If the disclosure to the NCA is only made after the person has become involved in a transaction, the exemption applies only if there is reasonable excuse for the failure to disclose before becoming involved.[105] In any case, if there is intention to disclose and reasonable excuse, no offence is committed.[106]

Furthermore, the Act imposes positive duties to disclose information to the effect that failure to disclose is an independent offence. For credit institutions and financial institutions, the relevant duty is in Section 21A of the Act. Failure to disclose to a constable or nominated officer the information which came to a person in the course of a business in the regulated sector as a result of which the person knows or suspects, or has reasonable grounds for knowing or suspecting, that another person has committed an offence under Sections 15–18 constitutes an offence. For bank employees, the only exemption is the one of reasonable excuses. The offence of failing to disclose is punishable on indictment by imprisonment for a term not exceeding five years or a fine or both.

10.6 The internal process to generate a SAR

To comply with their positive duties to disclose information under POCA 2002 and the Terrorism Act 2000 and to avoid criminal liability for themselves and their employees under the substantive ML and TF offences banks submit SARs to the NCA. This section will examine the processes followed by banks to generate SARs and how relevant bank practice has evolved to date.

Disclosures can be classified into two categories: required disclosures are those that are made in compliance with a duty to disclose imposed by POCA or the Terrorism Act, whereas authorised disclosures are those made to protect the person disclosing from criminal liability under one of the exemptions provided for in the legislation. Typically, when an authorised disclosure is made consent is sought to continue with the relevant transaction or arrangement. An additional category of disclosure is voluntary disclosure. In all these cases, a disclosure is not to be taken to breach any restriction on the disclosure of information (however imposed), and thus, this is a qualification to the common law duty of confidentiality.[107]

A recent Law Commission consultation gathered evidence through interviews on the internal processes followed by large UK banks.[108] Each bank has a central transaction unit headed by the bank's nominated officer. Once a bank employee has suspicions, for instance, due to observing unusual activity, the employee submits electronically a report to the bank's central transaction unit. Apart from such manual alerts received from employees, the central transaction unit also receives automated alerts, which are generated based on algorithms that identify unusual patterns of activity (e.g. high value transactions over a short period of time that are inconsistent with the customer's profile). When an alert is

---

104 Terrorism Act 2000, s 21ZA.
105 Terrorism Act 2000, s 21ZB.
106 Terrorism Act 2000, s 21ZC.
107 See Terrorism Act s 21B for required disclosures and s 21CE for voluntary disclosures made in good faith. See also POCA s 337 and 338 (4) and 339ZB (1).
108 'Anti-money Laundering: The SARs Regime' (above n 72) [2.2]–[2.9].

made usually a block is placed on the affected account in order to prevent the dissipation of funds until a decision is made on whether a SAR is to be made. All manual alerts and most automated alerts are then investigated by an investigator who acts as an alternate of the nominated officer. One of the largest UK banks confirmed to the Law Commission that it employs 150 investigators. Overall, UK banks have to process approximately 20 million alerts annually.[109]

The task of the investigator is to decide whether a SAR is needed and whether the consent of the NCA should be sought. To do so, investigators take into account the profile of the customer and of their transactional counterparties and check for any adverse media coverage on the customer. They may make further enquiries to see if there is a reasonable explanation of the suspicious activity (e.g. the customer recently came to a large sum of money). The investigator produces a reasoned report and, if appropriate, makes a required or authorised disclosure. In more complex cases, the matter may be referred to the nominated officer. Nominated officers oversee the overall process, but given the volume of alerts and SARs, they can realistically only maintain a high-level overview of the process.

SARs are submitted to the UKFIU which is part of the NCA either using the NCA's SAR online system or, in the case of large banks, via bulk data transfer. The same standard form is used for both authorised and required disclosures.[110] On average, the UKFIU receives 2,000 SARs per day, of which 100 include requests for consent.[111] Access to SARs is restricted to law enforcement officers who have received training in handling sensitive data. SARs are deposited on an electronic database known as ELMER for a period of six years. According to the Law Commission report, ELMER currently holds 2.25 million SARs.[112]

10.7 The bank-customer relationship after the submission of a SAR

Once a SAR has been submitted, the bank must refrain from proceeding with the relevant transaction until it has received consent by the NCA. During this period, the relevant account is likely to be blocked and the relationship between the bank and customer will come under considerable strain. The customer may sue the bank for breach of contract, although such litigation has few prospects of success, as the case law demonstrates.

We first examine the timeframe within which the NCA has to respond to a SAR. Once an authorised disclosure seeking consent to continue with a transaction or arrangement is made, the law imposes a seven working-day period on the NCA to respond.[113] If no response is given, the NCA is deemed to have consented and the relevant person can rely on the exemption from criminal liability and continue with the transaction or arrangement. In the case of ML, if consent is refused, a moratorium period of 31 days is imposed during which the bank must not engage in any transactions or arrangements. The court may extend the moratorium period in increments of up to 31 days and up to a maximum of 186 days in addition to the original moratorium.[114] This is at the court's discretion if it is satisfied that '(a) an investigation is being carried out in relation to a relevant disclosure (but has

109 Ibid., [4.1].
110 Ibid., [2.13].
111 Ibid., [2.14].
112 Ibid., [2.17].
113 See Terrorism Act 2000, s 21ZA (2)–(4); and POCA s 335 (3), (5) and (7) and 336 (3).
114 POCA, s 336A (4)–(8).

not been completed), (b) the investigation is being conducted diligently and expeditiously, (c) further time is needed for conducting the investigation, and (d) it is reasonable in all the circumstances for the moratorium period to be extended'.[115] As soon as an application is made to the court to extend the moratorium period, the period is automatically extended until the court determines whether to grant an extension or not, but for no longer than 31 days.[116] The combined effect of these provisions is that a bank customer may have her account blocked for a period of up to 224 days starting from the day after the submission of a SAR.

During the period that the customer's account is blocked the bank and its employees cannot disclose to the customer that a SAR has been submitted, as doing so would lead to criminal liability under the tipping off offences contained in both POCA and the Terrorism Act 2000. The two regimes are virtually identical, so the following discussion will cover both simultaneously. Section 333A of POCA and 21D of the Terrorism Act 2000 makes it an offence to disclose that a disclosure (SAR) has been made or that an investigation into allegations of an ML or TF offence is being contemplated or is being carried out, insofar as the disclosure would be likely to prejudice any investigation and the information came to the person making the disclosure in the course of business in the regulated sector. The *mens rea* element is that the person making the disclosure must know or suspect that the disclosure is likely to prejudice any investigation.[117] There are several exemptions covering disclosures to supervisory authorities, to law enforcement agencies and as part of court proceedings.[118] Disclosure is also permitted to another employee of the same undertaking and to another credit or financial institution that belongs to the same corporate group, insofar as it is situated in an EEA State or in a country or territory imposing equivalent AML and CTF measures.[119] Furthermore, a credit institution may disclose to another credit institution, which is situated in an EEA State or in a country or territory imposing equivalent AML and CTF measures, provided that the disclosure relates to a common client or former client, or to a transaction involving them both, or to the provision of a service involving them both, and only for the purpose of preventing an ML or TF offence.[120] A person guilty for tipping off is liable to imprisonment of up to two years or a fine or both.

The fact that customer instructions to make payments are refused without the provision of any explanation puts banks in a very difficult position, especially in modern times that electronic transfers of funds typically happen instantaneously, and can generate civil litigation, as the customer may sue the bank for breach of contract. The principle that applies in such cases is that the court will not order a bank to do anything that would constitute a criminal offence and that failure to honour a customer's instructions in circumstances where doing so would be an offence does not constitute breach of contract. In *K Ltd v National Westminster Bank Plc*,[121] the Court of Appeal confirmed the first instance court's refusal to grant an interim injunction forcing National Westminster Bank to comply with the payment instructions of its customer, K Ltd. The bank had formed a suspicion that funds in the customer's account were criminal property and made a disclosure to customs seeking

---

115 POCA, s 336A (1).
116 POCA, s 336C (1)–(5).
117 POCA, s 333D (3)–(4); and Terrorism Act 2000, s 21G (3)–(4).
118 POCA, s 333D (1)–(1A); and Terrorism Act 2000, s 21G (1).
119 POCA, s 333B; and Terrorism Act 2000, s 21E.
120 POCA, s 333C; and Terrorism Act 2000, s 21F.
121 [2006] EWCA Civ 1039.

consent so as to avoid criminal liability under POCA Section 328. As complying with the customer's instructions in the circumstances would have been an offence, the court ruled that there could be no breach of contract.

In *Shah v HSBC Private Bank (UK) Limited*,[122] the court dismissed Mr Shah's claim for damages exceeding US$300 million in breach of contract against HSBC Private Bank. Mr Shah was a wealthy businessman who at the relevant time resided in Zimbabwe. Four large payment instructions given by Mr Shah between September 2006 and February 2007 were executed with delay by HSBC. This was because HSBC had formed a suspicion that the transactions constituted ML and, as a result, it submitted SARs to the Serious Organised Crime Agency (SOCA)[123] and waited for its consent before executing each instruction. In fact, in three of the four cases, consent was given and the payment was eventually made, while in one case the instruction was revoked by the customer. Mr Shah claimed that HSBC was in breach of contract due to the delay in executing his instructions and the failure to explain the reason for not doing so. He also claimed that this resulted in him incurring losses in excess of US$300 million due to action taken by the Government of Zimbabwe.

Initially, in 2009, Hamblen J summarily dismissed the claim, on the ground that for Mr Shah to challenge HSBC's conduct he would have to assert that HSBC had acted in bad faith, which he had not. Therefore, there was no real prospect of success of the claim against HSBC. However, the Court of Appeal overturned the first instance decision and ordered that the case proceed to full trial.[124] The court held that Hamblen J was wrong to conclude that alleging bad faith was the only route open to Mr Shah. The court also held that it was for HSBC to provide evidence to establish that it had genuinely held a suspicion and confirmed that, in principle, undue delay in making a SAR could constitute a breach of a bank's duty of care to the customer. As a result, the case proceeded to full hearing at the High Court before Supperstone J. The judge ruled that there was an implied term in the contract between HSBC and Mr Shah that allowed HSBC 'to refuse to execute payment instructions in the absence of "appropriate consent" under Section 335 POCA where it suspected a transaction constituted money laundering',[125] and that HSBC was obliged to refuse to provide any information to Mr Shah until July 2007 to avoid contravening Sections 333 and 342 POCA. Supperstone J also ruled that the bank's conduct did not cause the defendant any loss, as the losses he claimed were remote and unforeseeable. Therefore, the claim failed.

The litigation in *Shah v HSBC Private Bank (UK) Limited* illustrates the steps that banks need to take to ensure that they avoid civil liability while complying with their obligations under the AML and CTF regime.[126] First, the state of mind of the bank's Money Laundering Reporting Officer (MLRO) or of any officer to whom the MLRO has delegated authority to investigate alerts and make SARs will be taken to constitute the bank's state of mind. If the relevant person is in bad faith the bank will be liable in breach of contract. Assuming that there is no bad faith, it will be sufficient for the bank's investigator to have formed a relevant suspicion, as defined in *R v Da Silva*, discussed in Section 10.4.1.

---

122 [2012] EWHC 1283 (QB).

123 This was the predecessor of the National Crime Agency.

124 [2010] EWCA Civ 31.

125 At [236].

126 Banks may also be held liable if customers complain to the Financial Ombudsman Service, especially as they will not be able to disclose that they have made a SAR to defend. See 'Anti-money Laundering: The SARs Regime' (above n 72) [2.97].

The bank, if challenged, will have to provide evidence to the court of its internal procedures and documents relating to the SAR in question to prove that it had indeed formed a relevant suspicion. It follows that banks should maintain a clear audit trail. Once forming a suspicion, a bank must submit a SAR without undue delay. Once the authority's consent is given, the bank must execute the customer's instruction without undue delay. The bank will have to provide relevant information to the customer at a future point when any criminal investigation has been completed. Although the court is likely to imply terms that protect the bank in this context into the contract, banks may well be advised to include express terms to the same effect into their contracts with customers.

From the perspective of bank customers, the current state of the law means that entirely innocent customers may be subjected to large financial losses for which they have no valid claim against the bank. This has been observed eloquently by Laddie J in *Squirrell Ltd v National Westminster Bank*: 'In the result, if Squirrell is entirely innocent it may suffer severe damage for which it will not be compensated. [...] Whatever one might feel were Squirrell guilty of wrongdoing, if, as it says, it is innocent of any wrongdoing, this can be viewed as a grave injustice'.[127] This situation also creates serious difficulties for bank branch staff who are occasionally faced with threats of violence or suicide by customers whose accounts are blocked.[128]

10.8 Evaluating the UK AML and CTF framework

This section engages critically with the current UK AML and CTF framework as it applies to banks and assesses the normative justifications for the substantive ML and TF offences as well as the effectiveness of the present legal regime.

Conventionally the AML regime is justified on four grounds: (a) crime prevention and crime detection; (b) maintaining the reputation, integrity and stability of the financial system[129]; (c) the avoidance of unfair competition and price distortions[130]; and (d) preventing capital flight to tax heavens. There are salient reasons to doubt the cogency of the second, third and fourth justification, as ML and TF are unlikely to threaten financial stability, and other areas of law are more appropriate to deal with unfair competition and tax avoidance.[131] Arguably, the most important objective of the AML regime, and the main objective of the CTF regime, is the prevention of the predicate offences that generate funds that need laundering and the prevention of terrorist acts as well as the detection of persons who have committed such offences. This can be achieved as a result of information that is contained in SARs that are submitted by banks. In the best case, such information can lead to the avoidance of terrorist attacks, the arrest of offenders and the disruption of criminal enterprises due to lack of funding, and can reduce incentives to commit predicate offences, such as drugs trafficking, to the extent that their proceeds cannot be reintegrated into the

---

127 [2005] EWHC 664 (Ch), [7].

128 'Anti-Money Laundering: The SARs Regime' (above n 72) [2.98].

129 This is emphasised by para 2 of the Preamble to the Fourth Money Laundering Directive: 'The soundness, integrity and stability of credit institutions and financial institutions, and confidence in the financial system as a whole could be seriously jeopardised by the efforts of criminals and their associates to disguise the origin of criminal proceeds or to channel lawful or illicit money for terrorist purposes'.

130 On this, see Brigitte Unger, *The Scale and Impacts of Money Laundering* (Edward Elgar 2007) 122–132.

131 As argued by Alldridge, who engages in an in-depth critique of the possible harm caused by money laundering activity. See Alldridge (above n 14) 34–38.

financial system and enjoyed by the perpetrators. These are public policy goals which few would challenge.

However, it does not follow that the present regime is well-designed to achieve these goals. One major concern is that – due to the UK's all crimes approach,[132] and the risk that bank employees may be held liable if they hold a suspicion even without having reasonable grounds to suspect, or if they did not form a suspicion but had reasonable grounds to do so[133] – an excessive number of SARs are submitted. If this is the case, then the current regime inevitably causes unnecessary compliance cost for banks, which is likely to be at least partially transferred to customers, and high operational cost for the NCA and other authorities, which is ultimately borne by UK taxpayers. An excessive volume of reports can also make it harder to identify these that truly need to be investigated further thus undermining crime prevention and detection. So, the crucial question to be asked is whether there is excessive production of SARs in the UK. It would appear that this is the case. Indeed, 634,113 SARS were received by the UKFIU between October 2015 and March 2017, of which 27,471 requested consent due to suspicion of ML and 422 sought consent due to suspicion of TF. Consent was refused in only 5.67% of ML SARs and in 6.87% of TF SARs that sought consent.[134] The refusal of consent is significant, as cases where consent is refused are likely to lead to further investigation and ultimately prosecution. It is interesting that in more than 95% of cases disclosures do not seek consent to proceed with a transaction and are therefore required disclosures on the basis of a very mild suspicion. And that when consent is sought, it is granted in nearly 95% of cases. An additional argument supporting the claim that the UK system leads to an excessive number of reports can be drawn from comparing the situation in the UK to the situation in other EU Member States. It is remarkable that 36% of all SARs in the EU are generated in the UK. Other large countries such as Germany and France generate much fewer SARs than the UK; there were 24,054 reports in Germany in 2015 and 64,815 in France in 2016.[135]

The cost of AML and CTF compliance for banks is staggering. Banks generated nearly 83% of UK SARs between October 2015 and March 2017, and the British Bankers' Association estimated that its members spend at least £5 billion annually on financial crime compliance.[136] In parallel, as was discussed in the previous section, the current regime often has devastating financial consequences for individuals and firms that have their bank accounts blocked pending consent by the NCA. Even when the suspected customers are entirely innocent of wrongdoing, there is no remedy for them to recover their losses. Furthermore, UK banks tend to terminate business relationships with customers that are perceived to

---

132 For a critique of the all-crimes approach in the context of the legal profession, see Sarah Kebbell, '"Everyone's Looking at Nothing" – The Legal Profession and the Disproportionate Burden of the Proceeds of Crime Act 2002' (2017) 2017 *Criminal Law Review* 741.

133 Bello, for instance, argues that the behaviour of MLROs can be understood through the lens of the self-protecting theory which posits that compliance officers are likely to do what is best to protect themselves from liability rather than to fulfil their functions properly. Bello argues that MLROs align themselves with the bank they work for rather than the regulator and are therefore likely to report information in a defensive manner to protect themselves and the bank against the regulator. See Abdullahi Usman Bello, *Improving Anti-money Laundering Compliance: Self-Protecting Theory and Money Laundering Reporting Officers* (Palgrave Macmillan 2016) Chapter 3.

134 'Anti-Money Laundering: The SARs Regime' (above n 72) [4.2]–[4.3].

135 Ibid., [4.10]–[4.13].

136 Ibid., [1.19]–[1.20]. However, it is worth noting that there are no reliable academic studies on banks' compliance cost and banks are not being transparent on the matter.

present high risk, a practice known as de-risking.[137] This can lead to financial exclusion, and is likely to affect most severely members of minority groups and foreign customers.

Overall, it seems that the UK AML and CFT framework is characterised by unusually high – by international standards – and increasing volume of disclosures, which tend to be of low intelligence value and of poor quality, as a result of defensive over-reporting. The compliance burden is high, and the impact on customers that are the subjects of investigations is severe. To improve the UK regime, it is pertinent to review the all-crimes policy and to pay careful attention to the statutory threshold of criminality and especially to the notions of 'suspicion' and of 'having reasonable grounds for suspecting'.[138]

Glossary of terms

- Money laundering: The practice of hiding the criminal provenance of funds and re-integrating them into the legitimate financial system so that they can be used by the perpetrators of the underlying criminal offence.
- Terrorist financing: The criminal practice of raising funds to be used for, or in support of, the purposes of terrorism.
- Criminal property: Property that represents the gain from criminal activity or that is used to fund terrorist activity.
- Financial Action Task Force (FATF): Intergovernmental organisation founded in 1989 with the aim of combating money laundering and terrorist financing.
- Minimum harmonisation instrument: EU directive that requires Members States to achieve a minimum level of legal protection or of another legal outcome but permits them to provide for a higher level of protection/outcome.
- Customer due diligence: Obligation of banks and other firms to take reasonable steps to establish the true identity of their customers and monitor transactions as part of the anti-money laundering and counter-terrorist financing framework.
- Politically exposed persons: Individuals who currently do, or in the recent past have occupied state positions of high authority (legislative, executive, judicial, military, etc.) and their close family members.
- *Actus reus* (Latin): Component of a criminal offence meaning 'guilty act', i.e. the act or omission that is required for a certain criminal offence to be committed.
- *Mens rea* (Latin): Component of a criminal offence meaning 'guilty mind', i.e. the state of mind (e.g. Intention, recklessness, knowledge, suspicion) in which the perpetrator of a guilty act must be in order for him to commit the relevant criminal offence; there are offences that do not require a *mens rea* element and are known as strict liability offences.
- National Crime Agency (NCA): National law enforcement agency of the UK that deals with the most serious crime such as organised crime, human trafficking, drug trafficking, terrorism and serious economic crime.

---

137 On this phenomenon, see Tracy Durner and Liat Shetret, 'Understanding Bank De-risking and Its Effects on Financial Inclusion: An Exploratory Study' Global Center on Cooperative Security (2015) <https://www.oxfam.org/sites/www.oxfam.org/files/file_attachments/rr-bank-de-risking-181115-en_0.pdf> (accessed 28 May 2020).
138 This also appears to be the view of the Law Commission. See 'Anti-Money Laundering: the SARs Regime' (above n 72) [1.29]–[1.30].

- Suspicious activity report (SAR): Disclosure made by a bank or other regulated firm to the NCA under the anti-money laundering and counter-terrorist financing legislation detailing the bank's grounds for suspecting that certain individual has engaged, or attempted to engage, in money laundering or terrorist financing.
- De-risking: Practice followed by certain UK banks whereby business relationships are not commenced or discontinued with individuals possessing certain demographic characteristics who are deemed to present a high level of money laundering or terrorist financing risk.

Practice questions

The harsh criminal penalties provided by UK law for failure to disclose a subjective suspicion of money laundering or terrorist financing have led to an overproduction of SARs of low quality: this is costly for banks and their customers and does little to contribute to the fight against ML and TL. Critically discuss.

You may also find it useful to review the chapter through the following questions:

- How did the anti-money laundering and counter terrorist financing regime develop in the UK, EU and internationally?
- What is the harm caused by money laundering?
- What processes must UK banks maintain to ensure compliance with the AML and CTF regime?
- What is the role of the FCA in preventing financial crime?
- What are the substantive money laundering and terrorist financing offences? Are they too broad compared to other jurisdictions?
- How are suspicious activity reports (SARs) generated?
- Is there any effective judicial protection for bank customers who suffer loss due to their accounts being frozen as a result of the submission of the SAR?

Part III
Preventing banking crises

This part explores the principal regulatory tools that aim to prevent banking crises in terms of capital, liquidity, risk-taking and governance. It also explores shadow banking and emerging forms of banking which may potentially threaten financial stability.

11 Regulation of bank capital and liquidity

11.1 Introduction

This chapter examines the most crucial aspects of micro-prudential regulation, namely, capital adequacy and liquidity standards. Such standards set by the Basel Committee on Banking Supervision (BCBS) aim to address the risk that banks will become unable to pay their debts as they fall due. The discussion will explore the previous iterations of these principles (Basel I and II) before focusing on the currently applicable standards set by Basel III as implemented by the EU Capital Requirement Directive IV and Regulations. The Basel III minimum capital and liquidity standards increased the resilience of the global banking system but did not adequately address the 'too big to fail' problems. The new rules leave authorities with the same choices should a systemically important bank again find itself on the brink of failure: accept financial and economic turmoil or inject taxpayer money to keep it afloat. The chapter will conclude with an overview of the proposals for a future Basel IV and a tentative discussion of the possible impact of Brexit on the capital adequacy of UK banks.

11.2 International bank supervisory standards

The international framework for bank supervisory standards indicates the set of rules, principles and guidelines for monitoring the business conduct of credit institutions, and it is generally analysed in connection with the independence of central banks and other authorities in the discharge of prudential supervision.[1] While central bank accountability with regard to monetary policy is typically 'explanatory' (unless the law of the central bank is amended or the governor is removed from office, there is very little room for granting redress with regard to monetary policy decisions), the accountability of the central bank or the supervisory agency in the field of prudential supervision and regulation is sometimes 'explanatory' and sometimes 'amendatory'. Several legal scholars have recently explored the issue of [state] liability for loss caused by the inadequate supervision of banks,[2] in the context of the damages action against the Bank of England for the failure of Bank of Credit

---

1 Rosa Lastra, *Central Banking and Banking Regulation* (Financial Markets Group, London School of Economics, London, September 1996) 10–12.
2 Mads Andenas, 'Liability for Supervisors and Depositors' Rights: The BCCI and the Bank of England in the House of Lords' (2001) 22 *The Company Lawyer* 88, 226–234; see also Mads Andenas and Duncan Fairgrieve, 'To Supervise or to Compensate? A Comparative Study of State Liability for Negligent Banking Supervision' in Mads Andenas (ed), *Judicial Review in International Perspective* (Kluwer Law International 2000) 333–334.

and Commerce International (BCCI).[3] The plaintiffs claimed, *inter alia*, that the Bank of England was liable in damages for breach of its supervisory obligations under EU law. Goodhart points out that providing accountability and transparency for banking supervisors is particularly difficult, since the information that they get is frequently confidential and since 'success' is often measured by the absence of financial failures.[4] The recent financial crisis provides ample evidence about the difficult task supervisors have at hand.

Following the collapses of Bankhaus I.D. Herstatt in Germany, Franklin National Bank in the US[5] and British-Israel Bank of London in the UK,[6] the international financial community focused its attention on banking supervision. In this context, the BCBS issued the 'Basle Concordat' in September 1975 outlining few key principles, recommendations and best practices, regarding the supervision of banks operating internationally through branches (which are integral parts of a foreign parent bank), subsidiaries and joint ventures.[7] It has been observed that 'the Basel Concordat of 1975 set forth basic expectations among supervisors regarding how they would work together in regulating transnational institutions'.[8] The Basel Committee aimed both to develop international banking supervisory guidance and to prevent foreign banking establishments from escaping adequate supervision.[9] It developed a system of soft law with best practice supervisory rules that national regulators implemented domestically.[10] The Basel Committee drafted the Core Principles for Effective Banking Supervision and the Principles for the supervision of banks' foreign establishments (Concordat). The Basel Concordat originally formulated in 1975 and revised in 1983 (further refined and redefined in 1992) represents the regulatory framework for the consolidated supervision of international banking groups.[11] As has been argued, 'the Concordat established an outline co-operation and co-ordination framework based

---

3 *Three Rivers District Council v Governor and Company of the Bank of England (No. 3)* [2000] 2 WLR 1220; [2000] 3 All E.R. 1; [2000] Lloyd's Rep. Bank 235, HL.

4 Charles Goodhart, 'Regulating the Regulator – An Economist's Perspective on Accountability and Control' in Eilis Ferran and Charles Goodhart (eds), *Regulating Financial Services and Markets in the Twenty First Century* (Hart Publishing 2001) 162–163.

5 The cases of Franklin Bank and Bankhaus Herstatt raised many questions in relation to banking supervision. Specifically, Franklin Bank was shut down following significant foreign exchange losses and after a managed rundown of its operations. In Germany, Bankhaus Herstatt suffered significant foreign exchange losses and closed down in 1974. At the time of its closure, Bankhaus Herstatt had failed to make Deutschmark payments on outstanding foreign currency contracts and its correspondent bank, Chase Manhattan in New York. These collapses provoked the first 'big crisis' in the international financial markets and payments systems. In academic circles, see Richard Dale, *The Regulation of International Banking* (Prentice Hall 1984) 156.

6 Ethan B. Kapstein, 'Resolving the Regulator's Dilemma: International Coordination of Banking Regulations' (1989) 43(2) *International Organization* 323.

7 Committee on Banking Regulations and Supervisory Practices, 'Report to the Governors on the Supervision of Banks' Foreign Establishments' BS/75/44e (September 1975).

8 Michael S. Barr and Geoffrey P. Miller, 'Global Administrative Law: The View from Basel' (2006) 17(1) *European Journal of International Law* 22.

9 The activities of the Basel Committee on Banking Supervision began with the international banking crisis in 1974; subsequently, the Committee evolved into a forum for harmonising national supervision and capital standards for banks. The Basel banking rules were designed within the Concordat and Basel Accords. Therefore, the Committee can be considered a forum for regular cooperation on banking supervisory matters.

10 On this point, Rhys Bollen, 'Setting International Regulatory Standards for Hedge Funds: Part 3' (2011) 26(4) *Journal of International Banking Law and Regulation* 175; see also Rhys Bollen, 'The International Financial System and Future Global Regulation' (2008) 23(9) *Journal of International Banking Law and Regulation* 469.

11 Consolidated supervision is based on the assumption that financial groups form a single economic entity.

on a number of principles of joint responsibility, with primary responsibility for solvency vesting with the host authorities'.[12] On this view, the Concordat can be considered the regulatory cornerstone for cross-border banking supervision.

The major aspects of the Basel Concordat are as follows: (1) the responsibility of the solvency of branches is accounted to the home or parent country supervisor; (2) the responsibility of the solvency of subsidiaries and joint ventures is accounted to the host country supervisor or country of incorporation. The parent country should take account of the exposure of their domestic bank's foreign subsidiaries and joint ventures because of the parent banks' moral commitments to those foreign establishments; (3) the responsibility of the liquidity of branches, subsidiaries and joint ventures is accounted to the host country supervisor. In this case, the home country should monitor the liquidity of its international banks. The Concordat considered banking supervision through three different aspects, namely, liquidity, solvency and foreign exchange operations and positions. In relation to these aspects, the BCBS recognised that there was an overlap, for instance, between liquidity and solvency aspects. With regard to 'solvency', the Concordat explained that for branches their solvency is indistinguishable from that of the parent bank as a whole; while for subsidiaries, the supervision of solvency is a joint responsibility of both host and parent authorities, and, for joint ventures, the supervision of solvency should normally, for practical reasons, be primarily the responsibility of the authorities in the country of incorporation.

Regarding 'liquidity', the host authority had responsibility for monitoring the liquidity of the foreign bank's establishments in its country, while the parent authority had responsibility for monitoring the liquidity of the banking group. Regarding 'foreign exchange operations and positions', there should be a joint responsibility of parent and host authorities. The Concordat underlined the importance for parent banks to have in place systems for monitoring their group's overall foreign exchange exposure and for parent authorities to monitor those systems. To improve the supervision of banks' foreign establishments and to implement the guidelines set out in the Report, the Basel Committee proposed: (1) to strengthen direct transfers of information between supervisory authorities; (2) to establish direct inspections by parent authorities of their domestic banks' foreign establishments; and (3) to introduce indirect inspections of foreign banking establishments by parent authorities through the agency of host authorities. Therefore, the Concordat aimed principally to remove the restraints on co-operation between home and host supervisory authorities. The Basle Concordat was revised in the aftermath of the collapse of Banco Ambrosiano Holdings in 1982.[13] The major question was the lack of host or home country supervision among countries and the division of responsibilities between banking supervisory authorities for monitoring the prudential conduct and soundness of the business of banks' foreign establishments. The new version of the Concordat was formulated because 'the principle that banking supervisory authorities cannot be fully satisfied about the soundness of individual banks unless they can examine the totality of each bank's business worldwide through the technique of consolidation'. For the first time, the Basel Committee proposed the consolidated supervision for cross-border banks. This technique of consolidation was founded on effective co-operation between host and parent authorities.[14] Alexander argued that

---

12 Anu Arora, 'The Global Financial Crisis: A New Global Regulatory Order?' (2010) 8 *Journal of Business Law* 676.

13 On this matter Marc Dassesse, 'Supervision of Credit Institutions and Banking Secrecy in the EEC' (1986) 1(4) *Journal of International Banking Law* 251.

14 The principle of consolidated supervision is that parent banks and parent supervisory authorities monitor the risk exposure – including a perspective of concentrations of risk and of the quality of assets – of the banks

'consolidated supervision means monitoring the risk exposure (including the concentrations of risk, the quality of assets and the capital adequacy) of the banking groups for which the home authority bears responsibility, on the basis of the totality of the business, wherever conducted'.[15] In substance, the 1983 Basel Concordat established the widely accepted home-host model, providing that 'host authorities are responsible for the operation of foreign banking establishments within their territories as individual institutions, while parent authorities are responsible for them as part of larger banking groups, where a general supervisory responsibility exists in respect of their worldwide consolidated activities'.[16] The principles of the Basel Concordat were under spot after the collapses of the BCCI in July 1991[17] and Barings Group in 1995.[18] The BCCI scandal raised many questions regarding the regulation of cross-border financial institutions and revealed the limitations and gaps of the 1983 Concordat rules.[19]

After the BCCI scandal, the Basel Committee issued a new set of rules for the supervision of international banking operations, the 'Minimum Standards for the Supervision of International Banking Groups and their Cross-Border Establishments'.[20] This document reinforced the principles of consolidated supervision, dual-key supervision and communications between supervisory authorities, and proposed the following standards: (1) all

---

or banking groups for which they are responsible, as well as the adequacy of their capital, on the basis of the totality of their business wherever conducted. In addition, the Concordat underlined that 'the implementation of the principle of consolidated supervision presupposes that parent banks and parent authorities have access to all the relevant information about the operations of their banks' foreign establishments, although existing banking secrecy provisions in some countries may present a constraint on comprehensive consolidated parental supervision'.

15 Kern Alexander, 'The Role of a Global Supervisor for International Financial Markets' 8(3) *Journal of Financial Crime* 237. The author also stresses the difference with 'dual-key supervision' that means that the regulatory authority of each nation concurrently assesses the ability of other national authorities to supervise and carry out their respective. On this matter, see also Dirk Schoenmaker, 'Internationalisation of Banking Supervision and Deposit Insurance' (1993) 8(3) *Journal of International Banking Law* 106. The author affirms that 'consolidated supervision enables the supervisor to get an overview of the total "group" exposure'.

16 Basel Committee on Banking Supervision, 'Principles for the Supervision of Banks' Foreign Establishments' (May 1983).

17 See Peter Truell and Larry Gurwin, *False Profits: The Inside Story of BCCI, The World's Most Corrupt Financial Empire* (Houghton Mifflin 1992) 67–68.

18 See Christopher Brown, 'Report of the Board of Banking Supervision Inquiry into the Circumstances of the Collapse of Barings' (1995) 10(10) *Journal of International Banking Law* 446–452.

19 BCCI was not subject to consolidated supervision by its home authorities, because its parent entity (BCCI holdings, a Luxembourg Holding Company) escaped regulation under foreign law (Luxembourg legislation) as it was not classified as a bank. Specifically, BCCI's two main subsidiaries were incorporated in Luxembourg and Cayman Islands, where supervision is weak and bank secrecy strong, and BCCI's main shareholders were in Abu Dhabi while the operating headquarters were in London. Additionally, host authorities of the countries where BCCI-conducted operations, such as the UK, were limited in their supervisory efforts by the fragmentation of regulatory responsibilities. In substance, BCCI evaded supervision by both home and host countries and demonstrated the difficulties of adequately supervising cross-border banks. As result, the national and global regulators imposed more stringent authorisation requirements on branches of foreign banks, based on an assessment of the quality and scope of home country supervision. On the main problems of consolidated supervision, see Richard Parlour and Tim Herrington, 'The Regulation of Global Trading and Investment' (1992) 7(1) *Journal of International Banking Law* 9–15; Ken McGuire, 'Banking Supervision after the Bingham Report on BCCI: The End of an Era?' (1993) 4(3) *International Company and Commercial Law Review* 118–119; Richard Dale, 'Bank Regulation after BCCI' (1993) 8(1) *Journal of International Banking Law* 14.

20 Basel Committee on Banking Supervision, 'Minimum Standards for the Supervision of International Banking Groups and their Cross-border Establishments' (July 1992).

international banking groups and international banks should be supervised by a home country authority that capably performs consolidated supervision; (2) the creation of a cross-border banking establishment should receive the prior consent of both the host country supervisory authority and the bank's and, if different, banking group's home country supervisory authority; (3) supervisory authorities should possess the right to gather information from the cross-border banking establishments of the banks or banking groups for which they are the home country supervisor; and (4) if a host country authority determines that any of the foregoing minimum standards is not met to its satisfaction, that authority could impose restrictive measures necessary to satisfy its prudential concerns consistent with these minimum standards, including the prohibition of the creation of banking establishments. These standards represent a first attempt to design an adequate normative framework for ensuring effective prudential supervision and regulation of transnational financial institutions.[21]

11.3 The role of bank capital

One of the most important achievements of global financial regulation in the last few decades is that the definition of bank capital has been subject to a substantial degree of harmonisation because of work promoted by the BCBS. As a general proposition, capital serves as a buffer to absorb unexpected losses as well as to fund ongoing activities of the firm.[22] Typically, firms choose to hold a mixture of equity and debt capital that meets the risk and reward preferences of equity shareholders and debt investors. An accepted definition of bank capital comprises the following: (1) capital acts as a buffer to absorb losses if a firm is wound up; (2) the capital acts to absorb the losses the firm incurs without causing disruption to consumers or increasing the likelihood of the firm defaulting on its liabilities; and (3) capital must be available to a firm when it is needed to absorb unexpected losses.[23]

Given the importance of deposits to consumers and the role of financial firms in maintaining economic stability, financial firms are subject to minimum capital requirements. Financial firms are not free to choose gearing ratios that would place depositors at undue risk: they must meet minimum capital ratios. As mentioned, the main purposes of capital are (1) to absorb losses while the firm is a going concern, both when the firm is in a state of financial health and during periods of financial stress, thus maintaining market confidence in the financial system and avoiding disruption to depositors; and (2) to absorb losses in a gone-concern scenario, protecting depositors in a winding up.[24] On this view, the main reasons for bank capital regulation are to address the systemic risk and to reduce information asymmetries (e.g. between firm management and key stakeholders, including depositors and investors) on the financial condition of the firm. These objectives are fundamental for market confidence and consumer protection. The key rationale for regulating bank capital is to promote the stability of the financial system, which could be threatened in the event

21 Timothy Polglase, 'New Basel Core Principles' (1997) 16(4) *International Banking and Financial Law* 42–43.

22 For an overview, among others, see Kern Alexander, *Principles of Banking Regulation* (CUP 2019) 90.

23 On this point Douglas W. Diamond and Raghuram G. Rajan, 'A Theory of Bank Capital' (2000) 55 *The Journal of Finance* 2431–2432.

24 Simon Gleeson, 'Bank Capital Regulation and Sovereign Debt Restructuring' (2018) 13(3) *Capital Markets Law Journal* 474; Paul Davies, 'The Fall and Rise of Debt: Bank Capital Regulation After the Crisis' (2015) 16 *European Business Organization Law Review* 492–493.

of widespread bank failures.[25] Bank capital regulations help a firm to remain solvent and contribute to its ability to withstand liquidity problems. It is worth noting that widespread banking failures have the potential to inflict heavy social costs, including reductions in credit availability, less effective monetary policy or the general collapse of market confidence. Regulatory capital requirements seek to address these problems by helping firms to remain solvent and reducing the social costs associated with a systemic crisis.[26] The regulatory capital can help to improve the liquidity of a firm. Regulations on capital have a role to play in reducing the risk of systemic failure in the financial services sector. The failure of a firm may have adverse impacts not only on the firm's own consumers, but may also cause losses to other firms, their consumers and the economy. Regulatory capital requires firms to meet a common standard that protects all depositors. Capital operates to protect depositors in two ways: by requiring financial institutions to hold capital capable of absorbing losses while the firm is solvent; if a firm does fail, capital acts as a buffer in protecting depositors' claims in insolvency.[27] In other words, regulatory capital identifies the amount of capital regulators require banks to hold.

11.4 The Basel Accords

The definition of capital and its sufficiency were first harmonised via the so-called Basel I Accord of 1988 (a soft law instrument: the report by the Basel Committee on 'International Convergence of Capital Measurement and Capital Standards').[28] The 1988 Basel Accord (Basel I) was published by the BCBS in order to require banks to hold regulatory capital against credit risk (i.e. the risk that its borrowers may default on their interest payments and/or principal repayments).[29] The genesis of this Accord can be traced back to the aftermath of the Latin American debt crisis.[30] Anxiety about the eroded capital levels of major international banks weakened through their lesser developed countries (LDC) exposures, as well as concerns about competitive equality, whereby Japanese banks had benefitted from 'underpricing' international loans because of their low capitalisation, were the main rationales behind the Accord. Its legal impact in developed and developing countries and its acceptance by market participants and by rating agencies as a test of bank solvency have been remarkable and unprecedented, despite its lack of direct legal binding force.[31]

---

25 Heidi Mandanis Schooner and Michael W. Taylor, *Global Bank Regulation: Principles and Policies* (Elsevier 2010) 132.

26 Frans de Weert, *Bank and Insurance Capital Management* (London: Wiley 2010) 79–80.

27 Nikoletta Kleftouri, 'Meeting the Rationale of Deposit Protection System' (2014) 22 *Journal of Financial Regulation and Compliance* 300–301.

28 See below n 37.

29 Charles Goodhart, *The Basel Committee on Banking Supervision. A History of the Early Years 1974–1997* (CUP 2011) 189–190.

30 In August 1982, 'the total risk to the nine money-center banks in New York was estimated at more than three times the capital of those banks. The regulators, analysts say, did not force the banks to value those loans at the fire-sale prices of the moment, helping to avert a disaster in the banking system. In other words, the nine biggest banks were all insolvent in the 1980s'. For an overview, see Karin Lissakers, *Banks, Borrowers and the Establishment. A Revisionist Account of the International Debt Crisis* (Harper Collins Basic Books 1991) Chapter 8.

31 Graciela Kaminsky and Sergio L. Schmukler, 'Emerging Market Instability: Do Sovereign Ratings Affect Country Risk and Stock Returns? (2002) 16 *The World Bank Economic Review* 172.

The Basel Committee chose a capital-asset ratio instead of a debt-equity ratio as a way of measuring capital. It also preferred a risk-adjusted capital framework over a simple leverage ratio of capital to total assets, because of its perceived greater fairness for making international comparisons between different banking systems, its consideration of off-balance sheet exposures and its positive assessment of banks' holdings of liquid low-risk assets.[32] The Committee selected credit risk as a pillar of the Accord, though other risks were subsequently added in the revisions of the Accord. As it will be discussed later in this chapter, we examine the evolution from Basel I to Basel III and beyond. We point out here that having a framework (albeit an imperfect one) is better than no framework at all.[33] By setting a prudential common denominator, it facilitated the equivalence of the objectives of national banking legislations, thus encouraging mutual trust in the assessment of the capital levels of major international banks. Uneven regulatory practices that could draw banks to the most permissive regimes were, at least regarding matters directly affecting the solvency of credit institutions, gradually phased out. However, capital regulation as conceived since 1988 is not per se a panacea for regulation.

Considerations of asset loss pervade the concept of capital adequacy; the quality of the asset portfolio was and is the key to sound banking. Capital requirements do not take into account the competence, depth and integrity of management, which also plays a crucial role in sound banking. Furthermore, the tax treatment of equity and debt, and accounting practices, can create competitive disadvantages among international banks (and between banks and non-bank investment firms) of the very sort that the Accord tried to prevent. The regulatory framework of the Basel Committee has evolved during the recent decades, particularly in implementing the maintenance of financial stability and the protection of retail depositors.[34] In particular, the Committee has set out new rules on banking supervision to enhance the resilience of the global banking system.[35] As has been noted, 'the regulation of banks and banking groups has been driven primarily by the content of two international frameworks: the Basel Capital Accord and Basel II'.[36] The Basel Committee of Banking Supervision has conducted work in two main areas: supervision of cross-border establishments (mainly international branches and subsidiaries) and capital adequacy. Consolidated supervision has become a premise of global banking: however, the 2007–2009 financial crisis has shown that consolidated supervision is not by itself the answer to major failures.

---

32 Basel Committee on Banking Supervision, 'Basel III Leverage Ratio Framework and Disclosure Requirements' (January 2014) available at <https://www.bis.org/publ/bcbs270.pdf> (accessed 25 June 2020).

33 The catalyst for the capital framework was a UK/US Accord of 1986; the Bank of England and the US Federal Reserve Board's announcement of a draft on capital adequacy triggered an acceleration of the proceedings of the Committee to arrive to an acceptable multilateral formula on capital adequacy in December 1987. After a period of consultation, on 11 July 1988, the governors of the G-10 central banks endorsed the proposals on the 'International Convergence of Capital Measurement and Capital Standards', in which a risk-based capital framework for international banks was developed. See Bank for International Settlements, '58th Annual Report' (1 April 1987–31 March 1988) 194 available at <https://www.bis.org/publ/arpdf/archive/ar1988_en.pdf> (accessed 29 June 2020).

34 In July 2008, the Basel Committee and the International Association of Deposit Insurers formulated an internationally agreed set of principles for effective deposit insurance systems.

35 Basel Committee on Banking Supervision, 'Strengthening the Resilience of the Banking Sector' Consultative Document (December 2009). According to the Executive Summary, 'a strong and resilient banking system is the foundation for sustainable economic growth, as banks are at the centre of the credit intermediation process between savers and investors'.

36 Steven McEwan, 'Improving the Regulation of Banks and Banking Groups' (2009) 24 *Journal of International Banking and Financial Law* 334.

In conclusion, consolidated supervision needs to be aligned with the resolution process: the lack of effective consolidated resolution poses a challenge to the future of banking sector. This issue will be examined in Chapter 14.

11.5 Basel I: credit risk and the capital adequacy ratio

As we saw, micro-prudential regulation seeks to reduce the likelihood that a systemic financial institution fails and, in the event of failure, to mitigate its consequences. As explained in Section 11.2, the principal tool used to reduce the likelihood of bank failures is the adoption of minimum capital rules which require banks to maintain a minimum level of equity capital available to absorb potential losses in tandem with their risk exposures. There is a substantial degree of international harmonisation due to the broad acceptance of the standards promulgated by the Basel Committee since the 1980s. To appreciate the significance of the reforms introduced post-crisis, it is expedient to explain briefly the development of the regulatory framework.

The 1988 Basel Accord (Basel I) followed a simple approach of standardisation of capital requirements in relation to the credit risk assumed by each bank.[37] In short, Basel I required banks to maintain own capital equal to at least 8% of their risk-weighted assets (RWAs).[38] So, for example, a bank with RWAs amounting to £100 million would have to maintain capital of £8 million. The concept of RWAs was introduced as a measure for banks' credit risk, so the relevant assets were a bank's claims against borrowers and bond issuers, sovereign, corporate and individual. Therefore, the two main components of the Basel I regime were the calculation of banks' RWAs, which was on the basis of dividing assets into four main risk-weighted categories, and the definition of what counted as banks' own capital, which was divided into two types, namely, Tier 1 and Tier 2.

The four main risk-weighted categories of assets were assigned multipliers of 0%, 20%, 50% and 100%, which meant that in the case of the 0% category no capital had to be maintained in relation to the asset.[39] This was based on common assumptions about the level of credit risk posed by different broad types of borrowers: the higher the risk, the higher the multiplier. For instance, it appears reasonable that a claim a bank has against a sovereign state in the state's own currency has minimal risk of not being fully repaid, as the state can always issue the necessary currency to repay its debt. Of course, the value of any currency may suffer due to inflation, and therefore, credit risk is only truly minimal in cases that the loan is funded by assets denominated in the same currency as the loan, such as deposits in the same currency. Another assumption was that developed countries, such as the members of the OECD[40] and banks incorporated in such countries, present a lower level of credit risk than developing countries and banks incorporated in developing countries. It also appeared reasonable that fully secured loans by mortgages on residential property present a significantly lower risk than unsecured loans. Thus, the four main categories of assets were constructed as follows:

37 Basel Committee on Banking Supervision, *International Convergence of Capital Measurement and Capital Standards* (Bank of International Settlements Publications 1988). From now on to be referred to as "Basel I".
38 Basel I, para 44.
39 Basel I, paras 28–41.
40 Organisation for Economic Co-operation and Development. It currently comprises all EEA Member States – except for Bulgaria, Cyprus, Croatia, Malta and Romania – and the following other countries: Australia, Canada, Chile, Israel, Japan, Korea, Mexico, New Zealand, Turkey and the US.

a 0% category: This included cash, claims on any central government in its own currency and funded in the same currency, and claims on OECD central governments and central banks, irrespective of currency. Claims against domestic public sector entities other than central governments could be given a multiplier of 0%, 10%, 20% or 50% at national discretion.

b 20% category: Claims on banks incorporated in an OECD country and claims on non-domestic public sector entities other than central governments (e.g. local authorities).

c 50% category: Loans that are fully secured by a mortgage on residential property.

d 100% category: Claims against all other borrowers (including individuals and private sector companies).

As holding own capital is expensive for banks,[41] Basel I generated incentives to structure loan portfolios in ways that the total value of RWAs is kept as low as possible. This could be achieved by lending more to certain types of borrowers and by selling riskier loans. It must also be noted that Basel I also included rules on certain types of off-balance sheet exposures, such as contingent liabilities arising from trade, general guarantees and standby letters of credit. In such cases, the bank may end up effectively lending an amount and thus incurring credit risk. These were given a credit conversion factor (of 0%, 20%, 50% or 100%) which was applied to the nominal principal amount of the transaction and then the standard risk-weighting was applied.[42]

Regarding what counted as own capital, Basel I introduced the distinction between Tier 1 capital and Tier 2 capital. From a UK perspective, all companies that are limited by shares must have shares of a specified nominal value.[43] The total nominal value of all paid-up shares constitutes the paid-up share capital.[44] If shares are allotted at a premium above their nominal value, the total amount raised through the premium constitutes the share premium account.[45] If the net assets of a public company (assets minus liabilities) exceed the company's share capital and any undistributable reserves, including the share premium account, the remaining value is accounted for as retained earnings (distributable profits) and can be used to pay dividends and to purchase the company's own shares.[46] Thus, a bank's paid-up share capital, share premium account, retained earnings and other reserves together constitute its equity, in other words, its net value which is by definition equals to its net assets.

Tier 1 capital consisted of issued and fully paid-up ordinary share capital, issued and fully paid-up perpetual non-cumulative preferred share capital[47] and disclosed reserves (such as

---

41 This is because holding more capital tends to reduce banks' earnings per share. On this, see Chapter 13.2 and Andreas Kokkinis, 'A Primer on Corporate Governance in Banks and Financial Institutions – Are Banks Special?' in Iris Chiu (ed), *The Law on Corporate Governance in Banks* (Edward Elgar 2015) 13–14.

42 Basel I, paras 42–43.

43 Companies Act 2006, s 542.

44 On statutory distinctions of capital, see Companies Act 2006, ss 546–548.

45 Companies Act 2006, s 610.

46 See Companies Act 2006, ss 830–831 on distributions and s 692 (2) (a) (i) on buying back shares.

47 This refers to preference shares. Preference shares typically confer to their holder a right to a fixed rate of dividend, calculated as a percentage of their nominal value. In the case of cumulative preference shares, if the company cannot pay the preferential dividend in a year, due to not having sufficient distributable profits, then that amount is added to the dividend owed to the holder the following year.

the share premium account and retained earnings).[48] At least 50% of banks' capital had to be Tier 1 capital, the remaining being Tier 2 capital.[49]

Tier 2 capital included certain types of accounting reserves, preference shares and subordinated debt that although not having the same loss-absorbing quality as Tier 1 capital, they could still serve to meet future losses.[50] The most important types of Tier 2 capital were revaluation reserves (reflecting unrealised profits arising from an increase in the market value of a bank's assets), general loan-loss reserves (amounts earmarked to cover possible future losses), cumulative preference shares and perpetual subordinated debt, such as bonds with no maturity date. There was also an additional category of subordinated term debt instruments with a minimum maturity of five years, which could not exceed 50% of Tier 2 capital and thus 25% of total capital. This category included subordinated bonds issued by banks with a maturity of at least five years. Such instruments were subject to a 20% discount per year during the last five years to maturity.

Basel I was amended in 1996 to include market risk as part of the exposures against which capital must be maintained.[51] This reflected the increasing involvement of banks in investment banking activities, such as underwriting corporate securities, advising and arranging mergers and acquisitions and restructurings, running collective investments schemes, acting as brokers and trading in their own name (proprietary trading) in securities. A measure of market risk was calculated by summing four components, namely, interest rate risk,[52] equities trading risk,[53] foreign exchange risk[54] and commodities risk.[55] The market risk measure was weighted at 12.5% and then added to RWAs for the purposes of applying the 8% capital ratio. Further details on market risk will be provided as part of the discussion of Basel II.

11.6 Basel II: flexible capital requirements and market discipline

The Basel II Accord in 2006 reformed the overall regime to the direction of flexibility and heavy use of meta-regulation.[56] Basel II consists of three pillars. Under Pillar 1, banks have to maintain minimum capital equivalent to 8% of their total risk exposure, which consists of credit risk, market risk and operational risk. As under Basel I, half of the capital ought to be Tier 1 capital, i.e. shareholders' equity and disclosed reserves, while the rest could be Tier 2 capital.[57] Credit risk is the risk that borrowers may default; market risk is the risk

---

48 Basel I, para 12.
49 Basel I, para 14.
50 Basel I, paras 15–23.
51 Basel Committee on Banking Supervision, *Amendment to the Capital Accord to Incorporate Market Risks* (Bank of International Settlements Publications 1996).
52 This is the risk that the interest paid by the bank to fund a loan will increase, thus reducing the bank's net income from the loan.
53 This is the risk that equities traded by the bank will reduce in value, and hence, the bank will suffer a loss.
54 This is the risk of changes in the value of foreign currencies that can lead to losses for a bank under certain contracts.
55 This is the risk that commodities in which a bank trades will reduce in value, and hence, the bank will suffer a loss.
56 See Basel Committee on Banking Supervision, *International Convergence of Capital Measurement and Capital Standards: A Revised Framework, Comprehensive Version* (Bank of International Settlements Publications 2006). From now on to be referred to as 'Basel II'.
57 Basel II, paras 40 and 49 (i).

that financial assets traded by a bank, such as securities, may suffer a reduction in value; and operational risk is the risk of losses due to failed internal processes and systems, rogue employees and external events. Credit risk is calculated as a percentage of the actual value of a bank's relevant assets, whereas market risk consists of a risk-weighted market risk measurement, and operational risk is calculated by reference to a bank's income. Pillar 2 requires banks to have in place internal processes to assess their own capital adequacy regarding any residual risks not covered by Pillar 1, and gives regulators the duty to supervise banks' processes and the power to demand banks to hold additional capital and to intervene early in cases of breach.[58] Pillar 3 requires banks to disclose relevant information to enable market participants to assess banks' capital adequacy, thus reinforcing market discipline.[59]

The following paragraphs will set out the Basel II framework to calculate banks' exposures to credit, market and operational risk. These rules continue to be important as they form the basis of the Basel III framework – with certain crucial modifications that will be examined in Section 12.7. Basel II introduced two methodologies to assess credit risk, namely, the Standardised Approach and the Internal Ratings-Based (IRB) Approach, the latter being available for banks, only with the explicit consent of their regulator.[60] A similar approach was taken with regard to the other two types of risk. We will first examine the standardised approaches for the three types of risk and then the more flexible approaches.

Under the Standardised Approach for credit risk, assets are risk-weighted based on their falling within broad categories prescribed by Basel II, i.e. claims on sovereigns, public bodies, banks, companies, mortgages, etc. The multiplier to be used for certain traded assets (e.g. bonds) depends on their credit rating. So, sovereign bonds can be weighted at 0%, 20%, 50%, 100% or 150%, while corporate bonds can be weighted at 20%, 50%, 100% or 150%. Residential mortgages are weighted at 35%. Non-performing loans are weighted at 150%. It is notable that Basel II introduced risk weightings of 150%, exceeding the actual exposure of banks in the cases of particularly high-risk debt.[61]

The Standardised Approach for market risk remained the same as under the 1996 amendment for equities trading risk, foreign exchange risk and commodities risk, but was amended in relation to interest rate risk. While before Basel II interest rate risk-weightings for each type of loan depended only on the type of borrower and ranged from 0% to 8%, under Basel II, they also depend on the credit rating of the borrower and ranged from 0% to 12%.[62] Equities trading risk is calculated by reference to the value of a bank's equities portfolio, applying a weighting of 8% to account for general market risk and an additional weighting of either 4% or 8% to account for specific portfolio risk (4% if the portfolio is fully diversified and liquid). Foreign exchange risk is calculated at 8% of a bank's net long currency positions, or net short currency positions or net gold positions, whichever the higher. Commodities risk comprises two components: 15% of the net position of the bank in each commodity and 3% of the gross long and gross short positions of the bank on each commodity.[63]

---

58 See Basel II, Part 3: The Second Pillar – Supervisory Review Process.
59 See Basel II, Part 4: The Third Pillar – Market Discipline.
60 Basel II, paras 50–51.
61 See Basel II, Part 2, II. Credit Risk – The Standardised Approach.
62 See Basel II, Part 2, VI. C. Market risk – The standardised measurement method: 1. Interest rate risk.
63 See Basel II, Part 2, VI. C. Market risk – The standardised measurement method: 2. Equity position risk; 3. Foreign exchange risk; and 4. Commodities risk.

Regarding operational risk there are two off-the-shelf approaches. The Basic Indicator Approach, suitable for smaller banks with few lines of business, prescribes a weighting of 15% of a bank's annual gross revenues, averaged over a period of three years.[64] The Standardised Approach, suitable for banks with multiple business lines, distinguishes between eight different lines of business and assigns a separate weighting to the average revenue from each line of business, with weightings ranging from 12% to 18%. In particular, corporate finance activities, trading and sales, and payments and settlement are weighted at 18%; commercial banking and agency services are weighted at 15%; and retail banking, retail brokerage and asset management at 12%.[65]

Turning to meta-regulatory measuring approaches, for credit risk, there are two versions of the IRB Approach: the foundation and the advanced. Under the former, banks themselves calculate the probability of default of loans, but rely on their regulators for other factors, such as loss given default, exposure and maturity. Under the latter, banks autonomously calculate all of the above factors.[66] Banks were therefore given discretion, wider in the case of the advanced version, to calculate their own capital adequacy relating to credit risk. An Internal Models Approach is also available to calculate market risk, insofar as banks can convince their regulators that their models are robust.[67] In the case of operational risk, the equivalent approach was branded the Advanced Measurement Approach.[68] In all cases, banks following such approaches are required to set up an independent internal risk management department, to have a robust compliance policy, to ensure that there is board oversight and to have these systems independently reviewed, normally by external audit. They are also required to satisfy minimum technical parameters when constructing their methodologies for calculating the relevant risks. Furthermore, regulatory approval of these approaches and continuous supervision were relied on to place limits on banks' ability to bypass capital adequacy requirements, although with hindsight it is now evident that regulatory scrutiny of banks' internal models in the period before the global financial crisis was not sufficient.[69]

A significant feature of the Basel II framework – both under standardised approaches and within banks' own risk calculation models – was heavy reliance on credit ratings. Nevertheless, recent evidence suggests that Credit Rating Agencies (CRAs) may be consistently under-valuing the riskiness of certain debts,[70] due to the presence of conflicts of interest and the inherent limits of human rationality. The Eurozone sovereign debt crisis, for

---

64 Basel II, paras 649–651.

65 Basel II, paras 652–654.

66 Basel II, para 245.

67 See Basel II, Part 2, VI. D. Market Risk – The Internal Models Approach.

68 Basel II, paras 655–659.

69 On this, see Michael McAleer, Juan-Angel Jimenez-Martin and Teodosio Perez-Amaral, 'What Happened to Risk Management during the 2008–2009 Financial Crisis' in Robert W Kolb (ed), *Lessons from the Financial Crisis* (John Wiley 2010) 307. Several UK official reports on failed banks take similar views: Parliamentary Commission on Banking Standards, *An Accident Waiting to Happen: The Failure of HBOS* (2012–2013, HL 144, HC 705) 3–4; ibid., *Changing Banking for Good* (2013–2014, HL 27-II, HC 175-II) 82–83; and FSA, 'The Failure of the Royal Bank of Scotland: Financial Services Authority Board Report' (December 2011) 62–63, <http://www.fsa.gov.uk/pubs/other/rbs.pdf> (accessed 21 June 2020).

70 An analysis of the role and incentives of Credit Rating Agencies can be found in John P. Hunt, 'Credit Rating Agencies and the "Worldwide Credit Crisis": The Limits of Reputation, the Insufficiency of Reform, and a Proposal for Improvement' (2009) 2009 *Columbia Business Law Review* 109. For a detailed examination of the business model and conflicts of interest faced by CRAs, see Andrea Miglionico, *The Governance of Credit Rating Agencies: Regulatory Regimes and Liability Issues* (Edward Elgar 2019) Chapters 1–2.

instance, illustrates that borrowers who appear to be risk-free or of low risk (such as highly rated OECD countries) and hence banks face incentives to lend heavily to them may turn out not to be creditworthy, the most notable example being the government of Greece. Capital adequacy rules thus had negative unintended consequences and failed to influence banks' risk profiles to the intended direction. In addition, the requirement to keep capital against RWAs created incentives for banks to remove assets from their balance sheets. Extensive use of securitisation, for instance, was widely used before the global financial crisis to circumvent capital adequacy ratios by removing assets from banks' balance sheets.[71] In Section 11.7, we will see that certain steps have been taken, particularly at the EU level, to improve the quality of credit ratings and reduce reliance on them, but the extent to which they have mitigated the problem remains unclear.

11.7 Basel III and Capital Requirements Directive IV: enhanced capital and liquidity requirements

The global financial crisis highlighted the weaknesses of the Basel II framework and its misplaced reliance on banks' internal processes to calculate exposures and on market discipline.[72] Post-crisis capital adequacy rules have been strengthened, and new liquidity and leverage standards have been introduced to reduce the likelihood of bank failures by ensuring that there is adequate shareholder equity to absorb potential losses and by reducing shareholder incentives to encourage institutions' managers to take excessive risks. The Basel Committee's current recommendations, known as Basel III,[73] have been fully adopted by the EU, which adopted promptly the CRD IV[74] and Capital Requirements Regulation (CRR).[75] They are therefore an integral part of the UK's regulatory framework and will probably continue to be so post-Brexit, given the need to ensure that UK financial institutions have the broadest possible access to EU markets. Basel III did not increase the Basel

---

71 Orkun Akseli, 'Was Securitisation the Culprit? Explanation of Legal Processes Behind Creation of Mortgage-Backed Sub-prime Securities' in Joanna Gray and Orkun Akseli (eds), *Financial Regulation in Crisis? The Role of Law and the Failure of Northern Rock* (Edward Elgar 2011) 2–3.

72 On the limitations of market discipline and traditional shareholder governance to safeguard financial stability, see Emilios Avgouleas, 'The Global Financial Crisis and the Disclosure Paradigm in European Financial Regulation: The Case for Reform' (2009) 6 *European Company and Financial Law Review* 440; and Emilios Avgouleas and Jay Cullen, 'Market Discipline and EU Corporate Governance Reform in the Banking Sector: Merits, Fallacies, and Cognitive Boundaries' (2014) 41 *Journal of Law and Society* 28. For a comprehensive examination of the relationship between shareholder-centric corporate governance and financial stability, see Andreas Kokkinis, *Corporate Law and Financial Instability* (Routledge 2018).

73 Basel Committee on Banking Supervision, *Basel III: A Global Regulatory Framework for More Resilient Banks and Banking Systems* (rev edn, Bank of International Settlements Publications 2011). From now on, it will be referred to as 'Basel III'.

74 Directive 2013/36/EU of the European Parliament and of the Council of 26 June 2013 on access to the activity of credit institutions and the prudential supervision of credit institutions and investment firms, amending Directive 2002/87/EC and repealing Directives 2006/48/EC and 2006/49/EC [2013] OJ L176/338. From now on, it will be referred to as 'CRD IV'.

75 Regulation (EU) No. 575/2013 of the European Parliament and of the Council of 26 June 2013 on prudential requirements for credit institutions and investment firms and amending Regulation (EU) No. 648/2012 [2013] OJ L176/1. From now on it will be referred to as 'CRR'. The CRR has been amended by the EU Regulation 2019/876 amending Regulation (EU) No. 575/2013 as regards the leverage ratio, the net stable funding ratio, requirements for own funds and eligible liabilities, counterparty credit risk, market risk, exposures to central counterparties, exposures to collective investment undertakings, large exposures, reporting and disclosure requirements, and Regulation (EU) No. 648/2012 ('CRR 2').

II 8% capital ratio, but rather introduced a series of additional capital buffers – some of them applying to all banks and some applying only to systemically important banks, which have become fully effective since the beginning of 2019.[76] Further reforms in 2017, often described as 'Basel IV', introduced tight controls on banks' use of own methodologies to calculate credit and market risk, abolished the Advanced Measurement Approach for operational risk and adjusted the standardised approaches.

11.7.1 Improving the quality of capital

One area of reforms focused on improving the quality of capital that banks are required to hold. Since the coming into force of CRD (Capital Requirements Directive) IV, which implemented Basel III with effect from the beginning of 2015, Tier 1 capital must be no less than 6% of RWAs, while the core of it, Common Equity Tier 1 (CET1) must be at least 4.5% thereof.[77] CET1 consists exclusively of ordinary share capital,[78] retained earnings and disclosed reserves. It follows that preference shares do not qualify as CET1. The Prudential Regulation Authority (PRA) has also confirmed that, for the purposes of Pillar 2, capital should be of the same quality as the capital held to meet the Pillar 1 requirement, i.e. at least 56% of CET1, and no more than 25% Tier 2 capital.[79] Basel III and CRD IV also require that all new capital buffers, discussed below, consist of the highest quality CET1 capital.[80]

11.7.2 The capital conservation buffer, counter-cyclical buffer and Pillar 2 capital

The capital conservation buffer is a permanent buffer of 2.5% of RWAs, applying fully from the beginning of 2019.[81] It is the main permanent measure that effectively increases the capital ratio of 8%–10.5% for all banks. In parallel, Basel III recommends that banks hold additional capital during periods of financial growth,[82] and prescribes a counter-cyclical buffer of up to 2.5%.[83] CRD IV thus introduced the counter-cyclical buffer to constrain credit creation in times of economic growth. As such, its quantum reflects the phase of the economic cycle in which the economy is. It ranges from 0% to 2.5% in increments of 0.25%.[84] Each designated authority is expected to set for every quarter a buffer rate which should reflect any deviation of the ratio of credit-to-GDP from its long-term trend within the relevant national economy.[85] With regard to non-EU countries, the ESRB may

---

76 The new buffers generally apply from 1 January 2016 with the exception of the G-SII buffer which is coming into force gradually from 2016 and will be fully implemented by 2019. See CRD IV, art 162 (2) and (5).
77 See CRR, art 92.
78 Basel III, para 53. There is a list of criteria for the classification of an instrument as a common share.
79 See PRA, 'Strengthening Capital Standards: Implementing CRD IV, Feedback and Final Rules' (Policy Statement PS 7/13, 13 June 2013), para 3.6 <http://www.bankofengland.co.uk/pra/Pages/publications/imple-mcrdiv.aspx> (accessed 19 May 2020).
80 See CRD IV, arts 129 (1), 130 (5), 131 (4)–(5), and 133 (3).
81 CRD IV, arts 129 (1) and 160 (1) to (5). For 2017 the capital conservation buffer is set by the PRA at 1.25% and for 2018 at 1.875%. See PRA Rulebook, CRR Firms, Capital Buffers, 2.2.
82 Basel III, paras 122–135.
83 Basel III, paras 139–148.
84 See CRD IV, art 130, and 136–140.
85 CRD IV, art 136 (2).

recommend an appropriate buffer rate if the one set by the relevant country's authority is not sufficient to protect EU credit institutions.[86]

In the UK, the rate is set by the Bank of England's Financial Policy Committee and it currently stands at 1%. It must be further noted that for large banks that have credit exposures in various countries which have set the rate of the counter-cyclical buffer at various levels, CRD IV requires the national regulator of each bank to impose an institution-specific counter-cyclical buffer equal to the weighted average of the counter-cyclical buffers set in each country where a bank has exposures.[87] However, for non-EU countries that impose a maximum buffer exceeding 2.5%, the excess above 2.5% is not to be taken into account.

Basel III did not abolish the pre-existing Pillar 2 capital, which allows national regulators to impose additional capital requirements to each bank. In the UK, the PRA imposes Pillar 2A and Pillar 2B capital requirements on UK banks on an annual basis. Pillar 2A refers to credit, market and operational risk that is not captured under normal capital ratios. Pillar 2B, also known in the UK as the capital planning buffer, is forward-looking and can be reduced in times of stress.[88]

11.7.3 *Additional capital requirements for banks that pose systemic risk*

There is an additional capital buffer which aims to cover the risks that an individual institution poses to the financial system. If an institution is classified as a global systemically important institution (G-SII),[89] it is required to hold a special G-SII buffer the size of which depends on the systemic importance of the institution for the global financial system. The buffer can be 1%, 1.5%, 2%, 2.5% or 3.5% depending on the subcategory to which each institution belongs.[90] This depends on the categorisation made by the Financial Stability Board (FSB). The FSB issues a list of global systemically important banks (G-SIBs) in November of each year, classified into five buckets of ascending systemic importance, which correspond to the five rates of the buffer set out above.[91] Bucket 5 is currently empty. Bucket 4 contains only JP Morgan Chase. As far as UK banks are concerned, HSBC is in bucket 3, Barclays is in bucket 4 and Standard Chartered in bucket 5. If an institution is not a G-SIB but is still systemically important for the financial sector of the EU or a Member State, it qualifies as an 'other systemically important institution' (O-SII), a category that corresponds to the FSB's domestic systemically important banks (D-SIBs), and has to maintain a buffer of up to 2% of its RWAs.[92] Different buffers may apply to different corporate entities within a banking group, e.g. in the case of a group that is a G-SII and has one subsidiary in a different Member State which is an O-SII in that State, the G-SII buffer will apply

---

86 CRD IV, art 138.

87 CRD IV, art 140 (1).

88 On UK regulatory policy regarding Pillar 2A and 2B capital, see Bank of England, 'The Prudential Regulation Authority's Approach to Banking Supervision' (2018) paras 80–82 <https://www.bankofengland.co.uk/prudential-regulation/publication/2018/pra-approach-documents-2018> (accessed 15 June 2020).

89 The criteria to identify a G-SII include its size, interconnectedness, substitutability of the services provided, complexity and cross-border activity. CRD IV, art 131 (2).

90 CRD IV, art 131(9).

91 The Financial Stability Board was founded in 2009 as a successor of the Financial Stability Forum with a mandate to assess risks to the global financial system and promote the co-ordination of national authorities. It brings together the regulatory authorities of 23 countries and several international organisations such as the World Bank and the IMF. Its secretariat is located in Basel and hosted by the Bank of International Settlements.

92 CRD IV art 131 (3).

on a consolidated basis to the group and the O-SII buffer will apply on an individual or sub-consolidated basis to the subsidiary.

In parallel, CRD IV allows national regulators to impose a systemic risk buffer of at least 1% either on the financial sector as a whole or on certain subsets of the sector.[93] The systemic risk buffer captures non-cyclical macro-prudential risks. The buffer must escalate in increments of 0.5% and there is no upper limit, although Member States imposing a buffer in excess of 3% are required to justify their reasons to the Commission and await for its opinion before implementing the measure; if the opinion is negative they can still proceed but they have to give reasons.[94] The UK has imposed systemic risk buffers of up to 3% on large ring-fenced banks.[95] However, it must be clarified that the systemic risk buffer is not applied in addition to the G-SII or O-SII buffer. If a bank is either a G-SII or an O-SII it will have to maintain only one buffer, either the G-SII/O-SII buffer or the systemic risk buffer, whichever is higher.[96] The combined effect of the buffers introduced by Basel III is that – depending on their size and the phase of the economic cycle – banks will have to maintain CET1 capital ranging from 7% to 13% of their RWAs[97] and total capital ranging from 10.5% to 16.5% of their RWAs, plus any additional capital required by national regulators under Pillar 2. There are also two additional buffers that are calculated by reference to total exposures rather than risk-weighted exposures, as we will explain in Section 12.6.4. Table 11.1 summarises current capital requirements for UK banks.

Table 11.1. Overview of current capital requirements for UK banks

Type of entity	Capital requirement
All credit institutions	Capital ratio of 8% of RWAs (consisting of at least 75% Tier 1 and 56% CET1)
All credit institutions	Pillar 2A and 2B additional capital requirements (consisting of at least 75% Tier 1 and 56% CET1)
All credit institutions	Capital conservation buffer of 2.5% of RWAs (100% CET1)
All credit institutions	Counter-cyclical buffer 0%–2.5% of RWAs (100% CET1); set nationally but, for each institution, takes into account foreign exposures.
Credit institutions with deposits exceeding £50 billion	Counter-cyclical leverage ratio buffer of 35% of the counter-cyclical buffer, hence up to 0.9% of total exposures (100% CET1)
Systemically important institutions (G-SIIs, O-SIIs and institutions subject to systemic risk buffer)	G-SII buffer 1%–3.5%; or O-SII buffer up to 2%; or systemic risk buffer of 1% or more, if higher; all out of RWAs (100% CET1)
G-SIIs and O-SIIS	Additional leverage ratio buffer of 35% of the G-SII buffer/O-SII buffer, hence up to 1.225% of total exposures (100% CET1)

93 CRD IV, art 133.
94 CRD IV, art 133 (14).
95 PRA Approach to the implementation of the systemic risk buffer.
96 CRD IV, art 133 (4).
97 Indeed, the seven major UK deposit-taking institutions, namely, Barclays, HSBC, Lloyds Banking Group, Nationwide, Royal Bank of Scotland, Santander UK and Standard Chartered, have been expected by the PRA to maintain a CET1 capital ratio of 7% from 1 January 2016 unless a special capital plan has been agreed. See PRA, 'Capital Requirements for Major UK Banks and Building Societies' (Supervisory Statement SS3/13, November 2013), <http://www.bankofengland.co.uk/pra/Pages/publications/ss/2015/ss313update.aspx> (accessed 18 May 2020).

11.7.4 Leverage ratios and associated buffers

Basel III introduced a total leverage ratio to prevent the risk of excessive leverage. According to the new rules, Tier 1 capital must be no less than 3% of the overall exposures of a bank.[98] For these purposes, Tier 1 capital is defined in the same way as for the purposes of the capital ratio, so it must consist of at least 75% CET1 capital. Exposures include a bank's consolidated group assets as well as certain off-balance sheet items and commitments so that the regulatory leverage ratio of a bank tends to be lower than its equity to assets ratio.[99] The leverage ratio was introduced in the UK on 1 January 2016,[100] and applies to banks and building societies with total retail deposits of at least £50 billion either individually or on a group consolidated basis.[101] It is worth noting that from a EU perspective, the leverage ratio of 3% is not yet binding, but banks merely have to calculate their leverage ratio as required by Basel III and report it.[102] The 2016 proposal of the Commission to amend CRD IV and CRR includes the introduction of a binding 3% ratio.

Furthermore, regulators can impose leverage ratio buffers on systemically important banks and a counter-cyclical leverage ratio buffer at times of rapid economic growth.[103] In the UK, banks with deposits exceeding £50 billion must maintain a counter-cyclical leverage ratio buffer. The rate of the buffer is 35% of an institution's counter-cyclical capital buffer rate (currently 1% in the UK) rounded to the nearest tenth and is calculated as a percentage of the bank's total exposures. Therefore, the rate of the counter-cyclical leverage ratio buffer can reach up to 0.9% of total exposures. UK banks that are G-SIIs or O-SIIs must also maintain an additional leverage ratio buffer of 35% of their G-SII or O-SII capital buffer rate.[104] This means that the rate of the additional leverage ratio buffer can reach up to 1.225% of total exposures. Both these buffers must be supported by CET1 capital that is not used to satisfy any other buffer.

11.7.5 Regulation of bank liquidity

As a response to the liquidity shortages faced by major institutions during the 2007–2009 financial crisis,[105] CRD IV and Basel III include explicit rules on bank liquidity. Indeed, from 2018 banks are required to hold liquid assets adequate to cover the difference between their liquidity outflows and inflows under gravely stressed conditions for a period of 30 days, and thus maintain a Liquidity Coverage Ratio (LCR) of 100%.[106] In addition,

---

98 See Basel III, paras 153–164.

99 On the precise calculation of the leverage ratio, see CRR arts 429–430.

100 PRA Rulebook: CRR Firms: Leverage Ratio Instrument 2015 (PRA 2015/89), para E.

101 PRA Rulebook: CRR Firms: Leverage Ratio Instrument 2015 (PRA 2015/89), s 1.1.

102 CRR originally envisaged the introduction of a binding leverage ratio by the end of 2018 (CRR, Preamble para 94).

103 PRA Rulebook: CRR Firms: Leverage Ratio Instrument 2015 (PRA 2015/89), s 4.

104 Bank of England, 'Additional Leverage Ratio Buffer Model Requirements for G-SIIs' (2015) <https://www.bankofengland.co.uk/-/media/boe/files/prudential-regulation/supervisory-statement/2015/ss4515-vreq.pdf?la=en&hash=6C23E2FC69A86C381506AE0AAECD140DD89BB8DF> (accessed 25 June 2020).

105 For a policy discussion of the role of liquidity and liquidity ratios, see Markus Brunnermeier et al., *The Fundamental Principles of Financial Regulation: Geneva Reports on the World Economy 11* (Center for Economic Policy Research 2009) 39–48.

106 See Basel III paras 40–42 and CRR art 412. The requirement will be introduced gradually from 2015 and will apply fully from 1 January 2018. The Commission is empowered to specify the details of the requirement

banks must ensure that their long-term obligations are funded by a variety of stable funding instruments even under stressed conditions.[107]

There are detailed technical rules determining the types of assets that qualify as liquid and can thus form the liquidity buffer. In particular, Basel III introduced three types of liquid assets: Level 1, Level 2A and Level 2B. At least 60% of the liquidity buffer must consist of Level 1 assets, and no more than 15% can consist of Level 2B assets. Level 1 assets are taken on face value, whereas Level 2 assets are subject to discounts (haircuts) ranging from 15% to 50% for the purposes of satisfying the liquidity buffer. Level 1 assets include cash, central bank reserves and certain zero-risk-weighted securities. Level 2 assets include securities of higher risk.

The amount of net cash outflows within a 30-day period is calculated conservatively. Expected cash inflows are weighted at 75% to take into account that some borrowers and other obliged parties may fail to honour their obligations in times of stress. Expected cash outflows are also calculated on the basis of conservative assumptions. For instance, regarding typical individual deposits that are fully covered by a deposit guarantee scheme, it is assumed that there will be a 5% outflow.[108] Evidently, this still does not capture the scenario of a depositor run on a bank, and hence, if a depositors run occurs the LCR will not suffice to prevent a bank from facing a liquidity crisis. To further strengthen liquidity in the banking system, Basel III also introduced the concept of the net stable funding ratio (NSFR) which was originally intended to be introduced in the EU from 2018.[109] The aim of the NSFR will be to minimise the risk that disruptions of funding erode the liquidity position and thus threaten the viability of a bank.[110] This will be examined further in the next part of this chapter.

11.7.6 Capital adequacy rules for insurance firms

Finally, it is worth noting that although capital adequacy ratios are unique to deposit-taking institutions, there is a legal requirement for large insurance firms to maintain sufficient equity capital to ensure their solvency in view of calculable risks, by virtue of the Directive known as Solvency II.[111] Broadly speaking, an insurance undertaking, which falls within

---

(CRR art 460). See also Basel Committee on Banking Supervision, *Basel III: The Liquidity Coverage Ratio and Liquidity Risk Monitoring Tools* (Bank for International Settlements 2013).

107 CRR, art 413.

108 The technical rules on cash inflows and outflows are set by the Commission Delegated Regulation (EU) 2015/61 of 10 October 2014 to supplement Regulation (EU) No. 575/2013 of the European Parliament and the Council with regard to liquidity coverage requirement for Credit Institutions OJL 11/1.

109 See CRR, Preamble para 112.

110 The relevant consultation outlines the regime as follows. Banks' available amount of stable funding will have to eventually reach 100% of the required amount of stable funding. The latter is calculated by attributing a factor to each type of assets which seeks to measure the liquidity risk associated with the asset. For instance, all assets that are encumbered (i.e. are the subject matter of a security interest) for more than one year carry a factor of 100%, while cash and deposits in central banks carry a factor of 0%. See Basel Committee on Banking Supervision, *Basel III: The Net Stable Funding Ratio: Consultative Document* (Bank for International Settlements Publications 2014).

111 Directive 2009/138/EC of the European Parliament and of the Council of 25 November 2009 on the taking-up and pursuit of the business of Insurance and Reinsurance (Solvency II) (recast) [2009] OJ L335/1 to be abbreviated from now on as 'Solvency II'.

the scope of the Directive,[112] must review its capital on an annual basis[113] to ensure that it complies with the solvency capital requirement.[114] The latter includes the Basic Solvency Capital Requirement,[115] the capital requirement for operational risk and the adjustment for the loss-absorbing capacity of technical provisions and deferred taxes.[116]

11.8 The reforms known as Basel IV

The shortcomings of Basel III rules to address the failures highlighted by the global financial crisis have raised the attention of the BCBS to adopt amendments on the prudential regulatory requirements and banks' internal risk models. These amendments are generally referred to as the Basel IV framework which introduces reforms to the transparency and assessment of capital requirements among credit institutions.[117] Specifically, the Basel IV rules aim to reduce the weaknesses in risk evaluation by implementing a 'revised standardised approach' for credit risk; it also aims to enhance the credit valuation adjustment by reforming the internally modelled approach.[118] In the 'revised standardised approach', mortgage risk-weights relate to the loan-to-value ratio of the mortgage that should provide a better indication of the exposures of banks. This new approach strengthens the risk sensitivity of credit losses: for example, the internal ratings-based models will only apply to loss-given-default and exposure at default variables.[119]

The major reform introduced by the Basel IV is the 'aggregate output floor', a new layer of banks' RWAs no lower than 72.5% of their risk-weighted assets as produced in the Basel II standardised approach. The 'aggregate output floor', which is intended to be implemented by 2022, should limit the ability of banks to use their internal models to push downwards their RWAs.[120] The RWA is required to be generated under the standardised approach, and this figure has to be reduced by the use of IRB[121] internal risk-weightings. Under the Basel II framework, banking regulators allowed banks to use credit ratings from approved external credit assessment institutions (ECAIs) when setting their capital

---

112 Solvency II, art 2(1) defines its *prima facie* scope very broadly as applying to all life and non-life insurance undertakings established within the EU. However, articles 3–12 of the Directive exclude from its scope of application a range of insurance firms, *inter alia*: social security institutions, small undertakings, many mutual undertakings and the providers of funeral coverage.

113 Solvency II, art 102(1).

114 Solvency II, art 100.

115 This includes at least the following five individual risk modules: non-life underwriting risk; life underwriting risk; health underwriting risk; market risk; counterparty default risk [Solvency II, art 104 (1)]. Each risk module must be 'calibrated using a Value-at-Risk measure, with a 99,5% confidence level, over a one-year period' [Solvency II, art 104 (4)].

116 Solvency II, art 103.

117 Basel Committee on Banking Supervision, 'Finalising Post-crisis Reforms' (December 2017) available at <https://www.bis.org/bcbs/publ/d424.pdf> (accessed 26 June 2020).

118 Peter Yeoh, 'Basel IV: International Bank Capital Regulation Solution or the Beginning of a Solution?' (2018) 39 *Business Law Review* 181.

119 Ioannis Akkizidis and Lampros Kalyvas, *Final Basel III Modelling* (Palgrave 2019) 53–54.

120 Alexander (n 22) 122.

121 Basel Committee on Banking Supervision, 'Studies on the Validation of Internal Rating Systems' (May 2005) Working Paper No. 14, 7, available at <https://www.bis.org/publ/bcbs_wp14.pdf> (accessed 24 June 2020).

requirements.[122] Although this has been at least mitigated by Basel III, it has been argued that 'by giving banks the flexibility to adjust their regulatory capital according to a mix of rating agency ratings and the respective banks' internal models, Basel II outsources significant regulatory authority to the models of rating agencies and banks'.[123] Government use of CRAs has increased the practice of relying blindly on credit ratings' internal models to assess credit risks. The lower transparency and greater complexity in the securities markets ensured a heavy reliance by financial participants on rating agencies.[124] Governmental intrusion in rating activities could exacerbate excessive reliance on ratings particularly in cases where market participants can believe that these carry a governmental 'seal of approval'. Many investors did rely on these ratings and considered them not only to be expert opinions but authorised seals of approval. The problem that regulatory intervention runs the risk of exacerbating excessive reliance on ratings seems evident – particularly because of the high incentives for investors to rely uncritically on ratings as a substitute for independent evaluation.[125] Regulatory reliance on CRAs transformed these 'media opinions' into a sort of official approval for companies needing access to the capital markets. At the European level, Regulation (EU) No. 462/2013 introduced detailed rules in order to (1) reduce financial institutions' over-reliance on credit ratings[126]; (2) reduce European Supervisory Authorities' and the European Systemic Risk Board's over-reliance on credit ratings[127] and (3) reduce Union law's over-reliance on credit ratings.[128] These rules aim to address over-reliance on credit ratings by requiring financial institutions to

---

122 John Authers, 'Who Will Teach Responsibility in a Buck-Passing World?' *Financial Times* (London, 22 June 2014), where it is pointed out that 'the "Basel II" bank regulations gave investors a big incentive to buy anything stamped triple A by agencies. Ratings were only ever advertised as opinions, based on publicly available information: the agencies fell short when investment banks started trying to persuade them that products based on subprime mortgages should be rated triple A'.

123 Erik F. Gerding, 'Code, Crash, and Open Source: The Outsourcing of Financial Regulation to Risk Models and the Global Financial Crisis' (2009) 84(2) *Washington Law Review* 157.

124 Jonathan Katz, Emanuel Salinas and Constantinos Stephanou, 'Credit Rating Agencies' (October 2009) The World Bank Group Note No. 8, 3.

125 Sarah Pei Woo, 'Stress before Consumption: A Proposal to Reform Agency Ratings' (2012) 18(1) *European Law Journal* 77. The author observes that 'it is difficult to reduce reliance on ratings by market participants generally, as references to ratings and ratings triggers pervade investment guidelines, swap documentation, loan agreements, collateral triggers, and other important counterparty documents' (at 78).

126 Article 5a of Regulation (EC) No. 1060/2009 as amended by Regulation (EU) No. 462/2013 where it is stated that credit institutions, investment firms and insurance undertakings, reinsurance undertakings, institutions for occupational retirement provision, management companies, investment companies, alternative investment fund managers and central counterparties 'shall make their own credit risk assessment and shall not solely or mechanistically rely on credit ratings for assessing the creditworthiness of an entity or financial instrument'.

127 Article 5b of Regulation (EC) No. 1060/2009 as amended by Regulation (EU) No. 462/2013 where it is provided that the European Supervisory Authorities (European Securities and Markets Authority, European Banking Authority and European Insurance and Occupational Pensions Authority) 'shall not refer to credit ratings in their guidelines, recommendations and draft technical standards where such references have the potential to trigger sole or mechanistic reliance on credit ratings by the competent authorities, the sectoral competent authorities, the entities referred to in the first subparagraph of Article 4(1) or other financial market participants'.

128 Article 5c of Regulation (EC) No. 1060/2009 as amended by Regulation (EU) No. 462/2013 where it is stated that 'without prejudice to its right of initiative, the Commission shall continue to review whether references to credit ratings in Union law trigger or have the potential to trigger sole or mechanistic reliance on credit ratings by the competent authorities, the sectoral competent authorities, the entities referred to in the first subparagraph of Article 4(1) or other financial market participants with a view to deleting all references

strengthen their own credit risk assessment and not to rely 'solely and mechanistically' on external credit ratings.[129]

The Basel Committee argues that a key concern in the financial crisis was the fact that market participants relied excessively on external ratings instead of conducting the necessary due diligence in order to understand the risks underlying the rated instrument. In this light, Basel II explicitly allowed banking regulators to permit banks to use credit ratings from approved CRAs in calculating their net capital reserve requirements. Reliance on external ratings could undermine incentives to conduct independent internal assessments of the credit quality of exposures. As long as banks are permitted to make extensive use of ratings for capital adequacy purposes, their internal rating scales will continue to be dependent on the ECAIs' ratings.[130] In this context, the introduction of Basel IV standards could stimulate ECAIs to be accurate and transparent.[131]

In the light of the above reforms, the regulatory capital is expected to increase in tandem with the increase of RWAs: this means more stability in the banking sector and stricter standards for capital ratios.[132] Basel IV should reduce the appetite of banks on internal risk models to evaluate optimistically their regulatory capital and should strengthen the leverage requirements for systemically important financial institutions. Increasing capital requirements in the trading book will have the effect to ensure harmonised standards for banks and a level playing field in bank capital regulation. As noted, 'while finalising Basel III was an important milestone, work remains to (i) implement Basel III nationally in a full, timely and consistent manner; (ii) evaluate its effectiveness in reducing the excessive variability of risk-weighted assets (RWAs); and (iii) continue to monitor and assess emerging risks'.[133] However, the new framework can be affected by the future arrangements between the UK and EU on Brexit.[134] Specifically, the UK's views on the inadequacy of CRD IV in implementing Basel III remain a major issue although the wider global regulatory landscape highlights the possibility that Brexit may not necessarily undermine the effects of Basel IV.[135] The resilience on unstable funding of core assets of banks has been enhanced with the newly introduced 'Net Stable Funding Ratio' (NSFR).[136] As mentioned in Section 11.6.5, the NSFR aims

to credit ratings in Union law for regulatory purposes by 1 January 2020, provided that appropriate alternatives to credit risk assessment have been identified and implemented'.

129 Article 5c of Regulation (EC) No. 1060/2009 as amended by Regulation (EU) No. 462/2013 provides, *inter alia*, for the removal of any reference to credit ratings for regulatory purposes by 1 January 2020.

130 Angus Duff, 'The Credit Ratings Agencies and Stakeholder Relations: Issues for Regulators' (2009) 24(1) *Journal of International Banking and Financial Law* 11.

131 Basel Committee on Banking Supervision, 'Credit Ratings and Complementary Sources of Credit Quality Information' (August 2000) Working Papers No. 3, 4.

132 Marcel Magnus, Alienor Anne Claire Duvillet-Margerit, Benoit Mesnard and Alexios Korpas, 'Upgrading the Basel standards: From Basel III to Basel IV?' Economic Governance Support Unit, European Parliament Briefing Paper (2017) 9, available at <http://www.europarl.europa.eu/RegData/etudes/BRIE/2016/587361/IPOL_BRI(2016)587361_EN.pdf> (accessed 20 June 2020).

133 Stefan Ingves, 'Basel III: Are We Done Now?' (Keynote Speech at the Institute for Law and Finance Conference on 'Basel III: Are We Done Now?' Goethe University, Frankfurt, 29 January 2018) available at <https://www.bis.org/speeches/sp180129.pdf> (accessed 23 June 2020).

134 On 23 June 2016 citizens of the UK voted to exit from the European Union through the European Union Referendum Act 2015.

135 Andrew Henderson and James Burnie, 'Brexit and Basel III: An Invitation for More or for Less?' (2016) *Butterworths Journal of International Banking and Financial Law* 480.

136 BIS, 'Net Stable Funding Ratio (NSFR) – Executive Summary' (28 June 2018) available at <https://www.bis.org/fsi/fsisummaries/nsfr.htm> (accessed 10 July 2020).

to limit the banks' practice to rely on unstable and illiquid short-term wholesale funding: this should maintain a stable capital structure.[137] It is evident that the objective of NSFR is to support financial stability and avoid potential sources of systemic risk (i.e. by ensuring that funding shocks do not increase the probability of distress for individual banks). The NSFR formula is a ratio that relates the bank's available stable funding to its required stable funding: it requires banks to maintain a positive outlook in the short-term period and to cover credit exposures with liabilities once at times of stress. The rationale is to equip banks of reliable capital when in a distressed scenario without the recourse to funds arising from maturity mismatches between bank assets and liabilities (e.g. deposits and collaterals).[138] Despite some criticisms raised in the implementation of NSFR in the CRR and CRD IV, EU banks are now required to comply with the Basel Committee standards.[139]

Glossary of terms

- Basel Committee on Banking Supervision (BCBS): International standard setter in the area of banking regulation comprising the leaders of the central banks of most of the countries with the largest financial sectors; it has no legal personality and no formal powers; its secretariat is provided for by the Bank for International Settlements.
- Credit risk: The risk that a borrower will not repay interest and capital due under a loan contract timely and in full.
- Market risk: The risk that the market value of securities held by a bank will decrease.
- Operational risk: the risk that a bank will suffer losses due to failures in its operational systems, e.g. IT systems.
- Capital ratio: The ratio of a bank's capital to its risk-weighted assets. For example, if the value of the risk-weighted assets is 100 and the total capital is 8, the ratio is 8%.
- Capital buffer: Additional amount of capital that a bank must maintain under Basel III in addition to the basic 8% capital ratio.
- Standardised approach: Compliance option for the calculation of credit risk whereby banks assign pre-determined risk factors to different types of lenders.
- Internal Ratings-Based Approach: Compliance option for the calculation of credit risk whereby banks calculate credit risk autonomously on the basis of quantitative models with the approval of supervisory authorities.
- Organisation for Economic Co-operation and Development (OECD): Intergovernmental organisation comprising 36 developed countries, committed to the principles of democracy and market economy, that aims to stimulate economic progress and world trade.
- Leverage: The relationship between the equity and debt of a firm that can be expressed as a debt-to-equity ratio or equity-to-assets ratio; a firm that has relatively more debt than another is described as more highly leveraged; the concept is based on the accounting definition of equity as equal to total assets minus total debts.

---

137 Basel Committee on Banking Supervision, 'Basel III: The Net Stable Funding Ratio' (October 2014) 2–3, available at <https://www.bis.org/bcbs/publ/d295.pdf> (accessed 11 July 2020).

138 Iris H.-Y. Chiu and Joanna Wilson, *Banking Law and Regulation* (OUP 2019) 416–417. See also Michael R. King, 'The Basel III Net Stable Funding Ratio and Bank Net Interest Margins' (2013) 37(11) *Journal of Banking & Finance* 4144–4145.

139 Carla Stamegna, 'Amending Capital Requirements. The "CRD V Package"' (April 2019) European Parliamentary Research Service, 5, available at <http://www.europarl.europa.eu/RegData/etudes/BRIE/2017/599385/EPRS_BRI(2017)599385_EN.pdf> (accessed 2 July 2020).

Practice questions

Despite the significant strengthening of rules on bank capital and liquidity during the last decade, and the partial move away from meta-regulation in the calculation of bank's capital requirements, banks remain undercapitalised and susceptible to financial distress in the case of dramatic changes to external market conditions. Critically discuss.

You may also find it useful to review the chapter through the following questions:

*   How did international bank capital standards emerge? Why is international convergence important in this area?
*   According to the reforms introduced by Basel III to the Basel II framework, explain briefly what types of regulatory capital must banks currently maintain.
*   What are the different types of risk against which banks must maintain regulatory capital?
*   What instruments qualify as bank capital? Explain the difference between Tier 1 and Tier 2 capital.
*   What is the purpose of leverage ratios?
*   How is bank liquidity regulated?
*   Explain the rationale and content of regulatory proposals known as Basel IV.

12 The regulation of bank corporate governance, executive remuneration and senior managers accountability

12.1 Introduction

This chapter examines an area of prudential regulation which has come to the forefront of regulatory policy since the global financial crisis (GFC). As we have seen in previous chapters, due to systemic risk, there is a public interest in banks being managed in a safe and sound way to minimise the risk of failure. This is not easy to reconcile with the general UK corporate law and corporate governance regime which prioritises shareholder value maximisation and encourages efficient risk-taking. To this effect, new regulatory rules were implemented after the GFC relating to banks' board structure, risk management and executive remuneration. In parallel, the long-standing rules on the fitness and propriety of directors and senior managers have been strengthened. This chapter will first provide a concise overview of the standard UK corporate governance framework. Then the discussion will focus on the emergence of the policy debate and academic discourse on the specificity and regulatory significance of bank corporate governance. Having that background in mind, the chapter will then analyse the current regulatory rules on bank boards, risk management, executive remuneration, regulatory scrutiny of senior appointments and senior management accountability, and identify their rationales, strengths and weaknesses.

12.2 An overview of the conventional UK corporate governance framework

The UK corporate governance framework[1] is based on the Corporate Governance (CG) Code which is a document promulgated by the Financial Reporting Council and updated approximately every two years.[2] The most recent version of the Code will apply from 1 January 2019.[3] It consists of high-level principles and specific provisions. The Code has no legal force of its own but listed companies are required by Listing Rule 9.5.6 to disclose in their annual report how they implemented the principles and whether they complied with all the provisions of the CG Code. In the case that a listed company did not comply

---

1 For a comprehensive examination of corporate governance law and policy, see Marc T. Moore and Martin Petrin, *Corporate Governance: Law, Regulation and Theory* (Palgrave 2017).
2 The Code originates from the 1992 report of the Committee on the Financial Aspects of Corporate Governance chaired by Sir Adrian Cadbury, which is widely known as the Cadbury Report. Several other reports followed.
3 See <https://www.frc.org.uk/directors/corporate-governance-and-stewardship/uk-corporate-governance-code> (accessed 1 April 2020).

fully with the provisions it has to specify which particular rules it did not comply with and the duration of the non-compliance and to provide an explanation ('comply or explain approach'). Listing Rule 9.5.6 is based on the power given to the FCA by FSMA section 89O to regulate corporate governance in listed companies. The CG Code is based on the principle of effective corporate boards, and its most important provisions are discussed below.

The CG Code requires companies to have a majority-independent board, in the sense that half of directors (excluding the chairman) must be independent non-executive directors (NEDs). The chairman of the board must not be the same person as the CEO and must be independent at the time of appointment. An independent director is defined as a person who does not have – and has not had for a sufficient period of time prior to his appointment – any substantial relationship with the company on whose board he serves, as a shareholder, employee or business partner. The CG Code's independence criteria also capture family relations, interlocking directorships and other types of relationships.[4] Nearly all UK-listed financial institutions follow the CG Code's recommendations and have a high percentage of independent directors on their boards.[5] That being said, formal independence is only a proxy for actual independence of mind, which depends on the informal dynamics in the boardroom.

The CG Code requires the establishment of three board committees: audit committee (consisting of independent directors – Provision 24), remuneration committee (independent directors and possibly the chairman – Provision 32) and nominations committee (majority of independent directors – Provision 17). The audit committee is responsible *inter alia* for making recommendations to the board on the appointment and removal of the company's external auditor; for reviewing the company's internal financial controls and internal audit function and for monitoring the integrity of the company's financial statements (Provision 25). The remuneration committee is responsible for formulating the company's remuneration policy applicable to executive directors and for determining the actual levels of compensation of the chairman, executive directors and senior management (Provision 33). The nominations committee leads the process for board appointments and ensures sound succession planning for the board and senior management (Provision 17). Furthermore, as a response to the GFC, the 2010 version of the UK CG Code emphasised the importance of risk management as a key responsibility of boards.[6]

A useful way to understand the policy behind the CG Code is by reference to the economic concept of agency costs.[7] Economically speaking, a principal–agent relationship is a situation in which one person appoints another to act on her behalf and in her best interests.[8] In this sense, the relationship between (1) voters and members of parliament; (2) patients and doctors; and (3) shareholders and managers in a company are examples of

---

4 CG Code, Provision 10 contains a list of relationships and circumstances which are 'likely to impair independence'. For a critique of the notion of directorial independence, see Suzanne Le Mire and George Gilligan, 'Independence and Independent Company Directors' (2013) 13 *Journal of Corporate Law Studies* 443.

5 See Andreas Kokkinis, *Corporate Law and Financial Instability* (Routledge 2018) 64–66.

6 On this, see Marc T. Moore, 'The Evolving Contours of the Board's Risk Management Function in UK Corporate Governance' (2010) 10 *Journal of Corporate Law Studies* 279, 297–300.

7 Tackling the agency problem has been the *raison d'être* of the corporate governance movement since its inception. See Daniel R. Fischel, 'The Corporate Governance Movement' (1982) 35 *Vanderbilt Law Review* 1259.

8 Joseph Stiglitz, 'Principal and Agent' in *A Dictionary of Economics* (The New Palgrave 1987) Vol. 3, 966–971. See also Sanford J. Grossman and Oliver D. Hart, 'An Analysis of the Principal-Agent Problem' (1983) 51 *Econometrica* 7 and Frank H. Easterbrook, 'Managers' Discretion and Investors' Welfare: Theories and Evidence' (1984) 9 *Delaware Journal of Corporate Law* 540.

principal–agent relationships. An agency relationship gives rise to agency costs if the inter-ests of the agent and principal are not aligned, and there is information asymmetry between the two – the agent being in possession of superior information to the principal. In such cases, the principal cannot ensure that the agent will use his power in the principal's best interests. On the assumption that the agent is rational and selfish, it is to be expected that the agent will shirk his duties and will opportunistically transfer wealth and other benefits from the principal to himself.

In companies, it is the separation of ownership and control – first empirically observed by Berle and Means[9] – which gives rise to an agency relationship between shareholders (principals), and directors and senior managers (agents). The separation of ownership and control, which since the late 1960s is prevalent in the UK nearly as much as in the US, occurs when the ownership of shares is so dispersed that no shareholder – or small group of shareholders – holds a percentage of shares that would grant effective control of the com-pany. For current listed UK companies, for instance, controlling 30% of the shares is pre-sumed by the Takeover Code to secure control. This means that no individual shareholder (or small group) acting alone can determine the outcome of a shareholder vote.[10]

On these conditions, the costs faced by shareholders who seek to influence corporate decision-making (usually considered as 'activists') are significant. First, they have to invest time and resources in analysing relevant information. Second, they have to put together and maintain a coalition of shareholders. Third, they need to communicate with the board, and use the services of lawyers and other professionals. At the same time, the potential benefits from activism can be relatively small, as it is by no means certain that the activist sharehold-ers will defeat the board. Moreover, even if they are successful, any benefits will be equally spread amongst all shareholders. As a result, each shareholder faces a rational incentive to remain passive, a phenomenon described as the rational apathy of the shareholders.[11] The outcome is that the recommendations of boards are nearly always approved by shareholders, who routinely vote according to the board's advice. This also applies to the election of di-rectors, and thus, the boards of listed companies function as self-perpetuating organs, with the exception of the most evident cases of poor performance.[12]

Therefore, shareholders in companies with dispersed share ownership face agency costs. Primary agency costs include shirking by directors and senior managers (sub-optimal ef-fort) and behaviour that benefits directors and senior managers at the expense of the share-holders. Such behaviour may seek to provide agents with financial benefits (for instance, self-dealing, exploitation of corporate opportunities, misappropriation of corporate assets and excessive remuneration).[13] Alternatively, agents may serve their non-financial interests.

---

9 Berle and Means' empirical work confirmed that 44% of the 200 largest US corporations were managerially controlled, i.e. no single shareholder owned more than 5% of shares. See Adolf Berle and Gardiner Means, *The Modern Corporation and Private Property* (rev edn, Harcourt, Brace & World 1967) 108–109.

10 See Bernard Black, 'Agents Watching Agents: The Promise of Institutional Investor Voice' (1991–1992) 39 *UCLA Law Review* 811, 821–822.

11 For a modern explanation of the dynamics of shareholder voting and the rational apathy of the shareholders from a US perspective, see Christopher Gulinello, 'The Retail Investor Vote: Mobilizing Rationally Apathetic Shareholders to Preserve or Challenge the Board's Presumption of Authority' (2010) 2010 *Utah Law Review* 547, 573–576.

12 Berle and Means were the first scholars who observed the collective action problems faced by dispersed share-holders. See Berle and Means (n 9), 76–82 and 129–131.

13 On this, see Andrew Keay, 'Company Directors Behaving Poorly: Disciplinary Options for Shareholders' (2007) 2007 *Journal of Business Law* 656.

An example is corporate 'empire-building', i.e. the creation of inefficiently large corporate groups to secure personal power, prestige and security of office for directors and senior managers.[14]

Since investors anticipate the problem of agency costs, listed companies have to demonstrate to them that such costs will be kept low and investors may still wish to devote some resources to monitor corporate behaviour. In that sense, Jensen and Meckling classify agency costs into three categories, namely, (1) monitoring costs (incurred by shareholders); (2) bonding costs (incurred by companies) and (3) residual agency costs (primary agency costs).[15] Regarding bonding devices to signal to potential investors that agency costs will be held in strict control, American and British business practice made use of majority-independent boards. The role of independent boards is to monitor the performance of senior management and ensure that they act in the best interests of the shareholders.

In that sense, all the provisions of the CG Code regarding board independence and the role of board committees can be understood as devices to address agency costs. In particular, the three board committees tackle areas where the interests of senior management conflict starkly with the interests of shareholders. Evidently, regarding nominations, incumbent directors and managers want to be re-appointed, whereas shareholders only want that if the incumbents have performed well. Regarding remuneration, shareholders only want companies to pay as much as it is necessary to attract and retain talent, whereas it is in the interests of executives to be paid as much as possible. Regarding financial disclosures, it is in the general interest of investors for companies to disclose accurate information so that they can make well-informed investment decisions, whereas senior managers and executive directors face an incentive to hide negative information in order to protect their positions and remuneration. There is vast literature – both theoretical and empirical – on the importance of board structure and, in particular, on the degree of board independence, which is generally assessed based on the percentage of independent NEDs sitting on a board.[16] Empirical evidence indicates that board independence is positively correlated with CEO turnover, and thus, that independent boards lead to increase in CEO accountability.[17]

In addition, it is worth pointing out that the CG Code is only one of a range of legal devices used to control agency costs. Authoritative commentators identify five possible legal strategies, namely, (1) granting some decision-making power to the principal; (2) giving the principal the right to appoint the agent; (3) making the agent the trustee of the principal

---

14 Large corporations that run diverse businesses and operate in various markets are less susceptible to insolvency and hostile takeovers.

15 See Michael C. Jensen and William H. Meckling, 'Theory of the Firm: Managerial Behavior, Agency Costs and Ownership Structure' (1976) 3 *Journal of Financial Economics* 305, 308–310.

16 A review of general economic literature on the functioning of boards of directors can be found in Renee Adams, Benjamin Hermalin and Michael Weisbach, 'The Role of Boards of Directors in Corporate Governance: A Conceptual Framework and Survey' (2010) 48 *Journal of Economic Literature* 58 and Benjamin Hermalin and Michael Weisbach, 'Boards of Directors as an Endogenously Determined Institution: A Survey of the Economic Literature' (2003) 9 *Economic Policy Review* 7. See also Ada Demb and Friedrich Neubaurer, *The Corporate Board* (OUP 1992).

17 See Steven N. Kaplan and Bernadette A. Minton, 'How Has CEO Turnover Changed?' (2012) 12 *International Review of Finance* 57; Volker Laux, 'Board Independence and CEO Turnover' (2008) 46 *Journal of Accounting Research* 137; and Michael S. Weisbach, 'Outside Directors and CEO Turnover' (1988) 20 *Journal of Financial Economics* 431. On the psychological benefits of independent board chairmen, see Randall Morck, 'Behavioral Finance in Corporate Governance – Independent Directors, Non-executive Chairs, and the Importance of the Devil's Advocate' (2004) 12 *Journal of Management and Governance* 179.

who is prohibited from promoting his own interests; (4) rewarding the agent when he acts in line with the principal's interests and (5) ensuring that the principal can end his affiliation with the agent.[18] UK company law adopts all these strategies, and the CG Code is an example of the use of the reward and appointment devices through the medium of independent directors who are given the effective power to appoint and remove CEOs and senior managers and to decide the structure and level of their remuneration.[19]

12.3 Bank corporate governance: the Walker Review and the report of the Parliamentary Committee on banking standards

The failure of several major banks during the GFC highlighted corporate governance failures in the areas of risk management and board oversight.[20] For instance, the failure of boards to be involved meaningfully in strategy-setting, and the consequent complete delegation of strategy development to executive management was central to the failures of both RBS[21] and HBOS.[22] More broadly, the GFC raised the question of whether a shareholder-centric corporate governance system is appropriate for systemically important banks. The insolvency or even distress of a systemically important bank generates negative externalities and threatens the stability of the whole financial system. Running such institutions with a view to profit maximisation, which entails taking considerable risks, can thus be problematic from the perspective of the public interest in safeguarding financial stability.

Unsurprisingly, the GFC led to increased regulatory interest in the corporate governance of banks and other financial institutions. For instance, the OECD Steering Group on Corporate Governance stated that 'the financial crisis can be to an important extent attributed to failures and weaknesses in corporate governance arrangements which did not serve their purpose to safeguard against excessive risk taking in a number of financial services companies'.[23] The report identified three areas where bank governance failed: board oversight and risk management, executive remuneration and accounting standards. At the EU level, a 2009 Commission consultation led to a 2010 Green Paper on the corporate governance of financial institutions. The key normative finding of the Paper was that '[i]n the financial services sector, corporate governance should take account of the interests of other stakeholders (...), as well as the stability of the financial system, due to the systemic nature of many players'.[24] However, the Paper cautioned against regulatory-driven governance of financial institutions, and emphasised that the business strategy and risk appetite of banks should be decided by their boards under the supervision of shareholders.

---

18 Reinier Kraakman et al., *The Anatomy of Corporate Law: A Comparative and Functional Approach* (3rd edn, OUP 2017).

19 For further detail on this, see Kokkinis, *Corporate Law and Financial Instability* (n 5) 43–45.

20 This is widely accepted in the literature. See e.g. Jaap Winter, 'The Financial Crisis: Does Good Corporate Governance Matter and How to Achieve it?' in Eddy Wymeersch, Klaus Hopt and Guido Ferranini (eds), *Financial Regulation and Supervision: A Post-crisis Analysis* (OUP 2012).

21 See FSA, 'The Failure of the Royal Bank of Scotland: Financial Services Authority Board Report' (2011) paras 591–593 <http://www.fsa.gov.uk/pubs/other/rbs.pdf> (accessed 10 May 2020).

22 See Parliamentary Commission on Banking Standards, *An Accident Waiting to Happen: The Failure of HBOS* (2012–13, HL 144, HC 705) paras 91–92.

23 Grant Kirkpatrick, 'The Corporate Governance Lessons from the Financial Crisis' (2009) 2009 *OECD Journal: Financial Market Trends* 61, 61.

24 Commission, 'Corporate Governance in Financial Institutions and Remuneration Policies' COM (2010) 284 final, 2.

A further significant step in the development of harmonised principles in the area was the publication of the Basel Principles for Enhancing Corporate Governance in late 2010.[25] The Principles acknowledge that corporate governance is of great relevance[26] both at the micro-level of individual institutions and at the macro-level of financial system stability, as it can set proper incentives, facilitate supervision and foster market confidence. In parallel, the GFC is seen as partly due to governance failures, as poor governance led both to individual failures and wider problems, due to loss of confidence in financial markets.[27] The Principles place great emphasis on the role of supervisors who are expected to evaluate the corporate governance structures of financial institutions – including the expertise and integrity of prospective directors and senior managers – and to have formal powers to take remedial action.[28] In terms of governance procedures, the Principles focus on effective boards, sound risk management, executive remuneration, the simplification of group structures and transparency. They are modelled on the OECD Principles of Corporate Governance,[29] which are not specific to banks. Indeed, apart from the requirements for a board risk committee, a Chief Risk Officer (CRO) and the scrutiny of new products and mergers, the Basel Principles do not differentiate financial institution corporate governance from the governance of non-financial companies.

In the UK, the Basel Principles were anticipated by a comprehensive review by Sir David Walker[30] which proposed a set of corporate governance rules applicable exclusively to banks and other major financial institutions.[31] Following the approach taken by the UK Corporate Governance Code, the Review intended its recommendations to be enforced on a comply-or-explain basis.[32] Eventually, many of its recommendations were incorporated into the regulatory rules of the Prudential Regulation Authority (PRA) and Financial Conduct Authority (FCA). Specifically, the Review does not challenge the shareholder-value orientation of bank corporate governance but rather focuses on recommending several incremental changes to remedy perceived areas of weakness. These areas were the competence of independent directors, risk management and the remuneration of executive directors and senior managers. On this point, the report cautioned that:

> To dilute the primacy of the duty of the BOFI director to shareholders to accommodate a new accountability to other stakeholders would risk changing fundamentally the *contractual and legal basis on which the UK market economy operates.* It would introduce potentially substantial new uncertainty for shareholders as to the value of their

---

25 See Working Group on Corporate Governance of the Basel Committee, *Principles for Enhancing Corporate Governance* (Nouy Daniele and others and Bank of International Settlements Publications 2010).

26 Ibid., 1–2.

27 Ibid., 5.

28 Ibid., 30–32.

29 See Organisation for Economic Co-operation and Development, 'G20/OECD Principles of Corporate Governance' (2004) <http://www.oecd.org/corporate/oecdprinciplesofcorporategovernance.htm> (accessed 20 May 2020).

30 David Walker, 'A Review of Corporate Governance in UK Banks and Other Financial Industry Entities: Final Recommendations' (2009) <https://www.icaew.com/en/library/subject-gateways/corporate-governance/codes-and-reports/walker-report> (accessed 18 May 2020). To be abbreviated from now on as the 'Walker Review'.

31 Ibid., para 1.22.

32 Ibid., paras 2.16–2.19. It is notable that despite the original intention of Sir David Walker there is no formal obligation of banks to disclose whether they comply with the recommendations or not.

holdings and would be likely to lead to *shareholder exodus from the sector* and a rise in the cost of capital for BOFIs.

(emphasis added)[33]

In this sense, its recommendations remain within the traditional agency costs paradigm, dominant since the time of the Cadbury Committee. In any case, it would not be possible for a soft-law document such as the Walker Review to change the shareholder-centric orientation of bank corporate governance as it is partially embedded in statutory provisions applicable to all companies including banks.[34] However, the Review actively endorsed shareholder value maximisation as the key duty of bank directors and rejected the possibility of taking an alternative perspective on financial institution corporate governance.

A very different position on this matter was taken by the Parliamentary Committee on Banking Standards (PCBS). The Commission's report painted a grim picture of bank corporate governance during the years leading up to the GFC:

> The corporate governance of large banks was characterised by the creation of Potemkin villages to give the appearance of effective control and oversight, without the reality. In particular, many non-executive directors – in many cases experienced, eminent and highly-regarded individuals – failed to act as an effective check on, and challenge to, executive managers.[35]

More importantly, the PCBS called the government to initiate a consultation on the duties owed by bank directors by virtue of the Companies Act 2006 to ensure that the safety and soundness of banks is placed over and above the duties owed to bank shareholders.[36] As an interim solution before new legislation could be enacted, the PCBS recommended an amendment to the UK Corporate Governance Code which would acknowledge the tension between maintaining the safety and soundness of banks and pursuing shareholder wealth maximisation. The Government rejected the proposal to introduce 'a new primary duty on bank directors to promote the financial stability of their companies over the interests of shareholders'.[37] Part of the relevant academic literature is also against reforming company law duties only for financial institutions. For instance, Chiu argues that the company law framework for directors' duties and the prudential regulatory framework on senior managers serve distinct purposes and must remain separate.[38] Other commentators have

---

33 Ibid., Annex 3, 137.
34 See Companies Act 2006, ss 168, 171, 172, 304, 305, 314, 561 and 983.
35 PCBS, *Changing Banking for Good* (2013–2014, HL 27-I, HC 175-I), para 119.
36 Ibid., paras 702–708. Of course, the duty of loyalty is not owed to shareholder but to the company. Still, its formulation focuses on the benefit of the members as a whole.
37 See BIS, 'Transparency & Trust: Enhancing the Transparency of UK Company Ownership and Increasing Trust in UK Business: Government Response' (April 2014) para 249 available at <https://www.gov.uk/government/consultations/company-ownership-transparency-and-trust-discussion-paper> (accessed 18 May 2020).
38 Iris H.-Y. Chiu, 'Comparing Directors' Duties in the Financial Services Sector with Regulatory Duties under the Senior Persons Regime – Some Critical Observations' (2016) 27 *European Business Law Review* 261. See also Mads Andenas and Iris H.-Y. Chiu, *The Foundations and Future of Financial Regulation: Governance for Responsibility* (Routledge 2014), 392.

emphasised the potential value of harmonising the two areas and the benefits of private enforcement as a complement to regulatory enforcement.[39]

12.4 The regulatory framework on bank board structure and risk management

As most UK banks are systemically important and thus regulated by the PRA, the following discussion will focus on the PRA Rulebook. From a regulatory perspective, banks are required to have in place an effective governance system and to ensure that their governing body (board of directors) has overall responsibility for compliance with regulatory rules. This includes having a clear and transparent organisational structure, sound administration and accounting procedures and effective risk management processes.[40] The requirement to have in place appropriate systems and controls applies in a way that is proportionate to firm size, complexity, diversity of operations, volume of transactions and level of risk.[41]

As explained in the previous section, the Walker Review introduced a series of soft law recommendations regarding independent director competence. In particular, the Review recommended that a majority of NEDs possess relevant financial experience, and that NEDs are given individually tailored induction and training, and thematic business awareness sessions.[42] The Review also recommended that more time must be committed by financial institution NEDs than was previously the norm, and that in most cases this should mean 30–36 days annually, compared to approximately 25 days annually before the GFC.[43] Board chairmen were recommended to devote around two-thirds of their working time to their role.[44]

In parallel, Capital Requirements Directive IV (CRD IV) introduced several mandatory rules on the structure of bank boards. The Directive's approach to bank board composition is based on five general principles, namely, (1) sufficient collective knowledge; (2) time commitment; (3) adequate resources; (4) diversity and (5) honesty.[45] CRD IV precludes banks from combining the roles of CEO and chairman of the board without the consent of their regulator,[46] and requires nomination committees to consist exclusively of NEDs.[47] Although these requirements largely coincide with the recommendations of the CG Code[48] and – to a great extent – with the actual practice of UK banks, the transformation of the relevant rules from 'comply-or-explain' soft law to compulsory regulatory standards is significant. Furthermore, CRD IV imposes a cap on parallel board appointments so that the same person cannot hold more than either one executive and two non-executive appointments,

---

39 See e.g. Kokkinis, *Corporate Law and Financial Instability* (n 5). Armour and Gordon also propose reforming bank directors' liability rules. See John Armour and Jeffrey N. Gordon, 'Systemic Harms and Shareholder Value' (2014) 6 *Journal of Legal Analysis* 35.
40 See Directive 2013/36/EU of the European Parliament and of the Council of 26 June 2013 on access to the activity of credit institutions and the prudential supervision of credit institutions and investment firms [2013] OJ L176/338, art 74(1). From now on to be abbreviated as 'CRD IV'.
41 PRA Rulebook, CRR Firms, Risk Control 2.5.
42 Walker Review (n 30), paras 3.13 and 3.16.
43 Ibid., para 3.23.
44 Ibid., para 4.18.
45 See CRD IV art 91 (1), (2) and (7)–(9).
46 CRD IV art 88 (1) (e).
47 CRD IV art 88 (2).
48 See above Section 12.1.

or four non-executive appointments.[49] Appointments at not-for-profit organisations and charities are excluded from the cap,[50] and competent regulators have the discretion to allow bank directors to hold one additional non-executive position.[51]

Regarding risk management,[52] the Walker Review emphasised that the risk mitigation function of bank boards must not be confined to peripheral risks but rather must cover the risks that are intrinsic to banks' business. All the main recommendations of the Review on risk management are now included in the PRA Rulebook, and many are also mandated by CRD IV. Bank boards are expected to shape the risk appetite and tolerance of banks in a forward-looking manner.[53] Boards should establish risk committees of NEDs,[54] which should focus on major prudential risks[55] and encourage due diligence and in-depth risk scrutiny by the board of major strategic transactions, such as acquisitions and disposals.[56] Moreover, large financial institutions should be served by a CRO[57] to oversee risk-taking on an enterprise-wide basis. CROs must have a substantial degree of independence from CEOs, in the sense that they can only be removed from their post by the board and have direct access to the board.[58] Beyond this, the rules require the risk management function of banks, which is responsible for risk modelling,[59] to be independent from operational functions and able to report directly to the board.[60] At the European level, the European Banking Authority (EBA) amended in 2017 its guidelines on firms' internal governance to further emphasise the risk oversight duty of boards and risk committees.[61]

To conclude, the discussion in this section demonstrates that the prevalent regulatory approach to banks' internal risk management is to require credit institutions to have ultimate responsibility for the design and implementation of their processes, which is an example of meta-regulation.[62] In this context, the potential problem with meta-regulation is configured as the tension between the business purposes of financial institutions and the regulatory objectives.

---

49 The cap is effective since 1 July 2014. See CRD IV art 91 (3).

50 CRD IV art 91 (5).

51 CRD IV art 91 (6).

52 For a post-crisis critique of risk management, see Gabriele Sabato, 'Financial Crisis: Where Did Risk Management Fail?' (2010) 2 *International Review of Applied Financial Issues and Economics* 315.

53 Walker Review (n 30), para 6.22.

54 CRD IV, art 76 (3) implemented by PRA Rulebook, CRR Firms, Risk Control 3.1 (1).

55 Walker Review (n 30), para 6.21. The functions of risk committees are set out in detail in PRA Rulebook, CRR Firms, Risk Control 3.1 (2) and (3).

56 Walker Review (n 30), para 6.31.

57 For an early discussion of the role of chief risk officers, see Andre Liebenberg and Robert Hoyt, 'The Determinants of Enterprise Risk Management: Evidence from the Appointment of Chief Risk Officers' (2003) 6 *Risk Management & Insurance Review* 37.

58 PRA Rulebook, CRR Firms, Risk Control 3.5 and Walker Review (n 30), para 6.12.

59 For a discussion of risk models used by banks and a critique of their capacity to quantify extreme downward risks can be found in Christophe Bucher, 'Risk Models-at-Risk' (2014) 44 *Journal of Banking & Finance* 72.

60 PRA Rulebook, CRR Firms, Risk Control 3.4.

61 See EBA, 'Final Report on Guidelines on Internal Governance' (EBA/GL/2017/11, 2017) <https://www.eba.europa.eu/documents/10180/1972987/Final+Guidelines+on+Internal+Governance+%28EBA-GL-2017-11%29.pdf/eb859955-614a-4afb-bdcd-aaa664994889> (accessed 12 May 2020). The relevant consultation closed on 28 January 2017. See EBA, 'Consultation on Guidelines on Internal Governance(Revised)'(EBA/CP/2016/16,2016)<https://www.eba.europa.eu/regulation-and-policy/internal-governance/guidelines-on-internal-governance-revised-/-/regulatory-activity/consultation-paper;jsessionid=6A0D7509AA06AA3B77369D0CF89014BD> (accessed 1 June 2020)

62 On this, see Iris H.-Y. Chiu, 'Corporate Governance and Risk Management in Banks and Financial Institutions' in Iris H.-Y. Chiu (ed), *The Law on Corporate Governance in Banks* (Edward Elgar 2015) 191–192.

12.5 The regulation of executive remuneration on banks

As explained previously in this chapter, executive remuneration in banks attracted major policy attention after the 2007–2009 GFC. The current framework is a mixture of general company law and corporate governance rules that apply to all listed companies and specific regulatory rules that apply only to banks and some other financial institutions.[63] This section will first provide a brief overview of the general legal framework for executive remuneration before setting out the main regulatory rules in the area. These rules include the controversial cap on variable remuneration imposed by CRD IV.

12.5.1 *The general legal framework for executive remuneration in listed companies*

As we discussed in Section 12.1, the CG Codes recommend companies should have remuneration committees so that executive directors are not involved in setting their own remuneration. Turning to hard law, the Companies Act 2006 requires quoted (that is, listed) public companies to prepare a directors' remuneration report for each financial year which specifies the actual remuneration paid to individual directors and includes a remuneration policy detailing the principles and criteria by which remuneration is set.[64] In particular, remuneration policies typically set out the structure of executive remuneration packages in terms of breakdown by fixed and variable remuneration. Fixed remuneration includes a director's salary, pension contributions and benefits in kind. Variable or performance-based remuneration includes annual bonuses and performance shares which normally vest after several years. Regarding variable remuneration, remuneration policies specify the criteria used to determine whether to make a payment under a bonus scheme, the number of performance shares that can be awarded and the terms of such awards.

To empower shareholders with effective decision-making rights over executive remuneration, the Act requires listed companies to hold an annual advisory vote on their directors' remuneration report,[65] and a triennial legally binding vote on remuneration policy.[66] If shareholders do not approve the remuneration report as part of the advisory vote, the validity of payments made to directors is not affected but the company is likely to suffer a reduction in its share price due to reputational damage. In practice, even dissent by a significant minority of shareholders can force corporate executives to give up part of their remuneration, as happened in some UK banks in 2015 and 2016. Conversely, if a company changes its remuneration policy without shareholder approval, the change is ineffective, and any remuneration paid in contravention to the existing policy is void.

Furthermore, the Companies Act requires shareholder approval in certain circumstances where shareholder interests are considered to be at risk. Shareholders must approve any service contract for directors with a guaranteed term of employment which exceeds two

---

63 For an authoritative discussion of the legal framework for executive remuneration in banks, see Marc T. Moore, 'Design and Control of Remuneration in UK Banks' in Iris H.-Y. Chiu (ed), *The Law on Corporate Governance in Banks* (Edward Elgar 2015).

64 Sections 420–422A.

65 Companies Act 2006, s 439. This rule was first introduced in 2002.

66 Companies Act 2006, s 439A, inserted by s 79 of the Enterprise and Regulatory Reform Act 2013.

years.[67] Companies are also precluded from making any payments to directors for loss of office or due to retirement unless such payments have been approved on a case-by-case basis by the shareholders to whom the amount of the payment must be disclosed.[68]

12.5.2 *The regulatory framework for bank executive remuneration: general principles*

Reform impetus in the area of bank executive remuneration began with the Walker Review which recommended that remuneration committees' oversight be extended to cover remuneration policy at the group level[69] and approving the compensation of all high-end employees.[70] The report also recommended that half of an officer's variable remuneration be in the form of a long-term scheme, whereby half vests in no less than three years and half in five years. Bonus awards, meanwhile, should be paid over a three-year period.[71] Moreover, it was recommended that high-end employees and executive directors retain a shareholding in the company in proportion to their overall remuneration.[72] In terms of statutory reforms, FSMA 2000 section 139A, which was inserted by the Financial Services Act 2010 section 6, vested the PRA with new responsibilities on executive remuneration, including the duty to require regulated firms to adopt a remuneration policy consistent with the effective management of risks[73] and, most importantly, the power to prohibit relevant persons from being remunerated in a way that contravenes the above standards.

Significant reforms in the area were also introduced by CRD IV. The Directive clearly states that its policy is to prevent financial incentives for excessive risk-taking which are perceived as one of the main causes of bank failures and financial instability.[74] Indeed, the preamble to the Directive emphasises that 'Weaknesses in corporate governance in a number of institutions have contributed to excessive and imprudent risk-taking in the banking sector which has led to the failure of individual institutions and systemic problems in Member States and globally'.[75] To that effect, the Directive introduced a detailed set of rules on executive remuneration in banks falling within its scope.[76] In the UK, many of these rules were already in place before coming into force of the Directive. Regarding the range of senior managers covered, the scope of CRD IV remuneration rules is broad and covers all material risk takers including 'senior management, risk takers, staff engaged in control functions and any employee receiving total remuneration that takes them into the same remuneration bracket as senior management'.[77]

---

67 Companies Act 2006, s 188.
68 Companies Act 2006, ss 215–217.
69 Walker Review (n 30), para 7.7.
70 Ibid., para 7.10.
71 Ibid., para 7.34.
72 Ibid., para 7.35.
73 According to FSMA 2000, s 139A (3) (b), the policy must also be consistent with the 2009 Implementation Standards for Principles for Sound Compensation Practices issued by the Financial Stability Board.
74 For an academic critique of the mismatch between bank executive remuneration and long-term performance, see Lucian Bebchuk, Alma Cohen and Holger Spamann, 'The Wages of Failure: Executive Compensation at Bear Sterns and Lehman 2000–2008' (2010) 27 *Yale Journal on Regulation* 257.
75 CRD IV, Preamble para 53.
76 On the scope of CRD IV, see Chapter 11 of this volume.
77 CRD IV, art 92(2).

CRD IV requires banks to have a remuneration committee comprising NEDs.[78] The provision of guaranteed variable remuneration is prohibited other than to new staff and for the first year of their employment.[79] The fixed component of remuneration must be high enough to enable firms to not pay any variable remuneration at all when performance is poor.[80] Furthermore, the rules require that at least 50% of variable remuneration be paid in shares, share-linked instruments or capital instruments rather than cash.[81] The rules also require banks to defer at least 60% of variable remuneration for at least seven years, for persons performing a senior management function, which includes executive directors.[82] The deferred element must vest no faster than on a *pro rata* basis, i.e. equally on each anniversary of the grant, with no vesting taking place until three years after the award. Most crucially, banks are required to reduce any unvested deferred variable remuneration (malus) and to take reasonable steps to recover any vested variable remuneration (clawback) in case an individual senior manager is found guilty of misconduct, or failed to meet standards of fitness and propriety, or there is a significant failure of risk management.[83]

Another important aspect of the regulatory framework concerns the metrics used to measure senior managerial performance. Consistent with its overall emphasis on sound risk management, the PRA demands banks to risk-adjust any profit-related metrics used to assess financial performance.[84] As a result, all major UK banks currently use a variety of non-profit-related metrics alongside profit-related ones to determine the vesting of bonuses and performance share awards. Non-profit-related criteria include the following: capital strength, liquidity, minimisation of bad loans, customer satisfaction, compliance, risk management, corporate reputation and strategy development. In parallel, financial performance is no longer exclusively assessed by relative total shareholder return (TSR) and earnings per share (EPS), but rather some major UK banks use return on risk-weighted assets (RoRWA). The latter metric does not depend on a bank's leverage and therefore does not create any perverse incentive for senior managers to increase a bank's leverage in order to maximise the variable remuneration they receive.

12.5.3 *The regulatory framework for bank executive remuneration: the bonus cap*

In addition to the aforementioned provisions, CRD IV introduced a cap on all forms of variable remuneration paid to bank executive directors and senior managers as a percentage of their fixed remuneration. The rationale for the cap is evident in the Directive's preamble

---

78 CRD IV, art 95 implemented by PRA Rulebook, CRR Firms, Remuneration 7.4.

79 CRD IV, art 94(1)(d) and (e) implemented by PRA Rulebook, CRR Firms, Remuneration 15.7.

80 CRD IV, art 94(1)(f) implemented by PRA Rulebook, CRR Firms, Remuneration 15.9 (2).

81 CRD IV, art 94(1)(l) implemented by PRA Rulebook, CRR Firms, Remuneration 15.15.

82 PRA Rulebook, CRR Firms, Remuneration 15.17 and 15.18. All CRD IV regulated firms are expected to defer 40% of variable remuneration of all material risk takers. However, in the case of payments in excess of 500,000 euros and payments to directors of significant firms, 60% of remuneration must be deferred. The monetary limit was introduced by CRD IV, article 94 (1) (m). A discussion of the policy behind the seven year deferral period can be found in PRA, 'Strengthening the Alignment of Risk and Reward: New Remuneration Rules' (PRA PS12/15, 2015) 7–8 <http://www.bankofengland.co.uk/pra/Pages/publications/ps/2015/ps1215.aspx> (accessed 19 May 2020).

83 CRD IV, art 94(1)(n) implemented by PRA Rulebook, CRR Firms, Remuneration 15.22 and 15.23, respectively.

84 PRA Rulebook, CRR Firms, Remuneration 11.2–11.6 which also implement CRD IV, art 94(1)(a).

which states that 'in order to avoid excessive risk taking, a maximum ratio between the fixed and the variable component of the total remuneration should be set. It is appropriate to provide for a certain role for the shareholders, owners or members of institutions in that respect'.[85]

According to CRD IV, variable remuneration cannot exceed 100% of fixed remuneration,[86] unless the shareholders of a bank approve a higher ratio, up to 200% of fixed remuneration.[87] The cap refers to the maximum variable remuneration opportunity rather than the amount actually paid out in a given year. CRD IV prescribes the requisite process, majority and quorum in detail. All shareholders must be given a reasonable notice period in advance of the relevant general meeting and must be provided with a detailed statement by the bank on the impact of the proposed increase of variable remuneration on the bank's ability to maintain a sound capital base. The shareholder resolution approving the increase must be passed by at least 66% of the share capital, provided that at least 50% of the shares are represented at the meeting, or else by 75% of the share capital. Any shareholders who are directly affected by the decision (such as directors or managers of the bank) are disqualified from voting. All major UK banks have obtained shareholder's approval to extend variable remuneration to 200% of fixed remuneration.

In parallel, CRD IV enables Member States to allow banks to apply a discounted rate of up to 25% of variable remuneration,[88] in accordance with guidelines issued by the EBA, provided that variable remuneration is paid in instruments that are deferred for at least five years. The EBA Guidelines take into account four factors to calculate the rate for the discount rate, namely, (1) the national inflation rate; (2) the average interest rate paid on EU sovereign bonds; (3) the length of the deferral period and (4) any additional retention period requirement.[89] Major UK banks have not yet availed of this possibility.

The cap marks a significant departure from the previous practice of major UK banks.[90] Unsurprisingly, given that CRD IV imposes no restriction regarding the overall level of remuneration, all major UK banks have responded to the cap by introducing a new form of fixed remuneration to counterbalance its effect.[91] These payments, typically described as 'fixed pay allowances', are not made in cash but rather in shares which have to be retained for a specified period of time. Initially, banks' remuneration policies also provided for these allowances to be reviewed annually which was of questionable compliance with CRD IV's notion of fixed remuneration. According to EBA guidance, all components of fixed remuneration have to be pre-determined for the whole period of an employee's employment, irrespective of past or future performance, and therefore, any elements which

---

85 See CRD IV, Preamble para 65.

86 CRD IV, art 94(1)(g)(i).

87 CRD IV, art 94(1)(g)(ii).

88 CRD IV, art 94(1)(g)(iii).

89 See EBA, 'Guidelines on the Applicable Notional Discount Rate for Variable Remuneration' (EBA/GL/2014/01, 27 March 2014) <https://www.eba.europa.eu/regulation-and-policy/remuneration/guidelines-on-discount-rate-for-variable-remuneration> (accessed 19 May 2020).

90 For a detailed analysis of the way in which the remuneration practices of major UK banks changed due to the implementation of the bonus cap, see Andreas Kokkinis, 'Exploring the Effects of the Bonus Cap Rule: The Impact of Remuneration Structure on Risk-Taking by Bank Managers' (2019) 19 *Journal of Corporate Law Studies* 167.

91 This can be seen in the 2014, 2015 and 2016 Annual Reports and Accounts issued by Barclays, HSBC, Lloyds Banking Group, the Royal Bank of Scotland and Standard Chartered.

are subject to unilateral alteration at the employer's discretion must be classified as variable remuneration.[92]

The bonus cap was met with scepticism by the PRA which noted that the unintended outcome of the bonus cap, that is, the rise in fixed remuneration, is likely to weaken banks in times of crisis due to its less flexible nature.[93] In a similar vein, the Treasury launched in September 2013 an unsuccessful legal challenge against the bonus cap before the European Court of Justice on the grounds of lack of competence by the EU to legislate in the area.[94] There is also considerable academic opposition to the bonus cap rule pointing out that variable remuneration is a sound risk management tool,[95] and that the rule brings unintended consequences[96] and is likely to fail to achieve any reduction in risk-taking as it is a blunt tool which undermines the operation of maluses and clawbacks and is easy to evade by paying fixed pay allowances in shares.[97] Most academic contributions in favour of the cap are written from a perspective of distributive justice and reducing the total level of senior manager remuneration rather than from the perspective of its potential contribution to financial stability.[98]

12.6 The Senior Managers Regime

The Banking Reform Act 2013 introduced a new Senior Managers Regime which replaced the pre-existing Approved Persons Regime with effect from 6 April 2016.[99] The Commission on Banking Standards in its 2013 report criticised heavily the operation of the Approved Persons Regime, and proposed the introduction of a new more rigorous approval regime for systemically important institutions, distinct from that applied to other financial firms.[100] The Government responded to the report positively, and most of its recommendations were implemented by the Banking Reform Act 2013.[101] The new regime sits within the pre-existing statutory framework requiring senior employees in regulated entities to be fit and proper.[102] The Financial Services and Markets Act 2000 empowers the PRA/FCA to scrutinise and approve any person that performs a controlled function in an authorised

---

92 EBA, 'Guidelines on Sound Remuneration Policies under Articles 74(3) and 75(2) of Directive 2013/36/EU and Disclosures under Article 450 of Regulation (EU) No. 575/2013' (EBA/GL/2015/22, 2015) 120–123 <https://www.eba.europa.eu/documents/10180/1314839/EBA-GL-2015-22+Guidelines+on+-Sound+Remuneration+Policies_EN.pdf> (accessed 22 May 2020).

93 See Bank of England: Prudential Regulation Authority, 'Strengthening Capital Standards: Implementing CRD IV, Feedback and Final Rules' (PRA Policy Statement PS7/13, 2013) para 4.7 <http://www.bank-ofengland.co.uk/pra/Pages/publications/implemcrdiv.aspx> (accessed 17 May 2020).

94 Case C-507/13 *United Kingdom v Parliament and Council* [2013].

95 See e.g. John Thanassoulis, 'The Case for Intervening in Bankers' Pay' (2012) 67 *The Journal of Finance* 849.

96 Kevin J. Murphy, 'Regulating Banking Bonuses in the European Union: A Case Study in Unintended Consequences' (2013) 19 *European Financial Management* 631.

97 Kokkinis, 'Exploring the Effects of the Bonus Cap Rule' (n 90).

98 See Marc T. Moore, 'Corporate Governance, Pay Equity, and the Limitations of Agency Theory' (2015) 68 *Current Legal Problems* 431, 438–441 and Alan Dignam, 'Remuneration and Riots: Rethinking Corporate Governance in the Age of Entitlement' (2013) 66 *Current Legal Problems* 401.

99 This part is based on Kokkinis, *Corporate Law and Financial Instability* (n 5) 124–131.

100 See PCBS, *Changing Banking for Good* (n 35) Chapter 6.

101 Part 4 of the Financial Services (Banking Reform Act) 2013 amended Parts II and III of FSMA 2000. The relevant provisions were brought into force on 7 March 2016 by the Financial Services (Banking Reform) Act 2013 (Commencement No. 9) Order 2015 (SI 2015/490).

102 A detailed discussion of the evolution of the fit and proper test until early 2012 can be found in Andreas Kokkinis, 'The Reformed "Fit and Proper" Test: A Call for a Broader Rethink of Bank Corporate Governance? (2012) 9 *International Corporate Rescue* 5.

firm such as a bank.[103] FSMA identifies two groups of such individuals: (1) members of the governing bodies of financial firms (directors) and (2) senior managers to whom significant functions have been delegated. In deciding whether to approve a person, the Authority must assess her fitness and propriety.[104]

We will first examine the Approved Persons Regime applicable to FCA-regulated firms, which is similar to the one that used to apply to all financial firms (including systemically important banks) before the introduction of the Senior Managers Regime. According to the FCA Handbook (which is, in this respect, identical to the old FSA Handbook), when assessing whether a person is fit and proper, the Authority has regard to the proposed person's honesty, competence and financial soundness.[105] The Handbook contains detailed criteria for assessing honesty, such as prior convictions, disciplinary proceedings, regulatory breaches, dismissals from fiduciary positions and the insolvency of a company or partnership in which the candidate was concerned.[106] Conversely, scarce guidance is offered on competence; the relevant criteria included the person's training, experience and available time to devote to their post.[107] As regards the financial soundness of proposed persons, it is assumed to exist unless the relevant person has been declared bankrupt or entered similar proceedings.[108]

Prior to the GFC, the FSA concentrated heavily on the honesty and financial soundness of proposed bank directors and accepted any high-level general business experience as sufficient evidence of competence.[109] At board level, the role of bank directors was generally thought to be the same as the role of directors of any large company. Post-crisis, however, competence became a major regulatory concern and relevant financial experience is normally sought.[110] The lack of financial expertise on bank boards was broadly identified as one of the governance failures that contributed to the recent crisis,[111] and led to the Walker Review placing a substantial focus on directors' expertise.[112] Indeed, in 2010 the FSA clarified that it was prepared to scrutinise meticulously the competence of proposed individuals rather than merely rubber-stamping banks' decisions: 'Let me be clear – gone are the days when we receive a phone call to say that a firm wishes to appoint X to be the new chairman or CEO and expecting us to nod them through as approved within two days because that is when the firm wishes to publicly make the announcement'.[113]

103 FSMA 2000, s 59 (1).
104 FSMA 2000, s 61 (1).
105 FCA Handbook, FIT 2.
106 FCA Handbook, FIT 2.1.3.
107 FCA Handbook, FIT 2.2.1.
108 FCA Handbook, FIT 2.3.
109 For instance, Sir Frederick Goodwin, the CEO of RBS from 2001 to 2009, who is considered partly responsible for the unsustainable expansion of RBS and especially the merger with ABN AMRO, which precipitated its collapse, was a chartered accountant prior to moving to banking in 1995.
110 'We made clear that we are now seeking to ensure that firms are adequately assessing the individual's competence, particularly in terms of technical skills'. See FSA, 'Effective Corporate Governance (Significant Influence Controlled Functions and the Walker Review)' (FSA Consultation Paper 10/3, 2010) para 1.9 <http://www.fsa.gov.uk/pubs/cp/cp10_03.pdf> (accessed 19 May 2020).
111 For instance, the lack of a banking background of the CEOs of RBS and HBOS has been identified as a possible cause of their collapse. See Parliamentary Commission on Banking Standards, *Changing Banking for Good* (2013–2014, HL 27-II, HC 175-II), para 128.
112 See Walker Review (above n 30) para 3.6.
113 This is a quote from a speech given by FSA director Mr Ashley-Fenn. See Graeme Ashley-Fenn, 'Corporate Governance – An FSA Perspective' (Building Societies Association Corporate Governance Seminar, London, 2010) <www.fsa.gov.uk/pages/Library/Communication/Speeches/2010/0303_gaf.shtml> (accessed 19 May 2020).

The procedure which was followed by the FSA from 2008 until its abolition in 2013 included four stages, namely, (1) application by the relevant bank; (2) assessment of the candidate by the FSA; (3) interview of the candidate by the FSA and (4) ongoing review of the candidate's suitability. Interviews took place at the discretion of regulators depending on the size of the firm, the importance of the position that the candidate was proposed to assume and the candidate's record and qualifications. It follows that proposed bank directors were normally called for an interview.[114] Thus, the relatively light-touch approach followed up until the GFC was abandoned in favour of a more inquisitive and pro-active approach emphasising the competence of proposed bank directors and senior managers.

It is now pertinent to focus on the Senior Managers Regime which applies to PRA-regulated banks and other financial institutions. A senior management function is defined as a function that satisfies two criteria. First, that the relevant person will be managing one or more aspects of the affairs of a relevant authorised person (e.g. bank). This includes NEDs and directors of a parent company.[115] Second, that the activities of the relevant person involve a risk of serious consequences for the authorised financial institution or for business interests in the UK.[116] The Act ensures that, for all PRA-regulated firms, only persons exercising a senior management function will be designated as exercising controlled functions so that the two legal categories have been merged.[117] The regime thus covers the senior managers of all firms within the scope of CRD IV, including all UK-incorporated banks, building societies and credit unions, and some investment firms, which will be referred to as financial institutions, the term on this occasion excluding insurance firms for which there is a special Senior Managers Regime.[118]

A bank falling within the scope of CRD IV must not make an approval application unless it is satisfied that the relevant person is fit and proper to perform the senior management function,[119] and in doing so it has to consider the person's good repute, integrity, knowledge, experience, qualifications and training.[120] Crucially, financial institutions have to accompany each approval application with a statement of responsibilities detailing the particular aspects of their management that the candidate is intended to be responsible for.[121] If the functions of a senior manager change significantly, institutions have to submit to the regulator a revised statement of responsibilities.[122] These provisions aim to facilitate the apportionment of individual responsibility to senior bank managers in case of regulatory failures and thus enhance their accountability, as will be explained in the next section of this chapter.

114 The Walker Review (n 30) recommended (in paras 3.24–3.25) that the FSA holds interviews when proposed non-executive directors of banks do not bring relevant recent financial industry experience. In such cases, the interviewing panel should include at least one person with board-level (or just below board level) financial industry experience.

115 See Banking Reform Act 2013, Explanatory Notes, para 174.

116 FSMA 2000, s 59 ZA, inserted by Banking Reform Act 2013, s 19.

117 FSMA 2000, s 59 (6), inserted by Banking Reform Act 2013, s 18(3).

118 The meaning of the term 'relevant authorised person' is defined in Banking Reform Act 2013, s 33, which inserted s 71A into the FSMA 2000, as an institution with permission to accept deposits other than an insurer, or an investment firm with permission to deal in investments as principal provided that it is regulated by the PRA regarding that activity.

119 PRA Rulebook, CRR firms, Fitness and Propriety, 2.1.

120 PRA Rulebook, CRR firms, Fitness and Propriety, 2.6.

121 FSMA 2000, ss 60 (2A)–2C, inserted by Banking Reform Act 2013, s 20.

122 FSMA 2000, s 62A, inserted by Banking Reform Act 2013, s 24.

To that effect, the PRA has prescribed a list of senior management functions for which specific regulatory approval is required, including six executive functions (chief executive officer, chief finance officer, chief risk officer, head of internal audit, head of key business area and group entity senior manager) and five non-executive functions (board chairman, chairmen of the audit, remuneration and risk committees, and senior independent director).[123] The range of senior management functions is thus much more detailed now than it was before the GFC but still the role of NEDs who are not chairing a board committee is not recognised as a senior management function, contrary to what is the case for FCA-authorised firms.[124] However, when a CRD IV-regulated bank appoints NEDs who do not perform a senior management function it still has to provide the PRA with sufficient information to allow it to assess whether the director is fit and proper.[125]

In addition, the Banking Reform Act enables the PRA and FCA to approve a candidate for a senior management function subject to conditions or for a limited period of time and impose or vary such conditions at any time after approval is given. Each regulator must issue a statement of policy with regard to these issues.[126] Another innovation introduced by the Act is the duty imposed on banks and other relevant firms to ensure that all senior managerial candidates who apply for approval are fit and proper to perform the relevant function.[127] In particular, banks are required to have regard to the candidates' qualifications, past or current training, competence and personal characteristics.[128] To strengthen the effect of this provision institutions are also required to review annually the fitness of senior managers and to notify the regulator if they believe that there are any grounds on which the latter could withdraw approval.[129]

With regard to bank managers who do not perform senior management functions, but rather only perform a significant-harm function, the Banking Reform Act put in place a simplified regime whereby banks will be required to assess whether these employees are fit and proper persons to discharge significant-harm functions and issue a certificate.[130] A 'significant-harm function' is one that involves performing such duties that may cause significant-harm to the bank or its customers.[131] Certificates will have to specify the aspects of the affairs of the bank that the employee will be involved with, and will be valid for 12 months.[132]

The Senior Manager Regime and Certification Regime will also apply to all financial firms regulated solely by the FCA in the near future, probably on 9 December 2019.[133] At that point in time, the Approved Persons Regime will come to an end. FCA solo-regulated firms will be divided for the purposes of the Senior Manager Regime into three tiers: (1) the

---

123 PRA Rulebook, CRR firms, Senior Management Functions, 3.2–3.7, 4.2–4.6 and 5.2. These functions do not apply to credit unions, for which there is only the credit union senior management function (6.1–6.3).
124 FCA Handbook, SUP 10A.6.12. Indeed, there is a different range of controlled functions for FCA-authorised firms.
125 PRA Rulebook, CRR firms, Fitness and Propriety, 4.2.
126 FSMA 2000, ss 63ZD and 63ZE, inserted by Banking Reform Act 2013, s 27.
127 FSMA 2000, s 60A, inserted by Banking Reform Act 2013, s 21.
128 FSMA 2000, s 60A (2) (a)–(d).
129 FSMA 2000, s 63 (2A), inserted by Banking Reform Act 2013, s 25.
130 FSMA 2000, ss 63E and 63F, inserted by Banking Reform Act 2013, s 29.
131 FSMA 2000, s 63E(5).
132 FSMA 2000, s 63F(5).
133 For an overview of the forthcoming changes, see <https://www.fca.org.uk/firms/senior-managers-certification-regime/solo-regulated-firms> (accessed 20 June 2020).

core tier; (2) the enhanced tier (more complex firms) and (3) the limited scope tier (firms currently enjoying exceptions under the Approved Persons Regime).[134]

To conclude, the examination of the Senior Manager Regime reveals heavy reliance on meta-regulation techniques. Indeed, the onus is now on banks to assess the fitness and propriety of senior individuals and to communicate relevant information to the authorities. This approach reflects the costs and unintended consequences associated with any alternative interventionist regulatory approach to senior appointments. However, reliance on meta-regulation also raises the perennial issue of whether banks have sufficient incentives to co-operate with regulators and work towards the achievement of regulatory objectives.

12.7 Regulatory accountability mechanisms for bank directors and senior managers

In the financial sector, company law directors' duties are not the only available accountability device. The PRA and the FCA are empowered by FSMA to prescribe codes of conduct for the relevant approved persons[135] and to impose sanctions in case of breach.[136] The scope of these codes of conduct is broader than directors' duties as they cover all approved persons including senior managers. FSMA specifies the general process to impose regulatory sanctions.[137] If sanctions are imposed, the relevant person is allowed to appeal to the Upper Tribunal which can review the substance of the decision of the PRA or FCA.[138] Then a further appeal is allowed to the Court of Appeal on questions of law only.[139]

Indeed, the PRA Rulebook contains seven general principles of conduct for PRA-authorised persons. Banks must contractually require PRA-approved persons and NEDs to act with integrity and due skill, care and diligence (thus effectively replicating the company law duties of loyalty and care), and to co-operate with and disclose information to the regulators.[140] Banks must also contractually require PRA-approved persons to 'take reasonable steps to ensure that the business of the firm for which they are responsible' is effectively controlled and complies with regulatory rules, and that 'any delegation of their responsibilities is to an appropriate person and that they oversee the discharge of the delegated responsibility effectively'.[141] It is worth noting that they duty to oversee the discharge of delegated responsibilities does not apply to NEDs who do not perform a

---

134 FCA, 'Extending the Senior Managers and Certification Regime to FCA firms – Feedback to CP17/25 and CP17/40, and Near-Final Rules' Policy Statement PS18/14 (2018) <https://www.fca.org.uk/publication/policy/ps18-14.pdf> (accessed 10 May 2020).

135 FSMA 2000, ss 64–65.

136 FSMA 2000, ss 66–67. For a detailed analysis of the regulatory enforcement powers and a critique of the FSA's approach to enforcement, see Dalvinder Singh, *Banking Regulation of the UK and US Financial Markets* (Ashgate 2007) 121–135.

137 FSMA 2000, s 67.

138 FSMA 2000, s 67(7). The Financial Services and Markets Tribunal was established by FSMA 2000 s 132. Its powers were later transferred to the Upper Tribunal. See The Transfer of Tribunal Functions Order 2010 (SI 2010/22), s 2 (2). The proceedings before the Tribunal are regulated by FSMA 2000, ss 133–133B. It is worth noting that, given the availability of the special dispute resolution process provided for by FSMA 2000, judicial review of a PRA decision is not available save in the most exceptional circumstances. See *R (on the application of Davies) v Financial Services Authority* [2003] EWCA Civ 1128; and *R (on the application of Christopher Willford) v Financial Services Authority* [2013] All ER (D) 114.

139 Tribunals, Courts and Enforcement Act 2007, s 13.

140 PRA Rulebook, CRR firms, Fitness and Propriety, 3.1.

141 PRA Rulebook, CRR firms, Fitness and Propriety, 3.2.

senior management function contrary to the duty to supervise delegated function under the company law duty of care.

That being said, it must be kept in mind that the regulatory framework is not well-equipped to capture risky business decisions but rather dishonest behaviour and decision-making without following a reasonable process. Indeed, at the aftermath of the GFC, the FSA concluded that there was no reasonable prospect of success in seeking to impose regulatory sanctions on the former directors and senior managers of failed bank RBS as:

> Errors of commercial judgement are not in themselves sanctionable unless either the processes and controls which governed how these judgements were reached were clearly deficient, or the judgements were clearly outside the bounds of what might be considered reasonable. The reasonableness of judgements, moreover, has to be assessed within the context of the information available at the time, and not with the benefit of hindsight.[142]

As a result, there have been only a few instances of regulatory enforcement in banks on the grounds of mismanagement and excessive risk-taking in recent years, most notably, the enforcement case against a HBOS senior manager[143] and the enforcement case against the CEO and one senior manager of the Co-Operative Bank[144] which had to be recapitalised in 2012.[145]

However, the changes introduced by the Banking Reform Act 2013 have strengthened regulatory accountability for bank senior managers and have made it easier for the PRA to take enforcement action against individuals. Essentially, findings of misconduct by bank directors and senior managers will be facilitated due to the reversed burden of proof applicable when a regulated firm contravenes a conduct rule. The directors and senior managers who are responsible for the management of the firm's activities 'in relation to which the contravention occurred' will be guilty of misconduct unless they satisfy the PRA (or the FCA) that they took all steps that a person in their position could reasonably be expected to take to prevent the contravention.[146] Therefore, the requirement that each appointment of a person to perform a senior management function (which was discussed in the previous section) combined with the reversed burden of proof once a breach has happened with the scope of a manager's responsibility seeks to facilitate the attribution of liability to individual senior managers for regulatory breaches. This reform is indeed likely to facilitate taking enforcement action against bank senior managers in the context of future breaches of conduct of business rules. An example of such breach is the manipulation of London Interbank Offered Rate (LIBOR) which indeed led to enforcement action against several individuals.[147]

---

142 See FSA, 'The Failure of the Royal Bank of Scotland: Financial Services Authority Board Report' (2011) 9 <http://www.fsa.gov.uk/pubs/other/rbs.pdf> (accessed 19 May 2020). For a detailed discussion of the reasons for not imposing any sanctions, see ibid., 354–356 and 399–406.

143 For a discussion of the enforcement case against Peter Cummings, see Iris H.-Y. Chiu, 'Comparing Directors' Duties in the Financial Services Sector with Regulatory Duties under the Senior Persons Regime – Some Critical Observations' (2016) 27 *European Business Law Review* 261, 275–276.

144 A detailed examination of the two enforcement cases can be found in Kokkinis, *Corporate Law and Financial Instability* (n 5) 133–134.

145 For a vivid discussion of the near-failure of the Co-operative Bank, see Christine Mallin, 'The Co-operative Bank – What Went Wrong?' in Christine Mallin (ed), *Handbook on Corporate Governance in Financial Institutions* (Edward Elgar 2016).

146 FSMA 2000, ss 66A-66B, inserted by Banking Reform Act 2013, s 32.

147 See https://www.fca.org.uk/markets/benchmarks/enforcement (accessed 15 June 2020).

However, it is less likely to lead to successful enforcement action in cases where there is merely excessive risk-taking and poor board performance.

Finally, section 36 of the Banking Reform Act 2013, which came into force on 7 March 2016,[148] introduced a criminal offence relating to decisions causing a financial institution to fail, widely known as reckless banking.[149] The introduction of the criminal offence goes against the recent tendency of decriminalising regulatory offences.[150] The new offence applies to senior managers[151] of financial institutions that accept deposits and investment firms that are regulated by the PRA.[152] To establish that a person committed the offence the following elements must be proved: (1) that the institution has failed[153]; (2) that the failure was caused by the implementation of a particular decision; (3) that the defendant was a senior manager at the time the decision was taken; (4) that the defendant agreed to take the decision or failed to take all possible steps to prevent the decision; (5) that at the time the decision was taken, the defendant is aware of a risk that its implementation may cause the failure of the institution and (6) that the defendant's conduct with regard to the decision falls far below what could reasonably be expected of a person in his position.[154] Upon conviction on indictment, the offence is punishable by imprisonment for up to seven years and/or an unlimited fine.[155]

All the elements of the offence, with the exception of the failure of the relevant institution and holding the position of senior manager, are very difficult to establish, especially at the criminal standard of proof. In particular, establishing causation between a specific decision and the failure of an institution is a very difficult task. Recent experience demonstrates that it is usually a combination of a series of strategic decisions that contributes to the failure of a bank.[156] It follows that the 'but for' test of causation[157] will be particularly difficult to satisfy as it is often unclear whether a bank would have failed anyway if a particular decision had not been taken. Furthermore, proving that the defendant was aware of the risk posed by his decision to the viability of the financial institution will be a formidable task. In this context, given the complexity of financial institutions and the sophisticated risk management models in use, it will be very unlikely that a senior manager can be proved to have taken a decision being aware of such a risk, especially as the term 'risk' is construed by the courts as excluding very low probability events.[158] Similarly, establishing that the

---

148 See Financial Services (Banking Reform) Act 2013 (Commencement No. 9) Order 2015 (SI 2015/490).
149 This and the next paragraph are based on Kokkinis, *Corporate Law and Financial Instability* (n 5) 135–137.
150 An economic analysis of the use of criminal sanctions can be found in Steven Shavell, 'Criminal Law and the Optimal Use of Non-monetary Sanctions as Deterrents' (1985) 1985 *Columbia Law Review* 1232.
151 On the interpretation of the term senior manager, see Banking Reform Act 2013, s 37(7)–(8).
152 Banking Reform Act 2013, s 37 (2)–(6).
153 According to s 37 (9)–(10), an institution is regarded as having failed if it enters into an insolvency procedure or if the stabilisation powers of the Bank of England or the Financial Services Compensation Scheme are invoked.
154 Banking Reform Act, s 36 (1) (c).
155 Banking Reform Act, s 36 (4).
156 See e.g. FSA (n 142), 21–27, where a range of factors are identified as having contributed to the failure of RBS.
157 See *R v White* [1910] 2 KB 124.
158 According to Lord Diplock in *R v Lawrence* [1982] AC 510, 526, 'Recklessness on the part of the doer of an act presupposes that there is something in the circumstances that would have drawn the attention of an ordinary prudent individual to the possibility that his act was capable of causing the kind of serious harmful consequences that the section that created the offence was intended to prevent, and that *the risk of those harmful consequences occurring was not so slight* that an ordinary prudent individual would feel justified in treating them as negligible' (emphasis added).

defendant did not do all that he could have done to prevent the decision being taken will be complicated in the case of large banks where a number of management organs and committees share different responsibilities.[159] Most crucially, the offence imposes liability only if the defendant's conduct was grossly negligent.

12.8 Conclusion

This chapter canvassed the establishment of a detailed set of regulatory rules on bank corporate governance since the GFC, and sought to explain the policy behind legislative and regulatory intervention in bank corporate governance and to review academic contributions on these rules. It was observed that many of the new regulatory rules follow the meta-regulation technique of making the regulatory entity responsible for actively ensuring compliance with regulatory principles. Conversely, the use of prescriptive or inflexible rules has been mostly limited to the EU law-derived bonus cap and the criminal offence of reckless banking. The success of both of these provisions raises considerable doubts. From a policy perspective, while there is consensus that banks pose externalities which justify regulatory intervention in the way they are governed, there is still no consensus among policy-makers and academics on whether the regulatory framework and the company law framework ought to be harmonised or to remain distinct.

Glossary of terms

- UK Corporate Governance Code: Soft law code prescribing principles and standards of good corporate governance; UK-listed companies with a prime listing must disclose in their annual reports how they complied with the principles of the Code and whether they complied in full with all its provisions, and, if not, to specify which provisions they did not comply with, for how long and to provide an explanation for non-compliance.
- Separation of ownership and control: Economic phenomenon whereby the ownership of shares in a company (usually a listed public company) become effectively divorced from managerial control due to the high degree of dispersal of share ownership; as a result no shareholder or small group of shareholders has a majority of votes and the board becomes a self-perpetuating organ whose formal re-election is normally rubber-stamped by passive dispersed shareholders.
- Audit committee: Board committee, consisting exclusively of independent directors, responsible for leading the relationship between a company and its external auditor and for overseeing the company's internal audit and financial reporting processes.
- Remuneration committee: Board committee, consisting mostly of independent directors, responsible for deciding the structure of remuneration for executive directors and senior managers and for determining actual levels of pay-out depending on the achievement of predetermined targets and metrics.
- Nominations committee: Board committee, consisting mostly of independent directors, responsible for leading the process of recruiting new directors and for succession planning.

---

159 On this, see Lowry John and Edmunds Rod, 'Directors Duties and Liabilities: Disqualifying "Unfit" Directors at Banks? Political Rhetoric and the Directors' Disqualification Regime' in Iris H.-Y. Chiu (ed), *The Law on Corporate Governance in Banks* (Edward Elgar 2015) 96.

- Risk committee: Board committee, consisting mostly of NEDs, responsible for identifying the principal risks faced by bank, determining its risk appetite and tolerance, monitoring the overall risk taken and overseeing the operations of the risk management function of the bank; only banks are required to have a risk committee, although some other large corporations choose to do so.
- Chief Risk Officer (CRO): Senior executive in a bank who is responsible for leading the organisation's internal risk management function and who reports directly to the board of directors and has a degree of independence from the CEO.
- Fixed remuneration: Remuneration that is paid irrespective of the performance of the company; it may include salary, fixed pay allowance, benefits in kind and pension contributions.
- Variable remuneration: Remuneration that may be earned upon the achievement of certain goals relating to the financial (and for banks also non-financial) performance of the company, typically in comparison to the performance of similar companies; it may include performance shares (awarded under long-term incentive plans), share options and cash bonuses.
- Bonus cap: EU law rule that prohibits a bank from paying certain senior executives variable remuneration that exceeds 100% of their fixed remuneration; the upper limit can be extended to 200% with approval by a 66% majority of shares voted, provided that a quorum of 75% was met at the relevant shareholder meeting.
- Senior Managers Regime (also known as the Senior Managers and Certification Regime): Regulatory framework applicable to UK banks that seeks to ensure that senior managers are fit and proper, and requires banks to identify the individual responsibilities of each senior manager and ensure that persons are not appointed unless they have adequate knowledge, skills and experience.

Practice questions

Despite widespread reforms in the areas of executive remuneration, senior management appointments and senior management accountability, the directors and senior managers of large banks and other financial institutions are still under significant pressure to take risks that are excessive from society's point of view. Critically discuss.

You may also find it useful to review the chapter through the following questions:

- Explain the economic concepts of a principal-relationship and agency costs.
- What is the legal nature of the UK Corporate Governance Code and how effective is it?
- Why has bank corporate governance attracted special attention since the global financial crisis?
- How has executive remuneration in banks been regulated since 2010?
- Is the bonus cap rule likely to achieve its intended outcomes?
- What are the purposes of the Senior Managers Regime and Certification Regime and are they likely to be achieved?
- In the case of a bank failure or significant regulatory breach, what are the main legal and regulatory liabilities that directors and senior managers may face?

13 FinTech and automation in banks

13.1 Introduction

This chapter discusses the impact of digital technology in the provision of financial services in the UK and internationally. This innovation, often referred to as FinTech (financial technologies), comprises *inter alia* cryptoassets, online platforms, artificial intelligence (AI) and RegTech (i.e. applications of digital technology for regulatory purpose). The aim of the chapter is to examine the importance of the 'world of alternatives' – alternatives to money like virtual currencies, alternatives to credit like peer-to-peer (P2P) and crowdfunding platforms and alternatives to payments, such as shadow payments – from the perspective of financial innovation. In this context, the chapter analyses the evolution of FinTech in the banking sector with emphasis on blockchain and automating mechanisms. It also examines the implications of regulatory technology (RegTech) and its main effects in banking compliance. The structure of virtual currencies and digital platforms is examined in the light of the recent regulatory developments. The 'digital revolution' is discussed along its implications on monetary policy, prudential regulation and investor protection.

13.2 FinTech in banks: rules, principles and automation

FinTech aims to support regulation in the financial markets with the use of algorithm and computer systems (i.e. applications of digital technology by regulators).[1] FinTech also aims to reduce regulatory and compliance costs by enhancing operational efficiency and product development. This is evident in specific areas of financial services such as prudential regulation, customer protection, disclosure mechanisms, market integrity and competition regulation.[2]

A case in point of the application of FinTech is represented by the banking sector. The extent to which compliance with regulation can be automated and carried out by machines raises the question whether manual intervention is still required.[3] FinTech encompasses risk management and minimises reputational risk, legal risk and operational risk in financial

---

1 Douglas W. Arner, Janos Nathan Barberis and Ross P. Buckley, 'The Evolution of Fintech: A New Post-crisis Paradigm' (2015) 47 *Georgetown Journal of International Law* 1271.
2 Tom Butler and Leona O'Brien, 'Understanding RegTech for Digital Regulatory Compliance' in Theo Lynn, John G. Mooney, Pierangelo Rosati and Mark Cummins (eds), *Disrupting Finance FinTech and Strategy in the 21st Century* (Palgrave 2019) 85–86.
3 Bart van Liebergen, 'Machine Learning: A Revolution in Risk Management and Compliance?' (2017) 45 *Journal of Financial Transformation* 60–61.

markets: it provides innovative solutions to improve the regulatory framework and the compliant behaviour of financial firms (e.g. Natural Language Processing (NLP) and cognitive computing).[4] However, the adoption of cloud-based systems and data mining techniques in FinTech raises concerns on the necessary intervention of supervisors to avoid fraudulent activities and ensure data protection and privacy.

For example, the Financial Conduct Authority (FCA) has launched automated practices – i.e. 'sandbox' – to develop technologies in performing compliance programmes, particularly in areas such as anti-money laundering (AML) and 'know your customers' (KYC).[5] This section examines the impact of FinTech – automating regulation and supervision – in the financial market and considers whether the current rules are amenable to algorithmic treatment and what will be the impact on the quality of regulation and the exercise of judgement by the authority. In this context, the main aspects are international compliance using technology to address the challenge of making single contracts comply with multiple regulatory jurisdictions, and suitability of the current statement of rules and regulations for automation. Automating regulatory compliance does not apply mechanically, therefore it is relevant to investigate to what extent the Prudential Regulation Authority (PRA) can modify the regulation. The use of algorithmic regulation to guarantee fairness and appropriateness of insurance, ensuring there is contractual certainty to avoid poor outcomes for customers is a key aspect as well as the use of technology to ensure quality, suitability and competition in insurance products, e.g. at point of sale for consumer durables. A most interesting question is how FinTech affects firms' compliance functions – whether technologies improve or blindly rely on the algorithm, given that if the algorithm is not perfectly designed it may lead to problems – and whether the use of FinTech automatically excludes certain classes of consumers.

The prudential sourcebook for the UK financial industry offers evidence to discuss the extent to which these aspects can be addressed through principles and to examine which elements of regulation can potentially be most easily automated.[6] Specifically, it is relevant to consider whether the statements of these elements of regulation are 'algorithm ready', i.e. they are presented in a way that would allow automated software-based compliance and reporting compliance.[7] This means to investigate under what circumstances should we entrust 'x', 'y', 'z' tasks to algorithmic decision-making and under what circumstances should we entrust 'a', 'b', 'c' issues to human decision-making. A further issue concerns the generation of new risks that derive from the use of FinTech. It is worth considering the role of supervisory judgement and how it will be affected by the introduction of FinTech applied to banking sector, and whether automation will reduce or support the role of judgement and the application of principles in banking regulation.[8]

---

4 Mats Lewan, 'The Role of Trust in Emerging Technologies' in Robin Teigland, Shahryar Siri, Anthony Larsson, Alejandro Moreno Puertas and Claire Ingram Bogusz (eds), *The Rise and Development of FinTech* (Routledge 2018) 111–112.

5 Financial Conduct Authority, 'Regulatory Sandbox' available at <https://www.fca.org.uk/firms/regulatory-sandbox> (accessed 27 June 2020).

6 FCA, 'Prudential Sourcebook for Banks, Building Societies and Investment Firms' (June 2019) available at <https://www.handbook.fca.org.uk/handbook/BIPRU.pdf> (accessed 16 June 2020).

7 Bernardo Nicoletti, *The Future of FinTech: Integrating Finance and Technology in Financial Services* (Palgrave 2017) 261–262.

8 Veerle Colaert, 'RegTech as a Response to Regulatory Expansion in the Financial Sector' *Oxford Business Law Blog* (16 July 2018) available at <https://www.law.ox.ac.uk/business-law-blog/blog/2018/07/regtech-response-regulatory-expansion-financial-sector> (accessed 26 June 2020).

FinTech aims to provide clarity and create a shared understanding around rules and data through virtual platforms: rules are transformed into code, and automating the process allows regulators to request data and firms to quickly and simply share it without the need to interpret the data.[9] While machines can process data far more quickly than humans, they typically rely on more limited types of information. The challenge is how financial firms ensure that the machine has enough information about the world within which it is operating and how machines make critical decisions.[10] In this context, it is important to explore whether regulation is machine readable into programmes to determine whether data processing and computer code can ensure adequate consumer protection. Arner et al. argue that the focus of FinTech should be on transforming financial regulation as well as achieving efficiency gains.[11] Lastra and Allen observe that FinTech tools are an essential component in the regulatory response to virtual currencies and associated developments, such as 'smart contracts'.[12] Although machines may be more reliable than humans, new risk can be generated into systems.[13] Financial institutions face substantial difficulties in complying with regulation in different jurisdictions; therefore, the question arises whether the current statements of regulatory provisions are suitable for automation.

13.2.1 Risks and challenges of FinTech

The range of digital technologies used in financial services is very broad, including, for example, household and small business lending, online and mobile payments, insurance, capital market transactions, wealth management and regulatory reporting and compliance. Likewise, a wide range of digital initiatives seek to promote 'financial inclusion', i.e. widening access to banking and insurance services both for vulnerable households and small businesses, in both the global North and South.[14] Access to technology enacts financial inclusion that 'denotes banks' provision of basic financial services at affordable costs to those that need and qualify for them'.[15]

With the advent of FinTech, it has been said that lenders will have more information to assess the credit quality of borrowers and to make decisions on whether (and how much) to lend more quickly.[16] This raises the following points: (1) impact of FinTech on financial

---

9 Vasant Dhar and Roger M Stein, 'FinTech Platforms and Strategy' (2017) 60(10) *Communications of the ACM* 32–33, available at <https://cacm.acm.org/magazines/2017/10/221331-fintech-platforms-and-strategy/abstract> (accessed 29 June 2020).

10 Marshall W. Van Alstyne, Geoffrey G. Parker and Sangeet Paul Choudary, 'Pipelines, Platforms, and the New Rules of Strategy' (April 2016) 94 *Harvard Business Review* 54–55.

11 Douglas W. Arner, Jànos Barberis and Ross P. Buckey, 'FinTech, RegTech, and the Reconceptualization of Financial Regulation' (2016) 37 *Northwestern Journal of International Law & Business* 371.

12 Rosa Maria Lastra and Jason Grant Allen, 'Virtual Currencies in the Eurosystem: Challenges Ahead' European Parliament, Monetary Dialogue (July 2018) available at <http://www.europarl.europa.eu/cmsdata/150541/DIW_FINAL%20publication.pdf> (accessed 26 June 2020).

13 Ross P. Buckley, Douglas W. Arner, Dirk A. Zetzsche and Rolf H. Weber, 'The Road to RegTech: The (Astonishing) Example of the European Union' (2019) 20 *Journal of Banking Regulation* 2–3.

14 Daniela Gabor and Sally Brooks, 'The Digital Revolution in Financial Inclusion: International Development in the Fintech Era' (2017) 22 *New Political Economy* 423–424.

15 Emily Lee, 'Financial Inclusion: A Challenge to the New Paradigm of Financial Technology, Regulatory Technology and Anti-money Laundering Law' (2017) 6 *Journal of Business Law* 473–474.

16 Lord Hodge, 'The Potential and Perils of Financial Technology: Can the Law Adapt to Cope?' The First Edinburgh FinTech Law Lecture, University of Edinburgh (14 March 2019) available at <https://www.supremecourt.uk/docs/speech-190314.pdf> (accessed 28 June 2020).

industry structure, organisation and business models; (2) household and business attitudes to financial services and adoption of FinTech; (3) promoting financial inclusion using financial technology in low and middle-income countries, for example, the use of mobile phone payments and the promotion of financial inclusion in East Africa[17]; (4) the consequences of new forms of data and algorithmic processing in financial services; and (5) regulatory applications of FinTech, for example, how it might be used to support regulatory objectives and whether it can be used to manage financial instability.

Stakeholders and policy-makers are paying close attention to developments in FinTech, both because of the perception that they should support domestic capacity in what is a nascent and rapidly growing new industry with potential global impact, and because digital technology can address some of the perceived shortcomings of the traditional financial services industry (e.g. lack of consumer protection, weaknesses in governance, gaps in compliance and improved provision to previously underserved regions or customer groups). The UK Government has issued an updated Fintech Sector strategy which includes the formation of a Cryptoassets Task Force[18] – consisting of HM Treasury, the Bank of England and the FCA – with the aim of helping the UK to be at the forefront of harnessing the potential benefits of the underlying technology, while guarding against potential risks.[19]

In parallel, the European Commission has launched a wide-ranging 'Fintech Action Plan' and is expected to put substantial resources into supporting the development of FinTech across the EU.[20] Supervisory authorities are also taking steps to support innovation with a leading role played by 'Project Innovate' and regulatory sandbox programmes at the FCA in the UK and elsewhere in Europe, which allow automated machines to reduce the manual intervention of regulators.[21] The question is to what extent these and wider associated developments will have implications for the structure of the financial services industry, the way it relates to its customers and performs its core functions and the way it is regulated.

The UK is a leading centre for new financial technology companies, challenging incumbents and offering substantial business process improvements in banking, insurance, asset management and investment advice as well as wholesale capital markets. UK public policy towards these recent developments has focused on practical support for technology-based start-ups and the 'eco-system' that supports them, e.g. the FCA's 'Project Innovate' providing supportive advice on the complexities of financial regulation and for some firms a limited relaxation of rules in their 'regulatory sandbox'.

As mentioned, issues arising from digital technology and financial inclusion are wide ranging and require regulatory attention, especially in the context of AML, combating the financing of terrorism (CFT) and KYC requirements. These issues underline several economic, regulatory, legal and social concerns beyond finance (cybercrime, data protection, privacy, adequate dispute settlement mechanisms and crisis management procedures, surveillance of migrants, particularly to understand the physical barriers in communities

---

17 It is referred to mobile payments technologies in emerging markets, mostly relating to the successful MPesa network in East Africa.

18 HM Treasury, 'Cryptoassets Taskforce: Final Report' (October 2018) 11–13, available at <https://www.gov.uk/government/publications/cryptoassets-taskforce> (accessed 30 May 2019).

19 HM Treasury, 'Fintech Sector Strategy: Securing the Future of UK Fintech' (March 2018) 9–10, available at <https://www.gov.uk/government/publications/fintech-sector-strategy> (accessed 30 June 2020).

20 European Commission, 'FinTech Action Plan' (March 2018) available at <https://ec.europa.eu/info/publications/180308-action-plan-fintech_en> (accessed 19 June 2019).

21 FCA, 'Project Innovate' available at <https://www.fca.org.uk/firms/fca-innovate> (accessed 16 June 2020).

of immigrants).[22] It can be argued that FinTech highlights challenges in the regulatory framework in terms of the interpretation of 'smart contracts', attribution of responsibility for the acts and omissions of robots and enforcement of contractual obligations. Financial technology raises major data issues that relate closely to the accompanying think piece on data infrastructure.[23] Identity, security, data privacy and their regulation are all central concerns for financial services firms. Enhancing the appropriate public policy on financial data and the availability of 'open data' for use by other financial firms, investors and other 'stakeholders' are the questions at stake.

Data accessibility and interoperability is a 'public good', in the economic sense of the term, that requires co-ordination at industry level and may sometimes also need policy intervention to ensure that the data needs of industry and policy-makers are met appropriately.[24] Similar 'public good' considerations apply to cyber security, nowadays a major concern for all financial services firms, in particular because of the possibility of substantial fines for breaches of data protection regulations or failure to protect customer data.[25] Combatting fraud, establishing counterparty identity and effective enforcement of KYC and AML regulation are also essential public interest goals that may be much more efficiently achieved through industry collaboration and government policy co-ordination, rather than through mere private initiative. This relates to challenges of effective regulation and governance.

Issues of data security and privacy are also central to the broad challenge of consumer attitudes to the new FinTech, for example, to open banking.[26] Payment technologies and payment regulation are rapidly evolving; these changes are occurring just as much in the regulated financial services space, through, for example, the EU PSD2 directive[27] and the Open Banking remedies being applied by the UK Competition and Market Authority, the Australian New Payments Platform and the dramatic shift to mobile payments in China, as discussed in Chapter 8.[28] Payment technologies are closely linked to the broader impact of technology on industry and public services and to wider issues of identity and data infrastructure.

22 Daron Acemoglu, Asuman Ozdaglar and Alireza Tahbaz-Salehi, 'Systemic Risk and Stability in Financial Networks' (2015) 105 *American Economic Review* 564–565.
23 Inna Romānova and Marina Kudinska, 'Banking and Fintech: A Challenge or Opportunity?' in Simon Grima, Frank Bezzina, Inna Romānova and Ramona Rupeika-Apoga (eds), *Contemporary Issues in Finance: Current Challenges from Across Europe*, Contemporary Studies in Economic and Financial Analysis, Volume 98 (Emerald 2016) 21–22.
24 Solon Barocas and Helen Nissenbaum, 'Big Data's End Run around Anonymity and Consent' in Julia Lane, Victoria Stodden, Stefan Bender, Helen Nissenbaum (eds), *Privacy, Big Data, and the Public Good: Frameworks for Engagement* (CUP 2014) 45–46.
25 Arben Asllani, Charles Stephen White and Lawrence Ettkin, 'Viewing Cybersecurity as a Public Good: The Role of Governments, Businesses and Individuals' (2013) 16 *Journal of Legal, Ethical and Regulatory Issues* 9–10. See also Benjamin Powell, 'Is Cyberspace a Public Good - Evidence from the Financial Services Industry' (2005) 1 *Journal of Law, Economics & Policy* 498–499.
26 Laura Brodsky and Liz Oakes, 'Data Sharing and Open Banking' McKinsey on Payments (July 2017) 2–3, available at <https://www.mckinsey.it/sites/default/files/data-sharing-and-open-banking.pdf> (accessed 26 June 2020).
27 Directive (EU) 2015/2366 of the European Parliament and of the Council of 25 November 2015 on payment services in the internal market, amending Directives 2002/65/EC, 2009/110/EC and 2013/36/EU and Regulation (EU) No. 1093/2010, and repealing Directive 2007/64/EC.
28 F.X. Browne and David Cronin, 'Payments Technologies, Financial Innovation, and Laissez-Faire Banking' (1995) 15 *Cato Journal* 103–104.

13.3 RegTech in the banking sector

RegTech can be considered as the new paradigm of supervision and enforcement in the financial sector. The emergence of RegTech – the use of FinTech to automate regulation and reduce the costs of regulatory compliance – represents a major opportunity for addressing the limitations of financial regulation.[29] RegTech aims to enhance the effective and consistent implementation of broad principles across financial institutions; for example, it may facilitate the monitoring of compliance with bank capital rules with the use of automated machines.[30] Supervisory authorities are exploring RegTech platforms to expedite regulatory and management controls, and mechanisms for the enforcement of private contracts. RegTech can mitigate the problem of unintended consequences of regulation. For example, the substantial increases in fines for breaching AML regulations leading to widespread 'de-risking', i.e. withdrawal of banks from international correspondent banking, in turn raising the costs of international payments, damaging already vulnerable economies and shifting international payments outside of regulated institutions and arguably making money laundering easier rather than more difficult.[31] However, the application of technological solutions to reduce compliance costs and avoid gaps in supervising financial activities may undermine the possibility of manual intervention by the regulators.[32]

The extent to which compliance with regulation can be automated and carried out by machine raises the question whether manual intervention will still be required. As previously mentioned, the FCA has launched automated practices – e.g. 'sandbox' – to develop technologies in performing compliance programmes. The adoption of RegTech in automating regulation and supervision, particularly in sectors such as AML and 'know your customer', implies a shift from principles-based to rules-based regulation.[33] In this context, RegTech can promote more substantive compliance processes, ensure information disclosure and contractual certainty and predictability as an incentive to prevent risk-taking and can reduce discretion, particularly in terms of guaranteeing an adequate level of enforcement of principles.[34]

Further, RegTech eliminates the possible risks of compliance failures that consist, on the one hand, of creative compliance (i.e. where although the letter of the norm is adhered to, it is sometimes interpreted over-generously by the regulated entity) and, on the other, of over-compliance (i.e. over-regulation or additional burdensome levels of compliance

---

29 Kristen Silverberg, Andres Portilla, Conan French, Bart van Liebergen and Stephanie Van Den Berg, 'Regtech in Financial Services' (2016) available at <https://www.iif.com/system/files/regtech_in_financial_services_solutions_for_compliance_and_reporting.pdf> (accessed 12 June 2020).

30 Philip Treleaven, 'Financial Regulation in FinTech' (2015) 3 *University College London Journal of Financial Perspectives* 114–115.

31 Barbara Casu and Ruth Wandhöfer, 'The Future of Transaction Banking -Moving into the Digital Age' (2017) available at <https://www.swiftinstitute.org/wp-content/uploads/2017/11/SWI12-Future-of-Transaction-Banking-Vfinal2.pdf> (accessed 28 June 2020).

32 Ganesh Sitaraman, 'Regulating Tech Platforms: A Blueprint for Reform' (April 2018) 'The Great Democracy Initiative 2018'. Vanderbilt University Law School Legal Studies Research Paper Series 18–64, available at <https://greatdemocracyinitiative.org/wp-content/uploads/2018/03/Regulating-Tech-Platforms-final.pdf> (accessed 14 June 2020).

33 Nizan Geslevich Packin, 'RegTech, Compliance and Technology Judgment Rule' (2018) 93 *Chicago-Kent Law Review* 207–208.

34 Petros Kavassalis, Harald Stieber, Wolfgang Breymann, Keith Saxton and Francis Joseph Gross, 'An Innovative RegTech Approach to Financial Risk Monitoring and Supervisory Reporting' (2017) 19 *The Journal of Risk Finance* 39–40.

taken by risk-averse regulated entities). At its best, RegTech can be well-functioning on the basis of trust and fair behaviours, which entails confidence, transparency and cogent acts, and it can strengthen substantive compliance that represents the key objective for fostering responsive regulation. In promoting a new compliance culture, RegTech encompasses risk management but it also reduces reputational risk, legal risk and operational risk in the banking industry and banking products.[35] Firms and financial institutions have recognised the importance of RegTech, particularly as regards internal controls, where the relationship between members of the board, managers and investors finds its best expression in a species of self-imposed rules designed to reduce the reputational risks posed by non-compliant behaviours. It has been argued that 'RegTech could make compliance easier: rather than writing rules in legal English the regulator could write rules in machine-readable English or prescribe particular software applications'.[36] Opportunistic behaviours by market participants could be avoided by means of the regulatory technologies, e.g. blockchains and smart contracts, as a measure falling within the category of internal self-controls, which could limit the need to regulate by hard law and reduce mandatory disclosure costs.[37]

RegTech can also be used to prepare regulatory reports (e.g. market conduct annual statements). The FCA launched an initiative for 'Model Driven Machine Executable Reporting' to prove that if parts of their handbook were coded (so they became machine readable) this could streamline regulatory reporting and not only save ambiguity (but not judgement) time and costs associated with this compliance activity but also allow more uniform and accurate reporting and allow both regulatory and industry participants to identify and manage associated risks.[38] In substance, while the disclosure regime reduces the costs of capital and information, RegTech enables closer to perfect alignment of manager and investor interests. On this view, the parameters of the RegTech become not only a legal norm, but, predominantly, a social norm; on the one hand, it is a legal norm for verifying that the corporate management has complied with the rules, on the other, it is social norm designed to transform risk prevention into benefits for investors and consumers.[39] RegTech not only assumes a normative value but also constitutes a useful measure for enforcing principles. The role of RegTech, as an *ex ante* legal measure to prevent the risks of statutory enforcement loopholes, becomes an important link between the rules-based and principles-based regulatory approaches by conveying these types of regulation into the risk-based regulatory regime.[40]

35 Yonghee Kim, Young-Ju Park and Jeongil Choi, 'The Adoption of Mobile Payment Services for Fintech' (2016) 11 *International Journal of Applied Engineering Research* 1058–1061.

36 Eva Micheler and Anna Whaley, 'Regulatory Technology – Replacing Law with Computer Code' LSE Working Papers 14/2018, 8, available at <http://eprints.lse.ac.uk/89550/1/Micheler%20SSRN-id3210962.pdf> (accessed 29 June 2020).

37 Iris H. Y. Chiu, 'A New Era in Fintech Payment Innovations? A Perspective from the Institutions and Regulation of Payment Systems' (2017) 9(2) *Law, Innovation and Technology* 190–191.

38 FCA, 'Model Driven Machine Executable Regulatory Reporting TechSprint' (20 November 2017) available at <https://www.fca.org.uk/events/techsprints/model-driven-machine-executable-regulatory-reporting-techsprint> (accessed 27 May 2020).

39 Mark Carney, 'New Economy, New Finance, New Bank' (Speech Given at the Mansion House, London, 21 June 2018) available at <www.bankofengland.co.uk/speeches> (accessed 25 June 2020).

40 Matthias Kröner, 'API Deep Dive: Who Will Thrive in an Open Banking World? Why Meeting Regulatory Requirements Is Not Enough for Banks to Remain Relevant' (2018) 2 *Journal of Digital Banking* 198–199.

13.3.1 The role of automation and AI in banks

FinTech holds the promise of addressing fundamental problems of resource misallocation and social and economic inequity in financial services.[41] Supporting the continuing 'information technology revolution' in financial services, especially in addressing barriers such as the constraints of legacy systems and need for co-operation, e.g. on standardisation and on effective digital identity solutions, is the new frontier of regulators.[42] However, there is little consensus among practitioners and policy-makers on how technological change can shape the industry in the longer term, both in terms of industrial structure and regulation.[43]

For example, processes for KYC compliance are costly and time-consuming with extraordinary fines for non-compliance. By implementing RegTech solutions such as a distributed shared ledger, a business can rapidly verify the identity of its clients and assess potential risks of illegal intentions for the business relationship.[44] RegTech can increase the speed of client on-boarding, reduce risk as a distributed shared ledger acts as an immutable assured audit trail of all KYC processes, enhance the customer experience (as little customer input is needed for on-boarding) and bring efficiency gains as RegTech enables businesses to scale higher customer volume more efficiently.[45] In this context, AI Natural Language Generation (NLG) can be used to automate the generation of regulatory AML reports, e.g. suspicious activity reports (SARs).[46] Large institutions generate thousands of SARs every year, so AML compliance costs can be substantial, as discussed in Chapter 10. NLG enables compliance teams to automatically identify the most interesting and important information trapped in structured data and produce language that provides situational context, explanations and potential next actions. With advanced NLG systems, like 'Narrative Science Quill', the SAR Narrative can be automatically generated, while communicating the key 'who, what, when, and where' aspects of the suspicious activity and can also be tailored to meet the needs of the intended audience.

In terms of fraud insights, AI can be used to reduce occurrences of fraud (internal and external) using NLP to uncover hidden patterns and anomalies in large quantities of text

---

41 Phil Mader, 'Microfinance and Financial Inclusion' in David Brady and Linda M. Burton (eds), *The Oxford Handbook of the Social Science of Poverty* (OUP 2016) 844–845.

42 Juan M. Sánchez, 'The Information Technology Revolution and the Unsecured Credit Market' (2018) 56 *Economic Inquiry* 914–915.

43 Ian Pollari, 'The Rise of Fintech: Opportunities and Challenges' (2016) 3 *The Australasian Journal of Applied Finance* 15.

44 Distributed ledgers operate through the maintenance of multiple shared copies of the database which avoids single point attack or failure as with existing large legacy IT systems. Distributed ledger technologies can be used to allow governments to collect taxes, deliver welfare benefits, issue passports and control immigration, maintain land registries as well as manage the supply of goods and services and ensure the integrity of government records and services. For an overview, among others, Kern Alexander, *Principles of Banking Regulation* (CUP 2019) 342.

45 Yvonne Lootsma, 'Blockchain as the Newest Regtech Application—The Opportunity to Reduce the Burden of KYC for Financial Institutions' (2017) 36 *Banking & Financial Services Policy Report* 16–17.

46 A typical SAR has five components; the first four can be auto populated by many case management systems, however the last portion, the SAR Narrative, cannot. In doctrine see Max Gotthardt, Dan Koivulaakso, Okyanus Paksoy, Cornelius Saramo, Minna Martikainen and Othmar M. Lehner (eds), 'Current State and Challenges in the Implementation of Robotic Process Automation and Artificial Intelligence in Accounting and Auditing' (2019) 8 *ACRN Oxford Journal of Finance and Risk Perspectives*, Special Issue Digital Accounting 32–33.

(outlier and drift detection) to flush out suspicious transactions or claims.[47] NLP can be used to extract regulations and identify regulatory and control requirements (i.e. legislation/regulation 'gap' analysis tools). Telephone conversations, face-to-face meetings and written correspondence provide invaluable information for optimising regulatory compliance, risk management, customer care and sales.[48] There are many practical implementations of computer 'neural networks' and other automated methods of data analysis for applications in credit, investment and trading decisions, sometimes with substantial industry impact (e.g. the rise of algorithmic and high-frequency trading in equity markets).[49] Using technology-based computation to improve regulation, for example, in detecting insider trading, is conducted primarily by private firms. Ensuring that the above-mentioned systems and controls are independently assessed and tested for effectiveness at an appropriate frequency and that there is a clear allocation of responsibilities in the first and second line for monitoring compliance are the main challenges regulators may face. As the rules currently stand, every firm is responsible for interpreting regulation and implementing its requirements thus bearing the risk of any technology it chooses to use. Shifting the responsibility for converting regulation into code to a central body would raise questions about the legal basis for the coded regulation as well as liability questions about who is responsible if there are errors in the conversion.

Regulators are only at the first stages of using technology in financial regulation, a major aspect of their work involving efforts to translate parts of the regulatory rule-book into machine-readable form.[50] While this provides a 'proof of concept', it is relevant to identify what parts of the current range of regulations can be translated into a machine-readable form that can then be enforced algorithmically for rethinking regulatory process to make it more suitable for automated compliance.[51] For example, there is widespread industry interest in using a shared third-party database for KYC regulations to share identity information and hence lower costs of on-boarding, but it appears that these can make limited progress as long as responsibility for compliance remains solely that of the firms that use them with no possibility of regulatory and legal indemnity.[52] The burden of regulatory compliance may though still be a major barrier to technology-based entry into financial services. However, RegTech can increase competition in the financial services to the benefit of consumers by lowering barriers to entry in the market for personal current account and payments systems (technological change in bank delivery channels, e.g. through ATM, telephone or online

---

47 For example, IDVision is a RegTech company developing a set of solutions to verify consumer identities to establish identity with greater confidence by verifying against a broad set of personal and digital data and authenticate consumers, securing every point of the customer's journey by validating the claimed identity is who they say they are. In literature, among others, see Mikko Riikkinen, Hannu Saarijärvi, Peter Sarlin and Ilkka Lähteenmäki, 'Using Artificial Intelligence to Create Value in Insurance' (2018) 36 *International Journal of Bank Marketing* 1145–1146.

48 Recordsure is a RegTech company currently pioneering tools that automate the assessment of a conversation and identify potential compliance risks: Insurers could analyse up to 100% of customer calls rather than the fraction of calls typically analysed by humans.

49 Alain P. Chaboud, Benjamin Chiquoine, Erik Hjalmarsson and Clara Vega, 'Rise of the Machines: Algorithmic Trading in the Foreign Exchange Market' (2014) 69 *The Journal of Finance* 2045–2046.

50 Mike Bennett, 'The Financial Industry Business Ontology: Best Practice for Big Data' (2013) 14 *Journal of Banking Regulation* 256–257.

51 Lawrence G. Baxter, 'Adaptive Financial Regulation and RegTech: A Concept Article on Realistic Protection for Victims of Bank Failures' (2016) 66 *Duke Law Journal* 570–571.

52 José Parra Moyano and Omri Ross, 'KYC Optimization Using Distributed Ledger Technology' (2017) 59 *Business & Information Systems Engineering* 411–412.

banking or on the network economics of card payments).[53] It can be argued that the new generation of FinTech is an opportunity for rethinking and substantially improving the entire framework of financial regulation. However, the disadvantages and risks of using RegTech can be summarised as follows: initial cost, risk of errors in the system, risk of over-reliance and increased systemic risk if all firms follow similar AI solutions that lead to highly homogeneous market behaviours (herding) and thus to several firms experiencing financial distress simultaneously.

13.4 The virtual banking markets: Bitcoin

The experience of the global financial crisis, where rapid innovation masked fundamental vulnerabilities, has naturally raised some concern that the latest wave of innovation in financial technology could be a precursor to future financial instability. This is not the only perspective, FinTech could be used to promote macroeconomic and financial stability, for example, allowing the practical implementation of full reserve banking to eliminate the negative consequences of credit expansions.[54] For instance, the rise of virtual currencies, such as Bitcoin, demonstrates the spread of alternative forms of money that circulate through digital platforms without the intervention of financial intermediaries.[55]

Virtual currencies are not regulated by any central bank or other form of governmental authority; Bitcoin, for example, is a P2P electronic cash system. In this sense, virtual currencies are a species of financial hybrid that defies straightforward placement in established categories and exacerbates 'border problems' between the regulated and unregulated space and between national jurisdictions.[56] Virtual currencies allow for anonymous ownership and include a public register of every transaction involving a particular blockchain to show the present owner.[57] The fundamental difference between digital currencies and conventional currency is that they avoid the need for intermediaries, including central banks and commercial banks, through the creation of a global collaborative endeavour.

Bitcoin uses a combination of private and public cryptographic keys. Private keys are always kept confidential within an individual's wallet. Bitcoin uses an Elliptic Curve Digital Signature Algorithm.[58] Bitcoin works as a payment network and as money. Blockchain-based payment network solutions provide a cheap and secure cross-border payment and settle-

---

53 Ioannis Anagnostopoulos, 'FinTech and RegTech: Impact on Regulators and Banks' (2018) 100 *Journal of Economics and Business* 7–8.

54 Thomas Philippon, 'The FinTech Opportunity' (August 2016) NBER Working Paper No. 22476, 15–16, available at <http://www.nber.org/papers/w22476> (accessed 22 June 2020).

55 Virtual currencies such as Bitcoin are digital in form: they are not created or issued by a single issuer but rather created directly in a network by a special algorithm.

56 Lastra and Allen (n 12) 6.

57 Fergal Reid and Martin Harrigan, 'An Analysis of Anonymity in the Bitcoin System' in Yaniv Altshuler, Yuval Elovici, Armin B. Cremers, Nadav Aharony and Alex Pentland (eds), *Security and Privacy in Social Networks* (Springer 2012) 197–198.

58 The private key will be a randomly generated number expressed as a single unsigned 256-bit integer (32 bytes). The public key is used to confirm that signatures are genuine and based on the private key although the private key cannot be determined from the public key. Signatures confirm signing with these being mathematically generated from the hash of the transaction to be confirmed and the private key. In doctrine see David Yermack, 'Is Bitcoin a Real Currency? An Economic Appraisal' in David Lee Kuo Chuen (ed), *Handbook of Digital Currency. Bitcoin, Innovation, Financial Instruments, and Big Data* (Elsevier 2015) 31–32.

ment framework.[59] Bitcoin has been lauded on the grounds that it creates a fast, secure and efficient money generation and payment system although the highly technical nature of the software used creates substantial technological dependence.[60] Bitcoin blockchain can be the foundation of future financial market infrastructure; however, there are doubts whether it is robust enough to form the base of payment, settlement, clearing and trading systems. Bitcoin as a software is vulnerable to attack, it has bugs and only few investors understand how it works; this means that operational risks make it unsuitable to serve as the base of the financial system.[61]

Another development has been the phenomenal rise of speculative investment in cryptocurrencies and, in the case of the associated opportunity for raising finance for start-ups through cryptocurrency, 'initial coin offerings' (ICOs) represent a truly transformative innovation. The consequent market valuations are large (despite a near 50% decline in valuations since late 2017, their total 'market cap' was still $454bn as of June 2019 but this remains small compared to the global market cap of traded equities of around $80,000bn).[62] Chohan argues that there is a greater risk of fraud in ICOs than Bitcoin: ICOs require traditional securities regulation but Bitcoin which is trust-less does not.[63]

Cryptocurrencies have risen up the regulatory agenda of global bodies (e.g. the Basel Committee),[64] but there is a clear distinction between cryptocurrencies, cryptoassets – i.e. the new experimental forms of finance that uses pseudo-anonymity (participation determined by internal network identifiers not real-world identity) and cryptographic security to operate entirely outside of the regulated industry – and the application of new technologies in regulated financial services. The first category ('cryptofinance' to distinguish it from the second category of mainstream 'fintech') is important as an inspiration and source of technical innovations, but the separation of cryptofinance and FinTech reflects a continuing real-world divide between radical exploration of possible technological alternatives to our existing financial institutions and the many more practically focused innovations and start-ups that are challenging conventional regulated financial services.[65]

---

59 Paolo Tasca, 'The Dual Nature of Bitcoin as Payment Network and Money' in Christian Beer, Ernest Gnan and Urs W. Birchler (eds), *Cash on Trial* (SUERF Studies, The European Money and Finance Forum 2016) 71–72, available at <https://papers.ssrn.com/sol3/papers.cfm?abstract_id=2805003> (accessed 18 June 2020).

60 The system is nevertheless arguably too complex with over 380,000 blocks already having been generated. The system is slow and only allows for two transactions per second with Visa allowing over 1,700 transactions per second. Substantial delays can occur in using transferred coin with payees having to wait up to one hour, therefore the value of Bitcoins have fluctuated widely. See Gerald P. Dwyer, 'The Economics of Bitcoin and Similar Private Digital Currencies' (2015) 17 *Journal of Financial Stability* 81–82.

61 Angela Walch, 'The Bitcoin Blockchain as Financial Market Infrastructure: A Consideration of Operational Risk' (2015) 18 *NYU Journal of Legislation and Public Policy* 883–884.

62 See <https://coinmarketcap.com/all/views/all/> (accessed 27 June 2019).

63 Usman Chohan, 'Initial Coin Offerings (ICOs): Risks, Regulation, and Accountability' (2017) Discussion Paper Series: Notes on the 21st Century, 3–4, available at <https://papers.ssrn.com/sol3/papers.cfm?abstract_id=3080098> (accessed 20 June 2020).

64 Morten L. Bech and Rodney Garratt, 'Central Bank Cryptocurrencies' (2017) 2017 *BIS Quarterly Review* 58–59.

65 Maria Demertzis and Guntram B. Wolff, 'The Economic Potential and Risks of Crypto Assets: Is a Regulatory Framework Needed?' (September 2018) Bruegel Report Policy Contribution Issue No. 14, 8–10, available at <http://bruegel.org/wp-content/uploads/2018/09/PC-14_2018.pdf> (accessed 24 June 2020).

Garratt and Wallace point out that the value of Bitcoin is that it rests on self-fulfilling beliefs.[66] It is assumed there is a fixed stock of Bitcoin that is valuable today only as it is believed others will treat it as valuable in the future, hence the difficulties in determining money prices in the one-money model and two-money world, including Bitcoin and standard fiat money. In substance, the problem of determining Bitcoin's value is due to the ease of creating perfect substitutes. Most interestingly, Milne investigates the potential improvement on monetary arrangements using time-ordered immutable transaction records (i.e. blockchains, mutual distributed ledgers) to record cryptocurrency transactions.[67] By putting money (government fiat money and bank money) off-balance sheet, a distributed ledger can ensure the integrity of money and payments arrangements in the event of bank failure. If successful, this could potentially mean central bank reserves would not be required for bank payments settlements and consequently no requirement for 'too big to fail' protection of banks.

As argued, Bitcoin operates as a speculative currency with excessive volatility: this raises the question whether Bitcoin and other blockchain-based networks are a decentralised infrastructure which suffers from lack of transparency.[68] The transparency problem is that individuals can obtain the history of all transactions and potentially sensitive information about others. There is, however, an element of in-built privacy, as individuals can transact with each other without disclosing their identity: cryptographic techniques can ensure transaction data remains confidential and users can uncloak their transaction data to a third party in a certified way. Like other forms of modern money that lacks inherent value, Bitcoin is a promise. However, it is a different promise than central bank issued money, a promise backed by an algorithm with expression in a digital P2P network.[69]

13.5 Blockchain and digital platforms

The possibility for technology-based change in the financial industry is demonstrated in the new delivery of financial services and in the business models and operations of intermediaries that provide them. This is illustrated by the case of China which has seen rapid shifts to both mobile payments (AliPay, Weipay) largely displacing notes and coins in urban areas,[70] and to non-bank loan intermediation through the dramatic growth in the Chinese version of P2P lending.[71] A displacement of banks and financial firms by decentralised technologies

66 Rodney Garratt and Neil Wallace, 'Bitcoin 1, Bitcoin 2,…: An Experiment in Privately Issued Outside Monies' (2018) 56(3) *Economic Inquiry* 1888–1889.
67 Alistair Milne, 'Cryptocurrencies from an Austrian Perspective' (2017) 13–14, available at <https://papers.ssrn.com/sol3/papers.cfm?abstract_id=2946160> (accessed 11 June 2020).
68 On this discussion see Primavera de Filippi, 'The Interplay between Decentralization and Privacy: The Case of Blockchain Technologies' (2016) 7 *Journal of Peer Production* 7–8, available at <https://hal.archives-ouvertes.fr/hal-01382006/document> (accessed 27 June 2020).
69 Bill Maurer, Taylor C. Nelms and Lana Swartz, '"When Perhaps the Real Problem Is Money Itself!": The Practical Materiality of Bitcoin' (2013) 23 *Social Semiotics* 261–262.
70 John Engen, 'Lesson from a Mobile Payments Revolution' (29 April 2018) *American Banker*, available at <https://www.americanbanker.com/news/why-chinas-mobile-payments-revolution-matters-for-us-bankers> (accessed 28 June 2020).
71 Kieran Garvey, Hung-Yi Chen, Bryan Zhang, Edward Buckingham, Deborah Ralston, Yianni Katiforis, Kong Ying et al., 'Cultivating Growth. The 2nd Asia Pacific Region Alternative Finance Industry Report' (September 2017) 57, available at <https://www.jbs.cam.ac.uk/fileadmin/user_upload/research/centres/alternative-finance/downloads/2017-09-cultivating-growth.pdf> (accessed 10 June 2020).

such as 'blockchain' would allow households and businesses to cheaply and conveniently exchange payments, provide loans and pool risks without the need for financial intermediaries.[72] That being said, in developed countries, FinTech changes reveal a proliferation of new mobile and internet-based financial services applications but their market share mostly still remain very small.[73] Where new services have become widely used, e.g. Paypal for on-line payments, this rests on a 'piggybacking' on existing financial services infrastructure.[74]

Blockchain algorithms specifically allow transactions, or transfers, to be aggregated into blocks and added to existing chains using public and private key cryptography.[75] Maurer argues that distributed ledgers do not only verify records of transactions but also verify them without apparent human intercession.[76] Blockchain has the potential to make paper-based records obsolete with transactions stored on the decentralised ledger. It can reduce error, improve efficiency and eliminate transactional risk. However, there are issues such as reducing latency, as distributed ledgers could lead to the practices of before 2008 of making risk-stratified products. Further, blockchain's smart contracts introduce economic agents that could be viewed as robots or as legal persons, in which case they could have the same rights as a natural person.

At this stage the main policy questions regarding blockchains include the following: (1) which elements of the financial services value chain or individual products and services can be provided individually and competitively by technology-based firms; (2) whether this undermines the competitive position of incumbents, perhaps leaving them with little except loss-making but unavoidable responsibilities for underlying infrastructure or regulatory compliance; (3) whether the new technology opens up new customer opportunities, overcoming contractual and other barriers that have limited access to many financial services; and (4) whether it instead worsens problems of access with FinTech 'cherry picking' profitable high margin opportunities and eliminating opportunities for providing access through relationship-based intermediation and cross-subsidy.

Another institutional issue is the sustainability of the role of traditional mutual forms of financial intermediary (such as building societies and credit unions; entities that operate as co-operatives without shareholders), as access to financial services is increasingly virtual rather than face to face. Therefore, the challenge is whether the new financial technologies are destructive of community bonds that have supported mutual finance and whether they can support alternative forms of economic organisation or social enterprises (such as activity that is already happening to at least a limited degree through donation-based or reward-based crowdfunding).[77]

---

72 Don Tapscott and Alex Tapscott, *Blockchain Revolution: How the Technology behind Bitcoin Is Changing Money, Business, and the World* (Penguin 2016) 283–284. See also Melanie Swan, 'Blockchain: Blueprint for a New Economy' (2015) available at <http://www.amazon.com/Bitcoin-Blueprint-New-World-Currency/dp/1491920491> (accessed 21 June 2020).

73 Marc Pilkington, 'Blockchain Technology: Principles and Applications' in F. Xavier Olleros and Majlinda Zhegu (eds), *Research Handbook on Digital Transformations* (Edward Elgar 2016) 226–227.

74 Roger W. H. Bons, Rainer Alt, Ho Geun Lee and Bruce Weber, 'Banking in the Internet and Mobile Era' (2012) 22 *Electronic Markets* 197–198.

75 Marco Iansiti and Karim R. Lakhani, 'The Truth about Blockchain' (January–February 2017) *Harvard Business Review* 9–10, available at <https://enterprisersproject.com/sites/default/files/the_truth_about_blockchain.pdf> (accessed 20 June 2020).

76 Bill Maurer, 'The Racial Capitalism of Blockchain: Alternative Markets for Human-Computer Flourishing or Computational Slavery?' Talk given at the University of Helsinki Anthropology (8 February 2019) available at <https://blogs.helsinki.fi/anthropology/2019/02/18/bill-maurer-the-racial-capitalism-of-blockchain/> (accessed 12 June 2020).

77 Crowdfunds are financial platforms that support direct holding of small investments in equity and debt, as an alternative to intermediation through banks and investment intermediaries. The most important categories

13.6 Towards banking disintermediation

Regulators have seen an explosion of new FinTech around the world, supporting the establishment of internet in banks, the crowdfunding of both consumer lending and small business equity and debt, a range of innovative online and mobile-based payments and far-reaching change in business processes across the banking, insurance, investment advice and other financial services. These new technologies have the potential to correct the economic inefficiencies in financial services evident, for example, in high levels of margins and employee remuneration, frequent financial instability and the difficulties faced by many households and small businesses in accessing external finance or protecting themselves from risks of financial loss.[78] As discussed in this chapter, the aim of FinTech is to reduce traditional forms of intermediation through virtual platforms although the development of online FinTech is linked with disintermediation and decentralisation.

Recent progress in blockchains suggests that one of the interesting potential applications of the technology is in 'disintermediation protocols', which remove the need of having trusted third parties in a collaborative environment involving many (potentially anonymous) stakeholders.[79] A UK Government report also suggests that the technology offers the potential, according to the circumstances, for individual consumers to control access to personal records and to know who has accessed them.[80] The aim of the report is to facilitate secure access and traceability to confidential financial records and messages focusing on the governance and assurance of access to records. The principal focus is on removing the need to have a trusted authority in order to lower the costs associated with the operation of the system, which allows for a strong business model for the deployment of the system.

FinTech is supporting a range of new forms of intermediation including loan-based and equity-based crowdfunding.[81] There is an emerging attention on these new forms of intermediation (for example, using the data created by these platforms) that are revolutionising business models. This raises the following challenges: (1) the impact of new technologies on information asymmetry and the alignment of interests between the firm and the customer and whether these contribute to or alleviate increased conduct risk; and (2) how new digital technology affects customer perceptions and customer behaviour and its impact on the behavioural biases that undermine the presumption of 'caveat emptor', i.e. the customer is responsible for ensuring they are not disadvantaged in financial transactions. It has been argued that 'one of the issues which the invention of virtual currency has brought into sharp focus is the possibility of disintermediating the entire banking sector'.[82]

---

are 'loan-based' and 'equity-based' crowdfunding (there is also donation-based crowdfunding). See Armin Schwienbacher and Benjamin Larralde, 'Crowdfunding of Small Entrepreneurial Ventures' in Douglas Cumming (ed), *The Oxford Handbook of Entrepreneurial Finance* (OUP 2012) 371–372.

78 Andrea Minto, Moritz Voelkerling and Melanie Wulff, 'Separating Apples from Oranges: Identifying Threats to Financial Stability Originating from FinTech' (2017) 12 *Capital Markets Law Journal* 429–430.

79 Hossein Kakavand, Nicolette Kost De Sevres and Bart Chilton, 'The Blockchain Revolution: An Analysis of Regulation and Technology Related to Distributed Ledger Technologies' (2017) available at <https://ssrn.com/abstract=2849251> (accessed 18 June 2020).

80 UK Government, 'Distributed Ledger Technology: Beyond Block Chain' (19 January 2016) 18–20, available at <https://www.gov.uk/government/publications/distributed-ledger-technology-blackett-review> (accessed 12 June 2020).

81 Robert Wardrop and Tania Ziegler, 'A Case of Regulatory Evolution – A Review of the UK Financial Conduct Authority's Approach to Crowdfunding' (2016) 14 *CESifo DICE Report* 25–27, available at <http://hdl.handle.net/10419/167260> (accessed 24 June 2020).

82 Simon Gleeson, *The Legal Concept of Money* (OUP 2018) 153.

In this context, the relationship between governance and technology in financial services implies the impact governance has both on technology adoption and the possibility of using technology to improve governance. This is a particularly prominent concern for financial services because weaknesses in governance and culture have been a major problem in the sector, an underlying cause of the global financial crisis and of the many recent failures of conduct in large financial institutions as discussed in Chapter 12. A related issue is excess short-termism, the problematic emphasis in financial intermediation on short-term rather than long-term performance.[83]

Weaknesses in governance and culture may also be a barrier to the full application of new technologies in financial services. This is for several related reasons. First, technology has until only a few years ago been regarded as a secondary, back office function, 'plumbing' that is required to support the marketing and trading activities that create returns, but not something that merits substantial attention from senior management. Nowadays much trading activity has been computerised and technology is increasingly employed for engaging with customers, but old attitudes and lack of understanding may persist with potentially negative impacts. There seems to be a shortage both at incumbent firms and among regulators, of individuals at senior management or board level with an in-depth understanding of the new technologies and their business application. A second issue is that emphasis on short-term profitability discourages the potentially large investments needed to replace or upgrade old legacy systems, especially when substantial amounts are already devoted to regulatory compliance. A third issue is that firms in financial services are very reluctant, when compared to other technology-based industries such as internet commerce or mobile telephony, to co-operate on technical issues such as standard setting.[84]

The central question on technology and the governance and co-ordination of financial services is the extent to which FinTech may themselves help address weaknesses of culture and governance in financial institutions. A fundamental characteristic of today's giant financial institutions is their lack of transparency. Senior management does not have direct contact or understanding at operational level, a weakness often exacerbated by the way they have grown through multiple acquisitions so that internally they run hundreds of different operational systems that do not communicate adequately with each other. Employing technology has the potential to unbundle and simplify financial intermediation, so that processes are broken up into easily understood elements, thus improving their governance. But this runs into incentive problems. If the market power of firms and the administrative power of senior management rests on lack of transparency and oversight, then they can be expected to exert substantial resistance to technological change that promotes transparency and increases competition.

13.7 Conclusion

Financial actors are grappling with the internal challenge of managing heightened regulatory standards and expectations; increased regulatory monitoring and inspections; increased

---

83 Andrew G. Haldane, 'Growing, Fast and Slow' (Speech at the University of East Anglia, Norwich, 17 February 2015) available at <https://www.bankofengland.co.uk/-/media/boe/files/speech/2015/growing-fast-and-slow.pdf> (accessed 18 June 2020). See also Alfred Rappaport, 'The Economics of Short-Term Performance Obsession' (2005) 61 *Financial Analysts Journal* 65–66.

84 Kevin Houstoun, Alistair Milne and Paul Parboteeah, 'Preliminary Report on Standards in Global Financial Markets' (2015) 26–28, available at <https://ssrn.com/abstract=2531210> (accessed 20 June 2020).

enforcement actions, fines and penalties; and multiple jurisdictions with complex or con-flicting regulations. All these are coupled with mutable regulatory requirements entailing significant operational and reputational impacts/risks for financial institutions. But with the use of RegTech a modernised compliance regime is approaching. The extent to which regulatory compliance can be automated and carried out by machine raises the question whether human judgement is still required.[85] Addressing the challenges of regulatory com-pliance with the use of technology can allow supervisory authorities to embrace speed and agility, supported by cost savings, resource optimisation and value creation.

The prudential and financial stability risks revealed by the global financial crisis and earlier episodes of instability, inadequate customer protection, crime and ineffective com-petition and resulting market power of major financial firms have led to dramatic expansion in the regulation of financial services over the past decade. This piecemeal response has arguably resulted in an extensive but also often incoherent framework for financial regula-tion.[86] At the same time, the high costs of regulatory compliance – with skyrocketing fines on financial firms and increasing compliance costs for many firms – has become a political issue.[87] RegTech solutions bear the promise of contributing to more effective and more efficient regulation, supervision and internal controls in the financial sector to the ultimate benefit of the users of financial services and society at large.

Glossary of terms

- Public good: A good which is non-excludable (everybody can use it) and non-rivalrous (it can be used by many or infinite persons without its value being depleted). Public goods are underproduced by markets, and thus, they are an example of a market failure. Some common regulatory strategies to ensure sufficient provision of public goods are state production, subsidies and regulation obligating private parties to produce them.
- FinTech: Financial innovation comprises cryptoassets, online platforms and artificial intelligence.
- RegTech: Applications of digital technology by regulation and compliance actors.
- Natural Language Generation (NLG): Technology that can achieve the automation of the generation of regulatory AML reports, e.g. suspicious activity reports (SARs).
- Natural Language Processing (NLP): Technology that can extract regulations and identify regulatory and control requirements (i.e. legislation/regulation 'gap' analysis tools).
- Virtual currency: Species of financial hybrid that defies straightforward placement in established categories and exacerbates 'border problems' between the regulated and unregulated space and between national jurisdictions.
- Bitcoin: A payment network and type of money. It is not generally accepted as a means of exchange, and therefore, transactions are not supported by deposit protection or other central bank lender of last resort facilities.

---

85 Iris H.-Y. Chiu, 'Fintech and Disruptive Business Models in Financial Products, Intermediation and Markets - Policy Implications for Financial Regulators' (2016) 21 *Journal of Technology Law and Policy* 90–91.
86 John Armour, 'Current State of the Fintech Industry and Its Challenges' (2017) available at <https://oxford-fls.org/> (accessed 22 June 2020).
87 Tom Groenfeldt, 'Taming the High Costs of Compliance with Tech' *Forbes* (22 March 2018) available at <https://www.forbes.com/sites/tomgroenfeldt/2018/03/22/taming-the-high-costs-of-compliance-with-tech/#e1182fb5d3f7> (accessed 11 June 2020).

- Cryptoassets: New experimental forms of finance that use pseudo-anonymity (participation determined by internal network identifiers not real world identity) and cryptographic security to operate entirely outside of the regulated sector.
- Blockchain algorithms: Technology that allows transactions, or transfers, to be aggregated into blocks and added to existing chains using public and private key cryptography.
- Central bank digital currency (CBDC):Digital currencies that may potentially be provided by central banks that offer a costless medium of exchange.
- Initial coin offerings (ICOs): Process of raising finance via cryptocurrency using virtual platforms.

Practice questions

Issues arising from digital technology are wide ranging and require regulatory attention, especially in the context of AML, CFT and KYC requirements. These issues raise several business, economic, regulatory, legal and social concerns (cybercrime, data protection, privacy and crisis management procedures). Specifically, FinTech raises challenges in the regulatory framework in terms of the interpretation of 'smart contracts', attribution of responsibility for the acts and omissions of robots and enforcement of contractual obligations. Critically discuss.

You may also find it useful to review the chapter through the following questions:

- Can digital technologies reduce fraudulent behaviour of financial firms and contribute to AML/CFT policies, while ensuring consumer protection and predictability of enforcement actions?
- Can digital technologies improve internal controls and more effective compliance processes in the governance of financial firms?
- Can digital technologies promote greater use of cryptocurrencies exchange expediting customers' purchases and cash payments?
- Are the current statements of rules and regulations suitable for automation, or do they need changing and if so how?
- Would the use of RegTech automatically exclude certain classes of consumers?

Part IV

Managing bank failures

The aim of the final part of the book is to examine regulatory tools to deal with ailing banks in a way that prevents contagion and ensures the continuity of critical banking services.

14 UK banking resolution and the EU Single Resolution Mechanism

14.1 Introduction

This chapter examines the resolution tools for failing banks in the UK regulatory framework and the main pillars of the European bank insolvency regime, namely, recovery and resolution plans, and the Single Resolution Mechanism (SRM). In particular, the analysis focuses on the interplay between the European Central Bank (ECB) and national authorities in bank supervision and resolution. The regulatory architecture of the EU Bank Recovery and Resolution Directive (BRRD) and the SRM introduced rules necessary to prevent financial instability and systemic risk contagion. However, the restructuring tools for distressed banks – i.e. bail-in, precautionary recapitalisation and resolving plans – are largely flexible to allow Member States to adopt domestic policy measures to rescue distressed institutions. This leaves broad discretion to national competent authorities to provide public financial support, a legacy of the bail-out programmes that can undermine the new EU bank resolution regime. The new resolution tools within the BRRD reduce the intervention of competent authorities, although they constitute a challenge for the restructuring policies of the Banking Union. Recent bank failures across Europe have demonstrated that credit institutions rely on bail-out programmes and State aid practices. Banks tend to follow national supervision and domestic enforcement and resolution systems, a practice that in the aftermath of the global financial crisis seems difficult to change.

14.2 Ensuring banks are resolvable: ring-fencing of domestic banking

One of the many explanations proposed for the 2008–2009 global financial crisis pointed to the combination of retail and investment banking activities in large financial conglomerates in the years leading up to the crisis.[1] The argument goes as follows. Retail banks are fundamentally simple to manage and low-risk businesses that – under appropriate regulation and a deposit insurance scheme – would be very unlikely to fail and cause a systemic crisis. Conversely, investment banks are, by their very nature, high-risk entities which

---

1 Mervyn King, the former Governor of the Bank of England, is a supporter of full separation of retail and investment banking. See Mervyn King, 'Banking: From Bagehot to Basel, and Back Again' (New York, 25 October 2010) <https://www.bankofengland.co.uk/-/media/boe/files/news/2010/october/banking-from-bagehot-to-basel-and-back-again-speech-by-mervyn-king.pdf?la=en&hash=C1A4CAD8BD9CF4D6419E-C588A81336E1C5391D8A> (accessed 10 July 2020).

engage in speculative investments and are hence prone to insolvency. Therefore, a degree of separation of retail and investment banking activities – which may also reduce the overall size of very large financial institutions – has been proposed as a vital reform to enhance financial stability and address the so-called too big to fail problem.[2]

Historically, a strict separation of retail and investment banking was followed in the US from the 1930s until the 1990s,[3] and in the UK until the mid-1980s.[4] Conversely, Germany and other European countries have traditionally supported financial conglomeration and universal banking under the assumption that it leads to greater stability. The global financial crisis led to a limited reinstatement of structural separation of banking activities in the US, where the 'Volcker rule' prohibits banks from engaging in proprietary trading of securities and from investing in hedge funds and private equity funds.[5] In parallel, the UK adopted a mild form of separation of retail from investment banking, known as ring-fencing, which will be the main focus of this section. On the EU level, in 2014 the Commission proposed the introduction of a rule similar to the 'Volcker rule' for large EU banks.[6] The Commission's proposal had a successful first reading at the Council in June 2015, but progress has since stagnated. The EU Parliament that resulted from the 2019 European elections is expected in due course to take a position on the matter before negotiations with the Council on a draft Regulation can commence.[7]

In the UK context, the Financial Services (Banking Reform) Act 2013 (the 'Banking Reform Act') established a framework for ring-fencing providing for the separation of core activities (deposit taking),[8] which must be carried out by ring-fenced bodies, from excluded activities (trading in investments). The Act followed the influential report by the committee chaired by Sir John Vickers.[9] In brief, each banking group is expected to incorporate its domestic retail banking activities as a separate legal entity, the ring-fenced body, which will have to meet separate capital requirements. Certain activities – most notably deposit

2 For a discussion of the benefits and limits of ring-fencing initiatives internationally, see Leonardo Gambacorta and Adrian van Rixtel, 'Structural Bank Regulation Initiatives: Approaches and Implications' (2013) BIS Working Paper 412, Bank for International Settlements Publications.
3 In the US, the Banking Act of 1933, commonly referred to as the Glass-Steagall Act, introduced the compulsory separation of retail and investment banking. The separation was abolished by the Financial Services Modernization Act of 1999 (known as the Gramm-Leach-Bliley Act) which allowed banks, brokerages and insurance companies to merge.
4 In the UK, until the mid-1980s, there was a uniform practice of separating retail and investment banking.
5 See Wall Street Reform and Consumer Protection Act of 2010 (Dodd-Frank Act), s 619.
6 See Commission, 'Proposal for a Regulation of the European Parliament and of the Council on Structural Measures Improving the Resilience of EU Credit Institutions' COM (2014) 43 final, esp Article 6. The proposal is based on the recommendations of the Liikanen Report. See Erki Liikanen, 'High-level Expert Group on Reforming the Structure of the EU Banking Sector: Final Report' (2012) <http://ec.europa.eu/internal_market/bank/docs/high-level_expert_group/report_en.pdf> (accessed 1 May 2020).
7 European Council, 'Structural Reform of EU Banking Sector: Improving the Resilience of Credit Institutions' (21 November 2018) <http://www.consilium.europa.eu/en/policies/banking-structural-reform/> (accessed 1 April 2020).
8 Section 4 of the Financial Services (Banking Reform) Act 2013 inserts a new Part 9B (sections 142A–142Z1) into the Financial Services and Markets Act 2000 ('FSMA') providing for ring-fencing. The ring-fencing rules came fully into force on 1 January 2019.
9 The Vickers Report recommended a mild form of separation of retail banking from investment banking known as ring-fencing of domestic retail activities, which are to be undertaken by a separate subsidiary with stronger capital and supervision. See Independent Commission on Banking, *Final Report: Recommendations* (Domarn Group 2011) esp. para 9.2.

taking,[10] money withdrawal facilities and overdraft facilities – offered in the UK[11] must be undertaken by the ring-fenced entity, while several other activities can be undertaken by it, with the exception of excluded activities such as proprietary trading.[12] The statutory aims of ring-fencing are to ensure the continuity of the provision of core financial services in the UK[13] and to protect depositors.[14] As envisaged by Vickers, ring-fencing is intended to facilitate the resolution of troubled banking groups and, in particular, to make it possible to allow the non-ring-fenced part of the group to fail, while securing the survival of the ring-fenced part and hence the undisrupted provision of key financial services.[15]

In February 2013, the Parliamentary Commission on Banking Standards proposed that the regulator should be given a reserve power to require full separation of retail and investment banking in the case of an individual banking group – the 'electrification' power.[16] 'Electrification' means that if a bank breaks through the fence the consequences could be severe, with the Prudential Regulation Authority (PRA) being able to step in and enforce separation by completely breaking up the bank.[17] The PRA is required to carry out annual reviews of the ring-fence regime as well as to enhance competition in the banking sector.[18] However, according to the Commission, the annual reviews of the operation of the ring-fence by the PRA would not be enough: there should be a statutory independent review held on a regular basis. As observed, 'the ringfence must be "electrified" if it is to stand a better chance of success—in other words if the banks test the ringfence too much, they will get a shock'.[19]

'Electrification' may represent a valuable tool for ensuring banks comply with the rules of ring-fencing and for reducing uncertainty that would accompany endless gaming of the rules. However, even if the ring-fence is 'electrified' financial firms will still have other means to satisfy their objective for risk and leveraging, including tapping the money markets as many of them did in the recent financial crisis.[20] Further, ring-fence strategy may lead to unintended effects such as dealing with higher costs of debt and equity for the part of the bank that falls outside of the ring-fence. For banking groups with ring-fenced and non-ring-fenced activities potential failure of the non-ring-fenced part could cause reputational damage to the whole organisation and still precipitate failure of the healthy part via

10 FSMA 2000 s 142B (2) inserted by Banking Reform Act s 4.
11 FSMA 2000 s 142C (2) inserted by Banking Reform Act s 4.
12 FSMA 2000 s 142D (2) inserted by Banking Reform Act s 4.
13 FSMA 2000 s 2B (3) (c) inserted by Banking Reform Act s 1.
14 FSMA 2000 s 142B (4) (a) inserted by Banking Reform Act s 4.
15 See Vickers Report (above n 9) paras 3.23 and 3.95–3.99.
16 HM Treasury, 'Financial Services (Banking Reform) Bill. Government Amendments: Group Restructuring Powers ("Electrification")' (October 2013) 1. The 'electrification' power allows the regulatory authorities to switch the ring-fence into a permanent separation if they detect misuse of discretion by banks in interpreting the ring-fence rules.
17 Andrew Shiels, 'The Banking Reform Bill: What Lies Ahead for the Banks?' (August 2013) available at <http://www.bluerock-consulting.com/pdf-new-site/the-banking-reform-bill---aug-2013.pdf> (accessed 23 June 2020).
18 Bank of England, 'The Implementation of Ring-Fencing: The PRA's Approach to Ring-Fencing Transfer Schemes' Policy Statement PS10/16 (4 March 2016) 7–8.
19 Andrew Tyrie, 'Electrify the Banking Ringfence' *Financial Times* (London, 27 January 2013).
20 Kris James Mitchener, 'Skin in the Game' University of Warwick Department of Economics (March 2013) available at <http://www2.warwick.ac.uk/fac/soc/economics/news/2013/3/bankingreg/#sthash.fd63tdjh.dpbs> (accessed 22 June 2020).

contagion.[21] It has been noted that 'electrification of the ring-fence may give the regulations more teeth, but it will not overcome ringfencing's unintended effects and complexities'.[22] Therefore, the success of 'electrification' strategy depends on the ability of ring-fencing to totally prevent another financial crisis.[23]

As far as secondary legislation is concerned, the UK Government issued 'The Financial Services and Markets Act 2000 (Ring-fenced Bodies and Core Activities) Order 2014', [24] which sets out the scope of the ring-fence, and 'The Financial Services and Markets Act 2000 (Excluded Activities and Prohibitions) Order 2014' which defines the range of activities that may not be carried on by ring-fenced bodies.[25] The Financial Services and Markets Act 2000 (Ring-fenced Bodies and Core Activities) Order 2014 defines the circumstances when accepting a deposit is not a core activity under section 142B of the Financial Services and Markets Act 2000 (FSMA) – as amended by the Financial Services (Banking Reform) Act 2013 – so that the deposits in question may be held by banks that are not ring-fenced bodies. It also exempts certain banks from the definition of ring-fenced body under section 142A of FSMA.[26] The Order provides that only banks above a certain size will be required to be ring-fenced. It creates an exemption, excluding banking groups with less than £25 billion of core deposits from the definition of 'ring-fenced body' (article 12). It also exempts classes of institutions, such as insurers and credit unions that are captured by the definition of ring-fenced body in the Banking Reform Act because they accept deposits.

The Excluded Activities and Prohibitions Order 2014 defines the forms of trading in securities and commodities that must be outside the ring-fence and imposes specific prohibitions on ring-fenced banks.[27] The Order creates exceptions for (1) ring-fenced banks' own risk management and funding, (2) transactions with central banks and (3) the provision of simple risk-management services to customers. The first exception is intended to permit ring-fenced banks prudently to manage their own risks. It therefore permits dealing in investments, including derivatives, provided that the sole or main purpose of the transactions is to hedge the risks of the ring-fenced bank or its subsidiaries. The second exception permits ring-fenced banks to trade with central banks, which will allow ring-fenced banks to access central bank liquidity in times of stress. The third exception permits ring-fenced banks to sell a narrow range of simple risk-management products to their customers. Complex derivatives will not be permitted inside the ring-fence and are typically used only by

---

21 Mike Nawas and George Lamaris, 'Ringfencing of Banks: A Permanent Cure or a Sticking Plaster?' (London, 12 February 2013) 4, available at <http://www.bishopsfieldcapital.com/sites/default/files/article/market-insight-0213-ringfencing-of-banks-a-permanent-cure-or-a-sticking-plaster.pdf> (accessed 25 June 2020).

22 Ibid.

23 Steven L. Schwarcz, 'Ring-Fencing' (2013) 87 *Southern California Law Review* 103–104.

24 The Financial Services and Markets Act 2000 (Ring-Fenced Bodies and Core Activities) Order 2014 (Draft SI 2014 No. XX).

25 The Financial Services and Markets Act 2000 (Excluded Activities and Prohibitions) Order 2014 (SI 2014 No. 2080).

26 The Order defines the scope of the ring-fence, those bodies that must be ring-fenced and the kinds of deposit that must be in the ring-fence. Section 142D of the Banking Reform Act provides that the Treasury has the power to determine that those holding investors' deposits can deal as principal in investments and the range can be extended further having regard to the risks involved.

27 The Financial Services and Markets Act 2000 (Excluded Activities and Prohibitions) Order 2014 No. 2080, available at <http://www.legislation.gov.uk/uksi/2014/2080/pdfs/uksi_20142080_en.pdf> (accessed 27 June 2020).

larger and more sophisticated corporate customers, which are often already multi-banked and so would have little trouble sourcing derivatives from a non-ring-fenced bank.[28]

The Excluded Activities and Prohibitions Order creates a further excluded activity: dealing in commodities (article 5). It also imposes a series of specific prohibitions on ring-fenced banks which are prohibited from having exposures to certain financial institutions. The prohibition protects ring-fenced banks against financial contagion in the financial system. The Order prohibits ring-fenced banks from having exposures to non-ring-fenced banks such as investment firms, globally systemic insurance firms and investment funds.[29] It permits exposures to other ring-fenced banks, building societies, credit unions, recognised clearing houses and central counterparties (CCPs), investment firms that only offer advice and banks that are subject to the same restrictions as ring-fenced banks, such as small retail banks.

The systemic importance of CCPs consists in the fact that they may be considered as a central hub for systemic risk management.[30] CCPs are useful risk mitigation tools for the market however, despite having showed their worth in the 2007–2009 financial crisis, they are not infallible transformers of risk.[31] Exposures to non-systemic insurers are also permitted as those firms, which engage only in traditional insurance business, do not pose contagion risks comparable to those from non-ring-fenced banks or investment banks. The exposures involved are permitted, subject to controls imposed by the PRA to address any prudential risks. To ensure that ring-fenced banks are able to access the payment systems that are critical to their business, the Order separately imposes restrictions on the extent to which they may use the services provided by inter-bank payment systems except as members of those payment systems.[32]

In general, ring-fencing is only a light-touch form of separation of retail and investment banking activities within banking groups, and hence, its potential contribution to financial stability should not be overestimated.[33] It has been argued that ring-fencing is unlikely to enable the government to allow the non-ring-fenced part of banks to fail.[34] Indeed, it appears unlikely that ring-fenced entities would be able to survive the failure of the rest of the relevant banking group even if they were separately capitalised. It must be kept in mind that retail banks depend on the confidence of their depositors for their survival and that a serious crisis of confidence can lead a retail bank to insolvency. Allowing the larger part of a banking group to fail would in all probability cause a creditors' run against the ring-fenced entity, which would then have to be supported by the government to prevent its collapse.

---

28 The Financial Services and Markets Act 2000 (Ring-fenced Bodies, Core Activities, Excluded Activities and Prohibitions) (Amendment) Order 2016 No. 1032, available at <http://www.legislation.gov.uk/uksi/2016/1032/contents/made> (accessed 17 June 2020).

29 Rebecca Brace, 'Electrifying the Ring-Fence – The View from the Transaction Banking Industry' *Euromoney* (10 January 2013) available at <https://www.euromoney.com/article/b12kjvpk84dq26/electrifying-the-ring-fence-the-view-from-the-transaction-banking-industry> (accessed 16 June 2020).

30 European Systemic Risk Board, 'Central Counterparties and Systemic Risk' *Macro-prudential Commentaries* (2013) No. 6, 7.

31 Matt Gibson, 'Recovery and Resolution of Central Counterparties' Reserve Bank of Australia Bulletin (December Quarter 2013) 39.

32 Bank of England, 'Ring-Fenced Bodies (RFBs)' Supervisory Statement SS8/16 (December 2017) 24–25.

33 For a critical analysis of ring-fencing, see Policy Exchange, *Ringfencing UK Banks: More of a Problem than a Solution* (James Barty ed, Heron, Dawson and Sawyer 2013).

34 Mads Andenas and Iris H.-Y. Chiu, *The Foundations and Future of Financial Regulation: Governance for Responsibility* (Routledge 2014) 304.

Taking into account that the collapse of Lehman Brothers and other investment banks led to systemic contagion in various banks across the world, it is likely that the collapse of the investment banking in a banking group would lead to devastating consequences for the ring-fenced entity. Moreover, the collapse of the non-ring-fenced part of a large banking group could trigger a systemic crisis *per se*, as the non-ring-fenced parts of groups are expected to include at least 2/3 and up to 4/5 of large banks' assets.[35]

As an alternative, some scholars have advocated a strict separation of retail and investment banking would entail the complete break-up of financial conglomerates, as investment and retail banking activities would have to be undertaken by completely separate corporate entities with no material share ownership links.[36] It follows that retail banking activities ought to be completely separate from investment banking activities so that the failure of an investment bank would have no immediate consequence on retail banks.[37] It is envisaged that under a regime of strict separation, the government would be able to allow investment banks to fail, and thus, market discipline would be restored. It is also argued that a strict separation would reduce contagion and systemic risk in the financial sector, and that the economic benefits of combining retail and investment banking activities are overstated. An argument in favour of this approach is that structural separation has the potential to restore public confidence in banking and to mitigate existing concerns about a perceived lack of legitimacy with respect to the enormous economic influence of financial conglomerates.[38] However, strict separation would also be very costly and it is not entirely clear that it would bring all the benefits that such views expect it to bring. In any case, current UK policy on this matter appears settled on the present regime of ring-fencing.

14.3 The UK Special Resolution Regime

From a UK perspective, among other regulatory weaknesses, the 2008–2009 global financial crisis exposed the inadequacy of the previously available regulatory tools to respond to bank distress and failures. To resolve this problem, the Banking Act 2009 introduced a special crisis management framework and special insolvency framework for banks. The crisis management/resolution framework focuses on rescuing banks' business and is known as the Special Resolution Regime, whereby the Bank of England exercises its stabilisation

---

35 The services that must be provided by ring-fenced entities amount to 18% of UK banks' assets, while those that may be provided by them amount to another 18%. The Vickers Report (above n 9) para 3.40. It can be reasonably expected that banks will keep ring-fenced entities as small as possible to avoid any additional regulatory burden.

36 For instance, Avgouleas advocates a three-tier separation as follows: banks that are only allowed to engage in retail banking; retail banks that can also engage in a limited set of capital market transactions and investment banks that cannot accept deposits. See Emilios Avgouleas, 'The Reform of the "Too-Big-To-Fail" Bank: A New Regulatory Model for the Institutional Separation of "Casino" from "Utility" Banking' (2010) <https://papers.ssrn.com/sol3/papers.cfm?abstract_id=1552970&rec=1&srcabs=1525670&alg=1&pos=6> (accessed 14 May 2020).

37 For instance, Kay has advocated the creation of narrow banks to fulfil retail banking functions that are completely separate from entities providing other financial services with the latter being allowed to fail and thus being fully subject to market forces. See John Kay, 'Narrow Banking: The Reform of Banking Regulation' (2009) <https://www.johnkay.com/2009/09/15/narrow-banking/> (accessed 15 July 2020)

38 In this vein, Zingales has argued that structural separation would promote competition and limit the lobbying power of large banks. See Luigi Zingales, *Capitalism for the People: Recapturing the Lost Genius of American Capitalism* (Basic Books 2012).

powers.[39] The Act has been extensively amended in line with the EU BRRD, which will be discussed in detail in the next section. There are four statutory conditions for the exercise of the stabilisation powers of the Bank of England, which must all be met. The PRA must be satisfied that a bank is failing or is likely to fail, and the Bank of England must be satisfied that it is not reasonably likely that action will be taken to address this; that the exercise of the power is necessary in the light of the special resolution objectives and that one or more special resolution objectives would not be met to the same extent by the winding up of the bank.[40]

The statutory objectives of the Special Resolution Regime are: (1) to ensure the continuity of banking services and critical functions; (2) to protect the stability of the UK's financial systems by preventing contagion and preserving market discipline; (3) to protect public confidence in the stability of the UK's banking systems; (4) to protect public funds; (5) to protect depositors and investors to the extent that they are covered by the Financial Services Compensation Scheme or an investor compensation scheme under EU law; (6) to protect client assets; and (7) to avoid interfering with property rights that are enshrined by the European Convention on Human Rights.[41] The seven objectives are not listed in order of priority, but rather they are to be balanced as appropriate in each case,[42] which allows broad discretion to be exercised by the Bank of England and Treasury. The Act empowers the Treasury to issue a Code of Practice on the Special Resolution Regime to provide the relevant authorities (mainly the Bank of England) with guidance on when and how to use the special resolution tools.[43] The latest version of the Code was issued in March 2017.[44]

The Special Resolution Regime originally consisted of three stabilisation tools, namely, private sector purchase, creation of a bridge bank as a subsidiary of the Bank of England and temporary public ownership.[45] A fourth tool, bail-in stabilisation, was added as a result of the Financial Services (Banking Reform) Act 2013, in line with the BRRD.[46] A fifth tool, the transfer of assets to an asset management vehicle, which can only be used in conjunction with one of the other tools, was added in 2014, again in compliance with the Directive.[47] The Act provides the Bank of England and Treasury with very broad powers to transfer securities and property and compensate third parties.[48] The tools can be used concurrently,

39 For a conceptual framework of the functions and objectives of special resolution regimes, see Gustaf Sjoberg, 'Banking Special Resolution Regimes as a Governance Tool' in Wolf-Georg Ringe and Peter Huber (eds), *Legal Challenges in the Global Financial Crisis* (Hart Publishing 2014). See also Andrew Campbell, 'Northern Rock, the Financial Crisis and the Special Resolution Regime' in Joanna Gray and Orkun Akseli (eds), *Financial Regulation in Crisis? The Role of Law and the Failure of Northern Rock* (Edward Elgar Publishing 2011).
40 Banking Act 2009, s 7 (1)–(5), as substituted by the Bank Recovery and Resolution Order 2014 (SI 2014/3329), art 12.
41 Banking Act 2009, s 4 (3A)–(9), inserted by the Bank Recovery and Resolution Order 2014 (SI 2014/3329), art 8.
42 Banking Act 2009, s 4 (10).
43 Banking Act 2009, ss 5–6.
44 HM Treasury, 'Banking Act 2009: Special Resolution Regime Code of Practice' (2017) <https://assets.publishing.service.gov.uk/government/uploads/system/uploads/attachment_data/file/602948/Special-Resolution-Regime-Code-of-Practice.pdf> (accessed 8 July 2020)
45 Banking Act 2009, ss 1 (3), 11–13.
46 Banking Act 2009 ss 12A–12B, inserted by Banking Reform Act 2013 Schedule 2, s 2.
47 Banking Act 2009, s 12ZA, inserted by The Bank Recovery and Resolution Order 2014 (SI 2014/3329), art 19.
48 Banking Act 2009, ss 14–62, as amended.

but shareholder equity must be cancelled to absorb losses in all cases[49] and bail-in must be applied on eligible debts, before any public funds are used, as will be explained in the next section. A private sector purchase refers to the sale of a troubled bank's business as a whole to a private sector purchaser. Bail-in consists of writing down the value of certain types of debt and/or converting them into equity. A bridge bank and an asset management vehicle entail the transfer of distressed assets and commensurate liabilities from the distressed institution to the bridge bank or vehicle in order to restore the financial health of the distressed institution. The bridge bank and asset management vehicle are expected to manage the assets transferred to them with a view to maximising their value.

The Bank of England is empowered to use all tools, apart from public ownership which can be exercised only by the Treasury. However, in the case of a private sector purchase, bridge bank or asset management vehicle, if financial assistance is provided to the failing bank, the Bank of England can only use these tools with the approval of the Treasury.[50] Regarding the asset management vehicle stabilisation tool, the Bank of England can only exercise its asset transfer powers if either of the following three conditions are met: (a) the condition of the relevant markets is such that following normal insolvency proceedings would have an adverse effect on these markets; (b) the transfer is necessary to ensure the proper functioning of the failing bank; or (c) the transfer is necessary to maximise the proceeds from the assets.[51] For the Treasury to be able to use the temporary public ownership tool, it must be satisfied that doing so is necessary either to resolve or reduce a serious threat to the stability of the UK's financial systems or to protect the public interest, where the Treasury has provided financial assistance to a failing bank.[52]

When it is considered that using the stabilisation powers is not necessary by reference to the relevant statutory objectives, and therefore the bank is allowed to go into insolvency, the special bank insolvency[53] and bank administration[54] procedures may be used instead of normal insolvency proceedings.[55] The Code of Practice states that the test of necessity, which applies to the exercise of all stabilisation powers, is a high one and that the Bank of England and Treasury must balance short-and long-term effects on financial stability, public confidence and depositor protection.[56] The Code acknowledges that it is for the Bank of England to choose between stabilisation options, but stipulates that the bank insolvency procedure is 'the default option unless the public interest considerations weigh in favour of an exercise of a stabilisation option' and emphasises the importance of market

---

49 Banking Act 2009, ss 6A–6D, inserted by The Bank Recovery and Resolution Order 2014 (SI 2014/3329), art 10.

50 Banking Act 2009, s 8, as substituted by The Bank Recovery and Resolution Order 2014 (SI 2014/3329), art 14.

51 Banking Act 2009, s 8ZA, inserted by The Bank Recovery and Resolution Order 2014 (SI 2014/3329), art 15.

52 Banking Act 2009, s 9.

53 Banking Act 2009, Part 2, as amended. An application may be made by the Treasury, Bank of England or PRA on grounds of failure to pay debts, public interest or fairness. The primary objective of a bank liquidator is to ensure that all eligible depositors either have their accounts transferred to another financial institution or receive compensation from the FSCS, the secondary objective being to achieve the best result for the bank's creditors as a whole.

54 Banking Act 2009, Part 3, as amended.

55 Normal insolvency proceedings include a voluntary winding up, winding up by the court, administration, a company voluntary arrangement and a scheme of arrangement. On UK insolvency law in general, see Vanessa Finch and David Milman, *Corporate Insolvency Law: Perspectives and Principles* (3rd edn, CUP 2017).

56 Special Resolution Regime Code of Practice (above n 44) [6.25]–[6.26].

discipline for banks and building societies that should not be immune from failure.[57] Out of the stabilisation options, the Code clarifies that a private sector purchase is normally the preferred option,[58] while temporary public ownership is the last resort.[59]

14.4 The Bank Recovery and Resolution Directive

The EU Banking Union with its articulated system of supervisory powers of the ECB and the innovative tools given by regulators to SRM and BRRD[60] constitutes the new regulatory framework of the bank insolvency regime.[61] The design of the Banking Union has determined a transfer to the European level of the regulatory and institutional framework for safeguarding the robustness and stability of the banking and financial sector.[62] In particular, the EU Banking Union introduces a common platform for regulation of (1) supervision, (2) resolution mechanisms and (3) deposit insurance.[63] At macroeconomic level, the establishment of a single, unique safety net within the Banking Union would address the 'vicious circle' between national governments and banks.[64] However, the BRRD applies to all EU Member States and not only to the Banking Union, and it is thus applicable to the UK where the Bank of England is the resolution authority.

The BRRD represents the cornerstone of the EU crisis management regime. It sets out common resolution powers and mechanisms for co-operation between resolution authorities in applying resolution tools to financial groups operating on a cross-border basis, with a significant role for the European Banking Authority (EBA). The main elements of the special resolution regime introduced by the BRRD can be summarised as follows: (1) its

57 Ibid., [6.31].
58 Ibid., [6.32]. It can be combined with the bank administration procedure.
59 Ibid., [6.52].
60 EU Bank Recovery and Resolution Directive (BRRD), Directive 2014/59/EU of the European Parliament and of the Council of 15 May 2014. These resolution tools require the establishing of a framework for the recovery and resolution of credit institutions and investment firms and amending Council Directive 82/891/ EEC, and Directives 2001/24/EC, 2002/47/EC, 2004/25/EC, 2005/56/EC, 2007/36/EC, 2011/35/ EU, 2012/30/EU and 2013/36/EU, and Regulations (EU) No. 1093/2010 and (EU) No. 648/2012, of the European Parliament and of the Council, OJ L 173 of 12 June 2014, 190. The BRRD has been amended by Directive (EU) 2019/879 of the European Parliament and of the Council of 20 May 2019 amending the Bank Recovery and Resolution Directive as regards the loss-absorbing and recapitalisation capacity of credit institutions and investment firms and Directive 98/26/EC ('BRRD II').
61 The Single Supervisory Mechanism (SSM) has been established by Council Regulation (EU) No. 1024/2013 of 15 October 2013 conferring specific tasks on the European Central Bank concerning policies relating to the prudential supervision of credit institutions, OJ L 287 of 29 October 2013, 63. The SRM has been introduced by Regulation (EU) No. 806/2014 of the European Parliament and of the Council of 15 July 2014 establishing uniform rules and a uniform procedure for the resolution of credit institutions and certain investment firms in the framework of a Single Resolution Mechanism and a Single Resolution Fund and amending Regulation (EU) No. 1093/2010, OJ L 225 of 30 July 2014, 1. The SRM has been amended by Regulation (EU) 2019/877 of the European Parliament and of the Council of 20 May 2019 amending Regulation (EU) No. 806/2014 as regards the loss-absorbing and recapitalisation capacity of credit institutions and investment firms ('SRMR II').
62 Daniel Gros and Dirk Schoenmaker, 'European Deposit and Resolution in the Banking Union' (2014) 52(3) *Journal of Common Market Studies* 529.
63 European Commission, 'A Roadmap towards a Banking Union' COM(2012) 510 final, Brussels.
64 See 'European Banking Union' by Rosa Lastra, Bernd Krauskopf, Christos Gortsos and René Smits, MO-COMILA Report to the ILA Meeting, Washington DC (April 2014) available at <http://www.ila-hq.org/en/ committees/index.cfm/cid/22> (accessed 26 June 2020).

scope should encompass, not just the bank itself, but the entire banking group, including the bank's parent holding company; (2) the resolution authority should be a public body and should have powers similar to those of an administrator or insolvency practitioner in a normal bankruptcy proceeding; (3) resolution should be initiated 'when a firm is no longer viable or likely to be no longer viable, and has no reasonable prospect of becoming so'; (4) the resolution authority should have a full range of tools at its disposal, including the right to bail-in creditors via write-down or conversion of their claim into common equity; (5) the resolution regime should assure that the entry into resolution does not trigger close-out of derivative contracts; (6) the resolution process must respect creditor hierarchy and provide compensation to creditors who are made worse off than they would have become under liquidation under the general law; (7) the resolution regime should assure that taxpayers do not bear the cost of bank failures. To this end each jurisdiction should provide for a means (e.g. via a resolution fund) for the industry at large to bear any costs of resolution that are not absorbed by investors; (8) the resolution regime should require the responsible authorities to co-operate with their counterparts in other jurisdictions in which the banking group operates, specifically via the formation of a Crisis Management Group chaired by the home country authority; and (9) the resolution regime should require banks to develop recovery plans and the resolution authority to develop a resolution plan.[65]

The main objective of the BRRD is to ensure that insolvent banks can be resolved in an orderly and uniform manner in the EU without State aid.[66] Further, the BRRD establishes the principle that private investors in banks must pick up the first costs arising out of banks' poor risk management, before EU countries and their taxpayers are called on for financial support.[67] The BRRD contains binding provisions on loss absorbency in the form of bail-in of shareholders, creditors and, if necessary, depositors not protected by law (deposits exceeding €100,000) up to a maximum of 8% of the institution's total assets, which in the past would have covered all eventualities.[68] The resolution authorities can decide to sell the bank as a going concern, create a bridge institution, hive off assets, bail-in creditors and adopt precautionary recapitalisation in a form of private bail-in or recourse to public support in a form of State aid.

The BRRD has been under criticism for lack of harmonised regimes in the application of bail-in tools: a proposal to amend the existing rules has been advanced to strengthen the harmonisation process of national bank insolvency procedures in order to facilitate orderly intervention and uniformity of regulatory treatment.[69] The proposal aims to create a minimum level playing field for banks and to foster prudential treatment of Non-performing

65 Thomas F. Huertas, 'From Bail-Out to Bail-In: Are Banks Becoming Safe to Fail?' (2014) 29(8) *Journal of International Banking and Financial Law* 494.
66 Karel Lannoo, 'Bank State Aid under BRRD and SRM' (2014) 17 *Financial Regulation International* 6.
67 Vincent O'Sullivan and Stephen Kinsella, 'A New Era for Crisis Management for EU Banks' (2014) 17 *Financial Regulation International* 1.
68 Ioannis Kokkoris and Rodrigo Olivares-Caminal, 'Resolution of Banks and the State Aid Regime' in Jens-Hinrich Binder and Dalvinder Singh (eds), *Bank Resolution: The European Regime* (OUP 2016) 304–305.
69 Proposal for a Directive of the European Parliament and of the Council amending Directive 2014/59/EU of the European Parliament and of the Council as regards the ranking of unsecured debt instruments in insolvency hierarchy, Brussels, 23 November 2016, COM(2016) 853 final; Proposal for a Directive of the European Parliament and of the Council amending Directive 2014/59/EU on loss-absorbing and recapitalisation capacity of credit institutions and investment firms and amending Directive 98/26/EC, Directive 2002/47/EC, Directive 2012/30/EU, Directive 2011/35/EU, Directive 2005/56/EC, Directive 2004/25/EC and Directive 2007/36/EC (Brussels, 23 November 2016) COM(2016) 852 final.

Loans (NPLs): banks should be incentivised to deal with NPLs at an early stage to avoid the origination of high volume of non-performing assets. As mentioned, the rules contained in the BRRD are largely flexible to allow Member States to adopt the policy measures necessary to protect the public interest, even if the Directive does not define the boundaries of 'public interest' in the context of deciding to provide public support.[70]

For instance, the precautionary recapitalisation of Banca Monte dei Paschi di Siena (MPS) raised doubts on the suitability of the public measures to restore the equity of the bank due to the lack of clarity of the interpretation of article 32(4)(d) of the BRRD about the necessary aid.[71] Specifically, the BRRD does not provide a clear definition of the 'interest to preserve financial stability and remedy a serious disturbance in the economy'.[72] In addition, the distinction between precautionary recapitalisation and extraordinary public support is not entirely clear, since article 32 of the BRRD considers these concepts interchangeable, while in theory they should be treated as different tools.[73] Article 32(4) of the BRRD provides criteria for the failing or likely to fail (FOLTF) credit institutions, and the concept of solvency should refer to these provisions.[74] However, the concepts of solvency and FOLTF do not coincide, raising doubts in the application of preventive measures to resolve distressed banks.[75] It can be argued that the BRRD rules open room for interpretation of the applicable regime in a way that may not be consistent with the public interest. Another key innovation of the BRRD is the requirement to designate resolution authorities (Bank of England in the UK) with all the powers necessary to apply the resolution tools to institutions and entities.[76] This includes the power to take control of an institution under resolution and exercise all the rights and powers conferred upon the shareholders. The resolution tools aim to preserve financial stability and to protect public funds by minimising reliance on extraordinary public financial support. The resolution authorities intervene if the determination that the institution is failing or is likely to fail has been made by the competent authority.

---

70 Stefano Micossi, Ginevra Bruzzone and Miriam Cassella, 'Fine-Tuning the Use of Bail-In to Promote a Stronger EU Financial System' CEPS Special Report No. 136 (April 2016) 16–17.

71 Benoit Mesnard, Marcel Magnus and Alienor Anne Claire Duvillet-Margerit, 'The Precautionary Recapitalisation of Monte dei Paschi di Siena' (European Parliament Briefing, 6 July 2017) 3. See also European Commission, *State Aid: Commission Authorises Precautionary Recapitalisation of Italian Bank Monte dei Paschi di Siena* (Press Release 4 July 2017) 2.

72 Rodrigo Olivares-Caminal and Costanza Russo, 'Precautionary Recapitalization: Time for a Review' European Parliament, Note provided in Advance of the Public Hearing with the Chair of the Single Resolution Board in ECON (11 July 2017) 10.

73 Christos V. Gortsos, 'Last Resort Lending to Solvent Credit Institutions in the Euro Area before and after the Establishment of the Single Supervisory Mechanism (SSM)' Paper presented at the European Central Bank (ECB) Legal Conference: 'From Monetary Union to Banking Union, on the Way to Capital Markets Union: New Opportunities for European integration' held in Frankfurt (1–2 September 2015) 6, available at <https://ssrn.com/abstract=2688953> (accessed 21 June 2020).

74 EBA Single Rulebook Q&A (2015_1777) available at <http://www.eba.europa.eu/single-rule-book-qa/-/qna/view/publicId/2015_1777> (accessed 19 June 2020).

75 World Bank-FinSAC, 'Understanding Bank Recovery and Resolution in the EU: A Guidebook to the BRRD' (April 2017) 106, available at <http://pubdocs.worldbank.org/en/609571482207234996/FinSAC-BRRD-Guidebook.pdf> (accessed 16 June 2020). It is pointed out that 'the FOLTF definition used under the BRRD is rather vague (and it will be difficult in practice to define the point of non-viability) but gives the required discretion to intervene early enough'.

76 Jens-Hinrich Binder, 'Resolution Planning and Structural Bank Reform within the Banking Union' (2014) SAFE Working Paper, No. 81, 7–8, available at <https://www.econstor.eu/bitstream/10419/106149/1/815411138.pdf> (accessed 29 June 2020).

In addition, all Member States must set up national resolution funds with resources which after ten years must amount to 1% of insured deposits.[77] The BRRD establishes a resolution fund financed by contributions from banks. The fund should reach at least 1% of the amount of covered deposits of all the locally authorised institutions, with the possibility to set target levels in excess of that amount (by 31 December 2024). The fund can only be used to resolve a bank and to contribute to a bank under resolution only after equity and liabilities equal to 8% of total assets have been bailed-in, and its use cannot exceed 5% of total liabilities (article 44.5). In this context, it is also pertinent to consider the functions of Single Point of Entry (SPE) and Multiple Point of Entry (MPE) resolution. In SPE case, the home authority resolves the entire bank from the top-level holding company. In MPE case, home and host authorities resolve different entities simultaneously, which is more adapted to banks with separately capitalised subsidiaries.

The BRRD provides other measures such as (1) early intervention, (2) the removal of management, (3) the appointment of a temporary administrator, (4) the bridge institution tool, (5) the sale of business tool and (6) the asset separation (bad bank) tool. Article 42.1 of the BRRD states that authorities will be vested with appropriate powers to be able to undertake these measures, 'without obtaining the consent of the shareholders of the institutions under resolution or any third party other than the bridge institution, and without complying with any procedural requirements under company or securities law'. On this point, the BRRD requires that shareholders and certain groups of bondholders will have to accept a write-down on their claims (bail-in) before a bail-out intervention. It is possible for Member States to inject further public funds in case of a systemic crisis in the form of guarantees for new lending or as a precautionary injection of capital. However, as has been observed, 'this would only reinforce the existing link between problems in the banking sector and the sustainability of member states' public debt'.[78] Further, the BRRD rules require a lengthy process of adoption, a gap that reveals potential difficulties of the new insolvency regime being suitable of resolving the future crisis.

The new regulatory architecture for failing banks raises doubt about the effectiveness of restructuring tools introduced in the EU bank resolution regime. The provisions on bail-in and precautionary recapitalisation show how credit institutions rely on national supervision and public financial support. As Donnelly noted, 'Banking Union still relies significantly on national rather than European administrative and financial resources to ensure local financial stability, so that resilience remains asymmetric'.[79] It can be observed that an international insolvency regime should address fruitfully these issues establishing a common regulatory toolkit resulting from the different prevailing models.[80]

---

77 John Raymond LaBrosse, Rodrigo Olivares-Caminal and Dalvinder Singh, 'The EU Bank Recovery and Resolution Directive—Some Observations on the Financing Arrangements' (2014) 15(3–4) *Journal of Banking Regulation* 218–219.

78 Sebastian Dullien, 'How to Complete Europe's Banking Union' European Council on Foreign Relations, Policy Brief (2 July 2014) 8.

79 Shawn Donnelly, 'Liberal Economic Nationalism, Financial Stability, and Commission Leniency in Banking Union' (2017) 21(2) *Journal of Economic Policy Reform* 170.

80 Matthias Lehmann, 'Bail-In and Private International Law: How to Make Bank Resolution Measures Effective across Borders' (2017) 66(1) *International & Comparative Law Quarterly* 108.

14.4.1 Recovery plans and resolution plans

The BRRD regulates recovery and resolution plans. Credit institutions need to draw up and update recovery plans to (1) assess potential vulnerabilities and (2) prepare measures to restore their financial position in case of 'significant deterioration' of financial position. Recovery plans are based on various scenarios including both idiosyncratic problems and market-wide stress (e.g. normal and adverse stress scenario), and they are assessed by competent supervisory authorities, which may require amendments to remedy 'material deficiencies'.[81] Articles 10–14 of the BRRD and articles 8–9 of the SRM Regulation regulate resolution planning. In this scenario, resolution authorities need to draw up and update 'resolution plans' to prepare swift and effective resolution action in case 'conditions for resolution' under BRRD are met. In addition, resolution authorities of home and host countries need to develop 'group resolution plans' to facilitate consistent approaches in case of groups.[82]

The BRRD and the SRM Regulation set the process for resolution planning: competent resolution authorities need to draft and update 'resolution plans' to prepare swift and effective resolution action in case 'conditions for resolution' under BRRD are met.[83] Since the key objective of the BRRD is to favour private sector loss absorbency for failing banks through a mechanism of eligible liabilities [minimum requirements for own funds and eligible liabilities (MREL) system],[84] resolution authorities maintain discretion to adopt alternative measures for recapitalising banks in crisis. The key provisions of BRRD are (1) preparation – recovery and resolution planning; (2) early intervention; and (3) resolution – objectives and triggers, tools, depositor preference and co-operation in group recovery and resolution. As mentioned in the previous section, the BRRD tools are (1) resolution, sale of business, bridge institution, asset separation and bail-in; (2) write-down or conversion of capital instruments and (3) government stabilisation – public equity support and temporary public ownership.

Under the 'preparation' head, firms would be required to draw up recovery plans and update them annually. Both supervisory and resolution authorities are involved in the preparatory stage. Under the 'early intervention' head, authorities would have the power to appoint special managers to a firm either to replace or to temporarily work with the firm's management to restore its financial soundness and to reorganise the firm so as to ensure its viability at an early stage.

Under the 'resolution' head, there are powers and tools to ensure the continuity of essential services and to manage the failure of a firm in an orderly way. The resolution tools include a sale of business tool, a bridge institution tool, an asset separation tool and a debt write-down (or bail-in) tool. During the resolution phase, the resolution authority would have power to (1) take control of a firm and exercise all the rights conferred on the shareholders or owners of the firm; (2) transfer shares and other instruments of ownership issued by the firm and debt instruments issued by the firm; (3) transfer to another undertaking or

81 Matthias Haentjens, 'Bank Recovery and Resolution: An Overview of International Initiatives' (2014) 3 *International Insolvency Law Review* 255–256.
82 Articles 15–16 of the BRRD introduce the 'assessment of resolvability' with comprehensive powers to remedy impediments to resolvability under Articles 17–18 of the BRRD and Article 10 of the SRM Regulation.
83 Jens-Hinrich Binder, 'Resolution: Concepts, Requirements and Tools' in Jens-Hinrich Binder and Dalvinder Singh (eds), *Bank Resolution: The European Regime* (OUP 2016).
84 According to the BRRD, all banks are required to meet a minimum requirement for own funds and eligible liabilities (MREL) to ensure that sufficient financial resources are available for write-down or conversion into equity.

person-specified rights, assets and liabilities of the firm; and (4) remove or replace the firm's senior management. The BRRD and the SRM state that a recovery plan should consider the systemic importance of the credit institution and its interconnectedness, and the degree to which support would be credibly available to address the deterioration.[85] Further, the resolution tools should be applied before any public injection of capital or equivalent extraordinary public financial support to an institution.[86] However, if the recovery and resolution plans aim to avoid the recourse to bail-out plans or State aid, in the case of MPS the national authorities demonstrated to rely upon government financial assistance to restore the viability of the bank.[87]

14.4.2 *The bail-in tool*

Looking at the BRRD rules, the major innovation is the bail-in rule of up to 8% of liabilities. The bail-in tool works when losses affect the minimum capital base: common equity Tier 1 items are reduced in proportion to the losses and additional Tier 1, Tier 2 instruments and certain other liabilities (e.g. senior debt) are converted into capital.[88] A bail-in requires that banks' balance sheets have sufficient liabilities that can be bailed-in, in a progressive and hierarchical manner. The bail-in tool is considered as a workable measure of write-down or conversion of debt to equity; it mirrors debt-equity swaps for non-financial companies without using conventional bankruptcy procedures; internalises the consequences of failure within a financial institution and its immediate counterparties; and reduces moral hazard and incentivises creditors to exercise market discipline. In this respect, the Financial Stability Board (FSB) published on October 2014 the report 'Key Attributes of Effective Resolution Regimes for Financial Institutions' that contains recommendations for a greater specificity with respect to write-downs of creditors' claims and which assets should be exempted from write-downs.[89] From a regulatory perspective, these recommendations should strengthen the predictability of the bail-in procedures under the SRM; however, the success and credibility of bail-in mechanism should be tested when unexpected losses may be not be absorbed by unsecured debt holders. In this regard, the question at stake is whether there is a need for relatively high capital buffers. In addition, the workability of bail-in tool should be tested in the presence of (1) inadequate levels of eligible liabilities; (2) liabilities governed by foreign law; (3) ability to issue requisite number of shares; (4) treatment of

85 Recital 21 in the preamble to BRRD Directive and Article 10(2) of the SRM.
86 Recital 55 in the preamble to BRRD Directive.
87 Benoit Mesnard and Marcel Magnus, 'Banca Monte dei Paschi di Siena: State of Play' Note for the Banking Union Working Group (8 February 2017) 1, available at <http://www.europarl.europa.eu/RegData/etudes/BRIE/2017/587392/IPOL_BRI(2017)587392_EN.pdf> (accessed 23 June 2020).
88 Lannoo (n 66).
89 FSB, 'Key Attributes of Effective Resolution Regimes for Financial Institutions' (15 October 2014) available at <https://www.fsb.org/2014/10/key-attributes-of-effective-resolution-regimes-for-financial-institutions-2/> (accessed 4 July 2020). The Key Attribute 3.5 provides that 'powers to carry out bail-in within resolution should enable resolution authorities to: (1) write down in a manner that respects the hierarchy of claims in liquidation equity or other instruments of ownership of the firm, unsecured and uninsured creditor claims to the extent necessary to absorb the losses; and to (2) convert into equity or other instruments of ownership of the firm under resolution (or any successor in resolution or the parent company within the same jurisdiction), all or parts of unsecured and uninsured creditor claims in a manner that respects the hierarchy of claims in liquidation; (3) upon entry into resolution, convert or write-down any contingent convertible or contractual bail-in instruments whose terms had not been triggered prior to entry into resolution and treat the resulting instruments in line with (i) or (ii)'.

derivatives; and (5) contingent and non-quantified liabilities, and set-off. In essence, the bail-in tool may be applied to all liabilities other than (1) covered deposits and secured liabilities; (2) liabilities arising through holding client assets; (3) liabilities to unrelated institutions; (4) liabilities arising from designated systems with residual maturity; and (5) liabilities to employees (except for bonuses), critical trade creditors, preferred tax and so-cial security claims.[90] By contrast, the limitations of bail-in include (1) the need to establish worst-case losses, (2) application to deposit-funded banks, (3) complexities of derivatives, (4) issues of foreign law debt and (5) potential for diverging incentives of home parent and host subsidiary authorities.[91]

A possible issue in developing an efficient bail-in mechanism is the risk of contagion from bail-in of a single institution, due to other financial institutions holding outstanding debt of the failed institution.[92] Another issue concerns the fact that 'bail-in regimes will fail to eradicate the need for an injection of public funds where there is a threat of systemic collapse, because a number of banks have simultaneously entered into difficulties, or in the event of the failure of a large complex cross-border bank, except in those cases where failure was clearly idiosyncratic'.[93]

The bail-in tool must ensure that financial instruments (sufficient amount of bail-inable debt)[94] can be written down or converted to equity to ensure an orderly resolution of the failing institution in all cases. Bail-inable debt can be defined as a tool issued *ex ante* and specially designed to absorb conversion or write-down losses subordinated debt.[95] In essence, bail-inable debt is a form of pre-paid insurance for bank failure.[96] As Huertas claimed, 'there is a need to be sure that bank has amount of reserve capital outstanding sufficient to recapitalise the bank'.[97] On this view, resolvability hinges on the structure of liabilities by ensuring that long-term illiquid assets, i.e. loans, can be converted into short-term liquid liabilities, i.e. deposits.[98] The bail-in is one of the options to resolve a bank.

However, resolution authorities may contribute to the institution under resolution to cover losses or shore up its capital (article 44 (4)). But this can only be done after the 8% bail-in threshold is reached, to an amount not exceeding 5% of liabilities. Member States can also provide extraordinary public financial support through additional financial stabi-lisation tools, such as equity support and temporary public ownership, but again as a last resort, after all other measures have been exploited, and following State aid rules (articles 56–58). Bail-in is a key resolution instrument in the BRRD and in the SRM: the rationale

90 On this discussion Chris Bates, 'Ending Too-Big-To-Fail in Europe' Lecture given at the Centre for Commercial Law Studies, Queen Mary University of London, London (25 November 2014).
91 Charles Randell, 'The Road to Cross-Border Resolution of Financial Institutions' Lecture delivered at the Centre for Commercial Law Studies, Queen Mary University, London (13 February 2015).
92 Thomas Conlon and John Cotter, 'Anatomy of a Bail-In' (2014) 15 *Journal of Financial Stability* 258–259.
93 Emilios Avgouleas and Charles A. Goodhart, 'A Critical Evaluation of Bail-In as a Bank Recapitalisation Mechanism' Centre for Economic Policy Research, Discussion Paper No. 10065 (July 2014) 19.
94 Charles Goodhart, 'Ratio Controls Need Reconsideration' (2013) 9 *Journal of Financial Stability* 449, where it is provided a definition of bail-inable bond as 'one which specifies in the contract how, and under what conditions, the holder shall be required to bear the costs of bank failure and/or to put up additional money to recapitalise the bank'.
95 Avgouleas and Goodhart (n 93) 7.
96 Jeffrey N. Gordon and George Ringe, 'Resolution in the European Banking Union: A Transatlantic Perspective on What It Would Take' Oxford Legal Research Paper Series No. 18/2014 (April 2014).
97 Thomas F. Huertas, *Safe to Fail: How Resolution Will Revolutionise Banking* (Palgrave Macmillan 2014) 113–114.
98 Ibid., 6.

is to provide a mechanism to return an insufficiently solvent bank to 'balance sheet stability' at the expense of some of its creditors without the necessity for external capital injection. On this view, Avgouleas and Goodhart argue that the 'bail-in regimes will fail to eradicate the need for an injection of public funds where there is a threat of systemic collapse, because a number of banks have simultaneously entered into difficulties, or in the event of the failure of a large complex cross-border bank, except in those cases where failure was clearly idiosyncratic'.[99] Since the BRRD leaves broad discretion to national authorities to adopt domestic policy measures to rescue failing banks, it is difficult to clear up the legacy of bail-out intervention.

14.4.3 *MREL and total loss absorbing capacity (TLAC)*

Bail-in is complemented and supported by requirements for banks, especially for systemically important ones, to structure their liabilities in a way that a sufficient part thereof consists of debts that can be converted into equity in the case the bank faces large losses that wipe out its regulatory capital. An example of such liabilities are contingent convertible bonds that are automatically bailed-in when their conversion threshold is reached and other subordinated bonds with a long maturity date that can be converted into equity via the exercise of bail-in powers by the relevant authorities. As we will see, the principle is for global systemically important institutions (G-SIIs) to have approximately as many loss-absorbing liabilities as the basic capital requirement of 8% of risk-weighted assets (RWAs) plus any Pillar 2A capital imposed by their regulator. This means that even if a G-SII suffers losses equal to the sum of its capital buffers, basic capital and Pillar 2A capital (thus reducing its equity to zero and leading to the cancellation of its shares), the conversion of the eligible liabilities into equity means that the G-SII can continue as a going concern. After the conversion, the recapitalised G-SII will have equity capital equal to 8% of RWAs plus its Pillar 2A capital requirement, and therefore, it will satisfy the minimum capital requirements and will be able to continue its business and then gradually rebuild its capital buffers.

On the international level, the FSB has introduced the concept of TLAC which is a requirement for globally active and systemically important banks (G-SIBs) to have equity and eligible liabilities equal to the higher of 18% of their RWAs or 6.75% of their total exposures.[100] This requirement encompasses the 8% basic capital requirement, and thus, Common Equity Tier 1 (CET1) capital, other Tier 1 capital and Tier 2 capital also count towards TLAC, but this is not the case for the part of CET1 capital that satisfies capital buffers. In other words, a G-SIB that satisfies its capital requirements must also have liabilities eligible to absorb losses equal to 10% of its RWAs. The implementation of TLAC is in two phases. The full requirement will apply from the beginning of 2022. A requirement to have TLAC equal to the higher of 16% of RWAs or 6% of total exposures applies from the beginning of 2019 until the end of 2021. The criteria for an instrument to qualify as an eligible liability are (i) it must be fully paid-up; (ii) it must be unsecured; (iii) it must not be subject to set-off or netting; (iv) it must have a minimum remaining maturity of at least one year; (v) it must not be redeemable by its holder prior to maturity; and (vi) it must not have been funded by

99 Avgouleas and Goodhart (n 93) 19–21.
100 FSB, 'Principles on Loss-absorbing and Recapitalisation Capacity of G-SIBs in Resolution: Total Loss-Absorbing Capacity (TLAC) Term Sheet' (2015) <https://www.fsb.org/wp-content/uploads/TLAC-Principles-and-Term-Sheet-for-publication-final.pdf> (accessed 1 July 2020).

the G-SIB itself or a related party to it. Certain liabilities are excluded even if they satisfy the above criteria, e.g. any protected deposits, any deposits with maturity of less than one year, any liabilities arising other than from contract or from derivatives and operational liabilities on which the performance of critical functions depends.

The EU pre-empted action by the FSB by introducing the concept of MREL, as part of the BRRD.[101] MREL goes beyond TLAC, and hence, compliance with the EU frame-work also constitutes compliance with the FSB's guidance. In principle, MREL applies to all EU banks. However, MREL consists of different components and only applies in full to G-SIIs, in line with the scope of TLAC. The component of MREL that applies to all EU banks is called the loss absorption amount which includes all regulatory capital and buffers and is satisfied by the same instruments.[102] In essence, this component does not impose any additional obligation on banks: any bank that satisfies its capital requirements, discussed in Chapter 11, automatically satisfies this component of MREL. Small banks, which can be allowed to go into liquidation without causing systemic risk, fall into this category. The second component of MREL is the recapitalisation component which must be sufficient to satisfy Pillar 1 (i.e. the basic capital ratio of 8% of RWAs) and Pillar 2A cap-ital requirements as well as any applicable leverage ratio requirement.[103] This component cannot be satisfied by using any capital that satisfies the first component or capital buffers. The third component which applies only if it is necessary to restore market confidence and is known as the market confidence charge is equal to the total capital buffers (but again it cannot be satisfied by the capital used for the buffers).[104] If fully implemented, it would mean that the institution, after the conversion of eligible liabilities into equity, would satisfy in full not only Pillar 1 and 2A capital requirements, but also the capital buffer requirements. The scope of MREL eligible liabilities is similar to that under TLAC but somewhat narrower.[105] TLAC instruments do not have to be legally subordinated to ordinary unsecured claims, but there must be some form of subordination to opera-tional liabilities, whereas MREL eligible instruments must rank below ordinary unsecured claims.[106] To that effect, the EU has introduced a class of non-preferred senior debt in the hierarchy of creditors in insolvency.[107]

The UK resolution authority, the Bank of England, has decided to implement MREL by applying the recapitalisation component to all UK-based G-SIBs and D-SIBs (domestic systemically important banks).[108] Thus, from the beginning of 2022, the total MREL re-quirements (first and second component) will be equal to the higher of the following: 2 × (Pillar 1 capital + Pillar 2A capital) or 2 × applicable leverage ratio requirement, or 6.75%

---

101 BRRD, art 45.
102 See Commission Delegated Regulation (EU) 2016/1450 of 23 May 2016 supplementing Directive 2014/59/EU of the European Parliament and of the Council with regard to regulatory technical standards specifying the criteria relating to the methodology for setting the minimum requirement for own funds and eligible liabilities (2016) OJ L 237/1, art 1.
103 Delegated Regulation (EU) 2016/1450, art 2 (5)–(6).
104 Delegated Regulation (EU) 2016/1450, art 2 (7)–(8).
105 The general eligibility requirements are set out in BRRV, article 45 (4).
106 FSB, 'Review of the Technical Implementation of the Total Loss-Absorbing Capacity (TLAC) Standard' (2019) 18–19 <https://www.fsb.org/wp-content/uploads/P020719.pdf> (accessed 1 July 2020).
107 Directive (EU) 2017/2399 of the European Parliament and of the Council of 12 December 2017 amending Directive 2014/59/EU as regards the ranking of unsecured debt instruments in insolvency hierarchy (2017) OJ L 345/96, art 1 replacing article 108 of Directive 2014/59/EU.
108 The relevant power is conferred on the Bank of England by the Banking Act 2009, s 3A (4).

of total exposures.[109] It is worth noting that the implementation of MREL by the Bank of England is in line with TLAC; this is also the approach recommended by the EBA so that the EU requirements are harmonised with international standards.[110]

The MREL/TLAC framework can potentially bring two types of benefits. First, it can facilitate the implementation of bail-in and hence the resolution of systemic institutions without recourse to public funds.[111] Second, it can increase market discipline on banks and their senior management, as it forces institutions to issue eligible debt instruments such as subordinated bonds, which tend to carry a high interest rate. This, in theory, allows the capital markets to price the level of risk posed by each systemic institution and incentivises institutions to manage their risks prudently to keep their cost of capital low. However, it is also subject to limitations. One possible limitation is that the relevant requirements are not robust enough, as argued by Admati and Hellwig who estimate that a ratio of up to 30% of RWAs is necessary.[112] Another limitation stems from the fact that its successful implementation relies on the availability of investors who are interested in purchasing eligible instruments and on the political context that determines the use of bail-in powers, as discussed later in this chapter. Finally, banks that issue bonds to satisfy MREL requirement may face legal risk if the eligibility requirements or bail-in rules change in the future, as indicated by the (unsuccessful) litigation faced by Lloyds in connection with its decision to redeem certain contingent convertible bonds that it had issued.[113]

14.4.4 The mechanics of SRM and the Single Resolution Board

The Banking Union introduces a centralised approach for dealing with Eurozone crisis management. The establishment of the SRM – which includes a 'Single Resolution Fund' (SRF)[114] – provides a unified bank resolution scheme and a standard regulatory framework

109 See Bank of England, 'The Bank of England's Approach to Setting a Minimum Requirement for Own Funds and Eligible Liabilities (MREL)' Statement of Policy (June 2018) [4.10] <https://www.bankofengland.co.uk/-/media/boe/files/paper/2018/statement-of-policy-boes-approach-to-setting-mrel-2018.pdf?la=en&hash=BC4499AF9CF063A3D8024BE5C050CB1F39E2EBC1> (accessed 11 July 2020).

110 EBA, 'Interim Report on MREL: Report on Implementation and Design of the MREL Framework' EBA-Op-2016-12 (2016) 12–18 <https://eba.europa.eu/documents/10180/1360107/EBA+Interim+report+on+MREL> (accessed 12 July 2020).

111 For instance, Chiu and Wilson opine that 'the MREL regime should be supported for its risk-sharing ethos'. See Iris H.-Y. Chiu and Joanna Wilson, *Banking Law and Regulation* (OUP 2019) 392.

112 See Anat Admati and Martin Hellwig, *The Bankers' New Clothes: What's Wrong with Banking and What to Do about It* (Princeton University Press 2014).

113 *BNY Mellon Corporate Trustee Services Ltd v LBG Capital No. 1 Plc* [2016] UKSC 29. Lloyds had issued contingent convertible bonds at a 10% interest rate per annum to satisfy regulatory requirements. One of the terms of the bonds allowed Lloyds to redeem them on the occurrence of a capital disqualification event. After a change in rules, the threshold of conversion of the bonds into equity was no longer satisfactory. Lloyds redeemed the bonds on the basis of the capital disqualification event clause. The bondholders challenged the redemption. At first instance, the court found for the bondholders. However, on appeal both the Court of Appeal and Supreme Court ruled that the redemption was not a breach of contract, as the relevant clause had to be construed in the light of the surrounding regulatory capital context. The decision therefore provides some assurance to banks regarding relevant legal risk.

114 The Single Resolution Fund (SRF) was established according to Regulation (EU) No. 806/2014 as a single financing arrangement for all the Member States participating in the Single Supervisory Mechanism and in the Single Resolution Mechanism. The SRF is foreseen as a common financial backstop. See Council Implementing Regulation (EU) 2015/81 of 19 December 2014 specifying uniform conditions of application of Regulation (EU) No. 806/2014 of the European Parliament and of the Council with regard to *ex ante* contributions to the Single Resolution Fund.

for cross-border resolvability.[115] This means common rules and pre-established procedures for failing financial institutions in the Single Supervisory Mechanism (SSM) area, while the BRRD applies to all credit institutions in the EU, including UK credit institutions.

The SRM is structured into a centralised resolution authority (Single Resolution Board or SRB) and a Single Bank Resolution Fund which provides mutualised private financing of bank resolution tools. In terms of supervision, the SSM places the ECB directly in charge as the supervisor for the largest Eurozone banking institutions.[116] The ECB also has the right to oversee smaller Eurozone banks that it does not supervise directly: in substance, the ECB is the direct supervisor of large cross-border banks for the entire Eurozone banking system.[117] The SRM applies the rules of the BRRD to those states covered by the SSM. The SRM Regulation is complemented by an Intergovernmental Agreement (IGA) between Member States that participate in the SSM on the transfer and mutualisation of contributions into the SRF.[118] The SRM has significant competences in defining resolution plans, organising its implementation and funding. As Hadjiemmanuil observed, 'the SRM's competences involve questions of legal and constitutional nature, having critical effects on the use of the public funds, which has fiscal implications. The excessive discretion provided for the SRM's operation goes beyond prudential policy and mere technocracy'.[119] The SRM should ensure that – not withstanding stronger supervision – if a bank faced serious difficulties, its resolution could be managed efficiently with minimal costs to taxpayers and the real economy.[120]

The BRRD and the SRM introduced a comprehensive set of resolution tools for application in all Member States and significantly reinforced the regime for cross-border co-operation within the EU.[121] The ECB is the competent authority responsible for supervising failing banks and works in relationship with other authorities, namely, the European Commission and national central banks. The BRRD and the SRM for Eurozone banks provide a regulatory framework for the resolution of banks that requires senior creditors to participate in losses, if necessary, instead of or ahead of a bank receiving sovereign support.[122] As a rule, group resolution efforts are to be co-ordinated by the consolidated

---

115 Rosa M. Lastra, *International Financial and Monetary Law* (OUP 2015) 366–370.

116 The SSM is composed of the ECB and the national competent authorities, with the ECB in charge of its effective and consistent functioning (Article 6.1). The scope of application of the SSM Regulation comprises all euro area Member States on a compulsory basis and non-euro area Member States that voluntarily enter into a 'close cooperation' with the ECB (Article 7). The SSM Regulation confers 'specific tasks' related to the prudential supervision of credit institutions to the ECB. See Commission release Statement/14/77 (20 March 2014).

117 Eilís Ferran and Valia Babis, 'The European Single Supervisory Mechanism' (2013) 13(2) *Journal of Corporate Law Studies* 255. The authors note that 'designing the SSM has been an exercise in sophisticated legal gymnastics to fit within the existing Treaty framework, as well as high stakes political maneuvering and pragmatic decision-making'.

118 The Intergovernmental Agreement (IGA) on the Transfer and Mutualisation of Contributions to the Single Resolution Fund was signed on 21 May 2014. See ECOFIN 342 (8457/14), 14 May 2014 for the publication of this IGA in the website of the EU Council. The IGA was signed by all EU Member States, except Sweden and the UK.

119 Christos Hadjiemmanuil, 'The Directive and the New European Regulatory Infrastructure' Paper presented at 'The International Symposium on Bank Recovery and Resolution in Europe – 'The EU Bank Recovery and Resolution Directive in Context', University of Tübingen (19 October 2013).

120 Charles Randell, 'European Banking Union and Bank Resolution' (2013) 7(1) *Law and Financial Markets Review* 30.

121 See BRRD, Titles V (on 'Cross-Border Group Resolution' within the EU) and VI (on 'Relations with Third Countries').

122 It is important to note that covered bonds are exempt from bail-in under BRRD and may benefit from resolution tools.

group level resolution authority, with only limited scope for independent resolution action by national resolution authorities for individual group companies.[123]

It is worth noting that the BRRD and the SRM have favoured the centralisation of bank supervision and resolution. The SSM and the SRM, within their respective mandates, should be able to efficiently deal with the proliferation of cross-border banking and any possible negative implications. However, the EU mechanism for resolving failing banks is still work in progress and needs to be fully tested. State-level deposit insurers are not viable inside a monetary union because the liquidation of small banks could overwhelm the capacity of national deposit insurance. Mutualisation of deposit insurance requires full harmonisation of insolvency laws because the effectiveness of the bank liquidation process will have an impact on the financial situation of the deposit insurance over which insured depositors have a legal claim. Nieto and Wall observed that 'given that the barriers to cross-border banking are likely to fall, the EU should consider what sort of banking structure would provide the best combination of an integrated financial system and a financial system in which the banks are neither too large to supervise nor too large to safely fail'.[124] On this view, rules will have impact on where banks shed operations due to cost factors of maintaining operations and risk will likely migrate to less regulated local entities in a risk race to bottom.

The SRM Regulation ('Regulation')[125] creates a 'Mechanism' and gives a fundamental role to the European Commission. According to article 2 of the Regulation, the SRM will apply to the resolution of (1) credit institutions; (2) parent undertakings established in one of the participating Member States, including financial holding companies and mixed financial holding companies when subject to consolidated supervision carried out by the ECB; and (3) investment firms and financial institutions established in participating Member States when they are covered by the consolidated supervision of the parent undertaking carried out by the ECB.

Article 16 of the Regulation regulates the resolution process: (1) the ECB signals when a significant bank or cross-border group in a participating Member State is FOLTF[126]; (2) the SRB[127] determines that there is no reasonable prospect of a timely private sector rescue and also that a resolution action is in the public interest; and (3) the SRB with the help of the relevant national resolution authorities prepares and adopts the resolution scheme.[128]

---

123 Jens-Hinrich Binder, 'To Ring-Fence or Not, and How? Strategic Questions for Post-Crisis Banking Reform in Europe' (December 2014) available at <http://ssrn.com/abstract=2543860> (accessed 16 June 2020). See generally BRRD, articles 87 (general principles), 88 (resolution colleges), 91 and 92 (procedural and substantive requirements for resolution action in relation to groups). On the conditions for independent action by host authorities in this context, see articles 91(8) and 92(4).

124 Maria Nieto and Larry D. Wall, 'Cross-border Banking on the Two Sides of the Atlantic: Does It Have an Impact on Bank Crisis Management?' FRB Atlanta Working Paper No. 2015-11, 21.

125 Regulation (EU) No. 806/2014 of the European Parliament and of the Council of 15 July 2014 establishing uniform rules and a uniform procedure for the resolution of credit institutions and certain investment firms in the framework of a Single Resolution Mechanism and a Single Resolution Fund and amending Regulation (EU) No. 1093/2010 OJ L 225 (30 July 2014).

126 The Single Resolution Board can also act on its own initiative in pulling this trigger.

127 The SRB is an EU agency with legal personality: It comprises a chair [a vice chair], four full-time executive members and a member appointed by each participating Member State, representing the national resolution authority.

128 The adoption of a resolution scheme shall inevitably involve a margin of discretion. On 8 October 2014, the EU Commission adopted a Delegated Regulation on the provisional system of instalments for contributions to cover the administrative expenditures of the Single Resolution Board under the Single Resolution Mechanism Regulation. The Delegated Regulation sets out (1) the system for the payment of instalments during

The Regulation provides specific rules on the predictability of loss allocation. Article 27.5 of the Regulation addresses the predictability of the values of claims on banks by stating that 'in exceptional circumstances, where the bail-in tool is applied, certain liabilities may be excluded or partially excluded from application of the write-down or conversion powers where (b) the exclusion is strictly necessary and is proportionate to achieve the continuity of critical functions and core business lines in a manner that maintains the ability of the institution under resolution to continue key operations, services and transactions; (c) the exclusion is strictly necessary and proportionate to avoid giving rise to widespread contagion, in particular as regards eligible deposits held by natural persons and micro-, small- and medium-sized enterprises, which would severely disrupt the functioning of financial markets...'. Closer examination of this rule suggests that the resolution authority can exercise discretion in the interpretation of the terms 'exceptional circumstances', 'strictly necessary' and 'severely disrupt'. It can be argued that the EU legislator has considered the 'exceptional circumstances' for balancing the benefits of predictability for creditors about conditions for write-downs of the value of their assets.[129]

In this context, a significant role is played by the SRB. The SRB aims to ensure a coherent and uniform approach to the operation of the resolution rules under the SRM, and it will be responsible for the effective and consistent functioning of the SRM[130] and for undertaking an assessment of an individual institution and to which extent it is resolvable.[131] Under the supervision of the SRB, national resolution authorities are responsible for the execution of the resolution scheme. The SRB monitors the execution of resolution decisions by the national resolution authorities. The SRB also has investigatory and sanctioning powers which it can apply directly to market participants in certain circumstances (SRM Regulation, Arts 32–37b). The SRF is set up under the ownership of the SRB to ensure the availability of medium-term funding support while a bank is being restructured. The SRF can be used for a range of purposes, including providing guarantees, making loans, purchasing assets and providing compensation to shareholders or creditors. It can also be used to provide capital to a bridge bank or asset management vehicle, but it must not be used directly to absorb the losses of a failing institution or for direct recapitalisation.[132] It can be observed that the regulatory framework established by the Banking Union is not fully addressing concerns over complexity and lack of accountability. This means that it seems difficult to realise a harmonious co-existence between the Banking Union and the Single Market since issues of 'jurisdictional domain' haunt the design of the Banking Union.[133]

---

the provisional period, including the methodology for determining instalments to be paid in advance by each significant entity and procedure for collection; (2) the general obligation to pay contributions to cover the administrative expenditures of the Board during the provisional period for all entities falling within the scope of the SRM; (3) the arrangement for the settlement of any difference between the instalments paid in advance on the basis of the provisional system and the contributions as calculated under the final system for administrative contributions; and (4) penalties applicable for late payment and enforcement of the payment obligation.

129 European Shadow Financial Regulatory Committee, 'Complexity and Credibility in the Single Resolution Mechanism' Statement No. 39, London (10 November 2014) 5.

130 Art 6a (1) of the SRM Regulation.

131 Art 8 of the SRM Regulation.

132 Eilís Ferran, 'European Banking Union: Imperfect but It Can Work' (2014) University of Cambridge Faculty of Law, Legal Studies Research Paper Series No. 30, 17.

133 Rosa M. Lastra, 'Banking Union and Single Market: Conflict or Companionship?' (2013) 36(5) *Fordham International Law Journal* 1195–1197. In particular, the euro area, the SSM area, the EU and the EEA

14.5 Stress testing

One of the principal regulatory tools to ensure early detection of financial distress in financial institutions is conducting periodic stress tests. Stress tests are part of the ongoing micro-prudential supervision of banks, and therefore technically, they are not part of the resolution framework. However, they are discussed here because they are closely connected to resolution: they can inform the design of recovery and resolution plans, and they may trigger an intervention by the authorities such as the recapitalisation of the Co-operative Bank in 2014 after it failed a stress test.[134] A stress test can be defined as a form of internal audit whereby a financial institution tests its resilience and capital position in the event of the occurrence of certain adverse scenarios, such as a reduction of real estate prices, currency devaluation, failure of another systemic institution and lack of liquidity in financial markets. A reverse stress test identifies the circumstances that would have to occur for a bank to fail. There are two main types of stress test: those conducted internally by banks themselves and shared with regulators but not with the public and those conducted externally by regulatory authorities which are also made public. Internal stress testing serves two main functions: a corporate governance function, as it can provide useful information to the board, especially independent directors, and improve the risk management function of a bank and a supervisory function as it provides crucial information to the regulator and can lead to an effective regulatory dialogue. External stress testing fulfils these functions as well as an additional one: as the results are made public it enhances market discipline.

Capital Requirements Regulation (CRR) requires EU banks to conduct internal stress testing on a quarterly basis.[135] It must cover at least counterparty credit risk.[136] Banks that have adopted internal models for the calculation of risk under the capital adequacy framework must also subject them to stress testing.[137] The EBA has issued comprehensive guidelines on internal stress testing.[138] In the UK, the PRA requires banks to conduct regular reverse stress testing.[139] There are detailed rules on the scenarios, data and methodologies to be used and on the governance of the process of stress testing, which will only be presented here in brief.[140] Scenarios must be severe but plausible; data must be accurate, timely and complete; and methodologies must not be limited to quantitative modelling but also encompass qualitative elements. The process must be approved and overseen by the board and senior management.

---

represent concentric circles of integration, subject to differentiation and conditionality. A major challenge for the EU is that the needs of a well-functioning single market in financial services cannot be disentangled from the design of the supervisory pillar.

134 Jill Treanor, 'Bank Stress Tests: Co-op Fails as Lloyds and RBS Scrape Through' *The Guardian* (London, 16 December 2014) <https://www.theguardian.com/business/2014/dec/16/bank-stress-tests-co-op-lloyds-rbs> (accessed on 10 July 2020).

135 CRR, art 177.

136 CRR, arts 287 and 290.

137 CRR, art 368.

138 Final guidelines were issued in July 2018. See EBA, 'Guidelines on Institutions' Stress Testing' EBA/GL/2018/04 (2018) <https://eba.europa.eu/documents/10180/2282644/Guidelines+on+institutions+stress+testing+%28EBA-GL-2018-04%29.pdf/2b604bc8-fd08-4b17-ac4a-cdd5e662b802> (accessed on 18 July 2020).

139 PRA Rulebook, Internal Capital Adequacy Assessment: Reverse Stress-Testing.

140 For a detailed discussion, see Chiu and Wilson (above n 111) 462–465.

The potential limitation of internal stress testing is that banks will use excessively optimistic scenarios and methodologies that present their resilience under a positive light in order to avoid regulatory sanctions and support their profit-seeking priorities. This touches on the broader issue of the misalignment of incentives between bank senior management, directors and shareholders, and bank regulators, discussed in Chapter 12. For internal stress testing to be effective and initiate a healthy dialogue with the regulator there must be a relationship of mutual trust between the regulator and the bank managers and personnel conducting the stress testing must internalise the objectives of the regulator and perceive their role as an integral part of the supervisory process rather than as an attempt to defend against compliance risk. Building such relationships and inculcating such internal cultures within financial institutions remains a formidable challenge.

Some of these limitations are mitigated by external stress testing conducted by the regulators. Capital Requirements Directive IV (CRD IV) requires national regulators to conduct annual stress testing for the financial institutions they supervise.[141] In the UK, the main banks that are subject to externally conducted stress testing by the PRA on an annual basis are Barclays, HSBC, Lloyds, Nationwide, RBS, Santander UK and Standard Chartered.[142] These banks are subject to an annual cyclical stress test and a biannual forward-looking stress test that seeks to capture emerging trends and risks.[143] The PRA urges institutions to use its stress test scenarios as the basis to build their own scenarios for the purposes of internal stress testing. Stress testing by the PRA began in 2014, and several issues were identified in certain institutions in 2014, 2015 and 2016. In 2017 and 2018, all PRA-regulated institutions passed the stress test.

In parallel, the EBA conducts stress tests of the whole EU banking system by testing a sample of banks from across the EU, on the basis of its general power to monitor systemic risk.[144] Such testing has been occurring on a biennial basis since 2014 and highlighted the weakness of the MPS bank in 2016 (discussed further in the following section), but only after relevant information had become public knowledge. The main benefits of EBA's EU-wide stress testing are that it permits the detection of trends and vulnerabilities in the EU financial market as a whole and that it supports the convergence of regulatory standards across the Member States. Still, the lack of clear consequences following from the results of EBA's stress testing raises doubts in relation to the effectiveness of this tool.

14.6 Precautionary recapitalisation and State aid

The BRRD provides for the precautionary recapitalisation of 'non-insolvent banks' that experience a distressed scenario. Recapitalisation could preserve financial stability – as a remedy to cover losses for failing banks – in the case of a rescue plan with strict conditionality guaranteed by a pool of investment banks. Recapitalisation aims to give the bank a

---

141 CRD IV, art 100.

142 See Bank of England, 'Financial Stability Report' (Issue 44, November 2018) <https://www.bankofengland. co.uk/-/media/boe/files/financial-stability-report/2018/november-2018.pdf?la=en&hash=7239DE596D-D5DB14BEB17E1141C2CDEB73A8623C#page=9> (accessed 10 June 2020).

143 For an overview of the Bank of England's approach and initiatives, see Bank of England, 'Stress Testing' (Bank of England, 24 June 2019) <https://www.bankofengland.co.uk/stress-testing> (accessed 12 July 2020).

144 For an overview of EBA's EU-wide stress-testing activities and results, see EBA, 'EU-Wide Stress Testing' (EBA) <https://eba.europa.eu/risk-analysis-and-data/eu-wide-stress-testing> (accessed 20 July 2020).

new positive outlook for profitability with the injection of new capital, although it can be interpreted as a sort of temporary public financial assistance.[145] If the equity capital increase fails, the failing bank could need to resort to State aid, which in turn would likely result in the write-down or conversion of the bank's subordinated debt. The recent episodes of bank failures (Venetian banks, Banco Popular Español S.A., Banco Espírito Santo and Piraeus Bank) are cases in point to demonstrate the applicability of bail-in rules to protect national interests.[146]

The controversial rescue plan of MPS highlighted the deficiencies of the Italian banking sector in preventing failures and intervening timely to address the disruptions of distressed credit institutions.[147] MPS started dealing with the non-performing exposures (NPEs) after the results of the EBA EU-wide stress test of 2016[148] that showed for MPS a strong reduction of its CET1.[149] However, the difficulties of the Italian bank are a legacy of the past, as the first aids and relevant restructuring plan evidenced weaknesses in its corporate governance structure and lack of realistic prospects of restoring long-term profitability.[150]

The precautionary recapitalisation of MPS through a special insolvency procedure under Italian law raised concerns about the credibility of bail-in rules.[151] The provision of a guarantee by the Italian government technically amounts to a preferential treatment granted to MPS senior bondholders, despite the fact that it is contingent and might never materialise (contingent State aid, as there is a contingent burden on state resources).[152] The fact that the provision of the guarantee by the government, which was required for the transaction to occur, would be carried out under commercial market conditions (i.e. a fee charged in exchange of a service that rather than being provided by a market participant would be provided by the State acting in its commercial capacity) led the European Commission to

145 Communication on the recapitalization of financial institutions in the current financial crisis: limitation of aid to the minimum necessary and safeguards against undue distortions of competition (Recapitalization Communication) OJ C 10, 15.1.2009.

146 Louise Bowman, 'Aggrieved Banco Popular Bondholders Train Their Sights on Banco Santander' *Euromoney* (17 April 2018) available at <https://www.euromoney.com/article/b17t71ls5hhvyp/aggrieved-banco-popular-bondholders-train-their-sights-on-banco-santander> (accessed 11 June 2020).

147 Benoit Mesnard, Marcel Magnus and Alienor Anne Claire Duvillet-Margerit, 'The precautionary recapitalisation of Monte dei Paschi di Siena' European Parliament Briefing (6 July 2017) 3.

148 The stress test does not have a threshold for success/failure but is designed as an informative element relevant for the supervision process. The results will then be used by the competent authorities to assess the capacity of the bank to meet the regulatory requirements in stressed scenarios on the basis of common methodologies and assumptions.

149 It indicates the bank's core equity capital compared with its total risk-weighted assets that are used to quantify a bank's financial strength.

150 Following the acquisition of Banca Antonveneta for €9 billion from Banco Santander, BMPS reported €5.5 billion of impairments in the balance sheet of 2011 and 2012. See European Commission, 'State aid n° SA. 36175 (2013/N) – Italy MPS – Restructuring' C(2013) 8427 final, available at <http://ec.europa.eu/competition/state_aid/cases/249091/249091_1518538_162_2.pdf> (accessed 21 June 2020).

151 European Commission, 'State Aid: Commission Authorises Precautionary Recapitalisation of Italian Bank Monte dei Paschi di Siena' (Press Release, Brussels, 4 July 2017) 2. See also Monte dei Paschi di Siena, 'BMPS: European Commission Approves the 2017–2012 Restructuring Plan' (Press Release) available at <http://english.mps.it/media-and-news/press-releases/2017/Pages/press_release_20170705.aspx> (accessed 16 June 2020).

152 Bank of Italy, 'The "Precautionary Recapitalization" of Banca Monte dei Paschi di Siena' available at <https://www.bancaditalia.it/media/approfondimenti/2016/ricapitalizzazione-mps/index.html?com.dotmarketing.htmlpage.language=1> (accessed 8 June 2020).

not qualify the guarantee as State aid.[153] Moreover, in the aftermath of the overhaul of the EU resolution regime, it is expected to favour bail-in. Therefore, the case of MPS can be considered as one where there is an attempt to avoid the unavoidable and might constitute an abuse of the State aid framework. As a result, it is difficult to understand the policy of the Commission as the main objective of the BRRD is to ensure that insolvent banks can be resolved in an orderly and uniform manner without generating financial instability (and minimising the use of State aid).[154]

The case of MPS also involved market dissemination of subordinated bonds to retail investors who were not presented with full disclosure of potential risks.[155] As a result, the Italian government introduced a compensating scheme for affected retail investors whereby they would be able to convert the subordinated debt securities into equity.[156] Even if such a political strategy might be desirable,[157] it can be deemed as a circumvention of the applicability of bail-in on junior debt holders, according to the burden sharing principle applying when granting State aid. As Yadav noted, 'Monte dei Paschi offers a cautionary example of what is at stake for regulators in seeking to solve the problem of too-big-to-fail banks. Post-crisis regulation requires banks to maintain thicker capital buffers-reserves of assets available to better ensure that banks can pay off depositors and other short-term creditors to prevent a crisis at one bad firm from spreading to others within the financial system'.[158] The ECB promoted the precautionary recapitalisation for MPS while it clearly stated in the guidelines on NPLs that the priority is to develop workout units and private debt restructuring agreements to write-off bad loans from the bank balance sheet.[159] It seems that the ECB proposals to establish private mechanisms to resolve troubled banks ended up in forms

153 Gert Jan Koopman, 'Market Based Solutions to Bank Restructuring and the Role of State Aid Control: The Case of NPLs' (Speech delivered at the ECMI Annual Conference, Brussels, 9 November 2016) 11–12, available at <http://www.eurocapitalmarkets.org/system/files/Gert%20Jan%20Koopman_Speech.pdf> (accessed 10 June 2020).

154 Karel Lannoo, 'Bank State Aid under BRRD and SRM' (2014) 13(4) *European State Aid Law Quarterly* 630–632. It is noted that 'Member States can also provide extraordinary public financial support through additional financial stabilisation tools, such as equity support and temporary public ownership, but again as a last resort, after all other measures have been exploited, and following State aid rules'.

155 European Commission, Press Release dated 1 June 2017 titled 'Statement on an Agreement in principle between Commissioner Vestager and Italian Authorities on Monte Dei Paschi di Siena (MPS)'.

156 The financing to buy the equity from the original retail investors will be obtained from new secure senior debt instruments. The Commission understands that such compensation scheme is an entire separate consideration to burden sharing under the State aid framework. See European Commission, Press Release dated 1 June 2017 titled 'Statement on an Agreement in principle between Commissioner Vestager and Italian authorities on Monte Dei Paschi di Siena (MPS)'.

157 In this line of thinking Martin Sandbu, 'Banking Union will Transform Europe's Politics' *Financial Times* (26 July 2017), who observed that in the recent banking failures 'Spain offered a glimpse into the future of bank regulation, while Italy clung to the bad habits of the past. On this discrepancy, Italy demonstrated greater ability to lobby for its case, however power is not all; it matters what one uses it for'. In particular, it is argued that banks in Italy are run by politically embedded foundations a scenario that show an incestuous relation between state and credit institutions. This phenomenon can determine the following effects: 'deep confusion between the national interest and that of the banking sector; hidden subsidies from taxpayers to banks, protecting both their managers and their investors; and gross inefficiencies in an allocation of capital driven more by political and personal priorities than economic logic'.

158 Yesha Yadav, 'We Need to Know Who Invests in Bank Equity' (2017) 70 *Vanderbilt Law Review En Banc* 284.

159 ECB, 'Guidance to Banks on Non-performing Loans' (2017) 19–20, available at <https://www.bankingsupervision.europa.eu/ecb/pub/pdf/guidance_on_npl.en.pdf> (accessed 27 June 2020).

of domestic bailout. Therefore, the mandatory implementation of the NPL guidance into the complex system of banking resolution would have been desirable.

The recourse to financial assistance increased reliance on State aid and undermined the BRRD rules. This implies that precautionary recapitalisation under the BRRD has been deliberately left as a loophole for cases where bail-ins cannot work. The liquidation of Venetian banks (Veneto Banca and Banca Popolare di Vicenza) also demonstrates the willingness to avoid bail-in and seek public support.[160] These two banks were considered by the ECB 'failing or likely to fail' and thus was a condition to access the resolution or liquidation tools in which State aid was the restructuring option. The winding-up of Veneto banks seems an exception to the aid regime and constitutes a precedent for manoeuvre from Member States. However, the decision on a bank's critical functions and potential adverse effects into the market is a matter for the SRB. In the case of the Venetian banks, the justification for the State aid originated from the government's own assessment of the local effects of liquidation. On this point, it has been pointed out that 'in the absence of clarity on what constitutes a serious impact on the regional economy, the rules on liquidation aid leave room for governments to effectively re-instate at the local level the public interest that the SRB has denied at national (or, in the Italian case, even at the regional) level'.[161] The SRB is the authority in charge of the assessment of public interest although the criteria for assessing a failing bank through resolution actions or national insolvency proceedings are still far from clear. In addition, the assessment whether a bank is non-insolvent and 'failing or likely to fail' leaves discretion to EU regulators (i.e. ECB and SRB) as inconsistent decisions have been taken for distressed credit institutions. In this context, Tröger argued that 'the bail-in tool under the BRRD and the SRM-Reg provides for a highly complicated and detailed regulatory framework that gives a multitude of authorities ample discretion in compelling private sector involvement and requires significant inter-agency cooperation and information sharing'.[162]

In the case of Banco Popular, the SRB considered the institution 'failing or likely to fail' and subjected it to a resolution scheme in the public interest.[163] Banco Popular was resolved by transferring all shares and capital instruments to Banco Santander S.A. with no involvement of State aid. In substance, Banco Popular was resolved through the sale of assets and the bail-in tools.[164] Since the BRRD does not provide a definition of 'public interest', there is risk of lack of consistency and different regulatory treatment in resolving

---

160 Benoit Mesnard, Alienor Margerit and Marcel Magnus, 'The Orderly Liquidation of Veneto Banca and Banca Popolare di Vicenza' European Parliament (25 July 2017) available at <http://www.europarl.europa.eu/RegData/etudes/BRIE/2017/602094/IPOL_BRI%282017%29602094_EN.pdf> (accessed 22 June 2020).

161 Silvia Merler, 'Bank Liquidation in the European Union: Clarification Needed' Bruegel Policy Contribution, Issue No. 1 (January 2018) 11, available at <http://bruegel.org/wp-content/uploads/2018/01/PC-01_2018.pdf> (accessed 17 June 2020).

162 Tobias H. Tröger, 'Too Complex to Work: A Critical Assessment of the Bail-In Tool under the European Bank Recovery and Resolution Regime' (2018) 4 *Journal of Financial Regulation* 38.

163 Commission Decision (EU) 2017/1246 of 7 June 2017 endorsing the resolution scheme for Banco Popular Español S.A., C (2017) 4038. The resolution of Spanish bank can be regarded as private bail-in capital without intervention of the state.

164 Benoit Mesnard, Alienor Margerit and Marcel Magnus, 'The Resolution of Banco Popular' European Parliament (28 August 2017) 3.

banks in crisis.[165] This raises concerns on the effectiveness of EU rules since wide powers are granted to supervisory authorities in evaluating the financial condition of failing banks. The question lies in the divergent assessment of investors in terms of equity and subordinated debt.[166] As Mayes argued, 'it is really up to the SRB to decide whether the risks and the resolvability are acceptable'.[167] This approach confirms that the bank resolution regime remains subordinated to the State aid framework: a scenario that incentivises domestic biases in favour of protecting national champions or other banks whose failure would cause political problems domestically.

14.7 Conclusion

In the aftermath of the 2008–2009 global financial crisis, the introduction of new resolving mechanisms for distressed banks has been lauded as a significant step forward in the EU bank resolution regime. The recent failures of fragile credit institutions in several EU Member States have demonstrated the need to strengthen the harmonisation process of restructuring measures to avoid inconsistency in the application of rules and discretion of supervisory authorities. The EU Banking Union represents a welcome approach in the regulatory framework of ailing banks: the BRRD and the SRM establish innovative tools to avoid the involvement of depositors into the rescue programs and to contain the disruptions of collapses. The new insolvency rules introduced under the BRRD, and SRM marked a significant shift towards co-operation, uniformity and efficiency of regulatory measures. The adoption of a new centralised system to resolve failing firms in the Eurozone can be considered a notable change to prevent systemic crisis and to reduce the use of taxpayers' funds to bail-out distressed credit institutions.[168] However, EU regulators leave wide discretion to national governments to adopt taxpayer-funded bail-outs which is a legacy of the past to protect financial stability in the public interest. The implications of Brexit on the UK's banking resolution framework and on the resolution of banks with cross-border activities between the EU and the UK will be examined in Chapter 17.

Glossary of terms

- Ring-fencing: Regulatory approach intended to facilitate the resolution of troubled banking groups and, in particular, to make it possible to allow the non-ring-fenced part of the group to fail, while securing the survival of the ring-fenced part and hence the undisrupted provision of key financial services.

165 David Mayes, 'Banking Union: The Problem of Untried Systems' (2017) 20 *Journal of Economic Policy Reform* 9.
166 Robert Smith, 'Banco Popular Serves as a Harsh Lesson for Coco Debt Holders' *Financial Times* (8 June 2018).
167 David Mayes, 'Banking Union: The Disadvantages of Opportunism' (2017) 2 *Journal of Economic Policy Reform* 139.
168 Nicolas Veron and Guntram B. Wolff, 'From Supervision to Resolution: Next Steps on the Road to European Banking Union' (2013) The Peterson Institute for International Economics, Policy Brief 13-5, 5–6. See also Angel Ubide, 'How to Form a More Perfect European Banking Union' (2013) The Peterson Institute for International Economics, Policy Brief 13–23, 2–3.

- Electrification power: Regulatory power that represents a valuable tool for ensuring banks comply with the rules of ring-fencing and for reducing uncertainty that would accompany endless gaming of the rules.
- Bank Recovery and Resolution Directive (BRRD): Directive that represents the cornerstone of EU crisis management regime. It sets out common resolution powers and mechanisms for co-operation between resolution authorities in applying resolution tools to financial institution groups operating on a cross-border basis, attributing a significant role to the European Banking Authority (EBA).
- Single Point of Entry (SPE): Model according to which the home authority of the top-level holding company resolves the entire banking group.
- Multiple Point of Entry (MPE): Model according to which home and host authorities resolve different entities simultaneously; it is more adapted to banks with separately capitalised subsidiaries.
- Recovery plans: Plans drawn by banks that are based on various scenarios including both idiosyncratic problems and market-wide stress (e.g. normal and adverse stress scenario); they are assessed by competent supervisory authorities, which may require amendments to remedy 'material deficiencies'.
- Resolution plans: Plans drawn by banks setting out swift and effective resolution action in case the 'conditions for resolution' under BRRD are met.
- Bail-in: Resolution tool that presupposes that banks' balance sheets have sufficient liabilities eligible to be bailed-in, in a progressive and hierarchical manner. It is considered a workable measure of write-down or conversion of debt to equity.
- Bail-inable debt: Subordinated debt issued *ex ante* and specially designed to absorb conversion or write-down losses.
- Recapitalisation: Remedy to cover losses for failing banks in the case of a rescue plan with strict conditionally guaranteed by a pool of investment banks.
- Total loss absorbing capacity (TLAC): It is a requirement for G-SIBs to have equity and eligible liabilities equal to the higher of 18% of their RWAs or 6.75% of their total exposures.
- Minimum requirements for own funds and eligible liabilities (MREL): Applies to all EU banks and consists of different components. The component of MREL that applies to all EU banks is called the loss absorption amount which includes all regulatory capital and buffers and is satisfied by the same instruments.
- Single Resolution Mechanism (SRM): A unified bank resolution scheme and a standard regulatory framework for cross-border resolvability within the Eurozone.
- Stress test: Form of internal audit whereby a financial institution tests its resilience and capital position in the event of the occurrence of certain adverse scenarios, such as a reduction of real estate prices, currency devaluation, failure of another systemic institution and lack of liquidity in financial markets.

Practice questions

The regulatory framework established by the EU Bank Recovery and Resolution Directive (BRRD) and the SRM has introduced rules necessary to prevent financial instability and systemic risk contagion. However, the restructuring tools for distressed banks – i.e. bail-in, precautionary recapitalisation and resolving plans – are largely flexible and allow Member States to adopt domestic policy measures to rescue distressed institutions. Critically discuss.

You may also find it useful to review the chapter through the following questions:

- What are the key elements of the BRRD Directive?
- What is systemic risk, and what are its implications for banking regulation?
- What are the legal and policy implications of bail-in measures?
- What are the effects of a precautionary recapitalisation for a failing bank?
- What are the main functions of recovery and resolution plans in the BRRD?
- What are the key features of the Single Resolution Mechanism?

15 Deposit insurance and banking stability

15.1 Introduction

The 2008–2009 global financial crisis which featured the depositor run on Northern Rock has demonstrated the need to introduce an effective depositor protection scheme to mitigate depositor losses. Further, the global crisis has shown that there is a vicious link between sovereign default and bank failures. Banks in the euro area, both inside and outside the country in distress, that hold large amounts of bonds issued by the defaulting country in their portfolios might lose access to the European Central Bank's (ECB) refinancing facilities and face severe liquidity shortages as a result of a collapse. Increasingly, complex mechanisms of assistance have been established under very complicated political and financial conditions [European Stability Mechanism (ESM), European System of Financial Supervision (ESFS) and European Financial Stabilisation Mechanism (EFSM)].

Along with the financial mechanisms established to restore the viability of fragile economies in the euro area, this chapter examines the structure of Single Deposit Guarantee Scheme (SDGS), a mutual insurance system whereby each member insures the others: basically, it operates as an insurance policy provided to certain depositors by the other banks in the national banking system.[1] The Scheme comprises a formal structure with staff, policy-making capability and a fund capable of being deployed, or, in broad terms, a notional entity whose resources and capability are called from the industry as and when required.[2] The form of the Scheme involves 'pre-funding', where contributions are levied on industry in advance: this increases costs and creates investment problems; 'post-funding', where levies are made on industry after the event: this creates problems of access to immediate cash.[3] The Deposit Guarantee Scheme (DGS) applies when a bank is experiencing a default and cannot allow deposit withdrawal which involves the resolution or insolvency procedures.[4] Depositor preference in the UK works as follows: (1) covered deposits with UK banks retain full insolvency preference; (2) retail and SME deposits above the insured

---

1 Some limitations apply in terms of entities subject to the DGS (retail, corporate or other banks) and which financial instruments fall under the system (deposits, bonds, derivatives). For an overview, see Nikoletta Kleftouri, 'Meeting the Rationale of Deposit Protection System' (2014) 22 *Journal of Financial Regulation and Compliance* 300, 301.
2 Rym Ayadi and Rosa M Lastra, 'Proposals for Reforming Deposit Guarantee Schemes in Europe' (2010) 11 *Journal of Banking Regulation* 210, 215.
3 Almudena de la Mata Muñoz, 'The Future of Cross-Border Banking after the Crisis: Facing the Challenges through Regulation and Supervision' (2010) 11 *European Business Organization Law Review* 575, 586–587.
4 On this point, see Iris H.-Y. Chiu and Joanna Wilson, *Banking Law and Regulation* (OUP 2019) 669.

amount get 'secondary insolvency preference'; and (3) both primary and secondary preference deposits rank before floating charge holders.[5]

This chapter also analyses the mechanics of the DGS in the context of the EU Banking Union. It discusses the regulatory framework and main issues for implementing the Scheme among EU Member States such as the use of DGS in resolution and treatment of deposits in insolvency, the use of resolution funds for solvency support and the mutualisation of losses between resolution funds. Further, the role of lender of last resort (LOLR) in bank crisis management is addressed along the creation of common deposit protection, and the possible advantages and synergies for the Deposit Guarantee Network in connection with the launched Capital Markets Union (CMU). It is pointed out that the need to establish well-designed deposit insurance schemes to deal with cross-border resolution problems represents a challenge for banking regulators and public authorities.

15.2 The European Financial Stability Facility

The European Financial Stability Facility (EFSF) is a company incorporated in 2010 by countries that share the euro currency.[6] The EFSF was created by the EU Member States in order to safeguard financial stability in the Eurozone and provide assistance to Member States within the framework of a macro-economic adjustment programme.[7] It arranges temporary liquidity to euro area Member States (EAMS) in difficulty. Specifically, the EFSF issues bonds or other debt instruments on the capital markets, and may intervene in the primary and secondary bond markets, act on the basis of a precautionary programme and finance recapitalisations of financial institutions through loans to governments.[8] Generally, the ESFS grants financial assistance in the form of (1) loan disbursements, (2) precautionary facilities, (3) facilities to finance the recapitalisation of financial institutions in a EAMS through loans including non-programme countries and (4) facilities for the purchase of bonds in the primary and secondary markets.[9]

The EFSF has a temporary duration and ranks *pari passu* among creditors[10]: in other words, the EFSF has the same standing as any other sovereign claim on the country. The lending capacity maximisation consists of a partial guarantee on securities issuances by Member States plus collective investment funds. The main aim of EFSF is to preserve financial stability within the Economic and Monetary Union (EMU). Under the Framework Agreement (on the constitution of the EFSF), there are several credit enhancer tools: guarantees, grossing up of guarantees, loan-specific cash buffer, cash reserve (the net

5 Daniel C. Hardy, 'Bank Resolution Costs, Depositor Preference and Asset Encumbrance' (2014) 22 *Journal of Financial Regulation and Compliance* 96, 97.

6 See <https://www.esm.europa.eu/sites/default/files/2016_02_01_efsf_faq_archived.pdf> (accessed 18 July 2020).

7 Amy Verdun, 'A Historical Institutionalist Explanation of the EU's Responses to the Euro Area Financial Crisis' (2015) 22 *Journal of European Public Policy* 219.

8 Ledina Gocaj and Sophie Meunier, 'Time Will Tell: The EFSF, the ESM, and the Euro Crisis' (2013) 35 *Journal of European Integration* 239, 240.

9 Douglas J. Elliott, 'Levering Europe: Alternatives for the European Financial Stability Facility' (2011) *Brookings*, available at <https://www.brookings.edu/research/levering-europe-alternatives-for-the-european-financial-stability-facility/> (accessed 19 May 2020).

10 On the concept of *pari passu*, see the seminal work of Lee C. Bucheit, 'The Pari Passu Clause Sub Specie Aeternitatis' (1991) 10 *International Financial Law Review* 11, 12.

present value of the margin of the EFSF loan) and other credit enhancement mechanisms as may be approved (article 5, EFSF Framework Agreement).[11]

A downgrade of a member country would not necessarily lead to a downgrade of EFSF securities. Guarantees are several, irrevocable, firm, unconditional and binding: if a guarantor did not respect its obligations, guarantees from others could be called in to cover the shortfall. The cash reserve and the loan-specific cash buffer are invested in very safe and liquid assets. The EFSF will only provide financial support if an EAMS loses access to markets: it could be agreed with an EAMS that funds are to be used to stabilise the banking sector.[12] The case of Greece illustrates the operational functions of the EFSF at times of sovereign crisis.[13] Another case is the economic adjustment programme adopted in Spain that aimed to recapitalise the Spanish banking sector and restore market confidence. The financing was committed under the EFSF and then transferred to the ESM without seniority status.[14] The conditionality criteria set in the programme were as follows: (1) diagnostic as regards the capital needs of banks, based on a comprehensive asset quality review and valuation process, and bank-by-bank stress tests; (2) segregation of impaired assets from the balance sheet of banks receiving public support and their transfer to an external Asset Management Company; (3) recapitalisation and restructuring of viable banks and an orderly resolution of ultimately non-viable banks, with private sector burden sharing as a prerequisite; (4) measures applied to individual financial institutions targeting the financial sector as a whole and reinforcement of regulatory and supervisory framework; (5) compliance with agreed EU surveillance recommendations; and (6) restructuring plans in line with EU State aid rules.[15]

The funds of the EFSF, together with the EFSM (as discussed in the next section) and the International Monetary Fund (IMF), have provided temporary liquidity assistance to several Member States of the euro area. The EFSF does not have any currency limitation for its funding activities. Further, the EFSF will not crowd other borrowers out of the market: it will only act as a market substitute covering the refinancing needs of a country that is unable to borrow at reasonable rates from the markets. Member States that are not

---

11 Carlos Closa and Aleksandra Maatsch, 'In a Spirit of Solidarity? Justifying the European Financial Stability Facility (EFSF) in National Parliamentary Debates' (2014) 52 *Journal of Common Market Studies* 826, 827.

12 In 2010, the ECOFIN Ministers, European Commission and the ECB agreed to provide a loan to Ireland to safeguard financial stability in the euro area and the EU. The total lending programme was estimated at €85bn, financed as follows: €17.5bn from Ireland (Treasury and the National Pension Fund Reserve); €22.5bn from the IMF; €22.5bn from the EFSM; €12.9bn from the EFSF; and €4.8 bilateral loans such as from the UK (€3.8 billion), Denmark (€0.4 billion) and Sweden (€0.6 billion). The programme consisted of three pillars: (1) strengthening and comprehensive overhaul of the banking system; (2) ambitious fiscal adjustment; and (3) growth-enhancing reforms, particularly on the labour market. For an overview, see Stephen Kinsella, 'Is Ireland Really the Role Model for Austerity?' (2012) 36 *Cambridge Journal of Economics* 223, 224.

13 The financial assistance of EUR 164.5 billion until the end of 2014 was arranged as follows: EUR144.7 billion were provided via the EFSF and EUR19.8 billion were provided by the IMF (part of a four-year EUR28 billion arrangement under the Extended Fund Facility for approved in March 2012). The release of the disbursements was based on observance of quantitative performance criteria and a positive evaluation of progress made according to policy criteria detailed in Council Decision 2011/734/EU of 12 July 2011 (as amended in November 2011 and on 13 March 2012) and the MoU setting the economic policy conditionality, which was signed on 14 March 2012. The programme was accompanied by strengthened monitoring of the implementation of reforms in Greece.

14 Loan covers estimated shortfall in capital requirements (EUR 51–62bn) and additional safety margin of EUR 100bn. Loan maturities will be up to 15 years with an average of 12½ years.

15 Daniel Gros and Cinzia Alcidi, 'Adjustment Difficulties and Debt Overhangs in the Eurozone Periphery' (2011) CEPS Working Document No. 347, 2–3, available at <https://www.ceps.eu/ceps-publications/adjustment-difficulties-and-debt-overhangs-eurozone-periphery/> (accessed 17 April 2020).

members of the euro area, such as the UK, cannot access the EFSF (Balance of Payments facility under Council Regulation (EC) No. 332/2002.[16] However, these policy initiatives were developed in an ad-hoc manner and on a temporary basis only and did not provide an adequate basis for dealing with all possible future debt crises in the euro area. It can be argued that the market approach with sovereign guarantees adopted by the EFSF is a temporary bail-out assistance that can increase the effects of moral hazard if a bank cannot restore its own viability.

15.3 The European Stability Mechanism

In 2011, the European Council adopted a comprehensive package of measures to respond to the ongoing crisis at the time, as well as to guard against such crises materialising in the future. The main features of this package relate to the strengthening of the preventive and corrective mechanisms to address internal and external imbalances, particularly fiscal imbalances and competitiveness problems of individual Member States. The Council set up a permanent crisis resolution mechanism, namely, the ESM.[17] This includes the establishment of a permanent crisis management mechanism as an *ultima ratio* safeguard against imbalances in individual countries.[18] The ESM is an intergovernmental institution established under public international law by a treaty signed by the euro area countries and based in Luxembourg.[19]

The ESM is the permanent crisis resolution mechanism, which has been set up to provide financial assistance, subject to strict conditionality, to Euro countries experiencing severe financing difficulties.[20] Specifically, the ESM provides assistance in the form of (1) loan disbursements; (2) precautionary facilities; (3) facilities to finance the recapitalisation of financial institutions in an EAMS through loans including non-programme countries; and (4) facilities for the purchase of bonds in the primary and secondary markets.[21] The ESM may also exceptionally intervene in the debt primary market under the same conditionality. The main aim is to safeguard financial stability in Europe by providing financial assistance to EAMS. It has indefinite duration and, in terms of ranking, preferred creditor status: in other words, the ESM enjoys preferred creditor status in a similar fashion to the IMF, while accepting the preferred creditor status of the IMF above the ESM.

Within the financial assistance programmes for the Eurozone, it is worth noting that the EFSM was created to provide financial support to EU Member States in financial difficulties.

---

16 Council Regulation (EC) No. 332/2002 of 18 February 2002 establishing a facility providing medium-term financial assistance for Member States' balances of payments [2002] OJ L53/1. Greece's financial assistance was arranged prior to the EFSF's establishment.

17 See Eurogroup, 'Preparation of Eurogroup and Economic and Finance Ministers Council, 11 and 12 July 2011' MEMO/11/493, Brussels (8 July 2011) available at <https://europa.eu/rapid/press-release_MEMO-11–493_en.htm> (accessed 19 March 2020).

18 Sandrino Smeets, Alenka Jaschke and Derek Beach, 'The Role of the EU Institutions in Establishing the European Stability Mechanism: Institutional Leadership under a Veil of Intergovernmentalism' (2019) 57 *Journal of Common Market Studies* 675, 680–681.

19 See the ESM Treaty available at <https://www.esm.europa.eu/sites/default/files/20150203_-_esm_treaty_-_en.pdf> (accessed 18 June 2020).

20 Rodrigo Olivares-Caminal, 'The EU Architecture to Avert a Sovereign Debt Crisis' (2011) 2 *OECD Journal: Financial Markets Trend* 13–14.

21 Michael Schwarz, 'A Memorandum of Misunderstanding – The Doomed Road of the European Stability Mechanism and a Possible Way Out: Enhanced Cooperation' (2014) 51 *Common Market Law Review* 389, 390.

The EFSM finances euro area countries with fragile economies by issuing bonds on behalf of the European Union.[22] It is a special purpose vehicle established as a 'société anonyme' incorporated under Luxembourg law. Under this mechanism, the Council may decide by qualified majority on a proposal from the Commission to grant assistance to Member States in the form of loans or credit lines, with a view to preserving the stability, unity and integrity of the euro area. The EFSM is based on the assistance clause in article 122(2) of the Treaty on the Functioning of the European Union.[23] The EU Commission is empowered to contract borrowings on behalf of the Union for the purpose of funding loans made under the EFSM according to article 2 of Council Regulation No. 407/2010.[24] The assistance is granted subject to a number of economic policy conditions that the Member State in question must respect in order to receive the loans or credit lines. In addition, the total amount for financial assistance under the EFSM is limited to the moneys available within the budget of the Union.

The ESM works closely with the IMF in arranging financial programmes: the active participation of the IMF (in all circumstances) is sought on a technical and financial level. The debt sustainability analysis is jointly conducted by the Commission and the IMF in liaison with the ECB. In parallel, the policy conditions attached to a joint ESM and IMF assistance are negotiated by the Commission and the IMF in liaison with the ECB. EAMS may participate on an ad-hoc basis alongside the ESM in financial assistance operations for EAMS. This means that the ESM would not require the credit enhancements of the EFSF to secure a Triple-A rating. In this context, article 136 of the EU Treaty provides that "the Member States whose currency is the euro may establish a stability mechanism to be activated if indispensable to safeguard the stability of the euro area. The granting of any required financial assistance under the mechanism will be made subject to strict conditionality".[25]

In summary, the financial assistance programmes work as follows: (1) the ESM Stability Support (ESS) requests from an EAMS; (2) the EU Commission together with the IMF and in liaison with the ECB assesses the actual financing needs of the EAMS; (3) the Commission, the IMF and ECB negotiate a macroeconomic adjustment programme with the EAMS in an MoU; (4) the EU Council endorses the macroeconomic adjustment programme and the Commission signs the MoU on behalf of the EAMS; (5) the ESM's Board of Directors then approve the financial assistance agreement containing the technical aspects of the assistance; and (6) the Commission, the IMF and ECB are responsible for monitoring compliance with the policy conditionality.

15.4 The Deposit Guarantee Scheme Directives

The lack of international convergence of deposit insurance schemes raised concerns among bank regulators and policy-makers, particularly after the failure of cross-border banks which

22 Council Regulation (EU) No. 407/2010 of 11 May 2010 establishing a European financial stabilisation mechanism [2010] OJ L118/1.
23 See the Consolidated version of the Treaty on the Functioning of the European Union [2012] OJ C 326/47.
24 Council Regulation (EU) 2015/1360 of 4 August 2015 amending Regulation (EU) No. 407/2010 establishing a European financial stabilisation mechanism [2015] OJ L210/1. In doctrine, see Rainer Palmstorfer, 'To Bail Out or not to Bail Out? The Current Framework of Financial Assistance for Euro Area Member States Measured against the Requirements of EU Primary Law' (2012) 6 *European Law Review* 771, 772.
25 Consolidated version of the Treaty on the Functioning of the European Union - Part Three: Union Policies and Internal Actions - Title VIII: Economic and Monetary Policy - Chapter 4: Provisions specific to Member States whose currency is the euro, Article 136 [2008] OJ C115/106.

highlighted the domestic prerogative of protection systems.[26] In response to this regulatory loophole, the EU legislature introduced the DGS Directive that set a comprehensive legal framework on depositor protection.[27] The directive is provided for substantial harmonisation of deposit insurance policies and enhanced the integration of retail banking.[28] The EU regulators amended the directive in 2009 abolishing co-insurance and introducing a coverage level set at euro 100,000, which also applies to the UK where the coverage level is set at £85,000.[29]

The amending directive of 2009 addresses cross-border issues providing that home state schemes cover deposits taken in any branch anywhere in the EU; host state schemes manage payments, but home state schemes must reimburse; and non-EU branches may accept deposits covered by their home schemes if those schemes are equivalent – otherwise they must join the host scheme.[30] It can be argued that these regulatory measures reflect the existing voluntary lending and borrowing mechanisms between EU DGSs, particularly once extraordinary contributions have been raised and in an amount not exceeding 0.5% of covered deposits of the borrowing DGS.[31]

In November 2015, the Commission published a Communication setting out the European deposit insurance scheme (EDIS) for bank deposits,[32] accompanied by a Proposal for a Regulation[33] that marked a notable step towards the creation of a third pillar of the Banking Union, namely the SDGS.[34] The intervention of the EU legislature culminated with the adoption of the Deposit Guarantee Scheme Directive (DGSD) of 2014 that introduces minimum standards for bank DGSs.[35] The main objectives of the DGSD are as follows: (1) to ensure financial stability in the banking sector after the global financial crisis, and (2) to recover deposits by mandatory bank contributions.[36] Although the political agreement among Member States for the establishment of the EDIS is still far from an overall consensus, the rationale of designing a common deposit protection scheme falls under the prudential supervision of credit institutions.[37] Specifically, the common deposit guarantee system aims to achieve uniform administrative practice resolution financing; to establish the

26 The scandal of the Bank of Credit and Commerce International (BCCI) in 1991 posed challenges for implementing a regulatory framework on cross-border banking supervision. See Nikos Passas, 'The Genesis of the BCCI Scandal' (1996) 23 *Journal of Law and Society* 57–58.

27 Directive 94/19/EC of the European Parliament and of the Council of 30 May 1994 on deposit-guarantee schemes [1994] OJ L135/5.

28 George McKenzie and Manzoor Khalidi, 'The EU Directive on Deposit Insurance: A Critical Evaluation' (1994) 32 *Journal of Common Market Studies* 171, 172.

29 Art 6 of the Directive 2009/14/EC of the European Parliament and of the Council of 11 March 2009 amending Directive 94/19/EC on deposit-guarantee schemes as regards the coverage level and the payout delay (OJ 2009 L 68, 3).

30 Ross Cranston et al., *Principles of Banking Law* (3rd ed., OUP 2017) 185–186.

31 Jessica Cariboni, Elisabeth Joossens and Adamo Uboldi, 'The Promptness of European Deposit Protection Schemes to Face Banking Failures' (2010) 11 *Journal of Banking Regulation* 196–197.

32 Communication from the Commission to the European Parliament, the Council, the European Central Bank, the European Economic and Social Committee and the Committee of the Regions 'Towards the Completion of the Banking Union' (COM/2015/0587 final).

33 Proposal for a Regulation of the European Parliament and of the Council amending Regulation (EU) 806/2014 in order to establish a European Deposit Insurance Scheme (COM/2015/0586 final).

34 European Commission, 'A Roadmap towards a Banking Union' COM(2012) 510 final, Brussels.

35 Article 5 of the Directive 2014/49/EU of the European Parliament and of the Council of 16 April 2014 on deposit guarantee schemes (OJ 2014 L 173, 149).

36 For an overview; see Kern Alexander, *Principles of Banking Regulation* (CUP 2019) 171.

37 Rosa M. Lastra, *International Financial and Monetary Law* (2nd ed., OUP 2015) 375.

reimbursement of a limited amount of deposits to depositors whose bank has failed; and to prevent depositors from making panic-driven withdrawals.

The EDIS should reduce the moral hazard effects of banks' misbehaviours as well as pooling the risk of unexpected failures; however, different views in the Eurozone and wide discretion of domestic authorities create serious obstacles in the achievement of an effective DGS.[38] In academic terms, it has been proposed to establish a European deposit insurance and resolution authority (EDIRA) 'financed by a fund fed through regular risk-based deposit insurance premiums from the banks, whose customers benefit from its protection'.[39] This proposal aims to incentivise the private sector to cover solutions to resolve banking failures and contain moral hazard. Private funds should be available for resolution based on the principle of (self-)insurance by the banking sector. In parallel, deposit guarantee schemes are regulated by the Bank Recovery and Resolution Directive (BRRD) which provides a system through domestic DGS to cover deposits up to euro 100,000. All Member States must set up national resolution funds with resources which after ten years must amount to 1% of insured deposits.[40] According to article 31(2) of the BRRD, where resolution has the effect of protecting depositors, a relevant EU DGS is liable for the amount by which covered deposits would have been written down had they been written down to the same extent as other creditors of equal priority.[41] However, the DGS liability shall not be greater than the amount which it would have had to pay out in a conventional insolvency, or 50% of its target pre-funding level. In case the DGS exposure turns out to be in breach of the 'No Creditor Worse Off than in Liquidation' (NCWOL) principle, the BRRD provides a mechanism for compensation.[42]

The Single Resolution Fund (SRF) funds operate as a back-up option when additional capital is needed, e.g. for the purposes of providing guarantees, making loans, purchasing assets, providing compensation to shareholders or creditors, providing capital to a bridge bank.[43] Further, SRF is not to be used directly to absorb losses of a failing institution or for direct recapitalisation. It can be noted that the DGS is relevant to bank resolution because credit institutions are funded primarily by deposits than are financed primarily by wholesale markets. As most retail deposits are insured, the strength of the DGS is ultimately based on

---

38 On this point, see David Howarth and Lucia Quaglia, 'The Difficult Construction of a European Deposit Insurance Scheme: A Step Too Far in Banking Union?' (2018) 21 *Journal of Economic Policy Reform* 190, 194–195.

39 Daniel Gros and Dirk Schoenmaker, 'European Deposit Insurance and Resolution in the Banking Union' (2014) 52 *Journal of Common Market Studies* 529, 536.

40 Raymond LaBrosse, Rodrigo Olivares-Caminal and Dalvinder Singh, 'The EU Bank Recovery and Resolution Directive—Some Observations on the Financing Arrangements' (2014) 15 *Journal of Banking Regulation* 218, 219.

41 Art 31(2) of the Directive 2014/59/EU of the European Parliament and of the Council of 15 May 2014 establishing a framework for the recovery and resolution of credit institutions and investment firms and amending Council Directive 82/891/EEC, and Directives 2001/24/EC, 2002/47/EC, 2004/25/EC, 2005/56/EC, 2007/36/EC, 2011/35/EU, 2012/30/EU and 2013/36/EU, and Regulations (EU) No. 1093/2010 and (EU) No. 648/2012, of the European Parliament and of the Council (OJ 2014 L 173, 190).

42 Simon Gleeson, 'The Single Resolution Mechanism and the EU Crisis Management Tools' in Lo Schiavo (ed), *The European Banking Union and the Role of Law* (Edward Elgar, 2019) 228–229. By explaining the concept of NCWOL, the author argues that 'the effect of any special bank resolution measure (including bail-in) should be to leave all creditors in no worse a position than would have prevailed in a case where the institution was liquidated under general insolvency law'.

43 Ioannis G. Asimakopoulos, 'International Law as a Negotiation Tool in Banking Union: The Case of the Single Resolution Fund' (2018) 21 *Journal of Economic Policy Reform* 118, 120–121.

its recourse to financing from the sponsor national government.[44] Finally, the use of deposit guarantee schemes in resolution involves liability to contribute up to the amount of losses that the schemes would have had to bear if the relevant institution had been wound up.[45]

15.5 The LOLR and deposit insurance schemes

As discussed previously, in the EU banking sector liquidation typically entails a system of depositor preference, i.e. depositors' claims are typically paid before those of general creditors. If the country has a deposit guarantee scheme, the insured depositors are paid off up to the insurance limit; uninsured depositors and other creditors are likely to suffer losses in their claims.[46] Insured deposits travel with the 'good bank', while all other creditors typically travel with the 'bad bank' and become claimants in the insolvency proceedings.[47] Bank crisis management comprises an array of official and private responses that extends beyond the insolvency proceedings that are the only tool typically available to deal with corporate bankruptcy in other industries.[48] Specifically, crisis management comprises *inter alia* the LOLR function, deposit insurance, resolution and bank insolvency proceedings.[49] In this context, illiquidity is always the harbinger of insolvency but not every illiquid financial firm is, or will become, insolvent. Access to the credit facilities of the central bank, known as the LOLR ('lender of last resort') function or ELA ('emergency lending assistance'), can solve a condition of illiquidity, but it cannot solve a condition of insolvency.[50] The LOLR role of the central bank and deposit insurance schemes are the regulatory responses of supervisory authorities when confronted with failed or failing banks. The timely availability of central bank credit (the central bank being the ultimate supplier of high-powered money) makes the LOLR particularly suitable to confront emergency situations. In practice, central banks often provide assistance to institutions that are already insolvent, thus diluting the first classic principle.[51] Specifically, LOLR provides market liquidity and individual assistance in the case of a general liquidity dry up – e.g. in the wake of a dramatic fall in stock prices, and

44 Rosaria Cerrone, 'Deposit Guarantee Reform in Europe: Does European Deposit Insurance Scheme Increase Banking Stability?' (2018) 21 *Journal of Economic Policy Reform* 224, 234–235.
45 Florian Brandt and Matthias Wohlfahrt, 'A Common Backstop to the Single Resolution Fund' (2019) 22 *Journal of Economic Policy Reform* 291, 298–299.
46 Angus Chan, Andrew Godwin and Ian Ramsay, 'Depositor Preference and Deposit Insurance Schemes — Challenges for Regulatory Convergence and Regulatory Coordination in Asia' (2018) 12 *Law and Financial Markets Review* 71, 72–73.
47 In the banking sector, resolution tools entail separating out a distressed firm into different parts: separating bad from good assets and separating essential from non-essential functions. The good and critical functions are sold and transferred to another bank or to a bridge bank (bank established by the government) pending such a transfer.
48 Andrew Campbell and Rosa M. Lastra, 'Revisiting the Lender of Last Resort' (2009) 24 *Banking and Finance Law Review* 453, 458–459.
49 Rosa M. Lastra, *International Financial and Monetary Law* (2nd edn, OUP 2014) 121. Also cross-reference our resolution chapter.
50 ELA is under the ECB competence according to article 18 of the ESCB Statute, article 127 TFEU and the principle of subsidiarity. Article 18 (ESCB) provided a legal basis for the ECB to provide the two forms of ELA/LOLR. According to article 5.3 TFEU (principle of subsidiarity): 'in areas which do not fall within its exclusive competence, the Union shall act only if and insofar as the objectives of the proposed action cannot be sufficiently achieved by the member states, either at central level or at regional and local level, but can rather, by reason of the scale or effects of the proposed action, be better achieved at Union level'.
51 Rosa M. Lastra and Geoffrey Wood, 'The Crisis of 2007–2009: Nature, Causes, and Reactions' (2010) 13 *Journal of International Economic Law* 531, 532.

in the case of illiquidity of a financial institution. Basically, the LOLR financial assistance is a safety net for banks that permit them to translate the risk to the insurer or depositor (for example, in the 'too big to fail' case).

In this context, deposit insurance schemes promote financial stability by reducing incentive on depositors to run for the exit, but only if coverage levels are adequate (e.g. Northern Rock experience with coinsurance).[52] Deposit insurance schemes also limit moral hazard by replacing implicit (open-ended) government guarantee of bank deposits with clearly defined (limited) guarantee, but only if there is a credible bank resolution framework. Paybox systems,[53] risk-minimising systems[54] and mixed systems,[55] and tackling the forbearance problem are addressed by the US Federal Deposit Insurance Corporation (a risk-minimising system) and by the UK Financial Services Compensation Scheme (a paybox system).[56] Funding and ranking of deposit insurance schemes require a compulsory membership and involve 'pay as you go' vs. pre-funded schemes as well as subsidy of weak banks through flat rate systems vs. risk-adjusted contributions. The global crisis showed the dangers of relying on wholesale funding: treatment of uninsured deposits and treatment of the deposit guarantee scheme have been regulated in the BRRD provisions. However, the implications of bail-in for the deposit-funded bank model raise concerns among credit institutions. Funding of resolution implies satisfaction of the liquidity requirements of the resolved entity and presupposes availability of collateral and absence of foreign currency liquidity issues. It also involves resolution costs such as national resolution funds and cross-border burden sharing and mutualisation.[57]

15.6 The Deposit Guarantee Network and the Capital Markets Union

The European system of financing arrangements set in the BRRD is characterised by the deposit guarantee schemes in resolution. National pre-funded schemes are financed by *ex ante* and extraordinary *ex post* contributions from firms and are able to borrow including from other schemes. The schemes apply for guarantees, loans, purchase of assets, capitalising bridge

52 International Association of Deposit Insurers, 'Core Principles for Effective Deposit Insurance Systems' (June 2009), available at <https://www.bis.org/publ/bcbs156.pdf> (accessed 18 June 2020).

53 The paybox system provides the deposit insurer with a more limited set of powers that facilitate the payment of claims to depositors. On this point, see Hervé Hannoun, 'Introductory Remarks at the International Association of Deposit Insurers 2011 Research Conference: "Financial Crises: The Role of Deposit Insurance"' (Basel, 8 June 2011).

54 A risk minimiser requires the authority to gather information – either directly from insured institutions or from the supervisory authority – to assess risks, the authority to limit risks through various means and the flexibility to access needed funding sources. On this point, see Federal Deposit Insurance Corporation, 'Guidance for Developing Effective Deposit Insurance Systems' (7 September 2001) 59, available at <https://www.fdic.gov/deposit/deposits/international/guidance/finalreport.pdf> (accessed 24 July 2020).

55 Under the mixed system, cross-subsidisation is measured as the ratio between the exposure of the European fund and the contributions paid to the European fund only. On this point, see Jacopo Carmassi, Sonja Dobkowitz, Johanne Evrard, Laura Parisi, André Silva and Michael Wedow, 'Completing the Banking Union with a European Deposit Insurance Scheme: Who Is Afraid of Cross-Subsidisation?' (April 2018) Occasional Paper Series No. 208, 44, available at <https://www.ecb.europa.eu/pub/pdf/scpops/ecb.op208.en.pdf> (accessed 24 July 2020).

56 The US federal deposit insurance is substantially pre-funded, while the UK Financial Services Compensation Scheme is funded after the event, so the UK Treasury has had to finance its interventions temporarily.

57 Willem Pieter De Groen and Daniel Gros, 'Estimating the Bridge Financing Needs of the Single Resolution Fund: How Expensive Is It to Resolve a Bank?' Centre for European Policy Studies (CEPS) Special Report No. 122 (November 2015), available at <https://www.ceps.eu/ceps-publications/estimating-bridge-financing-needs-single-resolution-fund-how-expensive-it-resolve-bank/> (accessed 19 May 2020).

banks, compensating creditors and contributing on a bail-in in lieu of write-down (but not direct recapitalisation). The main aim is to create a Deposit Guarantee Network and a fiscal backstop in which governments are involved in covering depositors from bank run.[58]

The importance of developing deposit insurance systems to complete the Banking Union is interlinked with the achievement of CMU.[59] This means creating a common framework for supervision, resolution and depositor protection in the euro area.[60] In this context, Véron recommended '[to strengthen] trust by setting up a fully integrated, country-blind deposit insurance system to break the vicious circle of the linkage between banks and sovereign debt'.[61] Europe is still characterised by bank-dominated financial systems: in order to unlock financing resources for companies and individuals, there is a need to develop strong and diversified capital markets in the EU. This will help realise a more diversified funding market.[62] As a reform agenda to expand the non-bank part of Europe's financial system, the Commission launched a set of proposals for a 'Capital Markets Union'[63] and for an 'Investment Plan for Europe'[64] aiming to establish 'a properly-functioning Single Market in capital by diversifying funding and improving investment opportunities across the EU'.[65] This new regulatory approach proposes (1) to mitigate system-wide risks, (2) to reduce banks' risk-taking incentives and (3) to remove regulatory barriers across jurisdictions.[66] The rationale for such reforms is to enhance non-bank credit provision and to make Europe's financial system more efficient and competitive, more resilient because of greater diversity, more responsive to monetary policy signals and more able to respond to the financing needs of a vibrant innovation-driven economy.[67] The Commission stated that:

> the Capital Markets Union (CMU) is a plan of the European Commission that aims to create deeper and more integrated capital markets among Member States. With the CMU, the Commission will explore ways of reducing fragmentation in financial

58 On this discussion, see Dirk Schoenmaker, 'On the Need for a Fiscal Backstop to the Banking System' in Matthias Haentjens and Bob Wessels (eds), *Research Handbook on Crisis Management in the Banking Sector* (Edward Elgar Publishing 2015) 42–44.

59 Poul M. Thomsen, 'On Capital Market Finance in Europe' Speech at the Conference on Capital Markets Union Organised by the Financial Markets Group, The London School of Economics and Political Science (14 June 2019), available at <https://www.imf.org/en/News/Articles/2019/06/25/sp061419-on-capital-market-finance-in-europe> (accessed 25 April 2020).

60 Vítor Constâncio, 'Synergies between Banking Union and Capital Markets Union' Keynote speech at the Joint Conference of the European Commission and European Central Bank on European Financial Integration, Brussels (19 May 2017) available at <https://www.ecb.europa.eu/press/key/date/2017/html/ecb.sp170519_1.en.html> (accessed 24 June 2020).

61 Isabel Schnabel and Nicolas Véron, 'Breaking the Stalemate on European Deposit Insurance' *Bruegel Blog* (5 March 2018) available at <https://bruegel.org/2018/03/breaking-the-stalemate-on-european-deposit-insurance/> (accessed 21 May 2020).

62 Huw van Steenis, 'Why the EU Capital Markets Union Matters for ECB Policy' *Financial Times* (23 April 2018).

63 European Commission, 'Building a Capital Markets Union' Green Paper COM (2015) 63 final, Brussels (18 February 2015).

64 European Commission, 'Communication from the Commission to the European Parliament, the Council, the European Central Bank, the European Economic and Social Committee, the Committee of the Regions and the European Investment Bank, An Investment Plan for Europe', COM (2014) 903 final.

65 House of Lords, 'Capital Markets Union: A Welcome Start' European Union Committee, 11th Report of Session 2014–2015, 4.

66 European Commission, 'Q&A on the Green Paper on Building a Capital Markets Union' Fact Sheet, Brussels (18 February 2015), 1.

67 Nicolas Véron, 'Defining Europe's Capital Markets Union' Bruegel Policy Contribution, Issue 2014/12 (November 2014), 2.

markets, diversifying financing sources, strengthening cross border capital flows and improving access to finance for businesses, particularly SMEs.[68]

The main areas of the Green Paper addressing the CMU are as follows: (1) improving access to financing for all businesses across Europe and investment projects, in particular start-ups, SMEs and long-term projects; (2) increasing and diversifying the sources of funding from investors in the EU and all over the world; and (3) making the markets work more effectively so that the connections between investors and those who need funding are more efficient and effective, both within Member States and cross-border.[69]

The Commission's proposals aim to build a unified European financing system by finding new and innovative ways to channel funds efficiently from those enjoying surplus resources to those best able to make use of those funds.[70] However, a proper pan-European regulation is needed to realise the CMU ambition of development of EU capital markets and non-bank intermediation. As Véron observed,

> CMU policy should not seek to freeze market structures in their currently underdeveloped form but, on the contrary, to create a favourable environment for the development of new intermediation segments and new financing contracts, with effective but not excessive safeguards against systemic risk.[71]

In February 2015, the House of Lords published the report 'The Post-crisis EU Financial Regulatory Framework: Do the Pieces Fit?' containing an overview of the current reforms launched by the Commission in order to create a common platform for the capital markets sector.[72] The report sets out a list of recommendations with respect to (1) the role of the EU institutions, (2) the role of the European Supervisory Authorities (ESAs), (3) the EU financial regulatory framework, (4) the international regulatory agenda and (5) the implications for the UK. One of the key elements of the post-2008 financial crisis legislative action is the fact that Member States have shown great reluctance to abandon local rules and dismantle normative barriers. In this context, the House of Lords observes that the Commission's proposals represent a necessary step to strengthen the 'Single Market' and to avoid regulatory arbitrage. However, the weaknesses of the supervisory architecture put in place by the ESAs hampered the need to rethink the regulatory approach for retail financial services. The report notes that these bodies lacked authority, had insufficient independence and exerted only a marginal influence over the shape of primary legislation, with insufficient flexibility in the correction of legislative errors and inadequate funding and resources. In this respect, appropriate scrutiny and accountability mechanisms can enhance the ESAs consultation procedures and their engagement with practitioners and regulators. It is essential to develop a more flexible and expedited mechanism whereby the ESAs can improve their function in the law-making process.

---

68 See <http://ec.europa.eu/finance/capital-markets-union/index_en.htm> (accessed 18 July 2020).
69 See http://ec.europa.eu/finance/consultations/2015/capital-markets-union/index_en.htm
70 Jon Danielsson, Eva Micheler, Katja Neugebauer, Andreas Uthemann and Jean-Pierre Zigrand, 'Europe's Proposed Capital Markets Union: Disruption will Drive Investment and Innovation' Vox CEPR's Policy Portal (23 February 2015).
71 Véron (n 67) 3.
72 House of Lords, 'The Post-crisis EU Financial Regulatory Framework: Do the Pieces Fit?' European Union Committee, 5th Report of Session 2014–2015 (2 February 2015) 5.

A key aim of the 'Capital Markets Union' is to improve consumer and investor protection. Consumers represent a large proportion of financial actors, and an adequate regulatory system is needed to protect the 'weaker party' to business transactions. A lack of understanding of the complexity of the financial sector and its interconnections was a key factor in the scale and depth of the 2007–2009 global crisis. The report recognises the efforts of the Commission's proposals to strengthen consumer protection: however, detailed disclosure requirements are unlikely to benefit consumers. In this respect, 'Capital Markets Union' provides an ideal opportunity for addressing securities law and considering the role of crowdfunding as a funding tool.[73] It is recommended that 'the impact of the new regulatory framework on the retail market should accordingly be carefully monitored by national regulators and the ESAs'.[74] A pan-European securities market poses new challenges in terms of legal analysis and regulation strategy. On the one hand, the concept of harmonisation permits the administrative costs of the duplication of provisions (i.e. home country and host country rules) to be reduced, thus favouring cross-border financial transactions. On the other hand, the introduction of the 'Single Market' allows for a flexible and innovative framework in which capital markets, as an alternative to bank funding, assume a pivotal role in the functioning of the EU economy.

One of the Commission's fundamental goals in the area of securities regulation is legislative harmonisation. A 'Capital Markets Union' aims to create a single system for cross-border transactions with an efficient integration of securities products in which market participants are clearly accountable for their acts.[75] The 'Capital Markets Union' proposals do not lay down specific rules regarding enforcement; this function is delegated to the network of co-operation within the EU institutions, which has to monitor firms' behaviours and create strong incentives to reduce the risk of confidence failures. The implementation of the post-crisis EU financial legislation has determined an innovative change in terms of transparency and responsibility to consumers: in this context, the 'Capital Markets Union' proposes a new common ground of provisions, while adopting a practical and flexible approach to rule-making.

15.7 Conclusion

This chapter provided an overview of the SDGS as part of the EU Banking Union. From the above analysis, the interplay between DGSs and the BRRD is still unclear pending further development of EDIS. Recent episodes of banking distress demonstrated that bank resolution has serious political repercussions (e.g. Italy, Greece, Portugal, Spain) with evident lack of confidence and trust. It is notable that a well-defined pan-European deposit guarantee scheme remains to be properly designed and that the interests of the institutions and regulators involved in banking supervision ought to be adequately represented. This implies a rethinking of the third pillar of the Banking Union, which should encompass the new mechanisms of bank recovery and resolution. The Banking Union represents a welcome approach in the regulatory framework for ailing banks: the DGS and the SRF establish innovative tools to avoid the involvement of depositors into the rescue programmes and to contain the disruption of collapses.

---

73 Ibid., 94.
74 Ibid., 52.
75 Konstantinos Sergakis, *The Law of Capital Markets in the EU* (Palgrave 2018) 10.

However, EU legislation leaves wide discretion to national governments to adopt domestic depositor protection schemes which is a legacy of the past to protect deposits and national financial stability under the public interest. As Yadav noted, 'post-crisis regulation requires banks to maintain thicker capital buffers-reserves of assets available to better ensure that banks can pay off depositors and other short-term creditors to prevent a crisis at one bad firm from spreading to others within the financial system'.[76] State-level deposit insurers are not viable inside a monetary union because even the liquidation of several small banks could overwhelm the capacity of national deposit insurance. Mutualisation of deposit insurance requires full harmonisation of insolvency laws because the effectiveness of the bank liquidation process will have an impact on the financial situation of the deposit insurance over which insured depositors have a legal claim.[77] Finally, the membership of DGS and resolution financing arrangements can be seriously affected by Brexit effects: cross-border transactions and depositor protection can be regulated by the local guarantee scheme. Further, according to the BRRD, third country-covered deposits will be preferred in terms of creditor ranking in insolvency proceedings. As will be discussed in Chapter 17, the impact of the withdrawal of the UK from the EU in the special resolution regimes for failing banks will require the DGS to ensure the adequate protection of Member States 'by assessing (where relevant) the equivalence of the UK's deposit protection regime at the date of Brexit, and should consider putting in place cooperation arrangements with the UK DGS after Brexit'.[78]

Glossary of terms

- Deposit Guarantee Scheme (DGS): Mutual insurance system whereby each member insures the others; it operates as an insurance policy provided to certain depositors by the other banks in the national banking system.
- European Financial Stability Facility (EFSF): Luxembourg-based company incorporated in 2010 by countries that share the euro currency. The EFSF issues bonds or other debt instruments on the capital markets and may intervene in the primary and secondary bond markets, act on the basis of a precautionary programme and finance recapitalisations of financial institutions through loans to governments.
- European Stability Mechanism (ESM): Intergovernmental institution established under public international law by a treaty signed by the euro area countries and based in Luxembourg. It is a permanent crisis resolution mechanism, which has been set up to provide financial assistance, subject to strict conditionality, to Euro countries experiencing severe financing difficulties.
- European Financial Stabilisation Mechanism (EFSM): Institution created to provide financial support to EU Member States in financial difficulties by issuing bonds on

---

76 Yesha Yadav, 'We Need to Know Who Invests in Bank Equity' (2017) 70 *Vanderbilt Law Review En Banc* 284.
77 Maria J. Nieto and Larry D. Wall, 'Cross-border Banking on the Two Sides of the Atlantic: Does It Have an Impact on Bank Crisis Management?' FRB Atlanta Working Paper No. 2015-11, 19.
78 EBA, Opinion of the European Banking Authority on issues related to the departure of the United Kingdom from the European Union (EBA/OP/2017/12), Part IV Resolution and deposit guarantee schemes, 12 October 2017, 16. In terms of recovery and resolution plans, the EBA clarified that 'once the UK leaves the EU, arrangements for resolution planning for entities based in the UK should be subject to the same standard as for any other third country, in the absence of an agreement to the contrary'.

behalf of the European Union. It is a special purpose vehicle established as a 'société anonyme' incorporated under Luxembourg law.

- Single Resolution Fund: Fund that operates as a back-up option when additional capital is needed by distressed banks, e.g. for the purposes of providing guarantees, making loans, purchasing assets, providing compensation to shareholders or creditors, providing capital to a bridge bank.
- Lender of last resort (LOLR): Function of central banks that provides market liquidity and individual assistance in the case of a general liquidity dry up – e.g. in the wake of a dramatic fall in stock prices, and in the case of illiquidity of a financial institution.
- Common deposit guarantee system: Framework that aims to achieve uniform administrative practice resolution financing; to establish the reimbursement of a limited amount of deposits to depositors whose bank has failed and to prevent depositors from making panic-driven withdrawals.
- Precautionary conditioned credit line (PCCL): Credit access which is limited to countries with a sound economic and financial situation, and there is a clear track record of access to capital markets.
- Enhanced conditions credit line (ECCL): Credit available to countries with moderate vulnerabilities that cannot access PCCL.

Practice questions

Where resolution has the effect of preventing losses to depositors, a relevant EU Deposit Guarantee Scheme (DGS) is liable for the amount by which covered deposits would have been written down had they been written down to the same extent as other creditors of equal priority. But DGS liability shall not be greater than the amount which it would have had to pay out in a conventional insolvency, or 50% of its target pre-funding level. Critically discuss.

You may also find it useful to review the chapter through the following questions:

- Why are Deposit Guarantee Schemes relevant to bank resolution?
- How are Deposit Guarantee Schemes used in the context of resolution and the treatment of deposits in insolvency?
- How do Deposit Guarantee Schemes work in the EU Banking Union?
- What is the level of interconnection between national DGSs?
- To what extent is the strength of a DGS ultimately based on its recourse to financing from the sponsor national government?

16 The regulation of non-performing loans

16.1 Introduction

In the aftermath of the global financial crisis (GFC), a degree of standardisation has developed when it comes to the liability side of banks and other credit institutions' balance sheets.[1] However, it is difficult to compare non-performing figures across firms because their definition can vary across time, regulatory jurisdiction and legal system. In general, different definitions of non-performing loans (NPLs) might specify different thresholds of the period by which repayment of interest and principal is past due; specify different definitions of NPLs for different types of loan (e.g. thresholds for non-performance depending on the purpose of the loan); include or exclude loans that have been restructured and draw the distinction between restructured loans differently.[2] During the GFC, the banking sector experienced a rapid rise in loan delinquencies and defaults driven by the limitations of the Basel rules and the adequacy of capital.[3] The crisis revealed that NPLs played a central role in the linkages between credit markets frictions and macroeconomic vulnerabilities.[4] Espinoza and Prasad observed that 'in 2009 NPLs increased sharply and credit stagnated, raising worries that the recovery could be slowed down by credit constraints'.[5] The regulatory and accounting treatments to assess asset quality highlight the lack of common practices to monitor NPLs and the fragility of banking institutions. In particular, there is

---

1 Basel Committee on Banking Supervision, 'Prudential Treatment of Problem Assets – Definitions of Non-performing Exposures and Forbearance' (2017) Guidelines, available at <http://www.bis.org/bcbs/publ/d403.htm>.

2 EBA, 'Guidelines on Credit Institutions' Credit Risk Management Practices and Accounting for Expected Credit Losses' (2017) Final Report EBA/GL/2017/06 available at <https://www.eba.europa.eu/documents/10180/1842525/Final+Guidelines+on+Accounting+for+Expected+Credit+Losses+%28EBA-GL-2017-06%29.pdf>.

3 Tara Sullivan and James Vickery, 'A Look at Bank Loan Performance' Federal Reserve Bank of New York (16 October 2013). It is pointed out that at the start of 2007, only about 1% of bank loan balances were 'nonperforming', meaning that the loan was at least 90 days past due or in nonaccrual status. By late 2015, however, the average level of NPLs across the EU banks is 5.9% while NPL ratios for the United States and Japan is less than 2%. See also World Bank, 'Bank Nonperforming Loans to Total Gross Loans' available at <http://data.worldbank.org/indicator/FB.AST.NPER.ZS>.

4 Mwanza Nkusu, 'Nonperforming Loans and Macrofinancial Vulnerabilities in Advanced Economies' (July 2011) IMF Working Paper, 4. The author observed a negative correlation between NPLs and various macroeconomic variables.

5 Raphael Espinoza and Ananthakrishnan Prasad, 'Nonperforming Loans in the GCC Banking System and their Macroeconomic Effects' (October 2010) IMF Working Paper, 4.

no consensus on the notion of NPLs across countries, firms or even within firms – different data definitions are used across subsidiary companies and business lines.[6]

In several jurisdictions and for various firms, an NPL is defined as a sum of borrowed money upon which the debtor has not made his or her scheduled payments for at least 90 days.[7] Broadly speaking, at some point after the debtor starts making payments again on an NPL, it becomes a re-performing loan, even if the debtor has not caught up on all the missed payments. On this view, it has been suggested that provisioning should be more forward-looking and that, in retrospect, had credit events been recognised before they occurred, this might have made banks better prepared for losses when they were realised.[8] However, the inherent pro-cyclicality of loan performance expectations by banks would probably have meant that banks would have still underestimated risk. The current regulatory approach to NPLs classification gives firms a wide degree of discretion, and the practical implementation of rules depends much on prudential treatment. In this context, the main problem is the lack of a harmonised framework to assess the obligors' ability to repay and whether a loan has become non-performing.[9] Recently, policy-makers and legislators have focused on creating a common classification of asset quality standards that should complement a classification of sources of banks' funding (i.e. equity and debt).[10]

This chapter examines the structure of NPLs in the context of the asset quality of banks. It considers the regulatory and accounting treatments of NPLs for the stability of the firm and the financial system. This chapter also discusses the different restructuring mechanisms, public and private, to resolve NPLs in the banking sector. The intervention of regulators and policy-makers reveals a cascade of soft law measures that create a grey area of non-binding provisions. This raises concerns for investors and financial institutions since there is a lack of a co-ordinated legislative framework for NPLs. In this context, increasing policy responses of supervisory authorities can be attributed to the following: (1) the

---

6 David Bholat et al., 'Non-performing Loans: Regulatory and Accounting Treatment of Assets' (April 2016) Bank of England Staff Working Paper No. 594, 3. It is argued that although NPLs are generally defined as a loan that is more than 90 days past due, different definitions remain among central banks and credit institutions.

7 For example, in Russia, there is no exact definition of 'non-performing loan' in the regulatory framework. NPLs are intended as 'overdue' loans or 'bad debt' as defined by the Bank of Russia Regulation No. 254-P, 'On the Procedure for Making Loss Provisions by Credit Institutions for Loans, Loan and Similar Debts'. Specifically, 'bad debt is a loan when the credit organization has undertaken all required and sufficient measures to recover debt and all necessary documents and acts are at the disposal of credit organization, if possible, revenue is not covered by costs of collection'. A loan is overdue if the repayment of the principle or interest was not paid in time based on credit contract condition. Most interestingly, in Georgia, NPLs are not expressly defined. According to Article 4 ('Asset Classification System') of the Decree N of the Governor of the National Bank of Georgia ('Regulation on Assets Classification and the Creation and Use of Reserves for Losses by Commercial Banks'), loans are classified into five categories: (1) standard loans; (2) watch loans; (3) substandard loans; (4) doubtful loans and (5) loss loans. Article 9 of the Decree provides that a loss loan is not collectable due to the borrower's insolvency and where 'payment of principal or interest has been delinquent for 180 days or more despite any collateral or hypothec'. From the wording of the provision, it seems that NPLs are considered as losses by commercial banks.

8 Samuel Knott, Peter Richardson, Katie Rismanchi and Kallol Sen, 'Understanding the Fair Value of Banks' Loans' (November 2014) Bank of England Financial Stability Paper No. 31, 7, available at <https://www.bankofengland.co.uk/-/media/boe/files/financial-stability-paper/2014/understanding-the-fair-value-of-banks-loans>.

9 David Bholat et al., 'Non-performing Loans at the Dawn of IFRS 9: Regulatory and Accounting Treatment of Asset Quality' (2018) 19 *Journal of Banking Regulation* 33, 35–36.

10 European Central Bank, 'Guidance to Banks on Non-performing Loans' (March 2017), available at <https://www.bankingsupervision.europa.eu/ecb/pub/pdf/guidance_on_npl.en.pdf>.

proliferation of market failures in the business of NPLs, namely information asymmetries, negative externalities and moral hazard; and (2) the poor incentives for investors and financial corporations to restructure non-performing exposures (NPEs) without public intervention. It is argued that although theoretically market failures are expected to exist in restructuring NPLs, empirically we do still find private resolving of bad loans occurring.

This chapter is structured as follows. Section 16.2 discusses the role of NPLs in banking and economic crises. While higher *ex ante* provisioning against expected loan losses lowers bank profitability in the short term, over the long term the constitution of loan loss provisions (LLPs) in good times reduces the chances of having a situation in crisis times where *ex post* NPL losses force a bank to raise capital. Forward-looking provisioning and timely recognition of loss represent the main challenges for financial stability. Section 16.3 examines the regulatory framework of NPLs in the light of the recent initiatives adopted at the international level to address the negative impact on lending during a financial crisis or period of stress. It also provides an overview of what is a market failure. On this view, it is investigated whether a market failure exists in NPLs. Section 16.4 addresses the heterogeneity of restructuring tools for NPLs across jurisdictions. The focus is on current differences between prudential supervisory authorities and regulators in terms of enforcement of NPL standards. In this context, the likely outcome in a free market without governmental intervention is explored. Section 16.5 analyses the resolution options for NPLs recovery such as the asset management companies (AMCs) and provides an assessment of the strategies adopted by the banks to recover the value of these loans that constitute a major concern for market actors. The last section concludes.

16.2 The implications of NPLs on bank balance sheets

The problems NPLs create for the banking sector are evident in the period since the start of the GFC in 2007, with the persistence of NPLs being a reason for the delay in the recovery from the crisis.[11] Rottke and Gentgen noted that 'while non-performing loans are a phenomenon that is permanently present in the balance sheets of banks and other lending institutions, the significant rise of non-performing loans in banks' balance sheets and the emergence of a non-performing loan market are a temporary phenomenon'.[12] Generally, a loan is considered non-performing when customer's payments are past due: this can be interpreted as an early warning signal of banking crisis. Indeed, the classification of loans represents a key indicator of the bank's credit quality.[13]

The fundamental problem is that the balance sheet counterpart of NPLs on the assets side may have a negative impact to bank capital, particularly for claims: one key ratio to track is the proportion of LLPs to NPLs (coverage ratio) constructed and commonly used by credit rating agencies.[14] The aim should be to have a level of provisioning commensurate with the initial expectations of the rate of recovery on loans (and therefore the pricing of

11 Mwanza Nkusu, 'Nonperforming Loans and Macrofinancial Vulnerabilities in Advanced Economies' (2011) IMF Working Papers No. 161, 20–21.

12 Nico B. Rottke and Julia Gentgen, 'Workout Management of Non-performing Loans: A Formal Model Based on Transaction Cost Economics' (2008) 26 *Journal of Property Investment & Finance* 59–60.

13 Karlo Kauko, 'External Deficits and Non-performing Loans in the Recent Financial Crisis' (2012) 115 *Economics Letters* 196.

14 Anne Beatty and Liao Scott, 'Do Delays in Expected Loss Recognition Affect Banks' Willingness to Lend?' (2011) 52(1) *Journal of Accounting and Economics* 19–20.

credit).[15] If this is not so, then the scale of losses may be so large that they cannot be covered by income, bringing a bank's capital below (or close to) the minimum required. At that point, banks might have to recapitalise when the system may be facing a distressed scenario where it is difficult for a bank to raise capital as profitability is deteriorating and general economic conditions are weak. This can have macroeconomic consequences, as the burden of debt felt by some results in their decreasing spending, with reduced income down the line for others, including even those not indebted.[16] Demertzis and Lehmann argued that 'efforts to reduce and remove NPLs from the balance sheets of creditors must simultaneously remove excess debt from the balance sheets of debtors'.[17] However, adequate provisioning for NPLs requires overcoming complex strategic incentives that banks have to either seek to keep LLPs low, or to avoid writing NPLs off from their balance sheets.

The timing of losses taken as a result of provisions or write offs, and the level of LLPs set aside for future NPLs on the balance sheet, are often part of a bank's strategy to smooth reported earnings and reported capitalisation.[18] Specifically, the Basel Common Equity Tier 1 (CET1) and Tier 1 capital adequacy ratio numerators include common stock and retained earnings. Higher level of LLPs can be accounted as losses and can reduce retained earnings: this may affect the CET1 and Tier 1 capital ratios with negative consequence for maintaining an adequate standard of LLPs. These factors are complicated by a Basel III CET1 capital requirement of 7% (comprising the minimum CET1 requirement of 4.5% plus a mandatory capital conservation buffer of 2.5%) of risk-weighted assets.[19] In this context, LLPs have the effect of reducing CET1 and therefore the numerator of those ratios.[20]

Since write offs mean that some loans and the provisions against them disappear from the balance sheet – and as some loans tend to have higher provisions raised against them as a proportion of the gross amount of the loan – it follows that a bank that elected to write off relatively more of its highly provisioned problem loans would show lower provisions as a percentage of overall loans. Full information about write offs, and further data on when a bank deems that such write offs take place are critical for users of financial statements to compare overall provision numbers from bank to bank. On this view, Jassaud and Kang pointed out that banks have delayed writing off highly provisioned loans as this would lower their overall provisioning ratio and possibly their credit rating.[21] It is noted that the International Accounting Standards (IAS 39) were not explicit on exactly when and how to

---

15 It can be observed that for collateralised lending, provisions under US GAAP and IFRS are net of the recoveries on liquidating collateral: when the provisions are compared to the gross amount of the non-performing loan, they can be adequate even if less than 100% if there is adequate collateral.

16 Perry Mehrling, *The New Lombard Street: How the Fed Became the Dealer of Last Resort* (Princeton University Press 2010) 7.

17 Maria Demertzis and Alex Lehmann, 'Tackling Europe's Crisis Legacy: A Comprehensive Strategy for Bad Loans and Debt Restructuring' (2017) Bruegel Policy Contribution, No. 2017/11, 1, available at <https://www.econstor.eu/bitstream/10419/173107/1/PC-11-2017.pdf>.

18 Paul J. Beck and Ganapathi S. Narayanamoorthy, 'Did the SEC Impact Banks' Loan Loss Reserve Policies and Their Informativeness?' (2013) 56(2) *Journal of Accounting and Economics* 64–65; see also Iftekhar Hasan and Larry D. Wall, 'Determinants of the Loan Loss Allowance: Some Cross-Country Comparisons' (2004) 39 *Financial Review* 129, 151–152.

19 Josè Gabilondo, *Bank Funding, Liquidity, and Capital Adequacy. A Law and Finance Approach* (Edward Elgar 2016) 102–103.

20 The precise effect or size of the reduction is indicated by the interaction of the accounting rules on provisioning with the capital framework.

21 Nadège Jassaud and Kenneth H. Kang, 'A Strategy for Developing a Market for Nonperforming Loans in Italy' (2015) IMF Working Paper No. 15-24, 16.

write off uncollectible loans. In this case, and in all situations, the more LLPs and related accounting policy decisions such as write offs are left to management discretion, the more difficult it becomes to compare meaningfully cross-firm and cross-border NPL and LLP figures.[22]

16.3 The regulatory treatment of NPLs

The definition of bank capital under the Basel rules has marked a notable achievement in the assessment of loan quality although substantive progress is required in consolidating the classification of assets in the balance sheet.[23] However, the lack of a level playing field for NPLs makes meaningful comparison of banks' assets difficult for investors and regulators. The UN System of National Accounts provides a global statistical definition of NPLs as 'a loan is non-performing when payments of interest or principal are past due by 90 days or more, or interest payments equal to 90 days or more have been capitalized, refinanced, or delayed by agreement, or payments are less than 90 days overdue, but there are other good reasons (such as a debtor filing for bankruptcy) to doubt that payments will be made in full'.[24]

In this context, the Basel Committee on Banking Supervision (BCBS) published guidelines in assessing credit risk for regulatory purposes.[25] Under the Basel II capital framework, the internal ratings-based (IRB) approach required credit firms to provide their own assessments of probability of default, amount of loss given default and exposure at default.[26] Specifically, default is defined as where an obligor is 90 days past due, or is unlikely to pay its credit obligations to the banking group in full, without recourse by the bank to actions such as realising security. In 2006, the BCBS issued guidance that mentioned loan classification recommending banks to implement asset quality systems on the basis of credit risk.[27] In addition, the BCBS also provided guidelines on the prudential treatment of problem assets aiming to set a common definition for the terms 'non-performing loan'

---

22   Provisions are no longer based on an 'incurred loss' (IAS 39) concept (i.e. taken against loans where an objective 'loss event' has occurred) but are based on forward-looking rules (IFRS 9) that involve an assessment whether 'significant deterioration' has occurred.

23   The definition of capital was first harmonised under the Basel I Accord of 1988 through a soft law instrument. See Basel Committee on Banking Supervision, 'Report on International Convergence of Capital Measurement and Capital Standards' (July 1988), available at <https://www.bis.org/publ/bcbsc111.pdf>.

24   United Nations System of National Accounts 2008, available at <https://unstats.un.org/unsd/national-account/sna2008.asp>. However, the UN statistical definition of a non-performing loan leaves scope for firm discretion since the meaning of certain terms such as 'objective evidence of impairment' is not precisely defined.

25   Basel Committee on Banking Supervision, 'Sound Practices for Loan Accounting and Disclosure' Basel Committee on Banking Supervision Paper (July 1999) 35, para 91.

26   Basel Committee on Banking Supervision, 'International Convergence of Capital Measurement and Capital Standards' Revised Framework (2004).

27   Basel Committee on Banking Supervision, 'Sound Credit Risk Assessment and Valuation for Loans' (June 2006), available at <https://www.bis.org/publ/bcbs126.pdf>. In a further Consultative Document issued in December 2014 on revisions to the standardised approach for credit risk, the BCBS suggested a definition of non-performing, whose threshold includes (among other criteria) 90 days past due for loans, and 30 days past due for securities. The purpose of these criteria is to calculate a 'non-performing asset' (NPA) ratio when assessing exposures to other banks. At the time of issue, the proposals in this consultation were described by the BCBS as 'at an early stage of development'.

and 'forbearance'.[28] The definition in this document applies to all credit exposures from on-balance sheet loans, including debt securities, and off-balance sheet items, such as loan commitments and financial guarantees. The definition of non-performing developed for this purpose combines three existing concepts: (1) all exposures defined as in default under the Basel definition quoted above are considered non-performing; (2) exposures determined to be impaired for accounting purposes are defined as non-performing; and (3) loans that are past due by 90 days or where it is determined that full repayment is unlikely[29] are also considered non-performing.

The BCBS clarifies that collateralisation does not influence past due status and should not be considered in the categorisation of NPEs.[30] In this context, forbearance is defined as 'a concession granted by a bank to a counterparty for reasons of financial difficulties that would not be otherwise considered by the lender'.[31] Basically, forbearance comprises concessions and waivers extended to any exposures in the form of a loan, a debt security or an off-balance sheet item due to the position of the counterparty. This definition covers exposures of performing and non-performing status before the granting of forbearance measures. The main purpose is to ensure a harmonised approach to the disclosure of modified loans and debt securities due to borrower's financial difficulties.[32]

NPLs have become a recurrent phenomenon in some financial institutions and have slowed down economic activity, especially for countries that rely mainly on bank financing, as is the case in the euro area.[33] For example, Italy and Greece registered a sharp rise of NPLs and large losses among domestic banks.[34] The Italian banking sector reported an outstanding stock of €189 billion of gross NPLs mostly accumulated during the financial and sovereign debt crisis.[35] In Greece, Law No. 4354/2015 regulates the assignment and the transfer of NPL claims.[36] The new legislation provides specific rules on (1) obtaining a license from the Bank of Greece for Debt Management Companies and Debt Transfer Companies (DTCs) for NPLs; (2) the agreements assigning the management of claims and (3) the sale and transfer of claims from NPLs and credit agreements. The law adopts a

---

28 These new definitions are intended to complement existing accounting and regulatory measures, and as reference points to promote comparability. See Basel Committee on Banking Supervision, 'Prudential Treatment of Problem Assets – Definitions of Non-performing Exposures and Forbearance' Guidelines (4 April 2017), available at <http://www.bis.org/bcbs/publ/d403.htm>.

29 This is similar to the definition developed by the EBA in the 'Final implementing technical standards (ITS) on supervisory reporting on forbearance and non-performing exposures under Article 99(4) of Regulation (EU) No. 575/2013' published in 2014.

30 The BCBS also notes that non-performing status should be applied at the level of the counterparty in the case of exposures to a non-retail counterparty, and at the level of each exposure in the case of exposures to a retail counterparty.

31 Basel Committee on Banking Supervision (n 1) 7.

32 The BCBS recommends banks not to use forbearance practices to avoid classifying loans as non-performing.

33 International Monetary Fund, 'A Strategy for Resolving Europe's Problem Loans' (2015) Staff Discussion Note, SDN/15/19 9, available at <https://www.imf.org/external/pubs/ft/sdn/2015/sdn1519.pdf>.

34 European Banking Authority, 'Risk Dashboard. Data as of Q4 2016' (2017) 30, available at <http://www.eba.europa.eu/documents/10180/1804996/EBA+Dashboard+-+Q4+2016.pdf/74c92eb4–3083-47fc-bd5d-6a8ac64e8393>.

35 Bank of Italy, 'Financial Stability Report' No. 1 (April 2020) 35. It is reported that the coverage ratio – provisions in relation to the whole stock of NPLs – reached 52.4%.

36 Law 4354/2015, 'Non-performing Loans Management, Wage Provisions, and Other Urgent Provisions Concerning the Implementation of the Fiscal Goals and Structural Reforms Agreement' (Government Gazette A'176).

90-day past due threshold to define non-performing assets; however, the NPL figures do not provide information about the level of provision held against these loans by banks.

It can be observed that high percentages of NPLs reduce profitability, increase funding costs and tie up bank capital, which negatively impacts on credit supply and ultimately economic growth. Addressing the rise of NPLs has become a key concern for the EU banking system, and the supervision of deteriorated assets requires comprehensive action to deal with these types of bad loans sitting on banks' books.[37] The European Central Bank (ECB) established a prudential regime to strengthen the capital rules and banking supervision since NPLs represent the major systemic threat that banks are facing as they may rapidly lead to bank and borrower insolvencies.[38]

In March 2017, the ECB produced qualitative guidance on NPLs, including consideration of how the 'unlikely to pay' criterion should be applied in practice, and how banks should manage and monitor forbearance, write offs and collateral valuation.[39] This supervisory toolkit aims to address the issue of identification and allocation of past due loans in the EU banking sector. The NPL guidance has been further developed in the prudential treatment for distressed assets through supervisory expectations on the classification of NPEs.[40] The ECB's supervisory expectations supplement the NPL guidance by specifying the regulatory actions when assessing a bank's levels of prudential provisions for NPEs. Although the guidance can be considered a form of principles-based regulation,[41] these regulatory initiatives provide some substantial degree of harmonisation, which permits international comparisons of the asset side and facilitates both loan classification and the definition of NPLs.

The gains from a harmonised approach would be to aid the comparability of firms, to quantify forbearance and have a better understanding of the relationship between NPLs, economic growth and financial stability. From this perspective, it can be argued that there might be a role for a more discretionary prudential policy since the international regulatory response to this issue has been concentrated on enhancing disclosure and provisioning. It can also be observed that the increasing number of policy responses of supervisory authorities is driven by the potential proliferation of market failures in the business of NPLs,

---

37 Bholat et al. (n 6) 9.

38 The question of asset quality classification has become prominent since the divergence in practice between firms and regulators in defining 'non-performing' has hampered the need for NPL harmonisation. Within the NPL category are comprised: (1) bad loans; (2) default loans and (3) distressed debt. The classification depends on several factors and varies across jurisdictions. In some countries, non-performing means that the loan is impaired while in others can mean that payments are past due. Nevertheless, a rather common feature of non-performing loans appears to be that a payment is 'more than 90 days' past due, especially for retail loans. The classification of the loan as non-performing by the bank and when the loan becomes 'bad debt' depends on domestic regulations. Further, the rising discrepancy between banks' overdue loan ratios and NPL ratios makes difficult to identify deteriorated loans that are not formally classified as non-performing. This problem is particularly evident in the Chinese banks where the fragility of loan loss provisions does not help to mitigate the NPL classification issue. See Yuan Yang, 'China Banks in Stand-Off with Regulators on Loan Loss Provisions' *Financial Times* (London, 30 October 2016).

39 ECB, 'Guidance to Banks on Non-performing Loans' (2017) 49–50, available at <https://www.bankingsupervision.europa.eu/ecb/pub/pdf/guidance_on_npl.en.pdf>.

40 ECB, 'Addendum to the ECB Guidance to Banks on Nonperforming Loans: Prudential Provisioning Backstop for Non-performing Exposures' (2018) 2, available at <https://www.bankingsupervision.europa.eu/ecb/pub/pdf/ssm.npl_addendum_201803.en.pdf>.

41 The NPL guidance contains soft law recommendations not binding and not enforceable that leave discretion to national authorities to implement them at the domestic level.

namely, information asymmetries, negative externalities and moral hazard.[42] Further, the poor incentives for investors and corporations to restructure NPEs and lack of expertise to deal with NPLs contribute to rely on the public intervention.[43] While the principles-based approach to loan classification has some merit, it gives firms wide discretion in the way they account for loan impairments. But even in the presence of a more prescriptive regime, the successful implementation of regulatory strategy in practice depends mostly on the adequacy of the enforcement system.

16.4 The restructuring regime of NPLs

In the wake of the GFC, the lack of an internationally harmonised accounting concept of impairment created a grey area with respect to forbearance and the restructuring of troubled loans. The restructuring regime for NPLs identifies a set of regulatory tools to recover the value of NPEs: the various mechanisms adopted by banks and regulators such as out-of-court proceedings raise concerns on the divergent implementation of these measures among jurisdictions. IAS 39 provided that restructuring is a credit event that might lead to impairment and impairments have to be calculated based on the difference between the original and modified conditions.[44] The standard does not rule out cases of restructuring where there is no impairment and there is ambiguity about whether once restructured, an exposure needs to continue being identified as impaired.[45] On this view, it has been argued that 'lenders choose to extend or otherwise modify the terms of loans that show evidence of financial stress, these loans might avoid arrears and as such might not be identified as impaired (or non-performing), despite underlying credit deterioration of the borrower'.[46]

In 2011, the FSA issued guidance on loan forbearance, raising concerns that 'certain accounting practices can have the effect of concealing the full effect of impairment and forbearance and thus may not present the true nature of credit risk within retail portfolios'.[47] In the US, the Financial Accounting Standards Board published a guidance on the definition of troubled debt restructurings with the aim of developing more consistent standards in determining whether a modification of a loan receivable constitutes a concession to a borrower that is experiencing financial difficulties.[48]

---

42 John Fell, Maciej Grodzicki, Reiner Martin and Edward O'Brien, 'Addressing Market Failures in the Resolution of Non-performing Loans in the Euro Area' Financial Stability Review, Special Features (November 2016) 134, where it is argued that 'public policy responses are warranted to reduce the cost and duration of debt recovery while also addressing information asymmetries between better-informed banks and potential investors'. See also John Fell, Maciej Grodzicki, Dejan Krušec, Reiner Martin and Edward O'Brien, 'Overcoming Non-performing Loan Market Failures with Transaction Platforms' Financial Stability Review, Special Features (November 2017) 130.

43 European Systemic Risk Board, 'Resolving Non-performing Loans in Europe' (July 2017) 28, available at <https://www.esrb.europa.eu/pub/pdf/reports/20170711_resolving_npl_report.en.pdf>.

44 Kees Camfferman, 'The Emergence of the "Incurred-Loss" Model for Credit Losses in IAS 39' (2015) 12 *Accounting in Europe* 17.

45 Charles W. Calomiris and Stephen H. Haber, *Fragile by Design: The Political Origins of Banking Crises and Scarce Credit* (Princeton University Press 2014) 4.

46 David Bholat et al. (n 9) 40. On this discussion, see also Shekhar Aiyar et al., 'A Strategy for Resolving Europe's Problem Loans' International Monetary Fund, Staff Discussion Note SDN/15/19 (September 2015) 5.

47 Financial Services Authority, 'Forbearance and Impairment Provisions – Mortgages' FSA Finalised Guidance (October 2011) 23, available at <https://www.fca.org.uk/publication/finalised-guidance/fg11_15.pdf>.

48 Financial Accounting Standards Board, 'Accounting Standards Update No. 2011–02, Receivables (Topic 310): A Creditor's Determination of Whether a Restructuring Is a Troubled Debt Restructuring' (April 2011) 1–2, available at <https://asc.fasb.org/imageRoot/05/7484705.pdf>.

For Central, Eastern and Southeastern Europe (CESEE), the 'Vienna Initiative' – a private-public sector forum formed by international financial institutions, international organisations, public authorities and private banks – has launched an action plan to establish a common platform to create the right conditions for Western banks to remain engaged in emerging eastern European economies.[49] The 'Vienna Initiative' aims to establish coordinated resolution policies for dealing with distressed assets as NPLs are considered a serious obstacle to economic recovery because they affect banks' lending performance.[50]

In terms of the accounting treatment of NPLs, regulators have been incentivised to delay the recognition of any losses until banks developed sufficient loan loss reserves.[51] If there is a place for forbearance as a resolution or macro-prudential tool in certain circumstances to prevent the worst of economic catastrophes, this suggests that the search for a single, deterministic definition of NPLs is misconstrued. Then the focus of regulators should be on establishing a global standard NPL definition and on getting banks, regulators, investors and other stakeholders to monitor asset quality in a more timely and transparent way. On this point, the European Banking Authority (EBA) recently issued the 'NPL transaction templates' in order to create comparable and standardised data on non-performing assets.[52] The main objective is to reduce the information asymmetries in the NPLs transactions and provide incentives to promote secondary markets for distressed loans.

At origination, lenders collect information about obligors: in liquidation procedures, courts collect information about defaulted obligors. However, in the interval in-between, in the absence of market pricing for non-traded loans, there is a need for continuing monitoring of asset quality by looking at the overall solvency of obligors, the progress of projects the loans are financing and any other key risks that are evolving are obligor-specific and macroeconomic.[53] As regulatory standards shifted from incurred to expected loss models, it can be argued that substantial co-ordination among resolving tools represents a way forward to establish a harmonised insolvency regime for NPLs.[54]

16.5 Resolution options for NPLs: AMCs

Resolving the NPLs problem necessitates allocating losses within the system that have to be borne by either banks' customers, banks themselves, investors or sovereign states.[55] The fact that there is no universal internationally accepted definition of NPLs – for instance,

---

49 European Bank Coordination Vienna Initiative, 'Vienna Initiative Pushes for Action Plan to Deal with NPLs in Central and South-Eastern Europe. Fostering an Effective Framework for NPL Restructuring and Resolution' (26 September 2014), available at <http://vienna-initiative.com/wp-content/uploads/2014/10/NPL-Press-Release.pdf>.

50 James Roaf, 'Non-performing Loans in CESEE' Vienna (23 September 2014), available at <http://vienna-initiative.com/wp-content/uploads/2014/11/Session-I-James-Roaf-IMF.pdf>.

51 Piers Haben, 'Standardising the Definition of Non-performing Exposure and Forbearance' (2015) EBA Case Study, available at <http://docplayer.net/20943532-Case-study-standardising-the-definition-of-non-performing-exposure-and-forbearance.html>.

52 European Banking Authority, 'EBA NPL Templates' (14 December 2017), available at <http://www.eba.europa.eu/-/eba-publishes-its-standardised-data-templates-as-a-step-to-reduce-npls>.

53 European Banking Authority, 'Draft Guidelines on Loan Origination and Monitoring' (19 June 2019) Consultation Paper EBA/CP/2019/04, 34–36 <https://eba.europa.eu/documents/10180/2831176/CP+on+GLs+on+loan+origination+and+monitoring.pdf/3bc64e01-a4d1-4c7e-92d4-1dd84f4b234c> (accessed 27 July 2020).

54 David M. Bholat, 'The Future of Central Bank Data' (2013) 14 *Journal of Banking Regulation* 192.

55 Benoit Mesnard, Alienor Anne Claire Duvillet-Margerit, Cairen Power and Marcel Magnus, 'Non-performing Loans in the Banking Union: Stocktaking and Challenges' European Parliament (18 March

as a sum of borrowed money upon which the debtor has not made his or her scheduled payments for at least 90 days – makes it difficult to assess which is the most viable option to resolve deteriorated assets.[56]

Various proposals to restructure NPLs have been advanced, namely, individual bank restructurings, bank-internal bad bank units and bank-specific AMCs.[57] Enria suggested establishing an AMC with government support to resolve NPLs selling the assets at their economic value.[58] Generally, the AMC is a special purpose limited liability company created to facilitate the transfer of NPLs from financial institutions and administer and dispose of acquired assets.[59] It is important that the AMC is insulated from political interference in the disposition and restructuring of assets since transparency with respect to all of its operations and its performance is critical for the AMC's political independence.[60] Where AMCs are established to manage assets from running (rather than defunct banks), the price for removing the assets is a critical operational issue that can delay restructurings where banks seek to avoid marking down their assets or transferring the potential upside to a third party.[61]

Baudino and Yun observed that 'effective communication on resolution measures are essential to provide clarity to market participants on the resolution tools and their timelines, build public support for the initiatives, and establish a reference point for ex post assessment of the NPL resolution strategy'.[62] Avgouleas and Goodhart proposed a new structure for a Pan-European 'bad bank' with virtually ring-fenced country subsidiaries to ensure burden sharing without debt mutualisation.[63] This proposal has been echoed in the 2018 Commission blueprint on national AMCs[64]; the document provides non-binding principles to guide Member States in the implementation of AMCs at the domestic level. These principles highlight the role of AMCs in removing troubled assets from banks' balance sheets and restructuring banks with high levels of NPLs. It is stated that 'AMCs can be private or (partly) publicly funded without State aid, if the State can be considered to act as any other

2016) 4, available at <http://www.europarl.europa.eu/RegData/etudes/BRIE/2016/574400/IPOL_BRI(2016)574400_EN.pdf>.

56 Luis Cortavarria, Claudia Dziobek, Akihiro Kanaya and Inwon Song, 'Loan Review, Provisioning, and Macroeconomic Linkages' (2000) IMF Working Paper No. 00/195, 11–12.

57 See Patrizia Baudino and Hyuncheol Yun, 'Resolution of Non-performing Loans – Policy Options' (2017) FSI Insights on Policy Implementation No. 3, 3–4, available at <https://www.bis.org/fsi/publ/insights3.pdf>.

58 Andrea Enria, 'The EU Banking Sector - Risks and Recovery. A Single Market Perspective' Luxembourg (2017) 16, available at <https://www.esm.europa.eu/speeches-and-presentations/esm-seminar-andrea-enria-eba-chairperson>.

59 Xinjiang Wei, 'Asset Management Company and Debit-Equity Swap Practice in China' (2002) 17 *Journal of International Banking Law* 296.

60 Stefan Ingves, Steven A. Seelig and Dong He, 'Issues in the Establishment of Asset Management Companies' (2004) IMF Policy Discussion Paper, PDP/04/3, 14.

61 Thomas Laryea, 'Approaches to Corporate Debt Restructuring in the Wake of Financial Crises' (2010) International Monetary Fund, SPN/10/02, 26.

62 Patrizia Baudino and Hyuncheol Yun, 'Resolution of Non-performing Loans – Policy Options' (October 2017) FSI Insights on Policy Implementation No. 3, 4, available at <https://www.bis.org/fsi/publ/insights3.pdf>.

63 Emilios Avgouleas and Charles Goodhart, 'Utilizing AMCs to Tackle Eurozone's Legacy Non-performing Loans' (2017) 2017 *European Economy Banks, Regulation, and the Real Sector* 103, available at <http://european-economy.eu/wp-content/uploads/2017/07/EE_1.2017.pdf>.

64 European Commission, 'AMC Blueprint. Accompanying the document Communication from the Commission to the European Parliament, the European Council, the Council and the European Central Bank. Second Progress Report on the Reduction of Non-performing Loans in Europe' Commission Staff Working Document, Brussels, SWD(2018) 72 final, available at <http://ec.europa.eu/finance/docs/policy/180314-staff-working-document-non-performing-loans_en.pdf>.

economic agent'.[65] The blueprint underlines the need to underpin the operation of AMCs by State aid rules, the Bank Recovery and Resolution Directive (BRRD)[66] and the Single Resolution Mechanism[67] to establish a common level playing field for banks on resolving NPLs. In this context, NPL provisioning treatment is still not sufficient in the absence of harmonised deposit insurance.

Converging towards a harmonised approach on recovery and resolution plans for NPLs is the question at stake.[68] This means that EU rules will have an impact on where banks shed operations due to cost factors of maintaining operations and risk will likely migrate to less regulated local entities in a risk race to the bottom. Barriers to the resolution of problematic loans such as legal or economic impediments to collateral realisation may also result in the inability or unwillingness of banks to write loans off in a timely manner. This can result in a higher number of highly provisioned loans remaining on these banks' balance sheets. Since there is a lack of harmonised insolvency proceedings and deposit insurance scheme, the proposals to establish AMCs and bad bank units seem flawed, although some commentators observe that 'the public sector involvement is necessary'.[69] However, policy-makers and investors could explore alternative solutions to restructure NPLs and 'public actors could efficiently use public resources to solve the NPL problem'.[70]

The methods of financing for AMCs present several implications in terms of public guarantee and government support. The recourse to public funds to deal with NPLs may face risks of sovereign instability, i.e. unexpected default or downgrading. This can determine macroeconomic vulnerabilities and affect investors of AMCs particularly in jurisdictions where the legal system makes it difficult to recover assets.[71] In case of a systemic crisis, the government may face the need to provide solvency assurances to depositors and commit public resources to recapitalise banks.[72] Further, public-funded AMCs have social

---

65 Ibid., 4.
66 EU Bank Recovery and Resolution Directive (BRRD), Directive 2014/59/EU of the European Parliament and of the Council of 15 May 2014.
67 The Single Resolution Mechanism (SRM) has been introduced by Regulation (EU) No. 806/2014 of the European Parliament and of the Council of 15 July 2014 establishing uniform rules and a uniform procedure for the resolution of credit institutions and certain investment firms in the framework of a Single Resolution Mechanism and a Single Resolution Fund and amending Regulation (EU) No. 1093/2010, OJ L 225 of 30 July 2014, 1.
68 Vitor Constâncio, 'Resolving Europe's NPL Burden: Challenges and Benefits' Keynote speech at the Event 'Tackling Europe's Non-performing Loans Crisis: Restructuring Debt, Reviving Growth' (2017), available at <https://www.ecb.europa.eu/press/key/date/2017/html/sp170203.en.html>.
69 Andrea Enria, Piers Haben and Mario Quagliariello, 'Completing the Repair of the EU Banking Sector- A Critical Review of an EU Asset Management Company' (2017) 1 *European Economy* 67, available at <http://european-economy.eu/2017-1/completing-the-repair-of-the-eu-banking-sector-a-critical-review-of-an-eu-asset-management-company/>.
70 Eleonora Broccardo and Maria Mazzuca, 'New Development: Can "Public" Market-based Solutions Restore the Banking System? The Case of Non-performing Loans (NPLs)' (2017) 37 *Public Money & Management* 515–516.
71 Ben Fung, Jason George, Stefan Hohl and Guonan Ma, 'Public Asset Management Companies in East Asia. A Comparative Study' (February 2004) Financial Stability Institute, Bank for International Settlements, Occasional Paper No. 3, 19, available at <https://www.bis.org/fsi/fsipapers03.pdf>.
72 Rym Ayadi, Giovanni Ferri and Rosa M. Lastra, 'Systemic Solutions to Systemic Crises. Dealing with NPLs in the Eurozone' (2017) 1 *European Economy*, 177, available at <http://european-economy.eu/2017-1/systemic-solutions-to-systemic-crises-dealing-with-npls-in-the-eurozone/>.

implications: bearing the costs of NPLs resolution can create negative externalities, such as an increase in taxes or fiscal constraints.[73]

Alongside these considerations, it can be argued that the AMC option resembles the bail-out programmes that mostly end up at the expense of taxpayers and depositors. Establishing institutional AMCs may not be efficient to work out the NPLs and may not be sufficient to prevent moral hazard problems, i.e. potential collusive behaviour between the AMC and government authorities.[74] As observed, 'NPLs and collateral are often long-term "parked" in an AMC, not liquidated'.[75] Specifically, AMCs can be affected by political instability and poor internal governance with the consequence of ineffective restructuring processes for bad loans. On the basis of the above analysis, it may be preferable from a policy perspective to find market-based solutions, such as private options, i.e. workout plans.

16.5.1 Out-of-court proceedings and securitisation mechanisms

An example of effective and timely resolution mechanisms for NPLs is found in the Italian piece of legislation (Law No. 132/2015),[76] amending the procedures for firms' liquidation and restructuring of assets. The law aims to increase the speed and efficiency of insolvency proceedings and property foreclosures, and to promote higher recovery rates for creditors. Another legislative initiative concerning NPLs recovery (i.e. non-possessory pledge and foreclosure of collateral) has been launched with the Italian insolvency law reform of 2016.[77] The legal framework introduced the possibility to include private enforcement clauses in loan contracts with firms, allowing creditors to take ownership of collateral out-of-court in case of a debtor's default.[78]

The out-of-court enforcement procedures for secured loans granted to enterprises amend the 'pactum marcianum' (the civil law equivalent to the common law doctrine for mortgages and charges) according to which the creditor takes over or disposes the collateral but needs to compensate the debtor for any excess value of the collateral once the loan is

---

73 Ralph De Haas and Stephan Knobloch, 'In the Wake of the Crisis: Dealing with Distressed Debt across the Transition Region' (January 2010) EBRD Working Paper No. 112, 12, available at <http://ssrn.com/abstract=1742286>.
74 John Bartel and Yiping Huang, 'Dealing with the Bad Loans of the Chinese Banks' (July 2000) Discussion Paper Series No. 13, APEC Study Center, Columbia University, 18, available at <https://www8.gsb.columbia.edu/apec/sites/apec/files/files/discussion/boninhuang.pdf>.
75 Stefan Ingves, Steven A. Seelig and Dong He, 'Issues in the Establishment of Asset Management Companies' (May 2004) IMF Policy Discussion Paper, 9–10, available at <https://www.imf.org/external/pubs/ft/pdp/2004/pdp03.pdf>.
76 Italian Law No. 132/2015 published in Italian OJ No. 192 of 20 August 2015 that converted the Law Decree No. 83/2015 published in Italian OJ No. 147 of 27 June 2015 available at <http://www.gazzettaufficiale.it/atto/serie_generale/caricaDettaglioAtto/originario?atto.dataPubblicazioneGazzetta=2015–08–20&atto.codiceRedazionale=15G00136&isAnonimo=false&normativi=true&tipoVigenza=originario&tipoSerie=serie_generale&currentPage=1>.
77 Italian Law Decree No. 59/2016 converted into Italian Law No. 119/2016. For a commentary, see Elisa Brodi et al., 'New Measures for Speeding Up Credit Recovery: An Initial Analysis of Decree Law 59/2016' (2016) Bank of Italy Notes on Financial Stability and Supervision No. 4, 3–4, available at <https://www.bancaditalia.it/pubblicazioni/note-stabilita/2016-0004/no4-note-financial-stability.pdf?language_id=1>.
78 European Commission, 'Italy – Review of Progress on Policy Measures Relevant for the Correction of Macro-economic Imbalances' (2016) 13, available at <https://ec.europa.eu/info/files/italy-review-progress-policy-measures-relevant-correction-macroeconomic-imbalances-december-2016_en>.

satisfied.[79] These enforcement rules should reduce court involvement and speed up the process of collecting bad assets: this would facilitate reaching agreement among creditors and enhance the marketability of NPLs.[80] In addition, the law introduces provisions to facilitate access to finance for small- and medium-sized enterprises (SMEs) enabling entrepreneurs to pledge movable assets while continuing to use them, and to enforce new non-possessory security interests over movable assets (i.e. floating charge). The main aim of these provisions is to enhance out-of-court restructuring agreements in view of a timely resolution of firms' crises.

The Italian out-of-court proceeding allows creditors of a firm that has filed for '*concordato preventivo*' to submit restructuring plans in competition with the one presented by the firm.[81] These reforms introduced a systematic approach in the resolution options to address bad loans, particularly in protecting creditors' interests to invest in distressed debt of viable firms and to pursue higher recovery rates.[82] The rules on non-possessory pledge and foreclosure of collateral can have a systemic impact in the restructuring of troubled banks as they can enhance legal certainty and confidence in the process of divesting NPLs portfolios. As noted by the ECB, 'the Italian supervisory regulation for NPLs is mainly principles-based with regard to the guidelines issued to banks on NPLs management practices'.[83] On this view, the Italian government developed a mechanism of double guarantees[84]: the guarantee to collateralise liabilities and sell the senior tranches under the State backed-scheme 'GACS' (Guarantee on Securitization of Bank Non Performing Loans),[85] and the guarantee to inject capital by purchasing shares. The State provides a double process of securitisation: (1) on the credit enhancement of senior notes and (2) on the collateralised losses of the

79　José Garrido, 'Insolvency and Enforcement Reforms in Italy' (2016) IMF Working Papers, 8, available at <https://www.imf.org/external/pubs/ft/wp/2016/wp16134.pdf>.

80　The Italian Insolvency law provides both in-court and out-of-court restructuring tools. See Monica Marcucci, Alessandra Pischedda and Vincenza Profeta, 'The Changes of the Italian Insolvency and Foreclosure Regulation Adopted in 2015' (2015) Bank of Italy Notes on Financial Stability and Supervision No. 2, 2. As observed, 'faster and more efficient insolvency and foreclosure procedures will have a twofold effect on the stock of NPLs. In the short term, they should reduce the discount required by NPL buyers, with positive effects on NPL prices and on the perspective of development of a market for these assets'.

81　Prior to the law reform, a firm filing for '*concordato preventivo*' had the exclusive authority to submit a restructuring plan. The '*concordato preventivo*' is an alternative procedure of the liquidation of enterprises, it allows creditors to participate actively in the sale of assets and, overall, in the reorganisation process.

82　José Garrido, Emanuel Kopp and Anke Weber, 'Cleaning-Up Bank Balance Sheets: Economic, Legal, and Supervisory Measures for Italy' (2016) IMF Working Paper, WP/16/135, 26–27.

83　ECB, 'Stocktake of National Supervisory Practices and Legal Frameworks Related to NPLs' (September 2016) 87, available at <https://www.bankingsupervision.europa.eu/legalframework/publiccons/pdf/npl/stock_taking.en.pdf>.

84　On April 2016, Italian Parliament enacted the Law No. 49 of 14.2.2016, converting Law Decree No. 18/2016 providing for a State Guarantee for NLPs securitisation transactions.

85　The Guarantee on Securitization of Bank Non-performing Loans (GACS) introduced by Italian Law No. 49/2016 is an aid-free scheme aiming to assist Italian banks in securitising and moving NPLs off their balance sheets. Basically, it is a State guarantee scheme open to all banks on a voluntary basis. The State guarantee consists in remunerating the senior notes at market terms according to the risk taken, i.e. in a manner acceptable for a private operator under market conditions. The Ministry of Economy and Finance (MEF) can issue a GACS guarantee to secure the payment obligations of Italian Special Purpose Vehicles (SPVs) in relation to senior tranches of asset-backed notes issued by the SPVs within the securitisation transactions of NPLs according to the Italian securitisation law No. 130/1999. It can be observed that Italian Law No. 49/2016 allows for the provision of State guarantees for NPLs securitisation transactions that would contribute to alleviate the pressure on banks' balance sheets.

junior bondholders.[86] The government guarantee should favour the coverage of the gap between the net book value and the market value of the NPLs with a view to encouraging trading in bad loans. It can be argued that the purpose of the GACS scheme is to involve a wide range of investors, stimulate banks to restructure NPLs and restore the necessary liquidity.

The solution adopted by the Italian regulatory authorities to address the NPLs issue is a welcome approach in the current legislative framework even if the guarantees mechanism constitutes an accounting makeup – as the losses cannot disappear – rather than a full resolution of problems. The European Commission observed that 'the State guarantee on the senior tranche will only become effective, if at least more than half of the non-guaranteed and risk-bearing junior tranche has been successfully sold to private market participants'.[87] The GACS system to resolve NPLs raises complex challenges linked to market conditions: a restructuring mechanism that reflects a regulatory compromise where the guarantees could be activated at the expense of taxpayer money.

16.5.2 *The EU regulatory initiatives*

In this context, the Commission published a proposal for a directive on minimum procedures for out-of-court settlement regarding NPLs.[88] This new proposal links the various supervisory initiatives taken by the Single Supervisory Mechanism (SSM) and EBA in addressing the NPLs issue.[89] In managing NPLs, the proposal aims (1) to foster debt recovery procedures through the implementation of a distinct common accelerated extrajudicial collateral enforcement procedure and (2) to create secondary markets for NPLs. The overall objective is to reduce the burden of NPLs in banks' balance sheets by introducing efficient out-of-court procedures to recover value from collateral and to lower the costs of resolving NPLs making them more competitive in the market.[90] As claimed, 'active NPL resolution measures are needed to bring NPL ratios on a firm downward trajectory over the medium term'.[91] The need to ensure consistency in the restructuring proceedings and to create a harmonised insolvency regime has been recognised by the EU Council in the action plan

---

86 It can be noted that Italian law does not require the consent of the borrower for the sale of a loan, only the notification of the borrower. Article 58 of the Italian Banking Act (No. 385/93) provides an exemption from the obligation to notify each debtor in the case of a bulk loan sale.

87 European Commission, 'State Aid: Commission Approves Impaired Asset Management Measures for Banks in Hungary and Italy' IP/16/279 (10 February 2016), available at <http://europa.eu/rapid/press-release_IP-16-279_en.htm>.

88 European Commission, 'Proposal for a Directive of the European Parliament and of the Council on Credit Servicers, Credit Purchasers and the Recovery of Collateral' Brussels, COM(2018) 135 final, available at <https://ec.europa.eu/info/law/better-regulation/initiatives/com-2018-135_en>.

89 EBA, 'Guidelines on Common Procedures and Methodologies for the Supervisory Review and Evaluation Process (SREP)' EBA/GL/2014/13 (19 December 2014). See also ECB, 'Addendum to the ECB Guidance to Banks on Nonperforming Loans: Prudential Provisioning Backstop for Non-performing Exposures' (2018) 2; ECB, 'Guidance to Banks on Non-performing Loans' (2017) 49–50; ECB, 'Stocktake of National Supervisory Practices and Legal Frameworks Related to NPLs' (2017).

90 Alexander Lehmann, 'Risk Reduction through Europe's Distressed Debt Market' Bruegel Policy Contribution, Issue No. 02 (18 January 2018) 5–6, available at <http://bruegel.org/wp-content/uploads/2018/01/PC-02_2018-100118.pdf>.

91 Kamiar Mohaddes, Mehdi Raissi and Anke Weber, 'Can Italy Grow Out of Its NPL Overhang? A Panel Threshold Analysis' (2017) 159 *Economics Letters* 186.

for NPLs.[92] The Council underlines the opportunity to set common principles and harmonised key elements of insolvency law, such as minimum standards for secured creditor protection.[93]

The Council's initiatives have been reinforced in the Communication on the 'Reduction of Non-performing Loans in Europe' where it is suggested for banks to hold sufficient loan loss coverage for newly originated loans if these become distressed exposures.[94] It is also highlighted that the problem of NPLs could be addressed by monitoring the temporal triggers in contracts, specific cash flow impairments (i.e. principal, interest past due) and collateral value. In the same direction is the Commission's proposal to establish 'preventive restructuring frameworks' for financially distressed firms.[95] The proposed directive complements the 2015 EU Insolvency Regulation[96] and aims to harmonise pre-insolvency restructuring mechanisms for NPLs among Member States. The draft directive intends to incentivise firms to reduce the volume of non-performing assets although 'it creates a refuge for failing firms that should be liquidated'.[97] However, the proposal does not define the ranking of claims (particularly for banks holding NPLs with collateral) in pre-insolvency proceedings, a serious flaw that can undermine the objectives of the directive.

For resolution tools to work in practice, there needs to be a full understanding of the true value of assets in a crisis situation and therefore of asset quality more generally. Adequate provisioning for NPLs requires overcoming complex strategic incentives that banks have either to keep LLPs low, or to avoid writing NPLs off from their balance sheets. The timing of losses following as a result of provisions or write offs and the level of LLPs set aside for future NPLs on the balance sheet are often part of a bank's strategy to smooth out reported earnings and reported capitalisation.[98]

16.6 Conclusion

Resolution options for NPLs represent a major challenge for bank supervisors and regulators: the accumulation of high volumes of deteriorated assets affects the solvency, liquidity and lending capacity of firms. Further, the presence of NPLs can have a systemic impact on the financial sector: this is exacerbated by a lack of harmonised definitions of NPEs and

92 ECOFIN Council, 'Action Plan to Tackle Non-performing Loans in Europe' 11173/17 (Brussels, 11 July 2017) 3, available at <http://data.consilium.europa.eu/doc/document/ST-11173-2017-INIT/en/pdf>.
93 ECOFIN Council, 'Report of the FSC Subgroup on Non-performing Loans' 9854/17 (Brussels, 31 May 2017) 61, available at <http://data.consilium.europa.eu/doc/document/ST-9854-2017-INIT/en/pdf>.
94 EU Commission, 'Communication from the Commission to the European Parliament, the Council and the European Central Bank. Second Progress Report on the Reduction of Non-performing Loans in Europe' COM(2018) 133 final, 8, available at <http://ec.europa.eu/finance/docs/policy/180314-communication-non-performing-loans_en.pdf>.
95 EU Commission, 'Proposal for a Directive of the European Parliament and of the Council on Preventive Restructuring Frameworks, Second Chance and Measures to Increase the Efficiency of Restructuring, Insolvency and Discharge Procedures and Amending Directive 2012/30/EU' COM(2016) 723 final, available at <http://ec.europa.eu/information_society/newsroom/image/document/2016-48/proposal_40046.pdf>.
96 Regulation (EU) 2015/848 of the European Parliament and of the Council of 20 May 2015 on insolvency proceedings (OJ 2015 L 141, 19).
97 Horst Eidenmüller, 'Contracting for a European Insolvency Regime' (2017) 18 *European Business Organization Law Review* 276.
98 Paul Beck and Ganapathi Narayanamoorthy, 'Did the SEC Impact Banks' Loan Loss Reserve Policies and Their Informativeness?' (2013) 56 *Journal of Accounting and Economics* 42. See also Iftekhar Hasan and Larry D. Wall (n 18) 129–130.

lack of co-ordination in the resolving policies. Specifically, the resolution toolkit varies among national supervisory authorities raising uncertainty on the viable resolving tool for distressed loans. Dealing with NPLs issues presents concerns in terms of accounting and regulatory treatment since countries adopt different standards for loan classification in their domestic markets. The key economic consequence of insufficient loan loss provisioning and the accumulation of NPLs on bank balance sheets is the combined threat of a capital crisis and a liquidity crisis.

The NPL problem is even more complicated because of the lack of consolidation of data and information disclosures that should be the primary source to identify the deterioration of asset quality at an early stage. Various proposals to restructure NPLs have been advanced in the banking industry; however, harmonisation of insolvency rules and proceedings seems to be the way forward to prevent the accumulation of bad loans. The fragility of the European banking sector and the weaknesses of the bank credit channel for monetary policy transmission highlight the widespread risk of NPLs.[99] New pieces of legislation have been introduced at the national level (e.g. in Italy) to reduce the fragmentation of insolvency regimes although such national responses leave broad discretion to competent authorities. Domestic intervention should be combined with internationally co-ordinated insolvency procedures such as workouts, preventative measures, securitisation mechanisms and AMCs. However, in the absence of a consolidated and universal definition of asset quality it seems difficult to establish a common approach regarding restructuring tools aimed at NPL recovery.

Glossary of terms

- Non-performing loans (NPLs): Sums of borrowed money in relation to which the debtor has not made his or her scheduled payments for at least 90 days. Described in EU legal instruments as non-performing exposures.
- Loan loss provisions (LLPs): Level of provisioning on the balance sheet commensurate with the initial expectations of the rate of recovery on loans (and therefore the pricing of credit).
- Write offs: Process by which loans and the provisions against them disappear from the balance sheet.
- Forbearance: A waiver (concession) granted by a bank to a counterparty for reasons of financial difficulties that would not be otherwise considered by the lender.
- Asset Management Company (AMC): Special purpose limited liability company created to facilitate the transfer of NPLs from financial institutions and administer and dispose of acquired assets.
- Pactum marcianum: Civil law principle according to which the creditor takes over or disposes of the collateral but needs to compensate the debtor for any excess value of the collateral once the loan is satisfied. Similar to the common law concept of foreclosure.
- Guarantee on Securitization of Bank Non Performing Loans (GACS): Introduced by Italian Law No. 49/2016 is an aid-free scheme aiming to assist Italian banks in securitising and moving NPLs off their balance sheets.

---

99 Nadege Jassaud and Edouard Vidon, 'European NPLs through the Crisis: A Policy Review' (2017) 25 *Journal of Financial Regulation & Compliance* 413, 416.

- Out-of-court procedures: Mechanisms to recover value from collateral without court involvement and to lower the costs of resolving NPLs making them more competitive in the market.
- Default: It is defined as where an obligor is 90 days past due or is unlikely to pay its credit obligations to the banking group in full, without recourse by the bank to actions such as realising security.

Practice questions

In the aftermath of the global financial crisis, a degree of standardisation has developed when it comes to the liability side of banks and other credit institutions' balance sheets. However, it is difficult to compare non-performing loans (NPLs) across firms because their definition can vary across time, regulatory jurisdiction and legal system.

Critically evaluate the EU regulatory framework of NPLs, considering the latest developments in its supervisory tools.

You may also find it useful to review the chapter through the following questions:

- What are NPLs? How are they treated globally?
- What are the main risks NPLs may pose?
- What are the supervisory tools to monitor NPLs?
- What are the resolving procedures for NPLs?

17 The impact of Brexit on the banking sector

17.1 Introduction

The Brexit vote[1] has raised several questions such as how to regulate a single banking licence,[2] mutual recognition[3] and home country control. It also raised a question: how to regulate the EU requirements for equivalence determinations in the financial sector. In this context, several proposals have been launched such as co-operation agreements, bilateral agreements, reciprocity and substantive compliance, the 'Norway model' based on the European Free Trade Association (EFTA), Member State of Reference and subsidiary vs. branch to establish common requirements for the recognition of third country regulatory regimes.

As the UK has left the EU, UK-based banks (including non-EU banks operating through UK subsidiaries) are expected to lose access to the passport regime.[4] The equivalence arrangements will give the possibility to remove and re-modulate EU laws: a solution that will allow the UK to establish a new regulatory framework or, as observed, a 'Financial Centre' model.[5] A new financial platform poses risks in terms of supervision as home-supervised 'systemic branches' to the host market are all the greater where the branch is of a third country firm, such as a post-Brexit UK firm, which operates outside the EU's supervisory governance and co-ordination requirements.[6] This framework shows a grey area on which the City might continue to thrive as a global financial centre in Europe.[7]

---

1 See the European Union Referendum Act 2015. The legislative framework for Brexit consists of the European Union (Notification of Withdrawal) Act 2017, the European Union (Withdrawal) Act 2018, as amended, the European Union (Withdrawal) Act 2019 and the European Union (Withdrawal) (No. 2) Act 2019, as well as a plethora of delegated legislation. For an overview of the Brexit process up to September 2019, see *R (on the application of Miller) v Prime Minister* [2019] UKSC 41 [7]–[15].

2 The single banking licence was introduced by the Second Banking Directive (89/646/EEC) to provide access to EU financial institutions to do business with each other. In this way, credit institutions which are authorised to operate in any Member State are allowed to establish branches and to provide cross-border services throughout the community on the basis of the principle of home country supervision.

3 Mutual recognition means harmonisation of a managed regulatory system. It implies mutual trust and adoption of common rules.

4 Dirk Schoenmaker, 'Lost Passports: A Guide to the Brexit Fallout for the City of London' Bruegel Blog Post (30 June 2016), <http://bruegel.org/2016/06/lost-passports-a-guide-to-the-brexit-fallout-for-the-city-of-london/> (accessed 25 July 2020).

5 Barnabas Reynolds, *A Blueprint for Brexit. The Future of Global Financial Services and Markets in the UK* (Politeia 2016) 27. The effect of a 'Financial Centre' model would be the development of an attractive, market-friendly regulatory framework, allowing banks and financial institutions to improve returns on equity.

6 Niamh Moloney, 'Brexit, the EU and Its Investment Banker: Rethinking "Equivalence" for the EU Capital Market' LSE Law, Society and Economy Working Papers 5/2017, 12.

7 Karel Lannoo, 'EU Financial Market Access After Brexit' (2016) 51 *Intereconomics* 255.

A scenario that, according to this view, demonstrates how Brexit will manifest more in form than in substance.[8]

However, the outcome of the Brexit negotiations process can lead to the relocation of some banking activities to other financial centres in the EU.[9] The uncertainty created in the aftermath of the controversial Brexit vote has been affecting any plans among international banking groups to expand their UK-based operations. Most interestingly, there are costs associated with the Brexit transition and 'most banks will be facing similar cost shocks, a large proportion of the additional costs are likely to be passed on to customers, rather than having a long-term impact on profitability'.[10] In addition, the impact of Brexit affects transaction costs as banking regulation can diverge from the EU legislative framework. Compliance with different regulatory regimes can create additional costs for banks, which are likely to be passed on to customers and retail investors. Until more clarity is provided, the UK financial services sector will continue to face the threat of losing business and jobs to the rest of the EU. To be sure, only relatively few jobs have been already lost to the City,[11] as most firms have established branches or subsidiaries with minimal staff. This, however, could easily change in the near future.[12] It is worth noting that, in 2017, the year immediately after the referendum, investment in the sector fell in the UK, while it rose in the EU overall and particularly in France.[13]

This chapter examines the position of the UK banking sector under different scenarios of the future relationship between the UK and the EU that currently appears more likely where UK banks will have to rely on equivalence determinations for access to the Single Market. It also discusses the consequences of the UK becoming a third country on two crucial areas, namely, bank branches and bank resolution.[14]

8 Wolf-George Ringe, 'The Irrelevance of Brexit for the European Financial Market' Oxford Legal Research Paper Series 10/2017 (April 2017) 36.
9 AFME, 'Implementing Brexit Practical Challenges for Wholesale Banking in Adapting to the New Environment' (April 2017) <https://www.afme.eu/globalassets/downloads/publications/afme-implementing-brexit-2017.pdf> (accessed 24 July 2020).
10 Luis Correia da Silva, 'Leaving the EU: Impact on Bank Customers' Oxford Law Faculty, Blog Series (7 April 2017) 3, <https://www.law.ox.ac.uk/businesslawblog/blog/2017/04/brexitnegotiationsseriesleavingeuimpactbankcustomers> (accessed 25 July 2020).
11 Estimates of the total number of jobs that would have been lost by 29 March 2019, the day of Brexit, put the figure at around 10,500. See Ben Chapman, 'Brexit: UK to Lose 10,500 City Jobs as 30 Percent of Firms Flag Plans to Move Staff' *Independent* (London, 11 December 2017) available at <https://www.independent.co.uk/news/business/news/brexit-latest-news-uk-city-job-losses-move-eu-frankfurt-paris-luxembourg-banks-europe-sam-woods-a8104176.html> (accessed 28 June 2020).
12 Senior officers in the Bank of England have been reported to have estimated that 75,000 jobs could be lost in the long term. See Kamal Ahmed, 'Bank of England Believes Brexit Could Cost 75,000 Finance Jobs' *BBC News* (London 31 October 2017), available at <https://www.bbc.co.uk/news/business-41803604> (accessed 12 April 2020).
13 According to EY research, foreign direct investment in the UK financial services sector reduced by 26% in 2017 while it grew by 13% in the EU as a whole. See Omar Ali, 'We Now Need Decisive Action to Prevent Brexit Uncertainty from Damaging the UK's Status as Europe's Leading Financial Services Hub' (EY Report, June 2018) available at <https://www.ey.com/uk/en/issues/business-environment/ey-attractiveness-survey-2018-uk-fs> (accessed 11 April 2020). In addition, London has for the first time been surpassed by Paris as the most attractive city for foreign direct investment in the sector. See EY, 'Game Changers EY's Attractiveness Survey Europe June 2018' (2018) available at <https://www.ey.com/gl/en/issues/business-environment/ey-attractiveness-survey-europe-june-2018> (accessed 6 May 2020).
14 This chapter draws heavily on our previous work: Andreas Kokkinis and Andrea Miglionico, 'Dos and Don'ts of Brexit: The Future of the UK Financial Services Sector' (2018) 7(Part I) *Law and Economics Yearly Review*

17.2 The possible Brexit scenarios and their legal impact on the banking sector

Giving effect to the outcome of the referendum that was held on 23 June 2016, the UK Government triggered article 50 of the Treaty for the Functioning of the European Union (TFEU) on 29 March 2017. This led to the commencement of a prescribed two-year period until the UK exits the EU, within which it is necessary to agree the terms of its departure and its future relationship with the EU.[15] This period was initially due to expire on 29 March 2019; it was subsequently extended until 31 October 2019 and then further until 31 January 2020.[16] A withdrawal agreement determining the conditions of the UK's exit from the EU but not the nature of their future relationship was reached on 21 October 2019 and signed on 24 January 2020 by both parties.[17] It was then approved by the European Parliament and UK Parliament and the UK exited the EU on 31 January 2020. According to articles 126–127 of the withdrawal agreement, a transition period takes effect until 31 December 2020 during which Union law is applicable to and in the UK.[18] Article 132 of the Agreement provided a possibility to extend the transition period by a decision of the Joint Committee taken by 1 July 2020, but this did not take place. Therefore, at the end of 2020 either a new agreement between the EU and the UK will have been agreed determining the nature of their relationship or EU law will cease applying to the UK without any agreement in place, a scenario widely known as 'no-deal Brexit'. However, despite the lapse of the deadline under article 132, an extension of the transition period remains theoretically possible through a new treaty between the EU and the UK.

The impact of Brexit on UK's financial services and markets is difficult to foresee with any satisfactory degree of accuracy, as the future relationship between the UK and the EU will be largely determined by the political situation in the UK.[19] It is widely assumed that the UK will leave the Single Market because the Government[20] has insisted on multiple occasions that this is the only way to give substantive effect to the decision of the British people to leave the EU.

Irrespective of how politically plausible they are, the legally possible forms that the relationship of the UK with the EU may take in the future are as follows: (1) combined European Economic Area (EEA) membership and Customs Union membership, (2) EEA membership, (3) access to the Single Market via bilateral treaties (Swiss model), (4) Customs Union membership, (5) exiting the Single Market and Customs Union with a free trade agreement with the EU and (6) exiting the Single Market and Customs Union without a free trade agreement.

48–72. We are thankful to the editor of the Law and Economics Yearly Review for permitting us to reproduce parts of that article.

15 Henning Berger and Nikolai Badenhoop, 'Financial Services and Brexit: Navigating Towards Future Market Access' (2018) 19 *European Business Organization Law Review* 679–680.

16 Henry Mance, 'Who Wins from the UK's Extension of Article 50?' *Financial Times* (11 April 2019).

17 Agreement on the withdrawal of the United Kingdom of Great Britain and Northern Ireland from the European Union and the European Atomic Energy Community (2019/C 384 I/01) [2019] OJ CI384/1.

18 During the transition period market access of UK banks and financial firms to the EU is not affected. On this, see EBA, 'Opinion of the European Banking Authority on Deposit Protection Issues Stemming from the Withdrawal of the United Kingdom from the European Union' EBA-Op-2019-01 (1 March 2019), available at <https://eba.europa.eu/-/eba-recommends-maintaining-protection-of-depositors-in-case-of-a-no-deal-brexit> (accessed 10 June 2020).

19 For an overview of the areas of agreement and disagreement between the two sides and of the available models for the new relationship between the UK and the EU, see European Union Committee, *UK-EU Relations after Brexit* (HL 2017–19, 149).

20 HM Government, 'The Future Relationship between the United Kingdom and Europe' (Cm 9593, 2018) 1.

From the perspective of banking and the financial services, it is worth noting that there are effectively three models of the future relationship between the UK and the EU: EEA membership, a free trade agreement covering the financial services and ordinary third country status. Whether the UK will be part of the Customs Union or not does not matter for the financial services as its importance is limited to trade in physical goods.

Regarding the Swiss model, although it is a distinct blueprint for an institutional arrangement with the EU, from the perspective of the financial markets and services, it would amount to little more than ordinary third country status. This is because much of the Single Market acquis does not apply to Switzerland. Although EU law that is based on the free movement of persons (natural and legal) applies, most EU law on financial services and financial markets does not apply.[21] Moreover, the bilateral treaties between the EU and Switzerland do not provide for the incorporation of new pieces of EU legislation.[22] This has led the EU Council to state that no further bilateral treaties will be concluded and to request Switzerland to agree an appropriate institutional framework to ensure the coherence of the Single Market.[23] In any case, in the area of financial services, Swiss policy in recent years has focused on making Swiss law mirror EU law, so that Swiss firms can benefit from equivalence determinations and gain some access to the Single Market, rather than on new bilateral treaties.[24]

Whether the UK eventually concludes a free trade agreement with the EU only matters directly for the banking sector if financial services are included in the free trade agreement. If not, the legal position will be the UK having the status of a third country and thus UK firms having to rely on equivalence determinations to access the Single Market. Politically, an exit without a withdrawal agreement might affect the willingness of the Commission to make equivalence determinations. Therefore, the following three parts of the chapter examine in detail the likelihood and potential consequences for the banking sector of EEA membership, a free trade agreement covering the sector and simple third country status.

17.3 EEA membership and the banking sector

The purpose of this part is to set out the legal nature of the EEA[25] and to examine the implications of adopting this model for the UK banking sector.[26] As observed, 'if the UK became a member of the EEA it would retain the right to assign "passports" to companies, but

---

21 However, a special bilateral agreement allows Swiss general insurance firms to set up agencies and branches in EEA States and vice versa: agreement between the European Economic Community and the Swiss Confederation of 26 July 1989 on direct insurance other than life insurance [1991] OJ L205/3.

22 Indeed, any expansion of Switzerland's participation in the Single Market can only be achieved by concluding additional bilateral treaties, which has led to a proliferation of treaties, now in excess of 120.

23 Aydan Bahadir and Fernando Garcés de los Fayos, 'The European Economic Area (EEA), Switzerland and the North' (2016), available at <http://www.europarl.europa.eu/atyourservice/en/displayFtu.html?ftuId=FTU_6.5.3.html> (accessed 10 April 2020).

24 Kern Alexander, 'The UK's Third-Country Status Following Brexit: Post-Brexit Models, Third-Country Equivalence and Switzerland' in Kern Alexander et al. (eds), *Brexit and Financial Services: Law and Policy* (Hart Publishing 2018) 143–145.

25 The European Economic Area was created by the Agreement on the European Economic Area [1994] OJ L1/3. It is an international treaty originally between the 12 EU Member States and the European Free Trade Association States. These were at the time the following: Norway, Lichtenstein and Iceland (which are still members of EFTA and the EEA), Austria, Sweden and Finland (which joined the EU in 1995) and Switzerland, which never ratified the Agreement due to its rejection by a referendum in December 1992.

26 Andreas Kokkinis, 'The Impact of Brexit on the Legal Framework for Cross-Border Corporate Activity' (2016) 27 *European Business Law Review* 963–966.

that would leave the UK having to comply with EU laws with no say in the decision-making process'.[27] This section will briefly explain the EEA option. The Single Market's territorial extent is broader than the EU, as it also encompasses three of the EFTA Member States,[28] and – to a limited extent – Switzerland through bilateral treaties.[29] Those areas of EU law that derive from the fundamental Treaty[30] freedoms of movement of goods, services, capital and persons are equally applicable to countries that are not part of the EU but are part of the Single Market. All the EU acquis that is relevant to financial services and markets fall in that category.

The EEA Agreement covers in particular: (1) the free movement of workers, (2) recognition of professional qualifications, (3) the right of establishment, (4) financial services, (5) services in general, (6) the free movement of capital and (7) EU company law rules. It follows that, if the UK joins the EEA, little will change, in the first place, for the UK financial markets and firms and all the economic benefits that UK firms currently enjoy, including passporting rights, would continue as they stand.[31] However, in the long term, the EEA model may not be suitable for the fast-changing regulatory challenges of the financial sector, this means that if the UK seeks to join the EEA, it would need to ensure at least some mechanism to improve implementation speed for financial services measures.[32]

The benefits of broad access to the Single Market under the EEA model would come at the cost of the UK having to follow any new EU rules in these areas, without having anymore any official voice and power to shape such rules. If an EEA model is adopted in the outcome of Brexit negotiations, the UK will have an observer status, basically 'the UK will lose a channel for influencing international financial governance'.[33] Indeed, EEA countries are legally obliged to implement all new EU law rules that fall within the scope of the EEA Agreement subject to their approval by special joint committees that include representatives from the EU and EEA. New EU legislation is incorporated into the EEA Agreement by consensus of all EEA states. The process is facilitated by a number of institutions, including the EFTA Standing Committee (of ambassadors to the EU), the EFTA Surveillance Authority and the EFTA Court.[34] The process is led politically by the EEA Council (foreign

---

27 Norman Mugarura, 'The "EU Brexit" Implication on a Single Banking License and Other Aspects of Financial Markets Regulation in the UK' (2016) 58 *International Journal of Law and Management* 477.

28 The European Free Trade Association is an intergovernmental organisation established by a Convention on 4 January 1960.

29 The ten bilateral treaties granting Switzerland partial membership of the Single Market were signed in two phases, the first seven in 1999 and the last three in 2004. They cover areas such as the free movement of persons, technical trade barriers, public procurement, agriculture, air and land transport, and Switzerland's participation in the Schengen and Dublin agreements. For a discussion of the position of Switzerland in the Single Market, see Stephan Breitenmoser, 'Sectoral Agreements between the EC and Switzerland: Contents and Context' (2003) 40 *Common Market Law Review* 1137.

30 Consolidated Version of the Treaty for the Functioning of the European Union (TFEU) [2012] OJ C236/47, Art 26(2).

31 See e.g. Alexander (n 24) 118–121. Armour has also argued that a 'soft' Brexit is the safest option for the City. John Armour, 'Brexit and Financial Services' (2017) 33(suppl.) *Oxford Review of Economic Policy* 54.

32 John Armour, 'Brexit to the European Economic Area: What Would It Mean?' Oxford Business Law Blog (19 July 2016) <https://www.law.ox.ac.uk/business-law-blog/blog/2016/07/brexit-european-economic-area-what-would-it-mean> (accessed 26 July 2020).

33 Niamh Moloney, 'International Financial Governance, the EU, and Brexit: The "Agencification" of EU Financial Governance and the Implications' (2016) 17 *European Business Organization Law Review* 473.

34 An analysis of the jurisprudence of the EFTA Court can be found in EFTA Court (ed), *The EEA and the EFTA Court* (Hart Publishing 2015).

ministers of the EEA States and of the EU Member State which holds the presidency). The actual decision to incorporate applicable EU legislation has to be taken unanimously by the EEA Joint Committee, which consists of the EFTA Standing Committee and the European External Action Service.[35] The Joint Committee examines each piece of legislation to ensure it falls within the scope of the EEA Agreement. EEA countries have the theoretical right to refuse the application of new EU law, but such right has never been exercised since doing so would give the EU the right to terminate the whole EEA Agreement. This explains the strong resistance of many UK politicians to EEA membership as it would effectively bind the UK to follow EU rules without being represented on the EU institutions and fora. Of course, in such a scenario the UK, given its technical expertise and the size of its financial market, would retain the possibility of influencing the direction of EU law in soft ways through lobbying Member States' governments, providing technical assistance to EU authorities and contributing to international financial regulation such as the Basel Committee and IOSCO.

17.4 UK-EU free trade agreement covering financial services

It is now pertinent to examine the possibility of financial services to be included in a future free trade agreement between the UK and the EU. It is theoretically possible for the UK and EU to conclude a free trade agreement with a chapter on financial services that would grant access to each other's markets and provide for mutual recognition of each other's regulatory frameworks or parts thereof. Such an agreement would grant UK financial firms passporting rights (probably using different terminology) to operate in the EU and vice versa, and would include institutional arrangements to ensure that the regulatory frameworks of the UK and the EU do not diverge in the future within the scope of such rights of access.

Indeed, Philip Hammond, the former Chancellor of the Exchequer, consistently advocated this option as it would provide UK financial firms with the necessary legal certainty and clarity. He canvassed this scenario as follows:

> [T]he principle of mutual recognition and reciprocal regulatory equivalence, provided it is objectively assessed, with proper governance structures, dispute resolution mechanisms, and sensible notice periods to market participants clearly could provide an effective basis for such a partnership. And although we will be separate jurisdictions, we would need to maintain a structured regulatory dialogue to discuss new rules proposed by either side building on our current unparalleled regulatory relationships to ensure we deliver equivalent regulatory outcomes agreeing mutually acceptable rule-changes where possible.[36]

Tempting as this scenario may be for UK banks, the prospect of including the financial services within a future free trade agreement between the UK and the EU looks dim due to the firm position taken by the Commission and Michel Barnier. Their position is that

---

35 This is an Agency established for this purpose in 2010. Until then, the Commission represented the EU on the EEA Joint Committee.

36 Philip Hammond, Chancellor of the Exchequer, 'Speech on Financial Services at HSBC' (Speech at HSBC Headquarters, London, 7 March 2018), available at <https://www.gov.uk/government/speeches/chancellors-hsbc-speech-financial-services> (accessed 9 April 2020).

the UK will face a stark choice between EEA membership and a Canada-style free trade agreement covering (most) goods, but not services.[37] This was reluctantly accepted by the UK Government, which in its much discussed Chequers white paper conceded that access to financial markets will be a matter of equivalence rather than mutual recognition:

> This new economic and regulatory arrangement would be based on the principle of autonomy for each party over decisions regarding access to its market, with a bilateral framework of treaty-based commitments to underpin the operation of the relationship, ensure transparency and stability, and promote cooperation. [...] As part of this, the existing autonomous frameworks for equivalence would need to be expanded, to reflect the fact that equivalence as it exists today is not sufficient in scope for the breadth of the interconnectedness of UK-EU financial services provision.[38]

Evidently, the previous Government hoped for a governance framework that would be enshrined in a legally binding treaty but does not seek automatic mutual recognition, but rather unilateral equivalence granted autonomously, in line with current practice. So, it appears that, barring a major U-turn leading to the UK joining the EEA, the future —relationship between the UK and the EU in the area of financial services and markets will be based on autonomous and unilateral determinations of regulatory equivalence. In the worst case, from the UK's perspective, this will operate exactly as the current EU framework on equivalence. In the best-case scenario, there will be a binding treaty providing for an institutional framework for the making of such determinations on the basis of the following principles: regulatory dialogue, supervisory co-operation, transparent and objective assessment methodology and a presumption against unilateral changes that narrow the terms of existing market access regimes.[39]

It is worth noting that the political declaration for the future relationship between the EU and the UK clearly envisages that the financial services will be dealt with within the existing equivalence frameworks that the EU and the UK operate for third countries.[40] Still, it vaguely alludes to instituting a process for making such determinations[41]:

> This cooperation should be grounded in the economic partnership and based on the principles of regulatory autonomy, transparency and stability. It should include transparency and appropriate consultation in the process of adoption, suspension and withdrawal of equivalence decisions, information exchange and consultation on regulatory initiatives and other issues of mutual interest, at both political and technical levels.

---

37 Jim Brunsden, 'EU Rejects Brexit Trade Deal for UK Financial Services Sector' *Financial Times* (London, 31 January 2018), available at <https://www.ft.com/content/7f7669a4–067f-11e8–9650–9c0ad2d7c5b5> (accessed 9 May 2020). See also Jim Brunsden, 'Brexit Britain Faces Services Squeeze with Canada-Style Deal' *Financial Times* (London, 12 December 2017) available at <https://www.ft.com/content/30a358ac-dda6–11e7–8f9f-de1c2175f5ce> (accessed 8 May 2020).

38 HM Government, 'The Future Relationship between the United Kingdom and Europe' (Cm 9593, 2018) 30.

39 Ibid., 31–32.

40 'Political Declaration Setting out the Framework for the Future Relationship between the European Union and the United Kingdom' (2018) [38] <https://ec.europa.eu/commission/publications/political-declaration-setting-out-framework-future-relationship-between-european-union-and-united-kingdom_en> (accessed 11 June 2020).

41 Ibid., [39].

17.5 The UK as a third country: the equivalence framework and banks

The equivalence-based approach seems the way forward to maintain access to EU markets, as it is unlikely that the passporting[42] solution will be available, because it would require concessions on UK sovereignty.[43] The equivalence model, based on mutually reciprocal arrangements, can provide a fair agreement in providing access to the EU markets for branches of UK credit institutions and vice versa. In this context, the European Securities and Markets Authority (ESMA) has published sector-specific principles in the areas of investment firms, investment management and secondary markets, aimed at fostering consistency in authorisation, supervision and enforcement related to the relocation of entities, activities and functions from the UK.[44] The introduction of a third country equivalence regime in the Markets in Financial Instruments Directive (MiFID) activities would ensure that UK banks would be able to carry on investment business activities – including wholesale investment services cross-border to professional clients and eligible counterparties – under an equivalence decision.[45]

In terms of retail banking and private wealth management, UK banks will be able to carry on providing services which are MiFID activities to professional clients and eligible counterparties under the equivalence regime in MiFID II. However, the success of the equivalence-based model faces some doubts because of different incentives of the UK and the EU: different public policy objectives (for instance, to create a new Financial Centre) and uncertainties on supervisory powers are the main concerns at stake.[46] As Schoenmaker and Véron noted, 'many wholesale market activities will need to be relocated from the UK to the EU-27 so that financial firms can keep serving local customers within the single market: to address the supervisory risks, European leaders should reinforce the ESMA with significant additional resources and expanded responsibilities'.[47] It can be argued that MiFID represents the legislative framework to achieve mutual recognition among banks and to avoid the risk of de-regulation in the UK financial markets.

It is worth noting that, apart from MiFID, several pieces of EU financial legislation include equivalence clauses which effectively allow some degree of market access to the Single Market for firms that are governed by the law of third countries, provided that the legal

---

42 The EU passport system means that if a financial services firm is authorised to carry out activities by any Member State, it can freely trade in another Member State. The UK benefits from the EU's 'passporting' arrangements which govern access to the Single Market in financial services. Under EU financial governance arrangements, subsidiaries are supervised in the relevant domestic market in which the subsidiary is registered. Branches and cross-border services are supervised through the home Member State from which these services operate.

43 The passporting solution involves the following concerns: (1) rule-taking of EU regulations, (2) supranational bodies and (3) free movement and financial contributions.

44 ESMA issues sector-specific principles on relocations from the UK to the EU27, ESMA71–99–526 (13 July 2017), <https://www.esma.europa.eu/document/esma-issues-sector-specific-principles-relocations-uk-eu27> (accessed 24 July 2020).

45 The equivalence assessment may prove technically problematic because it is subject to the Commission discretion. In addition, issues may arise in relation to the supervisory and enforcement aspects of the MiFIR equivalence decision.

46 Moloney (n 6) 43–44.

47 Dirk Schoenmaker and Nicolas Véron, 'Brexit Should Drive Integration of EU Capital Markets' Bruegel Blog Post (24 February 2017) <http://bruegel.org/2017/02/brexit-should-drive-integration-of-eu-capital-markets/> (accessed 17 July 2020).

and regulatory framework of these countries is deemed to be equivalent to the European framework.[48] In these cases, the determination of equivalence is made for the whole of the EU by the Commission and is liable to be withdrawn at any time. However, the notion of equivalence is also used more broadly to determine compliance with EU rules for non-EU firms. In that sense, equivalence is not about market access but rather about allowing a third country firm to demonstrate compliance with any EU law provision which applies to it due to its operations in the EU. An example of that is the ability to treat certain exposures in a beneficial way in the context of capital adequacy regulation under Capital Requirements Regulation (CRR).[49] Furthermore, other pieces of EU legislation – especially in the areas of prospectuses, transparency, investment funds and alternative investment funds – empower the competent authority of each Member State to determine whether a firm from a third country is subject to equivalent legal requirements on a particular issue, in order to determine the firm's compliance with the requirements of EU law.[50] In the latter cases, the decision lies within the competent authority of the Member State where the third country firm seeks to obtain authorisation or undertake activities.[51] For the purposes of the present discussion, it is necessary to explore in more detail the instances where passport-like equivalence is granted centrally by the Commission.

This occurs in three areas, all of them belonging to the wholesale markets: (1) offering investments services to professional clients, (2) reinsurance activities[52] and (3) the operation of central clearing counterparties.[53] The former of these regimes is the most comprehensive

48 For an overview of various types of equivalence provisions in EU financial legislation and of the distinction between equivalence and passporting, see Directorate-General for Internal Policies (IPOL), 'Third-Country Equivalence in EU Banking Legislation' (Briefing Paper of the European Parliament PE 587.369, 12 July 2017) available at <http://www.europarl.europa.eu/RegData/etudes/BRIE/2016/587369/IPOL_BRI(2016)587369_EN.pdf> (accessed 7 July 2020). See also European Union Committee, *Brexit: Financial Services* (HL 2016–17, 81) 47–49. From the post-Brexit UK perspective, see Eilís Ferran, 'The UK as a Third Country Actor in EU Financial Services Regulation' (2017) 3 *Journal of Financial Regulation* 40.

49 Capital Requirements Regulation (EU) No. 575/2013 of the European Parliament and of the Council of 26 June 2013 on prudential requirements for credit institutions and investment firms and amending Regulation (EU) No. 648/2012 [2013] OJ L176/1, arts 107(3)–(4), 114(7), 115(4), 116(5) and 132(3).

50 Directive 2009/65/EC of The European Parliament and of the Council of 13 July 2009 on the coordination of laws, regulations and administrative provisions relating to undertakings for collective investment in transferable securities (UCITS) (recast) [2009] OJ L302/32, art 50(f). Directive 2003/71/EC of the European Parliament and of the Council of 4 November 2003 on the prospectus to be published when securities are offered to the public or admitted to trading and amending Directive 2001/34/EC [2003] OJ L345/64, art 20. Directive 2004/109/EC of the European Parliament and of the Council of 15 December 2004 on the harmonisation of transparency requirements in relation to information about issuers whose securities are admitted to trading on a regulated market and amending Directive 2001/34/EC [2004] OJ L390/38, art 23. Directive 2011/61/EU of the European Parliament and of The Council of 8 June 2011 on Alternative Investment Fund Managers and amending Directives 2003/41/EC and 2009/65/EC and Regulations (EC) No. 1060/2009 and (EU) No. 1095/2010 [2011] OJ L174/1, art 37.

51 The UK Financial Conduct Authority, for instance, has made equivalence decisions regarding disclosure rules for Switzerland, the US, Canada and Japan. See FCA, Equivalence of Non-EEA Regimes (2016) available at <https://www.fca.org.uk/markets/ukla/regulatory-disclosures/equivalence-non-eea-regimes> (accessed 5 May 2020).

52 Directive 2009/138/EC of the European Parliament and of the Council of 25 November 2009 on the taking-up and pursuit of the business of Insurance and Reinsurance (Solvency II) (recast) [2009] OJ L335/1, art 172 and 227. For a concise discussion, see Alexander (n 24) 142.

53 Regulation (EU) No. 648/2012 of the European Parliament and of the Council of 4 July 2012 on OTC derivatives, central counterparties and trade repositories [2012] OJ L201/1, Art 25(6). In brief, the Regulation stipulates that a third country CCP may provide clearing services to clearing members or trading venues

and thus warrants further examination. Indeed, in the area of investment services, the relevant framework is prescribed by articles 39–43 MiFID[54] and 46–49 MiFIR.[55] Recital 41 in the preamble to MiFIR states that 'the equivalence assessment should be outcome-based; it should assess to what extent the respective third country regulatory and supervisory framework achieves similar and adequate regulatory effects and to what extent it meets the same objectives as Union law'.[56] Articles 46(2)(a) and 47 of the MiFIR regulate the 'third-country firms' regime, and clarify that central to the requirements is the equivalence decision adopted by the Commission. After the end of the transition period, the UK will become a 'third country' within the current EU financial regulatory structure, this implies that future access to the EU's Single Market for UK-based financial institutions may be very limited.

Briefly speaking, a firm from a third country is allowed to provide investment services to professional clients in the EU without the need to set up a subsidiary or even a branch insofar as it is registered with the ESMA.[57] ESMA will only register a firm, if there has been prior adoption by the Commission of an equivalency decision regarding the legal and regulatory framework of the relevant third country. Notably, co-operation arrangements must be established between ESMA and the competent authorities of the third country. On the contrary, the provision of investment services to retail customers by third country firms remains within the discretion of Member States, which may impose a requirement that the firm sets up a branch or subsidiary in their territory.

As regards the decision-making process regarding equivalence under MiFID II/MiFIR, the Commission has to certify that the prudential and conduct of business framework of the third country is equivalent to the EU framework. This evidently entails a broad appraisal of the foreign framework. In particular, the Commission must be satisfied that the firm is subject to an authorisation requirement and ongoing supervision; sufficient capital requirements; sufficient organisational requirements and appropriate conduct of business rules; and that there are rules preventing market abuse.[58] In any case, the Commission's decision is discretionary. This process has not yet been tested as there have not been any determinations of equivalence under the mentioned rules at the time of writing, which is unsurprising given the short time that has lapsed since the implementation date for MiFID II/MiFIR.

However, there have already been determinations of equivalence under another provision of MiFIR which is not one granting market access, but rather falls in the category of determining compliance with substantive rules of EU law. Indeed, article 23 of MiFIR requires investment firms to ensure that any trade they undertake in shares which are admitted to trading on a regulated market or are traded on a trading venue only takes place on regulated markets or third country trading venues assessed by the Commission as equivalent. This means that if an investment firm wants to trade in a share which is listed on one of

established in the EU only if the CCP in question has been recognised by ESMA, which can only happen if an equivalence determination has been previously made by the Commission.
54 Directive 2014/65/EU of the European Parliament and of the Council of 15 May 2014 on markets in financial instruments and amending Directive 2002/92/EC and Directive 2011/61/EU (recast) [2014] OJ L173/349.
55 Regulation (EU) No. 600/2014 of the European Parliament and of the Council of 15 May 2014 on markets in financial instruments and amending Regulation (EU) No. 648/2012 [2014] OJ L173/84. From now on to be abbreviated as MiFIR.
56 Regulation 600/2014 on markets in financial instruments and amending Regulation (EU) No. 648/2012 [2014] OJ L173/84.
57 For a detailed discussion, see Alexander (n 24) 134–142.
58 MiFIR, art 47 (1) (a)–(e).

the EU stock exchanges it has to trade on this share only on an EU stock exchange or on an exchange of a country whose regime has been deemed to be equivalent. Apparently, this is practically significant in the case of dually listed shares which are listed on an EU exchange and a non-EU exchange. To date the Commission has determined that the legal and supervisory framework for national securities exchanges and alternative trading systems of the following countries is equivalent to the EU framework: Australia,[59] Hong Kong,[60] Switzerland[61] and the US.[62] These decisions need to be complemented by co-operation arrangements. The UK will be highly likely to achieve a similar determination in due course.

Regarding the policy of the Commission on its exercise of discretion under equivalence provisions in general, it recently described the criteria that guide its discretion as follows:

> [The Commission] takes into account objectives stemming from the empowering legislation and from the Treaty. These objectives may include in particular promoting the internal market for financial services and protecting financial stability or market integrity within the internal market. [...] In this context, factors such as the size of the relevant market, the importance for the functioning of the internal market, the interconnectedness between the markets of the third country and the EU, or the risks of circumvention of EU rules may play a role. The Commission also needs to factor in wider external policy priorities and concerns in particular with respect to the promotion of common values and shared regulatory objectives at international level. All these factors are indicative of the amount of risk to the financial stability or the need for adequate protection of financial market participants and other persons in the EU.[63]

It also emphasised that 'it follows a risk-based approach and the principle of proportionality'.[64] These statements indicate that fears that the Commission may refuse to grant equivalence to UK firms after the end of the transition period or withdraw such equivalence in a totally arbitrary manner are exaggerated.

However, references to the size of the relevant market, the interconnectedness between the third country and the EU and the risk posed to financial stability in the EU suggest that there may be some unpleasant surprises for the UK. The UK's financial market is huge by EU standard, highly interconnected to the EU market, and a systemic crisis in the UK would significantly reduce financial stability in the EU. These factors weigh negatively in

---

59 Commission Implementing Decision (EU) 2017/2318 of 13 December 2017 on the equivalence of the legal and supervisory framework in Australia applicable to financial markets in accordance with Directive 2014/65/EU of the European Parliament and of the Council [2017] OJ L331/81.

60 Commission Implementing Decision (EU) 2017/2319 of 13 December 2017 on the equivalence of the legal and supervisory framework applicable to recognise exchange companies in Hong Kong Special Administrative Region in accordance with Directive 2014/65/EU of the European Parliament and of the Council [2017] OJ L331/87.

61 Commission Implementing Decision (EU) 2017/2441 of 21 December 2017 on the equivalence of the legal and supervisory framework applicable to stock exchanges in Switzerland in accordance with Directive 2014/65/EU of the European Parliament and of the Council [2017] OJ L344/52.

62 Commission Implementing Decision (EU) 2017/2320 of 13 December 2017 on the equivalence of the legal and supervisory framework of the United States of America for national securities exchanges and alternative trading systems in accordance with Directive 2014/65/EU of the European Parliament and of the Council [2017] OJ L331/94.

63 Commission, 'EU Equivalence Decisions in Financial Services Policy: An Assessment' (Staff Working Document) SWD (2017) 102 final, 9–10.

64 Ibid., 8.

the context of equivalence decisions which means that the Commission is likely to examine the UK regime most carefully before making any equivalence determination. Even if the UK maintains full alignment with relevant substantive EU rules, this does not mean that the Commission will be automatically satisfied, as the ambit of its scrutiny also includes robust supervision and related enforcement. It is worth noting that a refusal to grant equivalence or a revocation of equivalence on ostensible grounds of protecting financial stability is very difficult to be challenged successfully at the fora of the World Trade Organisation as contrary to GATS.[65] This means that WTO law offers little effective protection for the UK in this area. Furthermore, there is currently pressure from the French Financial Markets Authority for the EU to tighten its MiFID equivalence regime in view of Brexit.[66] In particular, the French Authority emphasised the need for EU law to require firms from third countries which have achieved equivalent status to apply the MiFID rules on investor protection and market integrity, and the need to give ESMA a power to supervise third country firms that benefit from equivalence.

The preceding analysis suggests that the current regime on equivalence may well provide market access for UK financial firms in several areas, but will not attain the level of legal certainty that firms require.[67] This can only be achieved if an appropriate governance framework is put in place in the lines proposed by the UK Government. However, for the time being at least, the EU appears unlikely to consider entering into such an agreement with the UK as it views such a prospect as undermining the Single Market. It can be argued that some institutional framework may arise in the long term, especially one based on informal co-operation rather than hard law.[68]

17.6 Brexit and UK bank branches in the EU

Under EU law, any restrictions in the freedom of a national of a Member State to pursue economic activity in another Member State are prohibited including the rights to work as self-employed, and to set up a company, agency, branch or subsidiary.[69] This right is evidently enjoyed by companies or firms (other than those who are non-profit-making) whose

65 Andrew Lang, 'The "Default Option"? The WTO and Cross-Border Financial Services Trade after Brexit' in Kern Alexander et al. (eds), *Brexit and Financial Services: Law and Policy* (Hart Publishing 2018) 211–215.
66 Robert Ophèle, Chairman of the French Financial Markets Authority, 'From Brexit to Financial Innovations: New Challenges for Financial Regulation' (Speech at the Official Monetary and Financial Institutions Forum, London, 15 March 2018) available at <https://www.amf-france.org/en_US/Actualites/Prises-de-paroles/Archives/Annee-2016?docId=workspace%3A%2F%2FSpacesStore%2F02d32070-8a04–434a-a237-5b402bbf7139> (accessed 8 April 2020).
67 For instance, a recent House of Lords report concludes that the equivalence framework on its own would not provide a reliable foundation for the relationship between the UK and EU financial markets for the long term. See European Union Committee, *Brexit: The Future of Financial Regulation and Supervision* (HL 2017–19, 66).
68 An in-depth exploration of potential models can be found in Eilis Ferran, 'Regulatory Parity in Post-Brexit UK–EU Financial Regulation: EU Norms, International Financial Standards or a Hybrid Model?' in Kern Alexander et al. (eds), *Brexit and Financial Services: Law and Policy* (Hart Publishing 2018) 15–16. Regarding the feasibility of reaching a workable solution Ringe has optimistically asserted that a workable solution is highly likely to be found despite prevailing rhetoric on both sides as it is in the economic interest of both. See Wolf-Georg Ringe, 'The Irrelevance of Brexit for the European Financial Market' (2018) 19 *European Business Organization Law Review* 1.
69 TFEU, art 49.

registered office or centre of administration is within the EU.[70] As a result, a UK bank can establish itself, and operate an agency, branch or subsidiary in the territory of any other Member State and vice versa. A crucial aspect of the freedom of establishment is the right to set up branches in other Member States. Branches facilitate economic activity abroad as they ensure that a foreign company can acquire an establishment without infringing national laws and without having to set up a subsidiary company. This is important for the UK financial sector that is heavily export oriented. In parallel, London's position as a global financial centre is strengthened by the operation of branches of EEA banks and other financial institutions.

The concept of a branch, which derives exclusively from EU law, is somewhat obscure. The 11th Company Law Directive[71] which imposes a number of disclosure obligations to branches does not provide a definition. The European Court of Justice has not provided a definition of the term branch in the Treaty but has provided interpretations of the term as used in several directives. According to one such definition:

> [A branch] implies a centre of operations which has the appearance of permanency, such as the extension of a parent body. It must have a management and be materially equipped to negotiate business with third parties, so that they do not deal directly with the parent body.[72]

It follows that a branch must at least have a physical presence and include individuals with the authority to enter into transactions with third parties on behalf of the overseas company.

Regarding financial institutions, there is a special EU legal framework on overseas branches and on offering financial services directly abroad. Banks, insurance firms and investment firms that are authorised to perform regulated activities in one Member State can offer their services directly or through a branch in any other Member State,[73] insofar as the competent authority of the host State is notified, based on the provisions of the relevant piece of EU law regulating the activity in question.[74] The right to offer services

---

70 TFEU, art 54.
71 Eleventh Council Directive (89/666/EEC) of 21 December 1989 concerning disclosure requirements in respect of branches opened in a Member State by certain types of company governed by the law of another State [1989] OJ L395/36 (to be abbreviated as the '11th Company Law Directive') as amended by Directive 2012/17/EU of the European Parliament and of the Council of 13 June 2012, amending Council Directive 89/666/EEC and Directives 2005/56/EC and 2009/101/EC of the European Parliament and of the Council as regards the interconnection of central, commercial and companies registers [2012] OJ L156/1. The Directive is currently implemented in the UK by the Overseas Companies Regulations 2009 (SI 2009/1801) which requires branches or establishments of EEA companies to register with the Companies House.
72 Case 139/80 *Blanckaert & Wilems*, para 11.
73 This is governed by Council Directive 89/117/EEC of 13 February 1989 on the obligations of branches established in a Member State of credit institutions and financial institutions having their head offices outside that Member State regarding the publication of annual accounting documents [1989] OJ L44/40.
74 A number of Directives include passporting provisions the most significant of which are listed below: (a) Directive 2004/39/EC of the European Parliament and of the Council of 21 April 2004 on markets in financial instruments amending Council Directives 85/611/EEC and 93/6/EEC and Directive 2000/12/EC of the European Parliament and of the Council and repealing Council Directive 93/22/EEC [2004] OJ L145/1 (to be abbreviated as 'MiFID'); (b) Directive 2013/36/EU of the European Parliament and of the Council of 26 June 2013 on access to the activity of credit institutions and the prudential supervision of credit institutions and investment firms, amending Directive 2002/87/EC and repealing Directives 2006/48/EC

abroad without presence in the other Member State emanates from the free movement of services,[75] while the right to set up a branch emanates from the freedom of establishment.

A withdrawal of the UK from the EU and EEA would lead to the loss of the automatic freedom to set up branches and offer services to customers in other Member States for UK-based financial sector firms, which would be particularly alarming for the UK economy as financial services accounts for a considerable part of UK exports. It would also end the possibility of UK-incorporated companies to set up branches freely in the EEA and would probably make it necessary in many cases to set up subsidiaries in the relevant countries. Such changes would be particularly detrimental to the attractiveness of London as a place for non-EU financial institutions to set up their European headquarters. Currently, a non-EU multinational financial institution can set up a subsidiary in the UK and base its headquarters in London (to take advantage of London's professional services, multinational labour market and English legal system) and then set up branches in other EU Member States and pursue economic activities there. In other words, choosing London combines the benefits of the English legal system and City financial expertise with full and unfettered access to a huge market of more than half a billion consumers. If this possibility is lost and establishing elsewhere in the EU becomes more burdensome, the dominance of London as the preferred place for multinational financial institutions' European headquarters would be severely challenged.

17.7 Brexit and bank resolution

As previously discussed, after the end of the transition period the UK will most likely become a 'third country' within the current EU financial regulatory structure. In this context, the post-Brexit scenario will determine the re-arrangement of special resolution regimes for failing banks regulated by the Bank Recovery and Resolution Directive (BRRD).[76] This section considers the implications of Brexit in dealing with failing banks and highlights the potential outcomes of implementing domestic regulatory tools to resolve fragile credit institutions.

It is worth noting that the BRRD and the Single Resolution Mechanism (SRM) form the new European regulatory framework of the bank insolvency regime.[77] The SRM

and 2006/49/EC [2013] OJ L176/338; (c) Directive 2009/138/EC of the European Parliament and of the Council of 25 November 2009 on the taking-up and pursuit of the business of Insurance and Reinsurance (Solvency II) (recast) [2009] OJ L335/1; (d) Directive 2007/64/EC of the European Parliament and of the Council of 13 November 2007 on payment services in the internal market amending Directives 97/7/EC, 2002/65/EC, 2005/60/EC and 2006/48/EC and repealing Directive 97/5/EC [2007] OJ L319/1; and (e) Directive 2011/61/EU of the European Parliament and of the Council of 8 June 2011 on Alternative Investment Fund Managers and amending Directives 2003/41/EC and 2009/65/EC and Regulations (EC) No. 1060/2009 and (EU) No. 1095/2010 [2011] OJ L174/1.

75 TFEU, art 56.

76 EU Bank Recovery and Resolution Directive (BRRD), Directive 2014/59/EU of the European Parliament and of the Council of 15 May 2014. These resolution tools require the establishing a framework for the recovery and resolution of credit institutions and investment firms and amending Council Directive 82/891/ EEC, and Directives 2001/24/EC, 2002/47/EC, 2004/25/EC, 2005/56/EC, 2007/36/EC, 2011/35/ EU, 2012/30/EU and 2013/36/EU, and Regulations (EU) No. 1093/2010 and (EU) No. 648/2012, of the European Parliament and of the Council, OJ L 173 of 12 June 2014, 190.

77 The Single Supervisory Mechanism (SSM) has been established by Council Regulation (EU) No. 1024/2013 of 15 October 2013 conferring specific tasks on the European Central Bank concerning policies relating to the prudential supervision of credit institutions, OJ L 287 of 29 October 2013, 63. The Single Resolution

introduced a centralised resolution in a single authority (Single Resolution Board) and a single set of resolution powers for failing banks. In the context of BRRD rules, bail-in is a key resolution instrument: the main rationale is to provide a mechanism to return an insufficiently solvent bank to 'balance sheet stability' at the expense of some of its creditors without the necessity of an external capital injection. Bail-in should have put an end to taxpayer-funded bank bail-outs. However, the conditionality attached to the precautionary recapitalisation represents one of the major concerns in the current regulatory framework because of its interconnection with the provisions on State aid.[78] Recapitalisation could preserve financial stability – as a remedy to cover losses for failing banks – in the case of a rescue plan with strict conditionally guaranteed by a pool of investment banks.

Converging towards a harmonised approach on recovery and resolution plans is the key issue at stake. As has been observed, 'given that the barriers to cross-border banking are likely to fall, the EU should consider what sort of banking structure would provide the best combination of an integrated financial system and a financial system in which the banks are neither too large to supervise nor too large to safely fail'.[79] This means that rules will have an impact on where banks locate operations due to cost factors and that as a result risk will likely migrate to less regulated local subsidiaries. The rules contained in the BRRD are largely flexible to allow Member States to adopt the policy measures necessary to protect the public interest, even if the Directive does not define the boundaries of 'public interest' as a condition to provide public support.[80]

Withdrawal from the EU will allow the UK to adopt domestic policy measures to rescue distressed institutions. This will leave broad discretion to national competent authorities to provide public financial support and to implement restructuring tools, namely, bail-in, precautionary recapitalisation and resolving plans. Brexit can compound the risk of de-regulation for restructuring troubled banks: this complicates meaningful cross-border recognition when it comes to resolution or consolidated supervision.[81] It is instructive that the European Banking Authority (EBA) has warned that 'institutions and authorities need to assess their stock and issuance plans for instruments used to meet the minimum requirement for own funds and eligible liabilities (MREL) in the light of Brexit, and in particular their reliance on instruments issued under English law'.[82] This means that EU banks in the Eurozone will not be able to utilise any of their English law bail-inable debt towards

---

Mechanism (SRM) has been introduced by Regulation (EU) No. 806/2014 of the European Parliament and of the Council of 15 July 2014 establishing uniform rules and a uniform procedure for the resolution of credit institutions and certain investment firms in the framework of a Single Resolution Mechanism and a Single Resolution Fund and amending Regulation (EU) No. 1093/2010, OJ L 225 of 30 July 2014, 1.

78 Christos V. Gortsos, 'A Poisonous (?) Mix: Bail-Out of Credit Institutions Combined with Bail-In of Their Liabilities Under the BRRD – The Use of 'Government Financial Stabilisation Tools' (GFSTs)' paper presented at the Workshop of the Financial and Monetary Law Working Group of the European University Institute (EUI, Florence, 12 October 2016) on 'Suitability of the New Resolution Regime for Tackling Systemic and Structural Crises in the Banking Sector – Fine-Tuning Rules in Transition' 6, available at <https://ssrn.com/abstract=2876508> (accessed 10 June 2020).

79 Ibid., 21.

80 Stefano Micossi, Ginevra Bruzzone and Miriam Cassella, 'Fine-Tuning the Use of Bail-In to Promote a Stronger EU Financial System' CEPS Special Report No. 136 (April 2016) 16–17.

81 Francesco Capriglione, 'UK Referendum and Brexit Hypothesis: The Way Out Perspective and the Convenience to "Remain United"' (2016) 27(7) *European Business Law Review* 893–895.

82 EBA, 'Opinion of the European Banking Authority on Issues Related to the Departure of the United Kingdom from the European Union' (EBA/OP/2017/12) Part IV Resolution and Deposit Guarantee Schemes (12 October 2017) 16.

their pending regulatory requirements if future relationship agreement is reached.[83] In addition, as the EBA has pointed out, the Deposit Guarantee Scheme (DGS) shall ensure the adequate protection of Member States 'by assessing (where relevant) the equivalence of the UK's deposit protection regime at the date of Brexit, and should consider putting in place cooperation arrangements with the UK DGS after Brexit'.[84]

In the short term, the UK regime will continue applying existing domestic legislation for bank insolvency (e.g. the Banking Act 2009 that substantially anticipated the BRRD with respect to recovery and resolution plans).[85] As Mayes claimed, 'the resolution of the UK's banks will remain the responsibility of the Bank of England and purely national concerns will come first'.[86] Specifically, in terms of investment bank insolvency rules, Section 233 of the Banking Act 2009 provides that 'in making investment bank insolvency regulations the Treasury shall have regard to the desirability of—(a) identifying, protecting, and facilitating the return of, client assets; (b) protecting creditors' rights, (c) ensuring certainty for investment banks, creditors, clients, liquidators and administrators, (d) minimising the disruption of business and markets, and (e) maximising the efficiency and effectiveness of the financial services industry in the United Kingdom'.[87]

Over time divergences may appear and in fact new rules may be introduced to exploit new markets. As observed, 'a clear danger with adopting an early intervention model is still the timing issue, so whether a rules-based or a discretion-based approach is taken, its success will depend on its use and the timing, and not necessarily what shape it takes'.[88] However, the Banking Act 2009 faced criticism on the fact that it has the potential to cause significant interference with the rights of third parties, both by prohibiting the exercise of termination rights under a contract and, more generally, through the way that the assets and liabilities of an ailing bank are split.[89] One can argue that Brexit could lead to an increase in the complexities of resolution for groups that operate in the UK and rest of the EU, particularly if rules diverge. This could lead to conflicting resolving decisions on the applicable restructuring tool for failing bank: the application of the Banking Act 2009 can create inconsistency with other jurisdictions making these divergences challenging to resolve, particularly as the UK regime gradually diverges from the EU after the end of the transition period.

17.8 Conclusion

By way of conclusion it is worth reflecting on the likely future directions of UK financial regulation. The preceding analysis highlights the vital importance for UK firms of retaining alignment with EU financial legislation in order to maximise the chances of equivalence

83 Graham Bippart, 'English-Law Bonds Could be Excluded from MREL Post-Brexit' Euromoney (24 November 2017) available at <https://www.euromoney.com/article/b15rkx7999nk36/regulation-english-law-bonds-could-be-excluded-from-mrel-post-brexit> (accessed 13 May 2020).

84 EBA (n 82) 16. In terms of recovery and resolution plans, the EBA clarified that 'once the UK leaves the EU, arrangements for resolution planning for entities based in the UK should be subject to the same standard as for any other third country, in the absence of an agreement to the contrary'.

85 See Part II ('Bank Insolvency') of the Banking Act 2009.

86 David G. Mayes, 'Banking Union: The Disadvantages of Opportunism' (2018) 21(2) *Journal of Economic Policy Reform* 136–137.

87 Section 233 ('Insolvency regulations') of the Banking Act 2009.

88 Dalvinder Singh, 'The UK Banking Act 2009, Pre-insolvency and Early Intervention: Policy and Practice' (2011) 2011 *Journal of Business Law* 42.

89 Barney Hearnden and Jane Whitfield, 'The Banking Act 2009' (2009) 3 *Corporate Rescue and Insolvency* 96.

determinations. After the end of the transition period, the UK will most likely become a 'third country' within the current EU financial regulatory structure, which implies that future access to the EU's Single Market for UK-based financial institutions may be very limited. There is little doubt that the UK will continue to comply with MiFID/MiFIR and all other market infrastructure directives and with directives on banking and insurance prudential regulation. However, this is not to say that there will not be areas where the UK approach may diverge from EU law post-Brexit.

The potential impact of Brexit in the UK banking sector could open room for different regulatory scenarios. As with any predictions, the exact implications of Brexit and its effect on the UK banking sector are difficult to gauge. Without doubt Brexit matters, not only to the British banking sector, but also to the wider economy in the UK, mainland Europe and globally. Exactly how the challenges will manifest themselves is as yet unclear. It is certain there will be unexpected challenges, but there may also be unforeseen opportunities. Banking is a worldwide enterprise and a key question is whether the British banking sector will be able to recover quickly enough from the damage of Brexit to not just keep up with other global players, but to regain its preeminent position.

Glossary of terms

- Brexit: Withdrawal of the UK from the EU on 31 January 2020 following the referendum held on 23 June 2016 (under the European Union Referendum Act 2015) in which UK citizens voted that the UK should leave the European Union. The legislative framework for Brexit consists of the European Union (Notification of Withdrawal) Act 2017, the European Union (Withdrawal) Act 2018, as amended, the European Union (Withdrawal) Act 2019 and the European Union (Withdrawal) (No. 2) Act 2019, as well as a plethora of delegated legislation.
- Equivalence model: Based on mutually reciprocal arrangements provides a fair arrangement in providing access to the EU markets for branches of UK credit institutions and vice versa.
- EU passport system: Legal principle allowing a firm authorised to carry out certain activities by any Member State to freely carry out the same activities in any other Member State.
- Freedom of establishment: The right of a firm to provide services and set up branches in other Member States.
- 'Third country': A country that is not part of the EEA; future access to the EU's Single Market for UK-based financial institutions may be very limited.
- MiFID II third country equivalence regime: Ensures that UK banks would be able to carry on investment business activities – including wholesale investment services cross-border to professional clients and eligible counterparties – under an equivalence decision made by the Commission.
- Mutual recognition: Harmonisation of a managed regulatory system among two jurisdictions, it implies mutual trust and adoption of common rules.
- Single banking licence: Introduced by the Second Banking Directive (89/646/EEC) to provide access to EU financial institutions to access the markets of other Member States. In this way, credit institutions which are authorised to operate in any Member State are allowed to establish branches and to provide cross-border services throughout the EEA on the basis of the principle of home country supervision.

- Branch: Establishment without separate legal personality that implies a centre of operations which has the appearance of permanency, as an extension of the parent entity. It must have a management and be materially equipped to negotiate business with third parties, so that they do not deal directly with the parent entity.

Practice questions

If Brexit eventually leads to UK departure from the EU Single Market and a regime of equivalence applying to financial regulation, the UK financial industry will face long-term challenges and financial stability will be threatened. The only way to mitigate such challenges is close regulatory alignment with EU rules post-Brexit. Critically discuss.

You may also find it useful to review the chapter through the following questions:

- What are the different types of relationship that the UK may have with the EU post-Brexit and how do these impact banks and financial markets?
- Explain the concept of equivalence in EU financial legislation and especially under MiFID II.
- Does equivalence provide a satisfactory basis for the future relationship between the UK and EU financial sectors?
- How will Brexit affect branches of UK banks be established in other EU Member States?
- What is the likely impact of Brexit on the resolution of cross-border financial institutions?

Post scriptum

Temporary modifications to banking law and regulation in response to the Covid-19 public health emergency[1]

1 Overview of the global pandemic and its implications for the financial services

The Covid-19 crisis which erupted in early 2020 has severely impacted the financial sector in terms of its market activity and market prices, as a consequence of adversely affecting the real economy, i.e. firms and human capital. At the time of writing, the pandemic outbreak had forced national governments to announce extensive lockdowns of society and the economy. These lockdowns resulted in the freezing of business activity for many sectors, such as bricks and mortar retail (except groceries and pharmacies), travel and leisure, restaurants, public services and service-based industries that were adversely affected by social distancing such as transport, work-sharing facilities, leisure and hospitality. The freezing of business activity in these hard-hit sectors has had implications for their cash flow, servicing of debt, potential insolvency and hence their market valuation and credit ratings. Besides public finance packages for emergency help, such as furloughing, financial regulators' initiatives play a part in the overall mosaic to prevent systemic damage to the economy and to the financial sector's roles in risk and investment allocation.[2]

In the UK, the financial regulators, i.e. the Prudential Regulation Authority (PRA) and Financial Conduct Authority (FCA), released temporarily the application of certain regulatory laws and issued extraordinary measures to regulated entities to suspend the application of private contractual laws. In-built flexibility in law and regulation reflects the dynamic needs of policy and institutional tenets, and although regulated subjects, markets and stakeholders would theoretically be conditioned to expect the possibility of adjustment, the uncertain extent and duration of adjustment still raises issues in terms of the governance of regulatory discretion and external reactions. For instance, the PRA's guidance to its regulated entities in relation to cancellation of dividends was upsetting for banks and their shareholders[3] despite being part of the overall prudential regulation adjustment package.

---

1 This *post scriptum* is based on Section III of Iris H.-Y. Chiu, Andreas Kokkinis and Andrea Miglionico, 'Regulatory Suspensions in Times of Crisis: The Challenges of Covid-19 and Thoughts for the Future' (May 2020) ECGI Law Working Paper No. 517/2020. See also Iris H.-Y. Chiu, Andreas Kokkinis and Andrea Miglionico, 'Financial Regulation Suspensions in Times of Crisis' in Horst Eidenmüller et al. (eds), *Covid-19 and Business Law* (Hart Publishing 2020) Chapter 6, 29.

2 For an overview see Christos V. Gortsos and Wolf-Georg Ringe (eds), *Pandemic Crisis and Financial Stability* (EBI Press 2020) Chapters 1–3.

3 See 'PRA Statement on Deposit Takers' Approach to Dividend Payments, Share Buybacks and Cash Bonuses in Response to Covid-19' (31 March 2020) <https://www.bankofengland.co.uk/prudential-regulation/

On the other hand, the PRA's guidance on regulated entities drawing down their usually 100% mandatory liquidity coverage ratio[4] is somewhat 'unexpected' complement to in-built flexible regulatory measures such as the counter-cyclical buffer (CCyb). Further, the PRA's and FCA's guidance to payment holidays for consumers suspends clear and inflexible contractual frameworks that govern creditor-borrower relationships, feeding into the prudential treatment of defaults and non-performing loans (NPLs).[5] In this respect, the European Banking Authority's (EBA) similar guidance to national regulators[6] in the EU also manifests the bundling of regulatory suspensions, extending the aura of inherent flexibility to justify and legitimise the co-option of other adjustments not inherently envisaged. In parallel, the FCA introduced adjustments to mandatory procedural law for company meetings and mandatory disclosure for corporate fund-raising, accompanying the relaxation of pre-emption rights.[7]

The pandemic crisis revealed a key public policy concern: how would credit arrangements affect households and corporations that are either in debt or need financing by debt in order to meet financial needs during the challenging period. The package of responses from the PRA and FCA regarding banks' role in the crisis was intended to meet the policy goal of keeping credit lines flowing and providing liquidity for businesses and households.[8] This package comprises various measures designed to achieve two broad effects. One is to allow banks, as the main creditor of most households and corporations, to be able to treat their borrowers more leniently. This permits borrower battered by the lockdown to be relieved of the pressures of debt while regrouping themselves and surviving during the crisis. Two, the crisis-fighting regulatory measures would also allow banks to extend credit and finance to business borrowers during the crisis. This would help businesses avoid key social losses such as protecting jobs and inflicting knock-on effects upon their suppliers.[9]

2 Prudential regulatory suspensions to facilitate financing of the real economy

In order to anchor the package of measures introduced in a co-ordinated manner by the PRA and FCA, the Bank of England's (BoE) Financial Policy Committee (FPC) exercised its power to adjust an inherently elastic prudential regulatory measure known as the CCyb. The buffer was introduced in the wake of the global financial crisis of 2007–2009 as a

---

publication/2020/pra-statement-on-deposit-takers-approach-to-dividend-payments-share-buybacks-and-cash-bonuses>

4 PRA, 'Q&A on the Usability of Liquidity and Capital Buffers' (20 April 2020) <https://www.bankofengland.co.uk/prudential-regulation/publication/2020/buffer-usability-qanda>

5 PRA, 'Letter from Sam Woods 'Covid-19: IFRS 9, Capital Requirements and Loan Covenants' (26 March 2020) <https://www.bankofengland.co.uk/prudential-regulation/letter/2020/covid-19-ifrs-9-capital-requirements-and-loan-covenants>. See also 'Letter from Sam Woods "Covid-19: IFRS 9 and Capital Requirements – Further Guidance on Initial and Further Payment Deferrals"' (4 June 2020) https://www.bankofengland.co.uk/prudential-regulation/letter/2020/covid-19-ifrs-9-capital-requirements-further-guidance.

6 EBA, 'Our Response to Coronavirus (Covid-19)' (12 March 2020) <https://eba.europa.eu/coronavirus>

7 FCA, 'Technical Supplement – Working Capital Statements in Prospectuses and Circulars during the Coronavirus Epidemic' (8 April 2020) <https://www.fca.org.uk/news/statements/listed-companies-recapitalisation-issuances-coronavirus>

8 FCA, 'Joint statement by the FCA, FRC and PRA' (26 March 2020) <https://www.fca.org.uk/news/statements/joint-statement-fca-frc-pra>

9 Thomas Huertas, 'Here Is How Banks Can Help Save the Economy' *Financial Times* (11 May 2020) <https://www.ft.com/content/f02df444–8f78-11ea-bc44-dbf6756c871a>

measure to allow the macro-prudential regulator to impose capital cost on banks to miti-gate pro-cyclical creation of debt in bubbly times.[10] Prior to the onset of the Covid-19 cri-sis, the CCyb was set at 1% for UK banks and the plan was to elevate it to 2% by December 2020 as economic activity looked strong and it appeared that banks ought to be prevented from excessive risk-taking. This was abruptly adjusted to 0% during the Covid-19 crisis, freeing up for banks an estimated capital cost of £190bn.[11]

The regulatory elasticity in the CCyb reflects the need for micro-prudential supervision for banks, which uses capital cost tools in adjusting banks' incentives to create credit, to be flexible and agile depending on economic cycles and circumstances. Freeing up the cost of capital originally imposed by the CCyb does not however automatically result in either more lending or loan forbearance. During the Covid-19 crisis, borrowers' creditworthiness has been difficult to discern due to the uncertainties in relation to wider domestic and inter-national economic conditions, and this may impede banks from lending more. Behavioural tendencies such as risk aversion and impediments to efficient markets such as acute informa-tion asymmetry may also result in capital hoarding. Hence, the PRA and FCA introduced a raft of measures in areas where inherent elasticity is not present to steer more precise actions on the part of banks.

The PRA has clearly instructed UK banks that all elements of liquidity and capital buff-ers 'exist to be used as necessary to support the economy'.[12] This general pronouncement reflects the introduction of objectives in micro-prudential regulation that are different from the objectives in post-crisis regulatory reforms from 2010. Besides the inherent elasticity of the CCyb, the PRA guidance clarifies that banks can draw down their discretionary capital buffer in the first place and all other regulatory capital buffers if required, but the rates of the other regulatory buffers have been maintained.[13] As explained in Chapter 11, regulatory capital buffers such as the capital conservation, systemic risk, PRA buffer and buffers applying to systemically important banks have to be maintained as risk-constraining measures. Banks are also encouraged to build up a discretionary buffer on top of regulatory buffers. They are now encouraged to draw down their discretionary buffers[14] in order to maximise their capacity to lend. After exhausting any discretionary buffer, banks are able to draw down their regulatory buffers as well, starting from the PRA buffer which is individ-ual to each bank and not publicly disclosed, followed by any remaining CCyb, the capital conservation buffer and, finally, the systemic risk buffer.

A suite of micro-prudential regulatory measures in liquidity and leverage thresholds have been relaxed, many of these not thought to be inherently flexible as they relate to the risk moderation objective in shaping banks' asset creation conduct. Banks are encouraged to allow businesses with credit lines and undrawn credit to draw upon such lines, even if this means banks' liquidity ratios may fall below the mandatory 100% that they are sup-posed to maintain. In normal circumstances, the liquidity coverage ratio is intended to

10 Article 128(7), Capital Requirements Directive 2013/36/EU.
11 Bank of England, 'Bank of England Measures to Respond to the Economic Shock from Covid-19' (11 March 2020) <https://www.bankofengland.co.uk/news/2020/march/boe-measures-to-respond-to-the-economic-shock-from-covid-19>; see also PRA, 'Statement by the PRA Accompanying Measures Announced by the Financial Policy Committee' (11 March 2020) <https://www.bankofengland.co.uk/prudential-regulation/publication/2020/statement-by-the-pra-accompanying-measures-announced-by-the-fpc>
12 PRA (n 4) 1.
13 PRA, 'PRA Decision on Systemic Risk Buffer Rates' (9 April 2020) <https://www.bankofengland.co.uk/prudential-regulation/publication/2020/pra-decision-on-srb-rates>
14 PRA (n 4).

be maintained at all times at 100% which effectively means that a firm can meet its cash outflows for a period of 30 days to prevent liquidity-driven systemic crises. It is unclear to what extent banks can safely draw down their liquidity ratios, as this can cause liquidity hazards for them. However, the BoE's Coronavirus Corporate Financing Facility[15] which is designed to help businesses tide over liquidity squeezes through their bank could help prevent banks from being dragged into liquidity squeezes by corporate customers. Further, the PRA introduced a range of modifications to the calculation of the exposure measure for the liquidity ratio to support banks' market making activities in financial markets, so as to maintain liquidity conditions.[16]

In order precisely to steer banks' behaviour towards increased support for the real economy instead of perverse incentives such as rewarding shareholders, the PRA provided strongly phrased guidance to UK banks to suspend any capital distributions to shareholders including the payment of dividends and share buy backs as well as the payment of any cash bonus to certain material categories of staff.[17] Regulators' power over dividend restrictions is warranted under the Capital Requirements Directive IV (CRD IV)[18] in order to promote the resilience of banks and financial stability.

Further, the relaxation of micro-prudential requirements to incentivise lending, and hence overcome banks' potentially risk averse tendencies towards supporting the real economy, was complemented by suspension of externally administered stress testing. Stress tests are a vital exercise for supervisors to understand whether banks have enough capital to continue to intermediate and lend in disrupted scenarios.[19] The BoE normally runs the following stress tests: an annual cyclical scenario and a biennial exploratory scenario. Stress tests support the FPC in achieving the legislative mandates to identify risks to financial stability and take steps to contain such risks, as the tests are forward-looking and facilitate systemic judgements and cross-bank comparisons. The BoE has postponed the 2020 stress test[20]: this decision is intended to keep credit flowing to households and businesses and reduce pressure on banks induced by the stress test.[21] The drawback of such suspension is that information opacity may be exacerbated in relation to banks' strength at times of crisis to the detriment of those who invest in bank shares and bonds and of effective supervision.

15 Bank of England, 'Covid Corporate Financing Facility (CCFF): Information for Those Seeking to Participate in the Scheme' (17 March 2020) <https://www.bankofengland.co.uk/news/2020/march/the-covid-corporate-financing-facility>
16 Regarding the calculation of the total exposure measure for the purpose of the leverage ratio, firms have been permitted to apply article 429g of the Capital Requirements Regulation (CRR II), which would normally only become applicable in June 2021. The effect of this change is to encourage market making activity by banks and thus support the liquidity of capital markets, as such activity will no longer entail a risk that more equity capital needs to be raised.
17 Prudential Regulation Authority, 'PRA Statement on Deposit Takers' Approach to Dividend Payments, Share Buybacks and Cash Bonuses in Response to Covid-19' (31 March 2020) <https://www.bankofengland.co.uk/prudential-regulation/publication/2020/pra-statement-on-deposit-takers-approach-to-dividend-payments-share-buybacks-and-cash-bonuses>
18 Art 141 on restrictions of dividends that jeopardises the level of banks' CET1 capital ratio.
19 Donald Kohn, 'Stress Tests: A Policymaker's Perspective' (5 February 2020) <https://www.bankofengland.co.uk/speech/2020/donald-kohn-speech-at-2020-ecb-conference-on-macroprudential-stress-testing>
20 See 'Bank of England Announces Supervisory and Prudential Policy Measures to Address the Challenges of Covid-19' (20 March 2020) <https://www.bankofengland.co.uk/news/2020/march/boe-announces-supervisory-and-prudential-policy-measures-to-address-the-challenges-of-covid-19>
21 Delphine Strauss and Stephen Morris, 'BoE Cancels Stress Tests to Ease Pressure on Lenders' *Financial Times* (20 March 2020) <https://www.ft.com/content/7433d55c-6a89-11ea-800d-da70cff6e4d3>

3 Regulatory measures providing relief to personal borrowers

Regulatory suspension has been applied in relation to the repayment of loans granted to household borrowers. Payment holidays are applicable to consumer credit and mortgages and not to business loans. In terms of mortgages, FCA guidance requires firms to grant a payment holiday for three months to any customer who indicates that they may potentially experience difficulties.[22] This measure does not affect the accrual of interest on the loan, and firms are not required to investigate the individual circumstances of each customer, nor to assess affordability, although firms might carry out such investigations on their own initiative. In cases where a customer is in default, the guidance restrains firms from commencing or continuing repossession proceedings and any possession order already made must not be enforced. In parallel, the FCA required firms to offer a temporary payment holidays for personal loans and credit cards for a period of up to three months to any consumers negatively impacted by the pandemic crisis and, in the case of consumers with an arranged overdraft, to provide an additional interest-free overdraft facility of £500 for a three-month period. These measures were – at the end of June 2020 – extended until 31 October 2020 for the benefit of consumer credit customers.[23] The FCA has also taken temporary measures to freeze repayments within the context of high-cost short-term credit loans, initially for a period of one month from April 2020 but subsequently extended to deferral requests that may be made up to 31 October 2020.[24] Banks have warned that payment holidays are not the same as debt relief. Consumers benefiting from this may behaviourally postpone their troubles but may be storing up an amount of arrears and debt that may become even more unmanageable in the future.[25] Moreover, payment holidays exacerbate information asymmetry for banks in relation to borrowers' creditworthiness and banks may make increased loan loss provisions against these,[26] paddling back against the capital liberation measures that have been offered.

22 FCA, 'Mortgages and Coronavirus: Information for Consumers' (20 March 2020) <https://www.fca.org.uk/consumers/mortgages-coronavirus-consumers>. See also 'Coronavirus and Customers in Temporary Financial Difficulty: Draft Updated Guidance for Insurance and Premium Finance Firms' (24 July 2020) <https://www.fca.org.uk/publications/guidance-consultations/coronavirus-customers-temporary-financial-difficulty-draft-updated-guidance-insurance>

23 FCA, 'FCA Confirms Further Support for Consumer Credit Customers' (1 July 2020) <https://www.fca.org.uk/news/press-releases/fca-confirms-further-support-consumer-credit-customers>

24 FCA, 'Coronavirus: Information for Consumers on Personal Loans, Credit Cards, Overdrafts, Motor Finance and Other Forms of Credit' (3 April 2020) <https://www.fca.org.uk/consumers/coronavirus-information-personal-loans-credit-cards-overdrafts>; 'High-cost Short-term Credit and Coronavirus: Temporary Guidance for Firms' (24 April 2020) <https://www.fca.org.uk/publications/finalised-guidance/high-cost-short-term-credit-and-coronavirus-temporary-guidance-firms>. This is updated in 'High-cost Short-term Credit and Coronavirus: Updated Temporary Guidance for Firms' (3 July 2020) <https://www.fca.org.uk/publications/guidance-consultations/high-cost-short-term-credit-coronavirus-updated-temporary-guidance-firms>

25 Nicholas Megaw and Matthew Vincent, 'Lenders Sound Warning on Mortgage Holidays' *Financial Times* (25 March 2020) <https://www.ft.com/content/3a6b82b0–6e77-11ea-89df-41bea055720b>

26 Stephen Morris and David Crow, 'European Bank Investors Brace for Loan-Loss Provisions' *Financial Times* (27 April 2020) <https://www.ft.com/content/1d9d862a-df05–47c1–8245-cf798127165f>; Stephen Morris, Matthew Vincent and David Crow, 'BoE Warns Bank Loan Reserves Risk Choking Business Funding' *Financial Times* (26 April 2020) <https://www.ft.com/content/75767049-edfb-4074–942c-f9ce4d07f861>; Jon Rees and Mohammad Taqi, '"UK Banks" Loan Loss Provisions Soar in Face of Pandemic' *S&P Global Market Intelligence* (7 May 2020) <https://www.spglobal.com/marketintelligence/en/news-insights/latest-news-headlines/uk-banks-loan-loss-provisions-soar-in-face-of-pandemic-58478176>

In terms of loan loss provisioning, the accounting standard IFRS 9 requires banks to account for debt instruments at fair value unless they satisfy the contractual cash flow test and business model assessment requirement. Changes in fair value must be reported in the profit and loss account, e.g. a reduction in fair value is registered as a loss and thus reduces a bank's Common Equity Tier 1 (CET1) capital. The full application of IFRS 9 during the pandemic crisis would inevitably lead to a significant increase in expected credit loss provisions and hence a contraction of the ability of banks to grow their balance sheet by lending. To prevent excessive loan loss provisions, the PRA urged banks to consider longer-term outlooks for borrowers and pay due attention to the transitional nature of the crisis, nudging banks against excessive loan loss provisioning while refraining from discouraging prudence altogether.[27] The ECB, similarly to the PRA's approach, allowed banks to take a longer-term view of loan adversity so that banks avoid excessive loan loss provisioning.[28] Although the PRA has not explicitly provided guidance on NPLs, the EBA[29] encouraged banks to make use of existing flexibility in its guidelines on the management of non-performing and forborne exposures. To address the challenges caused by the economic shock, the European Commission has also proposed to delay banks' implementation of micro-prudential reforms not yet in force.

Looking at the regulatory measures in response to Covid-19, it can be noted that the FCA has not provided clear enough guidance to lenders on how to deal with requests for repayment holidays leaving to borrowers the burden of negotiating the exact terms of their debt for the period after the suspension of repayments. Another issue affecting customers is that the repayment holidays can trigger requests by lenders to customers demanding repayment of their debts because they will have gone into arrears, even though the loan holidays will have been agreed in advance.[30] Non-bank specialist lenders play a key role in financing small businesses and providing consumer finance such as point-of-sale credit.[31] The government has not included them in the emergency scheme for businesses which means they are not supported to originate new loans. Customers may be unable to switch to new deals at the end of their fixed terms even if they have kept up with repayments.[32] Further, BoE's 'Term Funding Scheme' which provides cheap funding to boost lending volumes only applies to

27 Bank of England, 'Bank of England Announces Supervisory and Prudential Policy Measures to Address the Challenges of Covid-19' (20 March 2020) <https://www.bankofengland.co.uk/news/2020/march/boe-announces-supervisory-and-prudential-policy-measures-to-address-the-challenges-of-covid-19>.

28 European Central Bank, 'ECB Banking Supervision Provides Further Flexibility to Banks in Reaction to Coronavirus' (20 March 2020) <https://www.bankingsupervision.europa.eu/press/pr/date/2020/html/ssm.pr200320~4cdbbcf466.en.html>. See also ECB, 'Opinion of 20 May 2020 on Amendments to the Union Prudential Framework in Response to the COVID-19 Pandemic' (CON/2020/16) 2020/C 180/04.

29 EBA, 'Draft Technical Standards' (27 March 2020) <https://eba.europa.eu/sites/default/documents/files/document_library/EBA-RTS-2020–03%20Final%20draft%20RTS%20on%20Risk%20factor%20modellability.pdf>. See also EBA, 'Guidelines on Legislative and Non-Legislative Moratoria on Loan Repayments Applied in the Light of the COVID-19 Crisis' (2 April 2020, updated June 2020).

30 Nicholas Megaw and Matthew Vincent, 'UK Loan Freeze Plan Leaves Customers Still Open to Arrears Letters' *Financial Times* (5 April 2020) <https://www.ft.com/content/7a533dc5–8cd8-4ef3–9963-d1f43e76ff47>.

31 Investment banks provide 'warehouse lines' to collateralised loan obligations managers that help them build portfolios of loans.

32 Stephen Morris, Nicholas Megaw and Daniel Thomas, 'Non-bank Lenders Push for Access to Emergency State Funding' *Financial Times* (24 March 2020) <https://www.ft.com/content/51340b70–6d28-11ea-89df-41bea055720b>

banks and building societies. Non-bank specialist lenders such as loan-secured warehouse facilities, which online lenders typically use as a source of cash to fund loans in good times, are unlikely to be available so long as portfolio losses remain a problem.[33]

4 Fiscal support for businesses raising debt financing during the emergency

As the Covid-19 crisis brings about uncertainties for business in relation to the macroeconomic effects of disruption, risk information regarding business creditworthiness is likely to be challenging for banks to price. The relaxation of micro-prudential requirements provides incentives to lend but banks are likely to be risk averse. In this context, the UK Government passed a new legislation, the Corporate Insolvency and Governance Act 2020, to give companies insolvency moratoria and directors relief from potential liability for wrongful trading.[34]

Most importantly, the UK Government has announced fiscal support for two business loan schemes. UK businesses with a turnover of less than £45 million can benefit from the 'Coronavirus Business Interruption Loan Scheme', which is administered by the government-owned British Business Bank and enables accredited lenders to provide loans and overdraft facilities of up to £5 million, guaranteed at 80% by the government, to be repaid over a period of up to six years.[35] UK small- and medium-sized businesses can also benefit from the 'Bounce Back Loan Scheme' that provides loan facilities of up to £50,000, guaranteed at 100% by the government to be repaid over up to six years with no payments in the first 12 months.[36] Lenders are expected to assess whether businesses should access such government-guaranteed finance, the principle being that loans should only be available to otherwise healthy businesses that need to trade through the short- to medium-term revenue loss caused by the lockdown.

In order to support the lending programme, the PRA has announced that loans made under the Bounce Back Scheme, which is 100% guaranteed, will be disregarded for the purposes of banks' leverage ratio.[37] The leverage ratio requires that the total leverage of banks

---

33 Todd Baker and Kathryn Judge, 'How to Help Small Businesses Survive COVID-19' in Katharina Pistor (ed), *Law in the Time of COVID-19* (Columbia Law School Columbia Law School) 120.

34 Sections 3, 6 and 7 of the Corporate Insolvency and Governance Act 2020 <https://www.legislation.gov.uk/ukpga/2020/12/contents/enacted>. See also Amir Licht, 'What's So Wrong with Wrongful Trading? On Suspending Director Liability during the Coronavirus Crisis' Oxford Business Law Blog (9 April 2020) <https://www.law.ox.ac.uk/business-law-blog/blog/2020/04/whats-so-wrong-wrongful-trading-suspending-director-liability-during>; Kristin van Zweiten, 'The Wrong Target? COVID-19 and the Wrongful Trading Rule' Oxford Business Law Blog (25 March 2020) <https://www.law.ox.ac.uk/business-law-blog/blog/2020/03/wrong-target-covid-19-and-wrongful-trading-rule>

35 Great Britain. Department for Business, Energy and Industrial Strategy, 'Coronavirus Business Interruption Loan Scheme' (23 March 2020) <https://www.gov.uk/guidance/apply-for-the-coronavirus-business-interruption-loan-scheme>

36 Great Britain. Business, Energy and Industrial Strategy Dept, 'Apply for a Coronavirus Bounce Back Loan' (27 April 2020) <https://www.gov.uk/guidance/apply-for-a-coronavirus-bounce-back-loan>

37 Bank of England, 'Statement on Credit Risk Mitigation Eligibility and Leverage Ratio Treatment of Loans under the Bounce Back Loan Scheme' (4 May 2020) <https://www.bankofengland.co.uk/prudential-regulation/publication/2020/pra-statement-on-crm-and-leverage-ratio-loans-under-bbls>

be supported by at least 3% of CET1 capital.[38] This is a measure that backstops bank lending and complements other capital adequacy measures that rely on risk-weighting, which can be discretionary and in the global financial crisis, proved to be inaccurate.[39]

The suspension of application of the leverage ratio to Bounce Back Loans is likely to fuel moral hazard as the urgent demand for such loans makes underwriting a time-sensitive process exacerbated by information asymmetry.[40] The government guarantee is likely to incentivise minimal underwriting diligence standards as banks do not have the financial incentive to price conservatively. Although the welfare needs of the real economy are immediately pressing, the suspension of hitherto mandatory micro-prudential standards creates problems for their future credibility. The difficult balance that must be struck is to ensure banks have both the flexibility needed to make sound commercial decisions and sufficient capital to remain robust in the face of highly uncertain circumstances.[41]

It may be argued that the hazards of compelling banks to support expanded credit in such emergency times may be overstated, as companies in need of capital also have the option of raising equity which is a more stable form of financing to navigate through the crisis. However, it is uncertain if the UK Government's policy choice to greatly expand commercial channels of financial support for businesses through banks is optimal, as the public interest needs underlying policy choice interfere with the delicate relationship between micro-prudential regulation and commercial decision-making. In essence, banks need to suspend much of their ordinary commercial decision-making standards, as supported by the removal of regulatory constraints, but regulators need to ensure that there is no boomerang effect upon banks due to poor commercial decision-making after normal micro-prudential regulatory standards are reinstated. Further, it is uncertain that the temporary boost of lending to businesses would not become a snare for borrowers in the future. The Bounce Back Scheme relieves businesses of payments for the first 12 months, but it remains uncertain if this period will be sufficient for businesses to recover, especially as the UK economy is only expected to reach 2019 GDP levels in 2023.[42] The government guarantee can also introduce perverse incentives for banks to accelerate treating Bounce Back borrowers as in default to call upon the guarantee and to remove these borrowers from banks' balance sheets. Banks are incentivised to appropriate any distributive advantage towards borrowers as soon as they are able to.

---

38 Arts 429, 430, Regulation (EU) No. 575/2013 of the European Parliament and of the Council of 26 June 2013 on prudential requirements for credit institutions and investment firms and amending Regulation (EU) No. 648/2012.

39 Financial Services Authority, 'The Turner Review. A Regulatory Response to the Global Banking Crisis' (March 2009) 88–92.

40 Peter Lee, 'CBILS Faulty: Sunak's Flagship UK Lending Scheme Looks Unfit for Purpose' *Euromoney* (24 April 2020) <https://www.euromoney.com/article/b11bgfwrx72nn3/cbils-faulty-sunaks-flagship-uk-lending-scheme-looks-unfit-for-purpose>

41 Patrizia Baudino, 'Public Guarantees for Bank Lending in Response to the Covid-19 Pandemic (2020) BIS Financial Stability Institute Briefs No. 5 <https://www.bis.org/fsi/fsibriefs5.pdf>; Pierre Schammo, 'Who Knows What Tomorrow Brings? Of Uncertainty in Times of a Pandemic' Oxford Business Law Blog (28 April 2020) <https://www.law.ox.ac.uk/business-law-blog/blog/2020/04/who-knows-what-tomorrow-brings-uncertainty-times-pandemic>

42 See EY, 'UK Economy Not Expected to Return to Its Late 2019 Size Until 2023, Says EY ITEM Club Forecast' (27 April 2020) <https://www.ey.com/en_uk/news/2020/04/uk-economy-not-expected-to-return-to-its-late-2019-size-until-2023-says-ey-item-club-forecast>

5 Concluding remarks

The management of the pandemic crisis required the PRA and FCA to work in a co-ordinated manner so that the FCA's regulatory suspensions in consumer credit could be co-ordinated with the PRA's approach to micro-prudential regulation. However, the effects of these temporary regulatory suspensions raised doubts on the sustainability of the policy objectives set by financial regulators against Covid-19. The suspension of the annual regulatory stress test will also cause a lack of information on bank resilience in the face of micro-prudential regulatory relaxation, especially as more risk is expected to be taken on. Moral hazard and increased risks for banks, systemic stability and both business and household borrowers may outweigh the short-term relief provided to the real economy by these measures.

Bibliography

D. Acemoglu, A. Ozdaglar and A. Tahbaz-Salehi, 'Systemic Risk and Stability in Financial Networks' (2015) 105 *American Economic Review*, 2.

V.V. Acharya, 'A Theory of Systemic Risk and Design of Prudential Bank Regulation' (2009) 5 *Journal of Financial Stability*, 3.

A. Acquisti, C. Taylor and L. Wagman, 'The Economics of Privacy' (2016) 54 *Journal of Economic Literature*, 442.

R. Adams, B. Hermalin and M. Weisbach, 'The Role of Boards of Directors in Corporate Governance: A Conceptual Framework and Survey' (2010) 48 *Journal of Economic Literature*, 58.

A. Admati and M. Hellwig, *The Bankers' New Clothes: What's Wrong with Banking and What to Do about It* (Princeton University Press, 2014).

AFME, 'Implementing Brexit Practical Challenges for Wholesale Banking in Adapting to the New Environment' (April 2017) at https://www.afme.eu/globalassets/downloads/publications/afme-implementing-brexit-2017.pdf.

K. Ahmed, 'Bank of England Believes Brexit Could Cost 75,000 Finance Jobs', *BBC News* (London, 31 October 2017) at https://www.bbc.co.uk/news/business-41803604.

K. Ahmed, 'RBS Reports First Profit in 10 Years', *BBC News* (London, 23 February 2018) at https://www.bbc.co.uk/news/business-43166560.

S. Aiyar et al., 'A Strategy for Resolving Europe's Problem Loans', International Monetary Fund, Staff Discussion Note SDN/15/19, September 2015.

I. Akkizidis and L. Kalyvas, *Final Basel III Modelling* (Palgrave 2019).

O. Akseli, 'Was Securitisation the Culprit? Explanation of Legal Processes Behind Creation of Mortgage-backed Sub-prime Securities' in Joanna Gray and Orkun Akseli (eds), *Financial Regulation in Crisis? The Role of Law and the Failure of Northern Rock* (Edward Elgar 2011) 5–6.

K. Alexander, 'The Role of a Global Supervisor for International Financial Markets' (2001) 8(3) *Journal of Financial Crime*, 237.

K. Alexander, 'Bank Resolution Regimes: Balancing Prudential Regulation and Shareholder Rights' (2009) 9(1) *Journal of Corporate Law Studies*, 63–64.

K. Alexander, 'Bank Capital Management and Macro-prudential Regulation – A Law and Finance Perspective' (2012) 24 *Journal of Banking Law*, 331.

K. Alexander, 'The ECB and Banking Supervision: Building Effective Prudential Supervision?' (2014) 33(1) *Yearbook of European Law*, 421.

K. Alexander, 'The European Central Bank and Banking Supervision: The Regulatory Limits of the Single Supervisory Mechanism' (2016) 13(3) *European Company and Financial Law Review*, 467.

K. Alexander, 'The UK's Third-Country Status Following Brexit: Post-Brexit Models, Third-Country Equivalence and Switzerland' in Kern Alexander et al. (eds), *Brexit and Financial Services: Law and Policy* (Hart Publishing, 2018) 118–120.

K. Alexander, *Principles of Banking Regulation* (Cambridge University Press, 2019).

K. Alexander, R. Dhumale and J. Eatwell, 'Managing Systemic Risk. The Rationale for International Financial Regulation' in Kern Alexander, Rahul Dhumale and John Eatwell (eds), *Global*

Governance of Financial Systems. The International Regulation of Systemic Risk (Oxford University Press, 2005).

K. Alexander, E. Ferran, H.E. Jackson and N. Moloney, 'A Report on the Transatlantic Financial Services Regulatory Dialogue' in *Harvard Law Discussion Paper Series*, John Olin Center for Law, Economics and Business, 2007, No. 1.

O. Ali, 'We Now Need Decisive Action to Prevent Brexit Uncertainty from Damaging the UK's Status as Europe's Leading Financial Services Hub' (EY Report, June 2018) at https://www.ey.com/uk/en/issues/business-environment/ey-attractiveness-survey-2018-uk-fs.

P. Alldridge, *What Went Wrong with Money Laundering Law?* (Palgrave Macmillan 2016) 11–12.

F. Allen and A. Santomero, 'What Do Financial Intermediaries Do?' (2001) 25 *Journal of Banking & Finance*, 271.

J.G. Allen and R.M. Lastra, 'Towards a European Governance Framework for Cryptoassets' SUERF Policy Note, August 2019 at www.suerf.org/policynotes.

I. Anagnostopoulos, 'Fintech and Regtech: Impact on Regulators and Banks' (2018) 100 *Journal of Economics and Business*, 7–8.

A.A. Anand, 'Is Systemic Risk Relevant to Securities Regulation?' (2010) 60 *University of Toronto Law Journal*, 980.

M. Andenas, 'Liability for Supervisors and Depositors' Rights: The BCCI and the Bank of England in the House of Lords' (2001) 22 *The Company Lawyer*, 88.

M. Andenas and I. Chiu, *The Foundations and Future of Financial Regulation: Governance for Responsibility* (Routledge, 2014).

M. Andenas and D. Fairgrieve, 'To Supervise or to Compensate? A Comparative Study of State Liability for Negligent Banking Supervision' in Mads Andenas (ed), *Judicial Review in International Perspective* (Kluwer Law International, 2000) 333–334.

J. Armour, 'Brexit to the European Economic Area: What Would It Mean?' Oxford Business Law Blog (19 July 2016) at https://www.law.ox.ac.uk/business-law-blog/blog/2016/07/brexit-european-economic-area-what-would-it-mean.

J. Armour, 'Brexit and Financial Services' (2017) 33(suppl.) *Oxford Review of Economic Policy*, 54.

J. Armour, 'Current State of the Fintech Industry and Its Challenges' (2017) at https://oxfordfls.org/.

J. Armour and J.N. Gordon, 'Systemic Harms and Shareholder Value' (2014) 6 *Journal of Legal Analysis*, 35.

D.W. Arner, *Financial Stability, Economic Growth, and the Role of Law* (Cambridge University Press, 2007) 73.

D.W. Arner, J. Barberis and R.P. Buckley, 'The Evolution of Fintech: A New Post-crisis Paradigm' (2015) 47 *Georgetown Journal of International Law*, 4.

D.W. Arner, J. Barberis and R.P. Buckley, 'FinTech, RegTech, and the Reconceptualization of Financial Regulation' (2016) 37 *Northwestern Journal of International Law & Business*, 371.

A. Arora, 'The Global Financial Crisis: A New Global Regulatory Order?' (2010) 8 *Journal of Business Law*, 676.

K. Arrow, 'Uncertainty and the Welfare Economics of Medical Care' (1963) 53 *The American Economic Review*, 941.

R. Arscott, 'LIBOR Floors in Leveraged Loans' (2018a) at https://papers.ssrn.com/sol3/papers.cfm?abstract_id=3073156.

R. Arscott, 'LIBOR Floors in Leveraged Loans' (2018b) at https://papers.ssrn.com/sol3/papers.cfm?abstract_id=3073156.

G. Ashley-Fenn, 'Corporate Governance – An FSA Perspective' (Building Societies Association Corporate Governance Seminar, London, 2010) at www.fsa.gov.uk/pages/Library/Communication/Speeches/2010/0303_gaf.shtml.

I.G. Asimakopoulos, 'International Law as a Negotiation Tool in Banking Union; The Case of the Single Resolution Fund' (2018) 21 *Journal of Economic Policy Reform*, 120.

A. Asllani, C.S. White and L. Ettkin, 'Viewing Cybersecurity as A Public Good: The Role of Governments, Businesses and Individuals' (2013) 16 *Journal of Legal, Ethical and Regulatory Issues*, 1.

P.S. Atiyah, *The Rise and Fall of Freedom of Contract* (Oxford University Press, 1985) Chapters 18–22.

J. Authers, 'Who Will Teach Responsibility in a Buck-passing World?' *Financial Times* (London, 22 June 2014).

N.W. Averitt and R.H. Lande, 'Consumer Sovereignty: A Unified Theory of Antitrust and Consumer Protection Law' (1997) 65 *Antitrust Law Journal*, 713.

Y. Avgerinos, 'The Need and the Rationale for a European Securities Regulator' in Mads Andenas and Yannis Avgerinos (eds) *Financial Markets in Europe: Towards a Single Regulator?* (Kluwer Law, 2003) 146.

E. Avgouleas, 'The Global Financial Crisis and the Disclosure Paradigm in European Financial Regulation: The Case for Reform' (2009) 6 *European Company and Financial Law Review*, 440.

E. Avgouleas, 'The Reform of the "Too-Big-To-Fail" Bank: A New Regulatory Model for the Institutional Separation of "Casino" from "Utility" Banking' (2010) at https://papers.ssrn.com/sol3/papers.cfm?abstract_id=1552970&rec=1&srcabs=1525670&alg=1&pos=6.

E. Avgouleas and J. Cullen, 'Market Discipline and EU Corporate Governance Reform in the Banking Sector: Merits, Fallacies, and Cognitive Boundaries' (2014) 41 *Journal of Law and Society*, 28.

E. Avgouleas and C.A. Goodhart, 'A Critical Evaluation of Bail-in as a Bank Recapitalisation Mechanism', Centre for Economic Policy Research, Discussion Paper No. 10065, July 2014, 19.

E. Avgouleas and C. Goodhart, 'Utilizing AMCs to Tackle Eurozone's Legacy Non-performing Loans' (2017) *European Economy Banks, Regulation, and the Real Sector*, 103 at http://european-economy.eu/wp-content/uploads/2017/07/EE_1.2017.pdf.

E. Avgouleas and A. Kiayias, 'The Promise of Blockchain Technology for Global Securities and Derivatives Markets: The New Financial Ecosystem and the 'Holy Grail' of Systemic Risk Containment' (2019) 20(1) *European Business Organization Law Review*, 82.

D. Awrey, 'Complexity, Innovation, and the Regulation of Modern Financial Markets' (2012) 2 *Harvard Business Law Review*, 2.

D. Awrey and K. van Zwieten, 'The Shadow Payment System' (2018) 43(4) *Journal of Corporation Law*, 796–797.

R. Ayadi, G. Ferri and R.M. Lastra, 'Systemic Solutions to Systemic Crises. Dealing with NPLs in the Eurozone' (2017) 1 *European Economy*, 177 at http://european-economy.eu/2017-1/systemic-solutions-to-systemic-crises-dealing-with-npls-in-the-eurozone/.

R. Ayadi and R.M. Lastra, 'Proposals for Reforming Deposit Guarantee Schemes in Europe' (2010) 11(3) *Journal of Banking Regulation*, 215.

I. Ayres, 'Making a Difference: The Contractual Contributions of Easterbrook and Fischel' (1992) 59 *University of Chicago Law Review*, 1391.

I. Ayres and R. Gertner, 'Filling Gaps in Incomplete Contracts: An Economic Theory of Default Rules' (1989) 99 *Yale Law Journal*, 87.

I. Ayres and J. Mitts, 'Anti-herding Regulation', Yale Law & Economics Research Paper No. 490 at http://ssrn.com/abstract=2399240.

V. Babis, 'Single Rule Book for Prudential Regulation of EU Banks: Mission Accomplished?' (2015) 26 *European Business Law Review*, 6.

A. Bahadir and F. Garcés de los Fayos, 'The European Economic Area (EEA), Switzerland and the North' (2016) at http://www.europarl.europa.eu/atyourservice/en/displayFtu.html?ftuId=FTU_6.5.3.html.

A. Bailey, 'The UK Bank Resolution Regime', Speech Delivered to the ICAEW Financial Services Faculty Breakfast, London, 26 November 2009.

A. Bailey, 'The Future of LIBOR' (Bloomberg, London, 27 July 2017) at https://www.fca.org.uk/news/speeches/the-future-of-libor.

S.M. Bainbridge and M. Todd Henderson, *Limited Lability: A Legal and Economic Analysis* (Edward Elgar Publishing, 2016).

R. Baldwin and J. Black, 'Really Responsive Regulation', LSE Law, Society and Economy Working Papers No. 15, 2007.

C. Bamford, *Principles of International Financial Law* (2nd edn, Oxford University Press, 2015) 247–248.

Bank of England, Working Paper No. 460, August 2012, 3–4.

Bank of England, 'Additional Leverage Ratio Buffer Model Requirements for G-SIIs' (2015).

Bank of England, 'The Implementation of Ring-Fencing: The PRA's Approach to Ring-Fencing Transfer Schemes', Policy Statement PS10/16, 4 March 2016, 7–8.

Bank of England, 'Ring-Fenced Bodies (RFBs)' Supervisory Statement SS8/16, December 2017, 24–25.

Bank of England, 'The Bank of England's Approach to Setting a Minimum Requirement for Own Funds and Eligible Liabilities (MREL)', Statement of Policy, June 2018, updated on December 2020.

Bank of England, 'Financial Stability Report' (Issue 44, November 2018).

Bank of England, 'The Prudential Regulation Authority's Approach to Banking Supervision' (2018), paras 80–82, at https://www.bankofengland.co.uk/prudential-regulation/publication/2018/pra-approach-documents-2018.

Bank of England, 'Stress Testing' (24 June 2019) at https://www.bankofengland.co.uk/stress-testing.

Bank of England, 'Interest Rates and Bank Rate' at https://www.bankofengland.co.uk/monetary-policy/the-interest-rate-bank-rate.

Bank of England: Prudential Regulation Authority, 'Strengthening Capital Standards: Implementing CRD IV, Feedback and Final Rules', PRA Policy Statement PS7/13, 2013, para 4.7 at http://www.bankofengland.co.uk/pra/Pages/publications/implemcrdiv.aspx.

Bank of England and Financial Services Authority, 'Instruments of Macroprudential Policy' (December 2011) at http://www.bankofengland.co.uk/publications/Documents/other/financialstability/discussionpaper111220.pdf.

Bank of England, HM Treasury and FSA, 'Financial Stability and Depositor Protection: Strengthening the Framework' (January 2008), 8.

Bank for International Settlements, '58th Annual Report' (1 April 1987–31 March 1988) at https://www.bis.org/publ/arpdf/archive/ar1988_en.pdf.

Bank for International Settlements, 'Report of the Committee on Interbank Netting Schemes of the Central Banks of the Group of Ten Countries (Lamfalussy Report)' (Basel, November 1990).

Bank for International Settlements, Committee on Payment and Settlement Systems, 'Core Principles for Systemically Important Payment Systems' (January 2001).

Bank of Italy, 'The 'Precautionary Recapitalization' of Banca Monte dei Paschi di Siena' at https://www.bancaditalia.it/media/approfondimenti/2016/ricapitalizzazione-mps/index.html?com.dotmarketing.htmlpage.language=1.

Bank of Italy, https://www.bancaditalia.it/compiti/stabilita-finanziaria/politica-macroprudenziale/documenti/OSII_2016_comunicato_en.pdf?language_id=1.

Bank of Italy, 'Financial Stability Report' (May 2019) No. 1, 25–26.

S. Barocas and H. Nissenbaum, 'Big Data's End Run Around Anonymity and Consent' in Julia Lane, Victoria Stodden, Stefan Bender and Helen Nissenbaum (eds), *Privacy, Big Data, and the Public Good: Frameworks for Engagement* (Cambridge University Press, 2014) 44–45.

M.S. Barr and G.P. Miller, 'Global Administrative Law: The View from Basel' (2006) 17 *European Journal of International Law*, 1.

J.R. Bartel and Y. Huang, 'Dealing with the Bad Loans of the Chinese Banks', Discussion Paper Series No. 13, APEC Study Center, Columbia University, July 2000, 18 at https://www8.gsb.columbia.edu/apec/sites/apec/files/files/discussion/boninhuang.pdf.

J.R. Barth, C. Brummer, T. Li and D. E. Nolle, 'Systemically Important Banks (SIBs) in the Post-crisis Era: 'The' Global Response, and Responses Around the Globe for 135 Countries' in Allen N. Berger, Philip Molyneux and John O.S. Wilson (eds) *The Oxford Handbook of Banking* (2nd edn, Oxford University Press, 2015) 617.

J.R. Barth, G. Caprio, Jr. and R. Levine, *Rethinking Bank Regulation: Till Angels Govern* (Cambridge University Press, 2006).

Basel Committee on Banking Supervision, 'Principles for the Supervision of Banks' Foreign Establishments' (May 1983).

Basel Committee on Banking Supervision, *International Convergence of Capital Measurement and Capital Standards* (Bank of International Settlements Publications, 1988).

Basel Committee on Banking Supervision, 'Report on International Convergence of Capital Measurement and Capital Standards' (July 1988) at https://www.bis.org/publ/bcbsc111.pdf.

Basel Committee on Banking Supervision, 'Minimum Standards for the Supervision of International Banking Groups and their Cross-border Establishments' (July 1992).

Basel Committee on Banking Supervision, *Amendment to the Capital Accord to Incorporate Market Risks* (Bank of International Settlements Publications, 1996).

Basel Committee on Banking Supervision, 'Sound Practices for Loan Accounting and Disclosure', Basel Committee on Banking Supervision Paper, July 1999, 35.

Basel Committee on Banking Supervision, 'Credit Ratings and Complementary Sources of Credit Quality Information', Working Papers No. 3, August 2000, 4.

Basel Committee on Banking Supervision, 'International Convergence of Capital Measurement and Capital Standards', Revised Framework 2004.

Basel Committee on Banking Supervision, 'Studies on the Validation of Internal Rating Systems', Working Paper No. 14, May 2005, 7 at https://www.bis.org/publ/bcbs_wp14.pdf.

Basel Committee on Banking Supervision, 'Sound Credit Risk Assessment and Valuation for Loans' (June 2006) at https://www.bis.org/publ/bcbs126.pdf.

Basel Committee on Banking Supervision, *Core Principles Methodology* (October 2006).

Basel Committee on Banking Supervision, *International Convergence of Capital Measurement and Capital Standards: A Revised Framework, Comprehensive Version* (Bank of International Settlements Publications, 2006).

Basel Committee on Banking Supervision, *Basel III: A Global Regulatory Framework for More Resilient Banks and Banking Systems* (rev edn, Bank of International Settlements Publications, 2011).

Basel Committee on Banking Supervision, *Basel III: The Liquidity Coverage Ratio and Liquidity Risk Monitoring Tools* (Bank for International Settlements, 2013).

Basel Committee on Banking Supervision, 'Basel III Leverage Ratio Framework and Disclosure Requirements' (January 2014) at https://www.bis.org/publ/bcbs270.pdf.

Basel Committee on Banking Supervision, 'Basel III: The Net Stable Funding Ratio' (October 2014) 2–3 at https://www.bis.org/bcbs/publ/d295.pdf.

Basel Committee on Banking Supervision, 'Finalising Post-crisis Reforms' (December 2017) at https://www.bis.org/bcbs/publ/d424.pdf.

Basel Committee on Banking Supervision, *Basel III: The Net Stable Funding Ratio: Consultative Document* (Bank for International Settlements Publications, 2014).

Basel Committee on Banking Supervision, 'Prudential Treatment of Problem Assets – Definitions of Non-performing Exposures and FORBEARANCE' (2017) Guidelines at http://www.bis.org/bcbs/publ/d403.htm.

C. Bates, 'Ending Too-Big-To-Fail in Europe', Lecture given at the Centre for Commercial Law Studies, Queen Mary University of London, London, 25 November 2014.

P. Baudino and H. Yun, 'Resolution of Non-performing Loans – Policy Options', FSI Insights on Policy Implementation No. 3, 2017, 3–4 at https://www.bis.org/fsi/publ/insights3.pdf.

C. Bauer and B. Herz, 'Reforming the European Stability Mechanism' (2020) 58(3) *Journal of Common Market Studies*, 636 version).

T. Baums and M. Gruson, 'The German Banking System--System of the Future?' (1993) 19 *Brooklyn Journal of International Law*, 1.

L.G. Baxter, 'Adaptive Financial Regulation and RegTech: A Concept Article on Realistic Protection for Victims of Bank Failures' (2016) 66 *Duke Law Journal*, 3.

A. Beatty and L. Scott, 'Do Delays in Expected Loss Recognition Affect Banks' Willingness to Lend?' (2011) 52(1) *Journal of Accounting and Economics*, 19–20.

L. Bebchuk, A. Cohen and H. Spamann, 'The Wages of Failure: Executive Compensation at Bear Sterns and Lehman 2000–2008' (2010) 27 *Yale Journal on Regulation*, 257.

M.L. Bech and R. Garratt, 'Central Bank Cryptocurrencies' (2017) *BIS Quarterly Review*, 58–59.

P. Beck and G. Narayanamoorthy, 'Did the SEC Impact Banks' Loan Loss Reserve Policies and Their Informativeness?' (2013) 56 *Journal of Accounting and Economics*, 42.

A.U. Bello, *Improving Anti-money Laundering Compliance: Self-protecting Theory and Money Laundering Reporting Officers* (Palgrave Macmillan, 2016) Ch 3.

J. Benjamin, *Financial Law* (Oxford University Press, 2007) 590.

J. Benjamin, P. Bowden and D. Rouch, 'Law and Regulation for Global Financial Markets: Markets as Rule-makers – Enforcement, Dispute Resolution and Risk' (2008) 2 *Law and Financial Markets Review*, 321.

J. Benjamin and D. Rouch, 'The International Financial Markets as a Source of Global Law: The Privatisation of Rule-making?' (2008) 2(2) *Law and Financial Markets Review*, 78.

M. Bennett, 'The Financial Industry Business Ontology: Best Practice for Big Data' (2013) 14 *Journal of Banking Regulation*, 3–4.

E. Benos, R. Garratt and P. Gurrola-Perez, 'The Economics of Distributed Ledger Technology for Securities Settlement', Bank of England Working Paper No. 670, August 2017, 27 at https://www.bankofengland.co.uk/working-paper/2017/the-economics-of-distributed-ledger-technology-for-securities-settlement.

G.J. Benston, 'Universal Banking' (1994) 8 *Journal of Economic Perspectives*, 3.

H. Berger and N. Badenhoop, 'Financial Services and Brexit: Navigating Towards Future Market Access' (2018) 19 *European Business Organization Law Review*, 4.

A. Berle and G. Means, *The Modern Corporation and Private Property* (Harcourt, Brace & World, 1967).

D. Bholat, 'The Future of Central Bank Data' (2013) 14(3/4) *Journal of Banking Regulation*, 192.

D. Bholat et al., 'Non-performing Loans: Regulatory and Accounting Treatment of Assets', Bank of England Staff Working Paper No. 594, April 2016, 3.

D. Bholat et al., 'Non-performing Loans at the Dawn of IFRS 9: Regulatory and Accounting Treatment of Asset Quality' (2018) 19(1) *Journal of Banking Regulation*, 33.

D.S. Bieri, 'Regulation and Financial Stability in the Age of Turbulence' in Robert W. Kolb (ed), *Lessons from the Global Financial Crisis* (John Wiley & Sons, 2010) 327.

J.-H. Binder, 'Resolution Planning and Structural Bank Reform Within the Banking Union' SAFE Working Paper, No. 81, 2014, 7–8 at https://www.econstor.eu/bitstream/10419/106149/1/815411138.pdf.

J.-H. Binder, 'To Ring-Fence or Not, and How? Strategic Questions for Post-crisis Banking Reform in Europe' (December 2014) at http://ssrn.com/abstract=2543860.

J.-H. Binder, 'Resolution: Concepts, Requirements and Tools' in Jens-Hinrich Binder and Dalvinder Singh (eds), *Bank Resolution: The European Regime* (Oxford University Press, 2016) 25–27.

J.-H. Binder, 'Governance of Investment Firms Under MiFID II' in Danny Busch and Guido Ferrarini (eds), *Regulation of the EU Financial Markets: MiFID II and MiFIR* (Oxford University Press, 2017) 60.

J.-H. Binder, 'Proportionality at the Resolution Stage: Calibration of Resolution Measures and the Public Interest Test' (3 July 2017) 20 at https://ssrn.com/abstract=2990379.

G. Bippart, 'English-Law Bonds Could be Excluded from MREL Post-Brexit', *Euromoney* (24 November 2017) at https://www.euromoney.com/article/b15rkx7999nk36/regulation-english-law-bonds-could-be-excluded-from-mrel-post-brexit.

BIS, 'Transparency & Trust: Enhancing the Transparency of UK Company Ownership and Increasing Trust in UK Business: Government Response' (April 2014), para 249 at https://www.gov.uk/government/consultations/company-ownership-transparency-and-trust-discussion-paper.

BIS, 'Net Stable Funding Ratio (NSFR) – Executive Summary' (28 June 2018) at https://www.bis.org/fsi/fsisummaries/nsfr.htm.

BIS Committee on Payment and Settlement Systems, 'Recommendations for Securities Settlement Systems', Report, November 2001, 8–10 at https://www.bis.org/cpmi/publ/d46.pdf.

W. Bishop, 'Negligent Representation through Economists' Eyes' (1980) 96 *Law Quarterly Review*, 360.

C.S. Bjerre, 'A Transactional Approach to the Hague Securities Convention' (2008) 3 *Capital Markets Law Journal*, 2.

B. Black, 'Agents Watching Agents: The Promise of Institutional Investor Voice' (1991–1992) 39 *UCLA Law Review*, 811.

J. Black, '"Which Arrow?": Rule Type and Regulatory Policy' (1995) 1 *Public Law*, 77.

J. Black, 'Using Rules Effectively' in Christopher McCrudden (ed.), *Regulation and Deregulation* (Oxford University Press, 1998) 101.

J. Black, 'Decentring Regulation: Understanding the Role of Regulation and Self-regulation in a "Post-regulatory" World' (2001) 54(1) *Current Legal Problems*, 103.

J. Black, 'Paradoxes and Failures: "New Governance" Techniques and the Financial Crisis' (2012) 75(6) *Modern Law Review*, 1037.

J. Black, M. Hopper and C. Band, 'Making a Success of Principles-based Regulation' (2007) 1(3) *Law and Financial Markets Review*, 191.

J. Black and D. Rouch, 'The Development of the Global Markets as Rule-makers: Engagement and Legitimacy' (2008) 2(3) *Law and Financial Markets Review*, 223–225.

R. Bollen, 'The International Financial System and Future Global Regulation' (2008) 23(9) *Journal of International Banking Law and Regulation*, 469.

R. Bollen, 'Setting International Regulatory Standards for Hedge Funds: Part 3' (2011) 26(4) *Journal of International Banking Law and Regulation*, 175.

R.W.H. Bons, R. Alt, H. Geun Lee and B. Weber, 'Banking in the Internet and Mobile Era' (2012) 22 *Electronic Markets*, 4.

R. Booth et al., *Money Laundering Law and Regulation: A Practical Guide* (Oxford University Press, 2011).

S.A. Booysen, 'Cheques: To Be or Not to Be?' (2018) 4 *Journal of Business Law*, 283.

S.A. Booysen, 'Payment Scams: Tidal Energy v Bank of Scotland and Recent Developments' (2018) 33 *Journal of International Banking and Financial Law*, 405.

M.D. Bordo and A.T. Levin, 'Central Bank Digital Currency and the Future of Monetary Policy. Technical Report', NBER Working Paper No. 23711, August 2017, 7–8 at https://www.nber.org/papers/w23711.pdf.

L. Bowman, 'Aggrieved Banco Popular Bondholders Train Their Sights on Banco Santander' *Euromoney* (17 April 2018) at https://www.euromoney.com/article/b17t71ls5hhvyp/aggrieved-banco-popular-bondholders-train-their-sights-on-banco-santander.

R Brace, 'Electrifying the Ring-Fence – The View from the Transaction Banking Industry' *Euromoney* (10 January 2013) at https://www.euromoney.com/article/b12kjvpk84dq26/electrifying-the-ring-fence-the-view-from-the-transaction-banking-industry.

L. Brainard, 'Supporting Fast Payments for All', Federal Reserve Board (3 October 2018) at https://www.federalreserve.gov/newsevents/speech/brainard20181003a.htm.

J.P. Braithwaite, 'OTC Derivatives, the Courts and Regulatory Reform' (2012) 7 *Capital Markets Law Journal*, 4.

P. Brandt, 'EMIR Regulations Continue to Impact Derivatives Markets in 2014' (2014) 131 *Banking Law Journal*, 3.

F. Brandt and M. Wohlfahrt, 'A Common Backstop to the Single Resolution Fund' (2019) 22 *Journal of Economic Policy Reform*, 3.

J. Breckenridge, J. Farquharson and R. Hendon, 'The Role of Business Model Analysis in the Supervision of Insurers', Bank of England Quarterly Bulletin (2014) Q1.

S. Breitenmoser, 'Sectoral Agreements between the EC and Switzerland: Contents and Context' (2003) 40 *Common Market Law Review*, 5.

S. Breyer, 'Judicial Review of Questions of Law and Policy' in Peter Cane (ed), *Administrative Law* (Routledge, 2002) 47–48.

C. Briault, 'The Rationale for a Single National Financial Services Regulator', FSA Occasional Paper Series No. 2, 1999, 18–19.

C. Briault, 'Revisiting the Rationale for a Single Financial Services Regulator', FSA Occasional Paper Series No. 16, 2002, 21–22.

British Bankers Association, 'The Banking Code and Business Banking Code' (31 March 2008).

E. Broccardo and M. Mazzuca, 'New Development: Can 'Public' Market-based Solutions Restore the Banking System? The Case of Non-performing Loans (NPLs)' (2017) 37(7) *Public Money & Management*, 515.

E. Brodi et al., 'New Measures for Speeding Up Credit Recovery: An Initial Analysis of Decree Law 59/2016', Bank of Italy Notes on Financial Stability and Supervision No. 4, 2016, 3–4.

L. Brodsky and L. Oakes, 'Data Sharing and Open Banking', McKinsey on Payments (July 2017), 2–3 at https://www.mckinsey.it/sites/default/files/data-sharing-and-open-banking.pdf.

C. Brown, 'Report of the Board of Banking Supervision Inquiry into the Circumstances of the Collapse of Barings' (1995) 10 *Journal of International Banking Law*, 10.

F.X. Browne and D. Cronin, 'Payments Technologies, Financial Innovation, and Laissez-Faire Banking' (1995) 15(1) *Cato Journal*, 101.

M. Brunnermeier et al., 'The Fundamental Principles of Financial Regulation; Geneva Reports on the World Economy 11', International Centre for Monetary and Banking Studies (ICMB), 2009 at http://www.princeton.edu/~markus/research/papers/Geneva11.pdf.

J. Brunsden, 'Brexit Britain Faces Services Squeeze with Canada-Style Deal', *Financial Times* (London, 12 December 2017) at https://www.ft.com/content/30a358ac-dda6-11e7-8f9f-de1c2175f5ce.

J. Brunsden, 'EU Rejects Brexit Trade Deal for UK Financial Services Sector', *Financial Times* (London, 31 January 2018) at https://www.ft.com/content/7f7669a4-067f-11e8-9650-9c0ad2d7c5b5.

R.A. Bryer, 'The Mercantile Laws Commission of 1854 and the Political Economy of Limited Liability' (1997) 50 *Economic History Review*, 37.

L.C. Bucheit, 'The Pari Passu Clause Sub Specie Aeternitatis' (1991) 10 *International Financial Law Review*, 11.

C. Bucher, 'Risk Models-At-Risk' (2014) 44 *Journal of Banking & Finance*, 72.

R.P. Buckley, D.W. Arner, D.A. Zetzsche and R.H. Weber, 'The Road to RegTech: The (Astonishing) Example of the European Union' (2019) 20 *Journal of Banking Regulation*, 2–3.

G. de Búrca, *The Constitutional Challenge of New Governance in the European Union* (2003) 28 *European Law Review*, 6.

S. Burgess, 'Measuring Financial Sector Output and Its Contribution to UK GDP' (2011) 51 *Bank of England Quarterly Bulletin*, 234.

D. Busch, 'Governance of the European Banking Union's Single Resolution Mechanism' (2017) 28 *European Business Law Review*, 4.

D. Busch, 'MiFID II and MiFIR: Stricter Rules for the EU Financial Markets' (2017) 11 *Law and Financial Markets Review*, 2–3.

D. Busch and C. van Dam (eds), *A Bank's Duty of Care* (Hart Bloomsbury, 2017) Chapter 12.

D. Busch and G. Ferrarini (eds), *Regulation of the EU Financial Markets* (Oxford University Press, 2017).

T. Butler and L. O'Brien, 'Understanding RegTech for Digital Regulatory Compliance' in Theo Lynn, John G. Mooney, Pierangelo Rosati and Mark Cummins (eds), *Disrupting Finance FinTech and Strategy in the 21st Century* (Palgrave, 2019) 86–87.

P. Callesen, 'Can Banking be Sustainable in the Future? A Perspective from Danmarks Nationalbank', Speech at CBS' 100 Years Celebration Event, 30 October 2017, 5–6 at https://www.bis.org/review/r171031c.htm.

C.W. Calomiris and S.H. Haber, *Fragile by Design: The Political Origins of Banking Crises and Scarce Credit* (Princeton University Press, 2014) 4.

K. Camfferman, 'The Emergence of the 'Incurred-Loss' Model for Credit Losses in IAS 39' (2015) 12(1) *Accounting in Europe*, 17.

D. Campbell, 'Reflexivity and Welfarism in the Modern Law of Contract' (2000) 20 *Oxford Journal of Legal Studies*, 477.

A. Campbell, 'Northern Rock, the Financial Crisis and the Special Resolution Regime' in J. Gray and O. Akseli (eds), *Financial Regulation in Crisis? The Role of Law and the Failure of Northern Rock* (Edward Elgar Publishing, 2011) 40–41.

A. Campbell and R. Lastra, 'Revisiting the Lender of Last Resort' (2009) 24(3) *Banking and Finance Law Review*, 453.

A. Campbell and R. Lastra, 'Revisiting the Lender of Last Resort - The Role of the Bank of England' in I. MacNeil and J. O'Brien (eds), *The Future of Financial Regulation* (Oxford and Hart Publishing, 2010) 161–162.

J. Canals, *Universal Banking: International Comparisons and Theoretical Perspectives* (Oxford University Press, 1997).

D. Capper, 'No Tort Liability for Breaching Freezing Orders' (2006) 65 *Cambridge Law Journal*, 3.

F. Capriglione, 'UK Referendum and Brexit Hypothesis: The Way Out Perspective and the Convenience to 'Remain United' (2016) 27 *European Business Law Review*, 887.

J. Cariboni, E. Joossens and A. Uboldi, 'The promptness of European Deposit Protection Schemes to Face Banking Failures' (2010) 11 *Journal of Banking Regulation*, 3.

J. Carmassi, S. Dobkowitz, J. Evrard, L. Parisi, A. Silva and M. Wedow, 'Completing the Banking Union with a European Deposit Insurance Scheme: Who Is Afraid of Cross-subsidisation?' Occasional Paper Series No. 208, April 2018, 44 at https://www.ecb.europa.eu/pub/pdf/scpops/ecb. op208.en.pdf.

M. Carney, 'New Economy, New Finance, New Bank', Speech given at the Mansion House, London, 21 June 2018 at www.bankofengland.co.uk/speeches.

A. Carstens, 'The Future of Money and Payments', SUERF Policy Note, Issue No. 66, April 2019, 5–6 at www.suerf.org/policynotes.

J. Casey and K. Lannoo, *The MiFID Revolution* (Cambridge University Press, 2009) 7.

F. Castagnolo and G. Ferro, 'Could We Rely on Market Discipline as a Substitute for Insurance Regulation? (2013) 21(11) *Journal of Financial Regulation & Compliance*, 5–6.

CEBS, 'Guidelines on Supervisory Disclosure – Updated' (March 2006), 4.

CEBS, 'Contribution to the Lamfalussy Review' (November 2007).

R. Cerrone, 'Deposit Guarantee Reform in Europe: Does European Deposit Insurance Scheme Increase Banking Stability?' (2018) 21 *Journal of Economic Policy Reform*, 3.

A.P. Chaboud, B. Chiquoine, E. Hjalmarsson and C. Vega, 'Rise of the Machines: Algorithmic Trading in the Foreign Exchange Market' (2014) 69(5) *The Journal of Finance*, 2045.

D. Chaikin, 'Adapting the Qualifications to the Banker's Common Law Duty of Confidentiality to Fight Transnational Crime' (2011) 33 *Sydney Law Review* 265.

C. Chambers, 'The Turner Review: A Verbose Attempt at Curbing the Cycle' (2009) 30(7) *Business Law Review*.

A. Chan, A. Godwin and I. Ramsay 'Depositor Preference and Deposit Insurance Schemes — Challenges for Regulatory Convergence and Regulatory Coordination in Asia' (2018) 12(2) *Law and Financial Markets Review*, 53.

B. Chapman, 'Brexit: UK to Lose 10,500 City Jobs as 30 Per cent of Firms Flag Plans to Move Staff' *Independent* (London, 11 December 2017) at https://www.independent.co.uk/news/business/ news/brexit-latest-news-uk-city-job-losses-move-eu-frankfurt-paris-luxembourg-banks-europe-sam-woods-a8104176.html.

Cheque & Credit Clearing Company at https://www.chequeandcredit.co.uk/information-hub/ facts-and-figures/key-facts-and-figures-0.

Cheque & Credit Clearing Company at https://www.chequeandcredit.co.uk/information-hub/history-cheque/what-next-cheque-clearing.

I. Chiu, 'Corporate Governance and Risk Management in Banks and Financial Institutions' in Iris H.-Y. Chiu (ed), *The Law on Corporate Governance in Banks* (Edward Elgar, 2015) 191–192.

I. Chiu, *Regulating (From) the Inside: The Legal Framework for Internal Control in Banks and Financial Institutions* (Hart Publishing, 2015).

I. Chiu, 'Comparing Directors' Duties in the Financial Services Sector with Regulatory Duties under the Senior Persons Regime – Some Critical Observations' (2016) 27 *European Business Law Review*, 261.

I. Chiu, 'Fintech and Disruptive Business Models in Financial Products, Intermediation and Markets - Policy Implications for Financial Regulators' (2016) 21 *Journal of Technology Law and Policy* 1.

I. Chiu, 'A New Era in Fintech Payment Innovations? A Perspective from the Institutions and Regulation of Payment Systems' (2017) 9 *Law, Innovation and Technology*, 2.

I. Chiu and J. Wilson, *Banking Law and Regulation* (Oxford University Press, 2019).

U. Chohan, 'Initial Coin Offerings (ICOs): Risks, Regulation, and Accountability', Discussion Paper Series: Notes on the 21st Century, 2017, 3–4 at https://papers.ssrn.com/sol3/papers.cfm?abstract_id=3080098.

S. Claessens, S.R. Ghosh and R. Mihet, 'Macro-prudential Policies to Mitigate Financial System Vulnerabilities' (2013) 39 *Journal of International Money and Finance*, 12.

C. Closa and A. Maatsch, 'In a Spirit of Solidarity? Justifying the European Financial Stability Facility (EFSF) in National Parliamentary Debates' (2014) 52 *Journal of Common Market Studies*, 4.

J.C. Coffee Jr., 'Market Failure and the Economic Case for a Mandatory Disclosure System' (1984) 70(4) *Virginia Law Review*, 717.

V. Colaert, 'RegTech as a Response to Regulatory Expansion in the Financial Sector', Oxford Business Law Blog (16 July 2018) at https://www.law.ox.ac.uk/business-law-blog/blog/2018/07/regtech-response-regulatory-expansion-financial-sector.

H. Collins, *Regulating Contracts* (Oxford University Press, 1999) Chapters 3–8.

M. Comana, D. Previtali and L. Bellardini, *The MiFID II Framework: How the New Standards Are Reshaping the Investment Industry* (Springer, 2019).

Commission, 'EU Equivalence Decisions in Financial Services Policy: An Assessment' (Staff Working Document) SWD (2017) 102 final.

Commission Communication of 11 May 1999 'Financial Services: Implementing the Framework for Financial Markets Action Plan', COM(1999) 232 final.

Commission Communication of 27 May 2009 'European Financial Supervision', COM(2009) 252 final.

Commission Communication to the Parliament, the Council and the Member States, COM(1980) 30 DEF, 24.1.80.

Committee of Wise Men, 'Initial Report of the Committee of Wise Men on the Regulation of European Securities Markets', Brussels, 2000.

Committee on Payment and Settlement Systems BIS/IOSCO, 'Principles for Financial Market Infrastructures' (April 2012) at https://www.iosco.org/library/pubdocs/pdf/IOSCOPD377-PFMI.pdf.

Committee on the Financial Aspects of Corporate Governance at https://www.frc.org.uk/directors/corporate-governance-and-stewardship/uk-corporate-governance-code.

Communication from the Commission on Intra-EU Investment in the Financial Services Sector, C/2005/4080, 21 October 2005.

Communication from the Commission to the European Parliament and the Council – A Roadmap towards a Banking Union, COM(2012) 510 final.

Competition and Markets Authority, 'Retail Banking Market Investigation', Final Report, 9 August 2016 at https://assets.publishing.service.gov.uk/media/57ac9667e5274a0f6c00007a/retail-banking-market-investigation-full-final-report.pdf.

C. Conceicao and R. Gray, 'Problems of Uncertainty' (2007) 26(6) *International Financial Law Review*, 42.

Conduct of Business Sourcebook at https://www.handbook.fca.or.uk/handbook/COBS.pdf.

T. Conlon and J. Cotter, 'Anatomy of a Bail-in' (2014) 15 *Journal of Financial Stability*, 258–259.

V. Constâncio, 'The Role of Stress Testing in Supervision and Macroprudential Policy' in Ronald W. Anderson (ed), *Stress Testing and Macroprudential Regulation: A Transatlantic Assessment* (Centre for Economic Policy Research, 2016) 53.

V. Constâncio, 'Synergies between Banking Union and Capital Markets Union', Keynote Speech at the Joint Conference of the European Commission and European Central Bank on European Financial Integration, Brussels, 19 May 2017 at https://www.ecb.europa.eu/press/key/date/2017/html/ecb.sp170519_1.en.html.

V. Constâncio, 'The Future of Finance and the Outlook for Regulation', Remarks at the Financial Regulatory Outlook Conference, Organised by the Centre for International Governance Innovation and Oliver Wyman, Rome, 9 November 2017, 4–5 at https://www.bis.org/review/r171110e.pdf.

V. Constâncio, 'Resolving Europe's NPL Burden: Challenges and Benefits', Keynote Speech at the Event 'Tackling Europe's Non-performing Loans Crisis: Restructuring Debt, Reviving Growth' (2019) at https://www.ecb.europa.eu/press/key/date/2017/html/sp170203.en.html.

Corporate Governance in Financial Institutions and Remuneration Policies' COM (2010) 284 final, 2.

L. Correia da Silva, 'Leaving the EU: Impact on Bank Customers', Oxford Law Faculty, Blog Series (7 April 2017) 3 at https://www.law.ox.ac.uk/businesslawblog/blog/2017/04/brexitnegotiationsseriesleavingeuimpactbankcustomers.

L. Cortavarria, C. Dziobek, A. Kanaya and I. Song, 'Loan Review, Provisioning, and Macroeconomic Linkages', IMF Working Paper No. 00/195, 2000, 11–12.

R. Cranston, E. Avgouleas, K. van Zwieten, C. Hare and T. van Sante, *Principles of Banking Law* (3rd edn., Oxford University Press, 2018).

A. Crockett, 'Why Is Financial Stability a Goal of Public Policy?' in *Maintaining Financial Stability in a Global Economy*, Symposium sponsored by the Federal Reserve Bank of Kansas City Jackson Hole, Wyoming, 28–30 August 1997, 9.

A. Crockett, 'Marrying the Micro- and Macro-prudential Dimensions of Financial Stability', Basel, 21 September 2000, 2.

S. Crown, 'Turner Review and Its Impact on the Future of Banking' (2009) 24(65) *Butterworths Journal of International Banking and Financial Law*, 243.

Cryptocurrency Market Capitalisation at https://coinmarketcap.com/all/views/all/.

R. Dale, *The Regulation of International Banking* (Prentice Hall, 1984).

R. Dale, 'Bank Regulation after BCCI' (1993) 8(1) *Journal of International Banking Law*, 14.

R. Dale, 'Risk Management and Public Policy in Payment, Clearing and Settlement Systems' (1998) 1 *International Finance*, 2.

R. Dale and S. Wolfe, 'The UK Financial Services Authority: Unified Regulation in the New Market Environment' (2003) 4 *Journal of International Banking Regulation*, 200.

J. Danielsson, E. Micheler, K. Neugebauer, A. Uthemann and J.-P. Zigrand, 'Europe's Proposed Capital Markets Union: Disruption will Drive Investment and Innovation', Vox CEPR's Policy Portal, 23 February 2015.

M. Dassesse, 'Supervision of Credit Institutions and Banking Secrecy in the EEC' (1986) 1 *Journal of International Banking Law*, 4.

K. Datla and R. Revesz, 'Deconstruing Independent Agencies (and Executive Agencies)' (2013) 98 *Cornell Law Review*, 769.

B. Davies, 'What Is the Extent of the Customer's Duty not to Facilitate Fraud?' (2009) 30(11) *Business Law Review*, 238.

P. Davies, 'The Fall and Rise of Debt: Bank Capital Regulation after the Crisis' (2015) 16 *European Business Organization Law Review*, 3.

H. Davies and D. Green, *Global Financial Regulation* (Cambridge University Press, 2008).

H. Davies and D. Green, *Banking on the Future. The Fall and Rise of Central Banking* (Princeton University Press, 2010).

H. DeAngelo and R.M. Stulz, 'Liquid-Claim Production, Risk Management, and Bank Capital Structure: Why High Leverage Is Optimal for Banks', Fisher College of Business Working Paper 2013-03-08, 2013 at http://papers.ssrn.com/sol3/papers.cfm?abstract_id=2254998.

S. Debbage and S. Dickinson, 'The Rationale for the Prudential Regulation and Supervision of Insurers', Bank of England Quarterly Bulletin, 2013.

W.P. De Groen and D. Gros, 'Estimating the Bridge Financing Needs of the Single Resolution Fund: How Expensive Is It to Resolve a Bank? Centre for European Policy Studies (CEPS) Special Report No. 122, November 2015 at https://www.ceps.eu/ceps-publications/estimating-bridge-financing-needs-single-resolution-fund-how-expensive-it-resolve-bank/.

R. De Haas and S. Knobloch, 'In the Wake of the Crisis: Dealing with Distressed Debt Across the Transition Region', EBRD Working Paper No. 112, January 2010, 12 at http://ssrn.com/abstract=1742286.

A. Demb and F. Neubaurer, *The Corporate Board* (Oxford University Press, 1992).

M. Demertzis and A. Lehmann, 'Tackling Europe's Crisis Legacy: A Comprehensive Strategy for Bad Loans and Debt Restructuring', Bruegel Policy Contribution, No. 2017/11, 2017 at https://www.econstor.eu/bitstream/10419/173107/1/PC-11-2017.pdf.

M. Demertzis and G.B. Wolff, 'The Economic Potential and Risks of Crypto Assets: Is a Regulatory Framework Needed?', Bruegel Report Policy Contribution Issue No. 14, September 2018, 8–10 at http://bruegel.org/wp-content/uploads/2018/09/PC-14_2018.pdf.

A. Demirgüç-Kunt, E. Detragiache and T. Tressel, 'Banking on the Principles: Compliance with Basel Core Principles and Bank Soundness', IMF Working Paper No. 242, 2006.

Department of Trade and Industry, *Consumer Credit: Report of the Committee (Crowther Report)* (Cmd 4596, 1971).

J. Devriese and J. Mitchell, 'Liquidity Risk in Securities Settlement' (2006) 30 *Journal of Banking and Finance*, 6.

M. Dewatripont and J. Tirole, *The Prudential Regulation of Banks* (MIT Cambridge Press, 1994).

B. De Witte, 'The European Treaty Amendment for the Creation of a Financial Stability Mechanism' (2011) 6 *European Policy Analysis*, 5–7.

V. Dhar and R.M. Stein, 'FinTech Platforms and Strategy' (2017) 60(10) *Communications of the ACM*, 32–33 at https://cacm.acm.org/magazines/2017/10/221331-fintech-platforms-and-strategy/abstract.

D.W. Diamond and R.G. Rajan, 'A Theory of Bank Capital' (2000) 55(6) *The Journal of Finance*, 2431.

K. Dickinson, 'Securities Depositories (CSDs and ICSDs)' in Keith Dickinson (ed.), *Financial Market Operations Management* (Wiley & Sons, 2012) 151–152.

A. Dignam, 'Remuneration and Riots: Rethinking Corporate Governance in the Age of Entitlement' (2013) 66 *Current Legal Problems*, 401.

Directorate-General for Internal Policies (IPOL), 'Third-Country Equivalence in EU Banking Legislation' (Briefing Paper of the European Parliament PE 587.369, 12 July 2017) at http://www.europarl.europa.eu/RegData/etudes/BRIE/2016/587369/IPOL_BRI(2016)587369_EN.pdf.

D.C. Donald, 'Securities Settlement Systems' in Gerard Caprio (ed.), *Handbook of Key Global Financial Markets, Institutions, and Infrastructure* (Elsevier Science & Technology, 2012) 558–59.

S. Donnelly, 'Liberal Economic Nationalism, Financial Stability, and Commission Leniency in Banking Union' (2017) 21(2) *Journal of Economic Policy Reform*, 170.

A. Duff, 'The Credit Ratings Agencies and Stakeholder Relations: Issues for Regulators' (2009) 24(1) *Journal of International Banking and Financial Law*, 11.

S. Dullien, 'How to Complete Europe's Banking Union', European Council on Foreign Relations, Policy Brief, 2 July 2014, 8.

E. Dunkley, 'Lloyds Back in Private Ownership After Government Sells Out', *Financial Times* (London, 17 May 2017).

P. Dupont, 'Rights of the Account Holder Relating to Securities Credited to Its Securities Account' in Pierre-Henri Conac, Ulrich Segna and Luc Thévenoz (eds), *Intermediated Securities. The Impact of the Geneva Securities Convention and the Future European Legislation* (Cambridge University Press, 2013) 91–92.

T. Durner and L. Shetret, 'Understanding Bank De-risking and Its Effects on Financial Inclusion: An Exploratory Study', Global Center on Cooperative Security (2015) at https://www.oxfam.org/sites/www.oxfam.org/files/file_attachments/rr-bank-de-risking-181115-en_0.pdf.

G.P. Dwyer, 'The Economics of Bitcoin and Similar Private Digital Currencies' (2015) 17 *Journal of Financial Stability*, 81–82.

F.H. Easterbrook, 'Managers' Discretion and Investors' Welfare: Theories and Evidence' (1984) 9 *Delaware Journal of Corporate Law*, 540.

J. Eatwell and L. Taylor, *Global Finance at Risk: The Case for International Regulation* (New York Policy Press, 2000).

EBA, 'Guidelines on Common Procedures and Methodologies for the Supervisory Review and Evaluation Process (SREP)' (EBA/GL/2014/13, 19 December 2014).

EBA, 'Guidelines on the Applicable Notional Discount Rate for Variable Remuneration' (EBA/GL/2014/01, 27 March 2014) at https://www.eba.europa.eu/regulation-and-policy/remuneration/guidelines-on-discount-rate-for-variable-remuneration.

EBA, 'Guidelines on Sound Remuneration Policies under Articles 74(3) and 75(2) of Directive 2013/36/EU and Disclosures under Article 450 of Regulation (EU) No. 575/2013' (EBA/GL/2015/22, 2015) 120–123 at https://www.eba.europa.eu/documents/10180/1314839/EBA-GL-2015-22+Guidelines+on+Sound+Remuneration+Policies_EN.pdf.

EBA, 'Interim Report on MREL: Report on Implementation and Design of the MREL Framework' (EBA-Op-2016-12, 2016) 12–18 at https://eba.europa.eu/documents/10180/1360107/EBA+Interim+report+on+MREL.

EBA, 'EBA NPL Templates' (14 December 2017) at http://www.eba.europa.eu/-/eba-publishes-its-standardised-data-templates-as-a-step-to-reduce-npls.

EBA, 'Final Report on Guidelines on Internal Governance' (EBA/GL/2017/11, 2017) at https://www.eba.europa.eu/documents/10180/1972987/Final+Guidelines+on+Internal+Governance+%28EBA-GL-2017-11%29.pdf/eb859955-614a-4afb-bdcd-aaa664994889.

EBA, 'Guidelines on Credit Institutions' Credit Risk Management Practices and Accounting for Expected Credit Losses', Final Report EBA/GL/2017/06 (2017) at https://www.eba.europa.eu/documents/10180/1842525/Final+Guidelines+on+Accounting+for+Expected+Credit+Losses+%28EBA-GL-2017-06%29.pdf.

EBA, 'Opinion of the European Banking Authority on Issues Related to the Departure of the United Kingdom from the European Union' (EBA/OP/2017/12), Part IV Resolution and Deposit Guarantee Schemes, 12 October 2017.

EBA, 'Risk Dashboard. Data as of Q4 2016' (2017) 30 at http://www.eba.europa.eu/documents/10180/1804996/EBA+Dashboard+-+Q4+2016.pdf/74c92eb4-3083-47fc-bd5d-6a8ac64e8393.

EBA, 'Guidelines on Institutions' Stress Testing', EBA/GL/2018/04 (2018) at https://eba.europa.eu/documents/10180/2282644/Guidelines+on+institutions+stress+testing+%28EBA-GL-2018-04%29.pdf/2b604bc8-fd08-4b17-ac4a-cdd5e662b802.

EBA, 'Draft Guidelines on Loan Origination and Monitoring', Consultation Paper EBA/CP/2019/04, 19 June 2019, 34–36 at https://eba.europa.eu/documents/10180/2831176/CP+on+GLs+on+loan+origination+and+monitoring.pdf/3bc64e01-a4d1-4c7e-92d4-1dd84f4b234c.

EBA, 'Opinion of the European Banking Authority on Deposit Protection Issues Stemming from the withdrawal of the United Kingdom from the European Union' (EBA-Op-2019-01, 1 March 2019) at https://eba.europa.eu/-/eba-recommends-maintaining-protection-of-depositors-in-case-of-a-no-deal-brexit.

EBA Single Rulebook Q&A (2015_1777) at http://www.eba.europa.eu/single-rule-book-qa/-/qna/view/publicId/2015_1777.

EBA, 'EU-Wide Stress Testing' (EBA) at https://eba.europa.eu/risk-analysis-and-data/eu-wide-stress-testing.

ECB, 'Overview of TARGET' (July 2005) at https://www.ecb.europa.eu/paym/pdf/target/current/targetoverview.pdf.

ECB, 'Guide to Banking Supervision' (September 2014), 14–15 at https://www.ecb.europa.eu/pub/pdf/other/ssmguidebankingsupervision201409en.pdf.

ECB, 'Stocktake of National Supervisory Practices and Legal Frameworks Related to NPLs' (September 2016) 87 at https://www.bankingsupervision.europa.eu/legalframework/publiccons/pdf/npl/stock_taking.en.pdf.

ECB, 'Guidance to Banks on Non-performing Loans' (March 2017) at https://www.bankingsupervision.europa.eu/ecb/pub/pdf/guidance_on_npl.en.pdf.

ECB, 'Stocktake of National Supervisory Practices and Legal Frameworks Related to NPLs' (2017).

ECB, 'Addendum to the ECB Guidance to Banks on Nonperforming Loans: Prudential Provisioning Backstop for Non-performing Exposures' (2018) 2 at https://www.bankingsupervision.europa.eu/ecb/pub/pdf/ssm.npl_addendum_201803.en.pdf.

ECOFIN Council, 'Action Plan to Tackle Non-performing Loans in Europe', 11173/17, Brussels (11 July 2017) 3 at http://data.consilium.europa.eu/doc/document/ST-11173-2017-INIT/en/pdf.

ECOFIN Council, 'Report of the FSC Subgroup on Non-performing Loans', 9854/17, Brussels (31 May 2017) 61 at http://data.consilium.europa.eu/doc/document/ST-9854-2017-INIT/en/pdf.

EFTA Court (ed), *The EEA and the EFTA Court* (Hart Publishing, 2015).

H. Eidenmüller, 'Contracting for a European Insolvency Regime' (2017) 18 *European Business Organization Law Review*, 273.

E.P. Ellinger, E. Lomnicka and C. Hare (eds), *Ellinger's Modern Banking Law* (5th edn, Oxford University Press, 2011).

D.J. Elliott, 'Levering Europe: Alternatives for the European Financial Stability Facility' (2011) *Brookings* at https://www.brookings.edu/research/levering-europe-alternatives-for-the-european-financial-stability-facility/.

J. Engen, 'Lesson from a Mobile Payments Revolution', *American Banker* (29 April 2018) at https://www.americanbanker.com/news/why-chinas-mobile-payments-revolution-matters-for-us-bankers.

A. Enria, 'The EU banking Sector - Risks and Recovery. A Single Market Perspective', Luxembourg (2017) 16 at https://www.esm.europa.eu/speeches-and-presentations/esm-seminar-andrea-enria-eba-chairperson.

A. Enria, P. Haben and M. Quagliariello, 'Completing the Repair of the EU Banking Sector- A Critical Review of an EU Asset Management Company' (2017) 1 *European Economy*, 67 at http://european-economy.eu/2017-1/completing-the-repair-of-the-eu-banking-sector-a-critical-review-of-an-eu-asset-management-company/

ESM Treaty at https://www.esm.europa.eu/sites/default/files/20150203_-_esm_treaty_-_en.pdf.

ESMA Issues Sector-Specific Principles on Relocations from the UK to the EU27, ESMA71–99–526 (13 July 2017) at https://www.esma.europa.eu/document/esma-issues-sector-specific-principles-relocations-uk-eu27.

R. Espinoza and A. Prasad, 'Nonperforming Loans in the GCC Banking System and their Macroeconomic Effects', IMF Working Paper (October 2010) 4.

EU Commission, 'Proposal for a Directive of the European Parliament and of the Council on Preventive Restructuring Frameworks, Second Chance and Measures to Increase the Efficiency of Restructuring, Insolvency and Discharge Procedures and Amending Directive 2012/30/EU', COM(2016) 723 final.

EU Commission, 'Communication from the Commission to the European Parliament, the Council and the European Central Bank. Second Progress Report on the Reduction of Non-performing Loans in Europe', COM(2018) 133 final, 8.

Eurogroup, 'Preparation of Eurogroup and Economic and Finance Ministers Council, 11 and 12 July 2011', MEMO/11/493, Brussels (8 July 2011) at https://europa.eu/rapid/press-release_MEMO-11-493_en.htm.

Europe Economics, 'Study on the Cost of Compliance with Selected FSAP Measures. Final Report' (London, January 2009).

European Bank Coordination Vienna Initiative, 'Vienna Initiative Pushes for Action Plan to Deal with NPLs in Central and South-Eastern Europe. Fostering an Effective Framework for NPL

Restructuring and Resolution' (26 September 2014) at http://vienna-initiative.com/wp-content/uploads/2014/10/NPL-Press-Release.pdf.

European Commission, 'A Roadmap towards a Banking Union', COM (2012) 510 final, Brussels.

European Commission, 'Communication from the Commission to the European Parliament and the Council: A Roadmap towards a Banking Union', COM (2012) 510 Final (September 2012) at http://eur-lex.europa.eu/LexUriServ/LexUriServ.do?uri=CELEX:52012DC0510:EN:NOT.

European Commission, 'State Aid No. SA. 36175 (2013/N) – Italy MPS – Restructuring', C(2013) 8427 final at http://ec.europa.eu/competition/state_aid/cases/249091/249091_1518538_162_2.pdf.

European Commission, 'Communication from the Commission to the European Parliament, the Council, the European Central Bank, the European Economic and Social Committee, the Committee of the Regions and the European Investment Bank, An Investment Plan for Europe', COM (2014) 903 final.

European Commission, 'Building a Capital Markets Union', Green Paper COM (2015) 63 final, Brussels (18 February 2015).

European Commission, 'Q&A on the Green Paper on Building a Capital Markets Union', Fact Sheet, Brussels (18 February 2015) 1.

European Commission, 'Italy – Review of Progress on Policy Measures Relevant for the Correction of Macroeconomic Imbalances' (2016) 13 at https://ec.europa.eu/info/files/italy-review-progress-policy-measures-relevant-correction-macroeconomic-imbalances-december-2016_en.

European Commission, 'State aid: Commission Approves Impaired Asset Management Measures for Banks in Hungary and Italy', IP/16/279 (10 February 2016) at http://europa.eu/rapid/press-release_IP-16-279_en.htm.

European Commission, 'State Aid: Commission Authorises Precautionary Recapitalisation of Italian Bank Monte dei Paschi di Siena', Press Release, Brussels (4 July 2017) 2.

European Commission, 'FinTech Action Plan' (March 2018) at https://ec.europa.eu/info/publications/180308-action-plan-fintech_en.

European Commission, 'Proposal for a Directive of the European Parliament and of the Council on Credit Servicers, Credit Purchasers and the Recovery of Collateral', Brussels, COM (2018) 135 final at https://ec.europa.eu/info/law/better-regulation/initiatives/com-2018-135_en.

European Commission 'Statement on an Agreement in principle between Commissioner Vestager and Italian authorities on Monte Dei Paschi di Siena (MPS)', Press Release (dated 1 June 2017).

European Commission, Second Progress Report on the Reduction of Non-performing Loans in Europe' Commission Staff Working Document, Brussels, SWD(2018) 72 final at http://ec.europa.eu/finance/docs/policy/180314-staff-working-document-non-performing-loans_en.pdf.

European Commission Statement 14/77, 20 March 2014.

European Council, 'Structural Reform of EU Banking Sector: Improving the Resilience of Credit Institutions' (21 November 2018) at http://www.consilium.europa.eu/en/policies/banking-structural-reform/.

European Deposit Insurance Scheme (COM/2015/0586 final).

European Economic Forecast Autumn 2013 (Commission, August 2013) 101 at http://ec.europa.eu/economy_finance/eu/forecasts/2013_autumn_forecast_en.htm.

European Financial Supervision, COM(2009) 252 final.

European Parliament, High Level Conference 'Towards a New Supervisory Architecture in Europe' (Brussels, 7 May 2009).

European Payments Council, '2019 SEPA Credit Transfer Rulebook Version 1.0', EPC125-05 at https://www.europeanpaymentscouncil.eu/sites/default/files/kb/file/2018-11/EPC125-05%20 2019%20SCT%20Rulebook%20version%201.0.pdf.

European Retail Payments Board, Statement Following the Second Meeting of the ERPB held on 1 December 2014 (ERPB/2014/018).

European Shadow Financial Regulatory Committee, 'Complexity and Credibility in the Single Resolution Mechanism', Statement No. 39, London (10 November 2014) 5.

European Systemic Risk Board, 'Central Counterparties and Systemic Risk', *Macro-prudential Commentaries* (2013) No. 6, 7.

European Systemic Risk Board, 'Resolving Non-performing Loans in Europe' (July 2017) 28 at https://www.esrb.europa.eu/pub/pdf/reports/20170711_resolving_npl_report.en.pdf.

European Union Committee, *Brexit: Financial Services* (HL 2016–17, 81).

L.T. Evans and N.C. Quigley, 'Shareholder Liability Regimes, Principal-Agent Relationships and Banking Industry Performance' (1995) 38 *Journal of Law and Economics*, 497.

T. Evens, 'A Brief Overview of Material Adverse Change Clauses in Credit Documents' (Lexology, 15 December 2016) at https://www.lexology.com/library/detail.aspx?g=8ad67d75-dccf-464e-a93b-b911956b6ba3.

EY, 'Game changers EY's Attractiveness Survey Europe June 2018' (2018) at https://www.ey.com/gl/en/issues/business-environment/ey-attractiveness-survey-europe-june-2018.

FATF, 'International Standards on Combating Money Laundering and the Financing of Terrorism & Proliferation; The FATF Recommendations; Updated October 2018' (2018) at http://www.fatfgafi.org/publications/fatfrecommendations/documents/fatf-recommendations.html.

FCA, 'Benchmark Enforcement' at https://www.fca.org.uk/markets/benchmarks/enforcement.

FCA, 'Project Innovate' at https://www.fca.org.uk/firms/fca-innovate.

FCA, 'Regulatory Sandbox' at https://www.fca.org.uk/firms/regulatory-sandbox.

FCA, 'Treating Customers Fairly: Towards Fair Outcomes for Consumers' (July 2006).

FCA, 'The Turner Review. A Regulatory Response to the Global Banking Crisis' (March 2009) 18–20.

FCA, 'Forbearance and Impairment Provisions – Mortgages', FSA Finalised Guidance (October 2011) 23 at https://www.fca.org.uk/publication/finalised-guidance/fg11_15.pdf.

FCA, Equivalence of Non-EEA regimes (2016) at https://www.fca.org.uk/markets/ukla/regulatory-disclosures/equivalence-non-eea-regimes.

FCA, 'FCA fines Deutsche Bank £163 million for Serious Anti-money Laundering Controls Failings' (31 January 2017) at https://www.fca.org.uk/news/press-releases/fca-fines-deutsche-bank-163-million-anti-money-laundering-controls-failure.

FCA, 'Model Driven Machine Executable Regulatory Reporting TechSprint' (20 November 2017) at https://www.fca.org.uk/events/techsprints/model-driven-machine-executable-regulatory-reporting-techsprint.

FCA, 'Protecting Consumers' (11 December 2017) at https://www.fca.org.uk/about/protecting-consumers.

FCA, 'Extending the Senior Managers and Certification Regime to FCA Firms – Feedback to CP17/25 and CP17/40, and near-final rules' Policy Statement PS18/14 (2018) at https://www.fca.org.uk/publication/policy/ps18-14.pdf.

FCA, 'FCA Mission: Approach to Consumers' (2018) at https://www.fca.org.uk/publication/corporate/approach-to-consumers.pdf.

FCA, 'Final Notice: Santander UK Plc' (19 December 2018) at https://www.fca.org.uk/publication/final-notices/santander-uk-plc-2018.pdf.

FCA, 'A Duty of Care and Potential Alternative Approaches: Summary of Responses and Next Steps: Feedback Statement' (2019) FS19/2 at https://www.fca.org.uk/publication/feedback/fs19-02.pdf.

FCA, 'High-cost Credit Review: Overdrafts Policy Statement' (2019) PS19/16 (1.8) at https://www.fca.org.uk/publication/policy/ps19-16.pdf.

FCA, 'Prudential Sourcebook for Banks, Building Societies and Investment Firms' (June 2019) at https://www.handbook.fca.org.uk/handbook/BIPRU.pdf.

FCA, 'The FCA Board' (13 June 2019) at https://www.fca.org.uk/about/fca-board.

Federal Deposit Insurance Corporation, 'Guidance for Developing Effective Deposit Insurance Systems' (7 September 2001) 59 at https://www.fdic.gov/deposit/deposits/international/guidance/finalreport.pdf.

J. Fell, M. Grodzicki, D. Krušec, R. Martin and E. O'Brien, 'Overcoming Non-performing Loan Market Failures with Transaction Platforms', *Financial Stability Review*, Special Features (November 2017) 130.

J. Fell, M. Grodzicki, R. Martin and E. O'Brien, 'Addressing Market Failures in the Resolution of Non-performing Loans in the Euro Area', *Financial Stability Review*, Special Features (November 2016) 134.

E. Ferran, 'Examining the UK's Experience in Adopting the Single Financial Regulator Model' (2003) 28 *Brooklyn Journal of International Law*, 257.

E. Ferran, *Building an EU Securities Market* (Cambridge University Press, 2004).

E. Ferran, 'The Break-up of the Financial Services Authority' (2011) 31 *Oxford Journal of Legal Studies*, 455.

E. Ferran, 'Crisis-Driven Regulatory Reform: Where in the World Is the EU Going?' in Eilís Ferran, Niamh Moloney, Jennifer G. Hill and John C. Coffee, Jr. (eds), *The Regulatory Aftermath of the Global Financial Crisis* (Cambridge University Press, 2012) 11–12.

E. Ferran, 'Regulatory Lessons from the Payment Protection Insurance Mis-selling Scandal in the UK' (2012) 13 *European Business Organization Law Review*, 247.

E. Ferran, 'European Banking Union: Imperfect, But It Can Work', University of Cambridge Faculty of Law Research Paper No. 30/2014 at http://ssrn.com/abstract=2426247.

E. Ferran, 'The UK as a Third Country Actor in EU Financial Services Regulation' (2017) 3 *Journal of Financial Regulation*, 40.

E. Ferran, 'Regulatory Parity in Post-Brexit UK–EU Financial Regulation: EU Norms, International Financial Standards or a Hybrid Model?' in Kern Alexander et al. (eds), *Brexit and Financial Services: Law and Policy* (Hart Publishing, 2018).

E. Ferran and V. Babis, 'The European Single Supervisory Mechanism' (2013) 13 *Journal of Corporate Law Studies*, 2.

E. Ferran and L. Chan Ho, *Principles of Corporate Finance Law* (2nd edn, Oxford University Press, 2014).

G. Ferrarini, 'Securities Regulation and the Rise of Pan-European Securities Markets: An Overview' in Guido Ferrarini, Klaus J. Hopt and Eddy Wymeersch (eds), *Capital Markets in the Age of the Euro. Cross-Border Transactions, Listed Companies and Regulation* (Kluwer Law International, 2002) 241–242.

G. Ferrarini, 'Single Supervision and the Governance of Banking Markets: Will the SSM Deliver the Expected Benefits?' (2015) 16 *European Business Organization Law Review*, 3.

G. Ferrarini, 'Regulating FinTech: Crowdfunding and Beyond' (2017) 2 *European Economy*, 139 at http://european-economy.eu/wp-content/uploads/2018/01/EE_2.2017-2.pdf#page=123.

G. Ferrarini and P. Saguato, 'Reforming Securities and Derivatives Trading in the EU: From EMIR to MiFIR' (2013) 13 *Journal of Corporate Law Studies*, 2.

P. de Filippi, 'The Interplay between Decentralization and Privacy: The Case of Blockchain Technologies' (2016) 7 *Journal of Peer Production*, 7–8 at https://hal.archives-ouvertes.fr/hal-01382006/document.

Financial Accounting Standards Board, 'Accounting Standards Update No. 2011–02, Receivables (Topic 310): A Creditor's Determination of Whether a Restructuring Is a Troubled Debt Restructuring' (April 2011) 1–2 at https://asc.fasb.org/imageRoot/05/7484705.pdf.

Financial Ombudsman Service, 'Bank Said Victim of Text Message Scam Was Grossly Negligent and Won't Refund Lost Money' at https://www.financial-ombudsman.org.uk/case-studies/bank-said-victim-text-message-scam-grossly-negligent.

Financial Ombudsman Service, 'The Banker's Duty of Confidentiality to the Customer' (April 2005) 45 *Ombudsman News*, 3 at https://www.financial-ombudsman.org.uk/publications/ombudsman-news/45/45.pdf.

Financial Services Consumer Panel, 'Consumer Panel Members' (Financial Services Consumer Panel, 2019) at https://www.fs-cp.org.uk/who-is-on-the-panel.

Financial Stability Board, 'Reducing the Moral Hazard Posed by Systemically Important Financial Institutions – FSB Recommendations and Time Lines' (20 October 2010) 1.

Financial Stability Board, 'Key Attributes of Effective Resolution Regimes for Financial Institutions' (October 2011) at http://www.fsb.org/wp-content/uploads/r_111104cc.pdf.

Financial Stability Board, 'Policy Measures to Address Systemically Important Financial Institutions' (4 November 2011) at https://www.fsb.org/2011/11/r_111104bb/.

Financial Stability Board, 'Global Systemically Important Insurers and the Policy Measures That Will Apply to Them' (18 July 2013).

Financial Stability Board, 'Key Attributes of Effective Resolution Regimes for Financial Institutions' (15 October 2014).

V. Finch and D. Milman, *Corporate Insolvency Law: Perspectives and Principles* (3rd edn, Cambridge University Press, 2017).

D.R. Fischel, 'The Corporate Governance Movement' (1982) 35 *Vanderbilt Law Review*, 1259.

J. Fisher, J. Bewsey, M. Waters, QC and E. Ovey, *The Law of Investor Protection* (Sweet & Maxwell, 2003) 18.

M. Flinders and C. Skelcher, 'Shrinking the Quango State: Five Challenges in Reforming Quangos' (2012) 32 *Public Money & Management*, 327.

C. Ford, 'Principles-Based Securities Regulation in the Wake of the Global Financial Crisis' (2010) 55 *McGill Law Journal*, 261.

FOS, 'Annual Reviews' at https://www.financial-ombudsman.org.uk/publications/annual-reviews.

FOS, 'Can you Look at Complaints about PPI, Now the Deadline Has Passed?' at https://www.financial-ombudsman.org.uk/faqs/questions-about-ppi/can-look-complaints-ppi-now-deadline-passed.

FOS, 'Case Studies: A Borrower Tells Us She Was Provided with a Loan She Couldn't Afford' at https://www.financial-ombudsman.org.uk/case-studies/borrower-tells-us-provided-loan-couldnt-afford.

FOS, 'Schedule of Matters Reserved for the Financial Ombudsman Service Board' (2018) at https://www.financial-ombudsman.org.uk/files/2481/schedule-of-matters-reserved-to-the-board-2018-02.pdf.

FOS, 'Time Limits' at https://www.financial-ombudsman.org.uk/consumers/expect/time-limits.

FOS, 'Who We've Helped' at https://www.financial-ombudsman.org.uk/consumers/who-weve-helped.

M. Friedman, 'The Role of Monetary Policy' (1968) 58 *American Economic Review*, 1.

FSA, 'Treating Customers Fairly: Towards Fair Outcomes for Consumers' (July 2006).

FSA, 'Principles Based Regulation: Focusing on the Outcomes that Matter' (April 2007).

FSA, 'Effective Corporate Governance (Significant Influence Controlled Functions and the Walker Review)' (FSA Consultation Paper 10/3, 2010) para 1.9 at http://www.fsa.gov.uk/pubs/cp/cp10_03.pdf.

FSA, 'The Failure of the Royal Bank of Scotland: Financial Services Authority Board Report' (2011) at http://www.fsa.gov.uk/pubs/other/rbs.pdf.

FSB, 'Key Attributes of Effective Resolution Regimes for Financial Institutions' (15 October 2014) at https://www.fsb.org/2014/10/key-attributes-of-effective-resolution-regimes-for-financial-institutions-2/.

FSB, 'Principles on Loss-Absorbing and Recapitalisation Capacity of G-SIBs in Resolution: Total Loss-Absorbing Capacity (TLAC) Term Sheet' (2015) at https://www.fsb.org/wp-content/uploads/TLAC-Principles-and-Term-Sheet-for-publication-final.pdf.

FSB, 'Review of the Technical Implementation of the Total Loss-Absorbing Capacity (TLAC) Standard' (2019) at 18–19 https://www.fsb.org/wp-content/uploads/P020719.pdf.

B. Fung, J. George, S. Hohl and G. Ma, 'Public Asset Management Companies in East Asia. A Comparative Study' (February 2004), Financial Stability Institute, Bank for International Settlements, Occasional Paper No. 3, 19 at https://www.bis.org/fsi/fsipapers03.pdf.

G20 Leaders Statement: The Pittsburgh Summit, Pittsburgh, 24–25 September 2009 at http://www.g20.utoronto.ca/2009/2009communique0925.html.

J. Gabilondo, *Bank Funding, Liquidity, and Capital Adequacy. A Law and Finance Approach* (Edward Elgar, 2016).

D. Gabor and S. Brooks, 'The Digital Revolution in Financial Inclusion: Internationa Development in the Fintech Era' (2017) 22 *New Political Economy*, 4.

M. Gallant, 'AML: Maintaining the Balance between Controlling Serious Crime and Human Rights' in Barry Rider (ed), *Research Handbook on International Financial Crime* (Edward Elgar, 2015).

L. Gambacorta and A. van Rixtel, 'Structural Bank Regulation Initiatives: Approaches and Implications', BIS Working Paper 412, Bank for International Settlements Publications (2013).

R. Garratt and N. Wallace, 'Bitcoin 1, Bitcoin 2,... An Experiment in Privately Issued Outside Monies' (2018) 56 *Economic Inquiry*, 3.

J. Garrido, 'Insolvency and Enforcement Reforms in Italy', IMF Working Papers (2016) 8 at https://www.imf.org/external/pubs/ft/wp/2016/wp16134.pdf.

J. Garrido, E. Kopp and A. Weber, 'Cleaning-up Bank Balance Sheets: Economic, Legal, and Supervisory Measures for Italy', IMF Working Paper, WP/16/135 (2016) 26–27.

K. Garvey, H-Y Chen, B. Zhang, E. Buckingham, D. Ralston, Y. Katiforis, K. Ying et al., 'Cultivating Growth. The 2nd Asia Pacific Region Alternative Finance Industry Report' (September 2017).

E.F. Gerding, 'Code, Crash, and Open Source: The Outsourcing of Financial Regulation to Risk Models and the Global Financial Crisis' (2009) 84(2) *Washington Law Review*, 127.

A. Georgosouli, 'The Revision of the FSA's Approach to Regulation: An Incomplete Agenda?' (2010) 7 *Journal of Business Law*, 599.

A. Georgosouli, 'The FSA's 'Treating Customers Fairly' (TCF) Initiative: What Is So Good About It and Why It May Not Work' (2011) 38(3) *Journal of Law and Society*, 405.

A. Georgosouli, 'Judgement-led Regulation: Some Critical Reflections', Financial Services Authority Conference 'Academic Input for Better Regulation' (January 2012) at https://ssrn.com/abstract=2053505.

A. Georgosouli, 'The FCA, the PRA and the Idea of Resilience as a Narrative for Policy Coherence' (2012) at https://papers.ssrn.com/sol3/papers.cfm?abstract_id=2094569.

A. Georgosouli, 'Judgement-led Regulation: Reflections on Data and Discretion' (2013) 14(3–4) *Journal of Banking Regulation*, 209.

A. Georgosouli, 'The FSA-PRA Coordination Scheme and the Challenge of Policy Coherence' (2013) 8(1) *Capital Markets Law Journal*, 62–63.

N. Geslevich Packin, 'RegTech, Compliance and Technology Judgment Rule' (2018) 93 *Chicago-Kent Law Review*, 193.

B. Geva, 'Systemic Risk and Financial Stability: The Evolving Role of the Central Bank' (2013) 28 *Journal of International Banking Law and Regulation*, 10.

M. Gibson, 'Recovery and Resolution of Central Counterparties', Reserve Bank of Australia Bulletin (December Quarter 2013) 39.

S. Gilad, 'Accountability or Expectations Management? The Role of the Ombudsman in Financial Regulation' (2008) 30 *Law & Policy*, 227.

S. Gilad, 'Juggling Conflicting Demands: The Case of the UK Financial Ombudsman Service' (2008) 19 *Journal of Public Administration Research and Theory*, 661.

R.J. Gilson and R.H. Kraakman, 'The Mechanisms of Market Efficiency' (1984) 70(4) *Virginia Law Review*.

A.W. Glass, 'The Regulatory Drive Towrds Central Counterparty Clearing of OTC Credit Derivatives and the Necessary Limits on This' (2009) 4(suppl. 1) *Capital Markets Law Journal*, S79–S80.

S. Gleeson, 'Bank Capital Regulation and Sovereign Debt Restructuring' (2018) 13 *Capital Markets Law Journal*, 3.

S. Gleeson, *The Legal Concept of Money* (Oxford University Press, 2018).

S. Gleeson, 'The Single Resolution Mechanism and the EU Crisis Management Tools' in Lo Schiavo (ed.), *The European Banking Union and the Role of Law* (Edward Elgar, 2019) 216–217.

L. Gocaj and S. Meunier, 'Time Will Tell: The EFSF, the ESM, and the Euro Crisis' (2013) 35 *Journal of European Integration*, 3.

J. Goddard, P. Molyneux and J. O.S. Wilson, 'Banking in the European Union' in Allen N. Berger Philip Molyneux and John O. S. Wilson (eds), *Oxford Handbook of Banking* (Oxford University Press, 2012).

M. Goodfriend and R.G. King, 'Financial Deregulation, Monetary Policy and Central Banking' (1988) 74(3) *Economic Review Federal Reserve Bank of Richmond*, 5–6.

C. Goodhart, *The Evolution of Central Banks* (MIT Press 1988).

C. Goodhart, 'Regulating the Regulator – An Economist's Perspective on Accountability and Control' in Eilis Ferran and Charles Goodhart (eds), *Regulating Financial Services and Markets in the Twenty First Century* (Oxford Hart Publishing, 2001) 151–152.

C. Goodhart, 'The Regulatory Response to the Financial Crisis' (2008) LSE Financial Markets Group Paper Series, Special Paper 177, 9 at http://www.lse.ac.uk/fmg/documents/specialPapers/2008/sp177.pdf.

C. Goodhart, 'The Organisational Structure of Banking Supervision', FSI Occasional Papers No. 1 (2010), at http://www.sa-dhan.net/Adls/Dl6/Baselcommittee/TheOrganisationalStructure.pdf.

C. Goodhart, *The Basel Committee on Bankig Supervision. A History of the Early Years 1974–1997* (Cambridge University Press, 2011).

C. Goodhart, 'Ratio Controls Need Reconsideration' (2013) 9 *Journal of Financial Stability*, 445.

J.N. Gordon and G. Ringe, 'Resolution in the European Banking Union: A Transatlantic Perspective on What It Would Take', Oxford Legal Research Paper Series No. 18/2014 (April 2014).

G. Gorton and A. Metrick, 'Regulating the Shadow Banking System' (2010) *Brookings Papers on Economic Activity*, 261.

G. Gorton and F.A. Schmid, 'Universal Banking and the Performance of German Firms', NBER Working Paper No. 5453 (1996).

C. Gortsos, 'Competence Sharing between the ECB and the National Competent Supervisory Authorities Within the Single Supervisory Mechanism (SSM)' (2015) 16 *European Business Organization Law Review*, 3.

C. Gortsos, 'Last Resort Lending to Solvent Credit Institutions in the Euro Area before and after the Establishment of the Single Supervisory Mechanism (SSM)', paper presented at the European Central Bank (ECB) Legal Conference: 'From Monetary Union to Banking Union, on the way to Capital Markets Union: new opportunities for European integration' held in Frankfurt on 1–2 September 2015, 6 at https://ssrn.com/abstract=2688953.

C. Gortsos, 'A Poisonous (?) Mix: Bail-Out of Credit Institutions Combined with Bail-In of Their Liabilities Under the BRRD – The Use of 'Government Financial Stabilisation Tools' (GFSTs)', paper presented at the Workshop of the Financial and Monetary Law Working Group of the European University Institute (EUI, Florence, 12 October 2016) on 'Suitability of the new resolution regime for tackling systemic and structural crises in the banking sector – fine-tuning rules in transition', 6 at https://ssrn.com/abstract=2876508.

C. Gortsos, 'The Role of Deposit Guarantee Schemes (DGSS) in Resolution Financing', European Banking Institute Working Paper Series 2019 – No. 37, 18–19, at https://ssrn.com/abstract=3361750.

M. Gotthardt, D. Koivulaakso, O. Paksoy, C. Saramo, M. Martikainen and O.M. Lehner (eds), 'Current State and Challenges in the Implementation of Robotic Process Automation and Artificial Intelligence in Accounting and Auditing' (2020) 9 ACRN *Oxford Journal of Finance and Risk Perspectives*, Special Issue Digital Accounting, 90–91.

S. Green and J. Randall, *The Tort of Conversion* (Hart Publishing, 2009).

A. Greenspan, 'Statement Before the SUBCOMMITTEE on Financial Institutions and Consumer Credit, Committee on Banking and Financial Services' (United States House of Representatives, 13 February 1998).

J. Gren, D. Howarth and L. Quaglia, 'Supranational Banking Supervision in Europe: The Construction of a Credible Watchdog' (2015) 53 *Journal of Common Market Studies*, S1.

T. Groenfeldt, 'Taming the High Costs of Compliance with Tech', *Forbes* (22 March 2018) at https://www.forbes.com/sites/tomgroenfeldt/2018/03/22/taming-the-high-costs-of-compliance-with-tech/#e1182fb5d3f7.

D. Gros and C. Alcidi, 'Adjustment Difficulties and Debt Overhangs in the Eurozone Periphery', CEPS Working Document No. 347 (2011), 2–3 at https://www.ceps.eu/ceps-publications/adjustment-difficulties-and-debt-overhangs-eurozone-periphery/.

D. Gros and D. Schoenmaker, 'European Deposit Insurance and Resolution in the Banking Union' (2014) 52(3) *Journal of Common Market Studies*, 536.

S.J. Grossman and Oliver D Hart, 'An Analysis of the Principal-Agent Problem' (1983) 51 *Econometrica*, 7.

C. Gulinello, 'The Retail Investor Vote: Mobilizing Rationally Apathetic Shareholders to Preserve or Challenge the Board's Presumption of Authority' (2010) *Utah Law Review*, 547.

R. Guynn and M. Tahyar, 'The Importance of Choice of Law and Finality to Pvp, Netting and Collateral Arrangements' (1996) 4 *Journal of Financial Regulation and Compliance*, 2.

P. Haben, 'Standardising the Definition of Non-performing Exposure and Forbearance' (2015) EBA Case Study at http://docplayer.net/20943532-Case-study-standardising-the-definition-of-non-performing-exposure-and-forbearance.html.

C. Hadjiemmanuil, 'The Directive and the New European Regulatory Infrastructure', paper presented at the 'The International Symposium on Bank Recovery and Resolution in Europe - 'The EU Bank Recovery and Resolution Directive in Context', University of Tübingen, 19 October 2013.

M. Haentjens, 'Bank Recovery and Resolution: An Overview of International Initiatives' (2014) 3 *International Insolvency Law Review*, 255.

M. Haentjens, 'New Bank Resolution Regime as an Engine of EU Integration', Oxford Business Law Blog (14 June 2017) at https://www.law.ox.ac.uk/business-law-blog/blog/2017/06/new-bank-resolution-regime-engine-eu-integration.

A. Haldane, 'The Contribution of the Financial Sector: Miracle or Mirage?' (Future of Finance conference, London, 14 July 2010) 14–15 at http://www.bis.org/review/r100716g.pdf.

A. Haldane, 'Growing, Fast and Slow', Speech at the University of East Anglia, Norwich, 17 February 2015 at https://www.bankofengland.co.uk/-/media/boe/files/speech/2015/growing-fast-and-slow.pdf.

J. Hamilton, 'Depositor Protection and Co-insurance after Northern Rock: Less a Case of Moral Hazard and More a Case of Consumer Responsibility?' in Johanna Gray and Orkun Akseli (eds), *Financial Regulation in Crisis? The Role of Law and the Failure of Northern Rock* (Edward Elgar, 2011) 19–24.

P. Hammond, Chancellor of the Exchequer, 'Speech on Financial Services at HSBC' (Speech at HSBC Headquarters, London, 7 March 2018).

D.C. Hardy, 'Bank Resolution Costs, Depositor Preference and Asset Encumbrance' (2014) 22 *Journal of Financial Regulation and Compliance*, 2.

M. Harker and others, 'Benchmarking the Performance of the UK Framework Supporting Consumer Empowerment through Comparison against Relevant International Comparator Countries' (2008) at http://webarchive.nationalarchives.gov.uk/+/http://www.berr.gov.uk/publications/index.html.

I. Hasan and L.D. Wall, 'Determinants of the Loan Loss Allowance: Some Cross-Country Comparisons' (2004) 39(1) *The Financial Review*, 129.

D. Haubrich, 'The Development of Regulatory Requirements for Payment Services: The European Banking Authority and the revised Payments Services Directive' (2018) 7 *Journal of Payments Strategy & Systems*, 12.

B.W. Havey Harvey and D.L. Parry, *The Law of Consumer Protection and Fair Trading* (Butterworths, 2000) 50–51.

B. Hearnden and J. Whitfield, 'The Banking Act 2009' (2009) 3 *Corporate Rescue and Insolvency*, 96.

A. Heathman, 'This is How Much the PPI Scandal is Still Costing UK Banks' (Verdict, 28 July 2018) at https://www.verdict.co.uk/this-is-how-the-much-the-ppi-scandal-is-still-costing-uk-banks/.

S.K. Henderson, 'Regulation of Credit Derivatives: To What Effect and for Whose Benefit?' (2009) 11 *Butterworths Journal of International Banking and Financial Law*, 147.

A. Henderson and J. Burnie, 'Brexit and Basel III: An Invitation for More or for Less?' (2016) 8 *Butterworths Journal of International Banking and Financial Law* 478, 480.

D. Henry, 'Clarifying and Settling Access to Clearing and Settlement in the EU' (2006) 17 *European Business Law Review*, 4.

B. Hermalin and M. Weisbach, 'Boards of Directors as an Endogenously Determined Institution: A Survey of the Economic Literature' (2003) 9 *Economic Policy Review*, 7.

G. Hertig and R. Lee, 'Four Predictions about the Future of EU Securities Regulation' (2003) 3 *Journal of Corporate Law Studies*, 359.

M.W. Hesselink, 'The Concept of Good Faith' in Arthur S Hartkamp et al. (eds), *Towards a European Civil Code* (4th edn, Kluwer Law International, 2010) 619–620.

F. Hirsch, 'The Bagehot Problem' (1977) 45 *The Manchester School of Economic & Social Studies*, 241.

HM Government, 'The Future Relationship between the United Kingdom and Europe' (Cm 9593, 2018) 1.

HM Treasury, 'A New Approach to Financial Regulation: Judgement, Focus and Stability' (July 2010).

HM Treasury, 'A New Approach to Financial Regulation: Building a Stronger System' (February 2011).

HM Treasury, 'A New Approach to Financial Regulation: A Blueprint for Reform' (June 2011).

HM Treasury, 'Remit and Recommendations for the Financial Policy Committee', Letter from the Chancellor, George Osborne to the Governor of the Bank of England Mervyn King (30 April 2013).

HM Treasury, *Annual Report and Accounts 2012–13* (2013–2014, HC 34).

HM Treasury, 'Banking Act 2009: Special Resolution Regime Code of Practice' (2017) at https://assets.publishing.service.gov.uk/government/uploads/system/uploads/attachment_data/file/602948/Special-Resolution-Regime-Code-of-Practice.pdf.

HM Treasury, 'Fintech Sector Strategy: Securing the Future of UK Fintech' (March 2018) 9–10, at https://www.gov.uk/government/publications/fintech-sector-strategy.

HM Treasury, 'Cryptoassets Taskforce: Final Report' (October 2018) 11–13 at https://www.gov.uk/government/publications/cryptoassets-taskforce.

HM Treasury, 'Transposition of the Fifth Money Laundering Directive: Consultation' (2019) at https://www.gov.uk/government/consultations/transposition-of-the-fifth-money-laundering-directive.

HM Treasury Consultation Papers: 'A New Approach to Financial Regulation Judgement, Focus and Stability' (2010) and 'A New Approach to Financial Regulation: Building a Stronger System' (2011).

HM Treasury and Home Office, *National Risk Assessment of Mone Laundering and Terrorist Financing 2017* (2017) Chapter 4.

G. Hoggard, P. Jackson and E. Neir, 'Banking Crises and the Design of Safety Nets' (2005) 29 *Journal of Banking and Finance*, 1.

W.S. Holdsworth, 'The History of the Treatment of "Choses" in Action by the Common Law' (1920) 33 *Harvard Law Review*, 997.

D. Hou and D.R. Skeie, 'LIBOR: Origins, Economics, Crisis, Scandal, and Reform', Federal Reserve Bank of New York Staff Report 667 (2014) at https://papers.ssrn.com/sol3/papers.cfm?abstract_id=2423387.

House of Commons Treasury Committee, 'The Run on the Rock', Fifth Report of Session 2007–08, Volume I (26 January 2008).

House of Lords - European Union Committee - Fourteenth Report 2008–09, 'The Future of EU Financial Regulation and Supervision' (9 June 2009) at https://publications.parliament.uk/pa/ld200809/ldselect/ldeucom/106/10609.htm.

House of Lords, 'The Future of EU Financial Regulation and Supervision', Volume I (London, 17 June 2009) 12.

House of Lords, 'The Post-crisis EU Financial Regulatory Framework: Do the Pieces Fit?' European Union Committee, 5th Report of Session 2014–2015 (2 February 2015) 5.

House of Lords, 'Capital Markets Union: A Welcome Start', European Union Committee, 11th Report of Session 2014–2015, 4.

House of Lords, House of Commons, Parliamentary Commission on Banking Standards, 'An Accident Waiting to Happen: The Failure of HBOS', Fourth Report of Session 2012–2013 (4 April 2013) at https://publications.parliament.uk/pa/jt201213/jtselect/jtpcbs/144/144.pdf.

K. Houstoun, A. Milne and P. Parboteeah, 'Preliminary Report on Standards in Global Financial Markets' (2015) 26–28 at https://ssrn.com/abstract=2531210.

D. Howarth and L. Quaglia, 'The Difficult Construction of a European Deposit Insurance Scheme: A Step Too Far in Banking Union?' (2018) 21 *Journal of Economic Policy Reform*, 3.

D. Howarth and A. Spendzharova, 'Accountability in Post-crisis Eurozone Governance: The Tricky Case of the European Stability Mechanism' (2019) 57 *Journal of Common Market Studies*, 899–900.

HSBC, 'Personal Loans' at https://www.hsbc.co.uk/loans/products/personal/.

HSBC, 'Savings Accounts' at https://www.hsbc.co.uk/savings/.

HSBC Holdings Plc, 'Annual Report and Accounts 2018', 290 at https://www.hsbc.com/investors/results-and-announcements/annual-report.

A. Hudson, *The Law of Finance* (2nd edn, Sweet & Maxwell, 2013) 558–560.

T.F. Huertas, 'From Bail-Out to Bail-In: Are Banks Becoming Safe to Fail?' (2014) 29 *Journal of International Banking and Financial Law*, 8.

T.F. Huertas, *Safe to Fail: How Resolution Will Revolutionise Banking* (Palgrave Macmillan, 2014).

B.C. Hunt, *The Development of the Business Corporation in England, 1800–1867* (Harvard University Press, 1936) 96.

J.P. Hunt, 'Credit Rating Agencies and the 'Worldwide Credit Crisis': The Limits of Reputation, the Insufficiency of Reform, and a Proposal for Improvement' (2009) *Columbia Business Law Review*, 109.

M. Iansiti and K.R. Lakhani, 'The Truth About Blockchain' (January–February 2017) *Harvard Business Review*, 9–10 at https://enterprisersproject.com/sites/default/files/the_truth_about_blockchain.pdf.

P. Iglesias-Rodríguez, 'The Regulation of Cross-Border Clearing and Settlement in the European Union from a Legitimacy Perspective' (2012) 13 *European Business Organization Law Review*, 3.

Independent Commission on Banking, *Final Report: Recommendations* (Domarn Group, 2011).

S. Ingves, S.A. Seelig and D. He, 'Issues in the Establishment of Asset Management Companies', IMF Policy Discussion Paper, PDP/04/3 (2004), 14.

S. Ingves, 'Basel III: Are We Done Now?', Keynote Speech at the Institute for Law and Finance Conference on "Basel III: Are We Done Now?" Goethe University, Frankfurt, 29 January 2018 at https://www.bis.org/speeches/sp180129.pdf.

Inter-institutional Monitoring Group. Final Report Monitoring the Lamfalussy Process (Brussels, October 2007) 8–13.

International Association of Deposit Insurers, 'Core Principles for Effective Deposit Insurance Systems' (June 2009) at https://www.bis.org/publ/bcbs156.pdf.

International Monetary Fund, 'A Strategy for Resolving Europe's Problem Loans', Staff Discussion Note, SDN/15/19 9 (2015) at https://www.imf.org/external/pubs/ft/sdn/2015/sdn1519.pdf.

M. Ioannidis, 'EU Financial Assistance Conditionality after 'Two Pack' (2014) at http://ssrn.com/abstract=2398914.

E. Iossa and G. Palumbo, 'Product Quality, Lender Liability, and Consumer Credit' (2004) 56 *Oxford Economic Papers*, 331.

N. Jassaud and K.H. Kang, 'A Strategy for Developing a Market for Nonperforming Loans in Italy', IMF Working Paper No. 15–24 (2015) 16.

N. Jassaud and E. Vidon, 'European NPLs through the Crisis: A Policy Review' (2017) 25(4) *Journal of Financial Regulation & Compliance*, 416.

P. Jenkins and G. Thiessen, 'Reducing the Potential for Future Financial Crises: A Framework for Macro-Prudential Policy', Canada Commentary No. 351 (C.D. Howe Institute, May 2012) 2.

M.C. Jensen and W.H. Meckling, 'Theory of the Firm: Managerial Behavior, Agency Costs and Ownership Structure' (1976) 3 *Journal of Financial Economics*, 305.

C. Jolls, C.R. Sunstein and R.H. Thaler, 'A Behavioral Approach to Law and Economics' (1998) 50 *Stanford Law Review*, 147.

J. Jones, W. Lee and T. Yeager, 'Opaque Banks, Price Discovery, and Financial Instability' (2012) 21 *Journal of Financial Intermediation*, 383.

C. M. Kahn, J. McAndrews and W. Roberds, 'Settlement Risk under Gross and Net Settlement' (2003) 35 *Journal of Money, Credit and Banking*, 4.

D. Kahneman, 'New Challenges to the Rationality Assumption' (1997) 3 *Legal Theory*, 105.

D. Kahneman and A. Tversky, 'Prospect Theory: An Analysis of Decision Under Risk' (1979) 47 *Econometrica*, 263.

H. Kakavand, N. Kost De Sevres and B. Chilton, 'The Blockchain Revolution: An Analysis of Regulation and Technology Related to Distributed Ledger Technologies' (2017) at https://ssrn.com/abstract=2849251.

G. Kaminsky and S.L. Schmukler, 'Emerging Market Instability: Do Sovereign Ratings Affect Country Risk and Stock Returns?' (2002) 16(2) *The World Bank Economic Review*, 172.

H. Kanda, C. Mooney, L. Thévenoz, S. Béraud, T. Keijser, *Official Commentary on the UNIDROIT Convention on Substantive Rules for Intermediated Securities* (Oxford University Press, 2012) Chapter III.

S.N. Kaplan and B.A. Minton, 'How Has CEO Turnover Changed?' (2012) 12 *International Review of Finance*, 57.

E.B. Kapstein, 'Resolving the Regulator's Dilemma: International Coordination of Banking Regulations' (1989) 43(2) *International Organization*, 323.

J. Katz, E. Salinas and C. Stephanou, 'Credit Rating Agencies', The World Bank Group Note No. 8 (October 2009) 3.

K. Kauko, 'External Deficits and Non-performing Loans in the Recent Financial Crisis' (2012) 115(2) *Economics Letters*, 196.

P. Kavassalis, H. Stieber, W. Breymann, K. Saxton and F.J. Gross, 'An Innovative RegTech Approach to Financial Risk Monitoring and Supervisory Reporting' (2017) 19 *The Journal of Risk Finance*, 1.

J. Kay, 'Narrow Banking: The Reform of Banking Regulation' (2009) at https://www.johnkay.com/2009/09/15/narrow-banking/.

A. Keay, 'Company Directors Behaving Poorly: Disciplinary Options for Shareholders' (2007) *Journal of Business Law*, 656.

S. Kebbell, '"Everyone's Looking at Nothing" – The Legal Profession and the Disproportionate Burden of the Proceeds of Crime Act 2002' (2017) *Criminal Law Review*, 741.

C. Kelly, 'Failings in Management and Governance. Report of the Independent Review into the Events Leading to the Co-operative Bank's Capital Shortfall' (30 April 2014) 2–3 at https://robllewellyn.com/wp-content/uploads/2017/02/kelly-review.pdf.

J.A. Ketterer and G. Andrade, 'Digital Central Bank Money and the Unbundling of the Banking Function. Technical Report', Inter-American Development Bank, Discussion Paper No. IDB-DP-449 (April 2016).

J. Gadsden and A.D. Keyes, 'Revised Article 8 of the Uniform Commercial Code: Investment Securities' (1998) 115(4) *Banking Law Journal* 346, 348

Y. Kim, Y.-J. Park and J. Choi, 'The Adoption of Mobile Payment Services for Fintech' (2016) 11 *International Journal of Applied Engineering Research*, 2.

M. King, 'Banking: From Bagehot to Basel, and Back Again' (New York, 25 October 2010).

S. Kinsella, 'Is Ireland Really the Role Model for Austerity?' (2012) 36 *Cambridge Journal of Economics*, 1.

G. Kirkpatrick, 'The Corporate Governance Lessons from the Financial Crisis' (2009) *OECD Journal: Financial Market Trends*, 61.

N. Kleftouri, 'Rethinking UK and EU Bank Deposit Insurance' (2013) 24 *European Business Law Review*, 95.

N. Kleftouri, 'Meeting the Rationale of Deposit Protection System' (2014) 22 *Journal of Financial Regulation and Compliance*, 4.

S. Knott, P. Richardson, K. Rismanchi and K. Sen, 'Understanding the Fair Value of Banks' Loans', Bank of England Financial Stability Paper No. 31 (November 2014) 7 at https://www.bankofengland.co.uk/-/media/boe/files/financial-stability-paper/2014/understanding-the-fair-value-of-banks-loans.

J.S. Knudsen, 'Is the Single European Market an Illusion? Obstacles to Reform of EU Takeover Regulation' (2005) 11 *European Law Journal*, 4.

A. Kokkinis, 'The Reformed "Fit and Proper" Test: A Call for a Broader Rethink of Bank Corporate Governance?' (2012) 9(1) *International Corporate Rescue*, 5.

A. Kokkinis, 'The Financial Services Act 2012: The Recent Overhaul of the United Kingdom's Financial Regulatory Structure' (2013) *International Corporate and Commercial Law Review* 325.

A. Kokkinis, 'A Primer on Corporate Governance in Banks and Financial Institutions – Are Banks Special?' in I. Chiu (ed), *The Law on Corporate Governance in Banks* (Edward Elgar, 2015) 13–14.

A. Kokkinis, 'The Impact of Brexit on the Legal Framework for Cross-Border Corporate Activity' (2016) 27(7) *European Business Law Review*, 959.

A. Kokkinis, *Corporate Law and Financial Instability* (Routledge, 2018) 64–66.

A. Kokkinis, 'Exploring the Effects of the Bonus Cap Rule: The Impact of Remuneration Structure on Risk-Taking by Bank Managers' (2019) 19(1) *Journal of Corporate Law Studies*, 167.

A. Kokkinis and A. Miglionico, 'Dos and Don'ts of Brexit: The Future of the UK Financial Services Sector' (2018) 7(1) *Law and Economics Yearly Review*, 48–72.

I. Kokkoris and R. Olivares-Caminal, 'Resolution of Banks and the State Aid Regime' in Jens-Hinrich Binder and Dalvinder Singh (eds.), *Bank Resolution: The European Regime* (Oxford University Press, 2016) 304–305.

G.J. Koopman, 'Market Based Solutions to Bank Restructuring and the Role of State Aid Control: The Case of NPLs', Speech delivered at the ECMI Annual Conference, Brussels, 9 November 2016, 11–12 at http://www.eurocapitalmarkets.org/system/files/Gert%20Jan%20Koopman_Speech.pdf.

S.J. Kozey, 'The Hague Securities Convention: An Opportunity to Take the UCC Global' (2015) 46 *Georgetown Journal of International Law*, 4.

R. Kraakman et al., *The Anatomy of Corporate Law: A Comparative and Functional Approach* (3rd edn, Oxford University Press, 2017).

J.C. Kress, 'Credit Default Swaps, Clearinghouses, and Systemic Risk: Why Centralized Counterparties Must Have Access to Central Bank Liquidity' (2011) 48 *Harvard Journal on Legislation*, 1.

M. Krimminger and R.M. Lastra, 'Early Intervention' in Rosa M Lastra (ed), *Cross-border Bank Insolvency* (Oxford University Press, 2011) 62.

M. Kröner, 'API Deep Dive: Who Will Thrive in an Open Banking World? Why Meeting Regulatory Requirements Is Not Enough for Banks to Remain Relevant' (2018) 2 *Journal of Digital Banking*, 3.

H. Kronke, *Capital Markets and Conflict of Laws* (Academie de droit international de la Haye, 2001).

D. Kynaston, *The City of London – Volume IV: A Club No More, 1945–2000* (Pimlico Publications, 2002).

M. Labonte, 'Systemically Important or "Too Big to Fail" Financial Institutions', Congressional Research Service Report, 19 September 2014, 34–36 at https://www.fas.org/sgp/crs/misc/R42150.pdf.

J. R. LaBrosse, R. Olivares-Caminal and D. Singh, 'The EU Bank Recovery and Resolution Directive—Some Observations on the Financing Arrangements' (2014) 15 *Journal of Banking Regulation*, 3–4.

A. Lang, 'The 'Default Option'? The WTO and Cross-border Financial Services Trade after Brexit' in K. Alexander et al. (eds), *Brexit and Financial Services: Law and Policy* (Hart Publishing, 2018) 155–156.

K. Lannoo, 'Bank State Aid under BRRD and SRM' (2014) 13 *European State Aid Law Quarterly*, 4.

K. Lannoo, 'EU Financial Market Access After Brexit' (2016) 51 *Intereconomics*, 5.

K. Lannoo and D. Valiante, 'Europe's New Post-Trade Infrastructure Rules', ECMI Policy Brief No. 20 (2012) 5–6 at http://aei.pitt.edu/37320/1/ECMI_PB_No_20_PostTrade_Market_Infrastructure.pdf.

F.-C. Laprévote and A. Champsaur, 'Hand in Hand or Parallel Paths? Reflections on the Future Coexistence of State Aid Control and Bank Resolution in the EU' in François-Charles Laprévote, Joanna Gray and Francesco De Cecco (eds), *Research Handbook on State Aid in the Banking Sector* (Edward Elgar, 2017) 538–539 .

J. de Larosière, 'The High-Level Group on Financial Supervision in the EU Report' (Brussels, February 2009).

T. Laryea, 'Approaches to Corporate Debt Restructuring in the Wake of Financial Crises', International Monetary Fund, SPN/10/02 (2010) 26.

R.M. Lastra, *Central Banking and Banking Regulation* (Financial Markets Group, London School of Economics, London, September 1996).

R.M. Lastra, *Legal Foundations of International Monetary Stability* (Oxford University Press, 2006).

R.M. Lastra, 'Northern Rock, UK Bank Insolvency and Cross-border Bank Insolvency' (2008) 9(3) *Journal of Banking Regulation*, 165.

R.M. Lastra, 'Systemic Risk, SIFIs and Financial Stability' (2011) 6(2) *Capital Markets Law Journal*, 199–200.

R.M. Lastra, 'Banking Union and Single Market: Conflict or Companionship?' (2013) 36 *Fordham International Law Journal*, 5.

R.M. Lastra, *International Financial and Monetary Law* (2nd edn, Oxford University Press, 2015) 375.

R.M. Lastra, 'Systemic Risk and Macro-Prudential Supervsion' in Niamh Moloney, Eilís Ferran and Jennifer Payne (eds), *The Oxford Handbook of Financial Regulation* (Oxford University Press, 2015) 309–310.

R.M. Lastra and F. Amtenbrink, 'Securing Democratic Accountability of Financial Regulatory Agencies – A Theoretical Framework' in Richard V. de Mulder (ed.), *Mitigating Risk in the Context of Safety and Security. How Relevant is a Rational Approach?* (Erasmus School of Law & Research School for Safety and Security, 2008) 115–116.

R.M. Lastra and J. Grant Allen, 'Virtual Currencies in the Eurosystem: challenges Ahead' (July 2018) European Parliament, Monetary Dialogue at http://www.europarl.europa.eu/cmsdata/150541/DIW_FINAL%20publication.pdf.

R.M. Lastra, B. Krauskopf, C. Gortsos and R. Smits, MOCOMILA Report to the ILA Meeting in Washington, DC, April 2014 at http://www.ila-hq.org/en/committees/index.cfm/cid/22.

R.M. Lastra and G. Wood, 'The Crisis of 2007–09: Nature, Causes, and Reactions' (2010) 13 *Journal of International Economic Law*, 3.

V. Laux, 'Board Independence and CEO Turnover' (2008) 46 *Journal of Accounting Research*, 137.

E. Lee, 'Financial Inclusion: A Challenge to the New Paradigm of Financial Technology, Regulatory Technology and Anti-money Laundering Law' (2017) (6) *Journal of Business Law*, 473.

A. Lefterov, 'The Single Rulebook: Legal Issues and Relevance in the SSM Context', ECB Legal Working Paper Series 15 (October 2015) 31–33 at https://www.ecb.europa.eu/pub/pdf/scplps/ecblwp15.en.pdf?03b5c5c0a61bb0d01ab6067afa536f87.

M. Lehmann, 'Bail-In and Private International Law: How to Make Bank Resolution Measures Effective Across Borders' (2017) 66 *International & Comparative Law Quarterly*, 1.

A. Lehmann, 'Risk Reduction through Europe's Distressed Debt Mrket', Bruegel Policy Contribution, Issue No. 02 (18 January 2018) 5–6 at http://bruegel.org/wp-content/uploads/2018/01/PC-02_2018-100118.pdf.

S. Le Mire and G. Gilligan, 'Independence and Independent Company Directors' (2013) 13 *Journal of Corporate Law Studies*, 443.

Lending Standards Board, 'Standards for Lending Practice: Personal Customers' (2016) at https://www.lendingstandardsboard.org.uk/the-standards-for-personal-customers/#statement-of-lender-and-borrower-responsibilities.

Lending Standards Board, 'Contingent Reimbursement Model Code for Authorised Push Payment Scams' (2019) at https://www.lendingstandardsboard.org.uk/wp-content/uploads/2019/05/CRM-code.pdf.

M. Lewan, 'The Role of Trust in Emerging Technologies' in Robin Teigland, Shahryar Siri, Anthony Larsson, Alejandro Moreno Puertas and Claire Ingram Bogusz (eds), *The Rise and Development of FinTech* (Routledge, 2018) 111–112.

Libra Association Members, 'An Introduction to Libra', White Paper (July 2019) at https://libra.org/en-US/wp-content/uploads/sites/23/2019/06/LibraWhitePaper_en_US.pdf.

Libra Association Members, 'The Libra Blockchain' (July 2019) at https://developers.libra.org/docs/the-libra-blockchain-paper.Blockchain.

B. van Liebergen, 'Machine Learning: A Revolution in Risk Management and Compliance?' (2017) 45 *Journal of Financial Transformation*, 177.

A. Liebenberg and R. Hoyt, 'The Determinants of Enterprise Risk Management: Evidence from the Appointment of Chief Risk Officers' (2003) 6 *Risk Management & Insurance Review*, 37.

E. Liikanen, 'High-level Expert Group on Reforming the Structure of the EU Banking Sector: Final Report' (2012) at
http://ec.europa.eu/internal_market/bank/docs/high-level_expert_group/report_en.pdf.

H.F. Lingl, 'Risk Allocation in International Interbank Electronic Fund Transfers: CHIPS and SWIFT' (1981) 22 *Harvard International Law Journal*, 3.

K. Lissakers, *Banks, Borrowers and the Establishment. A Revisionist Acount of the International Debt Crisis* (Harper Collins Basic Books, 1991) Chapter 8.

D. Llewellyn, 'The Economic Rationale for Financial Regulation', FSA Occasional Paper Series 1 (April 1999) 10 at https://www.researchgate.net/publication/247849804_The_Economic_Rationale_for_Financial_Regulation.

Loan Market Association, 'About Us' at https://www.lma.eu.com/about-us.

Y. Lootsma, 'Blockchain as the Newest Regtech Application—The Opportunity to Reduce the Burden of KYC for Financial Institutions' (2017) 36(8) *Banking & Financial Services Policy Report*, 16–17.

Lord Hodge, 'The Potential and Perils of Financial Technology: Can the Law Adapt to Cope?' (The First Edinburgh FinTech Law Lecture, University of Edinburgh, 14 March 2019) at https://www.supremecourt.uk/docs/speech-190314.pdf.

J. Lowry and R. Edmunds, 'Directors Duties and Liabilities: Disqualifying 'Unfit' Directors at Banks? Political Rhetoric and the Directors' Disqualification Regime' in Iris H-Y Chiu (ed), *The Law on Corporate Governance in Banks* (Edward Elgar, 2015) 75–76.

J. Macey and M. O'Hara, 'The Corporate Governance of Banks' (2003) 9 *Federal Reserve Bank of New York Economic Policy Review*, 91.

I. MacNeil, 'The Trajectory of Regulatory Reform in the UK in the Wake of the Financial Crisis' (2010) 11 *European Business Organization Law Review*, 4.

I. MacNeil and J. O'Brien, 'Introduction: The Future of Financial Regulation' in Iain MacNeil and Justin O'Brien (eds), *The Future of Financial Regulation* (Hart Publishing, 2010) 2–3.

P. Mader, 'Microfinance and Financial Inclusion' in David Brady and Linda M. Burton (eds), *The Oxford Handbook of the Social Science of Poverty* (Oxford University Press, 2016) 844–45.

M. Magnus, A.C. Duvillet-Margerit, B. Mesnard and A. Korpas, 'Upgrading the Basel standards: from Basel III to Basel IV?', Economic Governance Support Unit, European Parliament Briefing Paper 2017, 9.

C. Mallin, 'The Co-Operative Bank – What Went Wrong?' in Christine Mallin (ed), *Handbook on Corporate Governance in Financial Institutions* (Edward Elgar, 2016) 35–36.

H. Mance, 'Who Wins from the UK's Extension of Article 50?', *Financial Times* (11 April 2019).

H. Mandanis Schooner and M.W. Taylor, *Global Bak Regulation: Principles and Policies* (Elsevier, 2010).

M. Marcucci, A. Pischedda and V. Profeta, 'The Changes of the Italian Insolvency and Foreclosure Regulation Adopted in 2015', Bank of Italy notes on Financial Stability and Supervision No. 2 (2015).

A. de la Mata Muñoz, 'The Future of Cross-borer Banking after the Crisis: Facing the Challenges through Regulation and Supervision' (2010) 11(4) *European Business Organization Law Review*, 575.

K. Matthews, V. Murinde and T. Zhao, 'Competitive Conditions among the Major British Banks' (2007) 31 *Journal of Banking & Finance*, 2025.

B. Maurer, 'The Racial Capitalism of Blockchain: Alternative Markets for Human-Computer Flourishing or Computational Slavery?' Talk Given at the University of Helsinki Anthropology (8 February 2019) at https://blogs.helsinki.fi/anthropology/2019/02/18/bill-maurer-the-racial-capitalism-of-blockchain/.

B. Maurer, T.C. Nelms and L. Swartz, '"When Perhaps the Real Problem Is Money Itself!": The Practical Materiality of Bitcoin' (2013) 23 *Social Semiotics*, 2.

T. May, Prime Minister, 'Mansion House Speech', Speech at Mansion House, London, 2 March 2018 at https://www.bbc.co.uk/news/uk-politics-43256183.

D. Mayes, 'Banking Union: The Disadvantages of Opportunism' (2017) 2(2) *Journal of Economic Policy Reform*, 139.

D. Mayes, 'Banking Union: The Problem of Untried Systems' (2017) 20 *Journal of Economic Policy Reform*, 9.

M. McAleer, J-A Jimenez-Martin and T. Perez-Amaral, 'What Happened to Risk Management during the 2008–2009 Financial Crisis' in Robert W Kolb (ed), *Lessons from the Financial Crisis* (John Wiley, 2010), 307.

S. McEwan, 'Improving the Regulation of Banks and Banking Groups' (2009) 24(6) *Journal of International Banking and Financial Law*, 334.

K. McGuire, 'Banking Supervision after the Bingham Report on BCCI: the End of an Era? (1993) 4 *International Company and Commercial Law Review*, 3.

M. McKee, 'The Unpredictable Future of European Securities Regulation: A Response to Four Predictions about the Future of EU Securities Regulation by Gerard Hertig and Ruben Lee' (2003) 18 *Journal of International Banking Law and Regulation*, 7.

G. McKenzie, 'The EU Directive on Deposit Insurance: A Critical Evaluation' (1994) 32 *Journal of Common Market Studies*, 171.

A. McKnight, 'The Banking Act 2009' (2009) 3(4) *Law and Financial Markets Review*, 325–331.

H. McVea, 'Financial Services Regulation under the Financial Services Authority: A Reassertion of the Market Failure Thesis?' (2005) 64 *Cambridge Law Journal*, 413.

P. Mehrling, *The new Lombard Street: How the Fed Became the Dealer of Last Resort* (Princeton University Press, 2010) 7.

S. Merler, 'Bank Liquidation in the European Union: Clarification Needed', Bruegel Policy Contribution, Issue No. 1 (January 2018) 11 at http://bruegel.org/wp-content/uploads/2018/01/PC-01_2018.pdf.

W. Merricks, 'The Financial Ombudsman Service: Not Just an Alternative to Court' (2007) 15 *Journal of Financial Regulation and Compliance*, 135.

Y. Mersch, 'Central Bank Independence Revisited' (2018) 18(4) *ERA Forum*, 636.

Y. Mersch, ECB Executive Board, Speech at the TIPS Launch Event, Frascati, Rome, 30 November 2018 at https://central-banks.economicblogs.org/ecb/2018/bank-yves-mersch-tips-future-retail-payment-solutions-europe.

Y. Mersch, 'Money and Private Currencies: Reflections on Libra', Speech at the ESCB Legal Conference, Frankfurt am Main, 2 September 2019 at https://www.bis.org/review/r190902a.pdf.

B. Mesnard, A.A.C. Duvillet-Margerit, C. Power and M. Magnus, 'Non-performing Loans in the Banking Union: Stocktaking and Challenges', European Parliament (18 March 2016) 4 at http://www.europarl.europa.eu/RegData/etudes/BRIE/2016/574400/IPOL_BRI(2016)574400_EN.pdf.

B. Mesnard and M. Magnus, 'Banca Monte dei Paschi di Siena: State of Play', Note for the Banking Union Working Group (8 February 2017) 1 at http://www.europarl.europa.eu/RegData/etudes/BRIE/2017/587392/IPOL_BRI(2017)587392_EN.pdf.

B. Mesnard, A. Margerit and M. Magnus, 'The Resolution of Banco Popular', European Parliament (28 August 2017) 3.

B. Mesnard, A. Margerit and M. Magnus, 'The Orderly Liquidation of Veneto Banca and Banca Popolare di Vicenza', European Parliament (25 July 2017) at http://www.europarl.europa.eu/RegData/etudes/BRIE/2017/602094/IPOL_BRI%282017%29602094_EN.pdf.

B. Mesnard, M. Magnus and A.A.C. Duvillet-Margerit, 'The Precautionary Recapitalisation of Monte dei Paschi di Siena', European Parliament Briefing (6 July 2017), 3.

E. Micheler, 'Intermediated Securities and Legal Certainty', LSE Law, Society and Economy Working Papers 3/2014, 20–21 at http://eprints.lse.ac.uk/55826/1/WPS2014-03_Micheler.pdf.

E. Micheler and A. Whaley, 'Regulatory Technology – Replacing Law with Computer Code', LSE Working Papers 14/2018, 8 at http://eprints.lse.ac.uk/89550/1/Micheler%20SSRN-id3210962.pdf.

S. Micossi, G. Bruzzone and M. Cassella, 'Fine-tuning the Use of Bail-In to Promote a Stronger EU Financial System', CEPS Special Report No. 136, April 2016.

A. Miglionico, *The Governance of Credit Rating Agencies: Regulatory Regimes and Liability Issues* (Edward Elgar, 2019) Chapters 1–2.

S. Miller, 'The LIBOR Scandal: Culture, Corruption and Collective Action Problems in the Global Banking Sector' in Justin O'Brien and George Gilligan (eds), *Integrity, Risk and Accountability in Capital Markets* (Hart Publishing, 2013) 111–112.

D.C. Mills, K. Wang, B. Malone, A. Ravi, J.C. Marquardt, A.I. Badev, T. Brezinski, L. Fahy, K. Liao, V. Kargenian, et al., 'Distributed Ledger Technology in Payments, Clearing, and Settlement', FEDS Working Paper No. 2016–095, 2016 at https://papers.ssrn.com/sol3/papers.cfm?abstract_id=2881204.

A. Milne, 'Cryptocurrencies from an Austrian Perspective' (2017) 13–14 at https://papers.ssrn.com/sol3/papers.cfm?abstract_id=2946160.

A. Milne, 'Fintech and Regtech as Tools for Financial Stability', presentation at the 'Rebuilding Macroeconomics Finance Hub 2nd Workshop', London, 24 January 2019.

A. Minto, M. Voelkerling and M. Wulff, 'Separating Apples from Oranges: Identifying Threats to Financial Stability Originating from FinTech' (2017) 12(4) *Capital Markets Law Journal*, 429–430.

K.J. Mitchener, 'Skin in the Game', University of Warwick Department of Economics (March 2013) at http://www2.warwick.ac.uk/fac/soc/economics/news/2013/3/bankingreg/#sthash.fd63t-djh.dpbs.

F. Modigliani and M. Miller, 'The Cost of Capital, Corporation Finance and the Theory of Investment' (1959) 48 *American Economic Review*, 261.

K. Mohaddes, M. Raissi and A. Weber, 'Can Italy Grow Out of Its NPL Overhang? A Panel Threshold Analysis' (2017) 159 *Economics Letters*, 185.

N. Moloney, 'Confidence and Competence: The Conundrum of EC Capital Markets Law' (2004) 4(1) *Journal of Corporate Law Studies*, 11–12.

N. Moloney, 'Financial Market Regulation in the Post-Financial Services Action Plan Era' (2006) 55 *International & Comparative Law Quarterly*, 4.

N. Moloney, 'Innovation and Risk in EC Financial Market Regulation: New Instruments of Financial Market Intervention and the Committee of European Securities Regulators' (2007) 32 *European Law Review*, 5.

N. Moloney, *EC Securities Regulation* (Oxford University Press, 2008).

N. Moloney, *How to Protect Investors. Lessons from the EC and the UK* (Cambridge University Press, 2010) 104.

N. Moloney, 'International Financial Governance, the EU, and Brexit: The 'Agencification' of EU Financial Governance and the Implications' (2016) 17 *European Business Organization Law Review*, 4.

N. Moloney, 'Brexit, the EU and Its Investment Banker: Rethinking 'Equivalence' for the EU Capital Market', LSE Law, Society and Economy Working Papers 5/2017, 12.

N. Moloney, *The Age of ESMA. Governing EU Financial Markets* (Hart Publishing, 2018) Chapter I.

Money & Pensions Service, 'Board Terms of Reference' (2018) at https://moneyandpensionsservice.org.uk/wp-content/uploads/2019/04/MAPS-BOARD-TERMS-OF-REFERENCE.pdf.

Money & Pensions Service, 'Business Plan 2019/20' (2019) 10 at https://moneyandpensionsservice.org.uk/wp-content/uploads/2019/04/19-20-Business-Plan.pdf.

Money Advice Service, 'Overdrafts Explained' at https://www.moneyadviceservice.org.uk/en/articles/overdrafts-explained.

Money Laundering and Terrorist Financing: Council Returns Draft List of High Risk Countries to the Commission (7 March 2019).

Monte dei Paschi di Siena, 'BMPS: European Commission Approves the 2017–2021 Restructuring Plan', Press Release at http://english.mps.it/media-and-news/press-releases/2017/Pages/press_release_20170705.aspx.

M. Moore, 'The Evolving Contours of the Board's Risk Management Function in UK Corporate Governance' (2010) 10 *Journal of Corporate Law Studies*, 279.

M. Moore, 'Corporate Governance, Pay Equity, and the Limitations of Agency Theory' (2015) 68 *Current Legal Problems*, 431.

M. Moore, 'Design and Control of Remuneration in UK Banks' in Iris H-Y Chiu (ed), *The Law on Corporate Governance in Banks* (Edward Elgar, 2015).

M. Moore and M. Petrin, *Corporate Governance: Law, Regulation and Theory* (Palgrave, 2017).

R. Morck, 'Behavioral Finance in Corporate Governance – Independent Directors, Non-Executive Chairs, and the Importance of the Devil's Advocate' (2004) 12 *Journal of Management and Governance*, 179.

N. Mugarura, 'The "EU Brexit" Implication on a Single Banking License and Other Aspects of Financial Markets Regulation in the UK' (2016) 58(4) *International Journal of Law and Management*, 477.

P.O. Mulbert, 'Corporate Governance of Banks after the Financial Crisis - Theory, Evidence, Reforms', ECGI Working Paper No. 130/2009 (2010) 11–12 at http://papers.ssrn.com/sol3/papers.cfm?abstract_id=1448118.

E.V. Murphy, 'Financial Stability Oversight Council: A Framework to Mitigate Systemic Risk', Congressional Research Service Report R42083 (21 March 2013) 1–2 and 4–6 at http://fas.org/sgp/crs/misc/R42083.pdf.

H. Murphy, 'Facebook Unveils Global Digital Coin called Libra', *Financial Times* (18 June 2019).

K.J. Murphy, 'Regulating Banking Bonuses in the European Union: A Case Study in Unintended Consequences' (2013) 19 *European Financial Management*, 631.

E. Murray, 'Lomas v Firth Rixson: 'As you were!' (2013) 8(4) *Capital Markets Law Journal*, 395.

NatWest, 'Overdrafts' at https://personal.natwest.com/personal/current-accounts/overdrafts.html.

M. Nawas and G. Lamaris, 'Ringfencing of Banks: A Permanent Cure or a Sticking Plaster?' (London, 12 February 2013) 4 at http://www.bishopsfieldcapital.com/sites/default/files/article/market-insight-0213-ringfencing-of-banks-a-permanent-cure-or-a-sticking-plaster.pdf.

M.W. Nelson, 'Behavioural Evidence on the Effects of Principles-and Rules-Based Standards' (2003) 17(1) *Accounting Horizons*, 91

D. Neo, 'A Conceptual Overview of Bank Secrecy' in Sandra Booysen and Dora Neo (eds), *Can Banks Still Keep a Secret?: Bank Secrecy in Financial Centres around the World* (Cambridge University Press, 2017) 4–5.

L.A. Newton, 'The Birth of Joint-stock Banking: England and New England Compared' (2010) 84 *Business History Review*, 27.

B. Nicoletti, *The Future of FinTech: Integrating Finance and Technology in Financial Services* (Palgrave, 2017).

M.J. Nieto and L.D. Wall, 'Cross-Border Banking on the Two Sides of the Atlantic: Does It Have an Impact on Bank Crisis Management?' FRB Atlanta Working Paper No. 2015-11, 19.

M. Nkusu, 'Nonperforming Loans and Macrofinancial Vulnerabilities in Advanced Economies', IMF Working Papers No. 161 (2011), 20–21.

L. Noonan, 'Fintechs Face Libra Challenge', *Financial Times* (24 June 2019).

I. Ofoeda, J. Abor and C.K.D. Adjasi, 'Non-bank Financial Institutions Regulation and Risk-Taking' (2012) 20 *Journal of Financial Regulation & Compliance*, 4.

U. Okonkwo Osili and A. Paulson, 'Bank Crises and Investor Confidence: An Empirical Investigation', Federal Reserve Bank of Chicago Policy Discussion Paper PDP2009-9 (2009).

R. Olivares-Caminal, 'The EU Architecture to Avert a Sovereign Debt Crisis' (2011) 2 *OECD Journal: Financial Markets Trend*, 13–14.

R. Ophèle, 'From Brexit to Financial Innovations: New Challenges for Financial Regulation' (Speech at the Official Monetary and Financial Institutions Forum, London, 15 March 2018).

Organisation for Economic Co-operation and Development, 'G20/OECD Principles of Corporate Governance' (2004) at http://www.oecd.org/corporate/oecdprinciplesofcorporategovernance.htm.

V. O'Sullivan and S. Kinsella, 'A New Era for Crisis Management for EU Banks' (2014) 17 *Financial Regulation International*, 1.

A.M. Pacces, 'Financial Intermediation in the Securities Markets Law and Economics of Conduct of Business Regulation' (2000) 20(4) *International Review of Law and Economics*, 479.

P. Paech, 'The Governance of Blockchain Financial Networks' (2017) 80 *Modern Law Review*, 6.

R. Palmstorfer, 'To Bail Out or Not to Bail Out? The Current Framework of Financial Assistance for Euro Area Member States Measured against the Requirements of EU Primary Law' (2012) 6 *European Law Review*, 771.

C. Parker, 'The Ethics of Advising on Regulatory Compliance: Autonomy or Interdependence?' (2000) 28(4) *Journal of Business Ethics*, 339.

Parliamentary Commission on Banking Standards, *An Accident Waiting to Happen: The Failure of HBOS* (2012–13, HL 144, HC 705).

Parliamentary Commission on Banking Standards *Changing Banking for Good* (2013–14, HL 27-II, HC 175-II).

R. Parlour and T. Herrington, 'The Regulation of Global Trading and Investment' (1992) 7 *Journal of International Banking Law*, 1.

C.A. Parlour, U. Rajan and J. Walden, 'Making Money: Commercial Banks, Liquidity Transformation and the Payment System' Ross School of Business Paper No. 1337, 2017 at https://papers.ssrn.com/sol3/papers.cfm?abstract_id=2892150.

J. Parra Moyano and O. Ross, 'KYC Optimization Using Distributed Ledger Technology' (2017) 59 *Business & Information Systems Engineering*, 6.

N. Passas, 'The Genesis of the BCCI Scandal' (1996) 23 *Journal of Law and Society*, 57–58.

H. Paulson, 'Reform the Architecture of Regulation' *Financial Times* (18 March 2009) 13.

M. Pauly, 'The Economics of Moral Hazard: Comment' (1968) 58 *The American Economic Review*, 531.

J. Payne, 'Intermediated Securities and the Right to Vote in the UK' in Louise Gullifer ad Jennifer Payne (eds.), *Intermediated Securities. Legal Problems and Practical Issues* (Bloomsbury, 2010) 187–188.

PCBS, *Changing Banking for Good* (2013–14, HL 27-I, HC 175-I), para 119.

S. Pei Woo, 'Stress before Consumption: A Proposal to Reform Agency Ratings' (2012) 18 *European Law Journal*, 1.

G. Penn, *Banking Supervision: Regulation of the UK Banking Sector under the Banking Act 1987* (Butterworths, 1989).

B. Penn and D. Measor, 'A Guide to the Banking Bill 2008' (2009) 3(1) *Law and Financial Markets Review*, 34.

A.K. Pennathur, '"Clicks and bricks": e-Risk Management for Banks in the Age of the Internet' (2001) 25(11) *Journal of Banking and Finance*, 2013.

PERG 8.28 'Advice or Information' at https://www.handbook.fca.org.uk/handbook/PERG/8/28.html.

R. Peston, 'HSBC to Pay $1.9bn in US Money Laundering Penalties', *BBC News* (11 December 2012) at https://www.bbc.co.uk/news/business-20673466.

T. Philippon, 'The FinTech Opportunity', NBER Working Paper No. 22476 (August 2016), 15–16 at http://www.nber.org/papers/w22476.

S. Picciotto, *Regulating Global Corporate Capitalism* (Cambridge University Press, 2011) 288–290.

M. Pilkington, 'Blockchain Technology: Principles and Applications' in F. Xavier Olleros and Majlinda Zhegu (eds), *Research Handbook on Digital Transformations* (Edward Elgar, 2016) 225–226.

S. Platt, 'Why Turner Got It Wrong' (June 2009) 21 *Compliance Monitor*, 1.

T. Polglase, 'New Basle Core Principles' (1997) 16 *International Banking and Financial Law*, 4.

Policy Exchange, *Ringfencing UK Banks: More of a Problem Than a Solution* (James Barty ed, Heron, Dawson and Sawyer, 2013).

P.S. Pollard, 'A Look Inside Two Central Banks: The ECB and the Federal Reserve', Federal Reserve Bank of St Louis (January–February 2003) at https://research.stlouisfed.org/publications/review/03/01/Pollard.pdf.

I. Pollari, 'The Rise of Fintech: Opportunities and Challenges' (2016) 3 *The Australasian Journal of Applied Finance*, 15.

R.A. Posner, 'The Economics of Privacy' (1981) 71 *American Economic Review* 405.

R.A. Posner, *Economic Analysis of Law* (8th edn, Wolters Kluwer, 2011) Chapter 1.

B. Powell, 'Is Cyberspace a Public Good - Evidence from the Financial Services Industry' (2005) 1 *Journal of Law, Economics & Policy*, 497.

M. Power, *Organized Uncertainty. Designing a World of Risk Management* (Oxford University Press, 2007).

PRA, 'Designation of Investment Firms for Prudential Supervision by the Prudential Regulation Authority' (Statement of Policy, March 2013) paras 8–12 at http://www.bankofengland.co.uk/publications/Documents/other/pra/designationofinvestmentfirms.pdf

PRA, 'Strengthening Capital Standards: Implementing CRD IV, Feedback and Final Rules' (Policy Statement PS 7/13, 13 June 2013), para 3.6 at http://www.bankofengland.co.uk/pra/Pages/publications/implemcrdiv.aspx.

PRA, 'Strengthening the Alignment of Risk and Reward: New Remuneration Rules' (PRA PS12/15, 2015) 7–8 at http://www.bankofengland.co.uk/pra/Pages/publications/ps/2015/ps1215.aspx.

C. Randell, 'European Banking Union and Bank Resolution' (2013) 7 *Law and Financial Markets Review*, 1.

C. Randell, 'The Road to Cross-border Resolution of Financial Institutions', Lecture delivered at the Centre for Commercial Law Studies, Queen Mary University of London, 13 February 2015.

A. Rappaport, 'The Economics of Short-Term Performance Obsession' (2005) 61(3) *Financial Analysts Journal*, 65.

P. Rawlings, 'Bank Reform in the UK: Part II-Return to the Dark Ages?' (2011) 8 *International Corporate Rescue*, 55.

P. Rawlings, 'Restrictions on the Transfer of Rights in Loan Contracts' (2013) 28 *Journal of International Banking and Financial Law*, 543.

N. Reich, 'Diverse Approaches to Consumer Protection Philosophy' (1992) 14 *Journal of Consumer Policy*, 257.

M. Reid, *The Secondary Banking Crisis, 1973–75: Its Causes and Course* (Macmillan Publishers, 1982).

F. Reid and M. Harrigan, 'An Analysis of Anonymity in the Bitcoin System' in Yaniv Altshuler, Yuval Elovici, Armin B. Cremers, Nadav Aharony and Alex Pentland (eds), *Security and Privacy in Social Networks* (Springer, 2012) 197–198.

C.R. Reitz, 'Reflections on the Drafting of the 1994 Revision of Article 8 of the US Uniform Commercial Code' (2005) 10 *Uniform Law Review*, 1–2.

Review Committee on Banking Services Law, *Banking Services: Law and Practice Report by the Review Committee* (R.B. Jack, Cm 622, HMSO 1989).

B. Reynolds, *A Blueprint for Brexit. The Future of Global Financial Services and Markets in the UK* (Politeia, 2016).

M. Riikkinen, H. Saarijärvi, P. Sarlin, I. Lähteenmäki, 'Using Artificial Intelligence to Create Value in Insurance' (2018) 36 *International Journal of Bank Marketing*, 6.

W.-G. Ringe, 'The Irrelevance of Brexit for the European Financial Market' (2018) 19 *European Business Organization Law Review*, 1.

J. Roaf, 'Non-performing Loans in CESEE' (Vienna, 23 September 2014) at http://vienna-initiative.com/wp-content/uploads/2014/11/Session-I-James-Roaf-IMF.pdf.

J.-C. Rochet, 'Systemic Risk: Changing the Regulatory Perspective' (2010) *International Journal of Central Banking*, 259.

I. Romānova and M. Kudinska, 'Banking and Fintech: A Challenge or Opportunity?' in Simon Grima, Frank Bezzina, Inna Romānova and Ramona Rupeika-Apoga (eds), *Contemporary Issues in Finance: Current Challenges from Across Europe*, Contemporary Studies in Economic and Financial Analysis, Volume 98 (Emerald, 2016) 21–22.

A.K. Rose and T. Wieladek, 'Too Big to Fail: Some Empirical Evidence on the Causes and Consequences of Public Banking Interventions in the United Kingdom', Bank of England, Working Paper No. 460 (August 2012) 3–4.

L. Rosenblum, 'The Failure of the City of Glasgow Bank' (1933) 8 *The Accounting Review*, 285.

N. B. Rottke and J. Gentgen, 'Workout Management of Non-performing Loans: A Formal Model Based on Transaction Cost Economics' (2008) 26(1) *Journal of Property Investment & Finance*, 59.

M. Ruffert, 'The European debt crisis and European Union law' (2011) 48 *Common Market Law Review*, 6.

C. Ryan, 'Transfer of Banking Supervision to the Financial Services Authority' in Michael Blair et al. (eds), *Blackstone's Guide to the Bank of England Act 1998* (Blackstone Press, 1998) 39.

G. Sabato, 'Financial Crisis: Where Did Risk Management Fail?' (2010) 2 *International Review of Applied Financial Issues and Economics*, 315.

J. Said, R. Snook, D. McWilliams and M. Pragnell, 'The Importance of Wholesale Financial Services to the EU Economy 2007', Centre for Economics and Business Research, City of London (May 2007) at http://www.cityoflondon.gov.uk/economicresearch.

P. Samuelson, 'The Pure Theory of Public Expenditure' (1954) 36 *Review of Economics and Statistics*, 387.

J.M. Sánchez, 'The Information Technology Revolution and the Unsecured Credit Market' (2018) 56 *Economic Inquiry*, 2.

M. Sandbu, 'Banking Union Will Transform Europe's Politics', *Financial Times* (26 July 2017).

P. Schammo, 'EU Day to Day Supervision or Intervention-based Supervision: Which Way Forward for the European System of Financial Supervision' (2012) 32 *Oxford Journal of Legal Studies* 4.

R. Schiller, *The Subprime Solution* (Princeton University Press, 2008).

I. Schnabel and N. Véron, 'Breaking the Stalemate on European Deposit Insurance', Bruegel Blog (5 March 2018) at https://bruegel.org/2018/03/breaking-the-stalemate-on-european-deposit-insurance/.

D. Schoenmaker, 'Internationalisation of Banking Supervision and Deposit Insurance' (1993) 8 *Journal of International Banking Law*, 3.

D. Schoenmaker, 'A Fiscal Backstop to the Banking System' in Matthias Haentjens and Bob Wessels (eds), *Research Handbook on Crisis Management in the Banking Sector* (Edward Elgar Publishing, 2015) 42–43.

D. Schoenmaker, 'Lost Passports: A Guide to the Brexit Fallout for the City of London', Bruegel Blog Post (30 June 2016) at http://bruegel.org/2016/06/lost-passports-a-guide-to-the-brexit-fallout-for-the-city-of-london/.

D. Schoenmaker and N. Véron (eds), 'European Banking Supervision: The First Eighteen Months', Bruegel Blueprint Series 2016, 4.

D. Schoenmaker and N. Véron, 'Brexit Should Drive Integration of EU Capital Markets', Bruegel Blog Post (24 February 2017) at http://bruegel.org/2017/02/brexit-should-drive-integration-of-eu-capital-markets/.

L. Schuknecht, P. Moutot, P. Rother and J. Stark, 'The Stability and Growth Pact: Crisis and Reform' ECB Occasional Paper No. 129 (2011).

S.L. Schwarcz, 'Indirectly Held Securities and Intermediary Risk' (2001) 6 *Uniform Law Review*, 2.

S.L. Schwarcz, 'Systemic Risk' (2008) 97 *Georgetown Law Journal*, 1.

S.L. Schwarcz, 'The "Principles" Paradox', Duke Law School Legal Studies Paper No. 205, 2008.

S.L. Schwarcz, 'Keynote Address: Ex Ante versus Ex Post Approaches to Financial Regulation' (2011) 15 *Chapman Law Review*, 1.

S.L. Schwarcz, 'Ring-Fencing' (2013) 87 *Southern California Law Review*, 69.

S.L. Schwarcz, 'The Functional Regulation of Finance', paper presented at 3rd CCLS Roundtable on Financial Regulation: 'Financial Markets: Impossible to Govern?', London, 26–27 June 2014.

S.L. Schwarcz and J. Benjamin, 'Intermediary Risk in the Indirect Holding System for Securities' (2002) 12 *Duke Journal of Comparative and International Law*, 2.

S.L. Schwarcz and Lucy Chang, 'The Custom to Failure Cycle' (2012) 62 *Duke Law Journal*, 767.

M. Schwarz, 'A Memorandum of Misunderstanding – The Doomed Road of the European Stability Mechanism and a Possible Way Out: Enhanced Cooperation' (2014) 51 *Common Market Law Review*, 2.

A. Schwienbacher and B. Larralde, 'Crowdfunding of Small Entrepreneurial Ventures' in Douglas Cumming (ed), *The Oxford Handbook of Entrepreneurial Finance* (OUP, 2012) 369–370.

H.S. Scott, 'The Reduction of Systemic Risk in the United States Financial System' (2010) 33 *Harvard Journal of Law and Public Policy*, 2.

K. Sergakis, *The Law of Capital Markets in the EU* (Palgrave, 2018) 10.

S. Shavell, 'Criminal Law and the Optimal Use of Non-Monetary Sanctions as Deterrents' (1985) 85 *Columbia Law Review*, 1232.

A. Shiels, 'The Banking Reform Bill: What Lies Ahead for the Banks?' (August 2013) at http://www.bluerock-consulting.com/pdf-new-site/the-banking-reform-bill---aug-2013.pdf.

K. Silverberg, A. Portilla, C. French, B. van Liebergen and S. Van Den Berg, 'Regtech in Financial Services' (2016) at https://www.iif.com/system/files/regtech_in_financial_services_solutions_for_compliance_and_reporting.pdf.

D. Singh, *Banking Regulation of the UK and US Financial Markets* (Ashgate, 2007).

D. Singh, 'The UK Banking Act 2009, Pre-insolvency and Early Intervention: Policy and Practice' (2011) *Journal of Business Law*, 42.

G. Sitaraman, 'Regulating Tech Platforms: A Blueprint for Reform', 'The Great Democracy Initiative 2018', Vanderbilt University Law School Legal Studies Research Paper Series (April 2018) 18–64 at https://greatdemocracyinitiative.org/wp-content/uploads/2018/03/Regulating-Tech-Platforms-final.pdf.

G. Sjoberg, 'Banking Special Resolution Regimes as a Governance Tool' in Wolf-Georg Ringe and Peter Huber (eds), *Legal Challenges in the Global Financial Crisis* (Hart Publishing, 2014) 187–188.

S. Smeets, A. Jaschke and D. Beach, 'The Role of the EU Institutions in Establishing the European Stability Mechanism: Institutional Leadership under a Veil of Intergovernmentalism' (2019) 57 *Journal of Common Market Studies*, 4.

R. Smith, 'Banco Popular Serves as a Harsh Lesson for Coco Debt Holders', *Financial Times* (8 June 2018).

R.C. Smith, I. Walter and G. DeLong, *Global Banking* (Oxford University Press, 2012) 27–28.

K. Spong, *Banking Regulation: Its Purposes, Implementation and Effects* (5th edn, Federal Reserve Bank of Kansas City Publications, 2000).

C. Stamegna, 'Amending Capital Requirements. The 'CRD V Package', European Parliamentary Research Service (April 2019) 5 at http://www.europarl.europa.eu/RegData/etudes/BRIE/2017/599385/EPRS_BRI(2017)599385_EN.pdf.

K. Stanton, 'The United Kingdom' in Sandra Booysen and Dora Neo (eds), *Can Banks Still Keep a Secret?: Bank Secrecy in Financial Centres around the World* (Cambridge University Press, 2017) 337–338.

H. van Steenis, 'Why the EU capital Markets Union Matters for ECB Policy', *Financial Times* (23 April 2018).

R. Steennot, 'Reduced Payer's Liability for Unauthorized Payment Transactions under the Second Payment Services Directive (PSD2)' (2018) 34 *Computer Law & Security Review*, 4.

J. Stiglitz, 'Principal and Agent' in John Eatwell, Murray Milgate and Peter Newman P. (eds), *Allocation, Information and Markets* (Palgrave Macmillan, London 1989) 241–242.

T. Stockwell and D. Petkovic, 'The Jack Committee Report on Banking Services: Law and Practice' (1989) 4 *Journal of International Banking Law*, 134.

R. Stones, 'The Special Resolution Regime: A Cherrypicker's Charter?' (2008) 23(10) *Journal of International Banking and Financial Law*, 523.

T. Sullivan and J. Vickery, 'A Look at Bank Loan Performance', *Federal Reserve Bank of New York* (16 October 2013).

M. Swan, 'Blockchain: Blueprint for a New Economy' (2015).

L.E. Talbot, 'Keeping Bad Company: Building Societies - A Case Study' (2009) 60 *Northern Ireland Legal Quarterly*, 4.

D. Tapscott and A. Tapscott, *Blockchain Revolution: How the Technology behind Bitcoin Is Changing Money, Business, and the World* (Penguin, 2016).

D. Tarullo, 'Regulating Systemic Risk', Speech at '2011 Credit Markets Symposium', Charlotte, 31 March 2011.

P. Tasca, 'The Dual Nature of Bitcoin as Payment Network and Money' in Christian Beer, Ernest Gnan and Urs W. Birchler (eds), *Cash on Trial* (SUERF Studies, The European Money and Finance Forum, 2016) 71–72 at https://papers.ssrn.com/sol3/papers.cfm?abstract_id=2805003.

M. Taylor, 'Twin Peaks: A Regulatory Structure for the New Century', Centre for the Study of Financial Innovation (CSFI), London, 1995.

G. Tett, 'Facebook's 'Stablecoin' Libra Raises Questions for Regulators', *Financial Times* (13 June 2019).

G. Teubner, 'Reflexive Law' (1983) 19 *Law and Society Review*, 239.

P. Thal Larsen and J. Hughes, 'Sants Signals More Muscular Regulatory Era', *Financial Times* (13 March 2009) 19.

J. Thanassoulis, 'The Case for Intervening in Bankers' Pay' (2012) 67 *The Journal of Finance*, 849.

The Banking Conduct of Business Sourcebook. 'Dealings with Customers in Financial Difficulty' at https://www.handbook.fca.org.uk/handbook/BCOBS.pdf.

The Committee on Payments and Market Infrastructures at https://www.bis.org/cpmi/.

The Economist, 'Bolting the Stable Door' (21 March 2009) 35.

The Financial Markets and Insolvency (Settlement Finality) Regulations 1999 at https://www.legislation.gov.uk/uksi/1999/2979/made.

The Financial Services and Markets Act 2000 (Ring-fenced Bodies, Core Activities, Excluded Activities and Prohibitions) (Amendment) Order 2016, 2016 No. 1032 at http://www.legislation.gov.uk/uksi/2016/1032/contents/made.

The Joint Money Laundering Steering Group at http://www.jmlsg.org.uk/industry-guidance/article/jmlsg-guidance-current.

The Lending Code. Setting Standards for Banks, Building Societies, Credit Card Providers and Their Agents, March 2011 (Revised 28th September 2015) at https://www.lendingstandardsboard.org.uk/wp-content/uploads/2016/06/The-Lending-Code-Mar-2011-revised-2015-1.pdf.

The Money Advice Service at https://www.moneyadviceservice.org.uk/en.

The PRA's Approach to Insurance Supervision (2012) at http://www.fsa.gov.uk/about/what/reg_reform/pra.

The Prudential Regulatory Authority at http://www.bankofengland.co.uk/pra/Pages/default.aspx.

The UK Cards Association, 'UK Card Payments 2017' (2017) 12 at http://www.theukcardsassociation.org.uk/wm_documents/UK%20Card%20Payments%202017%20%20website%20FINAL.pdf.

L. Thevenoz, 'Intermediated Securities, Legal Risk, and the International Harmonization of Commercial Law' (2008) 13 *Stanford Journal of Law, Business & Finance* 2.

M. Thiemann, M. Aldegwy and E. Ibrocevic, 'Understanding the Shift from Micro- to Macro-Prudential Thinking: A Discursive Network Analysis' (2018) 42 *Cambridge Journal of Economics* 4.

P.M. Thomsen, 'On Capital Market Finance in Europe', Speech at the Conference on Capital Markets Union organised by the Financial Markets Group, The London School of Economics and Political Science, 14 June 2019 at https://www.imf.org/en/News/Articles/2019/06/25/sp061419-on-capital-market-finance-in-europe.

P. Toffano and K. Yuan, 'E-shekels Across Borders: A Distributed Ledger System to Settle Payments between Israel and the West Bank' LSE Middle East Centre paper series (2019) at http://eprints.lse.ac.uk/100470/.

R. Tomasic and F. Akinbami, 'The Role of Trust in Maintaining the Resilience of Financial Markets' (2011) 11 *Journal of Corporate Law Studies*, 2.

J. Treanor, 'Bank Stress Tests: Co-Op Fails as Lloyds and RBS Scrape Through' (London: Guardian, 16 December 2014) at https://www.theguardian.com/business/2014/dec/16/bank-stress-tests-co-op-lloyds-rbs.

Treasury Committee, *The Future of Cheques* (HC 2010–12, 1147-I) and HM Treasury, *Speeding up Cheque Payments: Summary of Responses* (2014).

P. Treleaven, 'Financial Regulation in FinTech' (2015) 3(3) *University College London Journal of Financial Perspectives*, 114–115.

T.H. Tröger, 'Too Complex to Work: A Critical Assessment of the Bail-in Tool under the European Bank Recovery and Resolution Regime' (2018) 4(1) *Journal of Financial Regulation*, 38.

P. Truell and L. Gurwin, *False Profits: The Inside Story of BCCI, The World's Most Corrupt Financial Empire* (Houghton Mifflin, 1992) 67–68.

J.D. Turner, *Banking in Crisis: The Rise and Fall of British Banking Stability, 1800 to the Present* (Cambridge University Press, 2014).

A. Tyrie, 'Electrify the Banking Ringfence', *Financial Times* (London, 27 January 2013).

A. Ubide, 'How to Form a More Perfect European Banking Union', The Peterson Institute for International Economics, Policy Brief 13–23, 2013.

UK Banking Regulation under Parliamentary Scrutiny' (1996) 1 *Yearbook of International Financial and Economic Law*, 333.

UK Government, 'Distributed Ledger Technology: Beyond Block Chain' (19 January 2016) 18–20 at https://www.gov.uk/government/publications/distributed-ledger-technology-blackett-review.

Uncertificated Securities Regulations 2001 at https://www.legislation.gov.uk/uksi/2001/3755/regulation/1/made.

B. Unger, *The Scale and Impacts of Money Laundering* (Edward Elgar, 2007).

United Nations System of National Accounts 2008 at https://unstats.un.org/unsd/nationalaccount/sna2008.asp.

S. Valdez, *An Introduction to Global Financial Markets* (5th edn, Palgrave MacMillan, 2007) 303.

M.W. Van Alstyne, G. Parker and S.P. Choudary, 'Pipelines, Platforms and the New Rules of Strategy' (April 2016) 94 *Harvard Business Review* 4.

P.C. Van Duyne, Jackie H. Harvey and Liliya Y. Gelemerova, *The Critical Handbook of Money Laundering: Policy, Analysis and Myths* (Palgrave Macmillan, 2018).

M. Van Empel, 'Retail Payments in the EU' (2005) 42 *Common Market Law Review* 5.

P.W.J. Van Esterik-Plasmeijer and W.F. van Raaij, 'Banking System Trust, Bank Trust, and Bank Loyalty' (2017) 35 *International Journal of Bank Marketing*, 1.

K. Vanderheyden and T. Reucroft, 'Central Securities Depositories Regulation: The Next Systemic Crisis Waiting to Happen?' (2015) 7 *Journal of Securities Operations & Custody*, 3.

A. Veng Mei Leong, 'Anti-money Laundering Measures in the United Kingdom: A Review of Recent Legislation and the FSA's Risk Based Approach' (2007) 28 *Company Lawyer*, 35.

A. Verdun, 'A Historical Institutionalist Explanation of the EU's Responses to the Euro Area Financial Crisis' (2015) 22(2) *Journal of European Public Policy*, 219.

M. Vereecken, 'Reducing Systemic Risk in Payment and Securities Settlement Systems' (1998) 6 *Journal of Financial Regulation and Compliance*, 2.

N. Véron, 'Defining Europe's Capital Markets Union', Bruegel Policy Contribution, Issue 2014/12, November 2014, 2.

N. Véron, 'Charting the Next Steps for the EU Financial Supervisory Architecture', Bruegel Policy Contribution, No. 2017/16, 9 at https://www.econstor.eu/handle/10419/173112.

N. Véron, 'Precautionary Recapitalisation: Time for a Review?' (2017) Bruegel Policy Contribution No. 21 at https://www.econstor.eu/handle/10419/173117.

N. Véron and G.B. Wolff, 'From Supervision to Resolution: Next Steps on the Road to European Banking Union' The Peterson Institute for International Economics, Policy Brief 13–5, 2013, 5–6.

P. Voigt and A. von dem Bussche, *The EU General Data Protection Regulation (GDPR): A Practical Guide* (Springer 2017) 3–4.

A. Walch, 'The Bitcoin Blockchain as Financial Market Infrastructure: A Consideration of Operational Risk' (2015) 18(4) *NYU Journal of Legislation and Public Policy*, 837.

D. Walker, 'A Review of Corporate Governance in UK Banks and Other Financial Industry Entities: Final Recommendations' (2009) at https://www.icaew.com/en/library/subject-gateways/corporate-governance/codes-and-reports/walker-report.

G. Walker, R. Purves and M. Blair, 'European Financial Services' in George Walker and Robert Purves (eds), *Financial Services Law* (4th edn, Oxford University Press, 2018) 77.

E. Walker-Arnott, 'Company Law, Corporate Governance and the Banking Crisis' (2010) 7 *International Corporate Rescue*, 19.

R. Wardrop and T. Ziegler, 'A Case of Regulatory Evolution – A Review of the UK Financial Conduct Authority's Approach to Crowdfunding' (2016) 14(2) *CESifo DICE Report*, 25–27 at http://hdl.handle.net/10419/167260.

V. Waye and V. Morabito, 'Collective Forms of Consumer Redress: Financial Ombudsman Service Case Study' (2012) 12 *Journal of Corporate Law Studies*, 1.

F. De Weert, *Bank and Insurance Capital Management* (Wiley, 2010).

X. Wei, 'Asset Management Company and Debit-Equity Swap Practice in China' (2002) 17(10) *Journal of International Banking Law*, 296.

M.S. Weisbach, 'Outside Directors and CEO Turnover' (1988) 20 *Journal of Financial Economics*, 431.

J. Welch, 'European Financial Services' in Michael Blair and George Walker (eds), *Financial Services Law* (4th edn, Oxford University Press, 2018) 69–70.

M. Wheatley, 'The Wheatley Review of LIBOR: Final Report' (2012) at https://assets.publishing.service.gov.uk/government/uploads/system/uploads/attachment_data/file/191762/wheatley_review_libor_finalreport_280912.pdf.

T. Wilhelmsson, 'Varieties of Welfarism in European Contract Law' (2004) 10 *European Law Journal*, 712.

J. Winter, 'The Financial Crisis: Does Good Corporate Governance Matter and How to Achieve it?' in Eddy Wymeersch, Klaus Hopt and Guido Ferranini (eds), *Financial Regulation and Supervision: A Post-crisis Analysis* (Oxford University Press, 2012) 366–367.

L. Wissink, 'Challenges to an Efficient European Centralised Banking Supervision (SSM): Single Rulebook, Joint Supervisory Teams and Split Supervisory Tasks' (2017) 18 *European Business Organization Law Review*, 3.

H.W. Wolff, *Co-operative Banking. Its Principles and Practice*(BiblioBazaar LLC 2008) 2–3. (.

Working Group on Corporate Governance of the Basel Committee, *Principles for Enhancing Corporate Governance* (Nouy Daniele et al., eds., Bank of International Settlements Publications, 2010).

World Bank, 'Bank Nonperforming Loans to Total Gross Loans' at http://data.worldbank.org/indicator/FB.AST.NPER.ZS.

World Bank-FinSAC, 'Understanding Bank Recovery and Resolution in the EU: A Guidebook to the BRRD' (April 2017) 106 at http://pubdocs.worldbank.org/en/609571482207234996/FinSAC-BRRD-Guidebook.pdf.

E. Wymeersch, 'The Future of Financial Regulation and Supervision in Europe' (2005) 42 *Common Market Law Review*, 4.

E. Wymeersch, *Investor protection in Europe: Corporate Law Making, the MiFID and Beyond* (Oxford University Press, 2006).

E. Wymeersch, 'The Structure of Financial Supervision in Europe: About Sigle Financial Supervisors, Twin Peaks and Multiple Financial Supervisors' (2007) 8(2) *European Business Organization Law Review*, 237.

Y. Yadav, 'We Need to Know Who Invests in Bank Equity' (2017) 70 *Vanderbilt Law Review En Banc*, 284.

Y. Yang, 'China Banks in Stand-off with Regulators on Loan Loss Provisions', *Financial Times* (London, 30 October 2016).

P. Yeoh, 'Basel IV: International Bank Capital Regulation Solution or the Beginning of a Solution?' (2018) 39 *Business Law Review*, 181.

D. Yermack, 'Is Bitcoin a Real Currency? An Economic Appraisal' in David Lee Kuo Chuen (ed), *Handbook of Digital Currency. Bitcoin, Innovation, Financial Instruments, and Big Data* (Elsevier, 2015) 31–32.

D.A. Zetzsche, 'Fintech, Financial Inclusion and Sustainable Investment', presentation delivered at LSE Conference on Technology in Finance, Law and Regulation, London, 16 May 2019.

D.A. Zetzsche, R.P. Buckley and D.W. Arner, 'Regulating LIBRA: The Transformative Potential of Facebook's Cryptocurrency and Possible Regulatory Responses' (August 2019) at https://papers.ssrn.com/sol3/papers.cfm?abstract_id=3414401.

L. Zingales, *Capitalism for the People: Recapturing the Lost Genius of American Capitalism* (Basic Books, 2012).

Index

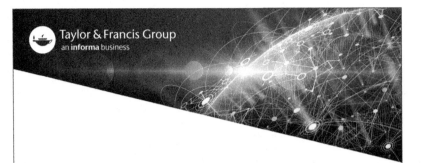

Printed in the United States
By Bookmasters